Thinkers
and
Tinkers

THINKERS AND TINKERS

✩ ✩ ✩ ✩ ✩ ✩ ✩ ✩ ✩ ✩ ✩ ✩

Early American
Men of Science

✩ ✩ ✩ ✩ ✩ ✩ ✩ ✩ ✩ ✩ ✩ ✩

Silvio A. Bedini

Illustrated with Photographs

CHARLES SCRIBNER'S SONS ✩ NEW YORK

Copyright © 1975 Silvio A. Bedini

Library of Congress Cataloging in Publication Data

Bedini, Silvio A
   Thinkers and tinkers: Early American men of science

   Includes bibliography, glossary, reference notes
and index
   1. Science—History—United States. 2. Scientist—
United States. 3. Research—United States. I. Title.
Q127.U6B33   509'.73   72-1174
ISBN 0-684-14268-6

1 3 5 7 9 11 13 15 17 19 V/C 20 18 16 14 12 10 8 6 4 2

Printed in the United States of America

To my wife,
Gale,
for sharing this work

Bright Science too, beneath our sacred dome,
Shall find a last retreat, a fav'rite home,
And, freed from schoolmen's trammels, shall impart
Her cheering influence to each useful art.
Diffuse her blessings, to the humblest cell,
And with the lowliest peasant deign to dwell.

"Verses on the commencement of the year 1789,"
American Museum, 1789

Contents

Illustrations

PART TWO

PART THREE

Preface

If the genesis of this work were to be traced to a single influence or inspiration, it would have to be to the discovery that I made more than twenty-five years ago, among remnants in the shop of a Connecticut antique dealer, of a rather disreputable and unattractive and apparently unwanted "scientific instrument." Although its components, design, and materials hardly recommended it either as a work of art or a useful tool of science, its nominal cost and my lack of knowledge of its purpose presented challenge enough to purchase it. The interest of this modest investment was increased substantially by the discovery that it was a wooden surveying compass, one of a relatively small number of surviving similar pieces made to serve the colonial American surveyor.

Identification of the venerable instrument subsequently led to the study of the work of the colonial American map makers and surveyors, their motivation, their accomplishments, their techniques and tools. Each new bit of information acquired aroused more questions, the answers to which could rarely be found in published works. Inevitably the story of the map maker and surveyor led to a study of the navigator, the maker of mathematical instruments, and the part-time science teacher, all closely associated in the fulfillment of related concerns but with minimal if any awareness of or relationship to one another, even when engaged in similar endeavors. Little by little the bits and pieces began to knit themselves together, and a picture of life in the colonial period began to emerge, in which each of these self-taught men engaged in a variety of scientific endeavors had a role. What they shared in common were the needs to which they responded, the practices and tools they applied, and the fact that most of them had had to teach themselves.

These men were "mathematical practitioners," a term coined in the sixteenth century to describe those engaged in such activities in England. It is doubtful whether any of the men so designated in this work were aware of the title, its meaning, or its application to them. Yet a remarkable chapter in American history, which has never previously been told or indeed acknowledged by historians, was the consolidation of the efforts of these scattered men which formed them into a movement. Only in retrospect can historical movements be identified and evaluated, and the threads of individual or combined achievement be woven into the fabric of history. Lack of recognition of the practitioners during the colonial period, during which the practical sciences were regarded as mundane endeavors unworthy of academic attention, is best expressed in *Memorials of My Life* by the seventeenth-century English mathematician Dr. John Wallis. "Mathematicks (at that time, with us) were scarce looked upon as *Accademical* studies," he wrote, "but rather *Mechanical*; as the business of *Traders, Merchants, Seamen, Carpenters, Surveyors of Lands*, or the like; and perhaps some *Almanack-makers* in London. . . . For the Study of Mathematicks was at that time more cultivated in *London* than in the Universities."

This view is further confirmed by J. Arbuthnit in an essay on the usefulness of mathematics published at Oxford in 1700. "The great objection that is made against the Necessity of Mathematics in the . . . great affairs of Navigation, the Military Art, &c.," he wrote, "is that we see those affairs carry'd on and managed by those who are not great Mathematicians: as Seamen, Engineers, Surveyors, Gaugers, Clock-makers, Glass-grinders, &c., and that the Mathematicians are commonly Speculative, Retir'd, Studious Men, that are not for an active Life and Business, but content themselves to sit in their Studies and pore over a Scheme or Calculation."

The dichotomy between the theoretical or "pure" disciplines taught in the universities on the one hand, and the practice, technique, and technology that were instrumental in the forging of a nation on the other, is an old and on-going difference. A useful discussion of it appeared in the Naval Tracts compiled in 1624 by the English naval commander Sir William Monson. "It is a question," he noted, "whether a man shall attain to better knowledge by experience or by learning? And many times you have controversies arise between a scholar and a mariner upon that point. The scholar accounts the other no better than a brute beast, that has no learning but bare experience to maintain the art he proposes. The mariner accounts the scholar but verbal, and that he is more able to speak than act."

Scholars nowadays continue to consider the practical sciences unworthy because they are not "pure." Moreover, few of the practitioners individually left a permanent mark by spectacular achievement. Nevertheless, it was they who charted the wilderness, navigated the unknown waterways inland and along the coasts, established the boundaries of personal properties and of provincial territories, made the instruments with which these tasks were accomplished, and instructed others in these skills.

A single volume cannot do more than encompass a brief account of the practitioners and their activities. But inasmuch as the combined efforts of all these "little men of science" made a significant impact on the formation of the early settlements and their unification first into colonies and then into a nation, and since in a true sense they were indeed participating members of a diverse scientific community, they deserve more than a footnote in history.

The isolated fragments that combined to produce their story were gleaned from many sources—the instruments themselves, the maps and charts and surveying plats produced, the texts with which they taught themselves, contemporary newspaper advertisements, and vital statistics in local archives. Little by little the endeavors of these men began to merge into accounts of life in their times and became integrated with its cultural, social, and military aspects.

A preliminary study published by the author in 1964 with the title *Early American Scientific Instruments and Their Makers* constituted a cursory survey of the tools of the early American men of practical science. It did, however, confirm the need for further investigation, which has culminated in the present work.

This book is not intended to be a comprehensive history of science in the British colonies of North America and the early years of the new nation, or a catalogue of all maps and charts compiled, surveys executed, or instruments made, or indeed a listing of the names of all engaged in these activities. It provides at most an overview of how the practical sciences were required and how they were utilized—with which and for what and by whom.

For the convenience of the reader a Selected Bibliography has been included, listing the major available works relating to the practical sciences and the mathematical instruments in Europe, England, and America.

The Glossary, arranged alphabetically, contains not only explanations of technical terms and phrases used in this work but also descriptions and histories of the mathematical instruments mentioned.

The title, *Thinkers and Tinkers*, was chosen to represent the two types of talent that contributed to the application of the practical sciences and their relationship to each other. The "thinkers" include not only the scientific leaders, some of whom have received respectful attention in scholarly works and individual biographies, but also the self-educated men who were concerned with the theoretical or experimental sciences as an avocation or for the purpose of teaching them. The "tinkers," on the other hand, were the vastly larger number of colonial Americans who applied the practical sciences, although not always scientifically, to solve existing problems. The term "thinker" therefore should require no further explanation. The term "tinker," however, has traditionally been loosely applied and may cause some confusion. By dictionary definition, a tinker is a mender of kettles and pans, an unskilled maker or mender, a botcher or bungler, a jack-of-all-trades; "tinkering" is an unskilled and frequently futile attempt to mend or improve something. Such indeed was the nature and result of the efforts of many of the early Americans. They did not, however, permit the task to defeat them; they returned to it again and again until they had improved themselves in whichever "art" they attempted.

The term "mathematical practitioner" has already been mentioned. It designated an individual who demonstrated technical skills in one or more of the practical sciences based on mathematics. These activities were frequently pursued part time in addition to another occupation. The greater number of the mathematical practitioners did not achieve the distinction that merits the title of scientist, but there were nevertheless reputable scientists or men of science among them, such as Benjamin Franklin, David Rittenhouse, and Andrew Ellicott. Even though their contributions frequently added to the knowledge of the physical world, only a few of them had any professional scientific training or earned more than half their total income from their scientific endeavors.

A "philomath," another term used in this work, is defined in dictionaries as "a lover of learning," or "a student, especially of mathematics and or allied sciences." These definitions do not, however, fully describe the activities of the early American philomaths, whose numbers included the amateur astronomers, the makers of almanacs, and the collectors of scientific books, instruments, and apparatus, as well as curiosities.

In general, the mathematical practitioners were an elusive lot, and their activities and achievements were frequently difficult and sometimes impossible to identify. The makers of mathematical instruments fortunately left tangible evidence of their work, which has survived in sufficient quantity to serve as a record of their skills. The map makers could be identified by means of surviving maps and charts, but the work of the surveyors generally had to be sought in local and state archives, where their plats and accounts are sometimes filed. Far more difficult was the quest for evidence of the work of the navigators. For the most part they were shipmasters and ships' mates, who, having learned seamanship before the mast, trained themselves in the art of navigation and in the use of instruments by experience at sea. Other than their instruments, the only records that survived them were their charts, sea journals and shipping records; their major achievement was their very survival. The teachers of the sciences revealed themselves in their newspaper advertisements and in the textbooks they used or compiled, while the philomaths occasionally perpetuated their work as published scientific papers, in almanacs, or with collections.

Until now the history of science in America as published and taught has concerned itself with the "naturalists"—the botanists and others who pursued the earth sciences—and a handful of major achievers in the mathematical and physical sciences. It is the intent of the present work to add yet another dimension by recording the remarkable development of a movement which was generated in response to the immediate needs of an unknown new world. In the words of Captain Samuel Sturmy in his *Mariner's Magazine* of 1669: ". . . all the Rules that have been laid down in the following Treatise, are most exact and easie to the meanest Capacity of such as are skilful in Arithmetick; but with a great deal of Labour, Study, Care, and Charge, in the Tryal of the Practice of them by our self: which may be considered by the Ingenuous Practicioners."

PART ONE

Settlement

1   Thomas Hariot (1560–1621). Painting in oils by an unknown artist, dated
1602. The figure holds a white ivory sphere covered with stars.

2   The coast from Chesapeake Bay to Cape Lookout. Watercolor drawing by John White as an addendum to his larger chart of the east coast entitled "La Virgenia Pars," drawn between 1585 and 1587.

3 Spherical compass horary ring, turned in ivory, such as Captain John Smith described. A compass fly is pivoted beneath a ring with a folding gnomon. Late sixteenth century.

4 Mariner's astrolabe dated 1603, believed to have been owned, used, and lost by Samuel de Champlain in his explorations of Canada in 1613.

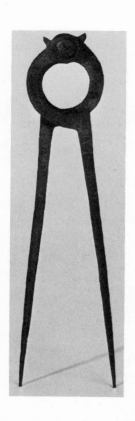

5 One-handed map calipers recovered from a sixteenth-century wreck.

7 Universal equinoctial ring-dial, English, seventeenth century.

6 Ring-dial made by Joan Paulus Gallucius, Saloensis, dated 1564.

8 Boxwood quadrant made for latitude 51° 30'. English, ca 1675.

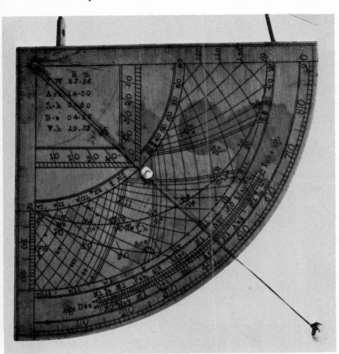

9 Marine compass card, from an illustration in *Practical Navigation* by John Seller (London, 1669); the hour numerals are marked on the outer ring.

10 Dry-card compass having compass fly pivoted inside a turned wooden bowl with glass cover sealed in putty. Made by William Davenport of Philadelphia, late eighteenth century.

11 Tell-tale or overhead compass, made by Iver Jensen of Copenhagen ca 1790. The form remained consistent without change from the seventeenth century.

12 "Sea-clocke," or marine time glass, with cord bights, eighteenth century.

13 Nocturnal for both the Great Bear and the Little Bear, made of mahogany, with a five-pronged brass pointer on the opposite side. American, eighteenth century.

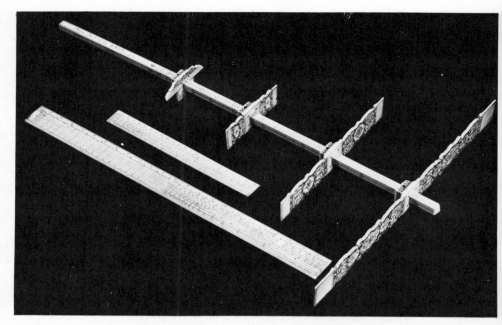

14 Cross-staff and Gunter's scales. A presentation set produced in ivory by Thomas Tuttell of London, ca 1700.

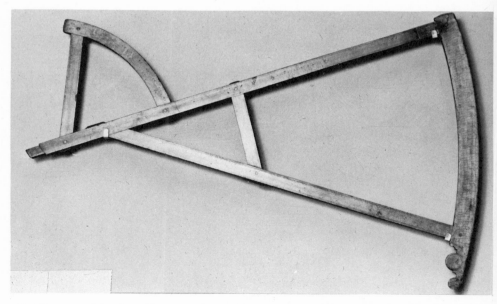

15 Pearwood backstaff, 1676, the earliest-known surviving mathematical instrument made in the American colonies. On the other side, the words "made by James Halsey" and the date "1676" are still legible; the owner's name may be "Thomas Swett."

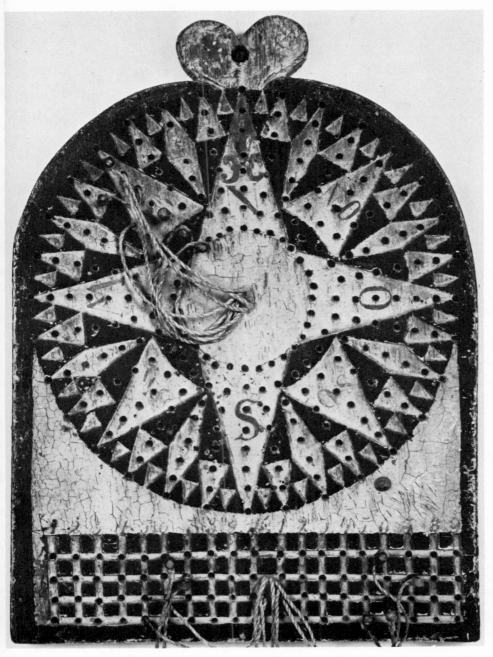

16 Traverse board, north European origin, ca 1800. Found on the island of
Barra, Scotland.

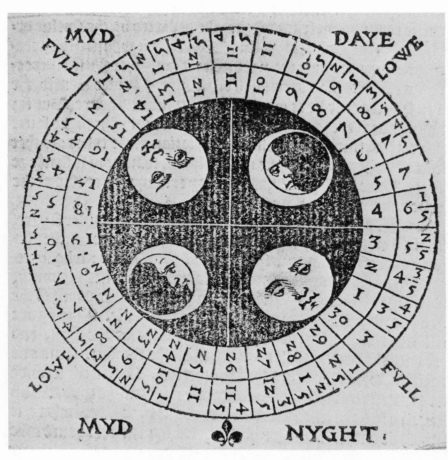

17   Table of the tides. Illustration from Richard Eden's translation of
The Arte of Navigation by Martin Cortes (London, 1584).

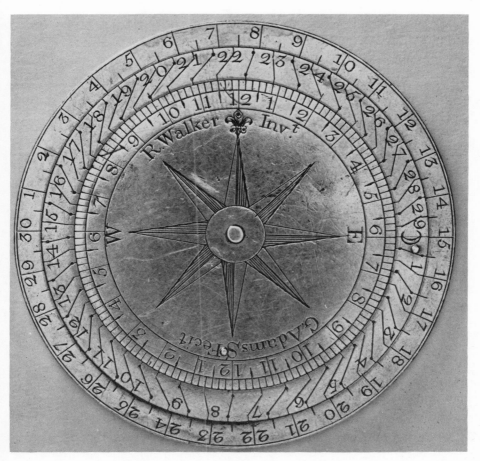

18   Tide calculator. Designed by Ralph Walker of Jamaica and London and made by George Adams, Jr., of London, ca 1780.

19 Lodestone bound in brass, eighteenth century.

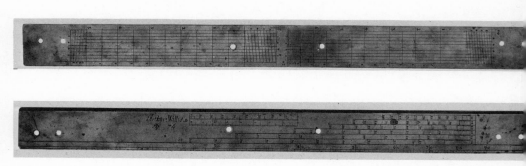

20 Brass plotting scale, probably used with a plane table. Inscribed "Arthur Willis 1674," and owned and used by the colonial surveyor Nathaniel Foote.

21   Plane table. Illustration from *The Compleat Surveyor* by William Leybourn
(London, 1653).

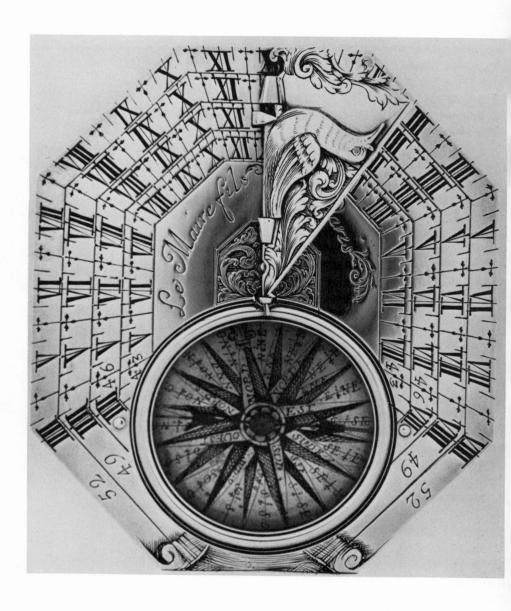

22, 23 Silver pocket compass sundial made by Lemaire fils of Paris in the early eighteenth century for use in northwest America: (*above*) top, showing the maker's name; (*opposite*) reverse, inscribed with the name of the owner and the names and latitudes of forts and locations in "New France."

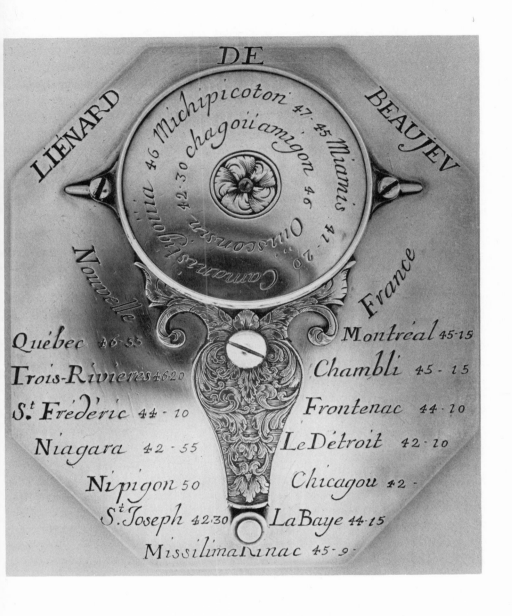

24 "The Surveyor." Oil painting on canvas by an unknown artist in the second half of the eighteenth century. The subject may be American. The instrument depicted is a brass theodolite of a type produced by Benjamin Cole
of London ca 1740–1750.

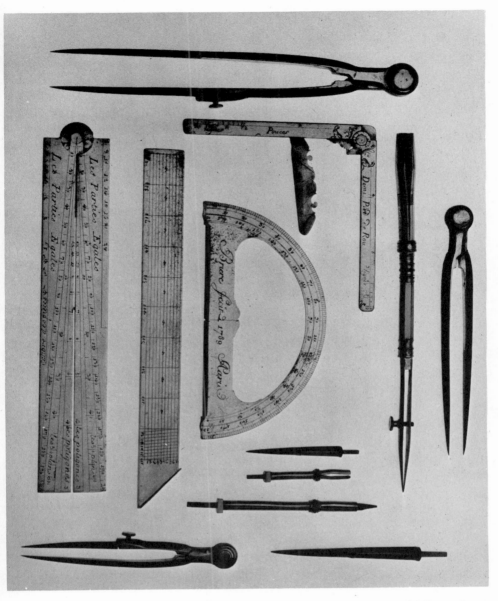

25 A set of drafting instruments made of silver by Briere, with a folding rule made by Nicholas Bion. Paris, early eighteenth century.

26 "Laying out Baltimore," an artist's conception of the survey in 1730. The instrument on the tripod at right is a plain surveying compass. From Charles C. Coffin, *Old Times in the Colonies* (New York: Harper & Bros., 1880).

27 Plain surveying compass of
brass made by Benjamin Cole of
London, early eighteenth century,
probably for use in the American
colonies.

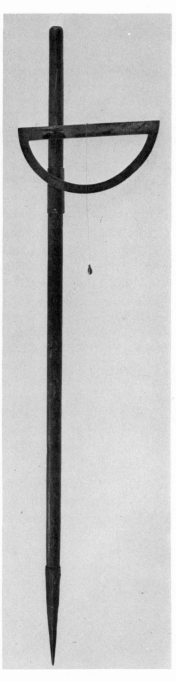

28 Brass instrument for determining grade
levels in surveying. American, eighteenth century, maker unknown.

I

☆ ☆ ☆ ☆ ☆ ☆ ☆ ☆ ☆ ☆ ☆ ☆

IN THEIR
BEGINNINGS

☆ ☆

Plantations in their beginnings have work ynough, & find difficulties sufficient to settle a comfortable way of subsistence,
there beinge buildings, fencings, cleeringe and breakinge up of
ground, lands to be attended, orchards to be planted, highways
& bridges & fortifications to be made, & all thinges to doe, as in
the beginninge of the world. Its not to be wondered if there
have not yet beene *itinera subterranea*. . . .

John Winthrop, Jr., letter to Henry Oldenburg (1668).

THE SEVENTEENTH CENTURY, one of the most creative periods in
world history, was marked by innovations in the arts and sciences,
political development, and man's view of the world. The effort to
discover a pattern or form within the apparent disorder of a world in
tumultuous change made considerable impact upon the sciences.
Man's new preoccupation with aspects of his world ranging from his
own bloodstream to the planets in the solar system led to the development of the science of dynamics, the invention of the calculus,

new knowledge of physiology and electricity, and the achievements of such giants as Galileo and Newton. The arts, in which a new artistic language was being developed, were dominated by the painters Rembrandt, Velasquez, Rubens, Van Dyck, and the architects Bernini and Wren. A new literature was created by Shakespeare, Milton, Molière, and Racine. A combination of music and drama appeared in the new forms of ballet and opera.

Political confusion and religious persecution, along with a desire to increase resources, caused a number of nations to attempt to gain footholds in the New World. In that eventful time, the establishment of a few modest English plantations on the North American continent seemed relatively insignificant, and the colonists' struggles for survival in the wilderness were minor when contrasted with the marching and countermarching of the armies of Europe. There was no vision, and little promise, that these embryonic settlements would in time emerge as a nation. The spirit that produced the great achievements of the century in other fields of endeavor and led to the establishment of colonial settlements did not extend to providing the support required to launch the English enterprise in the New World, and the settlers were compelled to find their own solutions. New strengths were born in the face of the need for survival, and a stubborn determination provided a response to immediate needs.

For each of the first settlements there were certain basic demands. The adjacent regions had to be investigated, and the important topographical features recorded in maps, which would be useful in avoiding dangers and seeking sources of sustenance. Navigation of waterways—inland rivers, the coastal waters, and the sea—was essential not only for transportation but to take advantage of a food resource. As each settlement was formed, boundaries had to be defined, first of individual properties, then of villages, and later of the colonies or provinces. For this work surveyors were required, as well as tools for their work and the skills necessary to produce these.

As the settlements developed into colonies, each basic need was proportionately magnified. The services of the occasional self-taught cartographer, navigator, or surveyor were not sufficient; skilled specialists were required in numbers, and teachers had to be found to train them. The result of these demands was the spontaneous development of a group of men pursuing the practical sciences. Self-taught for the most part, they emerged in substantial numbers throughout the new communities scattered along the east coast of

North America, and their combined skills not only produced the tools but provided the training. Gradually, over two centuries a movement of mathematical practitioners developed. The name, first applied by the members of a similar movement in England in the sixteenth century to distinguish themselves as a profession, is equally appropriate to the "little men of science" who were active in the New World.[1]

The mathematical practitioner movement formed one of three branches of science being pursued in the American colonies, each of which developed independently of the others. The first and best-acknowledged of these was theoretical or "pure" science, forming the discipline then entitled "natural philosophy," of which there were only a few proponents in the New World before the late eighteenth century. It was pursued in the early colleges and in urban centers by a small and select number of men, a few of whom emerged as major figures. The earth sciences, which constituted the second branch, were undertaken over a much wider range of the American continent, frequently with important results, by colonial naturalists, many of whom served as delegates of the Royal Society of London. The third branch consisted of the practical sciences developed by the cartographers, navigators, surveyors, and makers of mathematical instruments to support exploration and settlement. These men, together with the science teachers and the philomaths, constituted the mathematical practitioners.

The evolution of the practitioners in the colonies was the third manifestation of such a movement, and its development paralleled that of its predecessors, in Europe during the late Renaissance and in England in the sixteenth century.

The first practitioner movement emerged in Europe by the fifteenth century in response to the same stimuli which produced the Renaissance. The exodus of scholars from the Near East and the transfer of Byzantine manuscripts to Italy, following the fall of Constantinople, brought about an acceleration in intellectual pursuits and, in addition to the revival of interest in the arts and learning in general, a great change in the mathematical sciences. The invention of printing subsequently made available the works of the Greek geometers and popularized the study and application of geometry and trigonometry. The wide distribution of Ptolemy's concepts of geography reawakened concern with cartography and cosmography and advanced the art of navigation. A further stimulus was the search for new worlds in order to acquire territory, resources, and consequently greater world power. As maritime exploration became a subject of universal concern, the need for skilled navigators and for navigational instruments of greater precision became critical, but adequate instrumentation did not become available until the late sixteenth century. It was achieved by modification of the instruments used for astronomical observation, which in turn were developed after the newly evolved Copernican system of the universe had been expounded, the Julian calendar had been revised, and Arabic and Greek astronomy had become known to European scholars.

Similar needs for precision instruments were expressed in other areas. As improvement of the art of artillery called for the stronger defenses, instruments of greater precision for the design of fortifications and for gunnery became essential. Meanwhile, the first production of sheet brass, developed in the English armories, made possible a great variety of new products, including better instruments.

The decline of the feudal system in Europe and England had brought about changes in agriculture and in the relationship of the people to the land. Individual proprietorship became more widespread and by the beginning of the seventeenth century the manorial system had almost disappeared in France, the Netherlands, and England. The increase of the wool trade between England and the Netherlands caused more and more crop lands to be converted into sheep pasture, requiring enclosures and consequently boundaries. When the wool trade declined as a result of the war between Spain and the Netherlands, many of the large properties reverted to the common people, and the establishment of individual ownership increased the already critical need for property boundaries. These various developments created a demand for surveyors. There were few men capable of performing this work and no means of training others. Many amateurs attempted to make surveys, with unsatisfactory results. The increasing need for surveying skills finally led to the publication of popular works on the art, but adequate instruments with which to make the surveys were lacking. All of these factors, occurring more or less simultaneously, led to the development of a practitioner movement in England in the sixteenth century which reached its maximum influence in the two centuries that followed.[2]

With the establishment of settlements in the New World at the beginning of the seventeenth century, the same phenomenon occurred in the British colonies of North America. The rise of the practical sciences in the first American colonies coincided with the period of greatest activity in applied mathematics in England and in some of the European countries, and the parallels in achievement on the two sides of the Atlantic become the more impressive when the state of professionalism in America is compared with that of the Old World. In England the individual maker of mathematical instruments was a very small entity in the large framework of the guild system, the practices of which were established by tradition and restrained by stringent regulations. His training, his mode of life, and the quantity and quality of his work production were all carefully delineated, regulated, reviewed, and indeed restricted by the guild system. The colonial American instrument maker, on the other hand, only occasionally had any kind of specialized training and was subject to no guidance or regulation. Nevertheless, these colonial makers proved capable of producing most of the instruments and aids required by surveyors and navigators and eventually provided competition to their counterparts overseas. Furthermore, they accomplished this, not only without the traditional training, but often with makeshift tools and substitute materials.

Their achievements are even more remarkable in view of the difficulties of transatlantic communication and their remoteness from the scene where the major scientific discoveries and improvements were being made. Lacking too were the guidance and inspiration provided to the English practitioners by the giants of science. The few scientific leaders in the colonies consequently emerge as men of even greater stature in their time.[3]

The qualities which made these colonial achievements possible were assessed by Samuel Goodrich, a popular nineteenth-century American writer, in a manner that is descriptive of the attitudes which contributed to them. In connection with "this aptitude of our people, especially those of New England, for mechanical inventions," Goodrich wrote that it was based on a desire for improvement derived from a moral sense founded upon religious ideas, which made it a duty to be and do better as one advanced in life. The other principle, in his opinion, was "liberty, civil and social—actual and practical. New England is probably the only country in the world, where every man, generally speaking, has or can have the means—that is, the power—to choose his career; to say where he will live, what profession he will follow, what position he will occupy. It is this moral sense . . . cooperating with this liberty . . . which forms this universal spirit of improvement. . . . It is this which has conquered our savage climate, subdued our forests, and planted the whole country with smiling towns and villages. . . . The Yankee laborer has a mind that must be contented: he looks to the result of his labor; and if his tools or implements are imperfect, his first impulse is to improve them, and finally to perfect them." [4]

The practitioner movement in America—an excessively ambitious term for its early stages—was predicated upon the immediate needs for the practical sciences and the ability to respond to them. While the early settlements were being carved out of the wilds, a high priority was the exploration of the surrounding terrain for sources of food and other resources and of inland coastal waterways for the needs of communication and transportation. Cartographers, or map makers, undertook the task, thus representing the first advance of science into the unknown regions of the New World. It was in the cartographer's footsteps that soldiers, shipmasters, and settlers followed to establish the permanent communities. In general, the cartographers had no training other than experience in travel and survival under adverse conditions, and sometimes a knowledge of drafting. Most of them had to be capable of living and working alone for considerable periods of time, relying only upon their own ingenuity and endurance. Most of those who came to the New World had had military experience, and the discipline and austerity of military life served them in good stead during the weeks and months that they worked, alone or with a few companions, far from the settlements.

The great exploratory voyages of the fifteenth and sixteenth centuries were a natural outcome of the revival of learning during the Renaissance and the spirit of curiosity about the natural world and the achievements of men. As the hope of riches rose to fever pitch, ships were dispatched from European ports in frenzied competition. While the discovery that the New World was not the route to the treasures of the Orient deterred some, others realized that the unknown continent could be useful as a base for extending imperial domain and as a provider of much-needed natural resources. Some of the more practical minds speculated on the possibility of riches greater than gold and gems in the form of materials marketable for trade. It was partly the spirit of curiosity but even more the greed for gain that brought about the establishment of the first English plantations in North America. Subsidiary to these concerns were new resources for scientific study that would be provided by the flora and fauna not previously known. The New World had to be explored in order to capitalize on it.

The English explorations and settlements were primarily inspired by the successes of the conquistadors from Spain, who had fared forth in large numbers to seek, seize, and carry back great riches. While the coffers of the Spanish court were being filled with the treasures of Mexico and Peru, Spanish explorers collected other, more intellectual treasures in the form of scientific data. This endeavor bore its first fruit in a volume published in 1526 by Oviedo y Valdes and supplemented almost a decade later by a more ambitious work. An English translation of the earlier work, made by Richard Eden in 1555, was widely read and influential in directing English interest to the promise of the New World.[5] Among the English explorers who studied it was Sir Walter Raleigh.

Raleigh's half-brother, Sir Humphrey Gilbert, believed in the existence of a northwest passage to "Cataia" (Cathay, or China), and in anticipation of making the voyage, obtained in 1578 a royal patent to 200 leagues of North American coastline. His first voyage was a failure, but in 1583 he set out again to establish trading posts, advance naval bases, and permanent plantations for England.[6] For this venture Gilbert equipped himself with the most advanced scientific knowledge of his day. His party included a "colonial surveyor" named Thomas Bavin, who was provided with a variety of scientific instruments and with instructions for making a detailed survey of the North American coastline and for making observations of magnetic variations and for the determination of the longitude.[7] Gilbert arrived at what is now Newfoundland (Norimberga) and took possession of it in the name of Queen Elizabeth I. He then sailed southward to Nova Scotia and after a series of navigational errors and disasters turned homeward. His frigate, the *Squirrel*, grossly overloaded, was beset by foul weather and foundered, and Gilbert was drowned. While Bavin's fate is not known with certainty, it has been presumed that he also drowned and that his scientific records were lost.

After the tragic end of Gilbert's expedition, Raleigh attempted to bring his brother's dream to realization. Securing a similar patent from the queen for a six-year period, he equipped and dispatched two barks to inspect the New England coast and choose a suitable site between Newfoundland and Florida for the establishment of a plantation. This expedition reported that the best location was a site called Wococa situated off the coast of what is now North Carolina. Raleigh proceeded to assemble and equip a fleet of seven ships. His plans for a permanent settlement were well detailed and included an "engineer and traverse-master" to design a fort, a "geographer to make description of the landes discouered, and with hym an exilent paynter." Thomas Hariot, his tutor, was given the first of these appointments and John White was employed as the painter.[8]

After a successful voyage by way of the West Indies, the ships landed at Wococa. They had taken on water and stores at Puerto Rico and Hispaniola and moved up along the coast to settle on Roanoke Island, where they established "the Cittie of Raleigh." The region was explored during the first month of settlement, under the supervision of Hariot and White, who produced preliminary surveys, and the Englishmen made their first acquaintance with the Indians of the region. When the commander of the expedition, Admiral Sir Richard Grenville, sailed for England in August 1585, he left behind one hundred and nine men to form the first English colony in the New World.

In the months that followed, food became scarce and the Indians proved less friendly than had been anticipated. One hardship followed another, and when Sir Francis Drake anchored off the island on June 10, 1586, on his way home to England from a Caribbean voyage, many of the settlers insisted on returning with him. Shortly after his departure, the long-expected relief ship from Raleigh arrived, and two weeks later Grenville reached the colony with three ships filled with stores and new colonists. Leaving a small group of men on the island, he took the others, including Hariot and White, back to England. White returned as a leader of a new group of colonists in 1587 but was forced to go back to England for supplies. The attack by the Spanish Armada and other events delayed his return until 1591, and by that time the entire colony had disappeared.[9]

During the period of their stay, Hariot and White, the first two men of science on the North American continent, went about their assignments with dispatch and success. During the voyage from England it was clearly Hariot's assignment to act as consultant on navigation to Admiral Grenville and to take astronomical observations. After the colonists' arrival, he assumed the responsibility for studying the natives and supervising the mapping of the region. He was also required to make a comprehensive inventory of natural resources and to prepare a detailed report of his findings.

John White's assignment was to "draught," or sketch, a map of the region and to provide sketches of the animal and plant life and of the natives in their various activities. Hariot and White were provided with helpers to carry their equipment in the field and furnish other assistance as necessary. Hariot and White were to prepare "cardes," or sketch maps, illustrated by standard signs and symbols which indicated the location of natural resources, topographical features, and other useful information with appropriate notations entered both upon the map and in a journal.[10] Their instructions have not survived but were probably similar to those provided to Bavin for Gilbert's expedition.

Bavin's instructions required that the map maker be equipped with "a good store of parchments, Paper Ryall, Quills, and Inck, black powder to make ynck and of all sorts of colours to drawe all thinges to life, gumme, pensyll, a stone to grinde Colours, mouth glue, black leade, 2 payres of brazen Compasses, And other Instrumentes to to [*sic*] Drawe cardes and plottes." He was to be always attended by someone having pen and ink at hand and others having a universal dial, a cross-staff, and an ephemeris or other calculated tables with which he could determine the latitude. He was to mark places where oysters and other shellfish were to be found, note the distances of capes, headlands, and hills, havens, bays, and rivers, indicating their elevations and to compile similar data for inland features, such as lakes, pools, and woods. He was to note how the soil was "compassed," whether with hills, meadows, woods or "Champions," or with springs or bogs. The various types of trees were to be noted as they occurred. The plats were to be divided into several "cardes" or charts consisting of four sheets of "Paper Royall" according to the size of the table of the mapper's instrument (plane table). He was advised to divide the boundaries of the individual maps either by rivers, headlands, or the sea coast. Beginning at an established point on the coast, the "cardes" were to be numbered consecutively until the entire mapping operation had been completed. These would be later assembled in proper order and a single map or chart compiled.[11]

The cartographer was advised to use black leads or charcoal sticks for marking out general outlines and for making rough notes.

Black leads were sticks of natural graphite and were commonly used before the graphite pencil was developed in the late seventeenth century. Ground colors transported in powdered or compressed form were soluble in water and were used to denote such features as water, mountains, and forests by means of a "pensyll," which was a finely pointed brush made from animal hairs. Distances were taken and marked on the chart by means of a pair of wooden or brass dividers. "Brazen compasses" for drawing, which had a marking point of graphite or lead at the terminal of one of the legs so that a circle or desired part could be drawn, served a similar purpose.

The instructions given to Bavin provide a valuable listing of the drafting instruments in use for field work at the end of the sixteenth century. The paper used for map making consisted of thin, evenly textured white handmade paper, the surface of which had been rubbed with linseed oil on a piece of cloth. The paper was permitted to dry and then rubbed with gall or similar material to counteract the greasiness. This technique of preparation was used for centuries; substantial improvement of the process did not occur until relatively modern times.

The basic instrument for the map maker was the plane table, a triangulation instrument which underwent a period of evolution during the second half of the sixteenth century under a variety of names and forms. It was known as a "plaine" or "playne" table in England to indicate that it was as free as possible of all complications in its design and use.[12]

The portable magnetic compass was the explorer's only means for keeping a course through regions which provided no vista and of which he had no foreknowledge. The instrument was made in many types and sizes and provided for every need of colonization. The most common were small examples of gilded brass or silver combined with a simple sundial. Several of these small dials have been plowed up at early military fortifications and other sites of settlement where they were apparently lost by their owners. Although these pocket dials served the explorer or traveler they were not adequate for the map maker, who required a larger and more accurate instrument.

Although a wide variety of drafting instruments were available at the time, the first colonial map makers probably used only the most basic—the plane table, dividers, plotting scale, rules, magnetic compass, black leads, dried colors, and pensyll brushes. Their lack of professional skill was compensated for in practical ways. Each survey of a region required a number of days to complete, working constantly on the move. The map maker first made simple sketches of each area within sight or knowledge upon individual "cardes" or sketch maps, using the recognizable landmarks as coordinates so that the individual sketches could be compiled into a larger map or chart.

White, the first of the cartographers in the English plantations, fulfilled all the requirements of his assignment, including making sketches of the natives and of the flora and fauna and producing two maps. The first of these depicted the region between Chesapeake Bay and Cape Fear. The distances shown and the bearing noted were remarkably accurate considering the scale to which the map was drawn and the fact that it was probably compiled from small individual survey sheets. As far as is known, it was the first map of the New World to be based on a survey actually made on the site. White's second work was a general map depicting the southeastern part of the North American continent in its entirety. Parts of this were undoubtedly derived from existing Spanish and French maps, while other sections are clearly based on pure conjecture and incorporated distortions. Although White included notation of latitudes, there is evidence that the experimental observations he had made for the region actually surveyed were incomplete.

The first public use of White's work was a map engraved in 1590 by Theodore De Bry to illustrate Hariot's published report to Raleigh. The map as printed incorporated additions and modifications having no apparent basis in White's original work but provided important new information about the New World. It included the first available description of the coastal plain toward the Piedmont which some members of Raleigh's colony had crossed. Within the next several years De Bry's version of the map was incorporated into a great terrestrial globe produced by Emery Molyneux with the assistance of the instrument makers Edward Wright and William Sanderson and the cooperation of Raleigh and Hariot, who assisted particularly in the delineation of the North American coastline.[13]

Until the publication of White's map, the cartographic record of the New World had consisted of maps produced, not by cartographers working directly on the scene, but by Dutch, French, English, and other map makers and printers without personal experience of the areas plotted. Their products, based on data from manuscripts and published works of others, were less than reliable, since they frequently romanticized either to attract colonists or to compensate for information not known.

White was followed to the New World less than two decades later by another man of science who also made substantial contributions to its cartography. Captain John Smith has emerged as a highly romantic figure in the history of the British enterprise in North America, and with good reason. He had been active with the Virginia Company of London from its beginning, and was a member of the first band of colonists sent to establish a plantation. The ship dropped anchor thirty miles from the mouth of a waterway which became the James River, and the band of colonists made their landing on a small island in the river which they named "James Towne" after the reigning English monarch. Smith's first concern on arriving was to explore the surrounding region, and he made a comprehensive study of the terrain along the James River as far as what is now Richmond. His appointed task was trading with the Indians for provisions until supplies arrived from England, and he undertook a number of hunting and trading expeditions along the Chickahominy River. It was on such a journey that he was captured by the Indians.[14]

Smith published several versions of his capture and release, but the basic facts were essentially the same in all. The incident happened when he left his crew in his boat in a broad bay and proceeded with two companions and two friendly Indians in a canoe along the river. His men disobeyed and went ashore, were captured, and made to reveal the direction Smith had taken. The Indians found and surrounded him, and he was wounded and quickly overpowered. He was brought before the chieftain, Opechankanough, king of the Pamaunkees, "to whom he gaue a round Ivory double Compass Dyall. Much they marvailed at the playing of the Fly and Needle, which they could see so plainely, and yet not touch it, because of the glasse that covered them. But when he demonstrated by that Globe-like Iewell, the roundness of the earth, and skies, the sphaere of the Sunne, Moone and Starres, and how the Sunne did chase the night round about the world continually; the greatness of the Land and Sea, the diversitie of Nations, varietie of complexions, and how we were to them *Antipodes*, and many other such like matters, they all stood as amazed with admiration. Notwithstanding within an houre after they had tyed him to a tree, and as many as could stand about him prepared to shoot him, but the King holding up the Compasse in his hand, they all laide downe their Bowes and Arrowes, and in a triumphant manner led him to *Orapaka*, where he was after their manner kindly feasted and well used." [15]

The instrument which Smith claimed saved his life was a pocket compass sundial of a type then in common use. It was housed in a turned hollow ivory sphere made in two halves which screwed together and in which a magnetic compass and a sundial with collapsible gnomon were accommodated, protected by a glass cover. Fixed to the other half of the sphere was a lunar dial.

Smith remained a prisoner for approximately a month, during which period he was alternately feted and condemned to death. He was a prize of rare interest and was exhibited in one Indian village after another until he was finally permitted to return to his own people.

The exploratory journeys that Smith made soon after his arrival and later were motivated by instructions given in 1606 by the London Council: "You must observe, if you can, whether the river on which you plant [the settlement] doth spring out of mountains or out of lakes. If it be out of any lake, the passage to the other sea will be more easy, and is like enough, that out of the same lake you shall find some spring which runs the contrary way towards the East Indian Sea." [16]

He was particularly concerned with developing an accurate map of the entire region to send back to England. On June 2, 1608, he set off with a company of fourteen men in "an open barge of two tunnes burden" with which they crossed the bay from Cape Henry to the Eastern Shore, exploring every inlet and bay suitable for a harbor as they moved along the coast, and noting the many islands which they were unable to explore because of high winds and storms with which they were frequently beset. After "repairing our fore saile with our shirts" Smith and his party moved to the Western Shore which was more mountainous and barren, although the valleys were quite fertile. In the forests they found wolves, bear, deer, and other wild life. The party included a "Doctour of Physicke," a fishmonger, a fisher, and a blacksmith. Smith noted that ". . . they had not a Mariner or any other that had skill to trimme their Sayles, vse their Oares, or any business belonging to the Barge, but two or three. The rest being Gentlemen, or as ignorant in such toyle and labour, yet necessitie in a short time by their Captaines diligence and example taught them to become so perfect, that what they did by such small meanes, I leave to the Censure of the Reader." [17]

In less than two weeks, Smith's party explored almost 1,000 miles of coastline. Later that summer he made a second and more successful trip to seek the headwaters of the Chesapeake and explored the Rappahannock River as far as Fredericksburg, as well as a section of what is now Maryland as far as the present city of Elkton. During the following year he was making an exploring trip by canoe when gunpowder ignited accidentally and he was so seriously injured that he had to return to England in October 1609. Smith claimed that he had devoted almost five years of his life to the preparation of his map and that it had cost him more than 500 pounds sterling of his own resources, in addition to the considerable danger and misery that accompanied the effort.

Smith developed his own symbols, using outlines of houses to denote Indian villages and four different symbols for trees to indicate the varieties prevalent in the region. He stated: "In which Mappe observe this, that as far as you can see the little Crosses on rivers, mountains, or other places have been discovered; the rest was had by information of the Savages and are set down according to their instructions." [18]

The notes that Smith made in the field were compiled by one of his companions, Nathanael Powell, into a sketch map which was sent to the London Council and later published.

Smith's map provided the first detailed delineation of the Chesapeake Bay area and remained the only standard map of the region for more than half a century. It was copied in major works about the New World by Gerhardus Mercator, Jodocus Hondius, Willem Janszoon Blaeu, and Jan Jansson, among other European geographers.

Following his return to England in 1609, Smith devoted his boundless energies to the promotion of colonization of the North American continent. Returning to the New World in 1614, he made a survey of the New England coastline from Cape Cod (which he named Cape James) to Pembrocks Bay; he was the first to call the region "New England." As he described his effort, "I have draune a Map from point to point, Ile to Ile, and Harbour to Harbour, with the Soundings, Sounds, Rocks, and Land-Markes as I passed close aboord the shore in a little Boat. . . ." [19] His attempts to colonize the region were thwarted by his capture by French privateers in 1616, but the map had wide distribution, appearing first in his *Description of New England* published in that year, and in the various editions of his *Generall Historie* which followed. Subsequently he published two works on navigation designed specifically as practical manuals for colonists en route to the New World.

II

☆ ☆ ☆ ☆ ☆ ☆ ☆ ☆ ☆ ☆ ☆ ☆

IN SURGING
SEAS

☆ ☆

Whoso in surging-Seas, his season will consume,
And means thereof to make his onely trade to live
That man must surely know the shifting Sunne & Moone,
For trying of his Tides, how they doe take and give.
Robert Norman, The newe attractiue . . . (1581)

THE ART OF NAVIGATION achieved primary importance for the English plantations almost immediately after the arrival of the settlers. Although the colonists, except for the few navigators involved in their transport, were entirely without knowledge of the sea, they nevertheless approached this new challenge with the same practicality that marked all their endeavors and proceeded to master the sea as they did the wilderness.

The immediate need for experienced navigators and shipmasters rapidly increased in urgency. A navigator was defined as one capable of "conducting a vessel from one place to another in the safest, shortest, and most commodious way. He ought, therefore, to be well acquainted with the islands, rocks, sands, and straights near which he has to sail . . . the signs which indicate the approach of land . . . understand the nature of the winds . . . the motions of currents and tides. He must understand, also, the working of the ship, that is, the management of the sails, rigging, &c." Navigation was defined as being "either common or proper. The former is usually called coasting; that is, where the ships are on the same or very neighboring coasts; and where the vessel is seldom out of sight of land, or out of reach of sounding." In navigation requiring ocean passage, however, "a considerable skill in mathematics and astronomy is required, and an aptness in using instruments for celestial observations." Although the definitions appeared in an early-nineteenth-century "book of trades," they were equally applicable during the two preceding centuries.[1]

The experienced shipmasters played an important role in the development of marine resources, but they were far too few, and means for training others had to be found. The colonial navigator had to be skilled in the application of the basic procedures and instruments. For the most part he was an unromantic figure, a hardworking seaman in charge of fishing parties consisting of a wild crew of fishermen or seamen collected from the less desirable segments of the communities. Lack of facilities for formalized training caused the colonists to seek books on the subject, and to import from the mother country such as were available. A few important works had been produced in England, but basic texts for the training of seamen and navigators were lacking. Awareness of this fact led Captain John Smith to produce his two manuals on navigation. He was further inspired by another circumstance. In preparation for England's war with Spain, 10,000 English landsmen were pressed into military service in 1625. A proclamation by Charles I for "the well manning and arming of the ships of war belonging to this realm" resulted in the production by a hack writer named Gervase Markham of a manual for soldiers entitled *The Souldier's Accidence*. The demonstrated usefulness of this work encouraged Smith to compile the first manual for seamen to be published in England. He was not deluded, nor did he delude others, about his own competence as a navigator, but he collected and studied not only all available books on the subject but most recent navigational instruments. The knowledge thus acquired was substantially supplemented by his own experiences on shipboard.

Entitled *An Accidence* following its military counterpart, Smith's manual, aimed primarily at prospective colonists in the New World, provided many practical suggestions for young men following the sea. Smith, as he pointed out, did not attempt to present the art of navigation as such but primarily the use of instruments. He provided a list of published works, commenting, "to learne to obserue the Altitude, Latitude, Longitude, Amplitude, the variation of the Compasse, the Sunnes Azimuth and Almicanter, to shift the Sunne and Moone, and to know the tydes, your roomes [rhumbs], pricke your carde, and say your Compasse, get some of these bookes, but practice is best." [2] The manual was an instant success and he revised it into a larger edition which was published the following year as *A Sea Grammar*. [3]

Important navigational works which preceded Smith's included *The Lightning Columne, or Sea-Mirrour* of Theunisz Jacobsz, based on the *Spieghel der Zeevaert* by Lucas Wagenaer published in 1584. This was the first comprehensive work to include a treatise on navigation, an explanation of instruments, and a compilation of charts. [4] Richard Eden translated a Spanish work by Martin Cortes which he published in 1561 as *The Arte of Navigation*. [5] The sum total of sixteenth-century English navigational practice was summarized in Edward Wright's *Certain Errors in Navigation*, which appeared in 1599. [6] A skilled mathematician with considerable experience at sea, Wright developed a formula and tables for drawing charts on Mercator's projection, which its inventor first used in 1569. The greater accuracy of the curved Mercator projection, which replaced the parallel inscriptions of latitude and longitude on the traditional plane chart, substantially reduced the probability of error. For the first time navigation by means of calculation instead of day-to-day estimated or observed position became possible. Wright's innovation was of particular significance in the establishment of the English plantations in the New World and played an important role in the development of colonial American navigation. Another work worthy of mention was *The Seamans Secrets* by Captain John Davis, which provided the first instructions for maintaining a sea journal. [7] Davis described the calculation of the tides and suggested the use of terrestrial globes to determine the true distance and angle between positions, the circular motion of any course, and the latitude and longitude of places.

A skilled navigator, Davis is also recognized for his improvement of the backstaff, an instrument for observing the altitude of the sun at sea. The earliest known form was illustrated in a manuscript by Thomas Hariot and he may have tested it during Raleigh's expedition. An improved version was devised by Davis and tested by him in North American waters sometime between 1600 and 1604. This form of the instrument, which was known as the Davis's improved quadrant, came into common use on both sides of the Atlantic throughout the seventeenth and eighteenth centuries.

The instruments essential to water travel at the time that the New World was being settled were relatively simple devices which required more practice and experience than skill. The basic instrument was the mariner's compass, which was no more than the common magnetic compass adapted for use on shipboard.

In due course it was discovered that the needle of the mariner's compass did not indicate true north but pointed away to an angle which was later known as "magnetic north"; the phenomenon was called "magnetic variation." European navigators and compass makers had become aware of this variation by the late fourteenth century, and thereafter they frequently mounted the needle on the graduated compass card so that it pointed to the degree of variation, although the upper surface of the card was marked with the north point at magnetic north. Traditionally Christopher Columbus is credited with having discovered the compass's variation as it differed from one location to another on his original journey to the New World. The attribution cannot be made with certainty because manuscript sources have suffered extensively at the hands of translators and transcribers. Modern scholars are of the opinion that an easterly declination of the compass needle was already known in northwestern Europe prior to Columbus's voyage.

During the sixteenth century many efforts to accommodate the variation of the compass were made with mixed success, culminating with the dip circle invented by Robert Norman of England in 1581, which set the stage for Sir William Gilbert's great work on magnetism, *De Magnete*, in which he described his invention of the dip dial. This was basically the same as the dip circle. It was not successful because there were no means for producing it in quantity.

The mariner's compass was widely used in the British colonies and produced in numbers by colonial makers. For colonial navigators it constituted the only safeguard for finding the ship's way across the endless expanse of ocean. It is not surprising to find that many superstitions grew up around it, and it was used and maintained on shipboard with great care. An example of the legendry which governed its use was recorded by William Gilbert: "Steers men, and such as tend the Mariners Card are forbid to eat Onyons or Garlick, lest they make the Index of the Poles drunk. . . . But when I tried all these things, I found them to be false: for not onely breathing and belching upon the Loadstone after eating of Garlick, did not stop its vertues: but when it was all annonynted over with the juice of the Garlick, it did perform its office as well as if it had never been touched with it: and I could obserue almost not the least difference." [8]

The compass was used to determine the direction in which the ship was sailing. A simple device for keeping a record of the ship's course was the traverse board, which could be easily produced from a flat piece of wood. The upper portion was cut into the form of a circle; the lower section was square or rectangular. A compass rose of thirty-six points was marked on the face of the round portion. The traverse board was of ancient origin but was first described in England in 1577 by William Bourne, with the comment that in his time the "board" was used in place of "sheep-skinnes" or portolano charts by seamen for their reckoning when out of sight of land.[9] Smith also described it in his *Sea Grammar*.

A related device which came into use among the more literate of the early American seamen was the log slate, a panel of slate or wood, on which the seaman kept his daily record. The panel, which had a wooden frame, was permanently marked off into columns for hours, knots, fathoms, course, wind, and leeway, each indicated merely by the initial letter at the top of the panel. When a stone slate was not available, a pine plank coated with black paint was made to serve the purpose. Pencils or chalk were used for writing on the surface.

The running speed of a ship was measured by a device known as a log-ship-and-line, an ancient invention mentioned in the works of Vitruvius but not in common use in England until the mid-sixteenth century. It consisted of a triangular piece of wood weighted at one end and attached to a line. When dropped over the stern, the "ship" floated just below the surface, and as the vessel moved away from it, the speed was measured by means of a "running glass" on the basis of the length of line run out or the distance traveled in a specified period of time. This form of the time glass was first mentioned in late-sixteenth-century inventories of English royal ships as a "Rennying glass," as distinct from the "hour glasse" with which merchant ships were provided, which suggests that it was first used for naval purposes. At that time it measured ½ hour. A century later the period of measurement had been reduced to ½ minute. After the discovery early in the seventeenth century that the earth's circumference had been miscalculated, the running time of the glass for measuring the ship's speed under sail was reduced from 30 seconds to 28 seconds so as to maintain the same length of log line. The increased speed of vessels by the early eighteenth century led to further redesign of the running glass to measure 14 seconds to be consistent with the length of the log line, which by then had been reduced to one-half its traditional length. Log glasses of both 14 and 28 seconds' duration became regular issue in the British Navy during the eighteenth century, and both were commonly used by colonial American shipmasters.

Other glasses for measuring units of time were essential on shipboard and were in use from the fourteenth century until long after domestic timepieces came into common use. Ships were provided with three sizes of glasses, a "watch glass" which measured 4 hours, a "half-watch glass" which was capable of timing 2 hours, and a "half-hour glass." Each time the last-named timepiece was turned, the ship's bell was rung, giving rise to the system of ship's bells to measure the half-hours completed from one through eight for the duration of each watch.

One of the earliest-known instruments used in navigation was the seaman's quadrant, the first form of which was developed by Islamic mathematicians and brought to Europe in the Middle Ages. Designed for observation of vertical angles, it was probably first used for astronomical observations, then for surveying, and finally for navigation. Considerable confusion has resulted from the fact that several types of navigational instruments, which vary greatly in form and manner of use, are called quadrants. In addition to the sinical, horary, and Gunter's quadrants there were the Davis's improved quadrant and the Hadley's reflecting quadrant, both developed later. The form known as the sinical quadrant was inscribed for a single latitude and incorporated a plumb line and plummet for the indication of the altitude of the arc of the object being sighted. An improved version known as Gunter's quadrant was devised by an English mathematician, Edmund Gunter, in 1618 for use in time-telling at sea and for determining the sun's right ascension and declination.[10] This version was well known to colonial American navigators.

Another of the traditional instruments used by colonial navigators was the nocturnal, which had come into general use in Europe by the mid-sixteenth century. It served to tell time at night by observation of either the Great Bear or the Little Bear.

Next to the mariner's compass, the instrument most widely used at sea in the sixteenth and seventeenth centuries was the backstaff, already mentioned. The predecessor of the backstaff was the jacob staff, reputed to have been invented in Spain by an astronomer named Levi Ben Gerson in the late fifteenth century. It consisted of a simple wooden rod marked in degrees along which a wooden transom or panel could be slid. One end of the rod was placed just below the eye and the transom was slid along the rod until one end was aligned with the horizon and the other with the star being observed. The degree marked on the rod at the intersection with the transom indicated the star's altitude. As the instrument developed, it acquired the names "fore-staff" and "cross-staff" and became equipped with several transoms ranging in size according to the nature of the observations to be made.

The form known as the fore-staff or cross-staff was used not only on voyages to the North American continent but also by colonial American navigators, as were the backstaff and its improved version, the Davis's quadrant.

The nomenclature of the backstaff and of its variations has created considerable confusion for the historian, several names having been used interchangeably at different periods. In addition to the Davis's improved quadrant, other versions were the mariner's bow and the "plough." Although both these were prevalent during the period of colonization, the Davis quadrant was the instrument most commonly used and most frequently produced in the American colonies.

In addition to the more standard instruments, the shipmaster, when approaching port, also relied on the tide calculator. This was a navigational aid of respectable antiquity and ranged from simple forms accommodated on the compass card to mechanical devices. Derived normally from the tide tables printed in almanacs, the mechanical tide calculator consisted primarily of a compass dial marked with the sixteen points of the compass rose and having two or three movable dials superimposed one above another, representing the clock dial, the ages of the moon, and the compass points. Given the location of the "establishment of the port," and the moon's age, the time of high water for that port on any given day could be easily read by setting the moon pointer for the port location, and the sun pointer to indicate the rhumb, or compass point, equivalent to the hour of high water on the day corresponding to the age of the moon. Examples of the calculator were described by William Bourne and John Seller.[11]

A method of calculating the tides without using a mechanical calculator was by means of hour numerals inscribed on the outer edge of the compass card. This practice was imported into the American colonies from England. The monthly cycle of the tides and the times of high and low tides and their relation to the moon phases were a matter of common observation at sea. It was generally known that as the moon passed through its cycle of between 29 and 30 days there was an hourly lag of high water of 48 minutes, which the seaman measured as a rhumb (a point of the compass rose), or equal to 45 minutes. If the time of high tide for the new moon was known, the time of high tide on any day could be determined by counting the number of compass points around the compass rose to the moon's age and adding 45 minutes for each. Compass cards intended for such use are identified by having Roman numerals from I through XII twice continuously marked on the rhumbs. At least one such colonial American compass card has survived; it was produced by Daniel King of Salem in 1744. Examples of such compass cards were illustrated in works on navigation by John Seller and Samuel Sturmy, among others.[12] Sturmy also described and illustrated "An Instrument Shewing ye Changing of ye Tides and ye Variation of ye Compas," a simple form of tide calculator having three dials superimposed one upon the other. An American example of Sturmy's device was owned and used by Captain Christopher Waterman, commanding the sloop *King Hendrick*, in 1757.

Yet another form of tide calculator was a moon dial, having the division of "the dayes of the Moone," which was first illustrated in Richard Eden's translation of the navigational work by Cortes published in England in 1561. The reader was enjoined to "heede to the dayes of the Moone, howe many they are: as if she be in the coniunction, or if it be the fyrst or second of the Moone, &c. And the dayes beying knowen, then in the second circle whiche answeareth directly to the daye, shall be fynde when shalbe high water, or full sea: and consequently, the ebbe, or low water, which shalbe fyve sixe houres and one fyfth, after the full sea, and so lykewyse may be iudge when shalbe the halfe tyde: and this as well as the tyme when it encreaseth (whiche shalbe three houres and halfe a fyfth parte of an houre, before the full sea) as also when it decreaseth, which shalbe the halfe ebbe, three houres, and halfe the fyfth of one houre, after the full sea." [13]

The several forms of tide calculators continued in use through the eighteenth century, with the compass card marked with the hours the most prevalent.

Shortly after the Virginia Company's first colonists had established themselves at Jamestown, other English colonies were planted along the eastern coast of North America. The Plymouth Company's first abortive attempt to establish a colony at the mouth of the Kennebec River was followed by other equally unsuccessful ventures by the Reorganization Council for New England to develop settlements in the regions which are now the states of Maine and New Hampshire. Then in 1620 a group of English Separatists landed at Plymouth and made a permanent settlement. Ten years later a band of Puritans arrived on the shores of Massachusetts Bay and set up an independent self-governing group of settlements which they named the Massachusetts Bay Colony. From this nucleus other settlements were formed, including Providence and Portsmouth (Rhode Island) by 1635; Hartford, Wethersfield, and Windsor (Connecticut) a year later, and New Haven in 1637–38.

Also during the seventeenth century, the English proprietary colonies came into being. The first province was Maryland, with its earliest settlement at Saint Mary's City in 1634. The province of Carolina was established in 1663; its division into North and South Carolina occurred in 1729. The Dutch had meanwhile planted colonies on Manhattan Island, at Fort Orange, in the Jerseys, and in Delaware, all of which were taken over by the English in 1664. In 1682 William Penn undertook his "Holy Experiment" in Pennsylvania. The last of the English royal colonies, Georgia, was formed fifty years later.

Like the promoters in England, many of the colonists visualized vast riches readily available in the New World—valuable metals and other minerals, exotic plants and wildlife of commercial value, and other negotiable resources. They believed that it would be necessary only to locate and identify these riches in order to convert them for their own use and for trade with the motherland. The dream ended abruptly as the colonists discovered that they lacked the skill, knowledge, and experience to exploit such resources. They were faced instead with the more immediate priorities of mere survival, and being as practical as they were rugged, they proceeded to direct their energies to clearing land, both for the construction of temporary housing and to provide large open areas for protection from Indians and wild life. The virgin forests furnished a wealth of timber, and the temporary shelters were replaced with more elaborate buildings within the first few years. All the skills at the command of the settlers were brought into use as the embryonic communities began to take form. There were in each of the settlements representatives of a number of useful trades, such as blacksmiths, carpenters, farmers, brewers, and weavers, in addition to an occasional shipbuilder, tanner, wool comber, fustian maker, and tailor. The combined skills enabled the colonists to meet the challenges of their new homes. Wildlife and plants provided a source of food and were supplemented with an abundance of fish from the streams and coastal waters and the small amounts of grain planted and harvested by the colonists. The need for cooperation for the sake of survival throughout the entire period of colonization brought about a miraculous metamorphosis into a competitive new breed which was self-directed, independent, and generally successful.

All the first settlements were purposely situated near waterways; and as communities were established, shipping centers emerged rapidly, since the early colonists, though not in general seafaring people, promptly recognized the resources of the sea.

The need for ships was urgent, and the settlements situated on major waterways lost no time in turning to this endeavor. The first vessel known to have been built in the New World was a pinnace called the *Virginia*, which was completed and launched by the Popham Colony at the mouth of the Kennebec River by the summer of 1607. It sailed as far as the present city of Augusta, Maine, before departing for England with a small group of settlers when the colony was abandoned. Plymouth, because of its favorable location for developing sea industries, also gave shipbuilding high priority. In 1624, four years after first settlement, a ship's carpenter was brought from England and he completed three vessels before his premature death in the same year. Massachusetts Bay Colony Company was equally anxious to have ships, and in 1629 six shipwrights were sent from England with a shipload of equipment, tools, and materials. Two years elapsed before the first vessel, *The Blessing of the Bay*, was completed, but it was quickly put into service for trade with New Amsterdam. By 1634 Captain John Mason, a London merchant, sea officer, and governor of New Hampshire, informed the Admiralty in London that at least six of the more than fifty ships then trading with New England were owned in the colonies. The first vessels in the colonies were manned mostly by seamen who had deserted from ships bearing new contingents of settlers from England, or by runaway servants and unsuccessful emigrants.

Evidence of the importance assigned to maritime pursuits was an order issued by the Great and General Court of the Massachusetts Bay Company exempting all ships' carpenters and fishermen from compulsory military training. In Massachusetts alone 1,332 vessels were constructed between 1681 and 1714.

As the colonial communities emerged from their initial periods of hardship and privation, their horizons widened to encompass the development of trade, first with one another, then with other colonies, and finally with the motherland. The pioneer assumed the new role of merchant and as trade products became generally available attention was directed to new markets. The New England waters in particular were unusually rich in a variety of fish, and fishing for home consumption and for export became one of the most lucrative large-scale operations. Almost every segment of New England society came into contact with maritime trade in one form or another, and shipmasters became familiar figures in the communities. Those that achieved adequate wealth were accepted in the best circles; seamen in general ranked at the same social level as minor officials and skilled craftsmen.

The initiation of sea trade with the West Indies and other distant ports brought another generation of seamen into being. Young men in their early twenties moved to the port cities, fishing villages, and tidewater farms in search of wider opportunities. Many were attracted to life before the mast because of the strictness of the Puritan communities. Armored with youth and a desire for adventure, these recruits rapidly shaped into a new species of seamen, bold and alert, choosing to follow the sea as a career rather than merely as a way to earn a living. These qualities brought impressive success at sea, and the confidence that was evoked substituted for experience.

The emphasis on shipping and sea trade increased the need for nautical charts, or maps, of the waterways and the sea routes. At first professionally executed charts of harbors and shipping routes were produced by English military and naval officers stationed in the major shipping centers. Little by little colonial cartographers supplemented these with nautical charts of new areas, compiled from data accumulated by experienced pilots and shipmasters, and the work of the cartographer increased the capability of the navigator.

In Europe and England, the art of navigation had been professionalized for generations. It was taught in special schools by teachers experienced in the ways of the sea, or comparable training was acquired by apprenticeship on shipboard. In the colonies, however, neither time nor facilities were available to develop such programs and training was accomplished by firsthand experience. English navigational practices and instruments were adopted almost without change and the few available books and the equally rare charts of American waters were supplemented by apprentice training at sea.

The colonial navigator was further handicapped by the want of adequate tools. From the Middle Ages to the second half of the eighteenth century the seaman could only determine his east-west position at sea by means of dead reckoning. This consisted of measuring the ship's rate of speed at stated intervals and translating this rate into nautical miles. The distances and angular direction of the ship's course were marked on a traverse board and traverse tables applied to calculate the absolute distance traveled. The distance was then converted into degrees and marked on a chart at the correct latitude of the ship's last recorded position. The liability for error in this method was considerable and was further exemplified by the lack of accuracy of the navigational instruments then available, to which must be added the margin for error in the plane charts then in use. Until the late sixteenth century the plane chart was a network of parallels of latitudes, rhumb lines, and distances, drawn without providing any allowance for the curvature of the earth. The parallels of latitude were drawn as horizontal straight lines marked equidistantly, while the meridians of longitude were drawn as equidistant vertical straight lines. The rhumb lines, or bearings, bisected all meridians at the same angle because they converged at the poles. They were also straight lines, which resulted in gross distortion, particularly in large areas. Consequently the navigator was unable to establish his position with any degree of accuracy, even if he were capable of plotting it, which he rarely was.

The formula for drawing charts on Mercator's projection, first described in English by Edward Wright in 1599, provided greater accuracy, but it was some time before it was sufficiently well known to be adopted as a replacement for the plane chart.[14]

An invaluable aid for the navigator was the almanac, since its ephemeris, or compilation of astronomical data, provided him with the position of important stars at specific seasons. The value of these publications was appreciated from early times, although almanacs specifically for nautical use did not appear until the seventeenth century. On his voyage of discovery in 1492 Columbus utilized as a guide a copy of the *Almanach Perpetuum* produced by the Spanish sage Abraham Zacuto. The first English attempt to develop such an aid was made by John Tapp with *The Seaman's Kalendar*, first published in 1601, which proved to be one of the most significant and useful works for navigation in his time.[15]

The first almanac produced in the British colonies of North America was, appropriately enough, the work of an experienced shipmaster, Captain William Pierce of Plymouth. Between 1622 and his death in 1641 he commanded several ships, transported Governor Winslow and his cattle from England in the *Charity*, and in 1629 sailed from Holland with a shipload of Pilgrims on the *Mayflower II* for Plymouth. He also made trade voyages to the West Indies; it was on one such voyage that his ship was fired upon by the Spanish and he was killed. In 1638 Pierce calculated the ephemeris for an almanac for the year 1639 which was published as a single-leaf broadside by the printer Stephen Daye on his press in the basement of the Cambridge home of Henry Dunster, the first president of Harvard College. Entitled the *Almanack Calculated for New England, by Mr. Pierce, Mariner,* it was the second work to be printed in the British colonies after the introduction of the first printing press.[16] This was the first of a series of almanacs printed annually for a period of time at Cambridge, first by Daye and then by his successor, Samuel Green.

III

☆ ☆ ☆ ☆ ☆ ☆ ☆ ☆ ☆ ☆ ☆ ☆

WHERE WOLVES NOW HOWL

☆ ☆

> Not trackless Desarts shall thy Progress stay;
> Rocks, Mountains, Floods, before Thee must give Way:
> Sequester'd Vales, at thy Approach shall sing;
> And with the Voice of cheerful Labor ring.
> Where *Wolves* now howl, shall polish'd *Villas* rise;
> And towery *Cities* grow into the Skies.
>
> William Smith, *A general idea of
> the college of Mirania* . . . (1753)

AS THE FIRST SETTLEMENTS developed into communities, the division of land to define home lots, fire lots, and acreage for other uses became necessary. The measurement, marking, and recording of boundaries was the work of the surveyor, who also defined the areas and boundaries of tracts of land for provincial, territorial, and, later, state units. He was distinguished in this respect from the makers of maps, who "surveyed" unexplored regions and delineated their topographical features.

In Virginia and Maryland, the first surveyors were men professionally trained in England and brought to the plantations early. In the New England colonies, however, members of the communities had to be trained for this function. A basic knowledge and understanding of mathematics was required, and since no specialists with this particular ability were among the early settlers, individuals had to instruct themselves. The assignment consequently fell to the member of the community who was most capable of learning and applying the scientific principles and also had the time to do so. The one chosen or self-elected was frequently the schoolteacher, the minister, or some other adjudged to have more "book learning" than his fellows.

When a local surveyor had been appointed, he had to learn the work and provide himself with the required tools. A small number of texts on surveying had been published in England by the middle of the seventeenth century and some of these were imported into the colonies. Few of them, however, contained information useful in coping with the conditions of the New World, which were substantially different from those in Europe and England. In area alone, the American continent was overwhelming, and it was covered with almost impenetrable forests of virgin timber and threaded by waterways overgrown through centuries. Land had to be cleared for settlements and roadways and rivers opened for navigation, and surveying required techniques and instruments quite different from those traditionally used in England where the majority of areas were open.

The earlier texts on surveying dealt primarily with the responsibility of land stewards and provided a minimum of technical information. In that period geometry and trigonometry, on which surveying was based, were taught only to members of the upper classes. Prior to the application of triangulation with the plane table and the theodolite (an instrument for measuring horizontal and vertical angles), surveying was accomplished for the most part by measuring rod and cord or simply by viewing and estimating. The introduction of the estate map, a written plan of a completed survey, increased the accuracy and also the speed with which a survey could be made.[1] By the time the first English plantations were established, English surveying texts included trigonometrical tables as well as logarithms, and the decimal chain and an improved four-perch chain of one hundred links had come into use. A guide for new landowners in

Ireland and Virginia by William Folkingham, published in 1610, was circulated widely in Virginia. Richard Norwood's *Epitomie*, published in 1659, provided formulas and problems relating to location of courses on land and sea.[2] A basic work was *The Surveyor* by Aaron Rathborne, published in 1616, which furnished considerably greater detail than predecessor texts.[3] This in turn was superseded by *The Compleat Surveyor* by William Leybourn which appeared in 1653; this was written in a style that was readily comprehensible to the layman and consequently became very popular.[4]

It was not until 1688 that a surveying text was produced that was designed to meet the needs of men taking up land grants in the New World which they had to stake themselves. This was a work by John Love entitled *Geodaesia, or The Art of Surveying and Measuring of Land Made Easie.*[5] It was based on personal experience, for the author had served as a professional surveyor in North Carolina and Jamaica and understood the problems to be encountered and the type of information that was needed. He attempted to simplify the process of land surveying and recommended the chains devised by Aaron Rathborne and Edmund Gunter for the measurement of distances. For angle measurement he recommended that the colonial surveyor use the plane table, circumferentor, theodolite, and semi-circumferentor but provided cautions concerning their use under various conditions. For the densely wooded areas of the North American continent he recommended the circumferentor over other instruments. Love's work was widely used. At least eleven editions had been printed in England by 1792 and two editions were published in American cities shortly after that date.

The manner in which lands were distributed to the settlers in each plantation played an important role in the development of local surveying methods. The first colonists sponsored by the Virginia Company contracted to serve the Company for a period of five years. Upon emancipation each was entitled to one hundred acres of land within the colony to be chosen at will from land already reserved. If the tract so granted was developed by the addition of buildings or planting within three years, the owner could obtain a second grant of the same dimension, again with the proviso that it would be used within three years.

A different arrangement prevailed with those colonists who came to Virginia at their own expense. Each of these was allotted fifty acres, plus an equal amount for each member of his family traveling with him and for any other individual he imported at his own cost. These assignments were called "head rights." Each individual entitled to head rights made an affidavit of the facts upon which the claim was based; this statement was then examined, approved, and recorded and a warrant, or certificate, issued. The surveyor of the plantation or corporation of which the land was a part was required to survey and lay off the land, providing bounds either by natural boundaries or by marking trees on the lines of his courses. A copy of the survey map was returned with the certificate to the office of the Secretary of the province, and a patent was formally issued for the land. The patent was approved by the Governor and Council and recorded in the Secretary's office. When, as occurred frequently, the landholder was unable to plant the land within the specified period, he could apply for a new patent for the same land just before the expiration date.

The earliest grants were almost invariably situated on a watercourse. The surveyor ran a line from an obvious point along the margin of the watercourse for a distance in poles equal to one-half the number of acres in the grant. Using this as a base line, he ran another line of one statute mile (320 poles) from each terminal point inland at right angles, marking trees along it. The two terminals thus derived were connected and the course marked. Each succeeding survey was made in the same manner, so that the early surveys consisted of parallelograms fronted on the watercourse and extending inland one mile from the edge of the water.

This method was inexact and further subject to error because of the instruments used. According to an informed account: "The compass employed, at that day, was graduated as in a Mariner's Compass, the subdivisions of which extend only to a quarter of a point, or about 2°49′. Hence there must have been a constant source of error in the bearings of objects observed by such a compass, the mean of which errors could not be estimated at less than 1°25′, if measured by the surveyor's compass now in use [ca. 1849]. And the variation of the compass, if known to the old surveyors, was never noted by them in their surveys." [6]

In due course numerous disputes concerning the bounds arose, most of which could be traced to carelessness of the original surveyors. Further inaccuracies resulted from the need to have an object of a permanent nature to serve as a terminus for the lines drawn at right angles to the base line. When some condition of the terrain made this impossible or inconvenient, the surveyor might extend the line to the next permanent object in view. Although the line was generally represented on the survey drawing as one statute mile, it might in fact be shorter or longer. If forest growth or other features made it necessary to diverge from a straight line, this condition was not always recorded by the surveyor.

As the number of patents for great areas of land in the province of Virginia increased, it became necessary to provide some means of establishing definitive boundaries between them. Accordingly, in 1616 the Virginia Company detailed a surveyor from England to draw a plat of the lands to be distributed. This is the first known reference to a professionally trained surveyor in Virginia.[7] Richard Norwood, who later wrote the *Epitomie* as a text for surveyors, was considered for the position following his completion of a survey of the Somers Islands (the Bermudas), but instead William Claiborne was appointed in 1621.[8] After the abolition of the London Virginia Company, the position of Surveyor-General was created, the appointment to be made by the Solicitor-General in England. It was the Surveyor-General's responsibility to keep records of all surveys and to commission all surveyors in the province, and they in turn were required to report to him at Jamestown annually to have their books examined. Residence in the colony was not required of the Surveyor-General, and he customarily appointed a deputy living in the colony, but the delegation of authority led to problems. When a charter was granted to establish the College of William and Mary in 1692, it specified that the trustees of the College had the power to appoint surveyors in accordance with rules established for the Surveyor-General; if the trustees wished, they could delegate this authority. Candidates for the position of local surveyor were recommended by justices of the county courts, and a society of surveyors was formed at Jamestown to provide consultation in matters of dispute. In addition to appointed surveyors, leading landowners frequently served in that capacity.

After 1692 county surveyors were permitted to appoint deputies and all surveyors traditionally received their instructions from the Governor and the Council. A list of all surveys completed had to be submitted each April. The fee for surveyors was established at 20 pounds of tobacco for every 100 acres surveyed for tracts exceeding 500 acres in extent, or a total of 100 pounds if the area was smaller. The fee was modified by law in 1666 so that a surveyor could charge

40 pounds of tobacco for every 100 acres surveyed of areas more than 1,000 acres, or not over 400 pounds for areas that were less. Payment could be delayed until after the landowner had produced one crop of tobacco. The collection of surveyor's fees from the landholders was the function of the county sheriff.

Surveyors were required to return their plats to the office of the Secretary of the colony, and copies were filed in the office of the Surveyor-General. Eventually all plats were filed with the Secretary, and a clerk prepared the patent for the survey. It was signed by the Governor after presentation to the Council and then issued to the landowner. Throughout a long period in Virginia history the maintenance of survey records was haphazard at best and liable to considerable carelessness and neglect.[9] A number of laws were subsequently enacted to resolve the increasing number of disputes that emanated from inaccurate surveys, but even with the new laws problems remained.

One corrective measure was land processioning by view, which was first instituted in Virginia in October 1661. This was intended to define the limits of the parishes and was based on a traditional English practice held during Rogation Week with much ceremony and merriment. In Virginia, once every four years, all persons in each neighborhood were required to assemble at a given point and to march therefrom to examine and, if needed, renew terminal marks of all plantations in the area. The landholders were accompanied by two surveyors, who redrew the disputed lines when a disagreement arose between neighbors. Soon after processioning was instituted, the practice was enlarged to include personally owned lands as well as the limits of the parishes. At first the time of processioning was established to take place between Easter and Whitsuntide, but later in the century the time was moved to a period between September 7 and March 31. Heavy fines were levied on those who failed to participate. The purpose of the procedure was to settle the boundaries of the first half-century of Virginia colonization ". . . while men yet live that are acquainted with the first surveys, and while land is yet at a low[er] value, than it will be when time hath rooted out all knowledge to the bounds and added a greater value to the land." [10]

The land-processioning laws were reinforced several times within the next century. When the Church of England was disestablished in Virginia in 1785, the duty of processioning was transferred from the parish vestries to the overseers of the poor.[11]

Closely associated with the establishment of personal property boundaries was the construction of roads, one of the most difficult tasks faced by the colonists. The first roads laid out in any community were those connecting areas between which travel and transport of materials were most important: from the compound or village to the grist mill and the sawmill located on a river or stream perhaps several miles distant; to the wood lots set aside for each of the proprietors; to the river or ocean landing; to the meeting house which was the hub of community life; and to the meadows and pastures where livestock was kept and farming done. A sharp distinction was maintained between public thoroughfares and private roads. The latter were undertaken jointly by several neighbors and designed to serve their personal needs, often cut through unfenced private land. The use of private roads by others frequently caused problems with straying livestock and re-emphasized the importance of boundaries of private property. Such roads were sometimes "pent," or closed, by swinging gates at each end, erected by the owner at his own cost. Where there were no fences, the boundaries were marked by heavy brush or undergrowth adjoining the gates.

Roads had to be made wide enough to enable the passage of loaded wagons during harvesting of crops and for transporting goods to market and to the landings. Early roads were generally one rod (16.5 feet) in width. The removal of trees, stumps, and rocks after the underbrush had been cleared was a herculean task with the simple tools available. The numerous priorities of early settlement delayed the establishment of roadways, sometimes for decades, and they developed chiefly through travel until the settlers found them so difficult of passage that the community took a hand in their improvement.

Roads connecting communities with one another evolved in the same manner, haphazardly and slowly, and not until well into the eighteenth century did roadbuilding become a primary community concern. As late as 1704 the Boston Post Road connecting Boston and New York, two of the largest cities in the colonies, had its own particular problems despite the considerable use made of it.[12]

The laying out of public roads was a community responsibility, as was their continued maintenance. Although the specifics of laws related to roads varied from colony to colony, their general intent was much the same. The Connecticut law of 1643 specified that two surveyors be appointed in each town and empowered each year to call out all able-bodied men of the community between the ages of sixteen and sixty, with their teams of horses or oxen, for one day's labor on the town's roads. Anyone who failed to respond was subject to a penalty of 5 shillings, and in the early years no one was exempt. As the towns became established and the population increased, the law was relaxed and revised. In 1702 it excused "constant herdsmen and shepherds" and one miller from each grist mill. In 1762 the professional element of the community, including ministers, magistrates, physicians, ruling elders, commissioners, and schoolteachers, was exempted, and later it became necessary to exempt others as well. A later change of the law provided for the eligibility of slaves and servants in addition to Indians and mulattos to participate in road repair.

In 1679 the General Court of Connecticut designated roads leading from one plantation to another as "county roads" or "King's highways," and each town had to furnish labor for one day each year to clear them to the width of one rod.

Highways and roads, particularly those roads connecting counties, were equally subjects of concern in the middle and southern colonies. It was not until 1662, however, that the Virginia Assembly passed an act requiring the appointment of surveyors to establish a system of highways where such were lacking. Landholders were compelled to furnish labor from their plantations to establish and maintain public highways throughout the year.[13]

An unusual form of thoroughfare in Virginia and Maryland was the "rolling road." These roads were formed in a network that extended in all directions to connect tobacco plantations with one another and with landings in the river towns. The name "rolling road" was derived from the fact that hogsheads of tobacco served as their own means of transportation. Each of the containers had a pin, or gudgeon, fastened into each end, to which hoop shafts were attached and fastened to the collars of horses or oxen, which thus rolled the load from the plantation to the docks. Often a similar device was utilized to enable the hogsheads to be hauled by hand by slaves. In tobacco country these roads survived as the basis of the highway system.[14]

Quite distinct from the county surveyors in Virginia were the special commissioners appointed to run the boundary lines between counties and parishes, and sometimes between colonies. These men reported to the Assembly and were paid from quit-rents upon royal order; their warrants of payments were countersigned by the Lords of the Treasury and reviewed by the Governor.[15] Considerably more scientific skill was required of the commissioners than of the surveyors, and the surveying practices for establishing latitudes and longitudes had to be more sophisticated than before. The lack of such skills in the first century and a half of Virginia history is reflected in some of the provincial boundary disputes, such as the one between Virginia and North Carolina. After several abortive attempts to define the line, a joint commission again attempted a survey in 1710, only to discover that both sides lacked adequate instrumentation to perform it. Harry Beverley, one of the Virginia surveyors, owned a "Sea-Quadrant" which would have served the purpose, but Edward Moseley, a surveyor for North Carolina, claimed that it was defective and also sought to obstruct the commission in every other possible way. Later it was discovered that Moseley had secretly staked out claims of land in the area for himself, and the survey had to be abandoned for the time being. When it was next attempted, more problems ensued. Instruments owned by Moseley, which would have been acceptable for the project, did not arrive in time, and the Virginia surveyors suggested that they use a brass semi-circle which was available in the area. Moseley claimed that this was too small to take latitudes, and they finally resorted to Beverley's Sea-Quadrant for the purpose. It was cumbersome, being designed for use on shipboard.[16] One of the Virginia surveyors, Philip Ludwell, reported that, having arrived too late in the morning to begin the survey, "we had not time to fix ye quadrant to stand by it selfe, but we held it by hand rested by a stake of a fence, and standing on another stake; to this Mr. Moseley observed that it was liable to error and not so nice and certain as it ought to be (though it was more certain than an observation is taken at Sea where the Quadrant is held in hand and not rested)." [17] Attempts to establish the boundary continued and in 1713 Moseley and Beverley once again represented their respective provinces, this time using Beverley's brass semi-circle. The controversy over the boundary continued for some years.[18]

In the New England colonies at the time of settlement there was considerably less scientific capability than existed in the Virginia plantations. The English emigrants who first peopled Plymouth, the Massachusetts Bay Colony, and other settlements in New England came to the New World to seek religious freedom, to escape the government or the strictures of the motherland, and not as emissaries of the Crown as the first arrivals in Virginia had been. Collecting scientific data about the natives and flora and fauna of the region was not part of their mission as it had been at the Cittie of Raleigh and to a lesser degree at Jamestown. The only members of their parties having any scientific ability were the shipmasters who brought them to their destination. The capability for the pursuit of the practical sciences took much longer to develop in New England but in time it was achieved.

A contributing factor was the state of record keeping. For example, records of the Plymouth colony (in early records, Plimoth Plantation) were not formally maintained until 1632, more than a decade after the arrival of the Pilgrims. Prior to that date, records are fragmentary and incomplete. However, the very first entry made in the *Plimoths Great Book of Deeds*, in the handwriting of Governor William Bradford, relates to the division of land: "the meerstads and garden plotes of those which came first layd out 1620." The entry was followed by a listing of the lands allocated to the planters, entered in 1623, each noting approximate acreage but not the boundaries. The first record of a land sale which indicated boundaries was entered in 1627. It was concerned with the transfer of one acre from Philip Delano to Stephen Deane and noted that it was "bounded with the grounds of Moses Simmons on the north side and the said Stephen on the south side." No compass readings were noted, so it was presumably an approximate and arbitrary division. A land transfer recorded in 1630 was the first to include an indication of measure. It specified that the land extended "from yᵉ common passage by yᵉ Eele River side forty pole up into yᵉ land. . . ." [19] Even as late as 1699 the recorded land deeds of Plimoth Plantation did not provide accurate boundaries or dimensions, indicating that angle-measuring instruments had not been used. The measurement in terms of "poles" is of some significance, however, because it indicates that division was accomplished by means of a rod or pole of measured length and that the more sophisticated chain or line was not yet in use. An English work on surveying published in 1562 suggested that either a "rodde or lyne" could be employed for measuring land areas but advised that the latter was the quicker and more convenient method. [20] The origin of the "rod" or "pole" is derived from the name of the implement used. A wooden rod 16.5 feet in length was customarily used to measure distances on the ground, the length being as great as could be conveniently handled by an even moderately strong man.[21]

Shortly after the arrival of the colonists at Plymouth, the development of trade with other recently established settlements in the Massachusetts Bay Colony imposed upon them the need for greater agricultural production. This could be achieved only by making more land available, which was accomplished by the division of common lands for individual farming. In 1632 considerable acreage, consisting chiefly of land north of Plymouth, was distributed among the fifty-eight Purchasers, or original shareholders of the colony. The possibility of sharing in the new prosperity by enlarging their holdings led many of the settlers to move their homes to the new areas. This redistribution of land necessitated effective boundaries for the individual properties. Since there were neither trained surveyors nor appropriate instruments, the boundaries were run as well as possible with the rod, and terminal points were marked with mounds of rocks heaped around a stick projecting from the ground, on which the identity of the owner was marked. The mounds were placed at regular intervals at each angle of the divisions. The same procedures were followed in more important boundary surveys, such as the line between Plimoth Plantation and the Massachusetts Bay Colony, which was ordered by the General Court of the latter in 1640. Representatives of both colonies ran the course together but when they neared the termination, they discovered they had proceeded far south of the intended point. Instead of laying the line all over again, ". . . they made an angle and took a new course so far north to reach the true point." The area affected by this detour would have been part of Plimoth Plantation but was awarded to Massachusetts Bay instead; it included part of Mansfield and the towns of Norton and Wrentham.

When the General Courts of both colonies agreed in 1661 to make a new survey, they marked a black oak tree at the Neetmock River ". . . on four sides, viz., with an M. L. on the north side and a P. on the south side, and several letters under each of these, and on the east we set in figures the date of the present year." It was not until 1790 that the General Court of Massachusetts installed a permanent stone marker on the site of what had been traditionally known as the "Angle Tree." [22]

Although surveyors were lacking in early Plymouth, they were present and at work in Massachusetts Bay Colony at a relatively early period. In about 1624 the Massachusetts Bay Company initiated a fishing and trade enterprise at Cape Ann, and a fishing settlement was established by members of the colony. Among this group was Thomas Graves, who was described as being experienced not only in iron and salt works and mining but in surveying and fortification as well. His contract noted that he was skilled also in planning aqueducts and in drawing maps.[23] Another early surveyor was Captain John Sherman, who had settled in Watertown in 1636. He is believed to have worked as a surveyor in his native Dedham County in England and to have pursued this art in Watertown after his arrival. His personal property, inventoried after his death, included, in addition to books, ". . . instruments for surveying of land" valued at 5 pounds. Since a gun among his possessions was listed at 28 shillings, the comparison provided some indication of the scarcity of surveying instruments.[24]

Inventories of estates frequently serve as records of such instrumentation as existed in the early days of the first colonies. The inventory made of the properties of William Palmer the Younger of Duxbury in 1636 noted "1 Compasse dyal," while that of William Kempe of the same community, deceased in 1641, noted an "iron acar staff," which may have been a measuring rod or a jacob staff.[25] John Butcher, a distiller of Roxbury, upon his death in 1699, owned "Surveying bookes and old Surveying Instruments." [26]

Records of surveys in the late seventeenth century in Massachusetts were not always specific in identifying the instruments used, but Samuel Sewall noted the use of the plane table in a survey made in 1687 at Muddy River.[27]

Although professional surveys with appropriate procedures and instruments were not made in the New England colonies during the first part of the seventeenth century, the individuals responsible for laying out the land were known by professional titles. At Plimoth Plantation during the land division of 1627 the name used was "layers-out"; the term "surveighers" was also used but less frequently. Another title was "artist," a term derived from the fact that in the seventeenth century surveying was always described as "the art of surveying"; consequently anyone who practiced it was an "artist." An early use of the term occurred in the court records of Hampton, Massachusetts, for the new town of Salisbury, which on October 8, 1668, sued for trespass. The complaint entered was "for coming on their land and with several others of Haverhill and two men called *artists* ran a line, marked trees, heaped stones and so set a new bound mark between themselves and Haverhill."[28] The term appeared again with reference to the line established in 1642 between Massachusetts and Connecticut, which Massachusetts claimed was nearly if not entirely correct, because ". . . artists alike skilful may differ in a point or some minute thing but it is very improbable and unlikely the difference can be so great [as claimed by Connecticut]."[29]

An early known use of the term "surveyor" in Massachusetts was its application in 1674 to Jonathan Danforth of Essex County in relation to his work in that capacity in Newbury. He was mentioned on several later occasions as having made surveys also for various towns in that county.[30] In New England the position of surveyor was almost never a full-time occupation, and those so engaged usually pursued other endeavors, making surveys as the need arose. One of the earliest surveyors of record in Massachusetts was Joseph Lamson of Ipswich, a skilled stonecutter who cut gravestones in and around Boston during the late seventeenth century and also worked as a cordwainer and mariner.[31]

The earliest surveyor of record in the Connecticut colony was John Brockett who had migrated to Quinnipack in 1638. He had learned the rudiments of surveying in London, and soon after his arrival he laid out with impressive accuracy the original nine squares which later became the center of New Haven. He went on to lay out the Neck, or Fair Haven, and later worked as far west as New Milford and farther north and east. The surveyor occasionally found himself in the center of a conflict between property owners and frequently the target of both opponents. When in 1658 Brockett was called to Malbon's Cove to resolve such a dispute, one of the contestants was advised by the magistrate ". . . not to hinder the surveyor in his work when he came, but let him goe on quietly, and if his field that is fenced in falls out of ye line, it should be considered after; yet notwithstanding he hindered them, and when they set downe their sticks he pulled them up and threw them away and would not suffer them to go on, saying unless they bound him hand and foote and caryed him to prison, he would hinder. . . ."[32]

In New England a distinction was clearly made between the surveyor, who measured and laid out the land, and the "mathematician," who was a man of science capable of using mathematical instruments. John Harriman of New Haven was employed by the colonial government in 1647 as a "mathematician" to take the latitudes of points along the boundary between Massachusetts and Connecticut.[33] Several decades later, this title was applied in Massachusetts Bay Colony to James Halsey, the earliest known maker of mathematical instruments in the colonies.

County surveyors as distinct from local surveyors were first mentioned in New England public records in Connecticut for May 1700, at which time the General Assembly ordered and enacted that ". . . there shall be and is hereby appointed one person in each countie within this Colonie to be a Publick Surveyour for laying out of lands and for renewing the bounds of lands already laid out according to their originall grants as need shall require; who shall be sufficiently skilled in the surveyors art, and at his own charge furnisht with instruments suitable and sufficient for that service; who shall take the surveyors oath in that case provided."

The act then went on to define "the surveyors oath," which was formulated and prescribed for all who undertook the career of surveyor in public service and was continued in use until at least the middle of the eighteenth century. It required that: "You A. B. doe swear by the great name of ye living God that you shall faithfully attend to and discharge your office of Surveyor unto which you are appointed without favour or respect to persons." [34] A separate oath was required for the chainmen, which specified that: "You A. B. and C. D. Being desired to assist E. C.—Surveyer; in Carying the Chain, Do Swear by the Everliving God that you will faithfully assist the said Surveyer in his servis and that you will keep a true account of all Lines on measures by you taken and the same give up to said Surveyer at his desire according to your best Skill and ability. So help you God." A similar oath for chainmen was required in the province of Virginia in the seventeenth century. The use of such oaths was undoubtedly part of English surveying practice imported to the colonies.

Once the appointment of county surveyors had been established, the arrangement was apparently successful and was continued; it was subsequently supplemented by the General Assembly to exempt them from service in the militia.[35]

The art of the surveyor was only as professional as his practices and his instruments enabled it to be. Love's *Geodaesia* provided procedures which would be useful in the conditions encountered in the colonies, but the instruments available in England for surveying were not always adaptable. The one most commonly used was the plane table, which served the surveyor as well as the cartographer. The theodolite was already in use in England by the time the American colonies were established but it was not practical in the American forests.

The instrument upon which colonial surveyors chiefly relied was the "circumferentor," an instrument which was renamed the "plain surveying compass" or the "common compass" when used in the colonies. Extremely simple in design, it proved to be readily useful for taking bearings from one survey station to another, and furthermore it was relatively simple for colonial craftsmen to produce. In England, where the land was relatively open, this instrument was not much used, but according to the English instrument maker George Adams, writing in the late eighteenth century, ". . . in America where land is not so dear, and where it is necessary to survey large tracts overstocked with wood in a minimum time, and where the surveyor must take a multitude of angles, in which the sights of the two lines forming the angle may be hindered by underwood, the circumferentor is chiefly used." [36] Another instrument which also proved useful was the "semi-circle," or "semi-circumferentor," which was similar except that the scale was reduced to one-half of the full circle. [37]

As English colonies became firmly established in New England, the English Crown decided to create a series of plantations along the North American seacoast to form an Anglo-American frontier. It was hoped to accomplish this by publicizing the riches of the new regions and the unusual opportunities available to prospective investors and emigrants in England. Tracts, broadsides, and other forms of promotional material were published and widely distributed to advance the movement to the New World. English geographers contributed atlases and geographical publications and descriptive accounts of the new plantations. Despite the prevalence of these materials, the attempts to entice settlers encountered considerable difficulty. Among those who experienced this problem was Lord Baltimore, who undertook to overcome it by developing his own advertising. A pamphlet which he published in London in 1635 included a map of his colony, based on John Smith's map and produced by an unknown cartographer. [38] It incorporated many errors which were to have far-reaching results. A large section of the former Prince William County of Virginia was shown as part of

Maryland, and the main stream and source of the Potomac River were incorrectly located. These errors led to serious conflicts within the next several decades and propagated other misrepresentations in later maps.

Among those led into erroneous ways of depicting the colonies were John Ferrar, who had formerly served as Deputy Treasurer of the Virginia Company, and his daughter, Virginia. After moving from London, father and daughter became involved in the culture of silkworms with the intention of establishing the industry in Virginia. As part of their enterprise they compiled a tract about the colony of Virginia and included in it a map which showed the same distortion of the Potomac River that had appeared on Smith's map and on the one produced for Lord Baltimore.[39] "The happy Shoers" of Drake's New Albion (now California) were placed "in ten dayes march with 50. foote and 30. horsmen from the head of Jeames River." The "Sea of China and the Indies" were situated approximately in the location of the Allegheny Mountains.

In addition to the self-taught cartographers who worked in the early colonies, professional map makers began to appear on the scene. Among these was John Lederer, a young German medical student interested in the American Indians and the native resources of Virginia. He had emigrated to the colony at a time when its governor, William Berkeley, had become greatly interested in exploring the region beyond the tidewater settlements. With Berkeley's support, Lederer embarked on a voyage to find a way through the Appalachian Mountains, but his first venture was of short duration. Having been unable to find a passage through the Blue Ridge Mountains northwest of the present site of Charlottesville, he turned back. During the months that followed he made several more forays and was the first European to explore the Piedmont and the Blue Ridge and to leave an account of his work in addition to making a map.[40]

One of Lederer's party on his last expedition was Colonel John Catlett, well known in his time as a mathematician and surveyor. A report made to the Royal Society by the surgeon on the expedition, Thomas Glover, noted that ". . . one Colonel Catlet that was a good Mathematician, . . . with some other Gentlemen took a Journey to make some further discoveries of the Country to the Westward. . . ."[41]

Although Lederer's map was severely criticized in his own time for its obvious errors, it was nonetheless widely circulated by the

Lords Proprietors of the Carolinas to advertise their recently acquired province to prospective settlers. John Ogilby, cartographer to King Charles II, incorporated material from Lederer's map in one he prepared for the Carolina Proprietors, and other maps followed in short order which utilized the same material.[42] Ten years later a second map sponsored by the Lords Proprietors was produced by Joel Gascoyne, and errors made by Lederer were discovered and eliminated before publication.[43]

The next major contribution was by a Bohemian emigrant to New Netherlands named Augustine Herrman. An accomplished draftsman and a skilled surveyor, who had extensive military experience in his native land, Herrman was chosen by Peter Stuyvesant as his emissary to negotiate a treaty with Lord Baltimore, who was laying claim to Dutch possessions in Delaware. In the course of this mission Herrman became interested in the region and suggested to Stuyvesant that a map should be made to an exact scale with latitude and longitude of the South (Delaware) River and the Virginias with the land between the two. Stuyvesant was not interested in the proposal, and several months later Herrman made application to become a denizen of Maryland in order to own property in that province. He was accepted partly because, during his mission on behalf of Stuyvesant in 1659, he had "drawne a Mapp of all the Rivers Creekes and Harbours thereunto belonging." Developing the preliminary surveys made during his first visit, he further explored the shores of Chesapeake Bay in considerable detail and then spent several years in preparing a detailed map which was published in London in 1673.[44]

Herrman's map was an ambitious project, consisting of a land map of the colonies of Maryland and Virginia, in which he also included southern Pennsylvania, southern New Jersey, Delaware Bay, Chesapeake Bay, part of the Delaware River, and its tributaries. The shoals and channels of the Delaware Bay were delineated in extensive detail, an extremely useful feature since the bay had considerable local and foreign traffic and was a waterway of prime importance. Herrman's map extended from the fortieth parallel which ran through the city of Philadelphia, into North Carolina, and westward to near the source of the main rivers. Chesapeake Bay, its coastline, rivers and tributaries, hills and mountains, were featured, and the map also noted the location of Indian villages, plantations, settlements, with soundings for bays and harbors. Full ten years of travel and mapping through regions not yet inhabited were required to complete it and at considerable personal cost. It was one of the major cartographic achievements of its time and was extensively used by later map makers and figured prominently in the solution of boundary differences.[45] Between 1673 and 1752 at least eight adaptations or versions of it were produced in England and France.[46]

As new colonies emerged along the American coast, the need for maps increased and efforts were made in other areas to produce useful ones. A map of New Sweden, delineated in considerable detail with soundings of the Delaware Bay and River and reasonably accurate calculations of latitude and longitude, was compiled in 1654–1655 by a Swedish engineer, Peter Martensson Lindeström, on an expedition through the region made by boat and on horseback.[47]

The first map of New Jersey was compiled in England by John Seller, the Royal Hydrographer, who did not visit the region but based his map on existing sources. It represented the province as it appeared in 1674 and was the first map to show the names "New Jersey" and "New York." [48] In 1677, William Penn, who was Proprietor of New Jersey for four years before he received the Pennsylvania grant,[49] issued a promotional tract to encourage colonists to the province of New Jersey. The tract, which was produced by John Seller and William Fisher, contained a map depicting all of New Jersey from the Delaware Bay to the east coast, as well as part of Long Island and New York. A map of part of New Jersey, drawn and printed in 1688 by John Reid and engraved in London, depicted the extent of settlement of the provinces of East and West Jersey.[50]

Other early maps of the province included one compiled by John Worlidge of Salem, West Jersey, prior to 1698 and published in London in 1699 and the first authorized map of Burlington township, produced in 1696 by Daniel Leeds, a prominent almanac maker.[51]

Meanwhile Penn had received his grant for the lands in the region he named Pennsylvania, and among his first acts was the appointment of a surveyor-general. Captain Thomas Holme, the first to assume the position, produced two important maps, one of Philadelphia and another of the whole province. Although a man of considerable military experience and well equipped as a cartographer, Holme did not orient either of his maps, and the topography delineated left much to be desired.[52]

For the most part land maps and nautical charts of the British colonies were engraved and printed in England even when they had been drawn and compiled in the New World. The first map known to have been produced entirely in America was a map of New England compiled, drawn, engraved, and printed at Boston by John Foster in 1677. It was published as part of an account of King Philip's War by William Hubbard and may have been engraved from a drawing made by Hubbard. It was widely known as the "White Hills Map" because one of its topographical features, the White Mountains, was so designated.[53] Another version, known as the "Wine Hills Map," which is considered to be earlier, was prepared and published in London to illustrate the English edition of Hubbard's work in the same year. Foster developed his own series of conventional signs, using turreted buildings to mark settlements and decorating open areas with trees, wild life, hunters, and ships. The map was oriented to the west at the top. Foster, the son of the town brewer, graduated from Harvard College in 1667, established himself as a printer in Boston, and achieved note as an engraver. It was most unusual for a member of his social class and a Harvard graduate to pursue the crafts.[54]

Other maps of the colonies were produced from time to time in support of special projects or proposals. One such was a plan for opening an Indian route across the Virginia mountains, which was submitted to the colonial government by Cadwalader Jones, an important landholder and Indian trader. He proposed to establish a route from the falls of the Rappahannock River to the Great Lakes, based on explorations he had made in 1682 along the Great Fork of the Rappahannock as far as the Shenandoah below the Blue Ridge gap. In support of his proposal he submitted a map on which he had sketched the courses of the Rappahannock, Potomac, York, James, Appomattox, and Roanoke rivers and their branches.[55]

Charts of American coastal waters were badly needed for development of trade. The printed English and French charts that were available were less than adequate, and colonial navigators were forced to develop their own sailing directions and supplementary nautical data. In time they provided some of the most essential nautical charts. There had always been particular concern for the mapping and remapping of the Chesapeake Bay region because of its importance for trade. The first exclusively nautical chart of the bay region was produced in 1695 by two English hydrographers, John Thornton and William Fisher, published in *The English Pilot* of 1706, and reissued in its later editions.[56] The chart was based on data taken for the most part from Herrman's map.

Mapping activities were particularly encouraged in the Massachusetts Bay Colony. In the summer of 1665 William Reed of Boston was assigned by the General Court "together with some other gentlemen of the Court, to draw up an exact mapp of his majesties colonie of the Massachusetts." [57] Several decades later Philip Wells of Boston was earning his living as a map maker in New York in the service of Governor Thomas Dongan and also surveying private grants and holdings in the region. In 1684 he was assigned to make a map of Staten Island, and in the same year he served as one of the commissioners designated to run the line between New York and Connecticut. Among his achievements for the maritime community was "A sand draught of New-York Harbour," in which he delineated shoals, flats, bars, and some soundings. Later he was assigned by Governor Edmund Andros of Massachusetts to compile similar data about Boston harbor, which he executed in a manuscript chart.

The early endeavors were supplemented by the work of English military and naval officers stationed in the colonies. These men were primarily responsible for the military maps of the colonies used by the British during the Revolutionary War. Among the earliest of them was Colonel Wolfgang William Romer, a military engineer trained in the service of William of Orange, who arrived in New York in 1697 as the chief engineer to Lord Bellomont. His surveying assignments took him on many trips inland as well as along the New England coast and he became very familiar with the entire region. He also designed fortifications for seaport towns until 1706 when his tour of duty ended and he returned to England.

Another skilled British surveyor and cartographer was Captain John Bonner, who produced a detailed map of Boston in 1722. He was described at the time of his death in 1726 as ". . . a Gentleman very Skillful and Ingenious in many Arts and Sciences; especially in Navigation, Drawing, Moulding of Ships, &c. One of the best acquainted with the coasts of North America, of any of his time; of great Knowledge and Judgement in Marine affairs; was very much consulted, improved, and relied upon by the Government as a Principal Pilate, in our Marine Expeditions." [58] Bonner's map was published in cooperation with its engraver, Thomas Dewing, and the printer William Price. The latter retained the plate for more than forty years and with the assistance of another engraver, Thomas Johnston, reissued the map with alterations in at least five editions.

IV

DARK
HEMISPHERE

It comes! at last, the promis'd ÆRA comes!
Now *Gospel-Truth* shall dissipate the Glooms
Of Pagan-Error; and, in copious Streams,
O'er this dark *Hemisphere*, shed *saving Beams!*
For, lo! her azure Wing bright SCIENCE spreads,
And soft-approaches to these new-found-Shades . . .

> William Smith, *A general idea of
> the college of Mirania . . .* (1753)

IN CONTRAST TO THE self-taught men who struggled against the
forces of nature in the wilderness or on the sea, others in the colonies
pursued scientific endeavors indoors, as amateurs indulging personal
interests or less frequently on specific paid assignments. These amateurs are best characterized as the philomaths. Their numbers included professors teaching science in the early colleges, amateur astronomers also engaged in productive occupations, teachers who
supplemented their incomes by calculating ephemerides for al-

manacs, and collectors of natural and artificial curiosities for scientific study. Their activities were for the most part self-generated, and the modest fruits of their individual preoccupations occasionally combined to produce a significant achievement. The colonial American philomaths were chiefly led into scientific endeavors by the same motivation that also operated in Europe and England—consuming curiosity about the world around them.

In the Old World, however, the impetus for scientific activity had additional sources in the patronage of princes and prelates and wealthy amateurs, the needs of major figures in science for practical assistance from craftsmen, and finally the concerns of those who recognized the value of the sciences in furthering the aims of empire.

In the American colonies until the late seventeenth century there were few who had sufficient leisure to concern themselves with scientific endeavors not required by their daily activities. Then the first men of science began to emerge and to make contributions to knowledge. During this period also an occasional wealthy landowner or shipping merchant demonstrated his prosperity by acquiring a modest library and scientific apparatus or made the public gesture of donating such materials, or funds to purchase them, as a well-acknowledged gift to one of the early colleges. Such men, however, rarely became concerned with the sciences on their own behalf. For the most part the sciences remained a preoccupation of those having a little more education than was usual, such as the ministers and the schoolteachers and a few men of public position. To their numbers were added members of college faculties and some of the college graduates, who made occasional contributions of value. These teachers of "natural philosophy," by which term the physical sciences were then distinguished, were the aristocrats among the American practitioners, and to their numbers might be added the occasional experimental scientist of major proportion who emerged in the New World or found his way there. These philomaths were more concerned than were those who pursued the practical sciences with the natural phenomena which could hurt or serve their world, and the more curious and learned among them made collections of artifacts of nature and of other civilizations, assembled data concerning meteorological and other phenomena, and studied flora and fauna. Emphasis was frequently placed upon those natural elements which could be made to serve mankind.

"Natural philosophy"—which included all the physical sciences, astronomy, geology, meteorology, and mathematics—remained the preoccupation of a relatively small number of colonial Americans almost to the end of the eighteenth century; these subjects did not achieve a wider interest until popular lectures and the development of school curricula brought them to more general attention. The men who pursued the theoretical or pure sciences could seldom be truly identified as "scientists," because they rarely either had professional training or derived their income from these endeavors. Benjamin Franklin, although he lacked professional training, did not derive his income from science, and was concerned primarily with its utilitarian aspects rather than with the discipline, nevertheless deserved the title. Franklin's scientific involvement and his attitude toward the sciences were best described in his own words; in a letter to William Douglass written in 1752, he commented that ". . . business sometimes obliges me to postpone philosophical amusements. Whatever I have wrote of that kind are really as they are entitled, *Conjectures and Suppositions;* which ought always to give place, when careful observation militates against them. I own I have too strong a *penchant* to the building of hypotheses; they indulge my natural indolence. I wish I had more of your patience and accuracy in making observations, on which alone true philosophy can be founded." [1]

Among the first colonial Americans to turn their attention to science during the seventeenth century were the small number who became correspondents of the Royal Society of London. The Society had expressed considerable interest in England's overseas colonies, and early in its history it had established a Committee for Foreign Correspondence which circulated a series of "Enquiries for Foreign Parts" to members in the major countries of Europe and in the Americas as well. Support of the Society's interests was provided by English Secretaries of State who enabled its correspondence to be carried without charge on vessels of English trading companies.

Three American colonists in the seventeenth century became Fellows of the Society, the greatest scientific honor to be achieved on either side of the Atlantic in that period. Between 1663, when the Society was chartered, and 1783, when the British colonies in North America became the United States, fifty-three American Fellows of the Society had been elected. Although a few were chosen by virtue of their positions as governors of provinces, most of the American Fellows were elected on the basis of their scientific endeavors. As the Society's influence in the development of the sciences increased, its interest in the growing British colonies in North America expanded, and any colonist having legitimate scientific and technological interests, knowledge, or competence was encouraged to become a correspondent of the Society. Not only did the colonial members find themselves warmly welcomed when they visited London, but the Society attempted to provide assistance to them by furnishing published works, scientific instruments, and occasionally even funds for their pursuits. For colonial American members, however, membership in the Society was clearly an exchange, in which practical contributions were repaid by honors. Members were expected to promote scientific interests among other men of education in the New World, for the increase and diffusion of knowledge. This was clearly reflected in the Society's mandate issued in 1661 to its first American member, John Winthrop, Jr., when he was invited to become "the chief Correspondent of the Royal Society in the West." "You will please to remember," he was advised, "that we have taken to taske the whole Universe, and that we were obliged to do so by the nature of our Dessein. It will therefore be requisite that we purchase and entertain a commerce in all parts of the world with the most philosophicall and curious persons to be found everywhere." [2]

It is eminently clear that the Society's efforts, through its colonial members, were in fact a continuation of England's original aim in establishing plantations in the New World. The English were anxious to collect as much data as possible concerning their colonial possessions in order to determine the nature and extent of the natural resources and prospective products which would serve the motherland. The Society's shadow was shed fairly evenly over the colonies in the beginning, for nine of the first Fellows were elected from the Massachusetts Bay Colony, one each from Connecticut and Rhode Island, three each from Virginia and Pennsylvania, and one from the Carolinas.

John Winthrop, Jr., who was the oldest son of the first governor of Massachusetts Bay Colony, had trained for a career in law and had demonstrated at the same time considerable knowledge of the applied sciences. He had the distinction of being the first metallurgist and the first chemist in the New World and was proposed for membership in the Society in 1661, during his third visit to London. While in England he associated with many of the foremost English men of science. He brought home with him the first telescope owned in the New World, a small refracting instrument "3 foote and halfe with a concave ey-glasse" with which he subsequently made astronomical observations. With it he discovered, at Hartford on August 6, 1664, a fifth satellite of Jupiter. He reported the discovery to the Royal Society and it became the subject of considerable scientific discussion in the years that followed.[3] His observations were taken seriously by his English peers and he had their respect. He presented his telescope and its attachments to Harvard College in 1672; it was the first such instrument owned by that body of learning.[4]

Winthrop was an enthusiastic supporter of the Society's colonial efforts and on his visits to England he attended its meetings and brought interesting materials from America to show his fellow members. Among these were a self-feeding time lamp and samples of woods and of minerals, including lead, amethysts, and garnets, from New England. He subsequently presented a paper on the process of making pitch and tar, which was received with considerable interest. During this period he became involved with England's concern over the shortage of native timber for shipbuilding, and in a series of proposals presented to the Society in 1662 he called attention to the great forest resources in New England for this purpose. As he planned his return to New England, he asked the Society for a copy of its "Directions for Sea-men, bound for far Voyages," and for sounding leads and other apparatus so that he could attempt the experiments and observations on his return voyage. He did attempt them but they were unsuccessful.[5]

After his return Winthrop continued his association with the Society as eagerly as before and his contributions encompassed a wide range of subject matter, including a study on Indian corn, a report on beer brewed from corn bread, and various astronomical observations. His own endeavors ranged from salt making and exploring for new ores to observation of the tides. In 1669 he shipped to the Society four boxes of specimens, in which he included publications and reports, and followed this with a second shipment in the following year. One of the most popular exhibits Winthrop furnished to the Society was a starfish from American waters.

Winthrop's successor in his work in astronomy was Thomas Brattle, also a member of the Royal Society and a successful Boston merchant. Graduated from Harvard in 1676 with a degree of master of science, he published an almanac for the year 1678 and later made observations of the comet of 1680, using Winthrop's telescope. His observations were reported to the Royal Society and acknowledged by Isaac Newton in his *Principia*, although Brattle was not identified by name.[6]

During this period Harvard's lean store of scientific apparatus was supplemented with a "Brass Quadrant . . . with Tellescopick Sights" reported to have been ". . . the very same Dr. Halley used at St. Helena." In 1676 the English astronomer Edmond Halley, who was then twenty years of age, spent some time on the island of St. Helena preparing a catalogue of the stars of the Southern Hemisphere, a project requiring two years to complete.[7] The brass quadrant was part of his equipment, and how it may have been acquired by Harvard still remains a matter of speculation. It was more than a decade after the College's acquisition of the quadrant that Halley surveyed the harbor of Boston while making his return journey from St. Helena in the pink *Paramour*.[8] Halley's quadrant was used by Brattle on June 12, 1694, for observing a solar eclipse, which he subsequently reported to the Royal Society. By means of these observations Brattle hoped to determine the exact longitude of Boston, and by comparing his observations with those made at London, he determined the longitude to be 4 hours 43 minutes, or 70° 45' west of London, using an assumed latitude of 42° 25'. As was later determined, this value was only about 15 minutes short of the correct longitude, an amazing feat for that period.[9]

Brattle's records provide some of the earliest accounts of the use of astronomical instruments in the colonies. Early in 1700, for instance, he reported his observation of a lunar eclipse by means of a universal ring dial, which he used to adjust his clock, and a "4½ Foot Telescope, with all four Glasses in it."[10] He also submitted a report on his determination on April 5, 1707, of the variation of the magnetic needle at Boston, which he established to be 9 degrees west of north. His was the earliest-known precise observation of magnetic variation in the New World, a contribution of considerable significance because it established that the needle had returned to the position it had held two centuries before, proving that the variation is periodical.[11]

Also honored by membership in the Royal Society was Thomas Brattle's younger brother, William Brattle, who became a tutor at Harvard after graduation and produced an astronomical almanac for the year 1682. He published what was considered to have been the first book on logic, but this was in fact a re-issue of René Descartes' *Compendium Logicae*.

Another influential figure was Cotton Mather, who was elected to the Society in 1712. Consistent with his profession as a clergyman and with the mood of his times, he attempted to imbue the interest in and the achievements of science with religious significance, reflecting the derivation of much of his information from works on natural theology. His endeavors to promote inoculation against smallpox and his meteorological observations justified his membership in the Society.[12]

Other Royal Society members from Massachusetts were John Leverett, president of Harvard College; Paul Dudley, who submitted compilations on weather and earthquakes, an account of the Falls of Niagara, and various other matters; Zabdiel Boylston, a physician; and another John Winthrop, a grandson of John Winthrop, Jr.

The first fellows elected from other colonies were William Byrd II of Virginia, who was concerned with the flora and fauna of his region; John Mitchell, also from Virginia and a botanist and cartographer; and Benjamin Franklin of Pennsylvania.[13]

The presence at Harvard College in the early period of men of science who were concerned with mathematics and astronomy, and the continuity at the college of a program of related scientific endeavor, were to exert considerable influence on the evolution of the almanac in the colonies during the next century. Almanacs, which have been styled the first scientific journals published in America, became an academic project at Harvard, and the greater number of the almanacs produced in Massachusetts during the seventeenth century were by Harvard tutors preparing for an advanced degree. Of the known forty-four almanacs issued in Massachusetts before 1687, forty-one were the work of twenty-six Harvard graduates, of whom ten were teaching at the college at the time of their production. In almost all instances, these almanacs were published during the period of three years of graduate study, and it is plausible to assume that the work may have been part of the postgraduate course.

As Cotton Mather noted in 1683 about the almanac, "Such an anniversary composure comes into almost as many hands as the best of books." [14] The almanac has had an impressive history, tracing its origins to fourteenth-century Europe. Its primary components were a calendar of the months, which frequently identified days of historical and religious importance, feasts, and holidays; a listing of the dates of eclipses of the sun and moon; the times of rising and setting of the sun, moon, and certain stars; and data for the regulation of sundials at noon. Weather prognostication was occasionally included. The ephemeris, which provided the astronomical data, required knowledge of mathematics and astronomy for its preparation.

The words "almanac" and "ephemeris" were far more familiar to the American colonist than they are to the public today. The word "almanac" is believed to have been derived from "Almonaugh" or "Heed of all the Moons." William Brattle, in his almanac for 1682, described an ephemeris as "A Day-book, wherein the heavenly-minded Ephemeridist does keep an account of the Coelestial Motions."

From at least the sixteenth century, many almanacs incorporated a drawing of "the moon man" or "the man of the signs," which illustrated the influence of each of the twelve signs of the zodiac on specific parts of man's body. In order to treat an ailment of a certain part, it was necessary to know whether the moon was in that particular sign at the time of the ailment. The diagram was a graphic summary of astrological medicine as it prevailed at various points in history.[15]

The earliest American almanacs followed the format of their English counterparts and were frequently published as a single sheet providing the most essential information compiled in the ephemeris. Later this sheet was expanded into a pamphlet with a varying number of pages, which included other information presumed to be useful to a household. The scientific data was usually combined with theological and literary content. During the colonial period the emphasis was strongly theological; in the eighteenth century literary and educational materials assumed greater importance; and in the nineteenth the almanacs reflected political and specialized public interests.

Following the first colonial American almanac by Captain William Pierce (1639), already mentioned, came the series produced by Samuel Danforth, a Harvard tutor, for the years 1646 through 1649. Danforth became a minister but his interest in astronomy never diminished and he frequently noted meteorological and astronomical data with his records of births, marriages, and deaths. He viewed celestial phenomena in relation to his theological teachings. His treatise on the comet, published in his almanac for 1649, was praised by Cotton Mather because the author ". . . improves the opinion of a comet's being *portentous*, endeavouring, as it becomes a devout preacher, to awaken mankind by the portent, out of a sinful security." [16] Danforth emphasized his view of the importance and significance of comets and other celestial phenomena and attempted to provide evidence that comets moved in accordance with mathematical laws and that furthermore "comets are portentous signals of great notable changes . . . they have been many times heralds of wrath to a secure and impenitent world"—attributes which were reflected in several passages of "Compendium Physicae" by Charles Morton, a Charlestown minister, a work which had considerable influence on Harvard students during the late seventeenth and early eighteenth centuries. [17]

The concern with comets is reflected in a short account in the almanac for 1665 by Alexander Nowell, a Harvard tutor. When Halley's comet appeared in 1682, it provided Increase Mather (the father of Cotton Mather and also a clergyman) with the occasion to publish a discourse inquiring into the nature of "blazing stars," in which he presented evidence that they were portents of destruction. [18]

Another forewarning of divine displeasure which concerned the colonists, although it was not generally discussed in the almanacs, was the occurrence of "dark days" from time to time in New England. On these occasions the sky was pervaded by an increasing gloom which as the day progressed became so intense that artificial light was required, and the situation lasted for several days. The smell of smoke was prevalent and the imagination detected the odor of brimstone, as a portent that doom for sinners was imminent. It is now known that this phenomenon was caused by smoke from great forest fires occurring in the region that is now New York State and Canada. New England is believed to have constituted a meeting point for air currents from many parts of the country, and when such currents ran counter to opposing storms from the east or the northeast, smoke-laden air was banked to the degree that daylight was obscured. Notable among these dark days were May 12, 1706; October 21, 1716; August 9, 1732; and May 19, 1780. [19]

Social as well as physical phenomena were used as springboards for moralizing in early almanacs. In his almanac for 1676 the Reverend John Sherman included some comments on the state of moral degeneracy in New England and in that for the following year a sermon on the proper use of time for the good of eternity, which was followed by a description of calendar systems.

In almanacs produced in Massachusetts during the seventeenth century the first month of the year was March, a practice which prevailed in England until the Gregorian calendar was officially adopted in 1752. The laws of the Commonwealth of Massachusetts confirmed the practice in that colony, but it was not recognized in almanacs produced in other colonies during the same period, in which January was the first month listed. In his *Scripture Kalendar* for London for 1660 Henry Jessey noted that "The New England almanac sets them [the names of the month and day] down thus—the first month, the second month, &c. And such is the example of all the reformed churches in New England, and of some in London." On March 11, 1752, the English Parliament enacted legislation specifying that, whereas heretofore the year of our Lord began on the 25th day of March, after the last day of December 1751 the first day of January following that last day of December ". . . should be reckoned, taken, deemed, and accounted, and to be the first Day of the Year of our Lord, 1752, and that the practice was to continue thereafter and that January was to be constituted the first month instead of March." [20] Thereafter the "New Style" replaced the "Old Style" in England and its possessions.

Several of the earlier Massachusetts almanac makers emerged as important figures in science, chiefly as a result of their other science-oriented activities. Notable among them was Thomas Robie, who later practiced medicine. While a tutor at Harvard he compiled ephemerides for a series of almanacs which appeared annually with the title *An Ephemeris of the Coelestial Motions* and in which he included occasional essays on scientific matters. Among these were explanations of natural phenomena, including thunder, lightning, and hail; an account of the solar system; the sizes and distances of the sun and planets; and separate treatises on the Aurora Borealis and on chemical subjects. Because of Robie's interest in astronomy, considerable scientific apparatus was acquired by Harvard for the development of an observatory. [21]

Deserving special notice is John Foster, another Harvard graduate, who became the first printer in Boston and has already been mentioned as the maker of the first map wholly produced in America. Foster compiled the almanacs that he printed between the years 1675 and 1681. In the issue for 1675 he included an extensive account of the Pythagorean concept of the universe and developed arguments favoring the Copernican system, which had then only recently been proposed, in preference to the generally accepted Ptolemaic theory. His almanac for the following year provided two pages for each month and included a detailed discussion of weather signs. That for 1678 described the occurrence of eclipses and contained the first woodcut of "the man of the signs" to appear in an American almanac. In subsequent issues he also used woodcuts of elaborate astronomical diagrams and devoted attention to the tides, descriptions of the planets, and essays on comets, which he also described as ominous portents. Distinguished as a printer-engraver, chemist, almanac maker, and carver, Foster also studied and dabbled in medicine at a time when there were no professionally trained physicians in the colonies. His elaborate gravestone, which he ordered before his death, carried a couplet by Increase Mather and Foster's reply in a second couplet in Latin, which read, in translation:

Living thou studiest the stars; dying mayst thou, Foster, I pray,
  mount above the skies, and learn to measure the highest heaven.

I measure it, and it is mine; the Lord Jesus has bought it for me; nor
  am I held to pay aught for it but thanks.[22]

A preoccupation with astrology, which prevailed in New England throughout the seventeenth and early eighteenth centuries, was strongly reflected in the colonial almanacs, which also mirrored equally vehement opposition. The subject was of particular concern to navigators and seamen in England as well as in the colonies. John Dee of Mortlake, the astrologer-mathematician, and an Oxford scholar named Simon Forman produced forecasts based on compilations of ephemerides and frequently consulted with men of the sea for this purpose. On the basis of consultations between 1587 and 1604 Forman compiled a "Treatise on Sea-Astrological Practice" and gave wide distribution to his forecasts. Among the seafaring men who insisted on having horoscopes made for their ships before undertaking voyages were Sir William Monson and William Bayley, as well as countless others of less renown.[23] New England shipmasters engaged in the slave trade were especially likely to employ astrologers to cast horoscopes to determine the most auspicious day and hour for sailing, probably because of the excessive risks to be encountered in this trade.[24]

How influential English astrology may have been on colonial

Americans in other walks of life is difficult to estimate, although English publications on the subject found their way across the Atlantic. John Winthrop, Jr., "possessed some of the works on astrology so much esteemed at that time. Among these is a book with astrological figures set one on each page with the lower half of the page blank. These diagrams are for every four minutes of time, and by means of them 'any reasonable artist' in such things may give judgement of a question. On one page some reasonable artist has assayed to find out, by casting a horoscope, what was the ailment afflicting one Alice Wilkins in 1656." [25]

Some almanac makers, particularly those who coupled the titles "philomath," "astrophil," and similar distinctions with their names on the title pages, scorned the astrologers and assumed a strong position in opposition to the subject in their own publications. The author of the *Boston Almanac* for 1686 commented:

> *Judicial Astrologer* I am not;
> That *Art* (falsely so called) I loathe, I hate,
> Both *Name* and *Thing*, I much abominate.

Philomathemat (believed to have been Thomas Brattle) spoke strongly against astrology in his almanac for 1694, claiming that astrological predictions were ". . . serving onely to Delude and Amuse the Vulgar . . . not fitting to be Joyned with Astronomicall Certainties." [26] Increase Mather commented that "If men did with understanding read the Scriptures more, they would mind Judicial Astrologers less." [27]

At the same time almanacs chiefly astrological in content competed with those opposed; an example was one compiled by Samuel Atkins, "student in the Mathematicks and Astrology," and entitled *Kalendarium Pennsilvaniense, or, America's Messenger* . . . which was printed in Philadelphia in 1685 for the following year.

Among the most distinguished of the astrologer almanac makers of the same period was John Tulley, an English-born philomath of Saybrook, Connecticut. He arrived in New England as a youth and ". . . from the instruments and libraries of a few gentlemen in Saybrook he became acquainted with several branches of science." [28] He worked as a teacher of arithmetic, navigation, and astronomy in his community and compiled almanacs for the years 1681 to 1702. They were unique in New England in their time because they began the year with January instead of with March and introduced, for the

first time in the colonies, listings of religious feast days such as
Easter and saints' days, a daring innovation in the period of Puri-
tanism. Tulley utilized astrology to forecast future, and usually dire,
events. "The obscuring of the smaller stars is a certain sign of tem-
pest approaching, the oft changing of the winds is always a forerunner of a storm," he declared. His predictions were so often correct that he achieved considerable notoriety. Christian Lodowick, a
contemporary almanac maker, in his own almanac for the year 1695
criticized Tulley so severely for these predictions that Tulley apolo-
gized for them in his almanac for the following year.[29]

Evidences of the prevalence of astrology in the seventeenth century, which recurred persistently and with frequency, were the
adopted names of the almanac makers, occasional accounts in newspapers, and the habits of the farmer and the seafarer and others involved with battling the elements in the course of their occupations.
In rural communities the phase of the moon or the conjunction of
planets determined which medicine was to be administered, when
brushwood or timber was to be cut so that it would grow again, and
the timing for a great variety of agricultural chores.

In 1723 a self-taught mathematician of Abingdon, Pennsylvania,
Jacob Taylor, calculated the aspects of the planets for the time that
the city of Philadelphia had been founded, and expressed his results
in the following verses:

> Full forty years have now their changes made,
> Since the foundation of this town was laid;
> When Jove and Saturn were in Leo join'd,
> They saw the survey of the place designed:
> Swift were these planets, and the world will own
> Swift was the progress of the rising town.
> The Lion is an active regal sign:
> And Sol beheld the two superiors join.[30]

Taylor, who served as master of a small school, and as surveyor-
general of the Province of Pennsylvania for more than a quarter of a
century, compiled a series of almanacs for the years 1702 through
1745, which were well received because of the accuracy of his calculations.[31]

Interest in astrology showed a marked decline by the first
quarter of the eighteenth century but the subject continued to have
some adherents. In 1728 the Reverend Joseph Morgan, an amateur

of the sciences of Philadelphia, was brought before the Synod of the city on charges of "making experiments with judicial astrology." Although the charges were not proven and the case was dismissed, Morgan's position as a cleric suffered seriously.[32]

One of the features of the almanac which had increasing popular appeal was weather prognostication. Although experience had taught the readers that the forecasts were unreliable at best and were probably not based on legitimate calculations, they were avidly read and followed. First introduced in John Tulley's almanacs as "prognostica Georgica" or "The Country-man's Weather-Glass," the practice was adopted by others and became a standard feature. A variety of methods for weather forecasting were used, but few had any scientific basis. Nathanael Ames, one of the most prolific and popular of the almanac makers, in his second almanac, for the year 1727, advised his readers: "As to what I have predicted of the Weather, it is from the Motions & Configurations of the heavenly Bodies, which belongs to Astrology: Long Experience testifies that the Sun, Moon and Stars have their Influences on our Atmosphere, for it hath been observed for Seventy Years past, That the Quartile & Opposition of Saturn & Jupiter produce wet Seasons; and none will deny but that the Sun affordeth us his benign Rays & kind influence; and by his regular Motion causeth Spring, Summer, Autumn & Winter; and if the Moon can cause the daily Ebbing and Flowing of the Tide, and has the vast Ocean subject to her government, she can certainly change the Air which is Thin, and Tenuious. . . ."[33]

This authoritative statement undoubtedly impressed his readers even though they did not understand it, but from the point of view of practical application Ames's forecasts were dubious. He confessed as much in a statement to the reader in his almanac for 1745: "In all this Time I have carefully compared my Calculations with Observation, and endeavored to correct my Mistakes; and with Regard to my Judgement of the Weather, I have only this to say, namely, that I have endeavored to observe what Aspects of the Planet affect the Country most, & have the Advantages of this same 20 Years Experience, but after all, the Weather is uncertain even to a Proverb—*As fickle as the Wind*, or *as uncertain as the Weather*."[34]

The most valid sources from which weather forecasts were derived were compilations of daily records kept throughout the year by farmers and by the almanac makers themselves. It was a common practice, particularly among farmers and tradesmen, to preserve copies of the almanac from year to year, noting events of importance in the community or in their own lives, purchases made, crop records, as well as comments on the weather, on the printed pages or on interleaved sheets, which were then crudely sewed together as a permanent family record.

One of the most professional methods of weather prognostication employed by almanac makers was that used by the Daboll family of New London. Each of the almanac makers of this family maintained a daily journal, preserved over a period of decades, of the weather in that community. These records were then utilized in compiling the data of anticipated climatological phenomena at the same times of the year in the almanacs being prepared for each following year. Presumably the same procedure was utilized by other almanac makers as well. That this practice was prevalent is verified in an English work of the eighteenth century, which noted in its preface: "Many ingenious gentlemen in different and distant places, at home and abroad, have kept journals of the weather, air and its temperature, and their monthly and yearly quantities of rain; several abstracts of all which I have perused and computed at monthly mediums between the highest and lowest of mercury, or spirits in their tubes, or rain in its receiver; but these being fitter for speculation and amusement than any other useful purpose yet known, though if collected, compared and improved, might afford some not contemptible hints, therefore such journals should be deposited in some public museums where the curious might have access to them." [35]

No scientific compilation of weather data existed in published form until the nineteenth century, nor were there procedures, instruments, or institutions concerned with weather forecasting; in fact, there was no knowledge of the laws that govern weather. The earliest scientifically compiled records or accounts of weather phenomena included the observations on storms made by Benjamin Franklin in 1747, which were published by the surveyor Lewis Evans on his map of Pennsylvania and adjoining provinces in 1749; Charles Mason's weather notes recorded in his journal during the survey of the Mason and Dixon Line; and the careful records kept by David Rittenhouse, Andrew Ellicott, and other outstanding surveyors. Except the Evans map, however, none of these was published or available for the compiling of almanacs.

A method occasionally used was astronomical analysis of the moon's position, based on the assumption that the moon controlled the weather, a belief which enjoyed great popularity during the eighteenth century. The changes of the moon's phases every seventh day were presumed to be the cause of changes in the weather, which normally occurred once or twice during the same time span. By considering only the occasions when the moon's and the weather's changes were concurrent, and ignoring those when they were not, it was possible to develop a system for prediction. The moon was assigned the primary responsibility for weather changes in planetary meteorology, the basis for the recurrence of certain types of weather being the lunar cycle of nineteen years during which the new and full moons are repeated on corresponding days of the month. The daily changing weather was correlated with the daily changes of the moon's aspect, and the weekly change of the lunar phases was associated with the occurrence of storms.[36]

Readers of seventeenth- and early-eighteenth-century almanacs evidently did not take the weather predictions any more seriously than did the compilers, and contemporary writers occasionally suggested that the compiler pretended to knowledge he did not possess. One of the Overbury group of character writers in England in 1614 described the English almanac maker as "the worst kind of astronomer" and declared that ". . . for his judging of the uncertainty of the weather, any old shepherd shall make a dunce of him." [37] This attitude changed by the middle of the eighteenth century, however. Weather prediction and other related content of almanacs then gained greater credence and respect, particularly as a result of the efforts made by Nathanael Ames and his son of the same name, who attempted to provide predictions having some practical basis.

Eclipses, conjunctions, and meteors were also of interest to readers of the early almanacs, but the times of the sun's rising and setting, the changes of the moon, and the position of specific prominent stars were of greater consequence to daily living, particularly for men of the sea, for whom this information had practical application. The importance of astronomical data for navigational purposes is best reflected in the fact that between 1620 and 1640 approximately 26,000 persons voyaged from England to the American shores with safety, during a period when the ship's place could be calculated only within approximately seventy miles of its true position and seafaring men relied more on the stars than on the imperfect instruments and nautical tables then available. The author of the only New England almanac for 1656, believed to be Thomas Shephard, noted that "the stars are an universal living dyal appointed to divide between day and night and to be for signs and seasons."

The subject of timetelling was closely related to astronomical phenomena and frequently included by almanac makers in their publications. The almanac calculated for the year 1667 by Samuel Brackenbury of Cambridge included a short essay on "The use of the Table of Altitudes" which provided the following procedure: "Having obtained the Altitude of the ☉, look for his place on that day, which you shall enter this Table ["A Table of the Suns Altitude for every hour of the day, *for* N. E. Lat. 42. *gr.* 30 *m.* North," which appeared on the following page] and in that line in which you finde it, look for your Altitude, or the nighest to it, from whence ascending to the top, you shall have the exact hour of the day. . . . *By this Table are made all* Instruments, *and fixed* Dyals *that give the* hour of the Day *by the* Altitude *of the* Sun." [38] As an alternative, Nehemiah Hobart, in an almanac he calculated for the year 1673, noted the southing of two important stars for each month, "from which the time of the night may be guessed."

Sundials and time glasses were prevalent in the seventeenth century, and the almanacs reflected the need for determining the time without mechanical means. Surviving records show not more than thirty-six clocks as existing in Boston between the years 1645 and 1687, and in a survey of 111 inventories of personal property in Essex County, Massachusetts, between 1699 and 1702 not more than four clocks were noted.[39] By the beginning of the following century, clocks and watches became more numerous in the colonies, and some almanacs featured a special column entitled "Sun fast and slow," by means of which the sun could be used to regulate these mechanical timekeepers daily at noon.

What reference works the almanac makers used as guides for calculating their ephemerides has been the source of considerable speculation by modern scholars. Some of these sources have been identified, such as the ephemerides of John Gadbury calculated for the period 1682 to 1701, which were used by the almanac maker Samuel Atkins in the preparation of his almanac for 1686 to establish the daily positions of the sun, moon, and fixed stars. For the rise, southing, and setting of the moon Atkins relied on the method employed by the almanac maker Vincent Wing in his publication. Other resources included a work by John Holwell published in 1682 and Jacob Taylor's *Tenebrae* which appeared in 1698.[40] A more absolute identification of source was noted in the Boston press in advertisements of *Clough's Almanack* for 1705, which claimed that it was calculated according to the latest tables extant, namely, the *Scientia Stellarum*. [41]

A little known fact about the early American almanacs is that the man of science who provided the calculation of the ephemeris, tide tables, and other scientific data was usually not responsible for the literary or tabular content. The printer customarily selected suitable bits of poetry, adages and proverbs, and moral essays, which he excerpted from a variety of published sources, including the works of British poets and essayists usually without crediting the original. Among the exceptions to the rule were Nathanael Ames, father and son, and a few others who collected and frequently wrote their own literary and supplementary materials.

PART TWO

Development

29 David Rittenhouse (1732–1796). Painting in oils by Charles Willson
Peale, 1791.

30 Gregorian reflecting telescope owned and used by the astronomer John Winthrop and donated to Harvard College after his death in 1779. English, maker unknown, ca 1735.

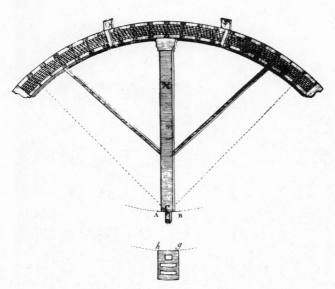

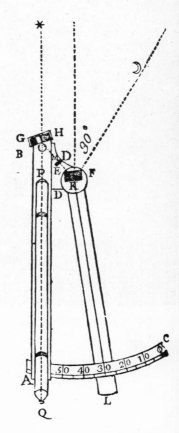

31 Thomas Godfrey's improvement of the mariner's bow. Engraving from the *Philosophical Transactions* of the Royal Society, no. 435, vol. XXXVII (1733–1734).

32 Thomas Godfrey's octant. Drawing from *The American Magazine*, 1758.

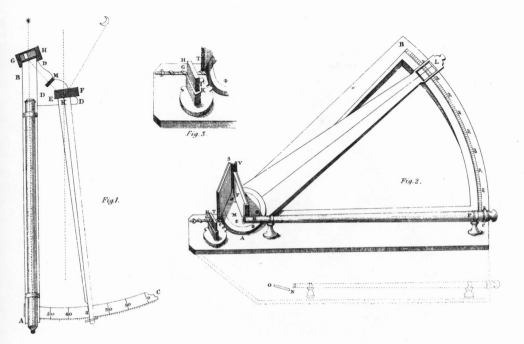

33 John Hadley's first version of his reflecting quadrant, or octant, with a telescope. Drawings from the *Philosophical Transactions* of the Royal Society, no. 420, vol. XXXVII (1731–1732).

34 Early octant with the scale in-scribed on an inset panel of box-wood. Probably American, eigh-teenth century.

35 Caleb Smith's Sea-Quadrant, made by Thomas Heath of London, ca 1735–1740. In this one of two known surviving examples the telescope and level are missing.

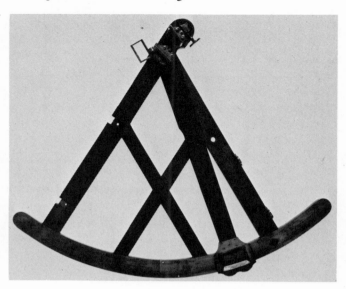

36 Sea-Quadrant, based on Caleb Smith's design, made by Benjamin King of Newport, Rhode Island, ca 1748.

37   A surveyor's field equipment, including tripod, plain surveying compass (made by Peregrine White of Woodstock, Connecticut) in its field case, combined ruler-protractor in wooden carrying case, and calipers. Eighteenth century. Owned and used by General Artemas Ward.

38   Thomas Greenough (1710–1785) of Boston. Portrait in oils by John Smi-
bert.

39 Wooden plain surveying compass with engraved brass scale inserted over engraved paper compass card, made by Thomas Greenough of Boston, mid-eighteenth century.

40   Vernier compass made by Benjamin Rittenhouse,
with specially designed socket joint. Shown in the original field case.

41   Special socket joint developed and produced by Benjamin Rittenhouse for use
with his plain surveying compasses to enable adjustment for declination.

42 Brass surveying level made by Benjamin Rittenhouse and believed to have been used in the development of the Washington Canal.

43 Clockwork odometer with case mountings, used for surveying in Salem, North Carolina, in the eighteenth century.

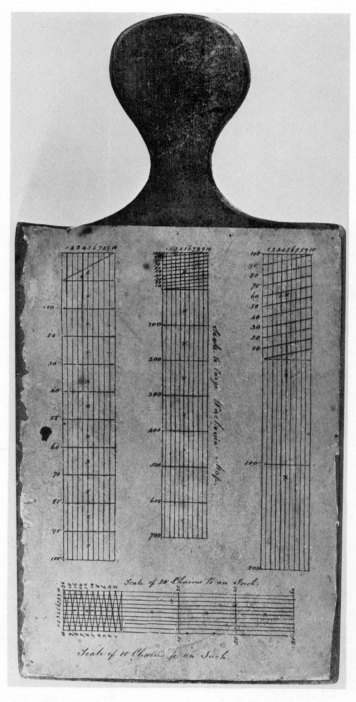

44 Surveyor's scale board for use in the field, made and used by Carl Ludwig Meinung (1743–1817) of Salem, North Carolina.

45   Christopher Colles (1738–1816). Portrait in oils by J. W. Jarvis, ca 1812.

46　The great orrery made by David Rittenhouse for the University of Pennsylvania.

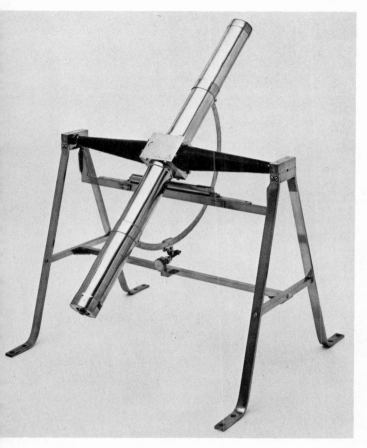

47 Astronomical transit constructed by David Rittenhouse for his own use in making observations of the transit of Venus in 1769 and used also in his observatory at Norriton, Pennsylvania.

48 Astronomical clock constructed by David Rittenhouse for observations of the transit of Venus in 1769 and maintained in his observatory at Norriton, Pennsylvania.

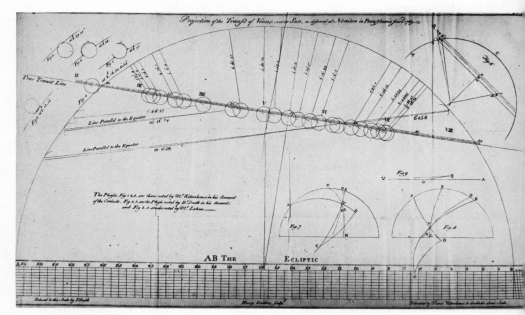

49 "Projection of the Transit of Venus, over the Sun, as observed at Norriton in Pennsylvania, June 3ᵈ, 1769." Engraved by Henry Dawkins and published in the *Transactions* of the American Philosophical Society, 1771.

50 Benjamin West (1730–1813) of Providence, Rhode Island. Portrait in watercolor by unknown artist.

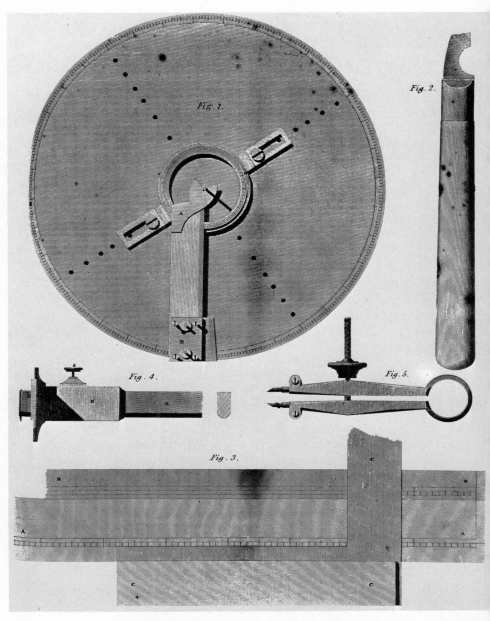

51 The tools of the mathematical instrument maker for graduating scales: circular dividing plate, cutting knife, and compass. Illustration from *The Edinburgh Encyclopedia*.

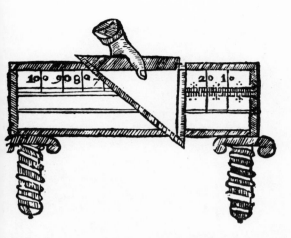

52   Scale of equal parts, for graduating scales on mathematical instruments, with iron screws for fastening. Illustration from Samuel Sturmy's *The Mariner's Magazine* (London, 1669).

53   Large instrument-maker's magnet, combining eight individual magnets within a brass housing, with keeper. Probably eighteenth century English or American.

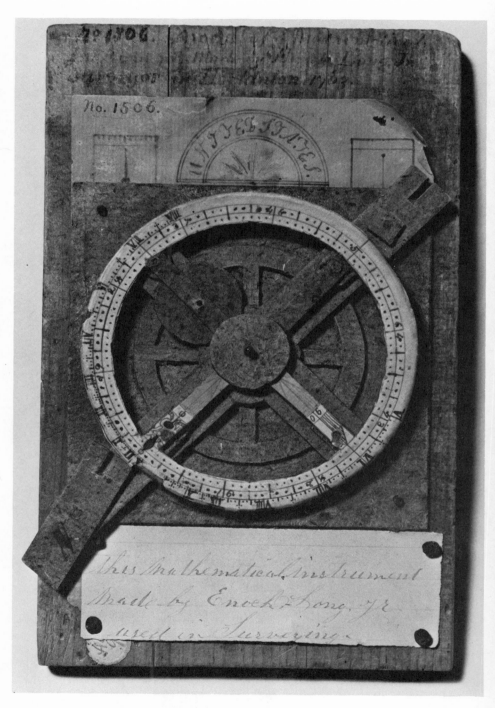

54   "Mathematical Instrument" made and used for surveying by Enoch Long,
Jr., of Hopkinton, New Hampshire, and dated 1763. Made of paper and cardboard attached to a wooden panel, the device combines among its features a
plain surveying compass and a horizontal sundial.

55 Unusual homemade surveying instrument having a bubble level, vertical scale, and plummet bob. The sighting bars are missing. Made to be used with a jacob staff or tripod. American, late eighteenth century.

56 Homemade wooden theodolite having a level on its upper surface, a pewter compass dial, and a hollowed-out telescopic tube.

57 Daniel King (1704–1790), maker of mathematical instruments at Salem, Massachusetts. Portrait in oils by an unknown artist.

58 Maplewood surveying compass, with an elaborate marine compass card
dated 1744, made by Daniel King of Salem, Massachusetts. The hour numerals
made the card useful for tide calculation. The figures engraved on the outer
circle are shown with navigational instruments.

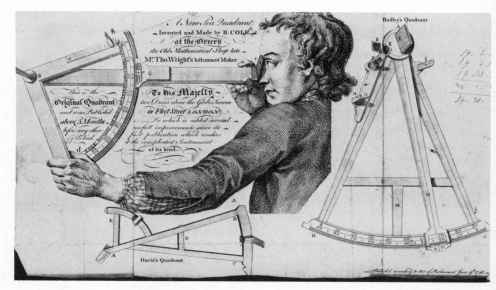

59 Advertisement of Benjamin Cole of London for a new type of Sea-Quadrant of his own invention, depicting also the backstaff (Davis's improved quadrant) and Hadley's reflecting quadrant. Dated June 9, 1748.

60 Battery of Leyden jars owned and used by Benjamin Franklin in his experiments with electricity and bequeathed to his friend Francis Hopkinson.

61 "Mercury," eighteenth-century shop figure carved by Simeon Skillin. It was displayed over the door of the Post Office on State Street at the southeast corner of Devonshire Street, Boston, and later by Frederick W. Lincoln, Jr., in his shop.

TO BE SOLD AT
WILLIAMS'S

Mathematical Shop, next Door to Major READ's, opposite the Town-House in *Marblehead*, A great Variety of Mathematical Instruments, Books, and Stationary, among which are the following Articles,

The largest Assortment of Hadley's and Davis's Quadrants ever in New-England.

ALSO,

Hanging and Standing Compasses, in Brass and Wood,

Gauging and Surveying Instruments,

Cases of Mathematical Instruments, with Steel Joints,

Half Cases Ditto,

Telescopes of various Lengths, in Ivory, Wood, and Fish-Skin,

Plotting Scales and Protracters,

Gunter Scales and Dividers,

Four and Two Pole Surveying Chains,

Artificial Magnets with Cases,

Sand Glasses, from Two Hours to a Quarter of a Minute,

Instruments of a new Construction to measure Boards,

An Assortment of Brass Pocket Compasses,

Box Rules,

Jack Knives,

Brass and Pewter Ink-stands,

Watch Keys,

Ass-skin Memorandum-Books, &c.

BOOKS.

West-India Pilot,

Strait and Mediterranean Ditto,

Southern Ditto,

Guinea Ditto,

Practical Navigation, by John Seller,

Mariner's Calendar,

Daily Assistant,

Wilson's Navigation,

Young Man's Best Companion,

Patoun's Treatise of Navigation,

Atkinson's Epitome,

A complete System Navigation, by John Barrow,

Large Charts of the English Channel,

Large Charts for the Coast of Guinea,

Di. for West-Indies,

Ditto for North and South-Carolina,

Nine Leaf Charts for the Straits and English Channel.

STATIONARY.

Writing Paper,

Dutch Quills,

Sealing Wax,

Wafers,

Slates,

62 Earliest-known illustrated advertisement of an American maker of mathematical instruments. It lists the products of William Williams and shows a caricature of his shop figure, "The Little Admiral" (from *The Salem Gazette and Newbury and Marblehead Advertiser*, July 15, 1774).

63 "The Little Admiral," a shop figure used for almost a century and a half by the Boston makers of mathematical instruments William Williams and Samuel Thaxter. Reputed to have been carved by John Skillin.

V

☆ ☆ ☆ ☆ ☆ ☆ ☆ ☆ ☆ ☆ ☆ ☆

MEN OF INGENUITY

☆ ☆

All civilized states have thought it their honour to have men of great ingenuity born or bred among them. Nor is it to be wondered that mankind be so generally eager in this respect since nothing redounds more to the honour of any state than to have it said that some science of general utility to mankind was invented or improved by them. Nevertheless it often happens that the true author of many a useful invention either by accident or fraud lose the credit thereof and from age to age it passes to the name of another. Thus it happened heretofore to Columbus and many others; and this also has happened to a native of Philadelphia. . . .

"On the invention of what is called Hadley's Quadrant,"
American Magazine and Monthly Chronicle (1758)

THE PRACTICAL SCIENCES in colonial America were based primarily upon the practices, texts, and instruments of the English, and the colonists demonstrated considerable energy and adaptability in mas-

117

tering these without the training required in the motherland. They proved equally skillful in modifying standard practices to their own particular requirements and in duplicating and developing mathematical instruments, using skills, tools, and materials borrowed from a variety of crafts. As colonial trade developed and experience increased, the colonists began to produce innovations, and occasionally inventions, which advanced the practices.

With the expansion of shipping on both sides of the Atlantic in the early eighteenth century, the limitations of existing navigational practices and instruments and the need for improvements became increasingly evident. One of the first responses caused an English-American controversy that lasted more than two and a half centuries. This was the invention of the octant, which was claimed simultaneously by John Hadley in England and Thomas Godfrey in the colonies.

Godfrey was an unusual figure in the history of the sciences in America. He had probably as much knowledge of science as anyone in his time in the colonies, and his achievements ranged widely. The son of one of Penn's maltsters of Bristol Township near Philadelphia, Godfrey was orphaned at an early age and sent to learn the trade of plumber and window glazier. Soon after completing his apprenticeship, he married and established a shop and a home for his bride in a building which Benjamin Franklin had leased and in which he and Hugh Meredith had opened a print shop. Godfrey paid rent to Franklin for his shop and home space, and Franklin and Meredith, both bachelors, boarded with the Godfreys. Godfrey was one of the founding members of the self-improvement society for young men which Franklin had instituted as the Leathern-Apron Club.[1] He devoted his leisure to the study of mathematics and astronomy and aroused the interest of James Logan, secretary to the Proprietors, who lent him books and instruments from his fine library. Godfrey calculated ephemerides for an almanac which Franklin printed and distributed for a time, and he also assisted Logan in making astronomical observations at his home.

As a result of his work in astronomy and his association with Philadelphia shipmasters, Godfrey learned of the inadequacies of the navigational instruments then available and directed his attention to their improvement. He studied the backstaff and the improved version called the Davis quadrant, both of which were in popular use for observing the altitude of the sun or a star. Having discovered from a study of Euclid's *Elements* that all angles at the periphery of a circle subtended by the same segment within it are equal on whatever part of the circumference that the angular point falls, he proposed that, instead of a quadrant, which constituted one-quarter of a circle, a semicircle, or half-circle, be graduated to 90 degrees, in which every 2 degrees were counted as 1, and an arc of the same circle be placed at the end of the diameter of the instrument. In this way every part of that opposite arc would serve equally for taking the coincidence of the rays required for the observation. He applied this information to the backstaff and discovered that, although such a modification was feasible in theory, the instrument became too cumbersome to handle when observing great altitudes, and the vanes could not be framed to stand perpendicular to the rays as was required.[2]

In the course of his experimentation, Godfrey applied his proposed improvement to the mariner's bow, another version of the backstaff, and attempted to resolve his problem by placing a curve at the center of a quadrant which would have adequate length to catch the coincidence of the rays. On the basis of his Euclidean formula, he was able to achieve observations having an error not greater than 57 seconds and was able to make his observation in one-fourth the time customarily required with the backstaff.

Godfrey continued to experiment, and while using a backstaff for taking the sun's altitude, he noted that although the shadow of the index should have coincided with the slit in the horizon vane, it was frequently indistinct. Seeking to correct this defect, he devised a transparent cylindrical glass lens which, when set at the proper focal distance, provided a well-defined light upon the horizon vane. He thereupon modified the horizon vane of the mariner's bow by cutting two apertures having rectilinear sides so that the sun's image was brought between them by means of a spherical lens fixed in the index vane. Such a lens had been proposed and applied by Edmond Halley in 1678; Godfrey's improvement consisted of the addition of the cylindrical lens. He reported his lens vane to the Royal Society in 1733, but it remained neglected for more than a century before being applied successfully for other purposes.[3]

From his experiments with the mariner's bow Godfrey returned to the backstaff, and in the summer of 1730 he made a major modification which resulted in the invention that he called the octant, a new instrument for taking angles at sea. Borrowing a backstaff from a seagoing friend, Godfrey temporarily attached to it five pieces of wood and mirrors to create a new instrument capable of being used to make a back observation. This new arrangement was successfully tested for him by the owner of the backstaff, who was first mate of the sloop *Trueman*, and by the captain of the same vessel, first on a voyage to the West Indies and later on one to St. John's in Newfoundland. They reported that with the modified instrument they made ". . . several observations of the Suns Altitude as also the direction of the Moon from the Stars . . ." and that it proved to be successful. The tests were made in November and December 1730 and again in August of the following year.[4] Godfrey demonstrated the instrument to his patron, James Logan, in about November 1730. Logan was so impressed that he sought to bring it to the attention of the Royal Society, with the intention of obtaining that body's acknowledgment of the invention. He was delayed in making the presentation, and it was not communicated to the Royal Society until 1732.[5] Then it caused a problem, because in the interim a claim to the same invention had been made by John Hadley, a vice-president of the Society and an optical innovator in the employ of the Admiralty.

Early in 1731 Edmond Halley had presented at a meeting of the Society a paper on the periodicity of the moon's motions, the regularity of which he claimed would make it possible to determine the longitude at sea.[6] At the next meeting Hadley described an instrument which he claimed he had devised and his brother, George Hadley, had constructed for him the previous summer, which accomplished what Halley proposed. Hadley later demonstrated a model of the instrument, which he named "a new instrument for taking angles," and subsequently described it in the Society's *Philosophical Transactions*.[7] In his description he referred to the instrument as a "reflecting quadrant," and it subsequently became widely known as "Hadley's reflecting quadrant." However, it was also called an "octant," and in principle it was identical with the instrument developed by Godfrey. Among Halley's papers after his death in 1742 was a drawing of an instrument embodying the same principle. It was similar to one which had been devised by Isaac Newton in about 1699, possibly based upon a concept by Robert Hooke. Newton had provided Halley with a drawing of his invention, which Halley presumably had forgotten.[8]

In 1734 Hadley obtained a patent for his reflecting quadrant which protected his exclusive rights to it until 1745 and its exclusive production by a London instrument maker named Joseph Jackson. Meanwhile, repeated communications to the Society from Logan and Godfrey had received no acknowledgment, and the Society published only those parts of Logan's communications that referred to Godfrey's improvement of the mariner's bow, ignoring his invention of the octant.[9]

Hadley's first version of his reflecting quadrant bore a remarkable resemblance to Godfrey's instrument, and the required accommodation to particular types of observation could be made by varying the angle of the horizon-mirror. Godfrey's instrument was less successful in practice than Hadley's because his horizon-mirror was based on the traditional form of the backstaff and retained all its inconvenience.

The announcement of the invention of Hadley's new instrument brought an immediate reaction from English makers of instruments, and an active competition ensued in an effort to capitalize on this revolutionary innovation without encroaching on Hadley's Crown patent. Instrument makers were forced to devise other improvements and modifications in order to market examples of their own manufacture. Consequently, for the next several decades the navigational world in England and France was frequently offered a new invention or an improvement on an old one. Of the numerous innovations proposed, very few were in fact improvements and an even smaller number true inventions.[10]

Among the earliest and most successful attempts to bypass Hadley's patent were those made in 1734 by a London insurance broker named Caleb Smith. He petitioned the Board of Longitude for an award for his invention of a new instrument in which he combined an "astroscope" and a "sextant" for observing the eclipses of Jupiter's satellites. The "sextant" of Smith's instrument was an astronomical sextant, not to be confused with an instrument which later replaced the octant. Smith published a pamphlet describing his instrument in which he claimed that it had been approved by such experienced navigators as Captain Christopher Middleton, Captain George Spurrel, and Joseph Harrison. These claims related to the use of the instrument in North American waters, for Middleton had served with the Royal Navy at the forts along Hudson Bay, where he tested the instrument.[11]

Sometime between 1740 and 1745 Smith announced the invention of a second instrument, described as a "Sea-Quadrant," which had been produced for him by the well-known London maker Thomas Heath. It was basically a modification of Hadley's improved reflecting quadrant equipped with a telescope, a bubble level, and a plummet. The object to be observed was viewed through one of two mirrors, whereas in the Hadley and Godfrey instruments one of the objects was viewed directly and the other by means of double reflection.[12] The Sea-Quadrant was known and used in the American colonies. Of two examples known to have survived, one was made and signed by Thomas Heath and was brought to Wachovia, North Carolina, in 1758 by Christian Gottlieb Reuter. Reuter had been Royal Surveyor to the Prince of Hanau and in America he laid out the communities of Lititz, Pennsylvania, and Wachovia and Salem, North Carolina, among others.[13]

Despite its promise, the Sea-Quadrant did not compete in popularity in England with Hadley's quadrant. Although significant modified versions of Hadley's instruments were produced and sold by several leading instrument makers, including George Adams and Benjamin Cole, the Hadley original continued to be the most used.[14]

Hadley's reflecting quadrant achieved instant popularity in the American colonies. Godfrey's octant was not likely to have become known in New England or elsewhere outside the Philadelphia area, whereas English shipmasters moving in and out of the New England port cities would have brought Hadley's version to American attention. At first American shipmasters attempted to acquire English-made examples, but by 1738 the Hadley quadrant was being produced in New England. The earliest-known advertisement of such production, in the Boston press in 1738, advised that being "Made and Sold by *Joseph Halsey* jun *Hadley's* New Invented Quadrant or the best and exactest Instrument for taking the Latitude or other Altitudes at Sea, as ever yet Invented." Joseph Halsey was a grandnephew of the James Halsey, "mathematician," who had made the earliest known instrument in the colonies.[15]

Godfrey's instrument was also produced, however; at least one colonial instrument maker, Anthony Lamb of New York City, made and sold it in preference to Hadley's version. Lamb was acquainted with Godfrey, and Lamb family records indicate that, after Godfrey had developed his invention, he visited Lamb in New York City early in 1731 to ask him to manufacture it for commercial distribution. Lamb featured Godfrey's octant in the advertisements listing his products, in which it was described as "Mr. Godfrey's new Sea Quadrant." According to this evidence, Godfrey's octant was being made, sold, and used aboard seagoing vessels several years before Hadley's reflecting quadrant was produced in accordance with the Crown patent, which was dated November 22, 1734.

In 1749 Lamb advertised in New York City newspapers: "The late invented and most curious Instrument call'd an Octant, for taking the Latitude or other Altitudes at Sea, with all other Mathematical Instruments for Sea or Land, compleatly made by Anthony Lamb in New-York. . . ." [16] Four years later he again mentioned the instrument in an advertisement of services offered by "Anthony Lamb, mathematical instrument maker, living on Hunter's Key, where may be had Godfrey's [sic] new invented quadrant, for taking the latitudes and other altitudes at sea. . . ." [17]

During the balance of the eighteenth century English instrument makers remained in the forefront in the advancement of navigational science, although the French and the Dutch were also in the race. Americans were not even in competition, because they lacked not only the extensive market but the capability to produce the precision instrumentation available in England.

Along with improved instruments, the development of navigation in the colonies required charts of American waters and sea routes, and efforts to provide them were made by the English and the colonists alike. The most important nautical charts produced by colonists were the work of Cyprian Southack, who emigrated from England to Boston in 1685. He became a privateer during the French and Indian wars, and commanded a number of vessels, including fifteen years as captain of the *Massachusetts Province Galley*. From these years of experience he gained extensive knowledge of coastal waters, and since harbor charts did not exist, and sailing charts were less than adequate, other ship captains drew on his stock of information. Urged to put his knowledge on paper, he produced during the next three decades a number of charts which had wide distribution. His first known work was a manuscript survey of New England, Nova Scotia, Newfoundland, and the "River of Canada" (Ottawa River), for which he received a reward from King William in 1694. Other manuscript works included charts of Boston Harbor, the St. John

River, and the St. Lawrence River. His first published work, which appeared in 1717, was "A New Chart of the English Empire in North America," which combined a chart with an essay in which Southack described the entire coastline from Labrador to the mouth of the Mississippi River. It was the first map or chart to be engraved on copper in the New World. Although the northern sections were presented in considerable detail, much of the data provided for the coastline below Long Island was inaccurate.[18]

Southack followed this map with published maps of Canso Harbor and a general chart from the Mississippi River to Cape Breton, Canso, and Casco Bay. His outstanding achievement was the compilation of a series of eight charts in a work entitled *The New England Coasting Pilot* published at an unknown date between 1718 and 1734, in which he included more than a hundred notes. Southack did not provide sailing directions on his charts but frequently noted safe harbors, tides and currents, and soundings. Despite the importance and wide distribution of his work, Southack was frequently the target of criticism. A contemporary writer, John Green, commented that his map of Nova Scotia and Cape Breton was in general "a very coarse and erroneous Draught, yet not without its use; and would have been more useful had he mentioned the parts which he viewed with most care, such as that of Cape Sable seems to be. It does not appear, however, that in making this chart he employed any instruments excepting the Log and Compass. . . . This is the first time perhaps that ever a person bred to the sea undertook to make a chart of so great an extent of coast, without ever taking a single latitude; and for the honor of navigators, as well as safety of navigation, I hope it may be the last." [19] Even harsher were the comments made in 1749 by William Douglass, a prominent Boston physician and writer. He wrote that Southack's ". . . large chart of the coast of Nova Scotia and New England being one continued error, and a random performance, may be of pernicious consequence in trade and navigation; therefore it ought to be publickly advertised as such and destroyed wherever it is found amongst sea charts." [20] These attacks did not in any way affect the sale of the work, which continued in wide use throughout the century.

Other charts produced in the following decades included a survey chart of Nova Scotia and its boundaries by a certain Harris, a new chart of the seacoast of New England from Cape Cod to Casco Bay made by a Captain Henry Barnsley in 1751; an anonymous chart of the Kennebec and Sagadahock rivers and part of eastern Massachusetts; a plan of the Four Governments of New England compiled from other surveys by Dr. William Douglass; a plan of the Hudson River surveyed by Timothy Clements; maps of Crown Point, the seacoast from Boston to Penobscot Bay, and all of the St. Lawrence River; and in 1761 a chart of the coast of North and South Carolina compiled by Daniel Dunbibin, advertised as being greatly esteemed by pilots of that region.[21]

While much attention had been given to mapping the shores of Chesapeake Bay and the Potomac River, it had not extended to the country west of the Blue Ridge Mountains. Following the settlement of the region west of the Shenandoah Valley with the support of Lord Fairfax, Maryland colonists moved westward, and the need for maps of the region became a priority. In the same period the ownership of a large tract of land between the Potomac and Rappahannock rivers had passed from Lord Culpeper to Lord Fairfax, and in 1733 the latter requested a survey of the territory granted by the Crown. A map in which the major branches of the two rivers were defined was completed by William Mayo, one of the surveyors, and submitted in 1737. Some concept of the conditions under which the cartographers of the period worked was provided in a statement by William Byrd, in which he noted ". . . here I think I ought to do Justice not only to the uncommon Skill, but also to the Courage and Indefatiguable Industry of Maj^r Mayo and two of the other Surveyors, employ'd in this long and difficult Task. Neither the unexpected Distance, nor the Danger of being doubly Starved by Hunger and excessive Cold, could in the least discourage them from going thro' with Their Work, tho' at one time they were almost reduced to the hard necessity of cutting up the most useless Person among them, M^r. Savage, in order to Support and save the lives of the rest. But Providence prevented that dreadfull Blow by an unexpected Supply another way, and so the Blind Surveyor escapt." [22]

Byrd was not exaggerating the field conditions which the cartographers encountered; he had participated in surveys and spoke from experience.

Another source for charts of American waters was British naval and merchant marine officers who sailed in them or were on assignment in the colonies. Among the most significant of these products was a large chart of the Chesapeake Bay and its principal rivers, provided with sailing directions for the regions depicted, which also

attempted to define the Gulf Stream and included a set of tables indicating the limits of the Stream to be encountered by ships bound
for the Virginia capes.[23] This chart was the work of Captain Walter
Hoxton, a British shipmaster sailing in the tobacco trade, who had
made twenty-three voyages to Maryland from England between
1699 and 1735. He had spent long periods ashore in Maryland with a
brother and a nephew who lived there and he had made trips to
study the bays, rivers, and harbors of the region. Hoxton distinguished between the elements on his chart based on personal observation and those not personally observed but based principally on
another map, probably one produced by the English publishers John
Thornton and W. Fisher in 1706. Hoxton's map was first published
in England in 1735, and a revised version, presented as a new and independent work by Anthony Smith, "Pilot of St. Mary's," appeared
in England in 1776. At least four more versions of the chart were
published before the end of the century.

The need for better communication and transportation between
the colonies and for fortifications and protective measures, which
became critical as the British conflict with the French assumed new
dimensions, focused attention on the production of more maps, particularly of Virginia and Pennsylvania. The establishment of new
counties and the widening of frontiers made a better map of Virginia
an immediate necessity. As early as 1710 Lieutenant Governor Alexander Spotswood considered the project, though no action was
taken, and in 1732 the Surveyor-General was assigned responsibility
for producing a new map, but the anticipated cost caused it to be
deferred again. Finally a map was completed by Joshua Fry and
Peter Jefferson in 1749 and published in 1751. Fry was a native of
Somersetshire who had arrived in Virginia in 1718 and served first as
Master of the Grammar School at the College of William and Mary
and then taught natural history and mathematics at the College until
1737, when he retired to devote himself to private enterprise in the
back country. Peter Jefferson, whose son became the third president
of the United States, was a neighbor and close friend of Fry. He had
learned the rudiments of surveying from William Mayo and had
emerged as a prominent land developer in the back country and a
well-known surveyor in his own right.[24]

Fry and Jefferson had worked together surveying the Northern
Neck boundary, which they mapped in 1746, and again in the westward extension of the Virginia–North Carolina boundary for which

they produced the 1749 map. Despite their professional competence, the map, hastily assembled from field notes in order to send it to the Board of Trade in London, incorporated inaccuracies which led to considerable criticism. Fry and Jefferson sent corrected drafts, which were subsequently incorporated into a revised and more accurate map published in 1755. This version proved to be one of the greatest colonial American cartographic achievements since John Smith's map a century earlier.[25]

Accurate definition of provincial boundaries, which continued to be a major concern of the colonists up to the eve of war with the motherland, could only be accomplished with precision instruments. This situation was dramatized by the saga of a historic astronomical instrument used for surveying, which became known as the "Jersey Quadrant" and figured in major boundary surveys for almost a century. The story began in 1719 when Allane Jarrette, a New York provincial surveyor working on the delineation of the boundary between New Jersey and New York, expressed dissatisfaction with the instruments available to him. A brass quadrant approximately 22 inches in radius with which he made observations for the latitude, was, he claimed, too small for the work, and he refused to proceed unless an instrument ". . . of five or Six foot Radius could be procured, Certified by able & skilful Mattematicants from Great Brittaine to be true and correct." His petition to the New York Provincial Council effectively disrupted the survey and postponed it for a long period, and it was suspected that such may have been his intention for personal reasons. Accusations and counteraccusations flew between the surveyors for the two provinces and their respective councils. Jarrette became a prime target for indulging in "capricios." It was suggested that, if he refused to proceed with the work, others be found to replace him, that they meet to examine the claim of defects of the instrument in question, amend them if possible, and if not, delay the work until a suitable instrument could be acquired ". . . but that it be not stopt upon the bare Whim or Credit of any one Visionary among them. . . ."

James Alexander, the Surveyor-General of East and West Jersey, was brought into the controversy, and he stated that even if a larger and improved instrument could be obtained, there would nevertheless be as much variation in the observations as had occurred with the smaller quadrant at hand. "It is impossible for the Art of Man," he declared, "to make an Instrument perfectly true and correct; and if the line be stay'd till one could be certified to be so, by able and skilful Mathematicians from *Great Britain*, it will be stay'd for ever; for the most that able and skilful Mathematicians can do, is to find out the Errors of it, and give a Table of Equations, how to correct it; which Capt. Jarret, if he will but take a little Pains, may easily make himself, for this Instrument. . . ."[26]

Alexander's advice appeared to be reasonable, and Cadwalader Colden, Surveyor-General of the Province of New York, was then ordered by the New York Council to examine the small quadrant and report on its accuracy. Meanwhile, those most directly affected by the controversy, the landholders in the area in question, requested that the survey be expedited by ordering an adequate instrument. Colden did not submit a report, and although a bill was formulated for purchase of an instrument, the Assembly failed to take further action. Numerous disorders continued along the border of the two provinces as the years went on and the line remained unresolved. In 1743 the Jerseys again passed an act to run and ascertain the boundary. The acquisition of a suitable instrument was immediately mentioned, and mindful of the controversy several decades earlier the Jersey Proprietors sought the advice of Alexander. He consulted with Colden, inasmuch as they both had been involved in the claimed deficiencies of the quadrant used by Jarrette. They agreed that a better instrument was required, and one was ordered from the foremost English instrument maker of that time, George Graham of London, through the agency of Peter Collinson of the Royal Society. A price for the instrument was established at 30 guineas, plus 10 more for testing it. Collinson then contracted with Jonathan Sisson, another London maker, to produce the instrument required, possibly because Graham was unable to do so at the time. Sisson advised that the latitude could best be determined by observations of the stars near the zenith, since they were free from refraction, by means of a new instrument called a zenith sector, which was first described in a work by the French mathematician Pierre Maupertuis, a copy of which Sisson forwarded to Alexander. Sisson had produced a number of these sectors, ranging in price from 60 to 120 pounds, according to their radius. Alexander decided that although a zenith sector might be desirable, it was beyond the means of the Proprietors and ordered instead a brass quadrant of 30-inch radius, since Sisson had specified that to observe the latitude to 1 minute, or 60 seconds, a quadrant of such a size would be required.[27]

The quadrant was constructed by Sisson and tested by comparison with an 8-foot mural arc at the Royal Observatory at Greenwich with satisfactory results. Seven pages of instructions for its use were compiled by John Bevis and James I. A. Short, two eminent English men of science, and were shipped to Alexander with the quadrant. The final cost was considerably greater than had been anticipated, £47.17.3, but it was paid by the Jersey Proprietors without great objection. This was the instrument which features in history as the Jersey Quadrant. During the next several years it was used in surveys by Alexander and Colden in their respective provinces, and after James Alexander's death it passed into the possession of his son, William, who succeeded him to the post of Surveyor-General of the Jerseys.

In 1756 William Alexander accompanied William Shirley, Governor of the Jerseys, to England as his aide and remained there until 1761 while he pressed his claim to the title of Earl of Stirling. The Jersey Quadrant remained in the colonies, but its story was not finished.[28]

VI

☆ ☆ ☆ ☆ ☆ ☆ ☆ ☆ ☆ ☆ ☆ ☆

THE WITTY

GEOMETERS

☆ ☆

The Shippes on the sea with Saile and with Ore,
    were first founde, and styll made, by Geometries Lore.
Their Compas, their Carde, their Pulleis, their Ankers,
    were founde by the skill of witty Geometers.
To sette forth with Capstocke, and eche other part,
    would make a great showe of Geometries art. . . .

> Robert Recorde, *The Pathway of Knowledge*
> *. . . First Principles of Geometrie,*
> *applied unto practice . . .* (1551)

No BOUNDARY IN THE HISTORY of the American continent was the subject of more prolonged controversy than the line dividing the provinces of Pennsylvania and Maryland. The charter issued in 1632 to Cecil, second Lord Baltimore, granted him the entire peninsula east of the Bay of Chesapeake and all the land "*hactenus inculta* [not yet husbanded or planted]," as far as 40° north. The grant made to William Penn by King Charles II in 1682 included the territory ly-

130

ing west of the Delaware River from 12 miles north of the town of New Castle to the 43° parallel. The two grants overlapped, inasmuch as New Castle and Pennsylvania itself lay south of the 40° parallel. The problem was further complicated by the fact that the peninsula had been settled by the Dutch before it was granted to Lord Baltimore. When the Dutch claims were relinquished, the land reverted to the English Crown, and in 1682 Penn acquired from the Duke of York the town of New Castle and surrounding territory for an area of 12 miles extending southward on the Delaware River to Cape Henlopen in what is now Delaware. Charles Calvert, the third Lord Baltimore, appealed to the king, and a committee of arbitration was established. The committee directed that the peninsula north of a line running west from what was then identified as Cape Henlopen (Fenwick Island) was to be divided between the two Proprietors. The division was made, and the Penn Proprietors added to their holdings the area which is approximately the present state of Delaware.[1]

As a first step to resolving the conflict by resurveying the line, the governor of Pennsylvania, William Markham, arranged to borrow a large astronomical quadrant owned by Colonel Lewis Morris of New York and had it shipped to New Castle. While awaiting Markham's arrival, the Maryland commissioners for the survey prevailed upon the captain of the sloop bearing the instrument to permit them to use it for establishing the latitude of New Castle, which was determined to be 39° 40'. Three weeks passed without word from Markham, and after making the observations for the latitude required by their Proprietors, the Maryland commissioners departed for home, just before he finally arrived.[2] Displeased with the latitude established, Markham openly accused the Maryland commissioners of knavery, which led to further unpleasant exchanges between the officials of the two provinces. Markham eventually agreed to meet Lord Baltimore at Upland (now Chester, Pennsylvania), and when Baltimore asked to examine Markham's instruments, it was discovered that one of them lacked necessary lenses. The Morris quadrant was functional, however; it was used jointly by the commissioners and the latitude was subsequently established to be 39° 47' 5". Later surveys established it to be actually 39° 51', placing an area of about 4½ miles in dispute. Markham and Baltimore were unable to agree concerning the continuation of the project, and each conference ended with increasing animosity.

Later in 1682 William Penn met with Lord Baltimore and discussed the establishment of an acceptable boundary at the latitude of 40°. The matter was not fully resolved, however, and many more meetings followed, with equally frustrating results. Meanwhile a cousin of Lord Baltimore, Colonel George Talbott, ran a line from the mouth of Octoraro Creek on the Susquehanna River eastward to Naaman's Creek on the Delaware. This line, executed carelessly without the use of instruments and marked only by the blazing of trees, was destined to become critically important in the contest between the rival Proprietors, for both claimed that it represented the approximate northerly boundary of Maryland as conceived by the third Lord Baltimore at the time that the controversy had begun. Talbott's line was in fact the first actual boundary run between the two provinces.[3]

Subsequent attempts to rectify the errors of Talbott's survey included an effort to determine the latitude of Palmer's Island (later named Watson's Island, and then Garrett's Island) in the Susquehanna River, made in 1683 with a "Sextant of about tenn foote Semidiamiter" and recorded to be 39° 0' 44".[4] The passage of time multiplied the conflicts relating to the provincial boundary, and a satisfactory survey of the 12-mile circle at New Castle was not achieved for half a century. As defined by Penn's charter, the southern boundary of Pennsylvania was the arc of a circle of 12 miles' radius with New Castle, Pennsylvania, as its center, a line established under a warrant from William Penn in 1701. Commissioners were appointed in 1732 and again in 1739 but repeatedly failed to reach an agreement.

At this juncture Benjamin Franklin ventured into map making and produced the so-called Franklin Map of 1733. This was in fact a copy of a map based on earlier work reproduced by John Senex of London for Lord Baltimore which had been proposed as the basis for the articles of agreement between the Pennsylvania Proprietors and Lord Baltimore to terminate five years of argument. When Lord Baltimore realized that the Franklin map was more favorable to Pennsylvania than it was to Maryland, he repudiated the agreement, and the case was referred to the High Court of the British Chancery in 1735.

A decision was finally made in 1750 which provided the basis for adjudication, and an agreement was signed in 1760 which specified that the boundary was to be a line drawn east-west across the peninsula from Cape Henlopen to Chesapeake Bay. From the exact middle of this line another line was to be drawn due north that would be tangent to the western arc of the circle of the 12-mile radius, measured westward from the town of New Castle until it intersected a parallel of latitude 15 miles due south of the southernmost part of the city of Philadelphia, thus providing the northeastern corner of Maryland as the point of intersection. From this point the line was to be run west on a parallel as far as it formed a boundary between the two provinces.[5]

Commissioners and surveyors were appointed for both provinces, and the next several years were spent in measuring the base and tangent lines between Maryland and the present area of Delaware. Meanwhile Thomas Penn, then Proprietor of Pennsylvania, but living in England, was being urged by his officials in the colony to acquire suitable instruments for this work. Penn, who had become acquainted with William Alexander, now Lord Stirling, during the latter's stay in England, remembered the Jersey Quadrant and sought to borrow it. Stirling agreed, but negotiations proceeded slowly because the instrument was in the Jerseys in his wife's possession. Late in 1761 Penn advised his secretary, the Reverend Richard Peters: "It is impossible for the Maryland Commissioners to agree to use a Quadrant 'till they see and examine it, so they must have it sent to Newcastle." In the following spring he notified Peters that he was sending from England ". . . a very fine Telescope in brass, as it will not be too liable to warp, with Cross-hairs, and three feet in length, which will be easily managed, having a swivel fixed to it, that can be fixed to a Staff." [6]

Of the Jersey Quadrant Penn noted that it "is a sufficient instrument, and M^r. Calvert [Lord Baltimore] appears very much pleased that we can have it. I cannot have any good opinion of an Instrument made in Pensulvania, even here there is not one in twenty, exactly graduated, and with such workmen as you have there they must be very faulty, so that I think you should be very careful how you use it, as to an Instrument propper for Stakes I think a Theodolite of which you have two very good ones of mine, the best. . . ." He also informed Peters that the commissioners appointed for Maryland had requested instruments to be sent from England but Lord Baltimore would be unable to forward them in time, so that they would have to depend on the Jersey Quadrant for the work.[7] As the correspondence between Penn and Peters developed, it became ap-

parent that both Penn and Lord Baltimore had been consulting usefully with English mathematicians and men of science and both had
become thoroughly informed about the instruments and other
requirements for the survey. Meanwhile, as negotiations to borrow
the Jersey Quadrant proceeded at an exceedingly slow pace, Penn
changed his mind and informed Lord Stirling that "we are advised to
send a Six feet [zenith] Sector to mark the points for running a parallel of Latitude; Lord Baltimore has sent one by Sisson and I have
bespoke one of Bird, that I hope to send about two months hence,
that he says will fix points to two Seconds." [8]

This represented an agreement between Penn and Baltimore to
acquire examples of the latest and most sophisticated—and expensive—instrument available. The zenith sector was comparatively rare
and could be produced only by the most skilled instrument makers
in England. One of these was George Graham, who had produced
the first professional examples—one for Samuel Molyneux in 1725,
one for the astronomer James Bradley in 1727, and one for the
French astronomers making observations in Lapland in 1736 which
was the instrument described by Maupertuis. The only two others
capable of producing zenith sectors of suitable precision were Jonathan Sisson, who made the Jersey Quadrant, and John Bird, both
former apprentices of Graham's. [9]

Early in 1762 Penn informed Peters and through him the Pennsylvania commissioners that work on the survey project should be
postponed until Bird had completed and delivered the zenith sector.
He confirmed that the sector would fix latitudes within 2 seconds,
whereas the Jersey Quadrant was liable to ½ minute of error, if not
more. In a later letter Penn urged: "If the Jersey Quadrant has not
been already used I desire you may stay 'til either Lord Baltimore's
or our sector arrives, for I cannot be of opinion that any Instrument
maker you have with you is fit to repair an Instrument that perhaps
no maker here but Bird or Sisson could be depended on for. . . . I
wish the Quadrant may not be injured by your cleaning of it, and
think the Sector I shall send will do that Business much better." [10]

The zenith sector being constructed by Bird for Penn was the
first example of the instrument to incorporate improvements previously suggested by the Astronomer Royal, Nevil Maskelyne, who
later noted: "Mr. Bird has contrived one [sector] of six foot length,
for settling the limits between Pennsylvania and Maryland, in which
the plumb-line is adjusted so as to pass over against and bisect a

small point at the center of the instrument." The modification of the plumb line, which was Maskelyne's suggestion, corrected a situation which had introduced an error of many seconds of angle.

In a letter to Lord Stirling, Penn made an interesting comparison of the two sectors being constructed for the rival Proprietors. "I have pressed Mr. Bird very much to finish the Sector," Penn wrote, "and yesterday Mr. Calvert, Dr. Bevis and myself saw it put together and examined it, the Doctor says it is very well executed and a most curious Instrument, much more so than that sent by Lord Baltimore, and will cost three times the price; there are some small things to it not quite finished." [11] To Governor Hamilton of Pennsylvania, Penn wrote that he expected to see Lord Baltimore again before the latter sailed for Maryland, adding: "I propose to send in conjunction with Lord Baltimore one or two persons with our Sector to take the observations if his Lordship will agree to it." [12] This letter confirms the fact that the suggestion to employ two English mathematicians or astronomers to run the provincial boundary had originated with Thomas Penn; it resulted in the appointment of Charles Mason and Jeremiah Dixon. Lord Baltimore was in Naples, however, and some time passed before Penn was able to obtain his concurrence to employ the two mathematicians jointly. [13]

The selection of Mason and Dixon for the scientific endeavor which was to resolve permanently the long-standing controversy was fortuitous: the two men, with their valuable combination of skills, happened to be available at just the moment that their services were required. Mason was an astronomer who had worked as assistant to James Bradley, the Astronomer Royal, at the Royal Observatory. Dixon was a mathematician who had become well known as a surveyor and amateur astronomer in his native county of Durham, England. The two men had worked together as a team sent by the Royal Society to the Cape of Good Hope to observe the transit of Venus in 1761 and had just returned to England when the new assignment was offered. [14]

Meanwhile the boundary survey was proceeding at the hands of local surveyors employed by Peters, including David Rittenhouse. They had been confronted with many difficulties and were eagerly awaiting the arrival of the English team. Rittenhouse was to make the necessary calculations and fix certain points of the 12-mile circle around New Castle. The problem was that neither the exact center of the town of New Castle nor the southernmost point of the city of

Philadelphia had been established, and it was furthermore not determined whether a certain arm of Chesapeake Bay was to be reckoned as part of the Bay. The middle point of the transverse line was finally established by the commissioners after considerable difficulty, and the problem that remained was to cut a tangent to the circle around New Castle. Two attempts, made at the expense of much time and cost, failed. Rittenhouse's involvement was not extensive, and in a letter to his friend William Barton, written the following year, he commented that Peters had "paid me for my attendance at New-Castle, and much more generously [six pounds] than I expected;—though I found it a very tedious affair; being obliged, singly, to go through a number of tedious and intricate calculations." [15]

Mason and Dixon, laden with scientific equipment, arrived at Philadelphia in November 1763. They met with the city authorities and the commissioners, then established a base near the southern point of Philadelphia. There they constructed a temporary observatory and, once settled into their base, they proceeded to set up both of the zenith sectors and make comparative tests of their accuracy. The sector purchased by Lord Baltimore from Sisson proved to be the less precise of the two. Mason noted in his journal that, after the sectors had been installed, they discovered that the nonius of the Sisson instrument would not touch the middle of the arc, and they abandoned it in favor of the Bird instrument, which they used exclusively for the remainder of the project. When they returned to England, they took the Sisson sector back with them, leaving the Bird sector in Pennsylvania.[16]

They first measured the zenith distances of eight stars selected from a star catalogue prepared by James Bradley, and observed as they passed the meridian. Corrections of apparent distances for refraction were made and reduced for precession, aberration, and nutation to January 1, 1764.

Mason and Dixon established the latitude of the South Point of the city of Philadelphia by January 6, 1764, and the following day they set out with a quadrant to locate a place in the Forks having the same latitude. They fixed a station near the house of John Harland, about 30 miles westward of the city, in Newlin Township, Chester County, Pennsylvania, and there they remained until April. They built a crude observatory building, established its latitude, and erected a permanent monument which has become known as "The

Stargazers' Stone," to which they returned again and again during the next four years to assemble more data.

In April they measured an arc of meridian southward from the Stone for almost 15 miles to a point in New Castle County and identified the latitude established on a marker. They then moved to the "Middle Point" between the Atlantic Ocean and Chesapeake Bay in the latitude of Cape Henlopen, a point determined by earlier surveys, and established the latitude of the Middle Point by October. The summer and autumn months had been spent in running an arc of a great circle almost 82 miles long slightly west and north of the Middle Point to produce a tangent line to the 12-mile circle having New Castle as its center, which had already been established. Mason and Dixon reported that they found no errors in the earlier surveys by Rittenhouse. They extended the radius from New Castle to intersect the arc of the great circle run from the Middle Point and then had to cease operations for the winter months. Work was resumed in March 1765, and from the Stargazers' Stone in Harland's field they ran the line which has memorialized their names, moving westward to the Susquehanna River. In June they returned to the tangent line and proceeded to extend and mark an arc of meridian northward to intersect the parallel.

With the major part of their project completed, Mason and Dixon then proposed to the Royal Society that they measure a degree of latitude and a degree of longitude and requested funds and instruments for the purpose. While awaiting approval, they spent the autumn of 1765 installing stone markers along the tangent line and establishing the latitude of the Middle Point, as well as the bearings of the arc of the great circle which they had run from that point the previous year.

The Society's favorable response finally reached them, and in December they reassembled the Bird sector at Harland's farm in the same parallel in which it had stood in 1764. The astronomical clock which the Royal Society furnished was now set up, in addition to a clock belonging to the Pennsylvania Proprietors. They undertook observations of the eclipses of the satellites of Jupiter for the determination of the latitude with the Society's clock, and by midsummer 1766 they had completed their observations at Harland's farm and moved westward to Fort Cumberland to extend the line of the parallel. Early in October they were halted by unfriendly Indians and forced to terminate their work, delivering their maps and notes to Peters for the Proprietors on January 29, 1767. There was still some other work which they wished to complete, however, and using some rectangular levels made for them by Joel Baily, a local member of their surveying party, they remeasured the five successive lines from Harland's farm to the Middle Point, continuing through the winter and spring until they reached the Middle Point in June. Their work in America was now finished, and after completing their records they departed for England in September.

Joel Baily was one of the few colonial members of the Mason and Dixon enterprise, and one whose role was of some significance. A farmer, gunsmith, self-taught clockmaker, sometime maker of surveying instruments, and surveyor, Baily lived in West Bradford, Chester County, three miles from the observatory on Harland's farm. He worked with the English surveyors from time to time as needed from 1764 through 1768 and occasionally produced specialized instruments and surveying aids for them. When measurement was begun of the courses from Harland's farm southward to the Middle Point, Baily constructed sturdy pine frames to support the brass-tipped fir rods 20 feet long serving as surveying levels. Each frame was fitted with a plumb line hanging within a tube at its center, set up with the rod in a horizontal position along the line being measured, and its position marked to $1/100$ inch on a stake placed at the lower point of the plumb bob. The next frame was placed in line end to end and aligned by the plumb line. The rods were periodically checked against a 5-foot brass standard of length which had been provided by the Royal Society.[17] The levels were used in this manner for a distance of almost 82 miles, a major undertaking which Baily accomplished competently. According to Mason's journal, Baily also recorded the daily temperature over a period of several months in 1767 with a Fahrenheit thermometer that was part of the equipment.[18] A plain surveying compass made by Baily in 1765, which has survived, may have been produced for the use of the Mason and Dixon party.[19] Many years later, in a letter to Franklin Bache, the naturalist William Darlington commented that ". . . at the time of Mason & Dixon's Survey, those gentlemen were encamped, & engaged for some time, in the neighborhood of Mr. Baily. His taste for Mathematics led to an acquaintance with Mason and Dixon, and I understand he rendered them considerable assistance, in their operations. This circumstance, I have no doubt, was the occasion of Mr. Baily's being introduced to the notice of the Philosophical Society. . . ." [20]

When the boundary established by Mason and Dixon, which came to be commonly known as the Mason and Dixon Line, was resurveyed in the twentieth century by a commission under the Superintendent of the Coast and Geodetic Survey, the work was found to have been accomplished with incredible accuracy and the latitudes determined by Mason and Dixon were only 2 or 3 degrees in error.[21]

In 1774 the Bird zenith sector, which Mason and Dixon left behind in Pennsylvania, was borrowed from the Proprietors by Samuel Holland and David Rittenhouse when they began the survey of the northern boundary of Pennsylvania, and was subsequently returned.[22] The instrument was stored at the Capitol in Harrisburg when the state capital was moved to that city after the War of 1812, and it remained there for most of the nineteenth century. It had been dismantled for cleaning at the time that the capitol building was destroyed by fire in 1897, and a report in 1909 stated that only a few parts of the instrument had survived. More recent research has failed to confirm the report or to locate the salvaged parts.[23]

Another instrument acquired by Thomas Penn in England for the boundary survey was an astronomical transit made by John Bird, which was to prove of considerable value later for colonial observation of the transit of Venus. Mason and Dixon frankly admitted that they preferred the Bird transit to one that belonged to John Bevis which they had brought with them to Pennsylvania. They considered the Bird transit a "less complex and more portable Transit Instrument" which would be more generally useful to them in running their lines.[24] The instrument was next mentioned as being loaned by the Penn family to the American Philosophical Society in 1769 for use at the observatory in Independence Square to observe the transit of Venus. At some time after these observations, which are described elsewhere, had been made, the instrument was removed to the tower of the State House in Philadelphia, where it was subsequently used to regulate the public clock in the tower. In 1912 it was discovered stored under the floorboards of a platform beside the old supports on which the Liberty Bell had formerly hung. The transit evidently had been mounted for many years on the heavy stone sill of the south window opening of the tower, in a position to take the meridian passage of the sun at noon, for regulating the tower clock. The instrument is presently owned by the City of

Philadelphia and is on loan to the National Park Service for display at Independence Hall.[25]

Meanwhile, the adventurous Jersey Quadrant, which had been set aside with the advent of the Bird zenith sector, had been returned to the Jersey Proprietors. It appears to have been borrowed again by the Proprietors of Pennsylvania for the use of David Rittenhouse for observing the transit of Venus at his observatory at Norriton in 1769; in his report of the observations he made, the list of the equipment in his observatory included "an Astronomical Quadrant two and one half f. radius, made by Sission [sic], the property of the East Jersey Proprietors; under the care of the Right Hon. William Earl of Stirling, Surveyor-General of that Province; from whom Mr. Lukens procured the use of it, and sent it up to Mr. Rittenhouse for ascertaining the latitude of the Observatory."[26] Thereafter the instrument was lost to record, and recent efforts to locate it have been without success.

The advent of these highly sophisticated astronomical instruments had a significant effect on the art of surveying, and Rittenhouse, for one, was inspired to duplicate some of them for use in his own endeavors as well as for the use of others. In due course he produced the most advanced scientific instrumentation achieved in America.

Following the completion of the Mason and Dixon survey and the observations of the transit of Venus, Rittenhouse moved his home and workshop from Norriton to Philadelphia, where he is known to have been at work in 1770. There he presumably achieved the first important modification of the plain surveying compass by inventing the form known as the vernier compass. The instrument was developed and first produced between late 1770 and the beginning of the Revolution.[27] Whether the invention is in fact rightfully attributed to David Rittenhouse cannot be documented, but the earliest-known examples of the new instrument are his work or that of his associates, including his brother Benjamin and Henry Voigt.

Some vernier compasses were made by David Rittenhouse in partnership with W. L. Potts of Bucks County, Pennsylvania, and Potts also produced this type of instrument under his own name. Vernier compasses made of wood with metal components were produced by Benjamin Hanks of Mansfield, Connecticut, and possibly by other makers.

Because the invention of the vernier compass was ascribed to

David Rittenhouse, it became known also as the "Rittenhouse compass," and was produced by Benjamin Rittenhouse as well as by David. Confirmation of this association of the instrument with the Rittenhouse brothers exists in a letter of 1798 from the Surveyor-General of Ohio, Rufus Putnam, to Thomas Worthington, who was conducting surveys in Chillicothe. Putnam wrote: "If you are not already, you must furnish yourself with a compass having a moveable band (Mr. Rittenhouse, near Philadelphia, makes the best I have seen). Our compasses must all be rectified to one declination in order that our Surveys may be not only correct but uniform. But without having a moveable band those small variations between different compasses which frequently exist cannot be corrected to any considerable degree of certainty. A compass therefore with a moveable band cannot be dispensed with. . . ." Putnam was referring to Benjamin Rittenhouse; David had died two years previously.[28]

The use of the plain surveying compass, which was the practice during this period, was subject to two primary sources of error. One was the deflection of the magnetic needle by iron-ore deposits in the area being surveyed, and the other was irregularity in the behavior of the needle, possibly due to infinitesimal particles of iron accidentally embodied in the instrument during the process of manufacture. These defects could be detected only by comparing readings made of the same locality with different instruments and for different parts of the graduated circle.

That these difficulties continued to be experienced by surveyors was attested in a report made by William Nicoll and Gerard Brancker in 1773 on their survey of the boundary between New York and Massachusetts. When the instruments of the parties representing their respective colonies were compared, it was discovered that the instrument of the Massachusetts surveyor would run the line considerably more to the east than that of the New York surveyors, but it was agreed to use it. After having run a distance of about twenty-five chains the surveyors examined the course that had been run and discovered a defect in the Massachusetts instrument. They exchanged it for the New York instrument ". . . but finding the Needle frequently affected by Minerals, the Massachusetts Gentlemen expressed a doubt whether we had continued on the true Course, it was here tryed on low Land, where we did not apprehend there was any Attraction, and after correcting a Back Monument or two, and satisfying both Sides, it was agreed to run by Stakes and

Back Sights only, (as we found the Needle was often affected as not to be depended on) for this purpose we used the Telescope of their Instrument. . . ." [29]

The same difficulties were found in surveys conducted in Virginia in this period, and various efforts were made to overcome them. One solution appeared to be the use of an instrument which was a form of the dip needle, which an advertisement in the Williamsburg newspaper in 1772 advised as available for sale by Edmund Dickinson and described as "Mr. THOMAS MARSHALL'S new invented Instrument for finding the VARIATION of the NEEDLE." The new instrument was represented to be simple to use and inexpensive in cost and "singularly serviceable to the Surveyors if the Act takes place [which] requires them to return, Plot and protract their Surveys by the true Meridian." The act to which the advertisement referred became effective on June 1, 1773. Under it, surveyors were required under penalty "*to return* (plat, or Protract) *new Surveys by the true and not by the artificial or magnetic Meridian*." The announcement of the amendment of the act went on to report that many methods had been proposed and practiced for finding the true meridian line, but that the simplest was that proposed by Thomas Marshall of Fauquier, who had in fact been the one who first proposed the amendment to the act directing surveys of land. [30]

Marshall was a well-known legislator and soldier and the father of the first Chief Justice of the United States. A frontiersman during most of his life, he had worked as George Washington's assistant on the survey of the estate of Lord Fairfax and was an accomplished land surveyor. [31] No description or identification of his instrument has survived, although Thomas Jefferson in his memorandum books noted the undated purchase of "Marshall's meridian instrument mahogany cin /20." [32]

Various efforts were made to utilize improved and more accurate instruments for surveys, particularly of provincial boundaries about which there was continued conflict. Such an instance occurred on the northern boundary between Massachusetts Bay Colony and Rhode Island Colony, which had been first established in 1649 and extended by mutual agreement in 1719. After three decades of quarrels over provincial jurisdiction of property, the General Assembly of Rhode Island in 1748 appointed commissioners to run the line again and urged Massachusetts to do the same. At the appointed time the Massachusetts commissioners failed to appear, and although the Rhode Island surveyors proceeded to survey the line, it had to be undertaken anew in the following year. New representations to the governor of Massachusetts failed to gain participation, and in the meantime the Rhode Island surveyors continued their work.[33] In 1750 the Rhode Island General Assembly commissioned Benjamin King, a maker of navigational instruments in Newport, to construct "an Instrement to Determin the Latt:ᵈ and Run the Line between Boston Gouernment and this Colony of Rhode Island and the Province of Massachusetts Bay." [34] The failure of Massachusetts to respond led the Rhode Island Assembly to petition the king in England to have the boundary established in accordance with the line now being run by Rhode Island. The Assembly also voted to pay its surveyors for their work and to pay Benjamin King 300 pounds for making the instrument.[35]

The price of the instrument, even in Rhode Island tender for the period, was considerable, and it is not surprising to find that the Assembly made every effort to maintain it safely. In September of the same year it was voted "that the mathematical instrument now in the colony house, and which was procured by Capt. Joseph Harrison [one of the commissioners appointed by Rhode Island for the boundary survey], for the use of the colony, be lodged in the Redwood Library; but so, nevertheless, that the property thereof, shall stand and remain vested in the colony." [36]

King's instrument was an example of Caleb Smith's Sea-Quadrant, already mentioned. In the pamphlet describing the instrument, Harrison was mentioned as one who had used and approved it, and he probably recommended it to the Assembly and arranged for King to produce it.[37] The instrument, which Smith had described as being equally useful at sea and in land surveys, was a noteworthy achievement for a colonial instrument maker of the mid-eighteenth century. In addition to requiring a precisely graduated scale, with a vernier scale for more accurate reading, it was equipped with a telescope fitted with cross hairs, for which King had to import appropriate lenses from England. The Sea-Quadrant was stored at the Redwood Library at least until 1769, when it was borrowed, with the Assembly's permission, for the observations of the transit of Venus.

By the second half of the eighteenth century, surveying instruments were available in greater numbers and were noted from time to time in inventories of property. Robert Oliver of Dorchester,

Massachusetts, deceased in 1763, owned "4 Maps," one "Prospect Glass" and "a Case of Instruments"; in 1768 William Bridge of Roxbury left among other possessions a "Surveyors Chain & Steelyards . . . £0.4.0"; and an inventory made the following year of the estate of Thomas Dudley, also of Roxbury, included "Surveyors Instrum^ts. & Chain . . .60/." [38]

The equipment of a professional surveyor working full time is best represented by that owned by George Washington, who learned the art of surveying from one of his boyhood teachers and had begun to run lines at his home and the neighboring plantations of his kinsmen at the age of thirteen. At Ferry Farm, the home of his brother Augustine, he had found surveying instruments belonging to his father, and by the time he was fifteen he had already achieved the required standard of proficiency to make surveys for remuneration, using those instruments. [39] They included a brass plain surveying compass, a jacob staff, a surveyor's chain and poles, and probably one of the English texts on the art. Subsequently he received further training from other surveyors in his region, such as James Genn, George Byrne, and George Hume, who were employed from time to time by the Fairfax estate or as county surveyors. [40] Records of specific instruments purchased by Washington begin in 1760, when he ordered and received from London an "18 Inch Circumferentor w. Sights to let down . . . £4.10.0, 1 Strong Chain . . . 0.7.6., 1 Loadstone Comp^t . . . ⌐2. 16. 6." [41] In 1766 he ordered a "twelve Inch brass Gunter, full and compleat, one side to have Inches and 10ths and on the other Inches and 12ths as usual. 1 brass sliding or parallel Rule to be made very true, &c." Still later Washington ordered "1 Case Surveyors Plottg. Instruments." [42]

An inventory of Washington's property made after his death listed a full range of instruments at Mount Vernon relating to his profession, including "1 Tin Canister of Drawing Paper (.50), 1 Case Surveying Instruments (10.00), 1 Case of Instruments, Parallel Rule, &c. (17.50)." [43] A similar inventory made after the death of his widow a decade later included many of the same items, as well as such additions as "2 (Surveyors) machines (6.00)," "2 Pocket Compasses (5.50)," "1 Theodolite (50.00)." [44]

Considerable productive activity in cartography and surveying took place in Pennsylvania during the first half of the eighteenth century, resulting in the production of several outstanding works. Rapid expansion of trade and development of new communities was frequently accomplished by combining the skills of map making and surveying, as is demonstrated in the work of a whole succession of Pennsylvania surveyors, several of whom had been founding members of Benjamin Franklin's Junto. Among these was William Parsons, an English-born shoemaker who also worked as a dyer and scrivener in Philadelphia. He was active also as a deputy surveyor and in 1741 he was appointed Surveyor-General of the Province, a position in which he continued until 1748, when he became unable to cope with physical hardships in the field. He laid out several new communities, including Easton, Pennsylvania, and his work demonstrated that he was well trained and equipped for the profession. His estate included a "compleat theodolite, circumferentor, and other instruments for surveying" and he was capable of making astronomical observations for establishing latitude and longitude.[45]

Parsons was succeeded as Surveyor-General by another member of the Junto, Nicholas Scull, who had formerly served as deputy surveyor of Philadelphia and Bucks County, having worked as a surveyor from 1722. Among his most notable achievements were a map of Philadelphia and surroundings, produced in 1752, and another, issued seven years later, entitled "A Map of the Improved Part of the Province of Pennsylvania," which included almost all the roads which had been surveyed and measured to that time. Scull's grandson, William Scull, succeeded him as provincial Surveyor-General and produced another map of the province, based primarily on earlier works.[46]

The colonization of Pennsylvania owed much to several figures whose works emerged among the most important cartographic achievements of the century, as well as to others who did not achieve the same recognition but provided invaluable resources for later cartographers. Particularly noteworthy in the second category was Christopher Gist, agent for the Ohio Company and intrepid frontiersman, who made three journeys of exploration into the wilderness of western Pennsylvania between 1750 and 1754.[47]

Much better known was Lewis Evans, a Welshman who had traveled widely before emigrating to Philadelphia in 1736. He soon became associated with Franklin, from whom he purchased books and instruments and occasionally borrowed money.[48] Evans was a gifted public speaker and presented a series of popular lectures on natural philosophy and electricity in Philadelphia, Newark, and New York City within a few years after his arrival in the colonies. In

1743 he joined the English naturalist John Bartram on an expedition to explore the region between Philadelphia and Onondaga and subsequently spent considerable time with the Swedish naturalist Peter Kalm during the latter's visit to Pennsylvania, providing substantial assistance to Kalm in the compilation of his reports on natural history.[49] During the course of these varied activities Evans also worked as a map maker. In 1737 he produced the first map of the region of Bucks County, Pennsylvania, and the Delaware River known as the Walking Purchase, which he published the following year. In 1749 he published what was to be the most famous of his works, "A Map of Pennsilvania, New-Jersey, New-York, And the Three Delaware Counties," for which he borrowed from existing maps by Nicholas Scull and others. He noted towns, roads, Indian villages, limits of tide water on the rivers, and related data. Despite the obvious usefulness of the map, Thomas Penn was disappointed in it because he considered it to be prejudicial to his family's land claims, while Cadwalader Colden, Surveyor-General of New York, disputed the accuracy of the astronomical observations on which it was based. Others suggested that Evans had deliberately erred to favor New Jersey in representing the southern limits of New York. While the controversy was going on, Evans completed a manuscript map of the back country and presented it to Penn, who found it more acceptable than the earlier one.[50] By 1750 Evans began advertising that he continued to survey and draw deeds and writings, and that he also drew and copied with utmost accuracy all types of maps, plans, sea charts, prospects, and machines.[51] In 1752 he published a revised version of his 1749 map with corrections and additions, and three years later "A general Map of the Middle British Colonies in America" and "of the country of the Confederate Indians." [52] This map was a major achievement because Evans had established the latitudes accurately with the use of instruments and computed the longitude on the basis of observations made earlier by Thomas Robie at Boston and by Evans himself with the assistance of Thomas Godfrey at Philadelphia. General Edward Braddock used the map in his campaign of 1755, and it served also as a reference in the settlement of boundary disputes. It was widely advertised and distributed during the next several years and was equally the subject of criticism and praise.[53]

A second contributor of major importance to colonial American cartography was Joshua Fisher. Fisher was a native of Lewes, Delaware, where he had worked as a hatter and merchant and served as deputy surveyor and justice of the peace, in addition to various other political appointments. As Deputy Surveyor-General of Delaware he acquired intimate knowledge of the region, and as the owner of a country store frequented by the more than sixty Delaware River pilots in his community, he amassed a great deal of information about the Delaware Bay and the Delaware River.

These waterways were critical to the trade of a wide region, a fact realized from the time of the first settlements. As early as 1644 William Castell, an English writer, described the Delaware as "another river not fully discovered, but bigger than the former [North River] called the South River. It lieth west by south, towards Virginia. The entrance into it is very wide, having Cape May to the east, and Cape Henlopen to the west." [54]

During his years at Lewes, Fisher was repeatedly urged to render his knowledge of the waterways into useful form, and shortly after moving to Philadelphia in 1736, where he established himself in the shipping business, he began to compile a chart of the bay and the river. He had made the acquaintance of Thomas Godfrey and this association advanced the project substantially. Fisher had taught himself some mathematics and may have attended one of Godfrey's evening classes in mathematics and navigation.[55] He enlisted Godfrey's assistance in establishing latitudes and longitudes for his chart with observations taken from at least two points with Godfrey's recently invented octant. One of these was the tip of Cape James (now Cape Henlopen) and another a land point on an island in the middle of the Delaware Bay which was not named in the chart, although clearly represented. The inscription at Cape James on the published chart stated that it had been "observ'd by the Author and T. Godfrey," so the observation must have been made before Godfrey's death in 1749, although the chart was not published until seven years later.

Fisher devoted almost two decades to the preparation of his chart. It was drawn with a high degree of accuracy and provided a wealth of data for the bay pilots, including soundings marked in feet and fathoms, place names along all shores, indications of the shore's character, identification of outlets, creeks, harbors, shoals, sandbars, and ship channels, as well as all major navigational risks.

The chart was engraved for Fisher by James Turner and printed by John Davis at Philadelphia in 1756. A group of shipowners and merchants had subscribed a total of 100 pounds to defray the costs of the project, but relatively few copies of the first version were distributed. This was due to the intervention of Governor Robert Hunter Morris and the Provincial Council, who expressed apprehension that a wider dissemination might allow the chart to fall into the hands of the French and enable French ships to make their way up the bay to Philadelphia. The danger was immediate and urgent, and Fisher was ordered to postpone publication. He protested the delay, partly on the basis of his obligation to his subscribers and partly because he claimed that a prospective enemy could easily avail itself of the services of expert bay pilots without the need for the map. Furthermore, he suggested, an enemy might be deterred from attempting to reach Philadelphia by the very complexities clearly demonstrated in his chart. Nevertheless, in the first edition the upper river channel to Philadelphia was not shown. While the discussions were in progress, Fisher distributed copies of the chart locally and in England, until he was prevented from disposing of the remainder of his stock.[56]

Sailing directions were not included in Fisher's first chart, but a separate printed guide produced anonymously was added when the chart was re-engraved at Philadelphia in 1775. The chart was subsequently re-engraved also in London in 1776 with a printed guide prepared by Captain James Campbell. Ten editions of the chart had been published by 1800, including editions produced in London and Paris.[57]

Another major figure in eighteenth-century cartography was Dr. John Mitchell, a British-born physician and botanist who had spent some years in Virginia. He produced a map which provided the most accurate contemporary indication of British territorial claims and rights, primarily in response to the allegation made by colonial American writers that maps of the New World produced by the French deliberately sought to depict the British territories as much smaller than they actually were. Mitchell's map was believed to have been compiled from original surveys of land grants deposited in the Plantation Office in London, and from drafts, charts, and actual surveys of various parts of the American colonies and plantations which had been furnished to the office of the Board of Trade by the governors of the individual colonies.[58] The map was first published in 1755; two years later an anonymous tract was added, which described the contents of the map and the British claim to the Ohio Valley country. The map was received very favorably, and

Peter Collinson of the Royal Society wrote to the Swedish botanist Carolus Linnaeus that it was "the most perfect of any before published and is universally approved. He will get a good sum of money by it which he deserves for the immense labour and pains he has put to perfect it." [59] The American clergyman and agriculturist Jared Eliot received one of the first copies from a London correspondent who described the map in glowing terms but commented nonetheless on the superiority of the map of New England by William Douglass, which had also been produced in London. Despite the general praise, Mitchell's map had some inadequacies which subsequently led to boundary disputes along the northern border. Furthermore Mitchell had misnamed the town of Worcester, Massachusetts, as Leicester, so that the colony appeared with two Leicesters. [60]

The preoccupation with territorial expansion and boundaries, as well as with maritime development, during the first half of the eighteenth century contributed substantially to the growth experienced by the colonies up to the advent of war. The practical sciences, particularly as represented by cartography, navigation, and surveying, were an essential ingredient in this growth. These sciences were supported by the skills not only of the instrument makers who provided the tools, but also of another category of the mathematical practitioners which came into being shortly before the beginning of the eighteenth century—the so-called science teachers, who taught in evening schools and helped to swell the small numbers of "thinkers and tinkers" already at work.

VII

☆ ☆ ☆ ☆ ☆ ☆ ☆ ☆ ☆ ☆ ☆ ☆

TO ROUSE
THE GENIUS

☆ ☆

Where is taught Reading, a grace of the schools,
Writing, Arithmetic by easy rules,
Book-keeping, Geometry, too very plain,
And Navigation to steer o'er the main;
Surveying and Mensuration as well,
With rare Algebra to make you excell.
All this—and more—he has got in his plan
To rouse the genius, and furnish the man.

Advertisement of M. Davis,
The Royal Gazette (1781)

ALTHOUGH ADEQUATE TRAINING in cartography, navigation, and surveying was rare in the American colonies prior to the nineteenth century, a partial solution to the problem was gradually developed
much earlier with the advent of part-time teachers and the establishment of evening schools. These came into being first in the major
shipping centers and then in other large communities throughout the

colonies. By the late seventeenth century occasional evening classes were provided, primarily for young men apprenticed to the trades who could not afford to surrender any part of their working day for self-improvement. A vastly different situation existed in the colonies than had prevailed in the mother country.

In England the art of navigation was taught chiefly by school-masters at sea, who had shipped on voyages for the purpose of instructing young gentlemen who went to sea at an early age, usually twelve or thirteen, to be trained for a professional maritime career. The sea-going schoolmaster was responsible for providing these boys with a general education as well as training in navigational practices and preparing them for their examination in seamanship and navigation in anticipation of a lieutenant's commission in the Royal Navy. Sometimes a schoolmaster was hired to tutor an admiral's son who was sailing with his father. Navigation and seamanship became an organized part of the curriculum of the teaching profession in England, and experienced naval schoolmasters frequently found remunerative employment on the faculties of special academies organized for such training. In time these schoolmasters established themselves on land as part of a separate group within the teaching profession. They operated from a variety of bases, ranging from private boarding schools to local taverns and coffee houses, and they also worked as tutors in private homes.[1]

In the American colonies no such provision could be made for the training of young seamen. Soon after settlement, however, the need for able navigators and shipmasters was recognized and steps were taken to train men for seagoing careers. No central organization existed for this purpose. Occasional courses were taught in the evening by schoolmasters otherwise fully employed in the daytime in schools and academies, or by experienced shipmasters retired from the sea.

The teaching of surveying in England was usually undertaken by private tutors for the fortunate few of more than average station in life. There was apprenticeship to a limited degree, but most of the surveyors were by necessity self-taught. The land surveyor generally combined several occupations, including teaching of mathematics, calculating ephemerides for almanacs, writing texts, and serving as a land steward when such positions were available. He trained others—paid students as well as working apprentices—in the art of surveying. Other scientific subjects taught by the land surveyor, as well as in the academies, included dialing, gunnery, and drafting.[2]

The scarcity of facilities and teachers for scientific training in the colonies was a reflection of the limitations of the colonial American educational system in general. Colonial schools were based on the Latin grammar school prevalent in England which met the public needs more effectively there than it could in the colonies. This form of education persisted in America as long as the colonists maintained strong ties with the homeland and tended to imitate its familiar institutions. After a few generations, however, there was an increasing concern for a more practical system of education. The English system restricted opportunity to the wealthier segment of society and to "the youth of better parts" who were destined for college education and careers in the ministry, law, and medicine. No provision was made for training the youth of the nonprofessional segments of society, which were achieving greater importance in eighteenth-century community life. Inevitably, as the nonprofessional classes became more prominent, there was increasing protest against the traditional emphasis on the classics.[3] A new form of institution which provided a limited solution was the academy, a secondary school reflecting colonial economic and social evolution. By the mid-eighteenth century private academies were established at Philadelphia, where Benjamin Franklin had been active in the movement which led to the establishment of the Philadelphia Academy, and at Newbury, Massachusetts, where Lieutenant Governor William Dummer bequeathed property in 1761 to establish the first college preparatory school with totally private support and control. Eventually the state legislatures one by one recognized academies as a valuable part of the public school system, which not only prepared students for college but provided general training for those not planning to enter college, thus serving all classes.[4]

Education could not be among the earliest priorities of the settlers; not until communities were reasonably well established could suitable provision be made, and then the facilities varied from colony to colony. The educational system in the Massachusetts Bay Colony had received a boost in 1642 by an act of the General Assembly which provided that the selectmen of each community become responsible for the supervision of the training of children in writing. Several years later the law was modified to require that each town having fifty or more householders was to establish a grammar school for the community. Greek and Latin were part of the standard cur-

riculum, but in time the colonists questioned whether the time allotted to such pursuits could not be more gainfully spent in mercantile studies, and by the beginning of the eighteenth century the
curriculum attempted to reflect a more practical course of studies,
particularly in the middle and southern colonies.

Competent schoolteachers were hard to find, especially
schoolteachers who were religiously inclined and relatively sober.
Science-related subjects were added to the curriculum only long
after the establishment of a school system. Although "ciphering" was
taught, it consisted primarily of the manipulation of integral numbers, and the schoolmasters themselves did not have knowledge of
fractions or even the rule of three.[5]

A factor contributing to this condition was the scarcity of textbooks, not only in the colonies but in England as well. The lessons
were generally dictated by the teacher to the students from a single
text, and making manuscript books for teaching reading and religious subjects was a common practice. Horn books were used until
the beginning of the Revolution, when slates became prevalent.
Printed texts were infrequently available before the middle of the
eighteenth century.[6]

Mathematical subjects were introduced only after mathematical
primers became available in England and were reprinted in the colonies. Among those that had a wide distribution were the elementary
works by George Fox, James Hodder, and Edward Cocker. The first
text of a similar nature to be produced by an American author was
Greenwood's Mathematick, compiled by Professor Isaac Greenwood of
Harvard College.[7]

By the end of the seventeenth century the rapid development of
commerce and the advancement of the trades and crafts created an
urgency for instruction in related subjects, but this was not available
in the public schools. The apprenticeship system, even where it existed, was unable to provide the theoretical training required. Copybooks and manuals for self-instruction (called "vade mecums") published in England were introduced into the colonies by writing
masters and, as soon as printing facilities were available, were
pirated and reprinted by Americans. Notable among these were the
works of George Fisher and John Jenkins. Fisher's work, which first
appeared in London prior to 1731 with the title *The Instructor*, was
reprinted in America with a revised title *The American Instructor*, and
went into at least sixteen editions prior to 1800. In addition to the

customary instructions for reading, writing, and arithmetic, Fisher's work provided an impressive range of useful information for the trades, including the use of the "Plain and Exact Rule" for carpenters, joiners, sawyers, bricklayers, plasterers, plumbers, masons, glaziers and painters, and of other tools and instruments, such as Gunter's Line and the slide rule, and "the Art of Dialling, and how to erect and fix any Dial. . . ." [8] By the time *The American Instructor* had reached its twenty-first edition, on the eve of the Revolution, there had been added to it "A Compendium of the Sciences of Geography and Astronomy, Containing a Brief Description of the Different Parts of the Earth, and a Survey of the Celestial Bodies." [9]

Meanwhile special evening classes for working youth became established as a pattern, which may have had its genesis in the New Netherlands, where such a facility existed in the seventeenth century. The instructions and rules for the schoolmaster Evert Pietersen prepared by the Burgomasters of New Amsterdam in 1661 specified the fees he could demand for students taught in the daytime and that "for those who come in the evening and between times pro rate a fair sum." This contract became fairly standard and similar provisions occurred in arrangements made with other schoolmasters by Dutch colonists prior to the period of English rule.

Science-related subjects were not at first part of the curriculum in government-administered New Netherlands schools, although schoolmasters sent out by the West Indies Company were required to be able to teach arithmetic. Occasionally a schoolmaster had special skills. Jacques Cortelyou, a private tutor of the Latin School of Curtius and Luyck, was well versed "in the mathermaticks of Descarters [*sic*]" and was said to have a sound knowledge of medicine and other sciences and to be a sworn surveyor.[10]

The Dutch evening schools had proved to be such useful institutions that the English government in New York continued them, as well as the practice of sending apprentices to such schools. The popularity of evening schools in New York led to the establishment of similar facilities in other cities and in Boston they began to flourish by the early eighteenth century.

At first such schools were conducted only during the winter months, but by the mid-eighteenth century they were continued also into the spring. The courses generally began in late September or early October and remained in session until mid-March. Some classes were held every evening, others two or three evenings a week. The hours of instruction were from five o'clock to sunset, or from six to eight o'clock, or from candlelight to nine o'clock. Subject matter varied from "Writing and Cyphering" to mathematical studies encompassing the full range from simple addition, subtraction, and multiplication to geometry, algebra, and trigonometry, with specific application to the trades. Bookkeeping was a popular subject, and languages offered included French, Italian, Portuguese, Spanish, and occasionally Latin and Greek. The curriculum was designed to serve both students requiring additional study before entering college and youth employed during the day and anxious to find better jobs. For the most part the students were apprentices and other young men aspiring to learn a trade or profession.[11]

Places of instruction were sometimes single rooms fitted for the purpose, sometimes the schoolmaster's lodgings, and sometimes facilities in existing day schools and academies. A number of schools were conducted in buildings erected for rental to schoolmasters, and other facilities included sail lofts and rooms in public buildings such as the local customs house.

Few of the night-school instructors were college graduates, but many had taught in day schools and academies. Others were men who had had professional experience in the practical sciences in the past or were currently working in these during the day.[12]

Shortly after newspapers became prevalent in the early eighteenth century, the first advertisements for schools appeared. The subjects listed reflected vocational needs. Courses in navigation and surveying were featured, along with related mathematical and other subjects. Both these sciences required fundamental knowledge of algebra, geometry, trigonometry, mensuration, cartography, and to some degree geography as well, in addition to instruction in the use of the mathematical instruments involved. Other scientific offerings were such less practical subjects as dialing, gunnery and fortification, astronomy, and natural philosophy. In many instances these more esoteric subjects may have been included to impress the potential student with the range of the teacher's erudition. Although courses in navigation and surveying were particularly emphasized, during this earlier period relatively few of the teachers provided evidence of technical training or experience.

In Boston in 1709 Owen Harris conducted a school opposite the Mitre Tavern in Fish-Street near Scarlett's Wharf, where the usual program was supplemented by courses in geometry, plain and spherical trigonometry, surveying, dialing, astronomy, navigation, "and the use of Mathematical Instruments." John Green, advertising a school at Cross-Street at the same time, emphasized "Merchants Accompts." [13] In March 1719 Samuel Grainger, a London-trained schoolmaster, established a day school in Boston with a program of studies that included the various mathematics and the full range of the practical sciences, ". . . with the use of the Globes and other Mathematical Instruments." Grainger exercised a significant influence on the Boston teaching profession. The jurist Samuel Sewall commented: "Col. Fitch express'd himself as much prizing Mr. Granger's Accomplishment to Teach Writing; never was such a Person in Boston before." [14] Grainger soon informed the public that "those whose Business won't permit 'em to attend the usual School Hours, shall be carefully attended and Instructed in the Evenings." [15] Grainger's school was a model for others, and after his death in 1734 it was continued by his widow and his son with the approval of the selectmen.

The first formalized academy was the free academy at Charleston, South Carolina, established in 1712, which taught commercial bookkeeping, the practical mathematics, navigation, and surveying.[16] In New York an academy was founded by John Walton, a graduate of Yale College, in 1723; it added to the standard curriculum "The Mariner's Art, both Plain and Mercators Way." Walton held evening as well as day classes from the first of October to the beginning of March.[17] These schools differed from the private academies formed later in the century in placing greater emphasis on practical subjects.

Some of the early teachers also produced texts which were used in their own schools as well as by others. Among these was John Vinal, who began teaching in Boston in 1727 and offered courses in navigation and mathematical subjects in his evening school, later conducted an evening school as part of the South Writing School from 1756 to 1764, then taught in Newburyport until 1781 when he returned to the South Writing School. In 1792 he published a text entitled *Preceptor's Assistant* which enjoyed a modest popularity.[18]

More formal scientific fare was offered by Isaac Greenwood, Hollis Professor of Mathematics and Natural Philosophy at Harvard College from 1727 to 1738. He gave evening lectures during the school year and conducted a private school during college vacation. His lectures were advertised as on "The Principles of Algebra, Sir

Isaac Newton's incomparable Method of Fluxions, or any of the Universal Methods of Investigation used by the Moderns, Conic Sections, the Doctrine of Curves; or any part of Speculative, or Practical Mathematicks, usually taught in the Schools or Colleges in Europe. . . ." After his dismissal from the college for insobriety, Greenwood conducted classes in rooms rented at the Duke of Marlborough's Arms in King-Street, featuring "any Parts of the Mathematicks whether THEORETICAL, as in the demonstrating Euclid, Appolonius, &c. or PRACTICAL, as Arithmetic, Geometry, Trigonometry, Navigation, Surveying, Gauging, Algebra, Fluxions, &c. Likewise any of the Branches of NATURAL PHILOSOPHY, as Mechanics, Optics, Astronomy, &c. . ." [19] He taught applied mathematics to tradesmen and apprentices for two years and from about 1744 conducted an evening school at the Surveyor's Office in Charlestown, holding daily classes from three o'clock in the afternoon until eight at night. [20]

Meanwhile the qualifications of teachers in the public schools and evening schools came under increasing scrutiny from the community. An article in a Boston newspaper of 1733 noted that "John Miller formerly Advertised the Publick he had set up a Mathematical School, at the House of Mr. Peter Barbour opposite to the North side of the Town House, was on Friday examined in the several Mathematical Arts and Sciences he Profess'd, by two Gentlemen (desired to make such an Examination by the Select men of this Town) and was by them Judged to be sufficiently Skill'd for an Instructor therein." [21] This may have been the John Miller who established a school for the practical sciences in New Haven in 1768. [22]

One of the most notable colonial schoolmasters was Theophilus Grew, who established a school on Second-street in Philadelphia in 1734, "over against the Sign of the Bible," where he conducted classes from nine to twelve o'clock, from two to five in the afternoon, and from six to nine in the evening. He specialized in "the Arts Mathematical, viz., Arithmetic in all its Parts, *Geometry, Mensuration, Surveying, Gauging, Trigonometry, Navigation, Dialling* and *Astronomy*, the use of the *Globes* and other *Mathematical Instruments*, according to the most approv'd Methods," as well as "*Algebra* and the *Analytical Art*, with the *Laws* and *Properties* of *Motion*, a thing absolutely necessary to the right understanding of the Modern Philosophy." [23] As his school progressed, Grew promised that his course could be completed within three months "provided the Person have a tolerable

Genius and observes a constant application." Later he featured "the use of Globes, Maps, Planispheres, Scales, Sliding-Rules, and all sorts of Mathematical Instruments." His fees per quarter ranged from 10 shillings for writing and arithmetic to 30 shillings for merchants' accounts, navigation, etc.[24]

Grew had distinguished himself as a mathematician and almanac maker in Maryland before he moved to Philadelphia, where his subsequent friendship with Benjamin Franklin brought him increasing patronage. In 1750, Franklin succeeded in obtaining Grew's appointment as professor of mathematics at the Philadelphia Academy. In 1753 Grew published a treatise on globes which was the first work of its kind to be produced in America.[25]

Among others with technical experience who taught practical sciences in Philadelphia during the same period was Thomas Godfrey, the inventor of the octant, who sought to supplement his income from his trade as glazier. An advertisement in Franklin's newspaper of 1740 informed the public that "THOMAS GODFREY Proposes during Winter Season, to teach Navigation, Astronomy, and other Parts of the Mathematicks, at his House in Second-Street." [26] Recent historians have claimed that the cartographers Lewis Evans and Joshua Fisher studied with Godfrey during this period, a reasonable assumption inasmuch as he was a prominent figure in the sciences in Philadelphia.[27] Another was Charles Fortesque, a schoolmaster who moved from Chester, Pennsylvania, and taught evening classes at his home in Taylor's Alley, including the range of the practical sciences.[28]

As the demand for instruction in the practical sciences increased, new evening schools developed, including one established in 1735 by Joseph Kent, Master of Arts from Nantucket, who taught young gentlemen in the mathematical sciences as well as "Sailing, Surveying . . . Calculation of the Eclipses . . ." [29] Master Job Palmer, claiming no firsthand experience, taught navigation, first at Middleborough and then at Roxbury, shortly after his graduation from Harvard.[30] Among those who had had a previous career at sea and whose teaching was undoubtedly of a more practical nature was Samuel Scammell, who had taught gentlemen volunteers in the British Navy before he opened a school for the mathematical sciences in Boston's North End in 1737. However, he had failed to obtain prior approval from the selectmen of Boston and for a time was refused permission to hold classes.[31]

Among teachers professing experience at sea were Captain George Mackay, who opened a school near the Meeting-House in New Boston in 1754,[32] and John Leach, who had spent several years in the British Navy and made three voyages with the East India Company before offering classes at the home of the Widow Robins in the North End of Boston. Leach was a qualified surveyor, producing land surveys for the town of Boston, and he also taught "Drawing, as far as is useful for a compleat Sea-Artist, as it respects taking Prospects of Land and surveying Harbours." During the British occupation of Boston in 1775, Leach was imprisoned by the British and kept in Boston Jail, and his school was marked to be torn down by the 52nd Regiment.[33]

A schoolmaster who established one of the important evening schools in Philadelphia shortly after 1750 was Andrew Lamb. He had had experience at sea, first in the Royal Navy and then in merchant shipping, and his school offered considerably more to the aspiring young student than did many of its contemporaries. He had taught navigation and had kept a journal for more than forty years. At his chambers at the tallow chandler's shop of John Johnston he conducted both day and evening classes. He featured "Dr. and Cr. [dead reckoning and circle sailing] Navigation in all its Parts, both Theory and Practice &c. Also Sphaerical Trigonometry, Great-Circle Sailing, Astronomy, Surveying, Gauging, &c. and a compleat Method to keep the Ship's Way at Sea, called a Journal, whereby I teach in my School, to find the Longitude at Sea every Day at Noon, by true Proportions; as sure as the Latitude by Observation of the Sun. . . . My Journals from England to Cape Henlopen [Cape James] in America; and from thence to the Lizard Point again, I have proved to be within one Degree of Longitude, (near 140 Degrees of West Longitude) as appears in my Journals to be produced, with others of like Sort, and are good Proofs of my Principles; although Sun and Stars should disappear for several Days and Nights, my plan will find both Latitude and Longitude at Noon every Day, or any other Hour." [34]

Because of their shipping interests, Boston, New York, and Philadelphia continued to be prime centers for special training in navigation. In each of these cities several schoolmasters occasionally joined together to offer a wider range of subject matter, and, after the middle of the century the teaching partnerships proved to be successful.[35] At the same time men professionally engaged in the prac-

tical sciences tried their hand also at teaching. Among these was
William Cockburn, a surveyor in New York City, who in 1763 advertised classes on the entire range of the mathematical sciences, although curiously he did not include surveying in his curriculum. In
the following year, however, he advertised that "Gentlemen may
also have their Estates surveyed, and plans made in the neatest Manner." [36] Samuel Giles, who had taught as a partner with his brother
James from 1759 to 1762, opened his own evening school featuring
mathematical subjects and noted in 1764 that "Draughts and Surveys
of Land are made, or copied by him in the neatest Manner, on Paper
or Parchment, and Writing done at reasonable Prices." [37]

Thomas Carroll in New York City in 1765 featured a course on
"Surveying in Theory, and all its different Modes in Practice, with
two Universal Methods to determine the Areas of right lined Figures, and some useful Observations on the Whole; . . . Navigation;
the Construction and Use of the Charts, and Instruments necessary
for keeping a Sea-Journal (with a method to keep the same, were the
Navigator deprived of his Instruments and Books &c. by any Accident) . . . and Astronomy; Sir Isaac Newton's Laws of Motion." [38]

The emphasis on surveying increased after the middle of the
eighteenth century. G. McCain of Philadelphia offered a class in
"The Theory and Practice of Surveying and Navigation, both according to the best Authors now in Print," and another schoolmaster, William Thorne, provided similar instruction in his evening
school.[39] In Boston William Corlett claimed that he could teach surveying and navigating within a period of forty-eight hours to students of modest capacity.[40]

As the competition in evening schools heightened, the qualifications of teachers of scientific subjects were correspondingly emphasized in their advertisements. James Lamb, who taught navigation in
New York City, claimed that he had served sixteen years at sea and
"flatters himself he can render Navigation (in some Measure) familiar
to the young Navigator the first Voyage." [41]

One of the best qualified teachers of the sciences was Robert
Patterson. He had emigrated from Ireland to Pennsylvania in 1768
and taught a day school in mathematics, surveying, and navigation
first in Buckingham, Bucks County, Pennsylvania, and then opened
a day school at Philadelphia, which he maintained successfully until
1774, when he was appointed principal of the Academy at Wilming-

ton, Delaware. After service in the Continental Army, in which he rose to the rank of Brigade Major, he returned to teaching and in 1779 was appointed Professor of Mathematics at the University of Pennsylvania, later becoming its Vice-Provost.[42]

Another Irish emigrant who distinguished himself in teaching the sciences, first at Philadelphia and then in New York City, was Christopher Colles. A native of Dublin, he had been extensively trained in mathematics and the sciences and had spent his early years in teaching. Upon his arrival in Philadelphia he first attempted to gain employment as the city hydraulic engineer but failing that turned to lecturing on scientific subjects. Several years later he advertised that he could construct mills, hydraulic machines, and buildings, as well as practice surveying. In the event that none of these forms of employment was offered, he added that he ". . . will Engage to instruct young Gentlemen, at their Houses, in the different Branches of the Mathematics and Natural Philosophy." This appeared to be the only employment available to him, and he established an evening school which he advertised extensively a month later with an incredible list of scientific subjects.[43] He also offered to board a few sober, well-disposed young men at reasonable terms, and certified that he ". . . will take particular care of the morals and behavior of such as are intrusted to his care." [44] The school failed to meet all Colles's financial needs, and he supplemented his teaching with public lectures on geography, hydraulics, and pneumatics in an effort to call attention to his many skills. His proposal for a city water-supply system was approved but its completion was interrupted by the Revolutionary War. Heavily in debt with no means of subsistence and a family of eleven children, Colles moved to New Jersey, where he is believed to have become an instructor in gunnery for artillery recruits of the Continental Army and to have continued in that occupation until 1777.

With the growing threat of war, new tutors continued to come upon the scene with offerings of instruction in the practical sciences. Two teachers named Maguire and Power joined forces in a school to provide instruction in the most useful branches of the practical sciences "and how to make maps." [45] A teacher named David Ellison advertised in 1771 that he taught "Navigation in all its branches, both with regard to theory and practice, with the construction and use of a true Sea Chart (according to the oblate spheroid figure of the earth) whereby the errors attending to other projections are avoided, and how to find the latitude at sea, by two altitudes of the sun, at any time of the day, and to find longitude at sea, by the altitudes and distances of the sun and moon, or a known fixed star and the moon." Two years later Ellison again emphasized the instruction he provided for "the solution of the problem of finding the longitude at sea by celestial observation; also to find the latitude by the moon's meridianal altitude." [46]

Evening schools featuring the teaching of navigation continued to spring up along the eastern seaboard in substantial numbers. Among these were the schools taught by James Conn at Elizabethtown, New Jersey; John Wilson at Newark, Delaware; and Charles Shimin in Salem, Massachusetts. [47]

VIII

☆ ☆ ☆ ☆ ☆ ☆ ☆ ☆ ☆ ☆ ☆ ☆ ☆

NEW PATHS
IN SCIENCE

☆ ☆

Tho' mild AMERICA prevails:
The maid new paths in science tries,
New gifts her daring toil supplies;
She gordion knots of art unbinds;
The Thunder's secret source she finds;
With rival pow'r her light'nings fly,
   Her skill disarms the frowning sky . . .
         "To Mr. URBAN . . . ,"
     The Gentleman's Magazine . . . (1753)

THE TEACHING OF THE practical sciences required certain types of scientific instruments for demonstrational purposes; popular lecturers also needed these to illustrate their presentations. Prominent among these adjuncts to teaching or lecturing were terrestrial and celestial globes, most frequently produced in pairs to show the dimensions and relations of the countries and continents of the earth and the wonders of the skies. The globes produced for the teaching of geography and astronomy, and for the personal use of amateurs of these sciences, were generally more decorative than utilitarian, and usually quite costly, since they had to be imported. In spite of the cost, globes existed in the colonies as early as the seventeeenth century. Among the possessions of John Jenney, a brewer of Norwich, Massachusetts, who erected the first grist mill at New Plymouth in 1636, was a "small globe." [1] Jenney served as assistant governor of Plymouth Colony from 1637 until 1640 and was described by William Bradford as "a godlie though otherwise a plaine man, yet singular for publicness of spirit." Despite his position, he was taken to task in 1638 "for not grinding well and seasonable."

After the mid-eighteenth century globes became a popular teaching device, and many of the academy and evening-school teachers incorporated instruction in their use in their advertised curriculums. One such teacher also published an important treatise on the subject. [2]

Among the amateurs of science globes were equally popular, sometimes because they made impressive conversation pieces, and at other times because they were put to good use. In 1752 Benjamin Franklin wrote to his London agent and correspondent William Strahan with the request to send him "another pair of Popple's Maps of North America . . . ; a pair of Mrs. Senex's improved Globes, . . . (or Neal's improv'd Globes, if thought better than Senex's) the best and largest that may be had for (not exceeding) Eight Guineas." [3] Part-time science teachers when noting in their advertisements that they taught use of the globes often also made certain that the reader was aware of the quality of globes used. In 1745 Charles Peale announced that he taught surveying and navigation in addition to arithmetic at the Kent County School near Chester, Pennsylvania, and that he used globes that were "the largest and most accurate Pair in America." [4]

When Reverend Nathan Prince of Boston advertised in 1743 that he planned, if provided with suitable encouragement, to open a school for young gentlemen at his lodgings, he listed a curriculum which ranged from theoretical mathematics and branches of natural philosophy to such practical pursuits as navigation, surveying, fortification and gunnery, as well as "Geography and Astronomy, With the Use of the Globes, and the several kinds of Projecting the Sphere." [5] Prince did not mention that he had been discharged from a professorship at Harvard College for disorderly conduct, had been refused reinstatement, and had been denied refuge in Boston until his brother, the pastor of the Old South Church, arranged for his admission as an inhabitant.[6]

Closely related to the new and growing interest in geography was a preoccupation with astronomy in the curricula of academies and evening classes. Interest in the subject prevailed at all levels of society, and it had long been part of the curriculum in the colleges and an avocation of amateurs. For the navigator and the surveyor, it was a necessity. Celestial globes provided an excellent means for describing the world of the skies but did not explain celestial movements. The orrery, an instrument invented by George Graham, the well-known London instrument maker, between 1705 and 1709, demonstrated the annual as well as the diurnal motion of the earth around the sun and the moon around the earth by means of three-dimensional orbs traveling on a surface operated by a hand crank or by clockwork-driven wheelwork. Subsequently more complicated versions were produced, which included the other planets and their motions, often rendered with considerable elaboration.[7]

The first example of such a mechanism to arrive in America was a gift made by Thomas Hollis in 1732 to Harvard College, where it was used during the next few years by Professor Isaac Greenwood in lectures which captivated the public imagination throughout the colonies. The press publicized the instrument widely, noting: "This one Engine opens a new Scene to our Imaginations, and a whole Train of useful inferences concerning the Weather and the Seasons and administers the pleasure of Science to any one who has as much Attention as is necessary in a Man to acquit himself in the ordinary business of any Profession or Occupation among Men of all Orders or Circumstances. And therefore it is hoped that in time not only each Province, but each principal Town in these parts will think it necessary to have an *Orrery*, as a publick Town Clock, the one gives the Time of the Day and Night, the other presents to our View the wonderful Works of the Deity." [8]

The second orrery in America was one constructed in 1743 by the president of Yale College, Thomas Clap, who had established himself as an amateur astronomer of note.[9] Approximately a decade later, David James Dove, an English teacher who had an evening school in Philadelphia, undertook a series of public lectures on the sciences in which, as he claimed in the press, "The astronomical part will be explain'd and illustrated by a curious large ORRERY." [10]

The lecture series was scheduled in Newark, New Jersey, and New York City, but Dove's appointment as English master at the Academy of Philadelphia forced him to cancel his schedule, and a professor of philosophy named Baron was found to replace him. Baron was shortly thereafter notified that he was to leave for England to be ordained by the Bishop of London, and the series was finally presented by the cartographer Lewis Evans. Realizing that he was not qualified for the role of "philosopher" which had been advertised for Dove and Baron, Evans made every effort to instruct himself in experimental philosophy prior to undertaking the tour; Franklin personally assisted with his training. Evans finally presented the lecture series in New York City in 1751. Despite a number of misadventures, the series was well received both in New York and Newark and led to even greater interest in astronomy not only for the general public but as part of the college curriculum.[11]

It was directly as a result of the Evans lectures that David Rittenhouse undertook the construction of an orrery, which was to be perhaps his most outstanding achievement. He discussed the project for the first time in correspondence prior to 1767 with his brother-in-law, the Reverend Thomas Barton, and spent considerable time contemplating the project before undertaking it, investigating all the various types of orreries and other planetary machines then in existence. His aim in building such an instrument was to advance his own standing in the sciences in the colonies and possibly abroad as well, and he realized that to achieve such an ambition his instrument would have to surpass those being produced by the foremost instrument makers of England and Europe.[12] After studying English and European works describing planetaria and the orrery in particular, he found a satisfactory concept of the machine in the works of John Rowning, an English writer on the sciences. This inspired him to design an orrery which operated, not on the horizontal plane, as all existing examples did, but on a vertical plane, and one which would represent the motions and orbits of the planets and the moon with greater accuracy than had been achieved to that time.[13]

By the spring of 1767 Rittenhouse had developed the details of his instrument and set to work. Before it was finished it had been announced to the press, after a description which he had prepared for the American Philosophical Society had been published in the famous first volume of the Society's *Transactions*.[14] This publicity immediately made Rittenhouse the subject of public interest. Reverend William Smith of the College of Philadelphia urged him to move from Norriton, Pennsylvania, where he then lived, to Philadelphia, promising to obtain a permanent position for him which would provide sufficient time for his scientific pursuits. Rittenhouse succumbed to the temptation and moved his family and his shop equipment to Philadelphia by the autumn of 1770. He was assured by Smith that the College would purchase the orrery as soon as it was completed and Rittenhouse gave the project top priority. Meanwhile Dr. John Witherspoon, the new president of the Presbyterian College at Newark, where Evans had lectured, visited Rittenhouse with a view to acquiring the orrery for his college. The outcome was that the Presbyterian College purchased the instrument before it was finished, paying Rittenhouse 300 pounds, which was twice the cost of the most expensive orrery being produced in England. News of the sale brought immediate reaction from Smith and other Philadelphia associates of Rittenhouse, who had hoped that the instrument would remain in that city. Rittenhouse refused to withdraw from his agreement with the college at Newark but reluctantly agreed to produce another orrery for the College of Philadelphia. Meanwhile he sought to appease his Philadelphia colleagues by permitting the first orrery, when it was completed, to be displayed at the College of Philadelphia in connection with a series of lectures, of which Rittenhouse presented two on the subject of astronomy. The Pennsylvania legislature agreed to pay him 300 pounds for his second orrery, which he completed in the summer of 1771. He planned to produce a third instrument, but although he may have done some preliminary work on it, it was never completed. Rittenhouse's two orreries provided admirable evidence of American capability to compete with English men of science and furthermore represented a number of improvements over the British form of the instrument. In America his achievement was recognized publicly by John Adams and Thomas Jefferson, among others, and brought Rittenhouse to the topmost rank of American men of science. Jefferson suggested in a bill proposed June 18, 1779, for amending the constitution of the College of William and Mary that the instrument should be renamed a "Ryttenhouse" in honor of its maker, and also expressed the hope that Rittenhouse would not only produce an instrument for that institution of learning, but also one that the American Philosophical Society could present to King Louis XVI of France, as evidence of American accomplishment and to honor an ally of the American

cause. Rittenhouse, however, was not interested in making more orreries and avoided as much as possible Jefferson's persistent efforts to
have him do so.[15]

Many of the science teachers engaged in other scientific activities, often as a source of additional income and sometimes as a matter
of avocational interest. These pursuits included calculating ephemerides for almanacs, making independent astronomical observations, and collecting natural and artificial curiosities for scientific
study. Among those who combined a number of these activities was
Thomas Godfrey, whose invention of the octant has been described.
Godfrey's almanacs for the years 1730 through 1732 were published
in a large sheet of "Demi Paper in the London manner" by Benjamin
Franklin.[16] Because of the limitation of size, these almanacs included
only the ephemeris; data on eclipses, lunations, the times of the rising and setting of the sun and moon; the rising, southing, and setting
of the prominent fixed stars; times of high waters; and some weather
prognostication. Published under Godfrey's name, the almanacs had
a modest success and had become recognized as an annual series,
which Godfrey and Franklin planned to continue.

It was during this period that Franklin and his printing partner,
Hugh Meredith, lodged with the Godfreys. Godfrey's wife, noting
Franklin's increasing success, sought to arrange a match for him with
one of her relatives. Franklin showed interest, but it was contingent
on whether the candidate for marriage could provide a suitable
dowry. An argument arose over the dowry expectations, and, as one
harsh word led to another, a rift developed which could not be
healed. The Godfrey family moved out in the autumn of 1732, and
Godfrey took with him his calculations for the almanac for the year
1733, which he promptly sold to Franklin's printing rival, Andrew
Bradford. It was published as *Bradford's Pennsylvania Almanac for the
Year 1733*. Godfrey continued to calculate ephemerides for Bradford's
almanacs through 1736.[17]

Since the parting of the ways came late in 1732, Franklin found
himself faced with the choice of abandoning his almanac series or
finding other means for producing it. He employed a local philomath,
whose identity is not presently known, to calculate the ephemerides
and himself added the customary information about the courts and
Quaker meetings, distances of highways and roads, a historical chro-
nology, and a listing of European kings and princes, in a pamphlet of
twenty-four pages. To ensure the success of his hurried new ven-

ture, Franklin duplicated a hoax which had been perpetrated by Dean Jonathan Swift against a certain John Partridge in England in 1707. He included a prediction of the time of death of Titan Leeds, his major rival as a publisher of almanacs. Leeds reacted as Franklin had anticipated and used the popular press to heap abuse on Franklin and on his almanac. The result exceeded Franklin's hopes, for he sold out not only the first edition of his almanac but a second and a third issue within three months.

Franklin named his publication *Poor Richard's Almanack*, borrowing a form from an almanac issued by his brother James Franklin, in Rhode Island, whose series *Poor Robin's Almanack* had become very popular. The name Richard was taken from a seventeenth-century English astrologer and philomath named Richard Saunders. Franklin filled the space in his pages with miscellaneous materials assembled from various sources. Unconcerned with dignity, he permitted his love for jokes and his satirical approach to life to run unleashed. He provided a refreshing contrast to the customary grim and somber theological content of the New England almanacs of his time by reporting the adventures and misadventures of the fictional Richard Saunders and his wife, Bridget. He converted memorable sayings by great writers of the past into maxims couched in the language of the common people of his time. He constantly reflected the contemporary concern for making the maximum use of time to achieve the common good and developed it into a philosophy which has remained associated with him.[18]

The combination of materials and the new approach rendered the Franklin almanac an instant success, and he sold as many as 10,000 copies of each issue. He compiled and published the almanacs until 1758, after which he continued as publisher only for eight years more. After 1766 *Poor Richard's Almanack* was produced by the printing firm of Hall & Sellers in Philadelphia.

Franklin's light-hearted approach occasionally crept into the more scientific parts of the almanacs. In his first issue, he stated under "Profitable Observations and Notes": "All Measures of Longitude are deduced from Barley-corns. Three Barley corns make an Inch, 12 Inches a Foot, 3 Feet a Yard, 5 Yards & one half one Pole or Perch, 40 Pearches make a Furlong, 5 Furlongs make a Mile, in a Mile are 320 Perches or Poles, 1066 Paces, 1408 Ells, 1760 Yards, 5280 Feet, 63360 Inches, 190080 Barley-corns."[19] In another issue he decided to eliminate the forecast of eclipses. "You must excuse me dear reader that I afford you no eclipses of the moon this year. The truth is I do not find they do you any good. When there is one you are apt in observing it to expose yourself too much and too long in the night air whereby great numbers of you catch cold, which was the case last year to my very great concern. However, if you will promise to take more care of yourselves you shall have a fine one to stare at the year after next." [20]

The preparation of calculations for almanacs was a respectable occupation for even the most distinguished men of science, as well as a lucrative source of income, and the names of some of the most eminent mathematical practitioners are to be found among those who calculated them. David Rittenhouse prepared a number of ephemerides for various printers, the first of them for *Father Abraham's Almanack* for the year 1759, the earliest of the Abraham Weatherwise series printed at Philadelphia and subsequently copied in other parts of the country. Rittenhouse also produced the ephemeris for *The Universal Almanack* for the year 1773, published by James Humphreys and advertised widely as Rittenhouse's work. He apparently sold the same ephemeris simultaneously to printers in various cities.[21] He was the author of the ephemeris for the 1773 *Virginia Almanack*, printed at Williamsburg; for *The Lancaster Almanack* issued by Francis Bailey for 1775, and for Bailey's *Der Gantz Neue Verbesserte Nord-Americanische Calendar*,[22] in addition to *Father Abraham's Pocket Almanac* for 1776, published by John Dunlap at Philadelphia.

Another important scientific figure who successfully produced calculations for almanacs during the same period was Benjamin West, a book dealer and self-taught mathematician. A native of Massachusetts, he had learned the art of navigation from a Captain Woodbury and taught himself mathematics and astronomy in his leisure time. He moved to Providence, Rhode Island, and after failing in many enterprises, became a successful clothing manufacturer for the Continental Army during the war, taught in public schools, and was finally appointed Professor of Mathematics and Astronomy at Providence College (now Brown University). The first ephemeris West produced was for the year 1763, calculated for the meridian of Providence and published there by William Goddard.[23] West then produced calculations for several series of almanacs simultaneously, including *The New England Almanack*, published at Providence from 1765 through 1781; and *Bickerstaff's Boston Almanack*, published at

Boston in 1768, 1779, and thereafter annually from 1783 through 1793. In 1769 he provided the ephemerides calculated for the meridian of Halifax, Nova Scotia, for a series which was published continuously except for the years of the war until 1812.[24]

Not all of the self-taught astronomers who attempted to calculate almanacs were successful. A failed philomath was Clark Elliott, maker of navigational instruments at New London, Connecticut, who, having observed, soon after his arrival in that city, the success of the almanacs published locally by the printer Timothy Green, decided to provide him with some competition. In 1766 Elliott attempted to establish a new series called *The Connecticut Almanack* and compiled the issue for 1767 entirely by himself. Encouraged by its modest success, he produced a second issue for the following year. In this issue, however, he made an error in his calculations for one of the eclipses, which raised questions concerning his competence. Although mortified by the experience, Elliott nevertheless produced an issue for 1769, but the printer, Timothy Green, found a plausible reason for not publishing it. Elliott then calculated an almanac for the year 1770, which he prefaced with a long and elaborate explanation of his error for the year 1768. It was published but it was the last to bear his name. The issue for 1772 appeared as the work of "Edmund Freebetter, Student in Physick and Astronomy." This has been generally assumed to have been produced by Elliott under a pseudonym, but it has also been suggested that the pseudonym was in fact that of Samuel Stearns, the acknowledged author of the *North-American's Almanack* published at Boston during the same period.[25]

Elliott's almanac endeavors at New London were followed by those of Nathan Daboll who entered the field in 1773 with the issuance of *The Connecticut Almanack* for that year. With the next issue he changed the title to *Daboll's New-England Almanack* for the year 1775, and the next year he joined forces with Timothy Green for the publication of *Freebetter's New-England Almanack* for 1776. Daboll's almanacs were calculated for the meridian of New London and other port cities. The series became very popular with the whalers of New England. Later Daboll deliberately adapted his almanacs for the use of "landsmen" as well, and their popularity continued. Other members of his family succeeded him in this endeavor without interruption for more than 125 years.[26] Daboll's son Nathan was for a time professor of mathematics at Wesleyan College and then for a quarter of a century conducted a school of navigation at New London.[27]

During the decade prior to the advent of war the almanac makers frequently concerned themselves with public affairs. One of the most outspoken was Nathanael Ames, who in his almanac for the year 1766, voiced the general protest against the Stamp Act in an address to the "Generous Reader" and in several verses. Benjamin West followed suit in his almanac for the same year in an essay entitled "A Short View of the Present State of the American Colonies," [28] and in the following year both almanac makers commented on the Declaratory Act by means of which Parliament asserted its right to tax the colonies. The colonial grievances after the Townshend duties were eloquently voiced by Ames in his almanac for 1768.

Almanacs by various authors issued during the succeeding years continued to reflect the political events and concerns of their times, reporting the results of meetings held on the subject of nonimportation, identifying the leaders of colonial dissension, and including articles on the growing reaction, such as one by West entitled "A Brief View of the present Controversy between Great-Britain and America" in his almanac for 1775. It is significant that West referred, not to the American Colonies, but to "America." [29]

A number of the mathematical practitioners who had been active in various other practical sciences as well as the calculation of almanacs also participated in an astronomical achievement which constituted one of the major scientific endeavors of the eighteenth century in several parts of the world. This was the observation of the transit of Venus in 1769. In the British colonies of North America alone, at least nineteen different groups or individuals participated. Professor John Winthrop of Harvard (a great-grandnephew of John Winthrop, Jr.), who had made observations of the transit of Venus which occurred in 1761, again observed the new transit from Cambridge, while two sets of observations were made at Newport and Providence, Rhode Island, by Reverend Ezra Stiles, assisted by the navigational instrument maker Benjamin King at Newport and by Benjamin West and Joseph Brown at Providence. Another philomath named William Poole observed from Wilmington, Delaware, while the almanac maker Titan Leeds made observations from Talbot County, Maryland. Most important among these activites were the several combined observations sponsored by the American Philosophical Society at Philadelphia and Norriton, Pennsylvania, and Cape Henlopen, Delaware.

Transits of Venus are among the rarest of recurrent and predictable celestial phenomena. A transit occurs when the planet Venus passes between the earth and the sun and brings about what is in effect an eclipse. Only eight such transits have been observed in the world's known history thus far: in 1518 and 1526, 1631 and 1639, 1761 and 1769, 1874 and 1882. The next are scheduled to take place in the years 2004 and 2012. The transits always occur in pairs eight years apart and in the months of June or December. Only three such transits had been observable since the establishment of English colonies in the New World. The first occurred in 1631 and the second in 1639. The 1761 transit was visible only in Newfoundland, where John Winthrop and Samuel Williams took an expedition to make observations. They were able to see only the end of the transit, and the expedition was not successful. Consequently the 1769 transit was being anticipated with considerable interest, and both the British and the French sent out expeditions of scientists to chosen sites for the occasion. The phenomenon provided an exceptional opportunity to demonstrate that competent men of science could make satisfactory observations in colonial America as well as in the motherland. Benjamin Franklin took a dim view of the enterprise, however, because John Winthrop was the only colonial American astronomer recognized in England. The Astronomer Royal, Nevil Maskelyne, pointed out that the only place known where the transit would be visible for its entire duration was in the region of Lake Superior, to which he hoped that the Americans would send observers, a suggestion which was supported by Winthrop.[30]

Meanwhile in Philadelphia, in spite of Franklin's reservations, considerable interest was being generated by members of the American Philosophical Society. A fourteen-member committee was organized, led by Reverend William Smith and Reverend John Ewing, both of the College of Philadelphia (later the University of Pennsylvania), to equip three stations from which observations were to be made. Smith was to observe with David Rittenhouse at the latter's observatory in Norriton, and Ewing was in charge of a similar group at an observatory to be erected on State House Square. Owen Biddle, a Philadelphia clockmaker, was to supervise observations at Cape Henlopen.

The most remarkable aspect of this enterprise was the ingenuity shown in collecting suitable instruments. The Pennsylvania General Assembly had agreed to provide adequate funds to purchase a telescope and to erect the observatory in Philadelphia. Although Franklin had stated that there was not a single instrument adequate for the observations in the entire province of Pennsylvania, four telescopes and several other instruments were collected in Philadelphia: a new telescope purchased with funds from the Assembly; a small reflecting telescope and a transit and equal altitude instrument borrowed by the Pennsylvania Proprietors from Joseph Shippen; a telescope and an accurate clock owned by the instrument maker Thomas Pryor; and a large telescope loaned by a Miss Polly Norris for the use of Dr. Hugh Williamson. At Norriton, Rittenhouse had assembled a number of other instruments that he had made or modified for the event. These included a transit and equal altitude instrument, a large refracting telescope, and an astronomical clock. Additional instruments were a telescope with a set of lenses, which had been purchased by Franklin for Harvard College but not been forwarded, and the famous Jersey Quadrant, borrowed from the Jersey Proprietors.

In preparation for the observations Rittenhouse in 1768 had erected a wooden observatory building on an elevated piece of ground adjacent to his house. The roof was designed to incorporate a sliding panel so that the telescope could be trained on the sky while the observer remained inside, where the astronomical clock and other instruments were maintained.

The Cape Henlopen party was equipped with the reflecting telescope owned by the Library Company of Philadelphia, which was modified by Biddle with the addition of an endless screw, and another refracting telescope was provided for the use of Joel Baily, who was to work with Biddle.

Meanwhile, much feverish activity was taking place at Providence, where the merchant, Joseph Brown, had consulted with Benjamin West and provided funds for the purchase of the needed instruments from England. These included a reflecting telescope, of 3 feet dimension with a micrometer and adjustable cross hairs. The Sea-Quadrant which Benjamin King had made for the boundary survey more than a decade earlier was borrowed from the provincial government, and two accurate clocks were also acquired. In a published description of the instruments, West noted that the telescope was equipped with horizontal and vertical wires (cross hairs) for taking differences of altitudes and azimuths, adjusted with spirit levels at right angles, and a divided arc for taking altitudes, as well as a helioscope with micrometer. He identified the King Sea-Quadrant as having been made under the direction of Joseph Harrison and mentioned that its limb was divided to 5 minutes, and by a vernier index to 5 seconds.[31]

At Newport, Ezra Stiles was having a difficult time in assembling the instruments required. Abraham Redwood, founder of the Library which bears his name, agreed to undertake the costs for the construction and purchase of instruments for Stiles's use, and Stiles prevailed upon King to duplicate his Sea-Quadrant, which Stiles described as "an astronomical sextant" in the several references he made to it in his diary. King interrupted the work he was doing and was able to complete the instrument in less than a week.[32]

John Winthrop did not experience any of the anxieties and problems concerning the acquisition of instruments that were the lot of the others, for he borrowed an astronomical clock and a reflecting telescope from the collections of Harvard College and a second reflecting telescope from a private owner in Boston. While making his preparations for the observations, Winthrop delivered two lectures at the college, describing the impending transit, which were later published.[33]

In addition to these major observing parties, other interested individuals made their own observations with whatever equipment they could assemble. Reverend Samuel Williams of Harvard joined Tristram Dalton of Newburyport at the latter's home; William Alexander, Earl of Stirling, used his own telescope at his home in New Jersey; and John Page at his Virginia estate, Roswell, used a pair of "perspective glasses" made by the English maker Ayscough and a Hadley reflecting quadrant. The instruments used by Leeds and Poole were not reported.[34]

On the day of the transit the weather was excellent. Large crowds collected to watch, silently and respectfully, the observers operating in public areas. The quality and value of the several observations varied considerably, depending on the instruments and skills available and the precision with which the observations were being made. As Venus neared the sun, what was reported as a dark tongue seemed to connect the planet and the sun before Venus actually reached the sun's perimeter. Those observing were confused as to exactly when the point of contact occurred, and the internal ingress contact was just as difficult to establish. The emotional reaction of the observers to the phenomenon was another factor which had to be taken into consideration. It was reported that even Rittenhouse became so excited when the moment of contact arrived that he was speechless and did not report it until a few seconds later.

Some of the observations, such as those from the American Philosophical Society's stations and those made by John Winthrop, were recorded in a scientific manner and reported. These, as well as summaries of the observations made by West and Leeds, were published in the *Transactions* of the American Philosophical Society and subsequently summarized in the Royal Society's *Philosophical Transactions*. Many of the other observations were published in newspaper accounts, and in West's case in a separate pamphlet.[35]

After Rittenhouse had moved permanently to Philadelphia in 1770, he was assigned the responsibility for maintaining the State House Square observatory which had been constructed at the same time as his own. When in 1781 the Pennsylvania legislature finally appropriated 250 pounds to Rittenhouse so that he could support his work in astronomy, the fund was used to erect another observatory at the corner of Mulberry and Seventh streets in Philadelphia where he pursued his work.[36]

One of the problems he encountered in the new location was the development of a satisfactory method to establish a meridian mark for his observatory. It was not until 1785 that he was able to resolve the problem, which he communicated in a letter to John Ewing that was published in the *Transactions*. At the time he had constructed his observatory, which was in the form of an octagonal brick building, Rittenhouse had placed a meridian mark at the northward side at a distance of about 1,200 feet, because the southward exposure was too close to other buildings. Subsequently additional buildings were erected directly north of the observatory, making distant vision with his transit impossible. He pointed out that a meridian mark was not essential if one had a good transit instrument, and could check it daily by the passage of the north star, but that a permanent mark would indeed be an added convenience. He finally devised a method whereby he fastened the objective of a 36-foot telescope to the wall on which the transit instrument was supported, placed opposite to and as convenient as possible to the objective of the transit when it was in a horizontal position. In the focus of the objective so attached, he screwed a piece of flat brass plate to a block of marble placed in his garden and supported on a brick pillar built for the purpose on a firm foundation. He painted several black concentric circles on the brass plate, the remainder of which was silvered. The circles could be seen distinctly through his transit, and the innermost circle, which was "about the size of a brevier O," served as the meridian mark to the center of which the cross hairs of the transit could be adjusted.[37]

As the scientific interests and endeavors in the colonies received encouragement from various directions, wealthy merchants and landowners began to share them. A few of these collected scientific apparatus for their own edification, formed modest libraries of works on the sciences, and collected natural and artificial curiosities. Evidence of these interests was reflected from time to time in the advertisements of auction sales of estates. Governor William Burnet of Massachusetts in 1729 owned "sundry Mathematical Instruments" which were sold with his household goods at public auction.[38] When an unidentified Boston householder returned to England in 1754 he placed on sale various properties including "a Universal single and double Microscope, with a Solar Apparatus, Frog Frame, &c., a Farenheit's [*sic*] Thermometer on Box, a four-foot Reflecting Telescope, the largest size, six Inches Diameter, and an Electrical Machine and two spare Globes," all complete and little used.[39] A public vendue of the furnishings of the home of the late Honorable Paul Mascarene of Boston listed "Sundry Mathematical Instruments, a good Thermometer, and a genteel made new invented Microscope, with its proper Apparatus. . . ."[40] "Sundry Mathematical Instruments" were also noted in the sale at the Province House of the possessions of the Massachusetts Governor, Sir Francis Bernard, Bart.[41]

Among important libraries that included scientific works supplemented with collections of related scientific apparatus was that of the Honorable William Byrd II of Virginia, who had assembled "near 4000 Volumes in all Languages and Faculties, contained in twenty three double presses of black Walnut, and also a valuable Assortment of philosophical Instruments, and capital Engravings, the Whole in excellent Order."[42] The library had been founded by the seventeenth-century tobacco planter and merchant William Byrd I and supplemented with philosophical apparatus by his son, who had been elected to membership in the Royal Society and became associated with the foremost men of science and world affairs of his time.[43]

Dr. Thomas Moffat of Newport, Rhode Island, not only collected a library of his own but was involved with the founding of the Redwood Library. Moffat established himself as a physician shortly after his arrival in 1729 and became closely associated with the English philosopher George Berkeley, who had migrated to Newport in the same year. In 1730 Moffat assisted Berkeley in organizing a Literary and Philosophical Society, and when Berkeley suddenly returned to England it was continued with the encouragement of Moffat and his friends. In 1747 it was incorporated by the provincial assembly under the name "The Company of the Redwood Library," which was subsequently housed in a building financed by the wealthy local merchant Abraham Redwood. The library was founded for the instruction "of the curious and impatient" as well as for "the bewildered ignorant." Moffat was appointed the first librarian, and the library was opened to the public in 1750. Within its first decade it had become an important institution with more than 1,500 volumes and pamphlets in its collections.[44]

Meanwhile Moffat had assembled an important collection of scientific instruments of his own and had devoted considerable attention to making microscopic observations. He became more and more involved in civic, social, intellectual, and political affairs of his community but began to fall into public disfavor because of his loyalty to the British Crown. In 1765 he supported the Stamp Act and as a consequence was burned in effigy before the Colonial House along with the effigy of the British tax agent. Angry citizens sacked the tax agent's house, then moved to Moffat's residence, which they despoiled of his valuable collections of books, furnishings, paintings, and scientific apparatus.[45] As the riots continued, not only in Newport but in Boston, Moffat fled to the protection of General Gage in Boston, and thence to England. The king recompensed him for his loyalty and his losses, and when Moffat died in England, the inscription on his gravestone read in part: ". . . here lies Thomas Moffatt, M. D., 21 March 1787: who left his gratitude to the King and British Nation, his prayers to the Loyalists, and pardon to the Rebels of America."[46]

Another noteworthy private library was that assembled by John

Camm at Williamsburg, Virginia. A clergyman of the Church of England, Camm replaced Reverend William Small as Professor of Moral Philosophy and of Natural Philosophy at the College of William and Mary in 1766, succeeding to the presidency of the College in 1777. The advertisement of the sale of his property in 1779 mentioned ". . . the very valuable LIBRARY and PHILOSOPHICAL APPARATUS of the Rev. *John Camm,* deceased." [47]

Of considerably greater importance than the private collections were those formed by organizations dedicated either to scientific endeavor or to the promotion of useful knowledge. Among such organizations were the scientific societies which evolved from modest beginnings late in the seventeenth or during the first quarter of the eighteenth century to assume national importance by the time that the colonies achieved nationhood. The movement was derived from the great societies formed in Europe, particularly Italy, Germany, France, and England, during the seventeenth century and from the influence that the Royal Society in particular exerted in the colonies.

The first learned society in the American colonies was the Boston Philosophical Society, formed under the leadership of Increase Mather in 1683. Although short-lived, the organization established a pattern copied elsewhere in the colonies later. At the society's headquarters "agreeable gentlemen of Boston" met every fortnight for intellectual discussion and to develop a collection of the materials of natural history. The society's concerns in that period were largely theological and political, however, and scientific matters were of secondary interest. [48]

The Boston Philosophical Society may have inspired the second such organization, which was initiated by Benjamin Franklin shortly after he returned to Philadelphia from England and Boston in 1727. This modest group was formed as the Leathern-Apron Club, later the Junto, by a group of young men who met for companionship and to improve their minds by the discussion of political, literary, scientific, and intellectual questions. It was not a secret society, nor was its primary concern the pursuit of the sciences. The members were young tradesmen and others having similar interests. Franklin described its purpose and activities in his *Autobiography,* in which he noted that the Junto met to discuss questions ". . . of Morals, Politics, or Natural Philosophy . . . and once in three months produce and read an essay." Its debates were "to be conducted in the sincere spirit of inquiry after truth, without fondness for dispute, or desire for victory; and to prevent warmth, all expressions of positiveness in opinions, or direct contradiction."

No formally trained scholars belonged to the Junto, but its founding members included two self-taught surveyors, a shoemaker who had trained himself in mathematics, one "gentleman of means," a merchant's clerk, a copiest of deeds, and a window glazier and plumber who had taught himself in mathematics, Latin, and astronomy.[49] The Junto continued to meet without interruption for several decades. In about 1736 it countered a proposal for its expansion with the suggestion that regional clubs be formed having the same framework as the Junto, and some of these were established in other cities.[50]

A direct outgrowth of the group was the Library Company of Philadelphia, established in 1733 by a number of the members of the Junto with the cooperation and some financial support of others. The company was designed to fill a gap in providing education to the public, with "an Endeavour however small to propagate Knowledge and improve the Minds of Men, by rendering useful Science more cheap and easy of Access." [51] The Company provided a library for the mutual use of its members, and additional support was sought from the Pennsylvania Proprietors. Thomas Penn responded by donating a piece of land, and John Penn sent an air pump from England, the first in the American colonies. Although Samuel Jenkins, an English gentleman well acquainted with "Natural Knowledge and the Mathematicks," offered to demonstrate the equipment, little use was actually made of it. The air pump presented problems immediately, for a special cabinet had to be made to house it, and the assembly of the equipment developed one crisis after another. More than two years passed before the pump was ready for use, and the first to demonstrate it publicly was Professor Isaac Greenwood, who used it in a course of lectures on the sciences in Philadelphia.[52]

Meanwhile the growth of the Company's book collection was impressive, and by 1740 the Company obtained the use of rooms at the State House in which the books and scientific apparatus were maintained together. Other gifts received as the Company developed included a pair of 16-inch globes, an electrostatic machine, and a telescope. During the same period Peter Collinson, on behalf of the Royal Society, sent a glass tube for experimentation, a gift which was to initiate Franklin's experiments with electricity.[53] In the course of time the books and scientific apparatus were supplemented with archaeological and American fossil specimens, including Eskimo utensils and relics, some mechanical equipment, and a particularly prized hand and arm of a mummy.[54]

In 1743 Franklin formulated a proposal for a society having greater scope and wider reach. This was to have monthly meetings to discuss scientific observations and experiments as well as correspondence from members on "all philosophical experiments that let light into the nature of things, tend to increase the power of man over matter, and multiply the conveniences or pleasures of life." A number of members of the Junto became founders of the new society, first known as the American Philosophical Society Held at Philadelphia for the Promotion of Useful Knowledge, and later simply as the American Philosophical Society. The original Junto became dormant, with only occasional meetings, until it was reorganized in 1766 as the American Society Held at Philadelphia for Promoting Useful Knowledge and in 1769 was united with the new organization, of which Franklin was the first president and was re-elected repeatedly until his death in 1790.[55]

The American Philosophical Society had an important influence upon political as well as scientific thought in its time. Its first fruit was the initial volume of *Transactions*, which was published on the eve of the Revolutionary War. Copies of the volume were distributed to learned societies and major libraries in Europe at the same time that the Declaration of Independence was announced. It may be said that the first volume of the *Transactions* constituted the New World's declaration of intellectual independence. The European world was curious about this new American society, and its formation did much to achieve acknowledgment of the American colonies as a distinct nation. Franklin, as its president, turned the Society's efforts away from specialization. Emphasis was placed on the practical and the immediate, and the Society directed its attention primarily to the study and improvement of agricultural, maritime, and commercial concerns of the colonists. Its role in the observations of the transit of Venus of 1769, already described, received international recognition.

Meanwhile, the forerunner of a number of state organizations for the promotion of useful knowledge had come into being in 1759 at Williamsburg, Virginia. Organized primarily for the purpose of developing manufacturing in Virginia, it authorized the General Assembly to offer bounties for discoveries and improvements. In May

1773, The Virginia Society for the Promotion of Useful Knowledge was formally established, with the well-known botanist John Clayton as its first president and John Page as its vice-president. Page, who had served first as Lieutenant Governor and then as Governor of Virginia, was greatly interested in scientific research. In 1779 he suggested the identity of magnetism with electricity and invented an instrument for measuring the fall of dew and rain to 1/300 inch.[56]

A further manifestation of the interest in the sciences and related subjects was the creation of the first formal museum collections in the colonies. The earliest of these was assembled at Norwalk, Connecticut, at the beginning of the eighteenth century by a man named Arnold, who displayed "a curious collection of American birds and insects," which was viewed by John Adams at Norwalk and again in London after it had been sold and shipped to England. Nothing more is known of Arnold and his collection except that it was deemed to be of importance in its time.[57]

The first museum in the sense of a public collection was the Charlestown Museum of the Charlestown Library Society in Charlestown, South Carolina, which was formally constituted as such on January 12, 1773. A special committee was appointed for "collecting materials for promoting a Natural History of this Province which was agreed to." Most of the members were young men educated in England and Scotland who had been active during the preceding three years in building the collection of books on scientific subjects, emphasizing the natural sciences. Within two months after its appointment the committee had formulated a firm outline of the purpose and scope of the project. Four curators, two of them physicians, were appointed, and a prospectus was issued to the press. During the early meetings the committee directed its attention to individual sciences, one of which was astronomy.[58] A special meeting was called to take immediate action to acquire an orrery, and it was voted to ask "M. Writtenhouse" for the first refusal of the next orrery he produced. Fear was expressed that Rittenhouse might move to England and the Society lose its opportunity. Much time was devoted during 1774 in negotiating for the orrery. David Rittenhouse finally agreed to construct one for the museum, similar to that at the College of Philadelphia and to deliver it in three years, but, as mentioned earlier, he was diverted by the advent of the war and never returned to the production of orreries.

Meanwhile the Charlestown Museum acquired other scientific

apparatus of significance. In 1774, soon after the museum was formed, a telescope was purchased and a microscope acquired, as well as electrostatic equipment and a camera obscura. The threat of war in 1775 caused the Society to make plans for the storage of its library and collections, but collecting continued unabated and in early 1778 a hydrostatic balance was acquired from a gentleman about to leave the state. Then disaster struck. On January 15, 1778, the Society's journal recorded that "the Library together with the Books instruments Charter Box and its contents, &c., the property of the Society and also the books of the late Mr. McKensie were all consumed by fire except the Books & instruments mentioned in the List delivered in to him." [59] Temporary quarters were found for the surviving materials, but not until 1785 was permanent housing in the Charleston State House acquired.[60]

These meager beginnings of the museum movement were augmented, particularly in relation to the practical sciences, from another quarter. During the latter part of the eighteenth century, marine societies were formed in New England as benevolent organizations to aid the widows and children of impecunious members and also to encourage aids to navigation. The Salem Marine Society, established in 1766, kept records of accurate data about the waters and coasts, which subsequently proved to be an invaluable source of information to fishing and shipping interests. The East India Marine Society, founded at Salem in 1799, proposed "to collect such facts and observations as may tend to the improvement and security of navigation," and in addition "to form a Museum of natural and artificial curiosities, particularly such as are to be found beyond the Cape of Good Hope and Cape Horn." This was the only museum founded by a marine society and its collections developed into an important repository which still survives as part of the Peabody Museum at Salem.[61]

IX

☆ ☆ ☆ ☆ ☆ ☆ ☆ ☆ ☆ ☆ ☆ ☆

SUCH
PLEASANT
INVENTIONS

☆ ☆

> I wyll not onely write of suche pleasant inuentions—but
> also will teache howe a great numbre of them were wroughte,
> that they may be practised in this tyme also. Whereby shall be
> plainly perceaued, that many thynges seme impossible to be
> done, whiche by arte may very well be wrought. . . .
>
> Robert Norman, *The Safeguard of Saylers* . . . (1584)

ONE OF THE MOST critical factors in the development of the practical
sciences in the colonies was the scarcity of mathematical instruments, the tools of the sciences. These were traditionally the
products of the highly specialized artisans who proudly described
themselves as "makers of mathematical instruments" and who occupied one of the upper levels of the hierarchy of the arts and crafts

in Europe and England. In the colonies the profession was not at first a separate craft, nor had it originally been such in Renaissance Europe or in England. It was a new occupation, created by combining a variety of skills borrowed from already existing crafts. Pressed into service were the talents of the joiner or cabinetmaker, the engraver, the brass founder, the tinsmith, occasionally the pewterer and the ironmonger as well. Later, the clockmaker and the silversmith played important roles. At first these craftsmen continued to ply their normal trades and as a sideline produced or repaired instruments to order as the need arose. They rarely had the time to make such items in anticipation of sales.

The trades and crafts listed in surviving records of the first groups of settlers did not include that of the instrument maker or those of the clockmaker, silversmith, or engraver. These more highly skilled artisans came later. Nevertheless, there were among the early comers men talented enough to repair such instruments as had been brought or were later imported. When and by whom the first instruments were produced in the New World cannot be determined, but it is unlikely to have been prior to the arrival of artisans with the required skills. The first clockmaker, for example, did not arrive in the English colonies until the late seventeenth century. The earliest-recorded maker of instruments was James Halsey of Boston, whose name was inscribed on a pearwood backstaff dated 1676. Whether this was a unique achievement is not certain; probably he also produced other instruments. Halsey's unusual position in the community was indicated by the fact that he was identified as a "Mathematician" in land records.[1] No other instrument maker working prior to the eighteenth century has been identified, but a few must have existed, since professions requiring instruments had been practiced for almost a century.

The few mathematical instruments brought or imported during the period of settlement were highly prized. As the need developed, means of production had to be found, since imported instruments were very costly by colonial economic standards and, furthermore English surveying instruments generally could not be adapted to the topography of the New World. These considerations led the colonists, by the early eighteenth century, to begin producing their own in some numbers.

The supply was first augmented by copying the available instruments as accurately as was possible with the skills, tools, and materials at hand. Wood was the material generally used for navigational instruments, most of which were traditionally made of selected hardwoods with scales and inscriptions impressed by engraving or stamped with metal dies. The metal used for occasional small fittings was brass, which was easy to cast and to work. Consequently the navigational instruments were the first to be reproduced.

Instruments required for surveying were more difficult to duplicate, however, because they were made of brass and required other techniques. The clockmaker and the brass founder were enlisted to produce the plain surveying compass and circumferentor, which were the instruments most commonly used, and a silversmith or engraver was capable of dividing and inscribing the scales. Such skills were still rare even in the early eighteenth century, and all brass had to be imported from England until the second quarter of the nineteenth century. Brass instruments, whether imported or made locally, were consequently expensive.

The makers of mathematical instruments were divided into several categories on the basis of the skills and materials required. Those who made the traditional instruments of the navigator were competent in the use of wood. The makers of instruments for the cartographer and surveyor required skill in metalworking. The much smaller group of highly skilled craftsmen that produced the limited number of instruments of extreme precision for astronomical observation and related endeavors worked in metal also and were at the same time mathematicians capable of designing new instruments or modifications instead of merely copying existing instruments. Finally, a separate group of makers produced science-teaching apparatus and other specialized instruments requiring yet other skills. Because of regional restrictions and requirements, the same maker frequently produced several types of instruments. An artisan in an inland community would not be called upon to provide navigational instruments but would produce surveying instruments and possibly compasses and sundials and occasionally some items of science-teaching equipment. A maker working in or near one of the major shipping centers was generally capable of making both navigating and surveying instruments as well as other scientific aids.

Since surviving business records of the colonial instrument makers are fragmentary when they exist at all, no estimate of instrument production can be made. Certainly a substantial number of navigational instruments was produced from the late seventeenth through the early nineteenth century. Surveying instruments were proportionately fewer until the beginning of the nineteenth century when the nation's expansion escalated the numbers considerably. The production of mathematical instruments in any period reflects the changing scientific priorities of the colonists and their ability to create with the skills and materials at hand substitutes for the more professional products which were out of reach because of distance, cost, and political concerns.

During the earlier periods the market for mathematical instruments was occasional at best and did not require full time production by the makers, and consequently did not provide sufficient income to warrant exclusive occupation. The craftsman could put his regular work aside to provide the instruments required locally by the surveyor and seafarer and then resume his more lucrative craft. As the need for these scientific tools became more regular and frequent, craftsmen began producing them as a full-time occupation. In the maritime centers this was particularly the case with navigational instruments since there was a steady demand for repair of instruments and for replacements of those destroyed or lost at sea. It was not long before the makers realized that they had an unusual specialty of a refined order and identified themselves with it. The title "maker of mathematical instruments" was used with obvious pride and even a little professional snobbism, indicating awareness of this unusual distinction and establishing beyond doubt that it was a profession distinguished in itself. The title was used lavishily on the artisans' shop signs, trade cards, and newspaper advertisements, and the distinction they claimed was in the upper hierarchy of the crafts.

A major deterrent to the development of the profession of the instrument maker was the shortage of labor in every field of endeavor, which effectively curtailed the formalization of craft guilds and prevented the development of a successful apprenticeship system.

The practice of apprenticeship was brought to the New World by the first colonists and existed in varying degrees in each of the colonies. As in England, apprenticeship not only was of social and economic importance but provided the basic educational institution for a large part of the community, since apprentices were more commonly young people. There were two classes of apprenticeship. One was voluntary, in which the apprentice bound himself "by his own free will and consent" to a master for the purpose of learning a trade;

the other was compulsory, in which poor children were bound out by town officials to masters who could provide support and give them training in a trade as well as an elementary education. The teaching of reading and writing was required, and when the masters were too illiterate to provide it, they were obliged to send their apprentices to a teacher who could do so.

The ready availability of labor in England enabled a master craftsman to employ as many apprentices as he could afford, to perform a wide range of tasks during their seven years of training. Parents could be required to pay a specified amount of money for the privilege of having a son trained, and in return the master was required to provide only a minimum, which included board, lodging, and training. In the colonies, however, a master craftsman willingly employed an apprentice without exacting a cash premium and agreed to feed, lodge, and clothe him and to provide him with an education. The period of training was furthermore shortened from the traditional seven years of the English system to from four to five years. All of these inducements were not sufficient, however, to entice boys in sufficient numbers to enter many of the trades and crafts voluntarily, and most of the apprentices trained were recruited by compulsory service. These recruits included illegitimate and orphaned boys supported by the community, as well as a smaller percentage of voluntary candidates, since by colonial law all children "not having estates otherwise to maintain themselves" were required to engage in some useful occupation. The community played an important role in the system, inasmuch as indentures were required to be made a matter of public record. The selectmen, church wardens, or other town officials were designated to serve as a board of overseers to ensure that the youth was fulfilling his requirements and that the master was providing his charge all he had promised.[2]

When the apprentice had satisfactorily completed his training period, he received two sets of apparel—"freedom clothes"—from his master, his indenture was recorded as having been completed, and he graduated to the status of a journeyman. He was now free to ply his trade or craft wherever he chose. A master might offer a competent apprentice the opportunity to continue to work in his shop at a standard rate of pay to their mutual advantage. More frequently the newly graduated journeyman chose to travel from town to town to find employment and to save as much of his earnings as possible to enable him to establish his own shop. The journeyman was also free to marry, and young men offered continued employment by their master often did so.

The trades and crafts in the colonies provided unlimited oppor- tunities, and the journeyman could usually find more lucrative employment in the shops of his former master's competitors, or even at an entirely new specialty if he chose.

The apprenticeship system functioned successfully in some trades and crafts, but less well among the more highly specialized skills, such as the making of mathematical instruments. In general, these men hired shop assistants and errand boys instead of maintaining formalized training for apprentices. Few of their shop assistants seem to have developed sufficient mastery of the art to enable them to pursue the craft as a career, unless they had been English-trained before employment, as was the case with John Dabney who worked for the wooden-pump maker Rowland Houghton, or Henry Dawkins, employed by the New York instrument maker Anthony Lamb. Probably the fact that instrument making was so frequently only a part-time endeavor equally deterred the maker from investing in an apprentice and the would-be apprentice from pursuing that career. Except for English-born-and-trained instrument makers who migrated to the New World, most others who had served an apprenticeship were sons or relatives of their masters, and they often moved on to other employment, frequently in other communities. In contrast with the traditional practice in the Old World, dynasties of instrument makers were the exception in the colonies. Among the few families known where more than one member pursued the profession were the Halseys, Greenoughs, Elliotts, Kings, Chandlees, and Rittenhouses.

The chief reason that the colonial instrument maker did not commonly develop a large establishment with the intent of perpetuating it was that there were so many challenging new opportunities to offer competition to the drudgery of family enterprise. Even in other crafts when such an enterprise existed and apprentices were trained, they frequently went into other fields after having completed their training. The clockmaking establishment of Thomas Harland, an English-trained clockmaker who settled in Norwich, Connecticut, late in the eighteenth century,[3] employed ten to twelve apprentices at one time, but only a few of these later distinguished themselves as clockmakers. Anthony Lamb trained his son John Lamb as his apprentice at the same time that he employed Henry Dawkins as an engraver, and later made his son a partner, but John Lamb subsequently became a wine merchant.[4]

In the maritime communities, throughout the eighteenth century, the shop of the instrument maker became a center for doing business and exchanging information. Its services were required by the shipmasters entering and leaving port, who had other needs besides instruments. The shop served not only to sell merchandise to the retail customer, but also as the proprietor's own workshop and stockroom. Frequently the instrument maker found himself functioning as a ship's chandler, maintaining a large stock of ship's supplies and providing services of the nature of banking and exchange. Of the local institutions so familiar today, such as banks, labor exchanges, employment agencies, and insurance companies, few existed in most communities of that period. Business records of some of the major maritime New England merchants engaged in import-export during the six years prior to the beginning of the Revolution indicate that the average number of their daily transactions was thirty-two, which provides some idea of the volume of waterfront trade.[5] Just as the local tavern served as the center for dispensing news from the outer world brought by travelers and sharing local gossip and political concerns, the waterfront shop of the instrument maker and ship's chandler became the communication center for the shipping world. The shop sign, "The Sign of the Quadrant" or a variation, became a beacon for shipmasters coming into port, who invariably needed to have navigational instruments repaired, or perhaps to purchase a new one which had been ordered during their last visit. The marine compass in particular needed to have the needle "touched," or remagnetized, or the shipmaster might be in need of a set of nautical charts, or waggoners. Other local merchants and shopkeepers, always avid for news about activities in other ports, made it their practice to visit the Quadrant when ships arrived in port or were about to depart. The neighboring shops were generally also closely related to the needs of the maritime trade and included the ship's chandlery, the ship's carver, the ship's smithy, the cooper, and the sailmaker, in addition to the inevitable tavern.

The instrument makers engaged in a number of civic and other activities. Thomas Greenough of Boston, a maker of navigational instruments, was the son of a shipwright and may have been trained in his profession by James Halsey. He served at various times as clerk of the markets, was elected constable, made the "Annual Visitations" to record the inhabitants and to assess properties, served as select-man for two two-year periods, as haywarden, and as overseer of the poor. He was at first a member of the Second Church and later served as a deacon. He was a member of the Ancient and Honorable Artillery Company, to which he was admitted as a private, and rose to the rank of captain of the fourth company of the Second Massachusetts Regiment, serving in the Cape Breton expedition. Throughout his career he was extremely active in real estate.[6]

Clark Elliott, the son of a Boston ship captain, served a formal apprenticeship with Greenough at Boston, then worked for him for a period as a journeyman, and in about 1767 established his own business in New London as an instrument maker, maintaining it until his death in 1793. In addition to producing a large number of navigational instruments during his career, he conducted a brisk business in the exchange of secondhand instruments, conducted classes in navigation, calculated ephemerides for almanacs, and was actively involved in real estate and in community affairs.[7]

The activities of Goldsmith Chandlee, a maker of surveying and other instruments in an inland community, were similarly varied and extensive. A native of Nottingham, Maryland, where he served an apprenticeship with his father as a clockmaker, he moved to Virginia where he became associated with a silversmith named William Richardson, whose shop was situated between Stephensburg and Winchester on the frontier. Chandlee subsequently built his own shop and brass foundry at Winchester and produced clocks, surveying instruments, sundials, surgical instruments, magnetic compasses, apothecary and money scales, and other items in gold, silver, pewter, brass, and iron. He was active in the Society of Friends, a founding member of a volunteer fire company, a conveyancer and writer of deeds and other legal papers, sat on the Bench of Justices at the hustings courts of Winchester, bought and sold bills of exchange, bonds, notes, military warrants, and such, and served as an executor for large and small estates on the frontier. Chandlee owned and operated the largest single manufactory other than coach, wagon, and carriage works in the region.[8]

The first mathematical instruments to be duplicated and produced in the American colonies were those required for navigation. In general, they were relatively easy to reproduce because they consisted of simple elements made of hard-grained tropical woods, carefully finished, and assembled with brass pins as necessary to provide maximum resistance against warpage caused by exposure to sea air. The only skill other than that of the woodworker that was required was for the inscription of a divided scale, which needed a knowledge of mathematics applied by an engraver. The scale had to be inscribed with maximum precision on wood or on ivory, mediums which were probably more difficult than the paper or metal with which the engraver customarily worked. Each line of the scale had to be incised deeply enough to survive abrasion and wear, and the lettering and numbering were accomplished by stamping with tiny sharp steel dies which marked the scale to a sufficient depth without disturbing the wood fibers around them.

For the brass instruments of the cartographer and surveyor, however, the graduated scales presented greater problems, which were resolved by the skills of other artisans, such as engravers or silversmiths. They used the traditional techniques of their own specialties to cast and finish the components of brass instruments, and applied the method called "common graduation" to divide and mark the scales. The inability of colonial American craftsmen to execute the more complicated and finely divided scales for the sextant, zenith sector, and other specialized instruments prevented them from competing with English and European makers, and these instruments were imported in almost every instance until the middle of the nineteenth century.

Instrument production in the early days was hampered by scarcity of materials. The main components of navigational instruments were made of selected tropical hardwoods. Common among these were lignum vitae, rosewood, mahogany, and ebony. The arcs on which the scales were engraved were made of boxwood because it combined a close grain with a light olive color, rendering the scales readable. Pearwood had similar characteristics and was often used for the same purpose. Boxwood and pearwood were locally available, but the tropical hardwoods were imported by European and English traders. They were in adequate supply for the English instrument makers, but for the colonies, they had to be re-imported from England until well into the eighteenth century. The cost was considerable, and consequently colonial makers were forced to seek substitutes. They experimented with the native hardwoods found in abundance particularly in New England, and although these proved useful for some purposes, they were not totally satisfactory. Among those favored were black walnut, rock maple, and several fruit-woods, such as pear, wild cherry, and apple. By the middle of the century some had already become scarce, as Peter Kalm noted, including the wild cherry and the curled maple, which the colonists were using in great quantity without replanting. Kalm also observed that even the black walnut, while in sufficient supply, was probably due for extinction because "careless people are trying to destroy it, and some peasants even use it as fuel." [9]

Although these woods were widely sought for cabinetmaking, they were not sufficiently close-grained for instruments used at sea and lacked the oils which, in the tropical woods, provided a degree of protection against salt water and sea air.

After the first quarter of the eighteenth century a small supply of tropical woods began to be available in the larger port cities. Some were still imported from England, some now came from the West Indies, and others were provided by privateering. The earliest importations of these rare woods in quantity were advertised in the Boston press: ". . . on the Long Wharffe Lignumvitee, Box wood, Ebony, Mahogany, Plank, Sweet Wood Bark, and Wild Cinnamon Bark" in August 1737, and in November of the same year a public sale was announced at the Exchange Tavern of "50 Pieces of fine Mahogany in 10 Lots." [10] A few years later an advertisement noted the arrival of a shipment of ". . . a parcel of Lignam vitae and 3½ in. Mahogany." [11] Among the early importers specializing in this commodity was John Waghorne of Boston who could supply "the best of Turnery Ware of Mehogany &c." in quantity for local trade and export by 1740. [12]

Meanwhile New England merchants had found another source for rare woods besides paid shipments from overseas. The cargoes of prize ships taken from the Spanish and the French and brought into the ports of Newport and Boston frequently included mahogany and lignum vitae, which were then advertised for public auction. [13]

After the middle of the eighteenth century, rare woods of considerable variety were available as a result of expanded sea trade, particularly with the West Indies. Clark Elliot, the New London maker of navigational instruments previously mentioned, maintained a complete record of all the backstaffs (also called quadrants or Hadley's quadrants in his records) which he had produced in his long career. For each of the 403 backstaffs he listed in his journal, he recorded the woods of which it was made. Either because of personal preference or availability, he used "green ebony" for the greatest number, 138 examples. "Iron wood" was next in order with 62, and black ebony, marblewood, and "speckled wood" followed in that order. Other woods he used included red wood, naked wood, plane, red stopper, bastard cocas, pearwood, brazeletomet, boxwood, cocas (cocuswood), lingoram, shittim wood, and individual examples noted were made of "torn wood [thorn], "Whales Jaw-bone," and "Particularium." He frequently combined two woods in the same instrument, and some of his favorite combinations were cocas and plane, naked wood and plane, green ebony and cocas. One instrument he produced in "speckled wood brown" with "Ivory arches and vanes." Some of the backstaffs made of black ebony had "Ivory Diamonds," or thin lozenges of ivory, added as decorative features at the joints.[14]

The green ebony used by colonial American makers was probably not the true green ebony (*Diospyros melanoxylon*) but wood from the West Indian granadilla tree (*Brya ebeneus*), which was also the source of cocas or cocuswood, imported for the most part from Jamaica and other regions of the West Indies. Black ebony came from a variety of sources. That acquired in billets of relatively small size from the Cape of Good Hope and considered inferior in color and grain to the ebony from Mauritius, or East Indian ebony, was available to English makers for mathematical and philosophical instruments.[15]

Ironwood was derived from a number of species and regions, and that used in the colonies was probably the species *Krugiodendron ferreum*, imported from the West Indies. A related wood was red stopper which was also called ironwood and came from the species *Reugenia rhombea* in the same region. Marblewood (*Diospyros quaesita*) was found in Ceylon, while braziletomete was obtained in Brazil by Portuguese and Spanish traders and imported to Europe, where it proved to be extremely desirable for furniture veneer. It was known by many names, including "brazilwood." [16]

By the beginning of the Revolution a number of merchants were specializing in the importation of rare woods, and a supply for the instrument maker was assured.[17]

A comparable difficulty existed with the production of instruments of metal. Because of the scarcity of the component metals, copper and zinc, brass was not produced in America until the second quarter of the nineteenth century. Some copper was mined in Connecticut after 1709 and in other regions later, but it was not until

1837 that zinc was mined and utilized for the mass production of brass. Brass was shipped from England in the form of ingots or sheets. The ingots were cast in sand while sheets were formed by pouring molten metal into forms made of slate shaped as large plates. These large sheets were then reduced to various thicknesses as required by beating with tilt hammers, usually water-powered. Some utensils were formed directly from the brass by the same methods. These production methods and the cost of transatlantic shipment made the price of brass so high that between the beginning of the Revolution and the end of the War of 1812 importation ceased completely.

Clockmakers and other craftsmen requiring brass for their work tried to help themselves by advertising good prices for broken or discarded brass and copper utensils, and every effort was made to reuse the old metal by a process called "cementation," a technique first used in England in the sixteenth century, which had become standard practice. Broken-up brass or copper was melted in crucibles with calamite (zinc carbonate) to create new molten metal which was then poured into sand or slate molds. Zinc carbonate was a mineral form of the zinc metal prevalent in England, where it was mined and the lumps ground into powder. However, the English were reluctant to share their monopoly or even to make available the raw brass produced by this method.

The scarcity of brass led the colonial instrument makers to seek substitutes, and by the early eighteenth century they had resorted to hardwoods. The instruments required for the surveyor were duplicated in wood from metal examples with considerable skill, and wooden surveying instruments came into common use. For the most part these were produced by professional instrument makers, although examples were also made during the winter or in leisure time by Yankee whittlers for their own use.

Daniel Burnap, clockmaker and instrument maker working in East Windsor and Coventry, Connecticut, made not only brass surveying compasses in two grades which he sold for 6 pounds and 4 pounds respectively, but also wooden surveying compasses at the comparatively modest price of 2 pounds.[18] Surviving examples of brass and wooden surveying instruments by the same makers confirm the prevalence of this practice.

The colonial American instrument maker was distinguished from his English or European counterpart by his skill in working with more than one material. Wooden instruments were also produced in England for navigation and other uses, but because of the guild system's restrictions these makers worked only in wood, while those making brass instruments worked only in brass.

The makers of navigational instruments customarily worked in wood, and therefore had no difficulty in producing surveying instruments in wood when the need arose. The plain surveying compass, which was the most commonly used, was relatively easy to produce in wood. It consisted primarily of a circular body flat on the top and bottom, which could be easily turned on a lathe with a cavity inside which would accommodate a compass card and needle which would be protected with a glass pane set in putty. From the central body two arms extended which were slotted at each end to receive sighting bars which were whittled and fitted into place but could be removed for travelling. A turned piece of wood with a circular opening in its center was attached to the center of the bottom of the instrument so that it could be attached to a tripod or jacob staff. The compass card was generally the type used for marine compasses and engraved with the compass rose. A cover was also provided, cut from pine or other inexpensive wood, with leather thongs with which it could be tied over the glass pane of the compass.

Oddly enough the wooden surveying compass, an instrument which was made and known only in America, was restricted to the New England colonies, although makers of wooden navigational instruments were prevalent in the middle and southern colonies as well. The production of wooden compasses exclusively in New England, as well as the later wooden-clock industry of Connecticut, seems to indicate that the craftsmen of that region developed a particular affinity for working in wood, although no direct connection apparently exists between the makers of wooden mathematical instruments and the makers of wooden clocks.

Wooden surveying compasses were produced in substantial quantities by a number of makers in New England from about 1740 through the first quarter of the nineteenth century. Few of the instruments were dated; the earliest-known example is a particularly fine one made by Daniel King of Salem with the date 1744 on the compass card. The advent of the wooden surveying compass may possibly be related to the first known record of the production of surveying instruments in the colonies. This is at the same time a record of the earliest invention and patenting of a mathematical instrument, indeed possibly the first surveying instrument produced in the British colonies of North America. The instrument was a "new Theodolate" invented and patented in 1735 by a wooden-pump maker of Boston named Rowland Houghton, who made and sold all forms of water-drawing equipment and was a skilled mechanician.

By an act of the General Court of Massachusetts Bay Colony, Houghton was awarded a patent for his invention, which granted him exclusive rights for its production and sale for a period of seven years. This was the second patent issued in the colonies. The theodolate was not described beyond the words in the petition which specified that Houghton had "with considerable trouble and expense, projected and made a new theodolate for surveying of lands, with suitable instruments, with greater ease and dispatch than any surveying instrument heretofore projected or made within this province." [19]

Houghton's invention was advertised two years later in the Boston press, where the inventor reported modification of the original form.[20] From 1738 Houghton employed as his assistant an English-born maker of mathematical instruments named John Dabney, who presumably assisted in the commercial production of the invention.[21] The distribution and use of Houghton's theodolate cannot be determined, and no example is known to have survived, but the assignment of a provincial patent confirms the need for surveying instruments.

The use of the word "theodolate" instead of "theodolite," the name of a surveying instrument invented and used in England, suggests that Houghton's invention differed from the theodolite, but that there was a similarity between the instruments. Inasmuch as Houghton was an artisan who specialized in working with wood, it is probable that the theodolate was made of wood. "Theodolate" may have been Houghton's name for a plain surveying compass made of wood, and in fact he may have produced the first wooden examples of this common instrument.

Local surveyors and the instrument makers themselves occasionally experimented with variations of instruments. An example is a theodolite made of hickory which combined the components of the circumferentor with small parts in brass and a pewter compass dial painfully stamped out with metal dies. Another was a sighting instrument made by John Sellers in the 1760s for use on his surveys in Pennsylvania and designed to be suspended from a taut line and held in balance by a wrought-iron rod weighted at its terminal with lead. The major component was a wooden block, the interior of which had been hollowed out to accommodate small ivory sighting bars which were attached at the terminal top ends of the block when in use.[22]

An interesting variation is a wooden sighting instrument having a pewter scale inscribed to 90 degrees in each direction from the center, which was read with a lead plummet suspended from a string. It was equipped with a bubble level, detachable wooden sighting bars, and a means of locking the alidade at any angle required. The instrument was used with a tripod or jacob staff.[23]

Even more representative of the work of the do-it-yourself school was a plain surveying compass made entirely of thin pieces of cardboard mounted on a small pine panel and supplemented with a compass needle on a brass pivot. The circle of the compass card was marked into the 360 individual degrees, and the outer rim of the same circle was marked off in Roman numerals for the hours V through XII to VII, making the device serviceable as a sundial while working in the field. This composite "mathematical instrument" which combined the magnetic compass, surveying compass, and sundial, was produced in 1783, made entirely by hand, with all the inscriptions marked with pen and ink, by Enoch Long, Jr., a New Hampshire surveyor.[24]

Working from examples of English-made navigational instruments, the colonial woodworker had little difficulty in reproducing the instruments identically and in their entirety. Great care was required in the selection of the pieces of wood to ensure that they had no faults which would later weaken them. The common backstaff, or Davis quadrant, required six pieces of wood for its frame in addition to three more pieces which constituted the vanes. The braces and main members were made of one of the tropical hardwoods and the two arcs were made of boxwood or pear. The individual parts of the frame were assembled with mortise-and-tenon joints held firmly in place with glue and brass pins. Since pin making was a craft in its own right, brass wire for the pins may have been purchased by the instrument makers from pin makers or others stocking such material. The wire was made by stretching a strip of brass by hand or with water power through an iron plate having holes of diminishing size. The wire was then cut into lengths, the points sharpened on grindstones, and the heads formed by one of several means and crimped by hand-powered drop hammers. Other small parts were cast in brass and hand-finished. The vanes and transoms for the backstaff and cross staff were produced from sawn blocks and shaped by hand.

The division and inscription of scales, which were the most important part of all mathematical instruments, required particular skill. The art of scale division and inscription had evolved fairly rapidly in Europe and England during the sixteenth and the following centuries, from the diagonal scale used by the astronomer Tycho Brahe to the vernier scale which provided greater precision and which was introduced by the early seventeenth century. The merit of the scale depended on the accuracy of its division into equal parts, which in turn was totally dependent upon the tools available to divide, mark, and inscribe it and the competence of the craftsmen who applied them.

Measurement, as applied to the practical sciences, was accomplished by means of circular or linear scales, divided equally into units based on accepted standards. With the requirement for increasing precision, the graduation of scales became a separate science which evolved over centuries of improvement from the first crude inscription to the remarkably accurate division made possible in the late eighteenth century by the invention of a dividing engine. It is impressive to discover that the early American craftsmen were capable of producing tools for scientific measurement comparable in quality and precision to those made by specially trained makers of the Old World.

Prior to the nineteenth century, graduation was accomplished by any one of three methods. "Common graduation," which had evolved slowly through the Renaissance, was the method most generally in use. For scales of greater precision, such as those for astronomical instruments, a method known as "original graduation" was developed by a small number of English craftsmen during the eighteenth century. Its application was limited, since it required the most strenuous control of the tools and an extraordinarily discerning eye. Finally, there was "machine graduation," which was first accomplished in the later eighteenth century by an English instrument maker, Jesse Ramsden, who invented the circular dividing engine. Colonial American makers, not having the techniques, training, or capability for the other methods, were concerned only with common graduation, which was accomplished entirely by hand with the use of combinations of eight simple instruments: the dividing plate, an index, dividing knife, beam compass, spring dividers, a dividing gauge, a pattern scale, and a dividing square.

The tools underwent little modification throughout this period except for improvements in the scales of the dividing plate and the dividing square, brought about by the increasing refinement of the art. These were the same tools and procedures employed by the colonial American instrument makers until machine graduation was made possible in America after the middle of the nineteenth century.

Guidance for the instrument maker attempting to undertake common graduation without previous training and experience was provided in some of the early texts on navigation and dialing published in England. These had the faults of popular works and generally left much to be desired, either because the authors were obviously unfamiliar with the techniques described and had copied them from other works, or because they assumed too great a knowledge on the part of the reader.

One of the most interesting and useful of these works was a well-illustrated volume entitled *The Mariners Magazine*, by Samuel Sturmy, published in London in 1669. The content strongly reflected the author's personal association with William Leybourn and Henry Phillippes, two of the most important mathematical practitioners in England who had a particular interest in scientific instruments and their use.

The second book of his work was devoted to "A Description of Instruments" and in it he included "those which are the Grounds and Foundation of all the rest, and are now the only Instruments in esteem amongst Navigators and Mariners at Sea." He described the instrument maker's tools for producing scales for mathematical instruments by common graduation in various materials. For graduating scales on instruments of wood Sturmy specified that a prime necessity was several scales of equal parts of varying lengths which had been divided with extreme care and exactness. Selecting a scale of the same length as the radius of the instrument to be graduated, the line was first divided into the equal parts required and each of the parts thus derived was partitioned once more into ten equal units, which were divided again until the resulting scale had been graduated into one hundred or two hundred and more units as required. The scale was to be inscribed upon a prepared piece of hardwood. Sturmy recommended boxwood because it was free of knots and blemishes: it was dry, straight, and could be smoothly planed. Another requisite for the process was a true wooden square with a brass ferrule "with a pair of Cramps made of Iron, with Screws to fasten the Scale of Equal Parts, and the Scale to be made together, so as they may not slip, whereby may be made no mistake in Graduating." For smaller scales the work piece could be fastened together with the scale of equal parts to a piece of inexpensive wood such as deal "with the Heads of Scuper Nails, so that they will not stir" and he required also "a Gauge made of Brass, with a good Steel Pin, for the drawing of straight Lines on your Scale, for the division of the Columns for Graduation." [25]

Sturmy noted that the maker must have "two or three Sorts and Sets of Steel Letters and Figures, and Figures for Ornament, with a neat Hammer to use with them: And the Figures, Letters and Ornament-Figures, set in an Alphabet-Box, with written Letters and Figures before them, for the ready finding of them; with Characters of the Signs, and Planets, in like manner." This was a unique description of the die stamps for the instrument maker and provided a useful account of the range and type in which they were available in the seventeenth century.

Sturmy's instructions for engraving the graduations specified that the edge of the dividing knife must be extremely sharp and thin and he also required a pair of brass compasses having an arch [bow] and four interchangeable points, two sets of dividers of different sizes, a "Hand-Vice, so made as to screw into the edge of the Board for your use, and to take out again; with three or four soets of small Files, for to file and make Pins, which you will have occasion for." [26]

For setting off the graduations to make them readily visible he recommended that the artisan "Take Charcoal, and beat it to a fine Powder, and temper it with Lynseed-Oyl; and let it be rubb'd on the Instrument newly made, and lie on it for some time, untill it be pretty dry; and then with some Sallet-Oyl rub the Instrument, and make it clean: So you will have the Graduation and Figures set off very neatly on Box Instruments, with Black." [27]

In a section on the art of dialing, Sturmy provided detailed instructions for their construction and finishing. He advised that "to paint them, you must first Prime them: The Prime is made thus. Take an equal amount of Bole Amoniack and Red Lead, well ground together with Linseed Oyl, and well rubb'd in with a Brush or Pensil into the Plane; that being dry, for the outside Colour, it is White

Lead or Ceruse well ground together with Linseed Oyl. How to know the best. Buy the White Lead, and grind it to a Powder, and put it into Water until it become as thick as Pap, and let it dry; then it is for your use. For the Hour Lines a Vermillion, and a part Red Lead, well ground together with Linseed Oyl, with a small quantity of Oyl of Spike, or Turpentine that will dure, and make the Lines shine." [28]

As the colonial maker progressed from the production of occasional instruments on demand to constant production, particularly in maritime centers, he became more professionalized with his experience supplemented from such works as Sturmy's and from other texts in which techniques and instrument design were provided.[29] Although little information about the tools and methods of the colonial American makers have survived, some data is available from existing inventories of their shops, such as that of Benjamin King, who worked as a maker of navigational and surveying instruments in Salem throughout the second half of the eighteenth century. He is not to be confused with a contemporary relative of the same name, who was a mathematical instrument maker working at Newport, Rhode Island.

After having served an apprenticeship with his father, Daniel King, he established his own shop first at Court Street and later moved to Lynde Street in Salem. He became a man of substance, very active in community affairs throughout his life.[30] At the time of his death on December 30, 1804, Reverend William Bentley noted in his diary that "[King] was a Mathematical Instrument maker, in that branch which immediately regarded practical navigation by Quadrant and Compass. He supported a very good character through life & was much esteemed." [31] King's business was subsequently continued by his son-in-law, Captain Jonathan Mason, at the same location. King died intestate, and an inventory of his real and personal property, which was completed and filed on June 30, 1806, revealed several interesting items relating to his business. His executors paid the sum of $50.00 for "John Jayne's freedom clothes," indicating that Jayne had served a formal apprenticeship with King and that his term had expired at approximately the time of the master's death, leaving the requirements of the apprenticeship contract unfulfilled. Other than personal property and household goods, the inventory compiled of King's shop with contemporary appraisal values provides an excellent view of the variety and quantity of stock maintained by an active instrument maker of the eighteenth century, including a record of tools, raw materials, and discards on hand:

2 Quadrants . . . $36.0   1 Ditto . . . $16.0
30 Board & Timber Rules . . . $7.50
50 Compass Covers . . . 50¢   16 lbs. old Brass . . . $2.70
62½ lbs. old Brass . . . $12.50   a sett of Types . . . $3.0
A Lot of Mathematical Instrument makers Tools . . . $7.00
13 old Compass Boxes . . . 50¢   2 old Cases $1.0
30 Compass Cards . . . 75¢   a Lot of new Brass work . . . $2.0
a lot of Wire . . . 50¢   Surveying Instruments . . . $8.0
1 Magnifying Glass . . . 50;   1 Slate . . . 6¢   2 Vises . . . $1.75
2 Anvils . . . $2.50   Shears . . . $2.0   Bench . . . 25¢
Shelves . . . 50¢
3 Brass Compasses . . . $9.0   87 Wooden Ditto . . . $108.75
pieces of Tin Foil . . . 75¢   1 Loadstone . . . $20.0
7 Compass Vanes . . . 75¢
Sundry Books . . . $3.0
24 Compass Boxes . . . $3.0   Old Iron, &c. . . . $6.0

Under records of debts paid were noted "4 Quadrants which did not belong to the Estate . . . $52.00; loss of a Loadstone . . . $10.00; loss on Compass sold at Auction . . . $3.50."

Noteworthy in this listing is the data concerning stock kept on hand, as well as parts and completed instruments, and identification of the shop equipment and tools. The "Sett of Types" valued at $3.00 represents the die stamps used to mark the scales and inscriptions on instruments. The item for 87 wooden compasses valued at $1.25 each obviously did not relate to completed instruments but to the turned bases. An item of apparently unusual value, probably indicative of its original cost, was the loadstone appraised at $20.00. This was an essential tool for the instrument maker, used for touching the compass needles of new instruments produced as well as those repaired.

The only other listing of an instrument maker's property on record is, curiously enough, that of a cousin of Benjamin King, Samuel King of Newport, Rhode Island, who distinguished himself as an instrument maker and as a portrait painter. The inventory of his estate, compiled after his death in 1820, included "1 very small microscope" valued at $4.00, a broken spyglass for $2.00, and six broken quadrants valued at $1.00 for the lot. Two boat compasses were listed for 75 cents, and a magnet and loadstone were valued at

$5.00. Miscellaneous rules and measures, which King either made for sale or used in his work, included "11 gauges and rods" for $10.00, "9 Board Measures" for $5.40, "5 Want Rods finished $1.66"; unfinished rules for 66 cents, 1 rule, 2 time glasses and a square valued at 10 cents, and "two old boxes and sign box twenty five cents." Mentioned also was a considerable number of tool chests, an old bench vise in poor condition, "1 set of letter types, 60 in number," a drill, and various small tools.[32]

X

A WORK
ADORNED

> A Worke adorned with varietie of matter, both pleasant and profitable, wherein those that please may finde to fit their fancies. Herein by the office of the eie and the eare, the minde may reap double delighte through wholesome preceptes, shadowed with pleasant devises: both fit for the vertuous, to their incouraging: and for the wicked, for their admonishing, and amendment.
>
> Geoffrey Whitney, *A Choice of Emblems* (1586)

IN CONSIDERATIONS OF the work of the instrument makers an aspect which has been largely ignored is the artistic quality of their products and advertisements. Surviving examples of instruments produced during the first two centuries of American civilization provide substantial evidence that the restraints resulting from limited tools and materials forced the evolution of a new artistic style, a style generally devoid of minute detail and somewhat austere because of its basic simplicity. Dominant lines were featured, evoking a feeling of strength and simple beauty which characterized American art and governed the production of utilitarian wares as well as custom-crafted products. The makers of mathematical instruments consequently contributed to the evolution of an art style that became uniquely American by the turn of the nineteenth century. The hopes and boasts of the Americans were clearly reflected in the shop signs and trade cards and advertisements as well as in the instruments. The pre-eminent aim was to set aside the artistic traditions of the mother country and establish a separate identity.

Most instruments of the practical sciences provided a minimum opportunity for decoration. For the most part they were made of wood, skeletal in form as required by the uses made of them, and consequently with limited surface. Furthermore, the colonial craftsman lived by the adage that time is money; he reduced the work and time spent on his products to the minimum required to serve its purpose. As a consequence instruments made by colonial American craftsmen achieved a certain austere elegance of their own, featuring slimness, simple design, and an absence of distracting decorative motifs. It was a natural, and not a deliberate, evolution. The instruments were intended to serve as practical tools, and any elaboration provided not only a distraction to the user's eye but an additional cost of workmanship which would be viewed critically by the canny Yankee purchaser. Frequently the need to use substitutes for traditional materials led to innovation of design. When instruments were copied from some of the available texts, such as the one by Sturmy quoted in the preceding chapter, the maker might dispense with unnecessary details and derive new shapes. When metal type and number dies were not available, letters and numbers were engraved instead of being stamped, giving an instrument unusual attractiveness. The braces of the austere backstaff were frequently scored with decorative double lines filled with a vegetable dye to emphasize the trim, slim appearance of the instrument. Decorative die stamps in the forms of fleur-de-lys, asterisk, or star were often lavished on the terminals of the arcs or on the name plates to embellish them discreetly. A few colonial makers followed the practice of English makers by adding inscribed ivory lozenges at the points at which the members of the backstaff were fastened together.

The octant, or Hadley reflecting quadrant, was rarely decorated, even though the frame of the earlier, larger examples provided ample surface. In English examples produced in the late eighteenth and early nineteenth centuries the brass index arm was occasionally engraved with floral motifs, but the practice was not duplicated by American makers.

The instrument which lent itself most readily to artistic license was the compass in its various forms, because of the opportunities offered by the compass card. The card of eighteenth-century marine compasses was generally engraved on a good quality of rag paper from a copper plate applied with black ink. The cardinal and subcardinal points, customarily left white, were designed as two sets of four points, one set superimposed upon the other. The tertiary points were shown of a much slimmer form and the farther points were depicted as tips around the outer dial. The North point was generally featured by the imposition of a large fleur-de-lys, and the East point was also decorated to make it more dominant on the card.

The fleur-de-lys, which was first added to the compass rose after the beginning of the sixteenth century, was borrowed from earlier forms that had served in Byzantine times. Its design was derived from the shape of the lotus and it was later adopted by the early French kings in the form of a field lily. Among English mariners it came to be popularly known as "the Prince of Wales feathers," because it formed part of the arms of the heir apparent to the English throne. Its addition to the compass rose may have resulted as an attempt to decorate the large letter "T" which had formerly been used to identify "Tramonte" (north) or the "Tramontana," the Italian name for the wind that blew from the north—across the mountains—or the "Stella Tramontana," the North Star.[1]

The decoration added to the East point also has an interesting origin. On early Italian compass roses the west and south winds were marked "P" for "Ponente" (western) and "M" for "Meridionale" (southern). The East point, however, was marked, not with "L" for "Levante" (eastern, or the Levant), but with a cross, because it was the direction of the Holy Land. In the course of time greater emphasis was given to this direction by the addition of scrolls and other motifs, a custom which survived in English and American compass cards.

The central portion of the compass rose (also known as the rose of the winds) provided the engraver with space for the display of his talents, an opportunity he rarely ignored. The area was customarily enclosed with a double ring within which was inscribed the name and place of the maker, and the central medallion was reserved for a decorative motif.

Occasionally New England instrument makers had the engraver add further elaboration, including the depiction of allegorical figures. A card engraved for Daniel King of Salem featured a large central medallion enclosing the figure of King Neptune being drawn across the sea in a scallop shell by two sea horses. The riband was inscribed with the name and place of the maker and an outer riband was marked with the twenty-four hours in Roman numerals from I through XII twice continuously. The eight cardinal points were outlined in red on their outer side, and enclosed within seven of them were allegorical figures, including Grammer with a key and book, Logick without a symbol, Astronomy sighting with a cross staff, Arithmetick holding a tablet inscribed with the date 1744, Geometry with calipers and a map, Rhetorick with the wand of Aesculapius, and Musick with a lute. The North point had the customary fleur-de-lys. A second set of figures was shown with navigational instruments, including a backstaff, a sounding lead, a small cross staff, dividers, and a mariner's astrolabe.[2]

Such elaborate compass cards were extremely rare, and only two other examples are known, one engraved for Joseph Halsey of Boston and one for North Ingham of the same city. The eight cardinal points of the Halsey card are represented with the seven female figures of Musicke, Rhetorick, Astronomy, Arithmetick, Geometry, Logick, and Grammer as in the King card, while in the Ingham card the points were represented by human figures identified as the planets then known, Saturn, Jupiter, Mars, Venus, Mercury, and the sun and moon, named Sol and Luna.[3] The figure of Britannia dominated the central medallion, indicating that the card was produced before the beginning of hostilities with England. Other themes borrowed from the motherland included a Tudor rose, which was the central motif on the card engraved for Joseph Halsey, and an elaborate crown within the central boss, such as was featured on the compass card used by James Halsey (2nd).

As hostilities with England moved the colonies toward war, colonial engravers and their patrons quickly abandoned motifs which symbolized the mother country and replaced them with obviously colonial themes. The change became particularly apparent after the Revolution, when compass cards were engraved with new symbols representing the new nation, crudely at first and later with greater refinement.

Marine themes were the ones most frequently featured. Typical were a shipmaster sighting with a backstaff on shore with a masted vessel visible offshore, as was used in the card of Thomas Greenough of Boston, or a harbor scene with a brigantine offshore and a lighthouse on a promontory, identified as the famous Gurnet Light on the tip of Duxbury Beach in Plymouth Bay, which was featured on the card of Benjamin Warren of Plymouth. The latter card may have been the work of Paul Revere, in whose Day Book appeared an entry: "1783 March 13. Benjm Warren Dr. Plimouth. To printing one hundred Compass Cards 0-18-0." [4]

Few of the engravers of eighteenth-century compass cards identified themselves on their work, although occasional exceptions have survived. Among the engravers who signed compass cards were Nathaniel Hurd, a well-known silversmith who engraved a card for the instrument maker Andrew Newell in Boston, and Joseph Callender, who produced several cards, among them those used by Thomas Salter Bowles and Gedney King. Callender had served an apprenticeship with Paul Revere and subsequently became a die sinker at the Massachusetts mint. Thomas Wightman, engraver of compass cards for the instrument maker John Trundy of Portsmouth, New Hampshire, and possibly for Samuel Thaxter of Boston, among others, was an English-born engraver who worked first at Salem and then in Boston.[5] In Philadelphia Thomas Clarke engraved a compass card for the instrument maker William Davenport. Another English-born engraver was Henry Dawkins, already mentioned, who had been Anthony Lamb's apprentice before moving to Philadelphia to establish his own shop.[6]

Many of the makers of navigational instruments also made wooden surveying compasses with engraved paper compass cards. Exercising the frugality for which the colonial New Englander came to be known, the makers designed the surveying compasses with the same diameter as the marine compasses, thus making it possible to utilize the same stock of compass cards for both purposes. This created an unusual situation. Traditionally the surveying compass dial had the East and West points reversed, so that the East point lay at the left of the North point and the West point at its right. Brass surveying compasses were engraved with this arrangement almost without exception. The reversal enabled the direction of the line of sight to be correctly read when the instrument was held in the customary position with the South point toward the surveyor's body. The dual-purpose cards could not accommodate this practice.

The compasses made of metal provided other and different opportunities for decoration, but the colonial maker generally preferred the utmost simplicity. Decoration was reserved to the dial, which was customarily silvered and the compass points and decorative elements rendered in black for the greatest legibility. The many brass surveying compasses that have survived reveal that there were several distinctive schools of metal decoration prevalent in the colonies, which were geographically defined during the second half of the eighteenth and in the early nineteenth century, although not in the earlier period.

The most important school of instrument decoration flourished in Pennsylvania from the middle to the end of the eighteenth century and included the work produced by David and Benjamin Rittenhouse of Norriton and Philadelphia, George Hoff and Frederick A. Heiseley of Lancaster, W. L. Potts of Bucks County, and the partnerships of the Rittenhouses with David Evans and with Potts at various periods. The consistency of the types of motifs used identified them with similar motifs and styles prevalent in England and Europe in the same period.

The resemblance in artistic rendering among the works of a number of makers during the same period in the same region suggests that there may have been design books for engravers of instruments from which the designs were copied and modified. Such guides were quite common abroad and were widely used by silversmiths and engravers for many purposes, ranging from the decoration of watch cases to designs for book plates and trade cards. Further evidence of the possible existence of such guides in the colonies occurs in an advertising brochure or catalogue published for or by Jacob Gorgas, a watch and clock maker of Ephrata, Pennsylvania, in about 1765. Gorgas's father was a clockmaker and may have also taught watch and clock making to the Rittenhouse brothers, who were relatives and neighbors. The twelve pages of the Gorgas brochure contained a variety of elaborate motifs and designs printed from intaglio engravings for the use of clockmakers and engravers.[7]

The instrument makers of the Pennsylvania school, as well as others, generally utilized wide cardinal points (north, east, south, and west) in their design of the compass rose and filled the areas with elaborate foliate designs in fine detail, with the subcardinal points (northeast, southeast, southwest, and northwest) generally reduced to four in number and cross-hatched or rendered in some other subtle manner. Some engravers made the central medallion the dominant feature. The style reflected an obviously traditional form, varied by the degree of detail and rendered almost identically with the decoration prevalent on the dials of surveying compasses produced by some English makers during the same period. As an example, the dial motifs of some of the surveying compasses made by Benjamin Rittenhouse duplicated in many details those produced by Benjamin Cole (2nd) of London during the first half of the eighteenth century.[8] The engraved compass dials made by Benjamin Rittenhouse were among the most attractive and elaborate produced in America, customarily featuring a well-proportioned design in which the eight cardinal points extended from the center to the edge of the graduated circle. A Tudor rose with elaborate foliation forming the standard central motif was enclosed in a riband in which his name was inscribed, often with the date of production. The four dominant points of the compass rose were featured with minutely executed foliation while the four remaining points were subdued.

The compass dials of instruments produced by David Rittenhouse ranged from the utmost simplicity to elaborate detail, in which they resembled those produced by Benjamin and the dials may have in fact been his work. Several instruments signed by the partnerships of Rittenhouse and Potts and Rittenhouse and Evans have the same detailed elaboration as the work of Benjamin Rittenhouse, suggesting that the partnerships may have been with Benjamin and not with David.

Distinctive decorative features became identified with specific makers and their imitators. Benjamin Rittenhouse and some of the other Pennsylvania makers of his time employed elaborately decorated compass roses, while Richard Patten of New York City featured a heavy leafy garland around the dial, and Goldsmith Chandlee of Winchester, Virginia, incorporated circular motifs that readily identified his instruments. The metal surveying compasses produced by New England makers in general had minimum decoration, if any at all, but their proportions gave them an attractive simplicity.

While the production of navigational and surveying instruments showed a remarkable development in the colonies during the first half of the eighteenth century, optical instruments and others requiring the use of glass were another matter. Thermometers and barometers were imported from England and France until after the Revolutionary War. England in particular had developed as a center for the production of these items, which were for the most part used for scientific purposes or sold to gentlemen amateurs of the sciences, and not for general domestic use. Italian glass workers had emigrated to England in great numbers in response to the demand for the production of scientific glass, and English makers found a ready market in the colonies where these instruments were imported by stationers and booksellers in the larger cities. George Washington and Thomas Jefferson purchased such instruments from the stationer John Sparhawk of Philadelphia. Franklin in 1754 received from Peter Collinson of the Royal Society a number of scientific items, including "3 Barometers, two of which came safe, but the Ball of the third broke to pieces and the Mercury gone." [9] Thermometric and barometric instruments were also stocked by some of the more prominent colonial instrument makers.

Occasionally American makers attempted to produce these glass instruments, but usually for experimental purposes rather than commercial sale. David Rittenhouse was greatly interested in the use of these instruments and experimented with their development. In about 1762 he made a finely graduated thermometer on which he engraved, at a mark at 22 below zero on the Fahrenheit scale, a reminder of an unusual event, "Jan. 2, 1762—Great Cold In Pennsylvania." [10] Although his biographer William Barton stated that this was a reference to an entry in the daily journal maintained by the surveyor Charles Mason which recorded that this was the degree of cold registered in the forks of the Brandywine River on the date noted, the date was obviously in error, since the observation was made at another time. [11]

Early in 1767 Rittenhouse designed and constructed a special thermometer which was based on the contraction and expansion of metals by heat and cold and had a glass-covered dial graduated with a semicircle. The degrees of heat and cold marked on the dial corresponded with those of the Fahrenheit scale and were designated by an index moving from the center of the arc. The thermometer was square or parallelogrammatic in form, flat, thin, and small in size, so that it could be readily carried in the pocket. Rittenhouse presented one of these to Richard Peters, secretary to the Pennsylvania Proprietors, in June 1767, and another which he had made for himself was subsequently used by William Barton. Barton tested it at Lancaster and later returned it to the maker.[12]

In the summer of 1771, Rittenhouse received from Barton a tube for a barometer which had been made for him at the Glass House, a manufactory operated at Mannheim, Pennsylvania, by Henry William Stiegel. "I am obliged to you for the glass tube," he wrote, "it will make a pretty barometer, though the bore is somewhat too small. I have compared it with an English tube, and do not think the preference can, with any reason be given to the latter." He then asked Barton to "procure for me from the glass-house some tubes of a size fit for spirit-levels. . . . The bore must be half an inch in diameter, and from four to eight inches in length; as straight as possible, and open at one end only." [13]

The Glass House subsequently changed hands several times, and there is reason to believe that at some time after 1778 Rittenhouse leased it to produce scientific vessels and glass required for his work.[14] It was not until after the war, however, and then at a manufactory in Maryland that optical and scientific glass was commercially produced in America.[15]

Optical instruments were imported, almost without exception, until the middle of the nineteenth century. Telescopes and telescopic elements of other instruments were occasionally made for specific uses by Rittenhouse and a few others, but even in such instances the lenses had to be imported because neither skills, equipment, nor materials were available to grind them in America.

The art of lens grinding was slow to develop even in Europe, despite the ever-increasing demand for telescopic and microscopical lenses throughout the seventeenth and eighteenth centuries. The techniques of the mirror polishers of Murano, Italy, which provided the first lenses for Galileo's telescopes, were gradually replaced by a series of improved lens-grinding lathes borrowed from the traditions of the lapidary workers, first in Italy and Holland, then elsewhere in Europe, and finally in England. The best optical glass was first produced at Murano and even late in the seventeenth century France, Holland, and England sought vainly to develop facilities for the production of glass of matching quality. It was not until the development of flint glass that England moved to the forefront with a number of individual improvements of techniques as well as materials.[16]

Telescopic instruments imported into the colonies consisted primarily of the hand telescope, or spyglass, used for observation at sea as well as by amateurs of science. Occasionally finer pedestal-type telescopes were imported for science teaching in the colleges or for the edification of wealthy amateur astronomers.

Although it did not achieve importance for nautical use until much later, the hand telescope for use at sea first came to popularity in the Netherlands early in the seventeenth century, and occasional references to its use on shipboard in other European as well as English vessels in the same period were also to be found. Such instruments of that period were excessively large and cumbersome to use, because collapsible tubes were not introduced until later. Frequently the help of an assistant was required to hold the instrument in place while making observations on shipboard. The problem was noted in various accounts of the time, including a manual for navigators by Joshua Kelley published in 1720. In describing an attempt to observe Jupiter's satellites to determine the longitude on shipboard, he complained about "the impracticability of managing a telescope twelve or fourteen feet long in the tossing, rolling motion of a ship at sea." [17] The portable telescope primarily served the watch officer to distinguish flag signals or occasional landmarks, and out of habit it eventually became a fashionable adjunct to the officer's uniform.

The instrument first evolved in a form much resembling that of a trumpet in order to accommodate the large object lens required; not until grinding techniques were improved could smaller lenses be produced. When collapsible tubes were developed, they were first made of cardboard, covered with vellum or decorated leather, to keep the weight low. The lenses were accommodated within cells of turned boxwood which screwed together and fitted friction-tight within the tubes. By the middle of the seventeenth century wood replaced cardboard for the construction of the body and tubes, but the additional weight made it unsatisfactory, although it became a standard material for the larger instruments used for astronomical observations. The vellum- or leather-covered cardboard tubes were particularly liable to deterioration at sea, and although wood was also permeable by sea air, coverings of leather or coatings of lacquer were developed to overcome this failing. By the middle of the eighteenth century brass tubing became prevalent, made of thin metal sheets soldered together. Wood was often retained as the material for the body tube, with mahogany preferred, though in inexpensive models a cheaper wood such as deal was commonly used.[18]

During the same period portable telescopes were frequently made with square heads to accommodate the object lens, so that telescopes of various powers could be readily obtained as the state of the weather and circumstances required; instruments of the same type were also produced in longer lengths for the use of the military on land.

From about the middle of the eighteenth century, England entered the field of telescope making, providing a gradually increasing competition for European makers. The state of telescope production was reported in that period by Edmund Stone, a mathematician and a protegé of the Duke of Argyll, in a supplement to his translation of a book on mathematical instruments by Nicholas Bion, a work of considerable importance in the field of scientific instrumentation. Stone described the hand telescope or spyglass as a perspective glass and noted that such instruments ranged in size from 4 to 6 inches in diameter and from 1½ to 5 feet in length.[19]

An innovation introduced in this period was the "night telescope" for use at sea, which was designed to provide a much larger image and to collect as much light as possible. This was accomplished by combining object lenses of considerable diameter with astronomical-type eyepieces or ocular lenses, effecting a change in the function of the instrument from terrestrial to astronomical. The night telescope continued to be popular for navigational use well into the nineteenth century.

One of the major achievements in the development of the telescope was the invention of the achromatic lens, which was achieved by Chester Moor Hall in England between 1729 and 1733 and marketed by John Dollond after 1758. This type of lens consisted of two lenses of different indices of refraction combined into a single unit. One of the parts was ground from flint glass and the other from crown glass, an arrangement which successfully effected achromatism. These lenses were produced in considerable numbers from 1760 to 1780 and represented a major advance in the technology.[20]

A number of portable telescopes for use at sea were imported into the colonies after the beginning of the eighteenth century, but there was little capability for their production or repair. However, in 1753 the New York City press advertised that "the Widow of Balthaser Sommer, late from Amsterdam," living next door to Mr. Laffert's on Pot-Baker Hill in Smith Street in that city, not only had a wide variety of optical instruments for sale, but also "grinds all sorts of Optic Glasses to the greatest Perfection, such as Microscope Glasses, Spying Glasses, of all lengths, Spectacles, Reading-Glasses for near-sighted People or others; Also, Spying-Glasses of three Feet long; which are to set on a common Walking-Cane, and yet be carried as a Pocket-Book; all at the most reasonable Rates." [21]

Meanwhile, in Norriton, David Rittenhouse, according to biographers, had attempted to make a telescope as early as 1756. In a letter in that year to Thomas Barton, Rittenhouse noted that at that time he was "so taken with optics, that I do not know whether, if the enemy should invade this part of the country, as Archimedes was slain while making geometrical figures, so I should die making a telescope." [22] Whether he succeeded in this endeavor is not a matter of record, but in 1769 he successfully constructed a transit instrument for the observations of the transit of Venus at his home observatory, the first such achievement in telescopic instrumentation in the colonies.[23] Rittenhouse described his instrument as "a transit telescope, fixed in the meridian on fine steel points: so that the hair in its focus could move in no other direction than along the meridian: in which are two marks, south and north, about 330 yards distant each: to which it could be readily adjusted in a horizontal position by one screw, as it could in a vertical position, by another." [24] It was mounted on a stand consisting of two A-frames which could be permanently attached to a bench or table; it was equipped with a semicircular scale attached to the bottom of the tube having a spirit level suspended from the frame. Since the cost of brass for the two tapered arms was prohibitive, Rittenhouse constructed them of sheets of wrought iron riveted together. The source for the lenses remains a mystery; it is doubtful that Rittenhouse would have attempted to grind them himself, and there was no one else in the colonies capable of doing so. He may have imported the lenses from England or, most likely, taken them from other instruments at hand.

For the same observation of the transit of Venus, Rittenhouse also made for his observatory a refracting telescope having a focal length of 42 feet. For this instrument he incorporated a pair of lenses ordered from London by Harvard College which had arrived at Philadelphia and had not been forwarded.[25] This was used in addition to another of his instruments having a focal length of 36 feet.

Finally, Rittenhouse constructed a transit and equal altitude instrument for use in his own observations of the transit of Venus. It incorporated an English-made refracting telescope having a focal length of 3½ feet with one horizontal and two vertical cross hairs fixed at its focus. The instrument was of simple design, and devised so that it could be rotated on a fixed outdoor mount on a north-south axis and on an east-west axis by means of individual screws. He marked the instrument with the designation "#4" when he completed it on March 20, 1769. He installed this as well as another smaller instrument out of doors outside his observatory because he did not have time to make the necessary accommodations for them inside.[26]

A related instrument requiring telescopic lenses was also attempted by Rittenhouse. This was a leveling instrument required for surveying, and David Rittenhouse produced at least two examples, Benjamin at least one and possibly others. The earliest record of such an instrument occurred in a letter from Benjamin Lightfoot, a merchant, landowner, and surveyor of Reading, Pennsylvania, to a Philadelphia merchant, Samuel Coates, requesting the latter to call upon David Rittenhouse for a "leveling Instrument" being made for him, pay for it, and send it on to the writer.[27] Rittenhouse made a second instrument of the same type for the Delaware and Schuylkill Canal Navigation Company many years later, in 1793, for which he was paid 100 dollars, whereas the one he made for Lightfoot was priced at less than 7 pounds.[28]

A fine leveling instrument was produced by Benjamin Rittenhouse for George Washington and used by the latter in laying out the Potomac Canal in about 1785, an endeavor in which he was closely associated with Colonel George Gilpin, to whom he later presented the instrument. It was equipped with a heavy brass telescopic tube having one draw tube and a long cylindrical bubble level encased in brass supported at the side. Increase and reduction of elevation were accomplished by an unusual hinged arrangement adjusted by a hand screw. The instrument incorporated several unique features which may have been original with David Rittenhouse and then duplicated by his brother. All these leveling instruments were similar and shared an original design which did not duplicate European or English prototypes.[29]

As the trades and crafts, including those of the mathematical instrument makers, developed in the American colonies, a parallel need arose for advertising both skills and products. The media used were those prevalent in England, such as trade signs, shop figures, trade cards, and newspaper announcements.

Two basic reasons for advertising existed even in colonial times. The first was the obvious one of providing information about the availability of the craftsman's skills and products to as wide an audience as possible. The second derived from the desire for recognition as a member of the specialized social group of the skilled craftsmen. This position in a privileged social class was to be carefully signalized and protected.

Until the advent of the first newspapers in British colonial America in the last decade of the seventeenth century, the only media available for advertising were trade signs, trade cards, and broadsides. Map makers, navigators, and surveyors were unable to avail themselves of these media because the nature of their work precluded a fixed place of business, and there were not enough of them for competition to develop. Consequently it was chiefly the instrument makers and the science teachers who required advertising. Frequently science teachers used the shop of an instrument maker as a place for advertising their services. It was not until the prevalence of newspapers that the teacher could advertise his skills in a more practical manner.

The earliest form of advertising for the instrument maker was the trade sign which signalized his place of business and his products and skills. The signboards were simple panels of wood, sometimes with a border molding, which were painted and lettered with the shopkeeper's name and the nature of his services and products. The signs were traditionally attached above the shop door or sometimes hung from a projecting arm of wood or the branch of an adjacent tree so that the sign would swing free in the breeze and attract attention of the passersby from both directions. In addition, the sign frequently incorporated a symbol representative of the proprietor's particular skill. During the first century of settlement, such signs were more frequently reflections of the tradition of the craftsman than practical attempts to advertise. Shop and tavern signs trace their origin to traders of the Roman empire who identified their shops by means of symbols denoting the products sold. By the Middle Ages the practice had spread widely. The choice of symbols increased, and devices developed from family arms and guild motifs were often added. When an apprentice had completed his training and established his own shop, he commonly designed a sign that combined the symbol of his former master with his own.

The painting of signboards became a trade in itself, practiced by itinerant and often illiterate sign painters who traveled from community to community. With the increase in trade and traffic, the signboards increased in size and ostentation and eventually became disproportionate for the narrow streets, where their numbers frequently cut off the sun entirely. Eventually legislation was introduced in England to control their size and use.[30]

Although the signboard was imported into the American colonies at an early period, the number of shops was not sufficient to create the same problems. These signs were also painted by itinerant sign painters, some of whom had emigrated from England. The names of some of the American signboard painters are known primarily from their advertisements in newspapers. Their numbers included coach painters, limners, and ship painters, as well as an occasional fine artist seeking to implement his income while furthering his professional career.

The favorite symbol of eighteenth-century makers of navigational instruments in the American colonies was the octant, or Hadley reflecting quadrant, and the shop sign most frequently encountered in the seaport cities was "At the Sign of the Quadrant." Among prominent American instrument makers who used such an identification were William Hinton and Edmund March Blunt in New York City, Chester Gould in Philadelphia, John Jayne of Salem, Aaron Breed in Boston, James M. Elford at Charleston, South Carolina, and William Hamlin in Providence, Rhode Island. Variations included "At the Sign of Hadley's Quadrant and Compass Card," used by Philip Dorsey of Baltimore, and "At the Sign of the Compass and Quadrant" by which Anthony Lamb's first shop in New York City was known, although in this instance the "quadrant" referred to the Davis quadrant or backstaff. Later Lamb's shop was designated "At the Sign of Sir Isaac Newton's Head."

Other symbols and names included "The Sign of the Mathematical Instruments," featured by Benjamin King of Newport; "At the Sign of Dr. Franklin," for the two shops maintained consecutively by Benjamin King Haggar of Baltimore; and "At the Sign of the Mercury and Quadrant" by Frederick W. Lincoln, Jr., of Boston. The designation "At the Sign of the Seven Stars," denoting the celestial constellation of the Great Bear, identified the tavern build-in $\jmath$ of Charles Kugler in Philadelphia, in which several shops were re:.ted to makers of mathematical instruments.

From shortly before the Revolution into the nineteenth century, the shop figure became increasingly prevalent in colonial shipping centers. A carved three-dimensional polychromed figure was displayed in front of the shop entrance to supplement the signboard overhead. The practice was borrowed from England, where it was particularly popular among the makers of navigational instruments. The figure served not only to identify the shop of a specific trade or craft but stood as a constant reminder to the passersby of the nature of the product. Even more, it served as a status symbol for the tradesman or craftsman owning one, for its very presence established the fact that the shop owner was not only a member of the social class of the skilled craftsman but affluent enough to afford such an elaborate device.[31]

The most popular form of the figure designating the shops of makers of navigational instruments was a shipmaster or seaman in traditional costume, either holding an octant or a Hadley reflecting quadrant in his hand or sighting through it. The prevalence of the practice in England was described by Charles Dickens in *Dombey and Son*:

"Anywhere in the immediate vicinity there might be seen . . . outfitting warehouses ready to pack off anybody anywhere, fully equipped in half an hour; and little timber midshipmen in obsolete naval uniforms, eternally employed outside the shops of nautical instrument makers in taking observations of the hackney coaches. . . . One of these effigies which might be called, familiarly, the woodenest . . . thrust itself out above the pavement, right leg foremost, with a suavity the least endurable, and had the shoe buckles and flapped waistcoat the least reconcilable to human reason, and bore at its right eye the most offensively disproportionate piece of machinery. . . ."[32]

Similar figures persisted in British shipping centers to recent times, although some of the shops had changed their character and purpose in the meantime. The shipmaster shop figure was equally popular in the American colonies, and a small number of eighteenth- and early-nineteenth-century examples have survived, each with its own history.

Probably the earliest and the best known of the examples that survive in museum collections is "The Little Admiral," as it was popularly known, which was a landmark on Boston's Long Wharf for almost a century and a half. There it identified first a tavern and then the shop of two makers of navigational instruments. The figure is believed to have been intended as a portrait of the English admiral, Edward Vernon, popularly known in English naval history as "Old Grog." He habitually wore grogam breeches and he was distinguished for having ordered the raw rum rationed to the British Navy to be diluted with water. The resulting concoction was named "grog" in resentment of his orders. The term has survived as the common designation of a seaman's rum ration in the British Navy and led to the term "grog shop" to identify a waterside tavern.

The figure of the Little Admiral may have been carved for the Admiral Vernon Tavern which stood at the corner of State Street and Merchant's Row on Long Wharf. It was the work of the Boston ship's carver Simeon Skillin and was probably produced early in the eighteenth century, for the tradition is that the figure was removed from the front of the Admiral Vernon Tavern in 1750 when the ownership changed and was installed in front of the Crown Coffee-House. When the original Crown Coffee-House was burned, the figure was salvaged and placed in front of the new building constructed in its place.[33] In its tavern days, the figure is thought to have held a noggin of grog.

When a maker of mathematical instruments, William Williams, in 1770 established his business on King-Street "two doors East of the Sign of Admiral Vernon, near the Head of Long-Wharf," his shop was without designation.[34] Four years later an advertisement which he published in the Salem and Marblehead newspaper was embellished with a woodcut of a comical figure, unquestionably a representation of the Little Admiral, but holding an oversize octant.[35]

Williams acquired the figure some time between 1770 and 1774 and probably converted it for his own use by substituting an octant for the noggin of grog. The figure stood in front of Williams's shop until he joined the Continental Army. It was retired during his absence but restored to its former place upon his return. Contemporary writers several times noted having seen it in place before his death in 1792, when his business and shop, including the figure, were acquired by Samuel Thaxter. Thaxter moved his place of business several times in the years that followed but the figure continued to designate it and that of his successors under the same firm name, until the business finally went out of existence in 1916.[36]

A figure of Admiral Vernon was mentioned in a short story by Nathaniel Hawthorne, "Drowne's Wooden Image," in which the wood carver Deacon Drowne, after venturing into love and fantasy, returned to complete the carving of "yonder figure of Admiral Vernon." Hawthorne continues: "Another work of the good deacon's hand—a reduced likeness of his friend Captain Hunnewell, holding a telescope and quadrant—may be seen to this day, at the corner of Broad and State Streets, serving the useful capacity of sign to the shop of a nautical instrument maker." [37]

It is interesting to speculate which—if either—of the figures Hawthorne referred to was the one known as the Little Admiral. At the turn of the twentieth century Thaxter's shop figure was noted by a Boston popular writer, who reported that she had observed "in front of a nautical instrument store at the corner of State and Broad streets, Boston, still a quaint wooden figure of an ancient naval officer resplendent in his blue coat, cocked hat, short breeches, stockings and buckles, holding in his hand a quadrant. The old fellow has stood in this place continually taking observations of the sun upwards of one hundred years." [38]

Similar to the Little Admiral was the figure that identified the shop of Samuel King on Pelham and Thames Streets in Newport, in the late eighteenth and early nineteenth century. King customarily carried the figure out of his shop each morning and placed it upon a shelf beside the door, four feet above the ground, where it remained until closing time. It represented a mariner holding an octant in his hands; he was dressed in a blouse, knee breeches, white stockings, and shoes with silver buckles. The head was adorned with a wig and a tricorn hat. Following King's death the figure was included in an inventory of his estate as "1 image with a quadrant in his hand" valued at $3.00.

There is a claim that King carved his shop figure himself and that he had also produced a similar figure used by James Fales, Jr., in front of his shop at 91 North Water Street in Newport and known as the "Little Navigator." [39] When Fales moved his business from Newport to New Bedford, Massachusetts, between 1820 and 1830, the Little Navigator was one of four shop signs he displayed simultaneously. One of these was the standard signboard over the door which identified him as a watch and clock maker; another a large wooden watch which hung above the front window, and the third a large wooden gun wired in place at the right of the shop door. The fourth, on a shelf directly above the door, was the Little Navigator.[40]

In 1878, the New Bedford press noted that the "ancient mariner" had identified Fales's shop at New Bedford for the past fifty years, and that "for nearly a score of years before coming to this city he was located in front of James Fales' shop in Newport, R.I., where he was created by a cumming [*sic*] artificer in wood named King. His costume is of the olden time and the ruffled shirt bosom, short jacket and hat of the decidedly stove pipe pattern indicate that he was modelled after some jaunty skipper of Auld Lang Syne." After Fales's shop was abandoned in 1888, this polychromed wooden figure was preserved and subsequently became the property of the Old Dartmouth Society and Whaling Museum in New Bedford.[41]

The stories of other shop figures, if not the figures themselves, have survived, and contribute to the history of the instrument makers. The mariner with an octant carved from a ship's spar, used by the ship's chandler William Rathbone in front of his shop on Thames Street in Newport at the turn of the nineteenth century, successively served a blacksmith and a boat builder before it disintegrated in about 1885; efforts to restore it were futile.[42]

A figure of the winged messenger, Mercury, was carved by Simeon Skillin, Sr., at the beginning of the nineteenth century to stand outside the door of the Boston Post Office on State and Devonshire streets. It was acquired after 1850 by Frederick W. Lincoln, Jr., Paul Revere's grandson, and used to identify his shop as an instrument maker which bore the sign "At the Sign of the Mercury and Quadrant" on Commercial Street.[43]

Samuel Thaxter, who used the Little Admiral to identify his place of business throughout his career, also acquired a figure of Father Time, carved by John Skillin, which he used as a decoration inside his shop.

Nautical shop figures disappeared from the scene soon after the beginning of the twentieth century, except for one lonely survivor, which was also finally removed in 1973 and preserved in the Philadelphia Maritime Museum. This was a life-sized carved wooden figure of an early-nineteenth-century American shipmaster with bushy sideburns and a handsome mustache, sighting through his octant

along the busy Philadelphia streets from his lofty position above the
doorway of the shop of Riggs and Brother at 310 Market Street.
This firm of navigational instrument and chronometer makers was
established in 1818 and continued at the same address for more than
a century and a half, and the figure dates from the early days of the
firm's history.

The most common form of advertising used by colonial American craftsmen was the trade card. Printed or engraved notices, customarily including the name, attainments, and shop address of the
craftsman or merchant, as well as a listing of the services or products
he offered, originated in the seventeenth century, although they did
not come into general use until the early eighteenth. The format
varied from relatively small-sized cards with a formal style and arrangement of text to others that were larger and carried extensive
text and elements of decoration. The trade card became increasingly
popular in the eighteenth century with merchants and business
houses offering specialized products. It featured the symbols that appeared on the craftsman's signboard or that were used to distinguish
a mercantile or business house. The instrument maker pasted these
cards inside the cases of the instruments he sold or over the card of
the original maker in the boxes of instruments he repaired, as a
reminder of his services and place of business.

Early trade cards reflect the attempts of the colonial printer to
duplicate the style and ornamentation of the cards of English merchants and craftsmen and reveal the limited supplies of type and decorative elements available to them. However, many of the early-
eighteenth-century cards provide evidence of a fine sense of design
and ingenious use of materials at hand. A great number of the cards
were the products of English-trained engravers and printers who
duplicated English motifs of design and decoration, often obviously
culled from design books.

Later in the eighteenth century the trade card evolved into a
larger size printed from a copperplate engraving to identify the
craftsman and his products, frequently featuring the symbols of his
signboard or those representative of his specialty. The elaborate bor-
ders, mantling, and scrollwork of the Chippendale style of English
trade cards was copied by American engravers until the Revolution,
and examples of their work frequently matched in quality the fine
design, excellent proportions, and sharp delineation of their English

peers. By the end of the war, however, the American trade card began to change its appearance radically. The size was reduced once more to one convenient for attaching to the inside of cases for instruments, or underneath or behind surfaces on pieces of furniture. Gradually the paper stock changed from fine rag paper to paper of cheaper quality and the use of pasteboard for card stock became increasingly prevalent.

A number of colonial American engravers and printers advertised trade cards as a specialty, as did Henry Dawkins, who produced one of the finest surviving broadsides for his former master Anthony Lamb before Dawkins removed to Philadelphia to establish his own business.[44]

After the end of the Revolution and particularly after the beginning of the nineteenth century American trade cards discarded the traditional English motifs and style and reflected the national climate and the feeling of hard-won independence and egoistic self-sufficiency which began to distinguish the new republic in a variety of ways. The spread eagle as a national symbol occurred frequently by 1800 and the mantling and foliated designs were displaced in favor of simple strong elements. The result was not always as tasteful but an original American style was unquestionably manifesting itself. Examples worth noting include a card engraved by Joseph Callender for the instrument maker Samuel Emery of Salem, which featured a bold spread eagle dominating the upper portion of the card, holding in its beak a shield and banner inscribed with the new American motto "E Pluribus Unum," and on the lower portion a ship tossed in a stormy sea, a box compass, a sextant, and a ship becalmed. Another noteworthy example was a card designed by James M. Elford, a dealer in nautical instruments in Charleston, South Carolina, and engraved for him on copper by Charles Curtis Wright. Again the design reflected the mood of the times, with an eagle with widespread wings, peering through a spyglass held to its eye. The eagle had come to dominate the American scene, and it was represented in every commodity from glass and hardware to popular prints. A card believed to have been engraved by Callender for Thomas Salter Bowles, an instrument maker of Portsmouth, New Hampshire, combined the eagle with Masonic symbols.

Though it developed considerably later, the next important means of making services and products known was the newspaper advertisement. As with trade signs and trade cards, colonial news-papers duplicated their English counterparts and evolved into the ma-jor means of communication. Advertising, however, did not become a profitable undertaking without a struggle. Colonial merchants were skeptical because the first newspapers were organs for official pro-paganda and news was often five to thirteen months behind time, both factors resulting in limited circulation. It was not until after the first quarter of the eighteenth century that the potential of news-paper advertisement was recognized and acknowledged. Benjamin Franklin was largely responsible for its success because of the in-novations in printing techniques which he introduced.[45]

In form, the colonial newspaper consisted of a journal of two leaves issued once weekly. Half of its space was devoted to news and the remainder to personal announcements and advertising. The news items were gleaned from exchanges and local sources and were rarely sufficient to fill the pages, so that the editor was often forced to resort to the inclusion of literary pieces produced by local citizens or excerpts from published writings. Consequently the purpose best served by the journal was advertisement. No daily newspaper ap-peared until after the end of the war, but thereafter dailies made their appearance in a number of American cities.[46]

The form of the advertisement underwent an evolution. At its first appearance, it was not separated from news items except by paragraphing. Eventually a two-line initial to mark the beginning of the advertisement was introduced and became standard practice. The separation of advertisements by intervening ruled lines came much later, and thereafter printers occasionally replaced the rule with type ornaments. When at last it became the practice to set off the advertisements, a different type was used to distinguish them from the news items.

In time the large-type initial was replaced by casting the first several words of the announcement in two-line type, and eventually the advertisement became more formalized by providing identifica-tion of the tradesman's name and his product separately from and in-troductory to the text. The practice of including illustrative wood-cuts to identify the service or product did not develop until the last part of the eighteenth century. The first such example for a maker of mathematical instruments was the advertisement of William Wil-liams in 1774 which included a small woodcut representing the Little Admiral. Although produced as a caricature, this was also probably the first published representation of the octant in the American colonies.[47]

The use of drawings of mathematical instruments in newspaper advertisements became more frequent by the last decade of the eighteenth century, and a particularly fine example was the advertisement of Philip Dorsey of Baltimore in 1793, which featured a woodcut delineating four navigational instruments of the period.[48] The purpose of the advertisement, the capability of the individual printer, and the cost of space and illustration were all important factors governing the size and format of advertisements. An announcement published by the Philadelphia instrument maker Thomas Whitney in 1798, for instance, was intended not only to remind the reader of Whitney's services and variety of products but also to advise of a change of address, of new services provided, and finally of the availability of a stock of other hardware for sale.[49]

Business directories and nautical publications, which first made their appearance late in the eighteenth century, provided the makers of and dealers in mathematical instruments yet another medium for the promotion of their products. Advertisements might range from a one-line listing to a full page or even a double-page spread.

Another form of advertisement widely used by instrument makers and dealers was the handbill or broadside. This was a printed sheet designed to be glued inside the covers of books or on the reverse side of maps and charts, or distributed by hand. It was found to be a useful source of income by colonial printers early in the eighteenth century and was used generally for announcements of large public auction sales, government notices, special proclamations, militia assembly announcements, political events, propaganda, arrival of ships with special cargoes to be sold publicly, and similar purposes. At first it was used less frequently by tradesmen to advertise wares or services but in due course of time it came to be recognized as a useful means of advertising when inserted in books or other goods sold, to publicize the availability of other products and services which might be useful at a future date to a particular group of clients such as shipmasters.

The trail of evidence left by the maker of mathematical instruments in the various types of advertisement he used, added to the surviving instruments he produced, provides an invaluable source of information about the past.

PART THREE

Revolution

64 "Washington at the Battle of Trenton." Portrait in oils by John Trumbull, depicting the General with one of the numerous spyglasses he used in the field.

65 Spyglass used by General Washington at Valley Forge and presented by him to his nephew, Major Lawrence Lewis, in 1799. The instrument, by an unknown maker, has a main tube of mahogany and three brass draw-tubes; its original leather field case is also shown.

66 Trade card of Isaac Greenwood (3rd), dentist and maker of mathematical instruments. Reproduced from John Isaac Greenwood, *The Greenwood Family of Norwich, England in America* (New York, 1934).

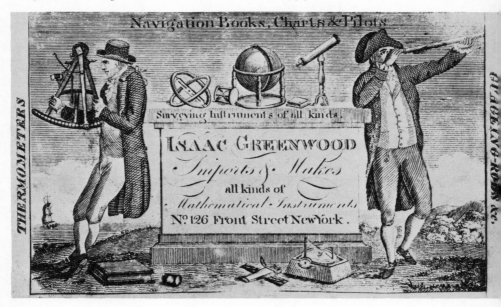

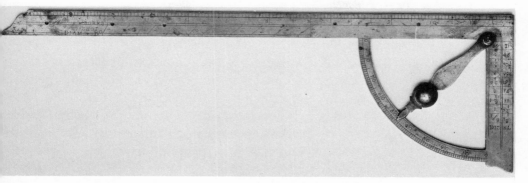

67, 68 Brass gunner's quadrant made by Isaac Greenwood (3rd) of New York City, eighteenth century, and detail, showing inscription on reverse.

69 Wooden gunner's quadrant, American, eighteenth century, maker not known.

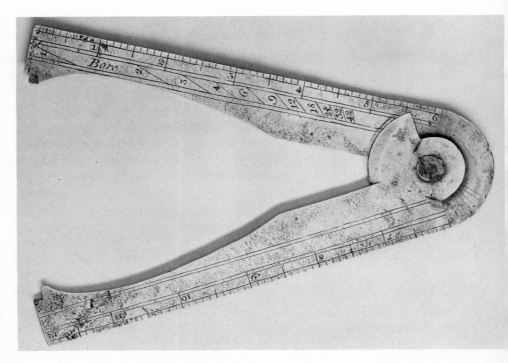

70, 71   Brass gunner's calipers, American, eighteenth century, believed to have been made and used by Paul Revere during the Revolution. (*Top*) Obverse; (*bottom*), reverse, showing the inscribed name of Revere.

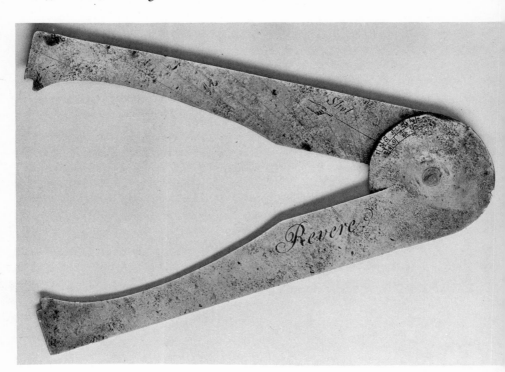

72   Marine barometer, made by Jesse Ramsden of London, ca 1800.

73   Part of a surveying instrument, possibly a plane table. Inscribed in ink inside the trough compass is "N. Bennet Middleboro° 1777."

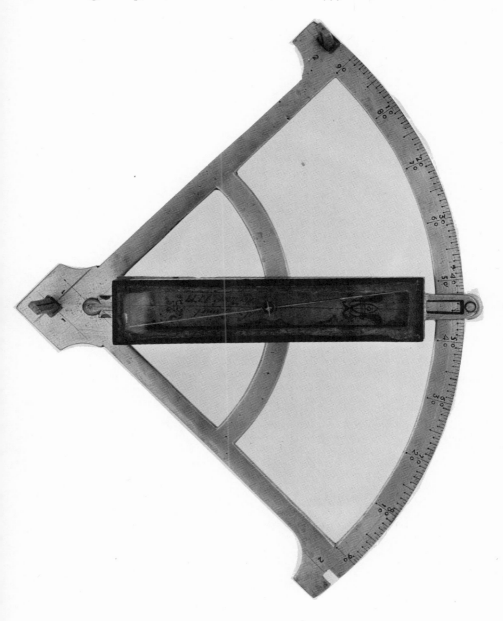

XI

☆ ☆ ☆ ☆ ☆ ☆ ☆ ☆ ☆ ☆ ☆ ☆ ☆

OF LIBERTY
AND LIFE

☆ ☆

> This is a land of ev'ry joyous sound
> Of liberty and life; sweet liberty!
> Without whose aid the noblest genius fails
> And science irretrievably must die.
>
> Philip Freneau and Hugh Brackenridge,
> "The Rising Glory of America" (1902)

HISTORIANS ARE generally agreed that when the American Revolution reached the stage of open conflict, one-third of the colonial population joined the patriot cause, one-third remained loyal to the British Crown, and the remaining third was indifferent. Despite affiliation, however, everyone was touched by the war to some degree. On the lives of many of the mathematical practitioners, it had an almost immediate effect. The skills of some were urgently and immediately required by the Continental Army if the practitioners were patriotically inclined, and by the British if they were loyalist, and many were forced to abandon their customary pursuits to re-

237

spond to military priorities. As the war continued, others discovered that their specialities were not required either for military purposes or civilian use, and they were forced to turn temporarily to other means of livelihood. Some whose skills were of critical value were reluctant to be associated with a rebellion so uncertain of success and found themselves in difficulty because of avowed or attributed loyalist attitudes. Few escaped the impact of war.

One of the first effects felt from the break with the mother country was the lack of a market for colonial trade products and the absence of a source of supply for materials previously imported from or through English merchants. Prices for all commodities rose to an alarming degree, making luxuries out of previous staples. A wholesale diversion had to be effected from the production of commodities to the provision of necessities. This change was reflected in some crafts more than in others. There was a pronounced decrease in the demand for clocks and related items, and many clockmakers were forced into other pursuits to make a living. Some basic materials could no longer be obtained from England, and new sources had to be found for them, or substitutes. The increasing demand for metals for many purposes and industries during the war led to the acceleration of mining and to the development of metalworking facilities in the colonies, but, as has been noted, these were unable to provide brass.

An unforeseen effect was the segmentation of skills into specialized crafts, and the makers of mathematical instruments found themselves in a variety of roles related to their chosen profession. A few, including the Rittenhouse brothers, were forced to set aside their crafts to assume administrative responsibilities related to the war. David Rittenhouse became a particularly important figure in the war effort for the province of Pennsylvania, serving as an engineer to the Committee of Public Safety from early 1775. He supervised the manufacture of gunpowder and the casting of cannon and experimented with rifling actions and the design of musket balls. He solved one metals crisis by ordering the substitution of iron for lead in clock weights because the former was more plentiful and the latter was needed for casting bullets. Totally in support of the patriotic effort and the Constitution of 1776, he was elected to the Pennsylvania Assembly and also held a position in the Pennsylvania Council of Safety. He played an important role in the 1776 Constitutional Convention, was elected treasurer of the province in 1777, was concerned with the fortification of Philadelphia, and even served for a time as a private in the Philadelphia militia.[1] Meanwhile he continued to be involved in the major boundary surveys of the province, particularly during the war years and the period of westward expansion that followed. In 1779, together with George Bryan and Reverend John Ewing, he represented Pennsylvania as a commissioner to resolve the dispute over the Pennsylvania-Virginia boundary and in 1783 served in the same capacity. He was instrumental in erecting an observatory at Wilmington and personally constructed the astronomical instruments required to make more than sixty observations of the satellites of Jupiter necessary for running the lines of the southwest corner of Pennsylvania. In 1786 he assisted in fixing the western boundary of the province.[2]

Meanwhile, Benjamin Rittenhouse, who was one of the most prolific makers of clocks and surveying instruments of his time, abandoned these activities for a military career early in 1776 when he was chosen captain of a company under the regulations of the Association of Inhabitants of Norriton. In the same year he was appointed superintendent of the gun-lock factory maintained at Philadelphia by the provincial government, and he continued in charge until the factory was closed in 1778. During the same period he saw active service under General Washington at the Battle of Brandywine and was wounded and taken prisoner.[3]

A Hanover, Massachusetts, clockmaker, gunsmith, and repairer of surveying instruments, John Bailey (1st) served as a lieutenant colonel in the regiment of Colonel John Thomas of Kingston and was subsequently promoted to chief colonel. He served at the Battle of Trenton under General Washington and is claimed to have fought at the Battle of Saratoga with General Gates. Ill health brought about his discharge in 1780.[4] The Boston instrument maker William Williams was a private in the company of Captain Mills in Colonel Jeduthan Baldwin's regiment of artificers during the years 1777 to 1779. In 1780 he served in Captain Pattin's company of General Knox's artillery stationed at West Point.[5] Nathaniel Chickering, a surveyor and later civil engineer of Dover, Massachusetts, marched into Lexington under Captain Battell and in 1776 fought in the Battle of Ticonderoga.[6]

One of the most colorful figures among the instrument makers to serve in the Revolution was Isaac Greenwood (3rd), who prior to the war had been trained as a dentist and maker of mathematical instruments and had established himself as a shipping merchant. As a boy of twelve he had witnessed the Boston Massacre while accompanying his father's young apprentice, Samuel Maverick, during the fighting on March 5, 1770. Maverick had just dropped Isaac's hand when he was fatally wounded. Greenwood also witnessed the destruction of the tea in Boston harbor three years later. Engaged as a merchant in Salem in 1775, he abandoned his shipping business to join the patriot cause, serving on armed private vessels. Tradition has it that he was captured by the British and imprisoned in the old Crown Street sugarhouse in New York City. He escaped by tunneling under the walls, across the street, and into the cellar of the building opposite. He then swam to Paulus Hook and after sleeping aboard an anchored sloop made his way to freedom. Greenwood served on privateers throughout the war, first on the brigantine *New Broom* under Captain Israel Bishop sailing from New London, then on the *Brutus* under Captain W. Coles sailing from Salem. He was again on duty on the *New Broom* in 1782 when the crew was captured in the West Indies and confined in a prison ship at St. John's, Antigua. When Greenwood was removed to a hospital on shore, he escaped in the uniform of a British naval officer and with the help of two friends took possession of a British sloop with which the three sailed to the island of Montserrat. Throughout his life Greenwood had the reputation of being an eccentric, and his father attributed his behavior to the effects of a saber blow on the head that he received during the war. After the war ended he moved from Salem, where he had sold ladies' umbrellas, to New York City, where he established himself as a dentist, and later he maintained businesses at Providence as a dealer in hardware and a maker of mathematical instruments.[7]

Other mathematical practitioners assumed significant responsibilities in providing weapons and gunpowder for the Continental Army. Paul Revere, in addition to producing inflammatory engravings and broadsides, was in charge of ordnance repairs for the Continental Army during 1775 and 1776 and engaged in various endeavors for the manufacture of gunpowder and the casting of cannon.[8] Isaac Doolittle, Sr., of New Haven, who was a well-known maker of clocks and surveying instruments, had served as Armourer of the Fourth Regiment of New Haven Colony in 1758 and was known as one of the most skillful mechanics in the colony. In 1776, in association with Jeremiah Atwater, he established a powder mill in West-ville, Connecticut, which produced a considerable supply of gun-powder for the war effort.[9] John Avery, a farmer, goldsmith, and maker of clocks and surveying instruments at New Preston, Connecticut, paid a substitute to serve for him in the Continental Army at the beginning of the war, but in 1776 he was appointed to a committee "to procure and purchase firearms in this state." [10] A third Connecticut maker of clocks and instruments who became involved with the production of arms was Gurdon Huntington of Windham. Being too young for military service, he worked in the manufactory for the repair of muskets and other arms which had been established by his father, Major Hezekiah Huntington.[11]

An armory for the manufacture and repair of muskets was established by Lebbeus Dod of Mendham, New Jersey, after he had served as a captain of artillery and distinguished himself at the skirmishes at Springfield and Elizabethport. Dod saw little other combat, because Washington detached him from active duty to develop the armory, which he managed with considerable skill. Prior to the war he had been well established as a clockmaker and maker of surveying instruments and had worked as a surveyor.[12]

Other weapons besides muskets were required. Another John Bailey, born and trained in England, was a cutler, swordsmith, and dealer in mathematical instruments in New York City at the beginning of the war. He became an ardent patriot and produced bladed weapons and other military equipment required by the Continental Army, including a dress sword for General Washington. When the British occupied the city in 1778, he moved to Fishkill, New York, where he continued his activities.[13] He was not related to the instrument maker of the same name who worked in Hanover, Massachusetts.

A number of distinguished practitioners played important roles in the provision of food and supplies for the Continental Army. John Fitch of steamboat fame, who had been trained as a silversmith and watch and clock maker, enlisted in the Continental Army at the beginning of hostilities and became a gunsmith for the Committee of Safety in New Jersey. Developing some personal conflicts in the course of his work, he left Trenton for Bucks County, Pennsylvania, just as the British forces approached and established himself as a silversmith in Warminster Township. There during the next several years he continued to supply the army with tobacco, beer, and other commodities. He also obtained a commission as a deputy surveyor and worked in that capacity until about 1780.[14]

Owen Biddle, the Quaker watch and clock maker of Chester County, Pennsylvania, who had distinguished himself during the observations of the transit of Venus and of the sun and was a founding member of the American Philosophical Society, took an active part in the events leading to war. He served as a delegate to the Provincial Conference of 1775 at which the resolution of non-importation was confirmed, was appointed a member of the Pennsylvania Council of Safety, was actively engaged in raising troops, and also served on a committee for the construction of boats and river defenses. He was one of the Philadelphia delegates to the Provincial Convention in 1776 and devoted the next several years to providing forage for the army. By the time the war ended, Biddle had been disowned by the Society of Friends for his military activities and had suffered a considerable loss of personal property, including three vessels operated by his shipping business. He was forced to assign his property to satisfy his creditors and was left in greatly reduced circumstances for the remainder of his life.[15]

Not all the colonial mathematical practitioners were patriots, however. Thomas Pryor, a Philadelphia instrument maker and man of property who had participated in the observations of the transit of Venus, showed his loyalist sympathies by advertising in 1778 in a Philadelphia newspaper published by the British during the occupation that he made, sold, and repaired navigational instruments.[16] Another acknowledged loyalist was Macock Ward, a lawyer, clockmaker, and maker and repairer of mathematical instruments in Wallingford, Connecticut.[17] William Hart, an instrument maker of Portsmouth, New Hampshire, spent most of the war years in prison for refusing to sign the Association Test in 1774. However, there were probably additional reasons for his imprisonment, since others in his community who had refused to sign were not confined.[18] William Hinton, a maker and dealer in mathematical instruments in New York City, remained active in business from at least 1772 to 1780, including the period of the British occupation.[19] Notable among the British sympathizers was Charles Oliver Bruff, a member of a distinguished dynasty of Maryland silversmiths, who also made mathematical instruments. Although in 1775 he advertised that he also made swords "for those Gentlemen who are forming themselves into companies in defense of the Liberties," his association with the patriotic cause was short-lived. When the British landed on Long Island, Bruff moved to Tarrytown, New York, and shortly thereafter joined the British forces in New York City where he was stationed until the British were evacuated. In 1783 he moved with other loyalists to the new community of Shelburne which they formed in Nova Scotia.[20]

In addition to the practitioners who were active on one side of the conflict or the other, there were others who conducted their businesses as usual, leaving military participation to associates or relatives. Benjamin King continued to work as a maker of navigational instruments at Newport until the city was occupied by the British forces, then moved with his family to North Kingston, returning after the end of hostilities.[21] King's one-time partner, William Guyse Hagger, moved his family to safety in Cranston in 1774. He served for a short period in 1778 with the Pawtuxent Rangers as a sentinel at Pawtuxent Fort, and then marched forward from Pawtuxent with the Continental Army.[22] Benjamin Condy, well-established maker of navigational instruments in Philadelphia, did not participate actively in the conflict but made himself useful to the patriot cause by making, repairing, and selling navigational instruments for some of the major shipping merchants.[23] Enos Doolittle, Jr., of Hartford, sold engraved views of the Battle of Lexington and Concord and maintained his watch and clock making business without interruption.[24] Anthony Lamb, although a strong and sympathetic supporter of the patriot cause, took no part in the war effort. When the British approached New York City in 1776 he moved his shop to New Haven. Three years later, when General Tryon swept into Connecticut for the second time, Lamb again found himself forced to flee. His son, John Lamb, who had been his partner as an instrument maker for a time, was a prominent patriot and from 1765 was extremely active as a leader of the Sons of Liberty in New York City. He served in several major engagements during the Revolution and in 1783 was brevetted as a brigadier general.[25]

Thomas Greenough of Boston did not participate in active combat because of his advanced age but was nevertheless one of the foremost patriots in his community. In 1774 he was a member of a committee collecting donations for "the relief of suffering inhabitants of Boston" and in 1776 was appointed to determine the damage sustained since the Boston Port Bill. He served on the Committee of Safety and other town committees before and after the British occupation of the city and was a member of the Revolutionary Committee of Correspondence. He had signed the Boston Non-Importation Agreement in 1769 and was active during the years of the war making, repairing, and selling navigational instruments to Boston shipmasters.[26]

Curiously enough, though most of the professional surveyors did military service, few practiced their specialty in response to the needs of war. General Washington's knowledge of surveying proved extremely useful in relation to the need for military mapping and was responsible for the considerable emphasis he placed on this endeavor, although he did not himself engage in it during this period. Thomas Marshall, a distinguished frontiersman and surveyor, served as a colonel in the Virginia State Regiment of Artillery.[27] Loammi Baldwin (1st) who had worked as a surveyor and engineer of New Bridge (now North Woburn), Massachusetts, enlisted in 1775 with Colonel Samuel Garrish's Foot Regiment, and rapidly advanced through the ranks to full colonel in charge of the main guard of New York City under General Washington, and retreated with Washington to Delaware. He also served with Washington at the capture of Trenton and in 1777 was honorably discharged for ill health.[28]

Joseph Frye, who was trained as a surveyor and engineer, was selected in 1775 by the Provincial Congress to command the forces of Cumberland County, Maine, in defense of the seacoast at Falmouth (now Portland) after that town was bombarded and burned by the British. Early in the following year he was appointed by the General Court to the rank of brigadier general in the Continental Army and subsequently rose to the rank of major general. In 1776 he resigned, claiming that he had been passed over for promotion in favor of others having less military experience; he also disagreed with some of Washington's plans. His oldest son, who was also a surveyor, served as a captain commanding a company at the Battle of Monmouth.[29]

Roger Sherman of New Haven, who emerged as one of the major figures in the achievement of independence, was originally a man of science. He had worked as a surveyor in Connecticut, had calculated ephemerides for a series of almanacs, was a member of the Connecticut legislature, and became a judge of the state supreme court. He was elected to the Continental Congress in 1774 and was a signer of the Declaration of Independence, the Articles of Association, the Articles of Confederation, and the Federal Constitution.

After the war he was a member of the Constitutional Convention at Philadelphia and was later elected to the House of Representatives and subsequently to the United States Senate.[30]

Most sought after of all of the categories of mathematical practitioners from the inception of the war were the cartographers. The few who were available responded promptly to the needs of war, and a handful emerged as major figures in the field that was the first to become professionalized. Among the most notable were Robert Erskine, Simeon De Witt, Thomas Hutchins, Bernard Romans, Abel Buell, Andrew Porter, and Rufus Putnam. Washington, because of his experience with the British Army, recognized at the outset of hostilities the critical role of the cartographer in his embryonic army. Maps were urgently needed for moving large bodies of troops and shipments of supplies over considerable distances and for charting undefined harbors and waterways for the movement of shipping. The cartographers were also sought for designing fortifications and other construction necessary to military operations.

In a letter to the Congress written on July 10, 1775, seven days after he assumed the office of commander-in-chief, Washington advised the president of the Congress, John Hancock, that "want of Engineers to construct proper Works and direct the Men" was one of his most pressing problems, in addition to the need for ordnance and adequate supplies of gunpowder. He elaborated: "In a former part of my Letter I mentioned the want of Engineers. I can hardly express the Disappointment I have experienced on this Subject, the Skill of those we have being very imperfect and confined to the mere manual exercise of cannon, whereas the war in which we are engaged, requires a Knowledge comprehending the Duties of the Field and Fortifications." He noted, furthermore, that not only was engineering skill lacking in his army, but that neither he nor his staff had any considerable knowledge of military matters and consequently were forced to compensate for it by their knowledge of men and by resorting to some books.[31]

During the period that Washington was vigorously searching for qualified personnel to undertake cartographic work, he announced his first achievement to a committee of the Continental Congress in 1776, reporting, "I accordingly have the pleasure to enclose you Colonel Gridley's report of the Harbour and Works of New London, with the several Plans he has taken, which appear to be accurate and well done." The map, prepared by Colonel Richard Gridley, was a simple outline on which soundings were noted but which otherwise included a minimum of physical or topographical features.[32]

The next several years continued to emphasize the critical scientific and technical needs of the Continental Army, and they were reflected in one of the first actions taken by Benjamin Franklin upon his arrival in Paris in December 1776 as minister plenipotentiary to the Court of Louis XVI. He made known to the French Minister of War the desire of the American Congress to "secure skilled engineers, not exceeding four," for it was Washington's opinion that with such a nucleus he could proceed to train others.[33] Four French officer engineers were selected, and as many more followed soon thereafter. They were commissioned by the Congress and were at work advising Washington and his staff in the development of general strategy and in the design of encampments such as Valley Forge, providings maps, and developing the Continental Army's engineering activities.

The French engineers had distinguished careers in America and made important contributions in the field of cartography in particular. Michel du Chesnoy, a captain in the Corps of Engineers, produced nineteen maps, or versions thereof, during his service. Chevalier Louis Duportail was appointed head of the Continental Army's Corps of Engineers and Companies of Sappers and Miners and was extremely influential in directing their activities. He assisted in laying out the defenses of Philadelphia, Fort Mifflin, and Valley Forge, as well as West Point. François de Fleury, a captain of engineers, distinguished himself with bravery in the field and later served with General Rochambeau. Etienne de Rochefontaine served with the Continental Army from 1778 to 1783, and Jean de Villefranche was involved with the fortification of the Delaware River, West Point, and the Hudson Highlands. The most outstanding of the group was Jean-Baptiste de Gouvion, who assisted in the planning of West Point and the redoubt at Verplanck's Point in the Hudson River. He participated in the siege and surrender of Yorktown and compiled a topographical map of the order of battle which in effect constituted a map of the surrender, a document which was subsequently transmitted to the Continental Congress.[34]

The need for cartographers and for the new type of professional designated by Washington as "engineers" became increasingly critical as the first months of war passed. Early in 1777 Washington again voiced his concerns to Hancock: "The want of accurate maps of the country which has hitherto been the scene of war has been of great disadvantage to me. I have in vain endeavoured to procure them, and have been obliged to make shift with such sketches as I could trace out from my own observations and that of gentlemen around me. . . . I really think if Gentlemen of known Character and probity could be employed in making Maps (from actual Survey) of the Roads, Rivers, Bridges, and Fords over them, the mountains and passes through them, it would be of the Greatest Advantage." [35]

Perhaps better than any other individual in his army, Washington understood the qualifications required for cartographers, as a result of his earlier experience in map making and surveying. He had produced several maps before the war, although only his "Map of the western parts of the colony of Virginia as far as the Mississippi" was published. It was inserted in the English edition of *The Journal of Major George Washington Sent by the Honorable Robert Dinwiddie, to the commandant of the French forces on the Ohio,* a small pamphlet originally published at Williamsburg in 1754 and reprinted in London in the same year.[36]

Washington's predicament was emphasized by the relative wealth of map materials which the British had acquired by the beginning of hostilities. With the support of the Lords Commissioners for Trade and Plantations, especially in relation to the acquisition of new lands after the French and Indian Wars, surveyor-generals had been appointed for the British colonies and possessions in North America. The most prominent of these were Captain-Lieutenant Samuel Holland, who had made surveys of New France, New England, and the province of New York from 1764 until the eve of the war, and William Gerard de Brahm, who had conducted surveys of Florida, South Carolina, and Georgia, an extensive project on which he was engaged until 1770.

In addition to these resources, the British had for their use not only *The English Pilot. The Fourth Book,* which was a standard work used throughout the war, but also a series of new coastal charts of the North American colonies based on the work performed by Joseph F. W. Des Barres from 1764 to 1775 and published as *The Atlantic Neptune.* For the following ten years Des Barres, working with a staff of more than twenty assistants, continued to compile maps from sketches and coastal surveys produced by British military and hydrographic engineers. As a result, *The Atlantic Neptune* ultimately included approximately 257 charts of American coasts and

harbors. This work was supplemented from private surveys of particular colonial companies as well as from records maintained by the
Lords of Trade.

Des Barres was a British officer of French-Swiss parentage, who
had studied mathematics under the Bernouilli family at Basel and
military art at Woolwich Academy before entering the Royal American Regiment, or 60th Regiment of Foot, with the rank of lieutenant. He was in active service in North America in 1757 and
1758, first at Schenectady against the Indians, then reconnoitering
Fort Carillon (Ticonderoga), which had just been completed by the
French, and finally serving as engineering officer at the siege of
Louisbourg, Nova Scotia.[37]

Samuel Holland, who became closely associated with Des
Barres, had gained considerable military and cartographical experience in the Dutch campaigns of 1747 and 1748 and later with the
British Army at Albany, Fort Edward, Ticonderoga, and eventually
Louisbourg. At the last-named station he met Captain James Cook
and taught him the use of the plane table and other surveying practices. Working together, Cook, Holland, and Des Barres produced
maps of the St. Lawrence River and Gulf and a chart of the approaches to the Gaspé Peninsula. Thereafter Des Barres and Holland spent much of their time along the Atlantic coast from Labrador
to Massachusetts in the service of the British Admiralty.[38]

The charts and descriptions of *The Atlantic Neptune* particularly
emphasized Nova Scotia and the St. Lawrence River and Gulf, but
gave rather meager hydrographic information about American ports.
They contained tables of the compass variation along the coast in
1775 and times of high water on days of the moon's changes, with
the vertical rise of the tide. They also included sailing directions
along the coast and colored engravings of numerous headlands and
harbor entrances. The charts were drawn in two scales, one for
coasting and the other for pilotage. This monumental work, which
had been assembled by the British Admiralty at a cost of approximately £100,000, proved inconvenient to use because of its unwieldy
size, and the charts were later issued individually with the sailing directions bound separately.[39] This resource would have been of considerable value to the Americans, but it was rarely available to them.
Copies were occasionally acquired from captured vessels, and individual charts were also available from time to time from other
sources, but since there were no facilities for duplicating them, their
use by the Continental Army was perforce limited.

The British also had a great many other cartographic works produced before the beginning of the war, covering a considerable part of the eastern coast of the North American continent. Among these were the charts of Newfoundland and Labrador issued between 1765 and 1768 from original surveys made by James Cook and Michael Lane, many of which were reproduced in a two-volume work, issued in 1777 as *The North-American Pilot* and *The West India Atlas* and again in 1778 as *The Western Neptune. An American Atlas,* including some of the maps published earlier, appeared in 1775, and a cartographic work designed for use by British officers in the field was published in 1776 as *The American Military Pocket Atlas.* An important contribution to British cartographic resources which appeared in 1777 was *The North American Atlas, Selected from the Most Authentic Maps, Charts, Plans, &c. Hitherto Published.*[40]

The British had thus amassed an impressive collection of hydrographic and topographic surveys of the British colonies of North America in a form which could be readily distributed to the field forces during the war. The concern with commerce had made it possible to develop by the mid-eighteenth century a center in London for the collection of survey data from British engineers in the individual colonies and trading centers. In this facility the data assembled were compiled by professionals and published in the form of maps to assist British commercial and military aims. By the time the American Revolution began, British military and naval forces were well equipped with maps, and valuable additions were made from time to time as the war progressed.

No counterpart to these important works was produced by the American colonists, and no such central cartographic facility was possible. Consequently the Continental Army was forced to rely on very limited resources. In general, the published British maps were not available in the colonies, although American navigators were occasionally able to acquire copies of French publications, such as G. L. Le Rouge's *Pilot Americain Septentrional* and the *Neptune Americo-Septentrional.*[41] Colonial American map makers had always relied on the English to engrave and publish their maps, and the colonies had no adequate facilities to engrave, print, or otherwise reproduce the few available maps in quantities sufficient for military activities in the field.[42]

Whereas the British maps of the period were consistently professional in quality, American maps during the Revolutionary period varied considerably in accuracy and quality. In addition to geographical surveys of a military nature, Americans produced maps of much more limited use—battle maps, sketch maps, and surveys of fortifications and camps. Of these the first were the most effective, particularly when produced by one of the few skillful cartographers in the Continental Army. The maps subsequently made by the French engineers were much more useful because they were the work of professionally trained men skilled in the art of mapping. However, even those maps that were competently compiled suffered when copied for distribution.

From time to time useful maps of the war and its progress appeared in some of the almanacs published in the colonies, and these received wide distribution. Notable among them were the maps included in *Bickerstaff's New-England Almanac* for 1776, the *North American Almanack* for 1777, and *Nathaniel Low's Astronomical Diary* for 1777. These were rarely sufficiently accurate for field use but served a function in informing the public of the war's progress.

Throughout the conflict there was continued concern for protecting information that might be useful to the enemy. The Continental Army was provided with a number of maps produced by what was virtually a spy network organized by Colonel Benjamin Tallmadge and conducted under the most dangerous conditions. Among the extremely useful products of the network were maps of New York City, Long Island, and adjacent areas.[43] The danger of having American cartographic resources fall into the hands of the British was kept constantly in mind not only by the military but by others as well. It was as a reflection of this concern that in 1777 Thomas Bond and William Smith, vice presidents of the American Philosophical Society, requested three of the Society's members, David Rittenhouse, Edward Duffield, and Pierre Eugene Du Simitière, to collect the copperplates that had been used for illustrations of the first volume of the *Transactions* and to place them in safekeeping. Their concern was particularly for what they described as "the Canal Plate," from which had been made copies of "A map of part of Pennsylvania & Maryland, intended to show, at one view, the several places proposed for opening a Communication between the waters of the Delaware and Chesapeake Bays . . . ," produced by Thomas Gilpin and used to illustrate an article about the proposed canal. In expressing concern for the safety of the plate, Bond and Smith noted that "it is the Theatre of War at present." [44] In fact, General Howe had by that time disembarked his troops and begun his march on Philadelphia from Elkton, Maryland. The map was well executed, for Gilpin was experienced in drafting and engineering and had devoted considerable attention to the improvement of roads and the development of the abortive canal project.[45]

Washington continued to reaffirm his cartographic needs whenever opportunity offered, and six months later, on July 19, 1777, he reminded the Committee of the Congress in a letter from his camp at the Clove in New York that "a good Geographer to Survey the Roads and take Sketches of the Country where the Army is to Act would be extremely useful and might be attended with extremely valuable consequences. He might with propriety have the chief direction of the Guides who must have a head to procure, govern, and pay them. If such a person should be approved of I would beg leave to recommend Mr. Rob.[t] Erskine who is thoroughly skilled in this business, has already assisted us in making maps of the country, and has (as I am informed) uniformly supported the Character of a fast friend to America." [46] The following week the Congress passed a resolution: "That General Washington be empowered to appoint Mr. Robert Erskine, or any other person that he may think proper, geographer and surveyor of the roads, to take sketches of the country, the seat of war, and to have the procuring, governing, and paying the guides employed under him. . . ." [47]

Erskine was officially appointed two days later as the Geographer-Surveyor of the Continental Army, and he proceeded to assemble a small staff of such assistants as were available. Some concept of the difficult nature of the work to be undertaken may be derived from Erskine's letter to Washington written shortly after his appointment. "In planning a country a great part of the ground must be walked over, particularly the banks of Rivers and Roads; as much of which may be traced and laid down in three hours as could be walked over in one; or in other words a Surveyor who can walk 15 miles a day may plan 5 miles. . . . Six attendants to each surveyor will be proper; to wit, two chain-bearers, one to carry the instrument, and three to hold flagstaffs. . . . Young gentlemen of Mathematical genius, who are acquainted with the principles of Geometry, and who have the taste for drawing would be most proper assistants for a Geographer." [48] Erskine's staff set to work immediately to prepare operational maps of the region from the Hudson Highlands to Philadelphia, concentrating on the mapping of upper New Jersey. Among their early achievements was a map of the battlefield of the Brandywine compiled on August 27, 1777, by James Brown. Consisting primarily of delineation of roads with their distances, the map provided Washington with useful intelligence for his order of battle.

In time Erskine developed a corps of more than twenty surveyors in addition to chain bearers and other field assistants. A number of the surveyors on his staff have been identified, including, besides James Brown, Lieutenant Benjamin Lodge, who mapped the route of the Western Army under General John Sullivan in 1779 and 1780, and Captain William Gray. Both the latter were attached to the Fourth Pennsylvania Regiment. Gray produced a number of maps of Colonel William Butler's line of march against the Iroquois Indians in 1778. The staff mapped the Continental Army's route from Easton, Pennsylvania, to Wyoming, Pennsylvania, along the Susquehanna River to the Genessee River in New York State.[49] Working closely with Erskine were David Pye, who provided valuable local knowledge of the region around Clarkstown, New York, and William Scull, Surveyor-General of Pennsylvania, who joined Erskine in 1779 and produced useful maps of Connecticut, New York, and New Jersey. John Watkins joined the staff in 1777 and subsequently made surveys of several parts of New Jersey and South Carolina. During 1779 and 1780 John Armstrong worked for Erskine in Morristown, New Jersey, executing several maps of the region. A map of the Farmington River was produced for Erskine in 1765 by Elijah Porter, a former surveyor of Hartford County, Connecticut. Jacob Brown, one of the few professional cartographers in the Continental Army, who had been trained as a surveyor after attending Wilmington's old Academy, made a regional map in 1777 which was used by Washington in the Brandywine campaign.

The most outstanding member of Erskine's modest corps of engineers and cartographers was Simeon De Witt, who eventually succeeded Erskine as Geographer and Surveyor-General. When De Witt's studies at Queen's College (now Rutgers University) were interrupted by the war, his uncle, Colonel (later General) James Clinton, encouraged him to join a volunteer battalion and later recommended him to Washington as a geographer. In 1778 he was appointed assistant to Erskine.[50]

Between the time of his appointment to the position of Geographer and his death in 1780, Erskine issued more than 130 different maps. The greater part of those produced during the Revolution, first under his direction and then that of De Witt, were plane-table sketches, only roughly finished, delineating the roads and major topographical features, as well as taverns and commanding elevations, generally made at a scale of 1 mile to the inch. Although crudely executed, the maps were surprisingly accurate, and most of them were subsequently compiled in a contracted form at scales varying from 2 to 8 miles to the inch, plotted on a grid of conic projection based on a prime meridian at New York City.[51]

The work of the cartographers was hampered not only by the hazards of weather and wildlife encountered in their fieldwork but by danger from the enemy. While Erskine's staff continued its mapping in the Hudson Highlands, Washington directed General James Clinton to move toward the enemy's lines in the vicinity of Kings Bridge "to cover the Engineers and Surveyors, while they reconnoiter and as far as time will permit, survey the grounds & roads in your rear, and in front of the Camp." [52]

A useful summary of the achievements that had been completed by early 1780 was furnished by Erskine to General Philip Schuyler. In it he noted: "From surveys actually made, we have furnished His Excellency with maps of both sides of the North River, extending from New Windsor and Fishkill, southerly to New York; eastward to Hartford, Whitehaven, &c. and on the west to Easton, Pennsylvania. Our Surveys likewise include the principal part of New Jersey, lying northward of a line drawn from Sandy Hook to Philadelphia; take in a considerable part of Pennsylvania; extend through the whole route of the Western Army under Genl. Sullivan; and are carried on from New Windsor and Fishkill northward, on both sides of the River, to Albany, and from thence to Schoharie. In short, from the Surveys made, and materials collecting and already procured, I could form a pretty accurate Map of the four States of Pennsylvania, New Jersey, New York and Connecticut, and by the help of a few magnetic and Astronomical Observations, with some additional Surveys, a very accurate one." [53]

The Continental Army's needs could not be met merely by the completion of accurate surveys of the regions that formed a field of war, however. Multiple copies of the maps were urgently needed for the prosecution of the war, and this proved to be an almost unsurmountable difficulty. The cartographer's or surveyor's small field sketches, supplemented by notes compiled hurriedly on the spot with many abbreviations, were submitted to professionally trained draftsmen who assembled the individual sketches into the required composite and then delineated a final map supplemented with the information from the field notes. Each of these maps was perforce an individual project and resulted in a single document. To provide additional copies required laborious and time-consuming duplication by draftsmen. Since the maps had to be kept out of enemy hands, the few copies available had to be restricted to officers of the highest ranks.[54]

The instruments used for conducting military surveys were those traditionally used throughout the eighteenth century for map making. The work was accomplished for the most part by the plane table and the plain surveying compass, with the common surveying chains and standards. Confirmation of this is provided by a letter from Peter R. Livingston written from New York early in 1781 to Colonel Timothy Pickering, who was then the Quartermaster General of the Continental Army. Livingston requested payment for a plane table which Erskine had purchased from him "for the use of the Surveying Department." [55]

Erskine's unexpected death in 1780, at the early age of forty-five, was a serious blow to the Continental Army's military cartographic project, but it did not interrupt the endeavor. Washington immediately appointed De Witt to succeed Erskine, and De Witt joined the Commander-in-Chief at his headquarters in New Windsor, New York, in mid-December 1780. He set to work to map the roads from New Windsor to other strategic points, including Trenton, New Jersey, and during this period he attempted to improve the quality of military map making by use of scientific aids as much as possible. In a request issued to all the newspapers published in New York, New Jersey, and Connecticut, De Witt appealed to "ANY MATHEMATICAL GENTLEMEN who can furnish the Subscriber with the correct *variation of the needle*, in any places in *Connecticut, New York, New Jersey* and *Pennsylvania*, shall have their services gratefully acknowledged; and as many observations of this kind as can be collected will be of use in performing maps formed of those parts of the country, for *His Excellency General Washington*.

"N.B. It will be necessary to mention the times and names of the places (also their latitudes if ascertained) at which the observations were made." [56]

This appeal reflected the needs expressed by De Witt in his report to General Schuyler, but despite the wide coverage given in the press to De Witt's request, there is no evidence that he received useful responses.

As the Continental Army began to develop its strategy for a southern campaign, Washington assigned De Witt the task of mapping the roads from Princeton, New Jersey, to Philadelphia, Delaware, and Maryland. He was particularly enjoined to remember the need to note "towns, Villages, and remarkable Houses and places." [57] Several months later Washington gave further instructions to map roads through Maryland and Virginia. De Witt and his staff accomplished the assignments sufficiently in advance of Washington's campaign at Yorktown to contribute measurably to its success.

Following the appointment of De Witt as Geographer-General of the Main Army under Washington, the new position of a Geographer-General of the Southern Army was created in July 1781, to which Captain Thomas Hutchins was appointed. Hutchins, a native of Monmouth County, New Jersey, was commissioned Ensign and Paymaster to the British forces in the western country before he was sixteen and soon rose to the position of deputy engineer in the British forces. He served in the Royal American Regiment, or 60th Regiment of Foot, and was appointed assistant engineer under Captain Brehm. He designed the fortifications of Fort Pitt, when it was taken over from the French in 1758. For some years thereafter he lived in Louisiana, a region he came to know extremely well. He made surveys of the country westward of the Allegheny Mountains on the Mississippi and Ohio and other rivers and lakes. These surveys with related descriptions were published in London after the war had begun.[58] Hutchins was in London in connection with their publication and remained until his map and pamphlet had been published but refused employment with the British government because his sympathies lay with his native country. He was arrested and jailed for a supposed correspondence with Benjamin Franklin in Paris and his considerable estate was seized. He was eventually set free and sailed to France and thence to Charleston, where he joined the Southern Army under General Nathanael Greene. He held the position of Geographer-General of that army from 1781 until his death in 1789.[59]

Hutchins is believed to have written an appendix to an account of the march made by Colonel Henry Bouquet from Philadelphia to Fort Pitt and other regions, which provided a general plan and details for the defense of western frontiers by a series of forts and military settlements. This appendix contains the genesis of the government survey of lands undertaken after the war, on which the plan of surveys put into operation by the government in 1785 was based.

Following the British defeat at Yorktown, De Witt and his staff continued their military service from a Philadelphia headquarters, preparing final versions of their field maps both to serve as a cartographic history of the war and to meet peacetime needs. De Witt's plan to provide "A Map of the State of War in America" was submitted to General Washington through the latter's aide John Trumbull and received the full approval of the Commander-in-Chief. However, it was rejected in 1783 in the Continental Congress, which agreed that, although the proposal was desirable, it could not be undertaken at public expense because of the reduced financial circumstances of the country. Nevertheless, a subsequent resolution of the Congress required that the Geographers of the United States be instructed that, in the interests of preserving the maps as a record of the war, a copy of each of the surveys made in their respective departments be deposited in the office of the Secretary of War.[60]

Early in 1784 De Witt again attempted to obtain the Congress's cooperation for the project. This time he suggested that from the materials he had at hand he could prepare a trial plate for a map to be published at his own expense, asking only that sufficient cash be advanced from the pay already due to him. Despite the encouragement of General Washington, now returned to Mount Vernon, no report was made on the project by the Congress, and it was discarded. Having failed to obtain the official support he required, De Witt resigned as Geographer-in-Chief of the United States on May 13, 1784, and accepted the appointment as Surveyor-General of the State of New York, a position he retained for more than half a century.[61]

With the conclusion of hostilities, the definition of national boundaries became a prime concern of a number of commissioners appointed to conduct the peace negotiations that resulted in the Treaty of 1783. American concern over these boundaries was reflected in a communication from Thomas Jefferson at New York to Benjamin Franklin early in 1790, in which Jefferson urged the latter "to communicate any Facts which your Memory or Papers may enable you to recollect and which may indicate the true River [the Bay of Passamaquoddy] the Commissioners on both sides had in their View, to establish as the Boundary between the two Nations. It will be of some consequence to be informed by which Map they traced the Boundary." [62] Franklin promptly assured him: "I remember distinctly the map we used in tracing the boundary was brought from England, and that it was the same that was published by Mitchell about 20 years before." [63] Mitchell's map of 1755 assumed considerable historical importance as the official map used to define the boundaries of the United States at the Treaty of Paris, but it had some basic inadequacies which subsequently led to several boundary disputes along the new country's northern border.

In the process of forging an acceptable government in which the individual states could function satisfactorily, a visual definition in the form of an official map of the republic as a single nation was one of the priorities, and this was only partially fulfilled by Mitchell's work. A major cartographic accomplishment shortly after the end of the war fitted these requirements and was also the first map of the United States to be compiled and engraved entirely by a native American. This was the work of Abel Buell of New Haven, completed in 1784.[64] It was admittedly a compilation made from other maps, including "A Map of the British and French Dominions in North America" based on the surveys made by John Mitchell, as well as "A New Map of the Western Parts of Virginia, Pennsylvania, Maryland and North Carolina," based on the published works of Thomas Hutchins, Lewis Evans, and others. It had been Buell's ambition to be the first to represent the political boundaries of the new country, but he was in fact anticipated by the work of several others, including maps published by Thomas Jeffreys in 1776 and by John Wallis in England in 1783.

Buell's map nevertheless was an important achievement as the work of a self-taught engraver, and it was possibly one of the first documents to be copyrighted in the United States. Its imprint stated that it was "Published according to Act of Assembly," referring to a general law passed by the Connecticut General Assembly in January 1783 for the protection of literary property, the first copyright law to appear upon the statute books of any American state.

Buell was an unusual individual with many skills and accomplishments. He worked at various times as a goldsmith, typecaster, inventor, engraver, printer, map maker, and maker and repairer of mathematical instruments. Not the least of his talents was that of counterfeiter, for which he served a prison sentence early in his career.

Among the cartographic endeavors inspired by the peace settlement of 1783 was a map claimed to have been compiled from the most accurate surveys and observations and individual maps made by others in the past, during and after the war. This was the work of William MacMurray, a cartographer of Carlisle, Pennsylvania, who had had a distinguished career in the Continental Army. He identified himself on his published map as "late Ass^t. Geographer to the United States," although such an appointment does not appear to be a matter of record.[65]

XII

☆ ☆ ☆ ☆ ☆ ☆ ☆ ☆ ☆ ☆ ☆

WAR'S
WEAPONS

☆ ☆

Since mongst all Nations *War* it self doth shew,
It Man behooves *Wars* Weapons for to know.
Who here may learn the *Gunner's* aiming *Arts*,
Which thy free Industry to all imparts.
The fittest Subject now it is by far,
At these times when such Rumors are of *War*.
Eulogy of Captain John Vincent,
Samuel Sturmy, *The Mariner's Magazine* (1669)

CARTOGRAPHY AND surveying were not the only skills that the practitioners contributed to the conduct of the war; other practical sciences, such as gunnery and military observation, were also required. Prior to the beginning of the conflict the Continental Army had little experience in the use of artillery weapons. There were few cannon in the colonies, inasmuch as they were of relatively little use in fighting the Indians and taming the wilderness. The advent of war found the colonists not only with almost no artillery weapons but also without trained gunners or practical means of training them, other than such theoretical knowledge as could be imparted by the few evening schools that included the subject in their curriculum. Consequently Washington's generals were forced to rely on the few available British manuals and texts and on occasional chapters on the subject included in some British works on navigation, surveying, and dialing. There were, however, several manuals that had wide distribution in the British Army and had been used in North America. One was John Muller's important *Treatise on Artillery*, which was first published in London in 1768, less than a decade before the outbreak of war.[1] Earlier English works on the subject which may also have been available in America were sixteenth- and seventeenth-century treatises by William Bourne, Thomas Smith, William Eldred, and Nathaniell Ney.[2]

Artillery or gunnery instruments used by the Continental Army were for the most part English in origin, although there were a small number of French instruments as well. Gunnery practices were based on English methods, which were well described in Muller's treatise. It explained military geometry and weights and measures related to gunnery but did not describe, illustrate, or explain the use of gunnery instruments. A more useful source for that purpose was the second edition of a treatise on mathematical instruments by John Robertson which included an appendix on the gunner's calipers.[3]

The most widely used of the artillery instruments, the gunner's calipers were designed for measuring the diameters of convex and concave objects, the weights of iron shot, the caliber of a cannon bore and the diameter of cannon balls. The instrument could be used to calculate windage and the tolerances between the ball and the bore and to estimate the service charge of powder for various guns. Some of the instruments could even be used as range finders. Only a few examples of the gunner's calipers were produced by American instrument makers, but one, which has survived, was the work of Paul Revere. This instrument was very similar to the British gunner's calipers except that it did not include all of the usual scales, lines, and tables. It was inscribed with the name "Revere" in the style used by the engraver in other examples of his work.

This pair of calipers was probably made by Paul Revere for his own use during the years 1775 and 1776 while he was in charge of ordnance repairs for the Continental Army and involved in various ventures relating to the manufacture of gunpowder and the casting of cannon for Washington's forces.[4] It may in fact be intimately associated with one of the major crises attending the decision of the colonies to embark on war with the motherland. At the beginning of hostilities, following Washington's appointment as commander-in-chief, a total of 80,000 pounds of gunpowder had been accumulated for his forces from private sources and from stores of the British crown that had been seized by the patriots. Half of this amount was shipped to Cambridge to General Washington, but much of it was wasted before it reached him. By the end of 1775 he had no powder for his artillery, and it was only after assembling a small stock from other sources that he was able to seize Dorchester Heights. Meanwhile the Continental Congress was forced to resort to emergency measures to develop a supply by importation and by manufacture undertaken by the various provincial governments. The Congress sponsored the publication of descriptions of systems or methods for the manufacture of gunpowder and even offered funding for the production of powder or saltpeter or both. The three colonial governments that responded most actively were those of Massachusetts, New York, and Pennsylvania. In December 1774 Massachusetts ordered the restoration of one of its abandoned powder mills as well as the construction of new ones. As part of this project, Revere was sent to Philadelphia to obtain plans for the construction of a mill as well as estimates of possible production and costs. A powder mill was constructed at Canton, Massachusetts, which was so successful that in less than one year's time it had developed substantial stockpiles of both gunpowder and saltpeter. Revere was directly involved with this project.[5]

Another artillery instrument related to the gunner's calipers was the proofing gauge, of which only a single example is known. This was a simple instrument made of boxwood and inscribed with tables of measure for proof and service charges for guns of various weights and calibers. Cannon were proofed to determine whether they were sufficiently strong and safe for use in the field. The tables also indicated the powder charges required for field use. These were inscribed by means of small metal dies, and several errors in the inscription are readily apparent. The tables expressed English usage and the instrument was designed for use in the armory as well as in the field. Because of the nature of its construction and the method of inscription which rendered it less than fully accurate, the instrument appears to have been produced, not by a professional English instrument maker, but by an American maker of navigational and related instruments, for use during the Revolution. No description or illustration in manuscript or published form of such an instrument is known, and the surviving example may have been one of a kind, made for an immediate need at a time when standard gunner's calipers were not available or readily produced. The inscription upon the wooden proofing gauge included only that part of a gunner's calipers that noted the names of the piece in poundage, with the diameters of bore of brass and iron guns separately, and the diameter of shot and the weights for the proofing and service charges of each.[6]

The most commonly used of the artillery instruments was the gunner's quadrant, an instrument designed to determine the angle at which a cannon was to be elevated for firing. Occasionally the instrument was equipped with scales for measuring gun bores and shot diameters, as well as tables for estimating elevations.[7] A surviving example of such an instrument was made in the colonies in the eighteenth century by Isaac Greenwood (3rd) of New York City, whose adventurous career during the war has already been described.[8]

The present rarity of such common instruments, which must have been widely used throughout the years of the war, leads to the speculation that many of them might have been made of wood instead of brass and were consequently discarded or destroyed. Furthermore, gunners were frequently forced to rely on makeshift appliances. A shot gauge was easily constructed by cutting circles of appropriate dimensions in a well-seasoned wooden board. Such a homemade gauge could also be readily produced by a blacksmith in wrought iron, and an example of the latter, made for a 12-pound shot, was recovered from the gundola *Philadelphia* which was part of Benedict Arnold's fleet on Lake Champlain in 1776.[9]

The lack of necessary instruments at the beginning of hostilities was repeatedly reflected not only in military dispatches but in newspaper advertisements. Sometimes the latter also featured instruments that were more gadgetry than practical, such as the haviland. In 1777 William Hinton, a maker of mathematical instruments whose shop was "facing the East Side of the New Coffee House" in New York City, advertised that "For the information of such military gentlemen who are not supplied with that useful instrument call'd a HAVILAND, the subscriber executes them with neatness and dispatch, at his shop at the sign of Hadley's Quadrant and Spy Glass, Beekman's Slip, New-York; where he has to dispose of, a portable plain table compleat, a neat microscope, and pocket camera obscura. He also continues to make and repair Hadley's and Davis's quadrants, compasses, &c., on the shortest notice, and will gratefully acknowledge all favors of the public. N. B. There is a book of directions for sale with the haviland." [10]

The instrument was described in an early-nineteenth-century military dictionary as "a brass machine for the purpose of fixing a military roster. It is so-called from General Haviland, who was the inventor." General William Haviland served with the British Army in North America prior to the Revolution and was known as the inventor of a type of pontoon for fording rivers. The haviland was not a new invention at the outbreak of war, for it had been produced and manufactured at least twelve years earlier by Anthony Lamb, another New York City instrument maker who has been mentioned earlier. In an advertisement of 1760 Lamb promoted it as "Suitable for Gentlemen of the Army. A Curious Instrument, useful for detaching of Men, (invented by Colonel William Haviland, of the 27th Reg.). It consists of two graduated Circles, one moving within the other, and it is so easy to be understood, that it needs no other Direction, than to place the Number of Men to be detached (from any Company or Regiment) on the inner Circle, opposite the Number they are to be detached from, on the outer Circle, and it shows directly the Number each Company or Regiment is to furnish, in a just Proportion, according to the Number of Men in each of them: It has on the Back of it, the Scheme for forming a Battalion, and is neatly made of Ivory, about three Inches Diameter, by Anthony Lamb of Hunter's Quay, where Gentlemen of the Army may be supply'd with large Pocket Compasses, with or without Dials, Mahogany, Japann'd and Shagreen Case Telescopes; with all Kinds of Mathematical Instruments in the neatest and best manner." No examples of the haviland are known to have survived, and it may not have been the most practical item in the officer's field kit. [11]

An instrument commonly used by British and French as well as by some of the Continental Army officers during the war was the pocket compass sundial. In a period when watches were not widely used because of their cost, these convenient small dials served the dual purpose of establishing direction in the field and of verifying the time during the daylight hours. The pocket dials carried by the British were more utilitarian than those used by the French. Generally, they were made in the form of a small round brass bowl in which a paper compass card was floated on a pin pivot and protected with a glass covering. A brass time scale was fitted over the glass with a hinged folding gnomon, and the whole was protected during travel with a screw-on brass cover. Tradition states that such a pocket dial, of French manufacture and made of silver, had been presented to Washington by General Braddock. Washington is known to have used pocket compass sundials during much of his time in the field. The inventory made of his possessions after his death included "1 Pocket Compass," valued at 50 cents, in his study at Mount Vernon, and in his iron chest two similar items were found, "1 Compass in Brass Case" valued again at 50 cents, and "1 Pocket Compass," valued at $5.00.[12]

General Philip Schuyler was equipped with a fine eighteenth-century ring sundial of English manufacture, inscribed with his name. Despite the apparently wide use of the compass sundial by military men, they were not produced for the purpose in the colonies; examples that have survived are English or French in origin, and presumably most of them were brought by the owners from the country of their origin.[13]

The French pocket dials were generally made in plates of gilded brass or silver combined with an inset compass engraved on an oval or hexagonal metal base or combining a separate card engraved with the sixteen points of the compass rose, and having a small decorative needle floating on a brass pivot and covered with a protective glass pane. The hours were engraved around the outer perimeter and were frequently made adjustable to a particular latitude by means of an additional part which supported the gnomon, frequently formed to represent a bird. The reverse side was inscribed with place names of the appropriate region in which it was to be used and the degree of latitude of each. A small number of these dials carried by French officers during the French and Indian Wars have been plowed up on the sites of early military fortifications, and others have been recovered from military sites of the Revolution, including Morristown, New Jersey, and Fort Ticonderoga, New York.[14]

Another instrument extensively used by military officers, both British and American, was the hand telescope, or spyglass. All examples existing in the colonies at the time of the outbreak of war were imported from England, or occasionally from France, generally by wealthy gentlemen of leisure. This type of telescope was also used by watch officers for observation at sea, but relatively few colonial American shipmasters were able to indulge in what was an expensive and not an essential instrument. Consequently, the hand telescope was available only in small numbers and was eagerly sought for the use of the military on land as well as at sea. Particularly in demand were portable examples with collapsible tubes.

The scarcity of these instruments can be inferred from occasional advertisements relating to them that appeared in the press prior to the war. The earliest-known advertisement, published in Boston in 1734, offered a reward by Captain Edward Ellis of Cold Lane, for the return of his "Prospective Glass, the Brass cap at the small end wanting," which he had inadvertently left behind him on the ferry boat from Charleston to Boston several nights before.[15] He assured the finder that there would be "no questions ask'd." In 1743 a Boston importer, William Price in Cornhill, announced the arrival of a shipment of prints, maps, looking glasses, "Prospect-Glasses," and a variety of other items which he would have for sale.[16] In 1754 "a four-Foot Reflecting Telescope, the largest size, six Inches Diameter" was among the furnishings being sold by a Boston gentleman leaving for Europe.[17]

There are few references to the use of telescopes for scientific purposes in the New World prior to the middle of the eighteenth century. An interesting incident, however, was reported in an account of a scouting expedition at Fort Edward during the French and Indian Wars. Captain Robert Rogers, who commanded the expedition, stated that he had "sent out Parties by Land, to look down the Lake with Prospect Glasses, which I had for that Purpose." [18]

The search for hand telescopes for military use intensified as the war developed, and both the British and the Continental armies made every effort to acquire as many as could be found. In the summer of 1777 David Rittenhouse advertised in the Pennsylvania newspapers for good pocket telescopes, undoubtedly with the intention of distributing them to officers of the Pennsylvania regiments.[19] The preoccupation with telescopes for the British military was reflected in an advertisement for "DOLLAND'S TELESCOPES" appearing in the New York press in 1778 while the city was under British occupation. It suggested that "Now the Military Gentlemen have taken their several posts, those not possessed of a portable SPY-GLASS, may be accommodated with this *Sine qua non* in RECONNOITERING the FOE, first invented by Mr. DOLLAND, a prime Optician. Please to apply to James Rivington; the prices from *Seven* to

Sixteen Dollars each. Those of supreme quality are fixed in strong cases, and flung over the shoulders, stand buff to all weather." [20]

General Washington made constant use of the hand telescope and was equipped with numerous examples of them during the years of the war and at home at Mount Vernon. He was extremely particular to have instruments of fine quality and was concerned with acquiring them long before the war. In 1763 he asked one of his London agents to send him "as good a spy glass as can be bought for 60/ of a good artist." The instrument he acquired may have been a long telescope made by Benjamin Cole (3rd), one of the most prominent London makers. The tradition is that Washington used it at Mount Vernon to observe life along the Potomac River and to watch for guests approaching his plantation. The telescope "was kept behind the hall door and his favorite amusement was to look over the river with it," according to Washington's sister, Mrs. Elizabeth Lewis. On a visit to Washington's home, Benjamin Latrobe produced an amusing sketch of his host watching for belated dinner guests with his telescope. [21]

Shortly after taking command of the army, Washington began to collect equipment for use in the field, and his account books recorded that on June 4, 1776, he paid cash in Pennsylvania currency for a collection of such items, including "Maps, Glasses, . . . for the use of my Command." On the same day he paid a Philadelphia stationer, John Sparhawk, for a collection of maps, and in the following spring his accounts noted a draft for 35 guineas to Colonel John Laurens for "Tin Plates—a Telescope &c. brought from France for my use." [22]

While in the field Washington preferred telescopes made by Dollond, and several of his orders to his London agents specified purchase of instruments by that maker. In 1778 he inquired from the quartermasters John Cox and John Mitchell concerning the availability of "any of Doland's best pocket Telescopes," and later in the same year he wrote to Major General William Alexander (Lord Stirling) at New York to request: "Could you procure me one of Dolland's best pocket telescopes from New York you would oblige me." [23] This may be the brass Dollond telescope with achromatic lens which Washington used in the field and later presented to Tobias Lear. [24] A fine hand telescope made by Henry Pyefinch of London was, according to Washington's records, "one of two spy-glasses which constituted part of my equipage during the late war"; he bequeathed it to his nephew, Lawrence Washington, with the observation that it would be useful where he lived in the Choptank region of Westmoreland County.[25] A smaller field glass with its original russet leather case, which Washington had used at Valley Forge, he later presented to his favorite nephew, Major Lawrence Lewis in 1799, the year of his death.[26]

A spyglass is included in the life-sized portrait *Washington at the Battle of Trenton* painted by John Trumbull in 1792. Trumbull had served as Washington's aide-de-camp during the war and commenting on the portrait, he noted: "He holds in his right hand his reconnoitering glass with which he is supposed to have been examining the strength of the hostile army pouring into and occupying Trenton. . . . Every minute scrap of dress down to the buttons and spurs, and every strap and buckle of the horse furniture, was carefully painted from the several objects." [27]

The best-known of Washington's hand telescopes presently hangs in the great passage at Mount Vernon. It was used by Washington in the field during the years of the war and when not in actual use it was always carried by his black body servant, Billy Lee. The instrument features in an amusing incident which occurred on the field at the Battle of Monmouth and was reported by John Parke Custis. "A ludicrous occurrence varied the incidents of the 28th June. The servants of the general officers were usually well armed and mounted. Will Lee, or Billy, the former huntsman, and favorite body-servant of the Chief, a square muscular figure, and capital horseman, paraded a corps of valets, and, riding pompously at their head, proceeded to an eminence crowned by a large sycamore-tree, from whence could be seen an extensive portion of the field of battle. Here Billy halted, and having unslung the large telescope that he always carried in a leathern case, with a martial air applied it to his eye, and reconnoitered the enemy. Washington having observed these maneuvers of the corps of valets, pointed them out to his officers, observing, 'See those fellows collecting on yonder height; the enemy will fire on them to a certainty.' Meanwhile the British were not unmindful of the assemblage on the height, and perceiving a burly figure well mounted, and with a telescope in hand, they determined to pay their respects to the group. A shot from a six-pounder passed through the trees, cutting away the limbs, and producing a scampering among the corps of valets, that caused even the grave countenance of the general-in-chief to relax into a smile." [28]

One of the pocket telescopes used by Washington during many years of the war was presented to President Andrew Jackson in 1830 by George Washington Parke Custis with a silver plate inscribed *"Erat Auctoris, est conservatoris, Livertatis, 1775–1783."* In his presentation Custis noted: "Although it was in itself but of little value, there was attached unto it recollections of the most interesting character. It had been raised to the eye of the departed Chief, in the most awful and momentous periods of our mighty conflict; it had been his companion from '75 to '83, and the toils, privations, the hopes, the fears, and the final success of our glorious struggle for independence; and, as the memorial of the hero who triumphed to obtain liberty, it is now appropriately bestowed upon the hero who triumphed to preserve it. Mr. C. requested that, as [the General] was childless, he would be pleased at his decease, to leave the telescope as Alexander left his kingdom—'to the most worthy.' " [29]

An unnoted instance relating to Washington's urgent need for telescopes led to unusual complications. In 1776 he had expressed the need for a powerful telescope with which he could observe the British maneuvers and detect the strength of their forces in New York. The only instrument known to him which he considered adequate was a pedestal telescope owned by King's College (now Columbia University) in New York City, which he had observed on a visit to his stepson, John Custis, when the latter was enrolled as a student in 1773. Remembering the instrument, Washington initiated steps to borrow it through the New-York Convention. On or about August 3, 1776, the Convention passed the following resolution: "Whereas his Excellency General *Washington* is in want of the use of a good Telescope; and whereas a good Telescope is absolutely necessary for the Commander-in-Chief of the Continental Army, to discover the arrangements and operations of the enemy: *Resolved,* That the Chairman of the General Committee of the City of *New-York,* with such other members of that Committee as he may think proper, take and deliver to his Excellency General *Washington,* for his use, the Telescope which belongs to, and is a part of the apparatus of the College at *New-York. . . .* That the Convention of this State of *New-York* will indemnify the governours of the College . . . for the use of his Excellency, General *Washington,* until the redelivery thereof to the said College. . . ." [30]

A letter to the chairman of the Secret Committee of the City for New York was drafted, read, and approved by the New-York Convention and forwarded to John Berrien, requesting that he call upon President Moore of the College, or such a Governor of the College having charge of the telescope, requesting delivery of it for the use of Washington. The letter went on to instruct: "If by that means you do not obtain the said telescope, then we desire that, in pursuance of the [foregoing resolution of the Convention], you cause the said telescope to be taken out of the City-Hall of the City, in the presence of yourself and some others of the Committee; and when, by either means, you have the said telescope, please to have it safely delivered to his Excellency, the General." [31] Berrien subsequently reported to the Convention that the telescope had been readily delivered by the Reverend Ingliss, the only Governor of the College then in the city. Berrien reported further: "The General must have been anxious for the receipt of it, for before it could be come at, from the number of boxes, &c., stowed in the small room it was put into at the City-Hall, his Aid-de-Camp, Colonel Webb, with some men, were ready to receive it, and it was delivered to him." [32] Washington acknowledged receipt of the telescope; that he used it for the purpose intended is indicated in a letter to General George Clinton from his New York headquarters reporting, "By intelligence received and movements observed of the enemy, we have the greatest reason to believe a general attack will be made in the course of a few days." [33]

The King's College telescope was an English instrument, and presumably the one presented by King George III in 1753 to the College when it was established and dedicated to the British monarch. It was first noted in the minutes of a meeting of the Governors of that institution held in 1763 at Queen's Head Tavern in which it was "ordered that the Reflecting Telliscope be sent home [to England] in order to be cleaned." [34] The instrument was presumably returned by Washington in due course, although no records relating to such action can be found. When Reverend Manassah Cutler visited the college in the early summer of 1787, he described the premises and noted the presence of "a small reflecting achromatic telescope," [35] but it may not have been the same.

Washington's extensive use of hand telescopes is reflected in the surprisingly large number of these instruments noted in the inventory made of his possessions at Mount Vernon following his death. There were "11 Spye Glasses" in his study, valued at $110.00; "1 Telescope" also in the study, valued at $50.00, which may have been the pedestal reflecting telescope he bequeathed to his physician, Dr.

David Stuart, who later married the widow of John Parke Custis; and "1 Spye Glass" in the passage, which was the one carried by Billy Lee,[36] valued at $5.00.

As the American colonies pursued the war, they recognized the importance of creating an official navy. However, because of restrictions imposed by England during the period prior to war the colonists had neither competence nor experience in the construction of large ships and men-of-war. Nonetheless, in late 1775 the Continental Congress ordered the building of thirteen large ships and at a later date increased that number by six more. The ships were built in various New England shipyards and equipped for thirty-two guns; because of the use of unseasoned timber, inadequate dry-dock facilities, lack of financial backing, inexperience in the construction of large ships, and the absence of knowledge or experience in sailing them, the results were unsuccessful.

What the colonial men of the sea lacked in skill with large vessels, however, they made up for in hardiness and daring, and their exploits came to be recognized and respected by their enemies as well as by their fellow patriots. From the initiation of hostilities the navigators played an important role in privateering endeavors as well as in the conduct of colonial shipping and naval activities.

Since the war closed off all avenues for the importation of navigating instruments and nautical charts, the colonial instrument makers assumed an ever-increasing burden in meeting the growing needs not only of the official navy, such as it was, but of the privateers and merchant vessels.

Some conception of the navigational aids required can be derived from inventories of privateers and American vessels engaged in supplying the army or otherwise supporting the army's activities. The first frigate of the Continental Navy to be launched, the *Raleigh*, was taken to France in 1778, and among the equipment and fittings listed in its inventory at that time were the following items:

Captain's cabin: 1 Hanging Brass Compass
Quarter Deck: 2 Bittacles, 1 Dog Vane & Staff
Small Stores: 2 Log Reels, 1 Deep sea Line Reel, 1 Chest for Compasses
  & glasses, 17 Half Hour Glasses, 28 Half & Quarter minute
  [glasses], 3 Four hours [glasses], 3 Two hours [glasses], 1 Azamuth
  Compass, 1 Amplitude [Compass], 2 Sailing Brass [Compasses], 4
  Sailing-wood [compasses], 20 Fishing Leads, 5 Deep Sea [leads].[37]

In contrast, the stores under the care of the several officers of the Continental frigate, *Alliance,* the last American frigate to remain in the service, John Barry commanding, included only:

> 2 Log Reels, 12 Log Lines, 5 Brass Compasses, 4 Wood Compasses, 1 Hanging Compass, 2 Two hour glasses, 12 Half hour glasses, 10 ½-minute glasses, 12 ¼-minute glasses, 3 Binnacles, 16 Hand leads, 4 Hand lines, 1 Deep Sea line, 6 Log Lines, 3 Deep Sea Leads.[38]

A comparison with similar equipment on a privateering vessel revealed yet another set of requirements. The inventory of "tackle, furniture and apparel" of a Connecticut privateer during the Revolution, compiled from papers that have been preserved, included the following scientific equipment:

> 1 Traverse Table, 1 Dipsey Line, 1 Compass, 1 Time Glass ½ hour, 1 pair dividers, 2 log books, 1 Lead line, 1 Log line and reel, 1 Quadrant, 1 28-second glass, an Almanack, 1 Bundle Quills, 3 quares paper, 2 dozen ink powders, 1 soapstone ink bottle.[39]

The primary navigational instruments used on shipboard were generally the personal property of the shipmaster and his officers and were not included in the ship's inventory. Nevertheless, the difference between the instruments listed for the privateer and those provided on official naval vessels is noteworthy.

Meanwhile, as the war progressed, the necessity for training in seamanship and in navigation increased constantly without engendering the response that had occurred in time of peace. Texts as well as training were urgently required, and the cessation of importation from England made the few that were available all the more prized. The first effort to supply a text was made by Thomas Haselden, who produced the first book on the subject of practical navigation to be authored and published in America. His work, which appeared in 1777, was immediately popular and was quickly reprinted in several editions.[40] A *Treatise on Practical Seamanship* by an English mariner named William Hutchinson published in the same year was useful and popular, but few copies reached the colonies until after the war. In 1790 Samuel Buckner of Newport, Rhode Island, published *The American Sailor: A Treatise on Practical Seamanship,* which was in fact an abstract of Hutchinson's work.[41] The most important American work of the period was not produced until 1794. It was a compilation of several treatises by Commodore Thomas Truxtun, based upon his own training and experience, and its superior quality did much to achieve recognition of American competence in shipbuilding and navigation by the close of the eighteenth century.[42]

Evening courses in navigation continued to be taught through the years of the war and provided training for at least some of the great numbers of young men who swarmed to a career at sea either in the Continental Navy or in privateering. Notable among the teachers at work in this period was Nicholas Pike, a Harvard College graduate who conducted his school at the Town House in Salem in 1776.[43] He emphasized courses in mathematics and navigation and in 1788 published a text on arithmetic which became the standard manual on the subject for many years to come. It was reprinted in numerous editions and served as a prototype for later publications.[44] Other texts on arithmetic followed in due course, two of them English texts revised by Benjamin Workman, an instructor of mathematics at the University of Pennsylvania. Workman was interested also in astronomy and calculated ephemerides for almanacs published in Baltimore, in addition to his other accomplishments.[45] His major contributions, however, were a revision of John Gough's arithmetic text and the production of a handbook on gauging, published in 1788, which constituted the first American work on the subject, although compiled for the most part from existing British practice adapted for use in America.[46] Workman's revision of Gough's arithmetic was again revised and published with a new title, *The American Accountant* . . . , later revised again by Robert Patterson.[47] It enjoyed wide popularity until it was replaced with a textbook produced by Nathan Daboll, teacher and almanac maker of New London.[48]

The production of ephemerides for almanacs by science teachers and others continued during the war and postwar years, and some of these had wide distribution. William Waring was prominent among mathematics teachers so involved.[49] Another popular series was produced by a self-taught black man of science, Benjamin Banneker of Baltimore County, Maryland. He calculated ephemerides for almanacs published in Baltimore, Philadelphia, Wilmington, and other cities from 1792 until 1797. So popular were the almanacs issued under his name that at least twenty-nine separate editions of the seven issues were published. Born a free Negro, with an interest in mathematical puzzles since boyhood, Banneker had a minimum of schooling and spent the major part of his life as a tobacco planter. At the age of fifty-nine he began to teach himself mathematics and astronomy with texts and instruments loaned by a neighbor. He progressed so well that within a year he had calculated the complete ephemeris for the year 1791, which he submitted to several printers, but without achieving publication. In the interim he became involved with the survey of the Federal Territory (now the District of Columbia) as scientific assistant to Major Andrew Ellicott and worked for him for several months. Upon his return to his farm he prepared the calculations for an almanac for the year 1792, which came to the attention of leaders of the abolition societies of Pennsylvania and Maryland. With their support the almanac was published with Banneker's name and had a wide success. The fact that the author was black was used to promote the anti-slavery cause, and the almanacs enjoyed great popularity as long as the abolition of slavery continued to be a major issue. With the diminishing interest in abolition, interest in the almanacs declined and they ceased to be published. Banneker, however, continued to compile his calculations for each year until 1802.[50]

The calculation of ephemerides for almanacs was not only a respectable preoccupation with the advantage of earning additional income, but identification as an almanac maker added status to the individual who was so engaged. At the same time the printer of the almanac found it lucrative to indicate the name of a prominent man of science as the source of the calculations he published, while the purchaser had the assurance that the work had been prepared with competence. This identification, in addition to the income, was undoubtedly influential in attracting to this activity such notable figures as David Rittenhouse, Andrew Ellicott, Benjamin West, and others.

PART FOUR

Nationhood

74 Major Andrew Ellicott (1753–1820). Miniature portrait painted on ivory "by a Spanish lady" in New Orleans, 1798–1799.

75 Brass portable quadrant made and used by Andrew Ellicott, ca 1780–1790. The tangent screw is a nineteenth-century replacement.

76 Achromatic telescope with vertical and horizontal motion accomplished by means of rack work, made by W. & S. Jones of London, late eighteenth century, and used by Andrew Ellicott on his major surveys.

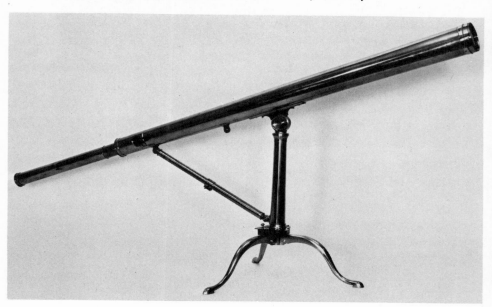

77 Astronomical regulator clock
designed for use by the surveyor in
the field. Painted dial plate signed
"David Rittenhouse," plain pine
case.

78 Wooden semi-circumferentor with brass cover plate and alidade, inscribed "Made by A. E. 1790." May have been made and used by Andrew Ellicott.

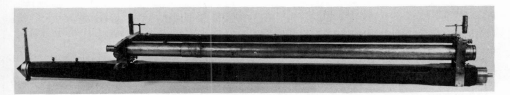

79, 80 Zenith sector having a focal length of 6 feet, made by David Rittenhouse, and modified and used by Andrew Ellicott on his major surveys, with detail of the fine adjustment mechanism.

81 Topographical map of the "Territory of Columbia" (now the District of Columbia) drawn by Andrew Ellicott, 1791–1793.

82 Two-pole surveying chain, wrought iron, American, eighteenth century.

83 Transit and equal altitude instrument made by Henry Voigt, with its original adjustable tripod.

84 Title page of *Bickerstaff's Boston Almanack*, for the Year of Our Redemption 1783, for which the ephemeris was calculated by Benjamin West. A woodcut by an unknown artist shows a figure making astronomical observations with an unidentifiable instrument and surrounded by other scientific instruments. This woodcut, first known from ca 1758, was reprinted several times.

85 Trade card of Samuel Emery, instrument maker of Salem, Massachusetts, engraved by Joseph Callender, early nineteenth century.

86 Sextant made and signed by Benjamin Stancliffe of Philadelphia, ca 1817–1833.

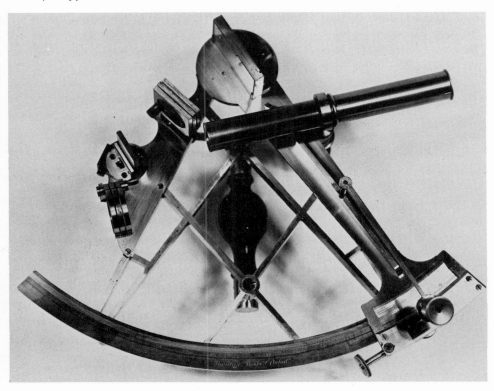

87 Circular dividing engine completed by Jesse Ramsden ca 1775, which made possible machine graduation of scales for scientific instruments.

88 The Trigonometer, an instrument for surveying invented and patented by Colonel George Wall of Bucks County, Pennsylvania. Frontispiece of his published work *A Description, With Instructions for the Use, of a Newly Invented Surveying Instrument, Called the Trigonometer* . . . (Philadelphia: Zachariah Poulson, 1788). From the copy owned by George Washington.

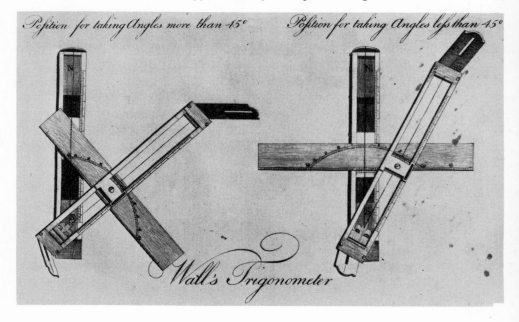

89 Detail of dial plate and table of a surveying compass made by Goldsmith Chandlee for T. Buck.

90 Surveying compendium made by Daniel Dod of Mendham, New Jersey, for Richard Loveridge, late eighteenth or early nineteenth century. Found in 1862 by Lieutenant J. G. Reeves while scouting for hostile Indians on the upper Sweetwater River in Wyoming.

91, 92 The first American-made chronometer, constructed by William Cranch Bond in Boston in 1812. Shown without its brass cylindrical case. (*Below*) Dial plate of the chronometer.

93 A ship's chronometer made by John Bliss & Co. of New York City, nineteenth century.

94 Rule and two gauging rods made and signed by John Jayne, instrument maker of Salem, Massachusetts.

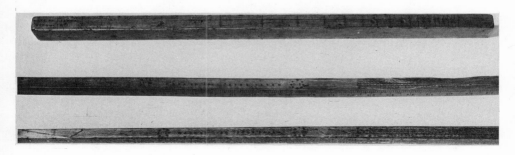

95   Surveying transit made by Edmund Draper of Philadelphia, ca 1830.

96   Solar compass invented by William Austin Burt and first produced by
William J. Young of Philadelphia in 1836.

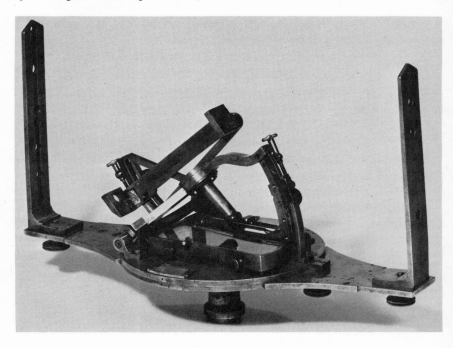

97   Pair of 3-inch globes, one celestial and one terrestrial, with matched
turned pedestal frames. Made by James Wilson ca 1822–1835.

98   Orrery by Joseph Pope, 6.5 feet in diameter and 6.5 feet high. Completed in 1787, it was purchased by lottery for Harvard College. The twelve corner figures, believed to have been carved by Simeon Skillin and cast in bronze by Paul Revere, represent Isaac Newton, Benjamin Franklin, and James Bowdoin, each repeated four times.

99 Wooden gearwork orrery, designed to be portable, presumably made for
a traveling lecturer. The flat upper surfaces are painted with designs of the
sun, a comet, the moon, and the twelve figures of the zodiac.

100   Electrostatic machine and attachments made by W. & S. Jones of London and owned by Moses Brown of Providence, Rhode Island.

101 Advertisement of Thomas Kendall, Jr., the first American to mass-produce thermometers. Reproduced from *Thomas's Massachusetts Spy, or Worcester Gazette* for February 25, 1817.

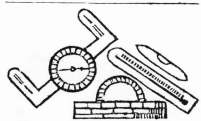

Thomas Kendall, jun.

INFORMS the Publick, that he has commenced the manufacture of THERMOMETERS of all descriptions, commonly used by Gentlemen, Distillers, Dyers, and those who make use of Lead or Oil in tempering Steel.—He also makes SURVEYORS' COMPASSES, SCALES, PROTRACTORS, SPIRIT LEVELS—and engraves Mechanicks' STAMPS.

From the time and expense he has devoted to scientifical knowledge and practical mechanism, he flatters himself he shall be able to give general satisfaction to those who may favour him with their patronage.

☞ Orders from a distance received through Oxford Post-Office, and articles forwarded by the assistance of Post-Riders, if requested.

Millbury, Feb. 25, 1817.

102 Broadside advertisement of Thomas Whitney of Philadelphia, ca 1820–1823, used as a trade card in cases for his instruments.

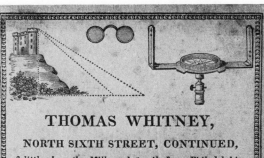

THOMAS WHITNEY,

NORTH SIXTH STREET, CONTINUED,

A little above the Mill-pond, 1 mile from Philadelphia,

MAKES

SURVEYING COMPASSES,

Principally, and many other kinds of Instruments occasionally. He has made near 400 Surveying Compasses, which are highly approved of, being of a firm and durable construction, tried and proved before they are offered for sale, and warranted good.—Also makes Optical Glasses, Glasses for Spectacles, &c.

T. W. now offers to the public, a new SURVEYING COMPASS, by which Vertical as well as Horizontal angles can be taken,—the price $10 more than the common kind. Likewise a new reflecting SEMICIRCLE or PROTRACTOR, by which angles may be taken by observation and instantly laid down on paper, and all cases of Trigonometry solved by construction.—Cases of Plotting Instruments, Measuring chains, &c. &c.

N. B. Orders, Letters, &c. left at No. 105, North Second street, will be promptly attended to.

Joseph Rakestraw, printer.

XIII

☆ ☆ ☆ ☆ ☆ ☆ ☆ ☆ ☆ ☆ ☆ ☆

ONE VAST REPUBLIC

☆ ☆

> At length, when all these contests cease,
> And *Britain* weary'd rests in peace,
> Our sons, beneath yon Western skies
> Shall see one vast republic rise . . .
>
> "To Mr. URBAN . . . ,"
> *The Gentleman's Magazine,*
> *and Historical Chronicle* (1775)

THE END OF THE War for Independence brought major changes to many walks of life in the former colonies. Some of these were immediately discernible, others became apparent only with the passage of time. The war had forged the "British colonial" into the "new American" in fact as well as in mood and attitude, but with the realization that the distinction worn with arrogant pride had been bought at great price. As a new national economy sought to stabilize itself, people returned to their former occupations or sought new ones, but most were concerned with resuming their lives where they had been interrupted. New skills developed in the pursuance of the war were put to use as new horizons loomed to be explored and exploited. A national effort redirected the skills of the cartographers, surveyors, and navigators to the demands of the westward movement. At the same time the makers of mathematical instruments exchanged their traditional hand-crafted procedures for multiple—not mass—production as a result of innovations learned from highly skilled immigrant craftsmen. This process was to culminate with the integration of the instrument maker into the coming American industrial development.

One of the most conspicuous effects of the successful end of the war was the emergence of the craftsmen, including the instrument makers, as part of a new class of American society. The ratification of the Constitution was celebrated in major cities throughout the country by great processions before and after the fact. In these an important role was played by the artisans, who sought in this way to achieve a group identification hitherto unknown. The earliest of the celebrations occurred in Boston in January 1788, when the artisans of neighboring towns joined the mechanics and craftsmen of the city of Boston in a procession led by John Hancock riding in a vehicle drawn by thirteen patriotic mechanics, followed by Paul Revere in a sleigh drawn by four horses.[1] Prominent in the parade was John Skillin, the carver of ships' figureheads and artisans' shop figures.[2]

In Philadelphia the celebration was held on July 4 of the same year, and in the grand procession the makers of mathematical instruments and scientific apparatus were grouped with the wood and ivory turners and the makers of Windsor chairs and spinning wheels. Columns representing the several branches of the craft of turning were featured, proudly carried by the turners Michael Fox and George Stow. Leading a group of sixty members of their specialized crafts with a display of mathematical instruments and turned workpieces were Thomas Mason, a turner, and Jacob Anthony, a turner and instrument maker. A similar procession of artisans was held in Baltimore but in this the makers of scientific instruments and apparatus were not specifically identified.

The most impressive of the celebrations was held in New York City on July 23, 1788. The mechanics and craftsmen of the city were led on parade by horsemen, an artillery company with field pieces, and 5,000 members of fifty-eight professions and trades, each bearing its distinguishing banners and insignia. The makers of mathematical instruments were grouped with the ivory turners and marched under the leadership of the turner Ahasuerus Turk, who had been a candidate for the New York Assembly in 1761.[3]

Although the war had forced some categories of craftsmen, particularly the clockmakers, into other fields of endeavor, because of the lack of market for their own products, it had the opposite effect on the makers of mathematical instruments. Their market did not suffer either during the war or in the period immediately following. The explosive land expansion westward also increased the need for various instruments of precision, most of which could not be provided by American craftsmen. The demand for the more common instruments alone led to the enlargement of shops and staff to increase production but these efforts were not sufficient. The required instruments could be readily imported from England and Europe at prices comparable to the American products, and the imported instruments were for the most part more professionally finished and satisfactory. Furthermore, the conviction that the imported product was superior persisted long after this had ceased to be true. The English and European trade had become aware of the new market, and in addition to supplying stocks to American dealers from abroad, a substantial number of makers and dealers immigrated to establish shops in the several major American shipping centers. There they imported, sometimes made, repaired, and sold a wide variety of instruments and related aids and supplies. This trend, already mentioned in connection with optical, barometric, and thermometric instruments, was equally apparent in charts and maps, octants, sextants, and other precisely graduated instruments. The growing competition was frustrating for the Americans who still employed the established hand-crafted methods of production.

With the cessation of hostilities, optical instruments, including telescopes, which had hitherto been so scarce, were imported in substantial numbers, primarily for maritime use. These instruments were advertised with increasing frequency during the final decades of the eighteenth century, by opticians, instrument makers, and stationers in the major American maritime centers, particularly New York City. Among those advertising such items in 1797 and 1798 were an optician named John Benson "at the sign of the Green Spectacles"; Richard Sause; and a wholesaler, David F. Launay.[4] John Grayson, "at the sign of the Spectacles," imported "telescopes for day or night, with night piece, aeromatic [sic] d°. for sea or land," in addition to other optical supplies and mathematical instruments.[5] In the same period "Day and night telescopes and others of the very best kind" were featured for sale by George Shipley, while Henry Gattey, a maker of and dealer in mathematical instruments, offered "warranted day and night Telescopes and others . . . [including] an excellent small reflecting Telescope." [6] In 1793 a Museum and Wax-works maintained by Gardiner Baker in lower New York City offered for sale "a good Reflecting Telescope made by an American Artist and magnifies 36 times." [7] If the claim to American workmanship is correct, this notice would be of considerable importance inasmuch as optical instruments were not commercially produced in the United States until after the mid-nineteenth century. A New York importer, not identified by name, listed for sale imported "Telescopes. A very handsome assortment: consisting of Day, Day and Night, Acromatic, Camp and Perspective Glasses. Also a few elegantly plated Telescopes and Perspective Glasses suited to the pocket." [8]

After the end of the war, there was considerable importation also of barometers and thermometers, which were utilized for making meteorological observations for scientific purposes as well as by amateurs, and for use on shipboard. Although barometers were not prescribed for marine use until the early nineteenth century, they were previously used for the purpose and were produced in England in quantity from the early eighteenth century. John Patrick, a well-known English maker, advertised a marine form of the barometer in an undated pamphlet produced about 1700, and in about 1710 such instruments of his manufacture were described by Zacharias Conrad von Uffenbach after a visit to Patrick's shop. He reported that among the instruments he had seen there were "barometers where the mercury can be screwed up, so that they may be conveniently carried about and used on board ship. The cheapest cost two guineas. Halley's ship-barometer with a blue liquor. They resemble thermometers with the degrees on a scale, on which the blue liquor can be used as a thermometer by means of a pointer; but that which the liquor registers above or below is shewn by the change of the barometer. Thus it is that this invention is much better than that with the mercury, since the latter dances about so prodigiously with the movement of the ship that no observation can be made." [9]

The Halley ship-barometer which von Uffenbach mentioned consisted of a spirit thermometer in which the sealed liquid rose as it expanded. This was combined with an air thermometer in which the liquid was depressed as the temperature increased and the air expanded. Halley had employed this form on his southern voyage of 1699–1701 and had described it in a publication.[10]

Marine barometers had been the subject of preoccupation among instrument makers and others from the late seventeenth century. One form described by Guillaume Amontons in 1695 [11] was widely distributed for use at sea, and during the second half of the eighteenth century some of the most prominent English instrument makers, including George Adams, Sr. and Jr., Nairne & Blunt, Thomas Jones, and W. & S. Jones, directed their attention to developing an improved form for marine use. The ship's barometer came more and more into use for foretelling storms at sea and was so advertised.[12] William Wales and William Bayley were among the first scientific voyagers to take official cognizance of glass instruments in relation to navigation, and in a report of their voyage toward the South Pole between 1772 and 1775 they noted that the instruments of this type used on shipboard were quite similar to the common form, in that they were of the cistern type. The major change was in the glass tube, which was of a relatively small bore for approximately 2 feet of its length, a feature designed to prevent the mercury from ascending as fast as it would naturally have done as a result of the motion of the ship. The larger bore of the upper part of the tube prevented the mercury which did rise from "having so sensible an effect as it would otherwise have had, on the motion of the mercury in that part of the tube." The barometer used on the Wales and Bayley voyage was suspended by the conventional type of gimbal attached halfway along the instrument's length, which, according to Wales, caused the mercury to stand higher, although the maker, Edward Nairne, claimed otherwise.[13]

As a result of these and other trials at sea, when the marine barometer came into general use it was fitted with a tube of small bore and a gimbal mounting to compensate for the constantly shifting angle of the ship.

The fact that all glass instruments had to be imported at great cost was the major deterrent to requiring the use of thermometers and barometers on American vessels at sea, and it was not until considerably later that they were generally used.

With the end of the war, however, a great change was brought about in which the importation of barometers and thermometers played a significant role. American makers of mathematical instruments discovered that the market for the common instruments had not declined with the end of hostilities, since commercial shipping was increasing and the new lands to the west were being developed. The general economic depression of the 1780s had no appreciable effect upon these craftsmen. The investment of commercial capital in land because of trade restrictions served to produce an explosive demand for the instruments of navigation and surveying. Craftsmen in shipping communities expanded their establishments and sought to increase their production by the employment of assistants but were still unable to compete with the active importation of instruments from Europe and England. Furthermore, as the European and English trade became aware of the growing new market in America, a substantial number of foreign makers directed their attention specifically toward it. Despite the tariff restrictions prevalent in most of the states, items that could not be produced in America found a ready market.

Even more disturbing than the competition in products was the increasing invasion of English and European makers and dealers, who began to migrate to the United States after the end of the war, and established themselves in business along the waterfront of major shipping centers. Particularly prominent among these were the makers and dealers of glass instruments such as barometers and thermometers, who arrived in Philadelphia and New York City in some numbers in the final decades of the eighteenth century.[14] A number of these were from Italy, where the working of glass for scientific purposes had become highly developed. Italian glass workers had migrated first to Holland and then to France, working frequently in menial capacities until they could establish their craft in the new country. Then England and Scotland became their focus, and they eventually succeeded in dominating the production of glass instruments in those countries.[15] It was inevitable that they would find their way across the Atlantic and establish their specialty in a new market. Among the first of the immigrant glass workers to come to public notice was John Denegan (also spelled Donegan) who advertised in Philadelphia in 1785 that he was lately from Italy and that he made thermometers, barometers, and scientific glassware.[16] In the same year a certain Joseph Donegany (or Donegani) who had migrated to Philadelphia moved to New York City, where he established a shop at Smith-street in which he "intends carrying on the business of Thermometer and Barometer making, in all its various branches, during his stay." [17]

Several years later Alloysius Ketterer, another glass worker, emigrated from Europe to Philadelphia and opened a shop in the house owned by Charles Kugler, who operated a tavern at the same location, identified as "at the Sign of the Seven Stars." Ketterer advertised in 1789 that he made and sold "the best Barometers, Thermometers and Glass Bubbles to prove spirits, of different kinds." [18] He moved his shop in the following year to the house of Nicholas Hess on Race-Street adjacent to the German Church. He was subsequently succeeded in business by Martin Fisher, who announced in the press in 1791 that he made pulse glasses and glassware for brewers and distillers, as well as thermometers and barometers. [19]

In 1794 a glassmaker named Joseph Gatty, who announced himself upon his arrival in New York City as "An Artist from Italy," opened a shop on Pearl Street where "he makes and sells all kinds of simple and compound Barometers and Thermometers and adjusts them to any scale," as well as repairing barometers. [20] By 1796 he had removed to Philadelphia with a shop on South Front Street, and by 1800 he identified himself as a "Weather Glass Maker." [21] An example of Gatty's work that has survived is a maximum-and-minimum thermometer based on an invention made by James Six of Canterbury in 1782, household versions of which had become the most popular meteorological instruments of the time. [22] Gatty made this thermometer of the Six type in about 1790, mounting the tubes on a mahogany board on which the scales were directly engraved. The surviving example is one that was purchased by Washington for Mount Vernon, where it has remained.

In 1800 the instrument maker Henry Gattey specialized in the manufacture and sale of compasses and other marine instruments with a shop on Water Street in New York City. [23] Whether there was any relationship between the men with similar names cannot be determined. Another cause for speculation is whether the names of some of the dealers and makers of glass instruments, such as Denegan and Donegany, Gatty and Gattey, may have been anglicizations of Italian names.

Meanwhile, occasional glass instruments had been produced in the colonies. One, a surviving fine barometer in the English style, was made by Thomas Dring in 1796. He had migrated from England to Westtown, Chester County, Pennsylvania, where he was listed on the town tax records in 1786 as an "optician." He also worked as a clockmaker and maker of mathematical instruments, and several of his clocks have survived. He had married a native of the region, and their only son, Jeptha Dring, was subsequently described as a carpenter by trade, a vagrant by inclination, and given to quoting Shakespeare. According to local legend, in about 1798 Thomas Dring collected money from a number of the townspeople of Westtown for the purpose of purchasing clocks for them in England. He set sail for his homeland with the money and never returned.[24]

The increasing trade in such relatively expensive instruments as thermometers and barometers during a period of economic stringency in the United States requires some explanation. These instruments, luxuries in the average home, had achieved popularity for use at sea and were among the status symbols of affluent merchants and plantation owners. When they began to be produced in less elaborate forms after the beginning of the nineteenth century, they also found their way into general domestic use. Makers of these glass instruments multiplied in response to the demand and commercial production in America finally developed.

Quantity production was first undertaken by Thomas Kendall, Jr., of Millbury, Massachussetts, in 1817, who announced in the local newspapers that "he has commenced the manufacture of THERMOMETERS of all descriptions, commonly used by Gentlemen, Distillers, Dyers, and those who make use of Lead or Oil in tempering Steel. ———— He also makes SURVEYING COMPASSES, SCALES, PROTRACTORS, SPIRIT LEVELS ———— and engraves Mechanick's Stamps. From the time and expense he has devoted to scientific knowledge and practical mechanism, he flatters himself he shall be able to give general satisfaction to those who may favour him with their patronage. Orders from a distance received through Oxford Post-Office, and articles forwarded by the assistance of Post-Riders, if requested." [25]

Despite the influx of imported instruments American instrument makers managed to retain an advantage over the importers in some areas, particularly in the production of instruments for surveying. The assignment of fire lands in the western regions in compensation for military service and for losses suffered from British depredation helped to direct national attention to the great areas remaining to be explored and developed and to the need to establish firm boundaries between the states, to achieve a geographical defini- tion of the United States, and to develop better means of navigation of the internal waterways.

In the autumn of 1784 the Pennsylvania legislature appointed David Rittenhouse, Thomas Hutchins, and the Pennsylvania sur- veyor Nathan Sellers to study the possibilities of water com- munications between the Susquehanna and Schuylkill rivers. Early in the following year Rittenhouse was a member of a commission ap- pointed to undertake the clearing of the Schuylkill River to make it navigable. During the summer and autumn he continued with the survey to establish the boundary between Pennsylvania and Virginia, working with instruments he had borrowed from the Col- lege of William and Mary and restored to working condition. Con- flicts which had arisen between Reverend John Ewing representing Pennsylvania and Reverend James Madison for Virginia were even- tually resolved and the work was completed in 1785.[26] Observations had been made of the satellites of Jupiter from the observatory which Rittenhouse and the other commissioners had erected at Wilming- ton, Delaware, in 1779 while running the line defining the south- western corner of Pennsylvania. From the observations taken at the observatory and from a point estimated to be 5 degrees of longitude west of the Delaware River, the beginning of the Pennsylvania– Virginia boundary was established.[27]

At the same time the commissioners extended the Mason and Dixon line to the west, and in 1785 another commission resurveyed and marked the line from the Ohio River to Lake Erie. The monu- ment installed on the north bank of the Ohio River during the defini- tion of the western boundary of Pennsylvania marked the point at which the first surveys for the division of public lands into towns and ranges were to be begun.

The next survey having a major priority was the boundary be- tween Pennsylvania and New York. On May 8, 1785, Rittenhouse advised Governor Dickinson of Pennsylvania that Simeon De Witt, Surveyor-General of New York, had suggested that the required in- struments be supplied by the Pennsylvania surveyors. Rittenhouse commented: "I believe there is no Instrument fit for the purpose in this part of America excepting the 6 feet [zenith] Sector belonging to Mr. Penn. But I have been for some time employed in making one which will be much more portable than that of Mr. Penn, and, I doubt not, equally accurate. It might soon be finished if I am not obliged to go to the westward." This was the first reference to the construction in America of a zenith sector, an achievement only two or three of the finest English instrument makers had previously accomplished.[28]

The lack of adequate instruments was reflected again and again in the major projects undertaken during the 1780s and 1790s. As he was about to undertake the running of the western line of Pennsylvania in 1785, Rittenhouse sought to borrow "a Small Astronomical Quadrant" which had been purchased by Pennsylvania for running the temporary line between New York and Pennsylvania. He commented to James Irvine that he wished to use it because "it is very Portable and would be useful on the Western Line, not for the purpose of running the Line or fixing the N. W. Corner but for correcting the Geography of the Country." Since the quadrant was public property then temporarily in his possession, Rittenhouse planned to take it with him if it was not needed by the surveyors of the temporary line.[29]

In 1786, when Rittenhouse and Andrew Ellicott, representing Pennsylvania, worked with James Clinton and Simeon De Witt, representing New York State, to establish the boundary between the two states, they had to furnish their own instruments. Since the Penn zenith sector was not then available for their use, Rittenhouse proceeded to complete the one he had under construction, basing its design on that of the Penn instrument made by Bird, which he had used in 1774 for the Pennsylvania–New York boundary survey.

When Rittenhouse completed his zenith sector, it was used jointly by the surveyors to obtain the latitude of points on a random line to run the eastern section of the northern boundary through a dense wilderness. Many years later, De Witt noted in a letter to Stephen Van Rensselaer: "I was so pleased with the ingenious construction and extreme accuracy of the instrument that I expressed a wish to have one like it, but of a more portable size, if such a one could be procured, whereupon M[r]. Rittenhouse promised to furnish me one, with he afterwards did. It is called a 30 Inch sector, but it appears that the distance from the centre to the graduated arch is only a little over 28 Inches. I cannot conceive that an instrument of the kind can be more accurately executed. The division on the arch are points hardly visible to the naked eye. M[r]. Rittenhouse explained to me his method of making them. A method I suspect entirely peculiar to himself, and observed that he had been so fortunate as to obtain a superior achromatic object glass for my sector; such glasses I suspect were not used in Mason & Dixons time. . . ." De Witt noted that the price for the instrument was $160.00.[30] Where Rittenhouse acquired the lens for the De Witt instrument cannot be ascertained, but it was undoubtedly imported from England, not ground by himself. He was capable of grinding lenses for spectacles, however, because in 1783 he had presented General Washington with a pair of spectacles as well as a pair of reading glasses, which the latter acknowledged and returned to Rittenhouse for repolishing and regrinding.[31] When possible Rittenhouse followed the usual practice of installing imported lenses into tubes of his own construction, although he sometimes attempted his own lenses. In a letter written in 1780, he requested James Searle, then en route to Europe, to procure for him good optical glass that he needed for grinding into lenses—presumably for astronomical instruments.[32]

Although he had become involved with the Pennsylvania–Virginia boundary survey in 1784, Rittenhouse continued his activities with the Treasury and Loan Office and pursued astronomical observations at his observatory in Philadelphia. It was during this period that he experimented with the addition of cross hairs to scientific instruments. Ever since instruments capable of making astronomical observations were produced, man had attempted to measure the relative distances of the stars and planets. The method of measure required the use of divisions of the lenses which was accomplished by means of cross hairs installed in the focus of telescopic instruments. Many materials were tested over the years, including animal and human hair and finely drawn wire, in an effort to achieve a line of the least diameter in a filament of sufficient durability. The problems encountered with the materials applied were twofold. Some were liable to change with variations in humidity and temperature and frequently loosened from their points of attachment or broke; others which were resistant to such variations were too thick in diameter for sufficiently accurate measurement.

After numerous experiments, Rittenhouse used spider silk successfully, becoming the first to make practical application of this material in astronomical instruments. Spider silk had previously been employed about 1754 by Felice Fontana, a noted Italian physiologist and naturalist, in an attempt to construct a level with two telescopes. Although this achievement was noted in a periodical in Italy in 1775,

the information did not reach the English-speaking world until recent times. Rittenhouse arrived at his own application of the material
independently.[33]

Rittenhouse reported his successful experiment in a postscript to
a letter to John Ewing, which was read before the American Philosophical Society in November 1785: "The great improvement of object glasses by Dollond has enabled us to apply eye glasses of so
short a focus, that it is difficult to find any substance proper for the
cross hairs of fixed instruments. For some years past I have used a
single filament of silk, without knowing that the same was made use
of by the European astronomers, as I have lately found it is by Mr.
Hirschell [sic]. But this instance, though far better than wires or hairs
of any kind, is still much too coarse for some observations. A single
filament of silk will totally obscure a small star, and that for several
seconds of time, if the star be near the pole. I have lately with no
small difficulty placed the thread of a spider in some of my instruments, it has a beautiful effect, it is not one tenth of the size of
the thread of the silkworm, and is rounder and more evenly of a
thickness. I have hitherto found no inconvenience from the use of it,
and believe it will be lasting, it being now more than four months
since I first put it in my transit telescope, and it continues fully extended, and free from knots and particles of dust." [34]

Rittenhouse undertook his experiment in June or July 1785.
Spider silk was subsequently tried by English instrument makers
with rewarding success, and in time its use for cross hairs became
universal. However, in 1813 Francis Wollaston, the English astronomer, was still using finely drawn platinum wire for the purpose. As late as 1824 Sir John Herschel commented: "I have in
vain attempted to find lines sufficiently thin to extend them across
the centre of the stars, so that their thickness might be neglected," [35]
although by that year spider silk filament had been successfully utilized by the foremost English instrument maker of the period, Edward Troughton, for cross hairs in micrometers forming part of a 5-
foot equatorial telescope used by John Herschel and Sir James
South.[36]

Spider silk was applied for other scientific uses—as filaments for
scientific equipment, for example—and has proved to be superior to
any other similar material to present times. Compared to the
thickness of the normal human hair, which is about 0.003 inch in diameter, the filament of spider silk is only 0.00015 inch; 400 strands

are required to equal the diameter of a single human hair. Although metals drawn to fine diameters were used prior to and subsequent to Rittenhouse's time, tests over prolonged periods proved that a spider-silk filament is stronger than one of steel having the same diameter, tested at approximately 60,000 pounds per square inch. Spider-silk filament not only is impervious to shock and changes of temperature and humidity but retains its elasticity for many years.[37]

Rittenhouse's development of superior cross hairs was only one among his achievements with astronomical instruments which could be compared favorably with those of the foremost European and English instrument makers. Notable also were the transit and equal altitude instruments which he developed and constructed at Philadelphia. The first of these was a prototype he had assembled for his own use while making observations of the transit of Venus in 1769; it proved successful, although crudely made. In 1789 he helped Andrew Ellicott produce a second and much improved transit instrument, which the latter used in surveys of the western boundary of New York State and later of the Federal Territory.[38] Ellicott had provided Rittenhouse with a design for the construction of the piece, patterned after one described and illustrated by Pierre Charles Le Monnier in his *Histoire Celeste*, except that Ellicott devised another style of frame.[39] Le Monnier drew the inspiration for his own instrument from one equipped with a movable telescope on a horizontal axis which had been used by Maupertuis. Le Monnier's instrument had been produced by George Graham and was used to determine the meridian line at Kittis mountain in Lapland. Le Monnier identified it as an "Instrument des Passages" or "transit instrument." [40]

The transit and equal altitude instrument proved well adapted for making boundary surveys, but because Rittenhouse and Voigt seem to have been the only makers capable of producing it—and possibly also because of its cost—the examples owned and used by Rittenhouse and Ellicott were among the few available until after the beginning of the nineteenth century.

Next to Rittenhouse, Andrew Ellicott was undoubtedly the most significant figure in American surveying in the second half of the eighteenth century. The son of Joseph Ellicott, a Quaker millwright and clockmaker of Buckingham, Bucks County, Pennsylvania, he had learned the craft of clock and instrument making from his father. He had received his first training in the mathematical sciences at a day school maintained in his community by the emigrant Irish teacher Robert Patterson who later became professor of mathematics at the University of Pennsylvania. Ellicott was only a youth when his father moved to Baltimore County, Maryland, to establish the new community of Ellicott's Lower Mills in 1772. Despite his Quaker affiliation, during the Revolution Andrew Ellicott joined the Elk Ridge Battalion and rose to the rank of major.[41] His first important assignment as a surveyor was as one of the commissioners for Virginia in the survey of the Pennsylvania–Virginia boundary in 1779 in the effort to extend the westward boundary of the Mason and Dixon line. This work had to be terminated because the Indians in the region viewed the astronomical instruments being used as "bad medicine." [42]

In 1784 Ellicott again surveyed for Virginia in running the line between that state and Pennsylvania. In the following year the Governor of Pennsylvania appointed him to serve as a commissioner with David Rittenhouse and Andrew Porter to establish Pennsylvania's western boundary. In 1786 he was a member of the commission for Pennsylvania which met with Governor Clinton and Simeon De Witt, commissioners for New York State, to fix the northern boundary of Pennsylvania. In the following year he worked with William W. Morris, commissioner for New York State, to establish the remainder of the boundary between the two states. In 1789 Pennsylvania Governor Mifflin assigned Ellicott and William Irvine the task of laying out a road from Reading, Pennsylvania, to the shore of Lake Erie, and to lay out a town at Presqu'Isle (now Waterford), Pennsylvania.[43]

In the same year President Washington named Ellicott Geographer of the United States and assigned him to run the line of the western boundary of New York State to determine whether or not the town of Erie was included within Pennsylvania or New York. The survey was completed in 1790. Ellicott established the line with the use of his transit and equal altitude instrument, and during this project he and Irvine saw Niagara Falls and made the first accurate measure of the full length of the Niagara River and of the falls and rapids.[44]

Ellicott had become recognized by this time as one of the most competent and skilled surveyors of the period and one of the few equipped with and capable of using the sophisticated astronomical instruments for determining latitude and longitude. He used two quite different methods for determining the longitude, both of which he performed with meticulous accuracy. By means of one method he recorded the time of the appearance, or eclipse, of one of Jupiter's satellites with the time of the same event that had been observed at Greenwich Observatory in England and then converted the differences into appropriate degrees of longitude. His second method was by observation of the lunar distances.

In 1790 Robert Morris employed Ellicott to define the line of the site of Geneva, New York, and adjacent lessee lands.[45] As he was completing this assignment, with his two younger brothers working as assistant surveyors, Ellicott was appointed by President Washington to undertake the survey of the 10-mile square of the Federal Territory in which the national capital was to be established.

In 1795 Ellicott laid out the towns of Erie, Franklin, and Warren in southwestern Pennsylvania, and in 1796 President Washington appointed him commissioner to establish the boundary between the United States and the Spanish possessions of Florida, a project which required four years to complete.[46] From 1802 to 1808 Ellicott served as secretary of the Pennsylvania Land Office and in 1811 he was selected to run the northern boundary of Georgia with North Carolina. He became professor of mathematics at the United States Military Academy at West Point in 1813 and held this position until his death in 1820. His last project for the government was a series of astronomical observations made in 1817 at Montreal to effect certain provisions of the Treaty of Ghent, which ended the War of 1812.[47]

With the establishment of the peace in 1783, and before a federal constitution was formulated, Congress turned its attention to the new territories, that great unmeasured and unknown wealth of land outside the confines of the United States. Thomas Jefferson was undoubtedly the greatest single force in focusing national attention on this land and its development, division, and assignment. He came to this concern as much by heritage as by his role as a statesman, for he had grown up on the edge of the frontier, the son of an active surveyor and land developer. From boyhood his mind had been filled with the romance of the wilderness beyond the frontier that lay awaiting exploitation. His preoccupation with land was increased by the inheritance of considerable land holdings at his father's death, some early training in surveying, and his love for his own estate, Monticello. He was also influenced by one of his boyhood teachers, Reverend James Maury, grandfather of the oceanographer Matthew Fontaine Maury, who was greatly preoccupied with the unknown

northwest territory and speculated on its physical features and resources. Maury visualized another great river beyond the western
mountains, corresponding to the Mississippi on the eastern side.[48]

More than any other American statesman, not excepting George
Washington, Jefferson was involved with the concerns of the mathematical practitioners; indeed he might be considered to have been
one himself. His copious correspondence with those engaged in map
making, surveying, and astronomical pursuits was filled with professional advice. He was receptive to every proposal, regardless of
source, which related to the practical sciences and to new methods
and instruments which would contribute to American scientific or
technological development. By Jefferson's definition, "science" embodied technology and included the earth sciences, or natural sciences, and agriculture, as well as invention.

Jefferson's awareness of the opportunities and needs of Americans was demonstrated in his remarkable *Notes on the State of Virginia*,
published in 1782. This work was originally intended to have been
a contribution to a compilation of information encompassing all
regions of the United States [49] which had been initiated by the
French politician François de Barbé-Marbois, later the negotiator of
the Louisiana Purchase. Jefferson assembled all available data on
Virginia's geography, waterways, topography, climate, natural resources, minerals, boundaries, people, commerce, military forces,
and social, cultural, and political life. Evaluating his fellow Virgin-
ians, he determined that they were ". . . all occupied in industrial
pursuits. They abound with persons living on the industry of their
fathers, on the earnings of their fellow-citizens, given away by their
rulers as pensions. Some of them, desirous of laudable distinction,
devote their time and means to the pursuit of science, and become
profitable members of society by industry of a higher order." [50]

One of Jefferson's principal concerns, reflected also in the *Notes*,
was inland navigation. He compared the advantages and disadvantages of the three waterways which could serve as links between the
Atlantic Ocean and the territory lying beyond the Allegheny Mountains and came to the conclusion that the Mississippi River was one
of the main arteries for transportation and communication, based on
the evidence that five-eighths of the country was watered by it and its
eastern tributaries. Jefferson's work, the first comprehensive study
made of any part of the United States, achieved immediate popular-

ity and had considerable impact on the thinking of leaders and the public about the land and its promise.

Jefferson was well aware that the mapping and division of western lands was being carried out in a haphazard manner by surveyors using indiscriminate techniques. He felt that it was imperative to develop a new and consistent plan of land division. Contributing factors to his concern were the rapidly expanding population along the eastern seaboard and the policy of awarding land in payment of military services. Following the peace, he organized a committee to develop such a plan, and the ensuing Land Ordnance of 1784 was based on the recommendations it prepared. This ordnance was succeeded by the Ordnance of 1785 and subsequently replaced by the Northwest Ordnance of 1787, which provided for greater democracy in the western territory.[51]

The Ordnance of 1785 was primarily concerned with the division of public lands, as well as the establishment of the geographical mile. It proposed a geographical pattern beginning northward from the 31st parallel. Each state to be formed included two degrees of latitude and was to be shaped as a rectangle, the eastern and western boundaries of which were to be defined by the appropriate degrees of longitude. Each of such units was to be named. The scheme was not adopted, chiefly because of objections raised by George Washington and James Monroe, among others.[52] Washington was concerned that the limited units would produce a sparse and scattered population, while Monroe believed that large segments of the land in the Northwest were extremely poor and consequently it was unreasonable to assign lots on such a basis.[53] As a result the ordnance was revised to define fewer but much larger areas to be constituted as new states. The rectangular land division scheme was nevertheless adopted for marking off individual lots of land, and the region was subdivided into a rectangular pattern, with individual units one mile square grouped into larger segments six miles square. The plan was based on several considerations. One was the custom prevalent in southern states of issuing land warrants from a land office, and another was the objective of imposing a grid pattern on all land regardless of topography or quality. The commitee's report to the Congress was subsequently embodied in the Land Act of 1796, which combined the warrant system of the southern states with the New England system of contiguous parcels of land already surveyed. The

units of 640 acres, designated as sections, were already combined
into larger rectangles forming townships 6 miles square, and a minimum price per acre, regardless of location or quality, was established. The process of selling the land was simplified by designating each unit by a number, which eliminated the need for and the
cost of definition of bounds.[54]

Captain Thomas Hutchins, who was credited with having provided the genesis for the plan of surveys adopted, had been appointed to the position of Geographer-General of the United States
in 1781. In that position, as the first official government surveyor, he
supervised the work undertaken under the new ordnance. The plan
called for assistant surveyors to be deputies from each of the states.
With the establishment of the Ordnance of 1785, Hutchins continued in office as surveyor-general of the public lands and was the
first to apply the new system in the region of the Seven Ranges in
eastern Ohio. He retained his title of Geographer-General of the
United States until his death in 1789, when he was succeeded by his
deputy, Major Andrew Ellicott.

The Ordnance of 1785 required that the lands in the public
domain be surveyed before sale and that all surveys be made in accordance with a consistent integrated system of lines oriented to the
true meridian, and furthermore that the land would be subdivided
into parcels that were approximately square. The townships, 6 miles
square, were to be divided by lines running due north and south,
and other lines crossing them at right angles. The first area to be surveyed was to extend in an east-west distance of the Seven Ranges
from the "beginning point," which was established at the intersection of the Ohio River with the western boundary of Pennsylvania.
The Geographer-General was required personally to undertake the
running of the first east-west line, and the resulting area, to be designated as the original Seven Ranges, was to be established by running
the first line due north and south, beginning on the Ohio River at a
point due north from the western termination of the southern
boundary of the state of Pennsylvania. The first east-west line was to
begin at the same point. It was designated the Geographer's Line
and would serve as the base line for succeeding surveys. The lands
to be surveyed were to extend from the base line westward for a distance of 42 miles. Various difficulties, ranging from the presence of
hostile Indians to unusual field conditions, delayed the work considerably. The plan was carried out in the privately subdivided tract of

the Ohio Company and in the region between the Miami and Little Miami rivers before it was discontinued.[55]

If the settlement of the western lands could have awaited formal survey, the proposed system of land division might have worked successfully. It was not feasible, however, to postpone the assignment of land until it could be surveyed by traditional methods, with the consequence that many areas became populated before the federal surveys were completed. Land already settled was frequently discovered to encompass more than a single quarter section, and local agencies were understandably reluctant to disturb the existing situation. Not until 1812 was a solution found in the formation under the Federal government of a General Land Office (later known as the Bureau of Land Management), which had the responsibility for developing standards for land measurement and for the subdivision of public domain.

One of the major problems encountered in the survey of the western territory was the determination of a true meridian line, based on the variation of the compass, which could be used by the ordinary surveyor with comparatively accurate results. Finding the azimuth of the sun by a single observation of its altitude required the use of a quadrant, as well as knowledge of the latitude or the hour at the time of observation, which the surveyor in the field might not have. The sun's azimuth could also be determined by taking equal altitudes before and after noon, but the necessary instruments were not generally available, nor was the time required always feasible. The third and most exact method known, that of measuring the time between the passage over the same vertical circle of two stars which differed substantially in declination but not in right ascension, was the most difficult of all for the surveyor in the field to undertake.

A new method proposed by Robert Patterson in 1786 involved the use of a table of the pole star, a method which required no additional calculation and could be applied with a common circumferentor or a theodolite. Provision was made in the table for the variation of the compass to a single minute of a degree with only one observation of the magnetic bearing of the pole star, and any variation could be corrected by repeating the observation. Patterson explained his table in considerable detail and provided helpful hints in the use of the instruments for the purpose. How widespread an application was made of his method cannot be determined, but it would have solved the problem.[56]

Another proposal for determining the meridian line with accuracy was published in a small pamphlet by Andrew Ellicott in 1796. He had prepared the work during the debates in Congress on the Land Office bill, in the expectation that if the bill were passed it would be necessary to have standards readily available for government surveyors. In his introduction, Ellicott reported: "Scarcely two compasses will trace with the necessary precision the same line, and for want of a general standard, by which the chains should be regulated, it is difficult to find two of the same length. To these sources of inaccuracy is to be added one other of much more importance, and therefore more necessary to be guarded against; I mean the variation of the magnetic needle." He explained that the easiest method was to make and return the surveys according to the true course instead of the magnetic, which necessitated finding the variation of the compass and making the necessary allowance required by the tracing of the true meridian. The difference between the true meridian and the meridian indicated by the magnetic compass was the variation.[57]

An accurate method of tracing the true meridian was not included in the published works on surveying, and knowledge of such a method was limited to the practical astronomer. For this reason Ellicott described several methods which he and his assistants used as standard practice.

The easiest method consisted of observing the greatest elongation of the pole star, which was accomplished by using two pieces of wood, one of which had a compass sight attached, and by supporting a plumb bob in a container of water by means of a makeshift apparatus resembling a well sweep. Because the greatest elongations of the pole star were invisible for several weeks at a time, Ellicott proposed a second method utilizing another star at the same time as the pole star. A third method consisted of running a true course by means of a surveying compass instead of a magnetic compass, by adjusting the compass card to the points of the needle. Ellicott expressed concern that "from the manner in which work has generally been executed in this country by the [surveying] compass, it may justly be doubted, whether it ought to be ranked among the most useful of instruments: a too implicit attraction varies several degrees in short distances, occasioned controversies without end. To prevent those consequences as much as possible (which are, however, in some degree inseparable from the use of the common compass), the artist should constantly examine the back sights in his line, to detect local variation, and whenever it appears, carry on the line by a plumb-line and a range of stakes. . . ." [58]

In 1796 the Congress passed another act which modified the system of numbering sections in the survey of public lands. Lines were to be drawn through townships at intervals of two miles, with the section corners placed at one mile intervals, establishing three corners for each section. The same act created the position of Surveyor-General, a position first occupied by Rufus Putnam, appointed in 1797. He was succeeded in 1803 by Jared Mansfield, who was followed by Edward Tiffin in 1810.

As part of a program to standardize weights and measures in the United States, the Congress by the same act of 1796 commissioned Benjamin Rittenhouse to construct a surveyor's chain which would serve as a standard for the U.S. Land Office, indicating that Ellicott was not alone in his concern with its inaccuracy. Rittenhouse produced a chain consisting of eighty links made of brass and measuring a total of 66 feet. It was specified to be the standard for surveyors' chains by an act of Congress regulating weights and measures, and the prototype was maintained at the U. S. Land Office in Washington. It was displayed at the Columbian Exposition in Chicago in 1893.[59]

Another innovation introduced during this period, which may or may not have been as the result of official action, was a new form of surveying compass. Goldsmith Chandlee, the Winchester, Virginia, instrument maker previously mentioned, developed the new form, on the dial of which he incorporated an outkeeper, manipulated from the underside by means of a knob, which enabled the surveyor to keep a visible record of the chains called to him by the rod man. The south limb of the instrument was engraved with a table for links and tenths. This form of the surveying compass was produced exclusively by Chandlee in his lifetime; instruments under production at the time of his death in 1820 were completed by his successor, George Graves.[60]

The significance of Chandlee's innovation has not as yet been thoroughly studied but it seems likely that it was devised to meet new needs arising from the requirements for surveying the western lands in accordance with the Ordnance of 1785. Chandlee at Winchester was situated at a critical point on the frontier, and his compasses may have been made specifically in response to new requirements imposed after the date of that ordnance. With only one known exception, which may in fact have been the prototype instrument, each of the special compasses was made to individual order and inscribed with the name of the purchaser. Among the surviving examples is one which Chandlee made for Washington's nephew, Lawrence Augustine Washington.

Chandlee's instrument-making shop and brass foundry were extremely active enterprises, but he was apparently unable to comply with all the orders he received as promptly as the needs dictated. Alexander White (3rd) of Winchester, in a letter addressed to the Ohio surveyor, Thomas Worthington, in 1796, reported: ". . . With respect to the Surveyors instruments, Mr. Chandlee says that he can at any time supply you with a chain and set of plotting instruments but it is extremely doubtful whether he can furnish a compass against the time you mention. He cannot do it unless some persons who have applied before you will agree to wait awhile. If he can get anyone to do that he will, and in that case your not taking one will be no disappointment to him. I believe you need not rely on his furnishing you with any degree of confidence. His price for a compass is £8:10. For a chain 15/0. For a set of instruments from £1:10 to £3." [61]

In the two decades following the establishment of the peace, the work of delineating the vast reaches of the western lands and of defining boundaries between the states as well as the geography of the new nation resulted in the achievement of professional status for surveyors in government service.

XIV

☆ ☆ ☆ ☆ ☆ ☆ ☆ ☆ ☆ ☆ ☆ ☆ ☆

THE TRUE

GEOGRAPHY

☆ ☆

A great deal is yet wanting to ascertain the true geography of our country; more indeed as to its longitudes than latitudes. Towards this we have done too little for ourselves and depended too long on the ancient and inaccurate observations of other nations.

Thomas Jefferson,
Notes on the State of Virginia (1781)

THE ROLE OF THE professional surveyor in the shaping of the United States became increasingly important as the new nation took its place among its older peers and sought identity not only by means of its new form of government but in its geographical definition as well. For achieving this definition, there were only a handful of men with the necessary skill, training, and experience in the field. The surveyor's life was a rugged one, requiring a strong constitution and good health as well as the willingness to forgo most of the luxuries of life and the comforts of a domicile. It has best been pictured in the records, journals, and correspondence of Andrew Ellicott.

Particularly revealing are Ellicott's letters to his wife, which he penned during his leisure hours after the day's work in the field was done. To her he described the details of the work performed and some of the obstacles encountered. Again and again he expressed his concern with the many hazards inherent in his work as well as his loneliness for his wife and children and for the family hearth. The inconveniences of camp life were always present, as well as constant . threats to life and limb from the nature of the work performed and from wild beasts, hostile Indians, weather, and illness. At one time he noted: "several of our Men have been hurt by the falling of Trees. one last friday got his arm broke in two places—he is in a likely way to do well. . . ." [1] On another occasion he reported: "We have had several of our Workman badly Hurt by the falling of Timber in our Line—One unfortunate person by the name of Cross, was caught under the Top of a Tree last Wednesday, and died on Friday—the same night we buried him in the middle of the Line, and raised a Monument of Logs—such a Circumstance in the Wilderness, is attended with an uncommon degree of Solemnity." [2]

At another time Ellicott commented: "We live considering our Situation very well; but by constantly shifting our encampment, it is out of our power to observe that regularity we are enabled to do at Home—When I say we live very well, it must be considered with regard to the many disadvantages under which a set of people in a Wilderness must labour. . . . These Hills are inhabited at present by Bears, Wolves, Deer, &c. and covered by tall Timber and Weeds; among the latter are many Serpents, particularly the Rattle Snake." [3]

Again he noted: "many unexpected difficulties arising from the want of knowledge of the Country, the death of our Horses and detention by the Indians." [4] He also complained: "The fleas begin to be extremely troublesome, and I dread them much more than the hardships attending such an expedition." [5] During the survey of the line between the United States and the Spanish territory of Florida in 1799, Ellicott reported: "The first year that I spent in this country I was three months confined with sickness—good nursing alone saved my life—and that of my son Andy—the one fourth of my people died within that period. . . ." [6]

The surveying teams lived on a variety of meats which they

hunted and killed, including bear, deer, and turkey, as well as some bacon they brought with them, and they were "supplied with an ample quantity of spirits and Whiskey." Occasionally they were unsuccessful in hunting and suffered periods of near want. A great delicacy was gooseberry tarts prepared from berries growing wild in the wilderness. They searched for new items of food to vary their fare, and while on the survey of the New York State boundary in 1795, Ellicott wrote: "We have cranberries in abundance, which we use with our bread in place of butter." [7]

The physical isolation of the surveyor in the field was made even more poignant by the fact that he received little news of events at home, in the country, or in the world, and that long after the fact. Ellicott commented in a letter to his wife: "Many are the solotary [*sic*] hours I spend in traversing these vast Woods and I never take a walk but I find the want of your Company and I have a thousand fears for your Health and the Health of our Children." [8] A decade later while on a field survey he wrote that, although he experienced frequent attacks of gout it did not keep him from his work; however, "owing to my anxiety about your welfare, and the health of our Children, added to so much hard labour falling to my share, I have lost much more than my superfluous flesh." [9]

These comments are particularly significant because Ellicott was not a demonstrative man and had been accused by his associates of lack of warmth. He was known to be a hard taskmaster, totally devoted to his work and scientific pursuits. Those employed by him on the surveys discovered that he was unrelenting in his dedication to his work, and that he drove himself even harder than he drove others on the project. His brother Joseph customarily ran the guide line for the axmen, or "choppers," and Andrew rarely spent more than four hours each day in putting marks on the line as it was developed. The rest of the time he spent making astronomical observations in the field camp, and if there was any suspicion of deviation or error he took the time to rectify the course by observations made at night.

Each morning Ellicott arose while it was still dark, breakfasted, and began his day in the field, working until bedtime seven nights a week. He customarily had a field crew of twenty men. Three or four of these served as assistant surveyors, and for many of his assignments he employed his younger brothers Joseph and Benjamin in this capacity. Ellicott worked from early spring until the beginning of winter, then closed his camp and spent the winter months at home with his family, returning to the field as soon as good weather prevailed.

Ellicott had professionalized his procedures to a considerable degree, learning with each new assignment. He preferred to establish his main encampment on a level area on top of the highest elevation of the region to be surveyed, and he generally sought the protection of trees or the edge of a forest when feasible. The focal point of the camp was the observatory tent, which he located by first carefully tracing a meridian. On his observation point he set up his large zenith sector, with his astronomical clock close by, and then erected the observatory tent over them.

The astronomical clock was a precision timekeeper which he had designed for use in the field and constructed entirely by himself in 1784. The clock was the item of equipment which caused the surveyor the greatest concern because it was liable to derangement from many causes. Among the most common were vibrations from movements on the ground nearby and changes of temperature and humidity. Ellicott learned to reduce these problems by keeping the clock off the ground; he usually found a convenient tree of adequate size, which he would have cut off at some distance from the ground to provide a shelf upon which the clock could be placed. The importance of the field clock in making surveys was emphasized again and again in Ellicott's field notes, where he expressed concern with its rate of going and the effect of changes in the weather. "Last night the weather was so extream cold that the Clock was stopped by the Oil losing its fluidity—set it going by my Watch—and took Equal Altitudes," he wrote in his notes of astronomical observations made at Baltimore in 1787. A short time later he recorded that he had "Cleaned the Clock and Oiled it with equal parts of Oil of Sweet Almonds and Olives—Olive Oil alone chilled with the cold and shortened the vibrations of the Pendulum—lowered the Pendulum Bob." [10] When it was not possible to find a suitable tree to make a shelf, Ellicott lashed the clock to a pole driven into the ground. During his survey of the Florida boundary with the Spanish possessions, he expressed repeated frustration with the necessity for adjustment of the clock's going rate. On one occasion the tent was blown down and fell on the clock. Once members of the surveying party leaned on the pole which had been set into sand for lack of firmer ground. At yet another time Ellicott reported: "At about 8 o'clock this morning the minute hand of the clock was moved by an impertinent young Indian. The glass having been unfortunately broken by which the hands were left exposed.—The clock was then set by my watch." [11]

The most important of Ellicott's field instruments, and one which was quite as sensitive as the clock, was a large zenith sector having a focal length of 5½ feet. It was a cumbersome piece, having to be supported on crude trunnions, and observations were made through the eyepiece at the bottom of the instrument, which required the observer to lie on his back. Even the heat of a nearby campfire made to keep the mosquitoes at bay was enough to affect the accuracy of the instrument, and "On account of the flies, and mosquitoes, which were so numerous, and troublesome . . . an observation which would require more than one minute, could not be made without great pain." [12] Nevertheless, this zenith sector was the most accurate and sophisticated scientific instrument on the North American continent in that period, and the only instrument then known having sufficient accuracy to trace a parallel of latitude, and Ellicott used it on a number of surveys.

The instrument traced its origin to the English-made zenith sector used by Mason and Dixon. When it was agreed early in 1786 between the states of New York and Pennsylvania to have their adjoining boundaries surveyed during the following summer, the need for a zenith sector was readily recognized, and David Rittenhouse and Ellicott set to work to make such an instrument together. The project was well under way when Ellicott was summoned urgently to his family home at Ellicott's Mills, and during his absence Rittenhouse completed the principal part of the work on the instrument. The telescopic component of the sector required an achromatic lens with a 5½-foot focus, with which stars of the second and third magnitude could be observed as they passed near the zenith any time of the day. It happened that such a lens was owned by Thomas Pryor, a Philadelphia instrument maker, who loaned it to Rittenhouse on the condition that the latter would subsequently replace it with a similar lens to be imported from England. Pryor did not need the lens at the time.

Ellicott used the sector on the survey of the New York–Pennsylvania boundary, made some modifications on it, and used it on subsequent surveys with considerable success. The instrument was housed under the observatory tent in the field, with the objective

projected through an opening in the canvas, and was used to determine the parallels of latitude by observing six or seven stars near the
zenith as they crossed the meridian at different hours of the night.
Ellicott would repeat the observations on a number of nights over a
given period of time. He discovered that when the stars were
very near the zenith they were affected by the varying refractive
powers of the atmosphere derived from the differing degrees of den-
sity. Ellicott learned that he could reduce the error of the visual axis
by taking zenith distances of the stars with the plane, or face, of the
sector alternately facing east and west. He averaged the figures
derived in this manner, made corrections for refraction, aberration,
and nutation, and then compared the results with data from published star catalogues. From this comparison, based on each of the
stars observed, he was able to establish the latitude.

He had assembled and packed the sector in readiness for undertaking the survey of the southern boundary of the United States in
1796, when he received a disturbing visit from Thomas Pryor. Pryor
inquired whether Ellicott intended to take the instrument with him,
and being answered in the affirmative, Pryor informed him that the
lens, which he had provided for it had never been replaced, and he
now demanded its return. Rittenhouse had apparently forgotten his
obligation to replace it. Ellicott, in a quandary because of his sched-
ules, refused to return the lens and referred Pryor to Timothy Pickering, then Secretary of State. Pickering offered Pryor any reasonable price for the lens so that the survey need not be postponed, but
Pryor was insistent and threatened to issue an attachment against the
instrument. Ellicott, being particularly averse to the processes of
law, then called upon Pickering and offered to give his own telescope
to Pryor in exchange for the lens, on condition that the telescope be
replaced by the government with one of equal quality and value. The
telescope was new, made to Ellicott's own specifications by George
Adams of London. Pickering approved the suggestion, and after de-
liberating for two days, Pryor agreed to the exchange. It then became necessary to borrow a telescope for Ellicott's use from the
collection of the American Philosophical Society. In due course a
new telescope was procured for Ellicott by Rufus King, then Minister to London.[13]

As a result of this exchange, Ellicott considered that the federal
government owned a percentage of the value of the zenith sector, as
represented by the lens and the telescope exchange and replacement,

and that the remainder belonged to Pennsylvania. The contemporary evaluation indicated that the state of Pennsylvania had an investment of 76 pounds and 5 shillings in the zenith sector and the United States government 43 pounds and 15 shillings.[14] When the survey was completed Ellicott left the sector, with all the other instruments belonging to the United States government, in the Continental Store, or United States Military Warehouse, maintained in Philadelphia by Samuel Hodgden.

In addition to the large zenith sector and the astronomical clock, Ellicott required a wide variety of other instruments. A second zenith sector, made for him by David Rittenhouse, which had a focal length of 19 inches, was a portable instrument which he used along the line of survey for observing the aberration of the stars and nutation of the earth's axis. In the field he was equipped with three telescopes, the largest of which was an achromatic instrument made by Dollond, having a terrestrial eyepiece of 60 magnification and three other eyepieces that could be used for celestial observation with magnifying powers of 120, 200, and 300 respectively. Two smaller achromatic telescopes made by W. & S. Jones of London were used for taking signals; these had sliding tubes, one of which could be drawn out to more than 4 feet and the other to 15 inches, with which Ellicott could observe the satellites of Jupiter. For taking horizontal angles, he used a circular plane table made for him in England by George Adams and based on an instrument described by Maupertuis. It had an 8-inch radius and was equipped with two telescopic tubes.[15]

Other field equipment included two common two-pole chains and three brass sextants. One of the sextants was made by Jesse Ramsden, an English instrument maker, and had a vernier scale divided to 20 seconds, which Ellicott used for taking lunar distances. Another basic instrument was a plain surveying compass, made for him by Benjamin Rittenhouse and inscribed with the names of the maker and owner and having an adjustable socket joint for turning the dial. Other items included two cased sets of drafting instruments, two fine stop watches having seconds hands which he used when the astronomical clock was not operative or readily available, a special device to secure the water for an instrument called an artificial horizon which protected it against the wind while in use, and two copper lanterns which he used for tracing meridians and giving the directions of lines determined at night by celestial observations.[16]

He also had a portable brass quadrant which he had constructed himself having a 12-inch radius with adjustable pedestal base, and which he used for making observations required to establish the western boundary of New York State in 1788.[17]

Used daily on his field surveys was the transit and equal altitude instrument which Ellicott had constructed himself. The importance of this instrument was confirmed again and again in Ellicott's correspondence and field notes. Referring to the survey of the 10-mile square of the Federal Territory, he reported: "These lines were measured with a chain, which was examined and corrected daily, and plumbed wherever the ground was uneven and traced with a transit and equal altitude instrument, which I constructed and used in running the western boundary of the State of New York. . . . This instrument was similar to that described by M. Le Monnier in his preface to *Histoire Celeste*, except in being accommodated to a firm portable triangular frame. The transit and equal altitude instrument is of all others the most perfect and the best calculated for running straight lines, and when the different verifications are carefully attended to, may be considered as absolutely perfect." [18] The superiority of that instrument was further verified during the next several decades, a period in which the common theodolite and the plain surveying compass proved inadequate for major surveys and the surveying transit had not yet been invented. When in 1794 it was desired to survey a large tract of land identified as the Pulteney Estate near Geneva, New York, the Surveyor-General, Simeon De Witt, reported "there were only two transits in the country, one owned by Andrew Ellicott, the other by Dr. Rittenhouse, neither of them available." [19]

When Isaac Briggs undertook the survey of the Mississippi Territory for the government in 1803, he sought to acquire such an instrument. Consulting President Jefferson, Briggs reported: "Henry Voight is engaged in making for me a portable transit—I hope in the course of ten days it will be finished, as this alone detains me. I have made an application to Andrew Ellicott for his Transit, but he absolutely refuses to sell it. I have drawn up a proposition, in writing to the American Philosophical Society to consent to the removal of their Observatory Transit to the City of Washington, to be used under their direction." [20] It was Briggs's intention, if he could not acquire a transit and equal altitude instrument, to borrow the Society's astronomical transit instead, but nothing came of his request. Meanwhile Voigt was greatly delayed in his work schedule, as

Briggs reported once again to Jefferson. "I must have misunderstood Henry Voight," he wrote, "or he must have deceived himself, in the probable time when my Transit Instrument would be finished; as he advanced in the work, the period of its completion seemed to be removed to a distance far beyond my expectation. Upon his informing me that it would probably require several months to complete it, I immediately packed up the remainder of my outfit. . . . Henry Voight is to send my Portable Transit and a Chronometer, immediately when finished, to Natchez." [21]

Voigt was probably the only available instrument maker capable of producing such an instrument, since David Rittenhouse had died and Andrew Ellicott was occupied with surveys. Voigt was an excellent mechanician, having been trained as a watch and clock maker as a young man and then employed at the Royal Mint at Saxe Gotha before emigrating to America. He had worked as Rittenhouse's assistant at Norriton prior to 1770 and in the production of the first orrery at Philadelphia. He was an important figure in the technology of his time, having established a wire mill at Reading, Pennsylvania, in 1780, then opening a shop as a clockmaker in Philadelphia. He was closely associated with John Fitch in about 1786, in 1787 became a shareholder in Fitch's steamboat company, and for a short time in 1792 was Fitch's partner in an enterprise to manufacture steam engines. In 1793 Voigt invented a process for making steel from bar iron, and in the same year he accepted the appointment as chief coiner of the United States Mint at Philadelphia, in which capacity he continued until his death. He was held in high esteem by all associates; despite a break in their personal relationship, Fitch described Voigt as "a plain Dutchman, who fears no man, and will always speak his sentiments, which has given offence to some Members of our Co., and some of them have effected to have a contemptable opinion of his Philosophic abilities. It is true he is not a man of Letters, nor mathematical Knowledge, but for my part I would depend upon him more than a Franklin, a Rittenhouse, an Ellicott, a Mancarrow, and Matlack, all combined, as he is a man of superior mechanical abilities, and Very considerable Natural Philosophy." [22] At the time that Briggs applied for his instrument, Voigt was employed at the Mint, while producing clocks and occasional instruments on the side. Although Briggs's correspondence did not report receipt of the transit instrument, it presumably was completed and shipped to the Mississippi Territory. [23]

Further evidence of the versatility of the transit and equal altitude instrument was provided by Ellicott after he had become Secretary of the Pennsylvania Land Office at Lancaster. He established an observatory at his home, and lacking fixed instruments, he converted his transit for the purpose. In 1802 he informed Jefferson: "I expect to get my transit instrument set up in three, or four weeks, by which I shall be able to increase the number and value of my observations. —————— I have with great difficulty, and patience, placed a reticule of spider's web (the first ever executed), in the focus of this instrument! and intend accommodating my Telescope with a diaphragm, to observe the eclipses of Jupiter's satellites,—this precaution appears necessary, and is strongly recommended by de la Lande in a late work." [24]

Ellicott subsequently came to the conclusion that he had completed the major surveys that would be required for the period, and he was concerned with perpetuating the special skills and the considerable experience he had amassed in the course of his work. David Rittenhouse was dead, and of those who had refined the techniques of practical astronomy in the field Ellicott alone remained. To his mentor, Thomas Jefferson, then president of the American Philosophical Society, he wrote, in 1801: "Being now the only native in the United States left, which time has not spunged away, and who has cultivated practical astronomy for the purpose of rendering it useful to commerce, to the division of territories, and the determination of the relative positions of the different parts of our own country, I feel a desire to keep the subject alive, till succeeded by some American, whose fortune may put it in his power to be more useful, by enabling him to devote his whole time to the improvement of so important a branch of science." [25]

Jefferson was responsive to the suggestion, and two months later Ellicott was offered the newly created position of Surveyor-General of the United States. Jefferson specified four requirements, however. The Surveyor-General was to determine the geographical position necessary for forming a chart or map by means of which the vacant lands belonging to the United States could be divided into districts and the surveying executed with accuracy. He was to appoint a sufficient number of capable deputies to perform the work in each district, in accordance with the prescription of the law. When not immediately engaged in the determination of the necessary geographical points that limit the several districts, he was to reside at the seat of government and be in charge of the public charts, surveys and drafts, not only of the various parts of the country but of the sea coast as well, to correct them as necessary and make copies available to the principal secretaries of the Cabinet and any others as required. He was to receive and examine the returns from the deputies and arrange them with all related documents for the use of the Cabinet officers.[26]

Reluctantly, Ellicott refused the appointment, primarily because of the regulations concerning its administration and the residency requirements which specified that the incumbent would have to live for some years "in the western Country" and otherwise at Washington. The annual salary of $2000.00 was an enticement that he found difficult to resist, because he had not yet received payment for his work on the survey of the southern United States boundary and had in fact been forced to sell his personal library and his theodolite in order to provide for his family.

In October 1801 Ellicott accepted an appointment as Secretary of the Pennsylvania Land Office and moved to Lancaster. There also he would be able to continue his astronomical observations and maintain his association with leading scientific figures of the time, particularly in nearby Philadelphia.[27]

Within the next several years concern with geographical expansion was reflected from the topmost levels of government. Thomas Jefferson in particular took a personal interest, and few attempts to explore or develop the new lands were undertaken without his involvement or assistance. He had long visualized the need to develop adequate transportation for the support of commerce on a national scale. It was this concern that led him as Vice President of the United States to negotiate with the Spanish government for free transit for American shipping into the Spanish-owned port of New Orleans. The same concern formed the basis for one of the greatest achievements of his presidency, the purchase of the Louisiana territory. This acquisition provided a new natural boundary on the Gulf of Mexico, included an outlet for the Mississippi River to the sea, and added more than a million square miles, nearly doubling the existing territory.

The Louisiana acquisition provided Jefferson with a reason for sending expeditions to explore and map the lands beyond the Mississippi. He assumed a personal role in the project and directed the surveys from afar, intimately involving himself in every stage from the planning and preparation to a review of the results.

Jefferson had already had some experience with expeditions into the new territory. While Minister to France in 1785 he had become acquainted with John Ledyard, an ambitious young adventurer from Connecticut who had accompanied Captain James Cook on his Pacific voyage. Jefferson proposed an exploration of the western part of the United States, beginning in Russia and then crossing the American continent. Ledyard was interested in the assignment and set out on the venture, only to be arrested by Russian police shortly after its beginning. Jefferson was also a co-sponsor with the American Philosophical Society in 1792 of an expedition undertaken by Captain Meriwether Lewis in company with André Michaux, the French botanist, to ascend the Missouri River and cross the mountains to the Pacific Ocean. The expedition had reached Kentucky when Michaux was recalled by order of his government and the project was unfulfilled.

These prior efforts provided Jefferson with a background for sponsoring the most famous and successful of the exploratory endeavors undertaken in his time, the Lewis and Clark expedition of 1803. The nominal purpose of the journey was to arrange for modification of the trade agreements with the Indians, but the greater mission was clearly defined by Jefferson. Captain Meriwether Lewis and Captain William Clark were to trace the Missouri River to its source, cross the highlands, and follow water communication to the Pacific Ocean. Jefferson brought his wide command of the sciences to the elaborate preparations for the project. His personal familiarity with surveying, navigating, and astronomy, and his interests in paleontology and botany were reflected in his detailed instructions to the explorers. Lewis was sent to Philadelphia to obtain instruction from Robert Patterson and Andrew Ellicott in mathematics and astronomy. In particular he received training in the procedures required for making observations of latitude and longitude; determination of the longitude was to be made by observation of the lunar distances. Aware of the need for a timekeeper, which would be subject to derangement in the course of travel over rough country, Jefferson had originally proposed instead the use of an equatorial telescope which employed a portable pendulum. This proved to be a complicated and uncertain procedure and he reluctantly abandoned the idea.

Ellicott responded with enthusiasm to Jefferson's request that he work with Lewis on the expedition's scientific needs. He suggested that in place of a clock Lewis be provided with a chronometer, specifying one made by John Arnold, one of the foremost chronometer makers of the period, as well as two sextants, a plain surveying compass, and an artificial horizon. A statistical table for astronomical observations, designed for use by Lewis and Clark in the field, was provided by Patterson.

Jefferson's final instructions to Lewis included several comments on instrumentation. He noted that "instruments for ascertaining by celestial observations the geography of the country thro' which you will pass, have already been provided. . . . Your observations are to be taken with great pain & accuracy, to be entered distinctly, & intelligibly for others as well as yourself, to comprehend all the elements necessary, with the aid of the usual tables, to fix the latitude and longitude of the places at which they are taken, & are to be rendered to the war office, for the purpose of having the calculations made concurrently by proper persons within the U.S. Several copies of these, as well as your other notes, should be made at leisure time & put into the care of the most trustworthy of your attendants, to guard by multiplying them, against the accidental losses to which they will be exposed. A further guard would be that one of these copies be written on the paper of the birch, as less liable to injury from damp than common paper. . . ." [28]

Lewis and Clark were to make observations for latitude and longitude, beginning at the mouth of the Missouri River, and "at all remarkable points of the river, & especially at the mouths of rivers, at rapids, at islands & other places distinguished by such natural marks & characters of a durable kind, as they may with certainty be recognized hereafter. The courses of the river between these points of observation may be supplied by the compass, the log-line & by time, corrected by the observations themselves. The variations of the compass, too, in different places should be noticed." [29] He also required that any interesting points of the portage between the head of the Missouri and the body of water offering the best communication with the Pacific should be fixed by astronomical observation, as should the course of that body of water to the ocean.

The story of the expedition is a familiar chapter in American history. Its success was rewarding beyond Jefferson's expectations and the materials returned for study were deposited with the Peale Museum in Philadelphia.

XV

☆ ☆ ☆ ☆ ☆ ☆ ☆ ☆ ☆ ☆ ☆ ☆

THE
PROMOTION
OF SCIENCE

☆ ☆

> I cannot forbear intimating to you the expediency of giving effectual encouragement to the introduction of new and useful inventions from abroad, and to the exertions of skill and genius in producing them at home . . . Nor am I less persuaded that there is nothing which can better deserve your patronage than the promotion of science. . . .
>
> George Washington, *First Annual Address to Congress* (1790)

AMERICAN MARITIME activity in the postwar years reflected the development of a new way of life in the established sailing and shipping communities. One aspect of this was that ship design and construction was no longer the prerogative of experienced shipwrights only; as the need for shipping increased, carpenters with varying amounts of training or experience boldly competed with professional ship-builders and met with reasonable success.

Although the wartime blockade which had throttled American shipping was ended, new factors impeded the restoration of sea trade. First a restriction on American shipping was imposed by European powers. Then the war between Great Britain and France jeopardized neutral commerce in the Atlantic. Consequently the West Indian trade was not resumed. The formerly profitable offshore whaling also diminished because the whales had moved farther afield.

Piracy, which was increasing rapidly throughout the shipping world, was another deterrent. So great did the problem become that in 1794 Congress had authorized the construction of a federal navy. A small number of warships were constructed and were soon supplemented by the addition of "gift" vessels and small vessels designed specifically for action against the North African freebooters.

The Embargo Act of 1807, forbidding international trade, and then the War of 1812 frustrated or terminated many of the new nation's ambitious plans for sea trade, although the war created an immediate need for more warships which American shipbuilding attempted to meet.

In the coastal communities of New England the fishing industries dwindled and many of the major shippers turned to the more lucrative opportunities of privateering. They discovered a new and larger world available to them, and greater markets than British restrictions had permitted prior to that time. Trade with China opened up with the arrival of the first ships at Canton in 1784, and Chinese demand for ginseng led to this product's being shipped from the American mainland in exchange for the exotic products of the Orient. New trade routes were developed to India, Java, the Philippines, and other areas of the Pacific, with Salem and Boston as the hub of the Oriental trade, while whaling and sealing out of Nantucket and New Bedford received new impetus. For the first time since colonization American men of the sea enjoyed the freedom of American waters.

New England shipmasters sought markets in other parts of the world, and within the next few years they were trading with Russia, Africa, and South America. The small shipping communities of New England began to emerge as major trading centers, dealing in spices, skins and hides, and such unusual commodities as ice, granite, and manufactured products. Boston became the principal city of New England, and in due course some of the wealth amassed by powerful shipping families was plowed back into worthy civic enterprises, such as the development of educational facilities, support of scientific endeavor, and improvement of the city.

The whaling centers also developed into extremely prosperous communities. At the same time other coastal communities of New England which had suffered extensive damage at the hands of the British rebuilt themselves slowly and became important maritime centers. The engagement in whaling farther afield and in trade with Europe and the Orient led to the development of a new type of vessel called a packet, which was capable of considerable speed. It was extensively used on regular runs between New Orleans and New York and between New York and European ports between 1830 and 1850, primarily for transport of cotton for European and English mills. Meanwhile, the China trade developed profitably, and although the trade in spices was relatively short-lived, it was replaced by the importation of tea, silk, and porcelain. The need for speed in this race for trade inspired the design of the vessel known as the clipper ship, which enabled American shippers to beat the British in reaching markets for tea and similar goods.

Ocean steam navigation was the goal and during the first several decades of the nineteenth century regular steam passage was firmly established around the American continent and across the Atlantic, with major ports competing for priority in the steam shipping race. This rapid evolution in transport brought with it a transformation of seacoast communities. As Boston and New York emerged as the principal centers of steam shipping, business in the small port towns declined. Shippers and merchants moved to the larger shipping centers. Little remained for the once famous waterfront communities but to replace their shipping enterprise with industrial projects. As the ship masts disappeared from the shorelines, they were replaced with the smoke stacks of factories, as more and more the coastal communities developed into centers for such specialized industries as textiles. The merchants and shippers who had moved to larger port cities were replaced by immigrants, who swarmed to work in the factories and rapidly brought an entire new character to the communities.

There were nevertheless frustrating deterrents to the modernization of navigational practices made necessary by the rapid advance of maritime enterprise. Primary among these was the American seaman's reluctance, and frequently inability as well, to accept and apply new navigational procedures and aids, as well as the concurrent inability of the American instrument makers to produce new instrumentation of adequate precision in sufficient quantity. These factors contributed materially to the long delay in the adoption of the sextant and the chronometer.

The numerous attempts in the mid-eighteenth century to improve the capability for accuracy of the octant inevitably led to the development of other instruments which in the course of time proved more adaptable and permitted greater precision. One of these was the sextant, which represented the ultimate fulfillment and refinement of the instrument maker's skills because it combined practicability in use with accuracy of readings. The invention and improvement of instruments of increased precision provided no assurance that they would come into immediate use, however. It was not until a half century after its invention in about 1757 that the sextant was adopted for general use. This delay was due to two major factors. Before the development of mechanical graduation, only the most skilled instrument makers could produce graduated scales of sufficient accuracy, and after the instruments became commercially available, shipmasters and seamen had to be taught the mathematical skills required in using them.

The sextant, which was to become the most common of the navigational instruments by the early nineteenth century, had its genesis in the reflecting circle, the first of a series designed specifically for the purpose of measuring greater angles required for determining the longitude by means of the lunar distances. Johann Mayer, a German astronomer, compiled the first tables of lunar distances in 1752.[1] Although the octant could take back observation angles to 180 degrees, Mayer was of the opinion that these observations could not be made with sufficient accuracy using the octant. He suggested the construction of an instrument designed for exactly this purpose, based on the principle of the octant but made in the form of a full circle and so constructed that both mirrors were adjustable. Mayer's plan was that by moving the mirrors alternately, a number of altitudes could be taken successively in such a manner that the instrument and not the observer performed the task of adding them together. The angle derived as the end result was then divided by the number of observations taken to obtain a mean reading.[2]

The evolution of the sextant from the octant through the reflecting circle came about as the result of an interesting series of circumstances. In the mid-1740s Captain John Campbell, a British naval officer, worked with Dr. James Bradley, the Astronomer Royal, in applying the octant, or the Hadley reflecting quadrant, as it was also called, for the actual measurement of distances. In about 1747 Campbell had used an octant made by the first licensee, Joseph Jackson, to measure the distances of several fixed stars for his own amusement. When Bradley saw a record of the measurements, he noticed that they corresponded exactly with the true distances of the stars in the heavens, and he thereupon proceeded to make additional observations of the moon's distance from the sun and the stars, and the relative distances of specific stars from each other. Meanwhile Edmond Halley's lunar tables had been further improved by Bradley in anticipation of making use of them to develop a system for determining the longitude at sea by measurement of the lunar distances from the sun and fixed stars.[3]

While these studies were in progress, John Bird, at that time England's foremost maker of precision instruments, had begun an active study of the octant and its defects with the intention of correcting them. Upon Jackson's death in 1746, Bird had become the official licensee in accordance with Hadley's patent, and Jackson's successor in the production of the instrument. He analyzed the octant's structural weaknesses and developed means to correct them. For example, the common complaint that the octant would bend when inclined out of a vertical position was corrected by adding a perpendicular bar to the face of the thin brass index arm. Even with this additional support, however, the instrument was still likely to bend in the direction of the plane of the angle to be measured. Campbell subsequently discovered that the defect was caused by the friction of the centerwork resulting from excessive tightness of the clamp fastening the index to the frame. Bird corrected this by adding a thin circular plate of hammered brass, beaten hollow on one side and cut around the edge with numerous slits, which acted as a spring. Bird later corrected the octant's defects further by reducing the radius of the instrument to 7 inches, and examples of the new size were used successfully by Benjamin Robins in 1750 on a voyage to the East Indies.

Bird meanwhile had been commissioned by the Board of Longitude to construct the first examples of the reflecting circle proposed by Mayer, and one of these was used by Campbell to test Mayer's tables on a voyage during the years 1757 through 1759. The reflecting circles proved to be so cumbersome in use that he discarded them in favor of one of Bird's improved octants. For his work Campbell needed an instrument having a scale divided to 60 degrees instead of that divided to 45 degrees which was part of the octant, and he commissioned Bird to produce such an instrument. This was the prototype of the sextant and proved to be considerably more accurate and satisfactory for making observations at sea. In this new instrument the octant's wooden frame was replaced with one of metal and the index arm was equipped with a vernier made in several scales which read variously from 10 seconds to 1 minute. Although the invention of the sextant is generally attributed to Campbell, examples of the octant graduated with scales to 120 degrees instead of 90 degrees had been produced in occasional examples by the instrument makers Jackson and Heath and Wing during the two decades prior to Campbell's contribution. Other unsigned examples made in the same period provide clear evidence that English instrument makers were experimenting with an early version of the sextant, possibly for use in surveying, within a decade after the invention of the octant in 1730–1732 and a decade before the date of 1757 which is usually attributed to the invention.

Simultaneously Sir Nevil Maskelyne, the Astronomer Royal, was attempting to simplify Mayer's lunar tables and the computation of lunar distances so that they could be used for determining the longitude at sea. Their adoption in the service of the East India Company encouraged him to publish a description of his methods as well as means for adjusting the octant.[4] He followed the publication with a strong appeal for producing a nautical almanac in published form for general use, and due largely to his efforts such a publication appeared for the year 1767 and was issued annually thereafter. The availability of the *Nautical Almanac* emphasized even more the shortcomings of navigational instruments, particularly in the generally inaccurate division of the scale.[5]

A mechanical dividing engine was invented in 1773 by Jesse Ramsden and proved a means of eliminating the factor of human error. Octants divided with this engine were found to be not more than 15 seconds of a degree in error, a great improvement over even the most accurate scales divided by hand.[6] Maskelyne then succeeded in correcting the speculum of the octant so that it eliminated errors due to parallelism.[7]

There was immediate enthusiasm for the sextant. Even earlier, in 1765 Dr. James Lind, physician to King George III and a well-known scientist, wrote to James Watt: "I am turned Longitude mad, and I have got a most novel Sextant made by my friend Ramsden with altho' only Six Inches Radius it is divided to half seconds. A magnificent magnifier, the nonnius and Telescope magnified the Observation." [8]

Although the sextant was recognized as a major improvement by men of science, it was slow to gain acceptance with men of the sea because it required considerable precision in use and more time and attention in its application than the shipmaster or seaman was inclined to give. From about 1770 to the beginning of the nineteenth century the octant and sextant flourished simultaneously, although the octant remained considerably more popular. The greater cost of the sextant was another factor affecting its popularity, for as late as the early nineteenth century it was priced for as much as 2 guineas. Eventually shipowners adopted the practice of fitting their vessels with both an octant and a sextant, the former for general use and the latter to be used only when particularly accurate observations were required.[9]

Samuel Eliot Morison noted that even in the early nineteenth century the position of a ship at sea was generally still determined by dead reckoning with the use of only a compass, log line, and deep-sea lead. Among examples of Atlantic voyages made by American vessels using these traditional methods, he reported that an American vessel was seized at Christiansand, Norway, because she had arrived in port without a chart or sextant. The ship was freed only after other American shipmasters in the port protested that they frequently sailed the width of the Atlantic without those aids, claiming that any competent seaman could do so.[10]

While this evolution of more precise navigational instrumentation was taking place in England, the Americans in general contented themselves with the octant. Prior to the War for Independence these instruments were chiefly imported from England but the onset of war drove American shipmasters to seek those produced by American makers. Relatively few were competent to produce them, and those who could were generally situated in the major port cities. Several proposals to improve the octant were made by American men of science, but in general they were academic in nature and did not result in modifications. The first such proposal was made by

Reverend John Ewing, Provost of the University of Pennsylvania, in 1767. Basing his study on an American-made example of Godfrey's octant, he discovered that the mirrors were not ground parallel to each other and that the instrument required adjustment virtually every time it was used. He suggested that the arc be extended from 90 to 120 degrees to enable the observer to measure larger angles for observations to be made with it, to equip the index arm with two specula instead of a single one at the center, and to incline both of these to each other at an angle of 60 degrees. Ewing suggested other modifications as well, including a handle at the back of the instrument, the attachment of a second octant directly opposite the middle of the first so that the single index could be continued to opposite arcs, and pivoting on the center for use in making observations on land.[11]

In 1784 the octant's shortcomings became the concern also of several others, including the mathematics teacher Benjamin Workman.[12] In 1788 a certain Daniel Byrnes submitted a proposal to the American Philosophical Society concerning "an Instrument . . . that wod take the altitude of the Sun and moon, and their Distances apart . . . for the determination of longitude." He subsequently proposed a second instrument, and the Society appointed a committee to review both but filed no report.[13] Finally, in 1794, the improvement of the octant became a concern also of Robert Patterson. He communicated his suggestions to David Rittenhouse, who read them before a meeting of the American Philosophical Society, but there is no evidence that further action was taken.[14]

In time the improvements in instrumentation inevitably created a demand for more specialized navigational training. Little by little shipmasters and seamen were forced to forgo instinct and traditional practices in favor of the increasingly sophisticated techniques. As the sextant became more widely used, its size was reduced for convenience in handling. By the late eighteenth century a silver scale and vernier were substituted for the earlier practice of inscribing the scale directly on the brass arc. Several English makers experimented with gold or palladium for the inscription of scales, because these metals were less liable to corrosion from sea air, although their cost limited their use. Meanwhile the efforts to perfect the octant did not cease, and as late as the mid-nineteenth century inventors sought patents for modification of the instrument.[15]

The reflecting instruments used in navigation required the horizon as one of the bases for measurement of the altitude of the sun or a star. When the natural horizon at sea was obscured, or when the instruments were to be used on land, it was necessary to provide a replacement. A mirror could be used for the purpose if set on a horizontal plane with sufficient precision, but that was rarely possible. It was discovered that a liquid, which automatically sought its own level, would serve the purpose admirably, and thus the "artificial horizon" was invented. History is vague about its origin, but one of the earliest descriptions is of one devised by John Elton in 1732, and another is of the mercury artificial horizon which was introduced by George Adams in 1738. One form, known as the whirling top or whirling speculum, was produced by J. Serson in 1752 and later improved by John Smeaton in a form called Smeaton's gyroscopic horizon.[16]

In 1830 an American, Phineas Spear of Portland, Maine, devised an artificial horizon in the form of a bubble level attached to the sextant, which was described in his patent application as consisting of "a fog glass, a horizon bar, and a level." [17]

An interesting American improvement of a navigational instrument was made by John Fitch and patented in England in 1793. The device, which he named "The Columbian Ready Reckoner," was an improvement on the traverse board, consisting of an engraved plate which replaced the perforated board. It was sold with a pamphlet of instructions prepared by the inventor. Fitch commented that he had been inspired to devise the Reckoner after observing seamen using the traverse board during the voyage on a British vessel on which he sailed to France in 1793. "This gave me an Idea that something more perfect might be made, in consequence of which, I went to work and formed the enclosed plate; which, as it appears to me, will reduce the art of navigation to the comprehension of the smallest capacity, and simplify it in such a manner as to save the masters of vessels much trouble in their reckonings." In his modest treatise, Fitch explained that the Reckoner could be made of metal, paper, skin, wood, or other materials which lent themselves to inscription and graduation. He compiled five tables to be used with the plate, and "being thus provided with these tables, and having a small plate, graduated similar to the first described table, put in a box and screwed down on the Binocle with 50 pins to keep the seaman's account." [18] Ironically, upon Fitch's return to the United States in the following year, his reduced circumstances forced him to work his passage homeward as a common sailor.[19]

Among other innovations and improvements in navigational aids being considered throughout this period, not the least important was the patent log. The log-ship-and-line and the Dutchman's log which had been traditionally used for centuries for measuring the speed of a ship within a given period became even less satisfactory as naval and commercial maritime activity increased on both sides of the Atlantic. There was considerable experimentation, particularly in England, with the development of a successful patent log and a number of noteworthy examples were produced. Among these were the "Marine Surveyor" patented by Henry de Saumarez in 1715 and further improved by John Smeaton in 1754; Joseph Gilmore's "Navivum" produced in the same period; Benjamin Martin's "Nautical Dromometer," and Edward Massey's patent log which was adopted by the British Admiralty as standard equipment for naval vessels from 1807 until 1815, when it was replaced with another known as Burt's Buoy and Nipper.[20]

The patent log also came under consideration by American inventors and instrument makers. In 1783 the American political leader and writer Francis Hopkinson, a friend of Thomas Jefferson, proposed a machine which appeared to constitute an improvement. It consisted of a palate attached to a long iron rod terminating in a gear turning other gears and wheels which activated an index on a dial which could be read aboard the ship. The brass palate was to be attached to the bow of the ship and would be pressed against a resisting medium with greater or less force depending on the progressive motion of the ship. Hopkinson noted that "an ingenious mechanic would probably construct this machine to better advantage in many respects." He hoped only to suggest a principle that others would develop, but nothing seems to have come of his idea.[21]

In 1796 a patent was granted to Amos Whittemore of Massachusetts for his invention of a nautical perambulator, which may have been a form of the patent log, but which did not seem to have been commercially produced.[22] Another patent log for which an American patent was claimed to have been issued was advertised in 1799 as a "Perpetual Log or Distance Clock" by the firm of Bulmain & Dennies of Water-Street in New York City, which served as agent for the device and displayed it at the Tontine Coffee-House.[23] The patentee could not be identified, and the log may have been the one devised by Edward Massey and adopted by the British Admiralty. When the Admiralty transferred its contract to Burt's Buoy and Nipper, considerable litigation ensued. The latter device was the invention of an English instrument maker named Peter Burt of Limehouse, London, and was commercially produced and marketed in 1813 by Chester Gould of Rome, New York. Because of Gould's role in marketing the apparatus, its name was changed to the Gould-Burt Buoy and Nipper. Gould was a London-born instrument maker and dealer who had established himself in Philadelphia in about 1794 and then moved to Rome, New York. He was responsible for having obtained Enlish patents on at least five navigational aids which he promoted, including a Patent Sea Log, a modified form of the artificial horizon, and an improved time glass.[24] Gould's Patent Sea Log was enthusiastically endorsed in New York City newspapers by John Galven, sailing master of the frigate *United States;* by a seaman named J. B. Davis of the ship *General Washington;* and by George Crowninshield, who used the device on his famous yacht, *Cleopatra's Barge,* in 1817.[25]

The marine compass, that most basic of all navigational aids, also came in for its share of consideration, and the need for its improvement was acknowledged by Americans as well as by the English. Among the early American proposals for an improved compass was one submitted in 1773 by the geographer Bernard Romans to the American Philosophical Society. Romans expressed concern with the unreliability of the brass bowl compass caused by the confinement resulting from the two brass rings of the gimbals, which restricted the movement of the bowl to two vertical motions at right angles to each other in the compass box, so that sudden concussions or a series of them would prevent the compass from recovering and result in the unshipping of the compass card as well. Romans experimented with some means to provide the box with a vertical motion at every degree and minute of the circle, and by compounding these motions with a horizontal motion of the box as well as of the card. A compass of this type, in which the bottom of the compass had a raised hollow cone instead of a bowl, was being produced in Holland.[26]

Other American makers and dealers concerned with the improvement of the compass included the New York City maker of glass instruments Henry Gattey, who in 1800 advertised the production and sale of a variety of compasses, including "a large elegant Azimuth Compass, storm, amplitude, and binnacle Compasses of the best quality, so contrived that the Compass will serve one or three, which saves cash and store room." [27] William Russell of New Bedford patented an improved marine compass in 1809, and in 1828 Lemuel Langley of Gosport or Norfolk, Virginia, patented an improved method of fixing the marine compass. He eliminated the need for a binnacle by proposing to install a two-faced marine compass within an opening cut through the deck above the captain's cabin, so that, by the addition of glass panes on the upper and lower sides of the box, it could be read simultaneously from the cabin and the deck. He suggested that the compass card be made of translucent material for easier reading.

This invention was received with enthusiasm by the editor of *The Journal of the Franklin Institute*. He noted that the glazed rim of the compass might be furnished with additional protection from cannon shot by the addition of a wide iron plate fixed somewhat higher than the rim, with the edges flush to the deck. At one time while Langley was attaching one of his compasses aboard an American vessel at Norfolk, the captain of a British ship then in port observed the invention and commented that he preferred it to the costly binnacle or the tell-tale compass with which his own ship was equipped. The editor of the *Journal* was convinced that the invention would probably be patented also in England, perhaps by others than the inventor, because "it is not there required that the patentee should be the inventor. Mr. Langley, we believe has not taken any measure to secure it for himself in that country. We frequently recognize the improvements made by our countrymen, in the accounts of British patents; of this we have no right or inclination to complain, but we cannot help feeling that justice requires that the credit of having made useful inventions, or discoveries, ought to be given to the country to which they belong." [28]

In 1830 Moses Smith of New York City patented a method for remagnetizing the needle of marine and surveying compasses by means of sliding caps of soft iron. He devised a compass needle substantially heavier than the conventional forms, having poles of uniform breadth and thickness to which sliding caps were fitted which could be moved toward or from the center of the pole's extremity. When an attraction foreign to the pole's attraction occurred, such as from the proximity of cannon or other iron, the caps were to be moved toward the points of the needle to lessen the effect of the foreign attraction. Smith went on to devise a brass electric rod for use in restoring the needle's magnetization.[29]

Another innovation which evoked interest in its time was the replacement of the conventional brass bowl of the marine compass by one made as a heavy glass hemisphere in which was accommodated a double-sided compass card, or fly. It became in effect a tell-tale compass which could be read from the top or the bottom with equal ease day or night. This invention by Jonathan Ball of Newry, Maine, patented in 1835, seemed to combine the best features of Langley's proposal with new ones.[30]

Meanwhile, the liquid compass, which had existed in a rudimentary form for centuries, again came to attention as potentially having general maritime use. An English watchmaker, Francis Crow, patented one in 1813 in which the compass card was fitted with a float in a bowl filled with liquid so that it floated up against a pivot on the underside of the glass cover. It was tested at sea but did not achieve sufficient popularity to make it marketable.[31] In about 1862 an American instrument maker, Edward Samuel Ritchie of Boston, while on a visit to England, observed a liquid compass in use and became enthusiastic about its possibilities. After his return to the United States he designed and produced an improved version which was officially adopted by the United States Navy, and with further modifications it was subsequently adopted by the British Navy. By the end of the nineteenth century it was to supersede all other forms of the compass at sea. Ritchie's compass, designed to withstand derangement from sudden shock, was not affected by change of the vessel's direction or from rough seas.[32]

From time to time instruments to aid the navigator and to replace traditional practices were devised, some of which were more successful than others. Among the former was the station-pointer, an instrument for fixing the ship's exact position on a chart, which was invented by an Admiralty surveyor named Murdoch Mackenzie prior to 1774. It was first described in Mackenzie's work on maritime surveying. The station-pointer came to the attention of American shipmasters and navigators soon after it had been commercially produced and eventually it came into universal use.[33]

Another instrument, which had a relationship to the station-pointer, was the trigonometer, an American invention made by William Bolles of Connecticut in 1824. It was a multi-use device, adaptable for trigonometry, mensuration, surveying, plane sailing, and for compiling a ship's course.[34] Eli Whitney noted: "This instrument is certainly ingenious and . . . enables the Navigator to keep his reckoning with more facility and less error," and the American chemist and geologist Benjamin Silliman described it as an instrument that would "be found valuable by surveyors and seamen in all cases in which expedition is required without much numerical accuracy." [35]

XVI

☆ ☆ ☆ ☆ ☆ ☆ ☆ ☆ ☆ ☆ ☆ ☆ ☆

FROM HIS KNOWN SHORE

☆ ☆

Th' acute *Geographer*, th' *Historian* sage
By thy Discov'ries clear the doubtful Page
From marked Eclipses, *Longitude* perceive,
Can settle Distances, and Æra's give.
From his known Shore the Seaman distant far,
Steers safely guided by thy *Polar Star;*
Nor errs, when Clouds and Storms obscure its Ray,
His Compass marks him as exact a Way.

Benjamin Franklin,
Poor Richard improved . . . (1756)

THREE CENTURIES and more elapsed between the first attempts to develop a method for determining the longitude at sea and the finding of a satisfactory solution, and then several more decades passed before that solution could be widely applied. A ship's exact position in relation to the nearest land is determined by calculating the latitude, or the ship's distance north or south of the equator, and by determining the longitude, or the ship's distance east or west of the point of departure. The latitude may be calculated by measuring the sun's altitude above the horizon at noon, or by measurement of the maximum altitudes of the moon, stars, or planets. Finding the longitude, however, presented considerable difficulty.

Basically, the difference in the longitudes of two given points is the difference between the clock time at each point, with 15 degrees reckoned as the difference of longitude to 1-hour difference of time. As a means of determining the longitude, the earth's surface is divided into 360 equal parts, each of which constitutes a degree of longitude. A line drawn from north to south through any point of the earth's surface is a meridian of longitude. Inasmuch as the revolution of the earth about its axis is completed in a period of nearly 24 hours, each degree of longitude is moved successively opposite the sun at a rate of 4 minutes between meridians.

The two principal methods for establishing the longitude of a given position east or west of a given meridian are with the use of timepieces, whereby the clock time between two points can be compared, or by comparing the time of the occurrence of an astronomical event, such as an eclipse, at two given points. For either method, an established prime meridian or datum point is required. In early Mediterranean maritime history, the point from which the longitude was measured eastward was a meridian through the Fortunate Isles, a name now believed to refer to the Canary Islands. Subsequently, prime meridians used included the meridian of Paris by French navigators, of Amsterdam by the Dutch, and of London by the English. It was not until the late nineteenth century that the prime meridian at Greenwich, England, was established for international use.

At least five different methods had been developed and utilized to determine the longitude, each of which was useful to some degree but all of which required instruments of more than usual precision and mathematical skill in their use. Each of the five major methods had been proposed in either the sixteenth or the seventeenth century and all continued to be re-invented in one form or another into the nineteenth century.

The methods proposed were dead reckoning, which was the most generally used until after the War for Independence; the employment of an accurate timekeeper, first suggested early in the sixteenth century and resolved almost two and a half centuries later with the invention of the marine chronometer; observation of the variation of the compass, first suggested by Henry Bond in England in 1662; observation of the lunar distances, first suggested in the early seventeenth century; and observation of the eclipses of Jupiter's satellites, proposed at approximately the same time.

The longitude could be determined by ascertaining simultaneously the difference in time between two meridians. Prior to the advent of the marine chronometer, this was accomplished only by establishing the apparent time of the same celestial phenomena at two different locations. Thomas Bavin, on his voyage to Newfoundland, and Thomas Hariot, on the voyage to Virginia, attempted to achieve this by the use of timekeepers kept in operation and verified with the sun at noon by means of a sundial, but neither had a sufficiently accurate timekeeper. Another method, first considered in 1514, was to establish the apparent time of the same celestial phenomenon, such as an eclipse of the sun or moon, at two different locations by observation of the motions of the moon among the fixed stars. The moon's motions could not be predicted in advance until precision instruments were available and a better theory of the moon's course was known, so that the observer at sea was able to compare his own observations of the moon with those indicated in an almanac. It was not until Newton's theory of universal gravitation had become generally known that such lunar distances could be predicted.[1]

The major achievement in the search for a method to determine the longitude at sea was the marine chronometer, which was invented by John Harrison, an English country clockmaker, in 1764, after thirty-six years of experimentation. He undertook the project in response to the offer made in 1714 by the English government of an award to be administered by the Board of Longitude. Harrison produced four timekeepers, each more precise than its predecessor, and the fourth one, which won the prize of 20,000 pounds, over a period of seven weeks at sea registered an error of 38.4 seconds, or 9.6 miles of longitude at the equator. Other clockmakers immediately set out to duplicate Harrison's achievement. Larcum Kendall, Thomas Mudge, John Arnold, and Thomas Earnshaw in England, and Ferdinand Berthoud and Pierre Le Roy in France, among others, added improvements, some of which subsequently had wide application.[2]

The measurement of lunar distances was perfected at about the same time as the production of a successful chronometer. Neither of these methods was practical for American navigators, however.

Many decades passed before chronometers were produced in sufficient numbers to affect the art of navigation. The computation of lunar distances required training, texts, and precise instruments. An American naval officer of the Revolutionary period thus described the problems: "After the mariner had studied and perfected himself in the use of all the necessary books and tables, . . . viz., The Nautical Almanac, The Requisite Tables and Shepherd's Tables, &c he should endeavour to get a complete sextant graduated to quarter minutes, or to half minutes, at most, with a screw to move the index along the arch; Ramsden's intire brass sextants are by far the best, but it is not easy to procure one of them, as I was four years after I had wrote for mine before I got it; and most people . . . have met with the same difficulty." [3]

As early as 1729 a certain John Smith of Cecil County, Maryland, announced in a local newspaper that he had discovered a new and useful method of determining longitude at sea, but no details were provided then or later.[4] New solutions continued to be proposed on both sides of the Atlantic throughout the eighteenth century, and among the most persistent proponents was another resident of Cecil County, John Churchman (3rd) of Nottingham, who had achieved local fame as a cartographer and surveyor. Not irrelevant to his proposal was his statement that he was self-taught on the subject of magnetism. In about 1785 Churchman produced a perpetual motion machine operated by magnetic power, which was constructed for him by Ellis Chandlee, a local clock and instrument maker. A surviving bond in the amount of 20,000 pounds, signed by Chandlee, stated that "Ellis Chandlee does always keep a secret and does not disclose same, the description of a machine invented by the said Churchman and supposed to move perpetually by the principles of magnetism," and he presumably was employed merely to construct a mechanism from Churchman's design.[5]

Churchman had conceived a new theory of the variation of the magnetic needle which led to his proposal that by observation of this variation another method for finding the longitude at sea could be derived. The first public announcement of his discovery was made in the Philadelphia press in 1777. He described his proposal as based on the theory that two satellites were revolving around the earth, one around the North Pole and the other around the South Pole. Neither of the satellites had ever been sighted because they were not visible from lower latitudes. He estimated the period of revolution of the northern satellite to be 463 years.[6] Early in 1787 Churchman presented a paper on his theory before the American Philosophical Society, and a committee was appointed to review it. The conclusion was that the theory was inconsistent with known principles and recorded observations, and Churchman's proposal was dismissed as a groundless whimsy.[7] David Rittenhouse, who had reviewed the proposal, wrote to Thomas Jefferson: "We have abundance of projectors and pretenders to new Discoveries, and many applications to the Legislature for exclusive priviledges, some of them ridiculous enough. The self-moving Boat, the Steam Boat, the Mechanical Miller, the improved *Ring Dial* for finding the Variations of the Needle. The *Surveying Compass* to serve 20 other purposes, and a project for finding the Longitude by the Variation of the Magnetic Needle. . . ." Although Rittenhouse's view of Churchman and his project was justified, time has disproved his estimate of some of the other proposals listed.[8]

Churchman, undeterred by the Society's response, asked Jefferson to use his influence to have his Memorial, a written presentation of his theory, read before the Royal Academy of Sciences in Paris.[9] Jefferson was sufficiently intrigued by the proposal and by the possibility of an American achievement in the sciences to mention it in correspondence with several of his friends.[10] His sometimes naive support of any new scientific endeavor was effectively cooled, however, by an evaluation provided by Francis Hopkinson: "This learned Man [Churchman] understands as much of Philosophy as can be acquired by practical Surveying; and as much of Navigation as can be obtain'd from paddling in a Canoe." [11] Nonetheless, Jefferson communicated Churchman's proposal to the Paris Academy and was informed that the presentation was not sufficiently explicit to enable that body to make a final decision.[12] Undaunted Churchman in 1789 published a request for support of his theory of magnetic variation, then communicated on the matter with Sir Joseph Banks, then president of the Royal Society and secretary of the Board of Longitude, and attempted to enlist the support of Benjamin Franklin and others.[13]

The repeated rebuffs that he received made Churchman all the more determined to prove his proposition. After further study, he reported that he was no longer certain that the satellites were situated above the earth, and he thought it possible that they were either rolling on its surface or lay beneath it. This led him to suggest that the United States government should undertake an expedition to Baffin Bay, where he had now decided the north magnetic pole was located. Surprisingly enough, he succeeded in enlisting support for this expedition from James Madison and went on to submit a request for its financing to the Congress, but this was rejected because of the country's economic difficulties at that time.[14]

Although the world of science tended to scorn Churchman's proposal, his *Magnetic Atlas* was published in four editions, one in Philadelphia, one in New York, and two in London.[15] In 1792 the author went to Europe, where he remained for four years. His proposal received a favorable response from the Imperial Russian Academy of Science. It was proposed for an award, which was not approved, but in 1795 Churchman was elected to membership in the Academy on the director's personal recommendation.[16] On a second voyage to Europe in 1802 he received permission from the Danish Admiralty to undertake magnetic observations aboard the Danish ship *Seyeren*, and sailed on that vessel to Kronstadt en route to Saint Petersburg.[17] In 1804 he was elected to membership in the Royal Society of Arts in London, and a paper on marine topographical survey which he presented was awarded a silver medal.[18]

Within a decade of Churchman's first announcement of his proposal, Benjamin Workman, who had become an instructor at the University of Pennsylvania, proposed another new solution for determining longitude. Francis Hopkinson described it to Jefferson as the work of a "semi-lunatic Projector" and went on to report that it "is nothing more than a convenient application of the *Ring Dial*, which finds the true solar Meridian; underneath this is the Magnetic Needle, and a graduated circle designates the Degrees and Minutes of Difference between the solar and magnetic Meridians." [19] This appears to have been the ring dial invention to which Rittenhouse had referred. Workman did not have Churchman's stamina, however, and he soon abandoned his project.

Yet another proposal for a solution of the longitude problem was submitted to the American Philosophical Society in 1789 by one Arthur Greer of Reading, Pennsylvania, but it was not pursued.[20] "New longitudinal discoveries" were claimed also by Captain Matthew C. Groves of Massachusetts in 1802, a proposal with which Jefferson and Robert Patterson became involved on behalf of the American Philosophical Society.[21] Although the proposal proved to be unsuccessful when tested, Groves attempted to obtain support for it through the press. In his newspaper statements he noted that he used a Godfrey octant fitted with an achromatic reflecting telescope for taking observations of Jupiter and its satellites, which he was able to accomplish with greater steadiness than was possible on shipboard.[22] During the next six years Groves used every means possible to find support and even wrote a play to raise funds for his project. Inevitably he returned to Jefferson for assistance, but the latter, in a kindly but firm letter, suggested that he discard the project.[23] As late as 1839 two gentlemen of Warrenton, Virginia, Messrs. Hitt and Pierce, advertised that they had invented a method for determining longitude which did not require even astronomical observations. However, this proposal was dropped shortly after it had been initiated.[24]

The marine chronometer proved the ultimate solution for determining the longitude at sea, but its general adoption was long delayed. In 1790 the ship *Massachusetts* sailed from Boston to the West Indies without a chronometer and with no officer on board who understood lunar observations. Navigational errors caused the ship to lose at least three weeks' time. In 1832 the shipping merchants, Bryant & Sturgis, reprimanded one of their East India shipmasters for having purchased a chronometer for $250.00 and advised him that he must pay for it personally. He was further admonished: "Could we have anticipated that our injunction respecting economy would have been so totally disregarded we would have set fire to the Ship rather than have sent her to sea." As late as 1827 a Massachusetts shipmaster, Nathaniel Silsbee, reported that he had sailed from Salem to Rotterdam by dead reckoning alone, without a chronometer or knowledge of lunar observations. The combined deterrents of high cost and limited production—since in this period each instrument had to be made entirely by hand by skilled clockmakers—were augmented by the unwillingness of shipping merchants and shipmasters to adopt a new and unfamiliar, as well as costly, navigational aid.[25]

Chronometers imported from England were offered for sale by American clock and watch makers in shipping centers from the beginning of the nineteenth century but at first there was little demand. By 1802 the New York City watchmaker David F. Launay advertised that, in addition to his normal trade, he also serviced "dead beat Seconds for astronomical observations, Longitudinal

Time Pieces, etc." At one time he offered for sale "An excellent Chronometer (or Timekeeper) its original cost 100 Guineas calculated to give the Longitude at sea—It has been tried on two voyages to the East Indies." [26]

Within the next several years other American watchmaking firms in port cities sold or repaired "Marine Time-Keepers Horizontal and Repeating Watches." [27] Little by little the American shipping world was becoming familiar with the instrument.

Among the earliest dealers to import chronometers for sale to the marine trade was William Bond, an English silversmith and clockmaker who had emigrated to Maine and then settled in Boston. It took him a long time to establish himself as an importer of chronometers and other timepieces, because he waged a constant struggle with poverty. However, his son, William Cranch Bond, constructed the first chronometer made entirely in America and went on to establish a chronometer-making business which continued in his family into the twentieth century.

Young William had demonstrated considerable mechanical skill at an early age; surviving family records relate that at the age of ten he had constructed an operable wooden clock and at fifteen he had produced an operating weight-driven chronometer. His inspiration for the latter had come from a French work which described the chronometer used by the eighteenth-century French explorer Jean François de La Perouse. While tending his father's shop in Boston, young William worked out the details of a reliable ship's chronometer and completed construction of the instrument with success. Unable to obtain a suitable spring for it, he powered the timekeeper by means of a falling weight.

In 1812, at the age of twenty-three, he completed the design and construction of the first successful American ship's chronometer. Again he experienced great difficulty in obtaining a mainspring. Mainsprings for clocks and watches were imported from England by watch and clock makers but the political situation at the time interfered, and equipment and practice for making them did not yet exist in the United States. Accordingly, Bond was forced to revert to the solution he had utilized in his earlier chronometer and substitute a weight for the mainspring for the maintaining power.

The production of this first American chronometer was acclaimed as a major achievement, and the instrument was tested on a voyage from Boston to Sumatra in the ship *Cyrus*, Captain Thomas B. Curtiss commanding. The tests indicated that it was quite as accurate as the majority of other chronometers available. The United States government offered Bond a large sum for the timekeeper but he would not part with it. It was carefully preserved in the shop by Bond and succeeding generations of his family.[28]

Meanwhile, Bond had become increasingly interested in the subject of astronomy and developed his own crudely made instruments for conducting celestial observations, in the course of which he independently discovered the comet of 1811. Throughout this period he continued to work with his father in the chronometer shop, and he rated most of the chronometers of ships sailing out of Boston harbor. He was commissioned in 1815 by Harvard College to visit English observatories to make a study of their work and equipment and brought back much valuable data about the observatory instruments he had seen.

Bond rated the chronometers brought to him for adjustment and testing by means of sextant observations. In 1819 he constructed a small observatory in his home at Dorchester and equipped it with astronomical and meteorological instruments, which enabled him to continue to earn his livelihood by making, repairing, and rating chronometers. Between the years 1825 and 1830 he diverted his energies to an investigation of the comparative rates of marine chronometers at sea and ashore, the results of which he published in 1833. His work dispelled the popular notion that chronometers, when brought on shipboard from shore, had an accelerated rate of operation because of the influence of iron in the ship's construction. Bond was able to prove that the same chronometers had an equally erratic rate on shore as on shipboard and he concluded that either the 226 instruments which he had tested were not well adjusted or that the effect resulted from some extraordinary cause.[29]

Bond continued to experiment with the chronometer and to study the influence on the performance of the instrument of changes of temperature, the presence of large surfaces of iron, and related problems. Many of his conclusions were at variance with acknowledged authorities of his time, but Bond was later proved to be correct. He communicated his findings to colleagues in England, and many of his suggestions for improvement of the chronometer were subsequently adopted and became essential to the instrument's performance.[30]

William Cranch Bond was the first to introduce the chronometer balance and the chronometer escapement to watches, and he was in fact the first to import chronometer watches from England. Working with his sons, he also invented an astronomical clock with a spring governor for registering astronomical observations by electricity. The Bond break-circuit, or circuit interrupter, and the chronograph were major contributions to the development of the chronometer and to its utilization in navigation and constituted the two most important additions to chronometry since Harrison's original invention.[31]

Among mathematical instrument makers as distinguished from clock and watch makers, one of the earliest to advertise the sale of chronometers was Thomas Biggs of Philadelphia, who informed the public in 1817 that he sold and repaired them. The firm of E. & G. W. Blunt of New York City did much to popularize the chronometer with the American shipping trade, and by 1833 it was American agent for the outstanding English makers, particularly featuring the products of Edward J. Dent of London.[32]

Among other American makers producing chronometers, one of the earliest after Bond, and the most important, was John Bliss, a New York City watchmaker who sold navigational instruments as well as chronometers from about 1835. As the nineteenth century progressed, many of the component parts of chronometers were mass-produced in England for sale to instrument makers in England and America, where they were assembled by skilled clockmakers and sold as their products. The plates, trains, fusees, chains, balances, and other elements were finished by the clockmakers, who produced the escapements and sometimes the balances and assembled the components into finished chronometers. In general, the clockmaker also made the dial and engraved it with his own name. Some of the less-known American clockmakers may have engraved the dials with the names of eminent English chronometer makers instead of their own, to realize a greater price for their product.[33]

During the half-century following the end of the war great strides were being made in the production of works on navigation by American authors and practitioners. In 1796, two years after the publication of Commodore Thomas Truxtun's significant work on navigation,[34] Edmund March Blunt, a publisher of nautical books in Newburyport, Massachusetts, and later in New York City, produced another important addition to the literature of navigation entitled *The American Coast Pilot*. The major part of the work was a compilation, made by Captain Lawrence Furlong, a Newburyport shipmaster, incorporating material from other works including John Norman's *The American Pilot*, Seller's *The English Pilot. Fourth Book*, and Bernard Romans's *Concise Natural History of East and West Florida*. Osgood Carleton, a science teacher, assisted in the preparation of the *Table of Latitudes and Longitudes*, and Blunt himself contributed information on tariffs, customs, and laws relating to the sea. The work had an immediate success and was reprinted again and again. In a fourth edition published in 1804 Blunt added new material which was apparently copied in part from the 1751 edition of *The English Pilot. Fourth Book*, and included sailing directions and eleven charts. Errors in courses and distances were inadvertently included and perpetuated before they were finally corrected in the edition of 1826. Publication of the work was carried on by Edmund and George Blunt, Edmund Blunt's sons, for a total of twenty-one editions, the last of which appeared in 1867. Blunt's *Pilot* was pirated and published in French in several editions.[35]

Blunt next undertook a modification of John Hamilton Moore's *New Practical Navigator* for use in American waters.[36] He selected the thirteenth edition of Moore's work for revision and contracted with Nathaniel Bowditch to make the corrections and additions. Bowditch was a competent mathematician and navigator of Salem, Massachusetts. He corrected numerous small errors as well as several major ones, which he discovered in Moore's work. Blunt engaged others to contribute to the project. One of the tables was provided by Nicholas Pike, mathematician and member of the American Academy of Sciences, who also found and corrected other errors. Notes for another table were provided by William Bowditch, Nathaniel's younger brother. The most important single addition was a chapter on finding the longitude at sea by observation of lunar distances, which Nathanial Bowditch prepared.[37]

Blunt's version of Moore's *Navigator*, published in 1799, met with immediate success and he produced a second edition with additional revisions and corrections by Bowditch. The American work soon began to supplant its English predecessor. Encouraged by the continuing sale, Blunt produced a third edition to which he gave a new title, *The New American Practical Navigator*, and cited Bowditch on the title page as author. Blunt arranged for a London printing firm to produce an English edition, which appeared simultaneously with the third American edition in 1802.[38]

In 1804 Blunt updated his earlier work by publishing a separate *Appendix*, which consisted of a compilation of the additional material which had been added to succeeding editions. Nathaniel Bowditch continued as editor of the *Navigator* until his death in 1838 and was succeeded in the project by his son, J. Ingersoll Bowditch. In 1867 the copyright and the plates were sold by George Blunt to the U. S. Hydrographic Office. The Blunt family had produced thirty-five editions of the work, which was undoubtedly one of the greatest single American contributions to the art of navigation.[39]

Although Bowditch's work was immensely popular with the navigational world, it did not escape censure. One of its most severe critics was a mathematician of New York City, George Baron, who gave a lecture in New York City in which he used a three-dimensional model to demonstrate how Bowditch had erred in his presentation of common navigation. A synopsis of the lecture was published as a small volume, and later in 1802 Baron produced and advertised for sale a set of tables of latitude and longitude.[40] Baron was unrelenting in his attack on Bowditch, and in the spring of 1803 he presented another lecture, again illustrated with a model to prove that Bowditch's *Navigator* was based on false principles of navigation.[41] Despite the support of the work from navigators all over the world, Baron's attacks became annoying to Bowditch and Blunt, and the latter offered a reward of $500 for proof that Bowditch's work had indeed been based on false principles as accused. Baron took up the challenge and the controversy continued without resolution, while Baron presented lectures on the subject and published announcements of them as late as the end of 1804.[42]

Meanwhile, Bowditch moved on to other achievements. When the first volume of the *Traité de Mécanique Céleste* by the French astronomer and mathematician Pierre Simon de Laplace was published in 1800, Bowditch immediately realized its significance as the latest and most authoritative work on astronomy. He accordingly undertook to translate it and took the volume with him on his voyages, preparing his notes while at sea. He continued to do this with each succeeding volume as it appeared, and in 1814 he began the preparation of a full translation. It was completed three years later, although the first volume was not published until 1829; the three subsequent volumes followed in succession within the next decade.[43]

Bowditch's English edition of the *Mécanique* was more than a translation, for he supplemented Laplace's work with unstated steps in the original author's demonstrations and annotated it throughout with copious commentary, including results of later observations and research as well as identification of the original discoverers of the facts included. Bowditch received considerable assistance, particularly in the compilation of the commentary, from Professor Benjamin Peirce of Harvard College.[44]

While the American maritime world was being provided with adequate navigational guides, concern on a national level for a government-supported effort to collect and make available information on American waterways was increasing. The establishment of a government-sponsored coastal survey was first proposed by Thomas Jefferson and supported by representations from members of the American Philosophical Society. Pressures from several directions led to an act of Congress in 1807, which authorized a systematic survey to be conducted of American coasts, under the administration of the Department of the Treasury. Despite the recognized need, it was not possible to implement the project immediately, and from time to time independent surveys were conducted by individuals, without official coordination of these efforts. Suggested plans of operation were solicited from American scientists and other interested persons, to be combined and formed into a basis for a nautical survey of national scope. This was a period of semi-official scientific activity by individuals in university observatories and civilian enterprises of a related nature, supported by financial assistance from shipping interests and prominent merchant families. Finally the time seemed appropriate for the formal establishment of a government endeavor.

A circular was issued by the Secretary of the Treasury, which was expected to result in a proposal for the establishment by astronomical observation of the positions of selected points from which to conduct a trigonometric study that would serve as the basis for an elaborate survey of the American coastline.

A reasonable response ensued, and among the plans submitted, the one proposed by Ferdinand Rudolph Hassler was accepted. Hassler was a Swiss engineer who had arrived in the United States in 1805 and taught mathematics at the United States Military Academy at West Point for several years. Delay followed delay in implementation of Hassler's plan, primarily because there were no adequate instruments available for making the survey. In 1811 Hassler went to Europe to purchase the instruments required, but the War of 1812 intervened and it was not until 1815 that he was back in the country once more.[45]

During this period of the Survey's enforced inactivity, several individual enterprises were successfully promoted. In 1810 Edmund M. Blunt undertook the first of what he planned to be a series of surveys of coastal waters. He selected surveys which had already been completed and published in England and had them re-engraved by his son-in-law, William Hooker. In 1812 he adapted and published a survey of New London made by the American Navy. When the British Navy blockaded that port, however, the American naval authorities impounded all copies of Blunt's re-issue and it did not become generally available again until 1815.

In 1816 Blunt initiated a program for publishing original surveys that were made for him by his son, Edmund Blunt. The first to be completed was of the harbor of New York City, made when the younger Blunt was not yet seventeen years of age. Encouraged by the response to this first venture, Edmund Blunt went on to make a survey of the Bahama Bank, a project which he completed in 1819 and 1820, with the assistance of his brother, George Blunt, and two officers of the United States Navy. In 1821 Edmund M. Blunt and his son Edmund conducted a survey of Nantucket and Georges Shoals and in 1824 one of the coast along the bay of New York. They completed other important surveys within the next several years, including a line of levels from the San Juan River to the Pacific Ocean, and one of Long Island Sound, executed between 1828 and 1830.[46]

Meanwhile, the U. S. Coast Survey had finally been activated in 1816, and Hassler was formally appointed Superintendent of the Survey of the Coast, as it was then termed. The first work of the new organization was initiated in the harbor of New York City, but only small units of the project could be completed before the Survey was forced by administrative problems to lapse in 1818. The employment of civilians was not permitted, and from 1818 to 1832 a cooperative arrangement was devised between the Army and Navy to enable the work to continue, but the product consisted of unrelated small surveys.

It was not until 1832 that the original act of 1807 was revived and the Survey reconstituted, under the Department of the Treasury as before, and again under the direction of Hassler. Two years later the Survey was transferred to the Department of the Navy, only to be returned in 1836 to the Department of the Treasury, where it continued for the remainder of the nineteenth century.

The chess game to which the Survey was submitted from the time it was first formalized did not add to the productivity of the project, but in spite of this Hassler organized it with brilliance and incorporated the most advanced scientific methods of the time. During the same period he produced standard weights and measures for the Department of the Treasury and served as Superintendent of Weights and Measures for the government. This position traditionally belonged to the Superintendent of the U. S. Coast Survey until the formation of the National Bureau of Standards in the early twentieth century.

The early years of the Survey were beset with many problems, due largely to Hassler's own impatience with administrative matters, his great concern for absolute precision, and criticisms from the Congress on costs, to which were added conflicts arising from the efforts of the Department of the Navy to acquire the Survey as a part of its own activities. Despite the problems and frustrations, the Survey made progress, and many Army and Navy officers, as well as scientists from the private sector, were enrolled in what gradually became an impressive corps of geographers, hydrographers, and surveyors. Its efforts in the field were being supported by and combined with work being independently carried on in astronomical observatories in colleges and universities, and this first major government support of science promised great achievement for the future.[47]

Young Edmund Blunt's reputation as an outstanding American hydrographer was well established and well earned by the time the Survey was reconstituted in 1832, and he was appointed Hassler's First Assistant in July 1833. Hassler and Blunt were well known to each other, as Blunt had been responsible for importing surveying instruments for Hassler in 1829. Their association became a productive one, although it was later beset with personal conflicts, a situation which occurred with almost everyone with whom Hassler became associated. Blunt's association with the Coast Survey continued more or less actively until his death in 1866. At the same time that Blunt was appointed to work in the Coast Survey, his father was employed to engrave and publish the charts produced for the U. S. Navy. The elder Blunt's son-in-law William Hooker had returned to work for him in 1817 and was primarily responsible for engraving most of the charts produced thereafter by the Blunt firm.

Despite their wide distribution, the reputation of the Blunt charts was occasionally attacked by shipmasters who had suffered losses and assigned the blame to inaccuracies in Blunt's surveys or publications. Blunt moved quickly on each such occasion to prove that the charges were unfounded, even chartering the vessel *Orbit* for a voyage to verify the accuracy of his surveys. The most serious attack was that of a competitor, the instrument maker Isaac Greenwood (3rd), who resented the increasing financial success of the Blunt enterprises. At first Greenwood's attack was relatively subtle, as reflected in one of his advertisements in the New York press in 1815, in which he announced the arrival of a shipment from London of "an assortment of Seamen's Charts, of the most approved publications. . . . They being taken from actual surveys and executed under the direction of men of Nautical Science, must be vastly superior to any copies of those charts printed in America, particularly by those who possess little or no information on the subject." [48]

This was followed in 1817 by a more open attack, in which Greenwood claimed that Blunt's charts were not original but were in fact copies of English and European works. In general, Greenwood's charges were based on truth, because it was not until after 1816 that the Blunt firm began to make its own surveys and to produce original charts of the coastal waters.[49] Greenwood had underestimated his opponent's strength, however, and he made the mistake of replying to a letter from a certain Captain Steinhauer with the statement that Blunt's charts were inaccurate and had been copied directly from British originals without authorization or acknowledgment. Steinhauer permitted Blunt to see Greenwood's letter, and Blunt promptly sued Greenwood. Other instrument makers and chart sellers became involved in the suit, including Richard Patten of New York City, who testified for Greenwood, and Erasmus Kutz who appeared on Blunt's behalf and nullified the testimony presented by Patten. The jury returned in less than five minutes and awarded Blunt the amount of $750 and costs.

Several years later Blunt sued Patten for infringement of copyright, undoubtedly in retaliation for the latter's role in the Greenwood-Blunt suit. In 1827 Patten had produced and sold a chart of the New England coast which included the relocation of the Nantucket South Shoal made by Edmund M. Blunt and Cheever Felch in 1821. The relocation added 22 miles to the channel used by ships to and from American ports and achieved a saving in time of as much as twenty-four hours in the passage. This discovery had been published and copyrighted by Blunt in 1821. On the publication of Patten's chart, Blunt brought suit. The case was tried before the U. S. Circuit Court in 1828, and although the decision was awarded to Blunt, there was much unfairness in the results of the trial.[50] It was well known that Blunt had habitually "borrowed" from English charts without acknowledgment during most of his career, and his suit against Patten for a similar act was viewed with some surprise. The importance of providing correct nautical data for the pursuit of trade traditionally placed such information within the public domain, and Blunt had no exclusive rights to the relocation of the shoal. He furthermore exercised questionable taste by publicizing the results of the lawsuits with Greenwood and Patten, and by including accounts from the court records of both in subsequent editions of the *Nautical Almanac* and in other publications which he produced.[51]

By this time the marine chronometer had achieved relatively wide distribution, but more accurate methods of timekeeping at sea were still needed. At the beginning and end of each voyage the instruments had to be "rated," or adjusted, by clockmakers or chronometer makers in shipping centers. This was an inconvenience, and eventually a system was evolved by which shipmasters could adjust their chronometers on shipboard without having to bring them ashore. This was accomplished by means of a time signal given from a signal station, or observatory, situated high above the harbor. These observatories, which usually consisted of simple wooden tower-like structures, had been created in several of the major ports during the early years of independence for the purpose of watching for and announcing the arrival of homecoming shipping. Generally the observatory was nothing more than a tall flagstaff, erected on the highest ground adjacent to the harbor and equipped with a lookout house from which an observer could survey the harbor with a spyglass. As an approaching vessel was identified, the observer raised a signal flag to inform the city, and the people would flock to the shore to greet the arrivals.

One of the earliest of these observatories was the Baltimore Observatory erected on Federal Hill in 1797 by Captain David Porter, Sr., and supported enthusiastically by the shipping community from the very beginning. Porter advertised his project in the press and obtained public subscriptions to support it. He devised a system of private flag signals which identified not only the type of vessel approaching but the owner as well. He also contemplated a project to drop a large ball made of canvas or basketwork to provide additional data about the ship arrivals, but this was never realized. No records relating to the Federal Hill observatory during the British invasion of Baltimore are available, but it managed to survive the War of 1812 and continued under Porter's administration until approximately 1830.[52]

These signal stations provided an excellent means for conveying accurate time signals from the clockmaker's shop, where correct time was maintained by means of regulator clocks checked periodically by observations made of the sun with a transit instrument. With the advent of the telegraph in the mid-nineteenth century, the problem was greatly simplified, but the signal station remained an interim solution. The conveyance of time signals was resolved by modification of a plan which Porter had conceived for Federal Hill, to drop a large ball—which would be visible in the harbor—at timed intervals from the flagstaff of the signal station. In due course time balls were installed in at least twenty American port cities.

The inspiration for the device came from the Royal Observatory at Greenwich, England. In December 1824 a proposal was made by Captain Robert Wauchope to the Lords Commissioners of the Admiralty that a system be installed at Greenwich which would provide the correct time by means of a signal. Similar signals had been installed successfully at the Cape of Good Hope as early as 1820. A time-ball signal was subsequently established at the observatory on the island of Saint Helena, and the first time ball was added to the observatory at Greenwich in 1833.[53] In the United States the first time-ball installation was made at the U. S. Naval Observatory in Washington, D. C., in about 1844.[54]

XVII

☆ ☆ ☆ ☆ ☆ ☆ ☆ ☆ ☆ ☆ ☆ ☆

THE BOOK
OF NATURE

☆ ☆

A large volume of the Book of Nature, yet unread, is open
before us, and invites our attentive perusal. . . . We stand on the
shoulders of our predecessors, with respect to the arts that depend
upon experiment and observation. The face of our country,
intersected by rivers, or covered by woods and swamps, gives
ample scope for the improvement of mechanicks, mathematicks,
and natural philosophy.

David Ramsay, "An Oration upon
the Advantages of American Independence,"
United States Magazine (1779)

DURING THE SAME period that government support was being provided to establish the United States Coast Survey in response to
maritime needs, the new profession of the engineer was coming into
being in America. This was accomplished with the establishment of
the United States Military Academy at West Point, which brought
to reality a vision of George Washington's. On March 16, 1802, the

Congress gave President Jefferson authority to create a corps of engineers, specifying that "the said corps when so organized shall be stationed at West Point, in the State of New York, and shall constitute a military academy." [1]

Training of engineers for war and peace was the stated purpose of the institution. An impressive faculty was appointed and a curriculum developed, with Jefferson's concern for the role of science in education strongly reflected in the planning. He greatly favored the French trend in mathematics in preference to that of the English schools, and his wishes prevailed. The physics department was particularly notable, but, curiously, the subject of geography did not become part of the curriculum until 1816 or later. [2]

The Academy flourished during its first years, but strong opposition, arising from the fear that it furnished the basis for a standing army, caused the Secretary of War to reduce his support. Early in 1812 the Academy was without a single instructor or student. By September 1813, however, it had largely recovered, chiefly because of the appointment of a new faculty, including Andrew Ellicott as professor of mathematics, which did much to restore it to a creditable basis. To logarithms, algebra, geometry, trigonometry, surveying, and conics, which Ellicott taught from the beginning of his appointment, he later added analytical trigonometry and calculus. In time he was provided with two teaching assistants, Charles Davis and Claude Crozet. Ellicott became noted for his rigorous examinations, which were claimed to have eliminated a large percentage of the candidates. After Sylvanus Thayer became superintendent in 1817, he introduced even more French engineering, including teaching techniques and texts which he had observed during his own studies in Europe.

Graduates of the Academy emerged not only as professional engineers, but also with training in the sciences which broadened their fields of endeavor. Many distinguished themselves on major surveys and related enterprises throughout the country, and during the early nineteenth century all government surveys were undertaken under their supervision. However, the number of canals and railway projects far exceeded the number of Academy graduates available, and men whose education was primarily derived from experience in the field were called upon to assume responsible positions on surveys and construction projects. Exhibiting the initiative, ingenuity, and perseverance which had characterized Americans from the beginning of settlement, young men who had served as axmen and rodmen rose in the profession to become distinguished engineers.

Before the graduates of West Point entered the field, the few full-time professional surveyors were men of general education who had made important contributions, despite their lack of an engineering training. Among the notable figures whose work, already described, placed them in the ranks of civil engineers, although without academic credentials, were Andrew Ellicott, Thomas Hutchins, Rufus Putnam, and Simeon De Witt. Others less well known included John Stevens of Hoboken, New Jersey, who had authored in 1812 an important pamphlet describing the advantages of the railroad over the canal; James Geddes, the first engineer to be engaged on the surveys of the Erie Canal in 1811; and General Andrew Porter, who had been a pupil of David Rittenhouse and later served as boundary commissioner and Surveyor-General of the State of Pennsylvania. The Honorable Benjamin Wright had been the chief engineer of the Erie Canal in 1817 and later of the Chesapeake and Delaware Canal, James River Canal, and Delaware and Hudson Canal. He became chief engineer of the Erie Railroad in 1851, when it was begun. Other distinguished figures were Canvass White, who became chief engineer of the Erie Canal in 1824,[3] and Isaac Roberdeau, who is best remembered as having been the assistant of Major Charles Pierre L'Enfant in preparing the design of the city of Washington, D.C. However, Roberdeau's important work came later. He was engaged in building canals in Pennsylvania when in 1813 he was appointed a topographical engineer in the United States Army with the rank of major. He was one of the engineers appointed to survey the boundary between Canada and the United States through the St. Lawrence and Niagara rivers and the Great Lakes. His final assignment was as chief of the Bureau of Topographical Engineering in Washington.[4]

With the professionalization of the cartographer and surveyor, there was renewed emphasis on more sophisticated instruments of greater precision. The faculty at the Military Academy incorporated into their teaching the latest types of instruments by the finest English makers. When Bernhard, Duke of Saxe-Weimar-Eisenach, visited the United States in the years 1824 and 1825, he was conducted by General Alexander Macomb of the War Office to the Topographical Office, which was then under Roberdeau's direction. He noted: "I found there several repeating circles, theodolites and telescopes, made by Troughton and Ramsden; also two transit instruments, destined for the observatory which was still to be built; an instrument by Troughton, which serves for measuring the ten-thousandth part of an English inch, and a model measure of the English yard, French metre and litre. This gentleman regretted that the old English measures and weights are retained in the United States, instead of adopting, as it has been done in the Netherlands, the new French standard, which is much better." [5]

The need for better instrumentation, particularly in national surveys and other government-related projects, had been anticipated by Hassler and other leading men of science. In addition to acquiring instruments by purchase abroad, Hassler imported skilled craftsmen from Europe to make, repair, and maintain instruments for the Survey. The first of these was William Wurdemann, a native of Bremen who had studied at Heidelberg. Upon his arrival in Washington in 1834 he became Hassler's assistant and continued to work for the Coast Survey until 1840, when he resigned to establish his own firm in Washington for the production of precision astronomical and geodetic instruments, many of them ordered for the Survey. Wurdemann was credited with numerous inventions in instrumentation, and the instruments he furnished to the Coast Survey and others were among the finest available in the United States at that time. [6]

Wurdemann was responsible for importing other skilled German instrument makers, and still others came independently. They continued the traditions of fine craftsmanship of their own country and employed and developed these techniques to create a totally new tradition of instrument making in the United States. These men were in large part responsible for establishing multiple production of precision instruments in place of individual handcrafting.

Meanwhile, other innovations in scientific instrumentation were being accomplished in America independent of the stimulus derived from government-sponsored scientific endeavors. The instruments now required could not be produced by the general maker of mathematical instruments who had furnished the simpler instruments used in the past century and earlier. Those now needed for making astronomical observations to determine latitude and longitude for boundary and territorial surveys were far more sophisticated, with scales divided by original graduation or machine graduation. Few men in America were capable of original graduation, and after the death of

David Rittenhouse only Andrew Ellicott and Henry Voigt, other than the German immigrants, might have qualified. Consequently, sextants, reflecting circles, and similar instruments remained the monopoly of England and Europe until the middle of the nineteenth century. Ramsden's circular dividing engine had initiated the age of mechanical graduation, and after other gifted English makers, such as John and Edward Troughton, John Stancliffe, and Samuel Rehee, were able to reproduce and use the circular dividing engine and train others in its use, the sextant and related instruments began to come into more general use on both sides of the Atlantic. Only after American makers could purchase or construct their own dividing engines could such instruments be produced in the United States, and even then it was difficult for them to compete in price with the imported instruments. Among the early importers of "Sextants, Quadrants with and without Tangent Screws warranted good" and "Elegant Metal and Black Ebony Sextants with Silver Arces" were the instrument makers John Jayne of Salem and Aaron Breed of Boston, as well as the New York chart maker Edmund M. Blunt. The latter's son Edmund began the construction of a dividing engine as early as 1831 but it was not until 1857 that it was sufficiently perfected to be capable of graduating instruments.[7] That the senior Blunt during the early decades of the nineteenth century did not in fact make his own instruments but imported them was slyly implied by his rival and competitor Isaac Greenwood (3rd), who also sold a variety of surveying and navigational instruments, some of which he constructed himself. Greenwood described himself as "a REAL Mathematical Instrument Maker," suggesting that his unnamed competitor was no more than an importer and dealer.[8]

Richard Patten, an instrument maker working variously in New York City, Washington, and Baltimore, advertised in his trade cards and labels that prior to 1841 he was "the only Manufacturer of Sextants and Quadrants in New York" and "All instruments in the above line made to order & warranted being divided on an Engine after the plan of Ramsden's."[9] Although the implication was that Patten produced his own instruments, many of the sextants and other instruments bearing his trade card or label in their cases were instruments produced by such English makers as Spencer, Browning & Rust. Patten may also have produced the framework and parts of sextants and imported graduated scales from English makers, since there is no evidence that he owned and used a dividing engine of his own. It is known, however, that before the end of 1845 he occasionally made use of the Troughton dividing engine owned by the U. S. Coast Survey in Washington, which had been modified by Wurdemann according to the designs of Joseph Saxton for the graduation of scales of the larger repeating theodolites that Patten produced for government use.[10]

Among the few sextants believed to have been made in the United States prior to the middle of the nineteenth century is a surviving example signed by the Philadelphia instrument maker Benjamin Stancliffe prior to 1834. It is possible, as is assumed with Patten, that Stancliffe made the major components of the instrument and added a scale engraved for him in England.[11]

The first American instrument maker known to have developed capability for mechanical graduation of instruments was William J. Young, who specialized in the production of surveying instruments at 224 South Second Street in Philadelphia. Born in Scotland, Young emigrated to Northern Liberties near Philadelphia with his family and was indentured in 1813 to serve an apprenticeship with Thomas Whitney, a prominent Philadelphia maker. Upon completion of his apprenticeship in 1820, Young apparently continued to work for Whitney as a journeyman for several years, during which period he produced instruments under his own name as well. After Whitney's death in 1823, Young established his own shop, probably acquiring some of Whitney's tools, stock, and trade at that time. His shop equipment included a dividing plate for common graduation, 18 inches in diameter, made by George Adams of London, which Whitney, who had been trained in London, may have brought with him from England.

Shortly after Young opened his own shop he undertook the construction of a circular dividing engine having a plate 24 inches in diameter which was operated by means of an endless screw and foot treadle. His engine must have been based on the description of Ramsden's machine prepared by the inventor for the Commissioners of the Board of Longitude in 1777, copies of which were deliberately distributed by the Board to encourage other instrument makers to make similar machines. In the early 1830s Young undertook a yet larger dividing engine to be used for more precise work, claiming to have introduced an important new principle, and later he modified the engine further so that it was automatically operated. Finally, some years later, he constructed a circular dividing engine having a

radius of 48 inches, which remained unequaled in the United States
for some time. Young used it for graduating the scales of engineers'
transits and of astronomical instruments. The most successful of
Young's endeavors, it was capable of dividing circular scales 44
inches in diameter.[12]

As more instrument makers became aware of the need for more
precise graduation, several American patents were issued for dividing engines of new design. Frequently the nomenclature created confusion; the machines patented may have been for linear and not
circular division. Among the American pioneers were Lemuel Hedge
of Windsor, Vermont, who was awarded a patent in 1827 for the invention of a machine for dividing scales, and Rufus Tyler of Philadelphia, who was granted a patent in 1828 for the invention of a
dividing engine. Whether Hedge or Tyler actually produced or used
their machines cannot be determined. About the same time that
Young successfully completed his second dividing engine, Edmund
Draper, another Philadelphia maker of mathematical instruments,
completed a dividing engine reputed to have great accuracy.[13]

Another graduating engine of this period was owned and used
from 1833 by the firm of D. Brown and Son, watch and clock
makers of Providence, Rhode Island. In addition to repairing timepieces, the Browns advertised: "They have a Dividing Engine for
making the most accurate graduations for Mathematical and Nautical
Instruments, and will attend to making and repairing such as are ordered. They intend to exhibit speciments of their own production
for sale. Dividing plates for all sized Engines graduated in the most
perfect manner." [14] The Brown shop subsequently developed into
the Brown & Sharpe Manufacturing Company, which has been producing machine tools ever since.

In the course of the endeavor to produce sophisticated instrumentation, an important innovation in surveying practice was
achieved with the invention of the surveyor's transit. This was not
derived from surveying experience in the field but created by an instrument maker working in his shop. The transit greatly modified
surveying practice from the early nineteenth century to modern
times. It evolved from another improvement of the surveying
compass known as the railroad compass, which was developed with
the advent of the railroad in response to the need to survey railroad
lines. Railroad surveys necessitated an instrument which would enable a surveyor or engineer to determine a number of angles in less

time and more accurately than was possible with the plain or vernier compass. The railroad compass was equipped with a vernier reading inside the compass dial. The surveyor's transit was evolved by the addition of a telescope to replace the sighting bars. The telescope enabled the horizontal and vertical angles of an objective to be measured simultaneously with reference to an assumed horizontal plane and an assumed azimuth direction. The outstanding feature of the transit which made it an improvement over the theodolite was that its telescope could be "transited," or completely revolved on its horizontal axis. Shortly after the instrument was first commercially produced in quantity in about 1830 by William J. Young, it achieved international use and has survived with virtually little change until the present.

The invention of the surveyor's transit has been variously attributed to William J. Young and to another instrument maker working in Philadelphia in the same period, Edmund Draper. Draper had produced transit instruments consisting of a plain surveying compass with a telescope. At the same time Young, who had been producing the railroad compass in great numbers, modified that instrument by the addition of a transiting telescope. A comparison of transits made by Draper and by Young reveals some basic differences. Draper's utilized an erecting telescope which was relatively weak in power. It also incorporated an arrangement for adjusting the telescope by shifting one end of the axle so that the cross hairs cut the same object as did the compass sights when reading the same magnetic bearing from the same point. His spirit levels were of a straight design. The early Young transits were designed to read with a vernier graduated to 3 minutes and were equipped with an outkeeper for tallying the number of chains measured. He incorporated a round spirit level and an inverting telescope of relatively low power.

The surveyor's transit was followed by yet another innovation which had considerable impact on the art of surveying and solved a number of the remaining problems. This was the solar compass, invented by William A. Burt of Michigan in 1836. The instrument was designed to overcome the difficulties experienced with magnetic declination in areas where iron deposits were prevalent. The solar compass was quite similar to the railroad compass except that the needle was replaced with a solar apparatus which enabled the surveyor to determine the meridian from the declination of the sun instead of by means of the magnetic needle. The instrument was first produced commercially by William J. Young and subsequently came into wide use, particularly for the surveying of government public lands.[15]

The design of the surveyor's transit and the solar compass provided greater ease or precision in use in the field and constituted a substantial improvement over the traditional English theodolite. These two instruments, which were important factors in the increasing professionalization of surveying, were the ultimate achievements of the "arte" of the instrument maker at the time that the role of the mathematical practitioner had reached its climax in America and was approaching its demise. The epoch of the handcrafted mathematical instrument was at an end; henceforth instruments would be multiple-produced by techniques made possible by mechanization.

An innovation introduced at about the same time that the circular dividing engine made its appearance in America was the linear dividing engine or ruling engine. Although rules for the trades were undoubtedly handmade by colonial American instrument makers by the process of common graduation, it was not until the beginning of the nineteenth century that commercial production of rules for all purposes became possible. Among the earliest-known rules and gauging rods produced by an American maker are several made by John Jayne of Salem. An instrument maker trained by Benjamin King, he established his own shop "At the Sign of Hadley's Quadrant" in 1805, in which he sold nautical charts and navigational instruments. He also specialized in the sale of a variety of rules and gauging rods, some of which he produced himself, possibly with a linear dividing engine imported from England.[16]

The first American maker of rules on a commercial scale was Thomas Belcher of New York City, who first advertised as a rule maker in 1823. Two years later he formed a partnership with his brother under the firm name of T. & W. Belcher & Co., and by 1829 the name had become Belcher Brothers, which continued as a firm of rule makers to modern times.[17]

Another pioneer of linear dividing was Samuel Darling of Portland, Maine, who established himself successfully as a specialist in rule making, producing rules and rods for general purposes with a linear ruling engine he constructed himself from the description in Ramsden's publication. Darling later joined the firm of Brown & Sharpe in Providence.

An instrument related to the rule was the protractor, the first of which were mass-produced in America in about 1840 by an instrument maker of Newburyport, Massachusetts, Thomas Tennent. Tennent had been trained in the workshop of William J. Young and later moved to San Francisco, where he sold nautical charts and navigational instruments, featuring instruments produced by Young. He subsequently published *Tennent's Nautical Almanac for the Pacific Coast* and the *California Tide Register, and Marine Digest.* He invented and patented a new type of artificial horizon, and continued in business until the end of the nineteenth century.[18]

Another aspect of the advancement of the practical sciences during the period of national expansion was reflected in the state of science teaching.

Navigation and surveying continued to be offered as prime subjects in evening schools throughout New England and the middle colonies, and the school masters sought to attract prospective students by every means at their disposal. M. Davis, whose school was on Maiden Lane in New York City, resorted to whimsical verse in his newspaper advertisements. The versification of the curriculum offered appears to have been successful, possibly because it provided a refreshing change in the newspaper columns. Davis invested in even more versified advertising to describe the subjects offered at his school, suggesting that

> These lively fields pure pleasure do impart
> The fruit of science, and each useful art,
> Which forms the mind, and clears the cloudy sense,
> By truth's powerful pleasing eloquence.[19]

He emphasized the teaching of "Practical Navigation by the most expeditious and approved methods, whereby the Navigator can never be at a loss upon any occasion to find the ship's place, by dead reckoning and celestial observation, and to this purpose also are taught the doctrine of the Orthographic and Stereographic Projection of the Sphere, Sphere Trigonometry, with its application to Astronomy."[20]

The New York schoolmaster M. Evans issued an advertisement in the same vein describing his evening courses in navigation held at his schoolhouse at Great-Dock Street, in which he specialized "particularly in finding the latitude by two altitudes of the sun, and the Longitude by the distance of the moon from the sun, &c., &c., as exhibited in John Hamilton Moore's Navigation."[21]

The chronometer remained too rare and costly for schoolmasters to use it in their courses on navigation until considerably later. They continued to teach the establishment of latitude by means of the "double altitudes" and the calculation of longitude according to the practices of lunar observation and dead reckoning. Meanwhile more mundane aspects of life at sea were also considered in some of the courses. In a school conducted by M. Morris "abaft the House of Messrs. Lockwood and Stoor, Merchants" on William-Street in New York City, in 1785, all the training required to enable a journal to be kept at sea was provided, to be completed in two weeks for $5.00. Morris claimed that many sailors who had attended his school returned again after making other voyages. He cited in particular a young seaman who had received instruction for only nine days and later reported that on a voyage to the West Indies he had erred no more than two miles in his reckoning upon making Sandy Hook! Morris taught from a manuscript journal based on Moore's *Navigation,* and his curriculum included "Amplitudes, Azimuths, and double Altitudes, from celestial observations taken by himself, from the Equator to the highest navigable latitudes." He taught the double Altitudes for a package price of $5.00, the construction of Mercator's Charts of any radius for $1.00, and for the price of 1 shilling he offered for sale a "Nautical Protractor" of his own construction, "which being applied to the edge of a ruler, gives the course from one place to another, without applying and damaging the chart with compasses." Morris also taught how to plan a ship's hold and provided instruction in taking observations. He enhanced his offerings by providing without cost to his students adjustment of their quadrants and silvering of the speculums and horizon glasses of the instruments as required. He also planned to publish a treatise of extracts from important works on practical navigation, but the work does not appear to have materialized.[22]

One of the surviving sources on the manner in which the subjects of navigation and surveying were taught in the eighteenth century are the manuscript copybooks used by teachers and maintained by students. In a time when texts on technical subjects were particularly rare and expensive, the practice of producing manuscript copybooks was developed, in which the teaching materials were carefully transcribed by hand from published texts with additional exercises to be completed by the student. The practice was widespread throughout the American colonies. The copybooks were generally bound blank volumes which the student usually divided into several sections, each identified with a heading, such as "Navigation," "Surveying," "Mensuration." The basic principles, presented in a most careful hand, were followed by related problems and exercises and their solutions. Frequently an entire volume would be reserved for a single subject. In many instances it is possible to trace the published text from which the guiding principles were copied. The sections on surveying in some of the surviving manuscript books clearly reflect the arrangement and content of John Love's *Geodaesia*. A unique example of considerable interest is a manuscript volume of thirty folio pages with a printed title page bearing the title *The Complete Mariner* . . . , the date 1731, and the name James Hubard, who may have been either the author or the owner.[23] Another manuscript book on navigation, prepared by Robert Patterson, first provided a series of definitions and then described plane and Mercator's sailing, middle latitude and great circle sailing, with problems and their solutions for each of the categories. It also included rules for keeping a journal of the ship's way at sea, with the record of a voyage from London to Madeira as an example.[24]

The practical sciences continued to flourish as subjects of private instruction in small communities as well as large cities. Reverend Levi Whitman of Wellfleet, Massachusetts, noted in 1794: "We have in the winter a number of private schools, by which means the greater part of the young men are taught the art of navigation." [25] A commentary on the subject occurred in the diary of Reverend William Bentley of Salem, in which he noted the death of a Captain G. West in 1802 in that community. Bentley described West as having been a "teacher of Navigation, for many years, & since he left off going to sea. The best master that I ever knew was a Mr. Smith, who had been a pensioner in the Greenwich Hospital, & who upon the death of his wife in 1791 returned to England. This Mr. Samuel Smith had great practical acquaintance with navigation, & a great fondness for mathematical studies, & had a reputation advantageous to the Town. Upon his departure Capt. G. West engaged, but he had not the same mathematical knowledge, but his success was sure with young seamen. Several persons undertook to teach navigation, but their success does not deserve to be named." [26]

The practical sciences were still not featured in the curriculum of the colleges. The most obvious reasons are that the colleges were directed primarily to young men seeking urban professions and there were not enough applicants for training in the practical sciences to make it feasible to offer the required courses. There seems to have been occasional consideration of the possibility that young gentlemen might have an interest in such subjects, but only for information, not professional training.

Although mathematics had come into prominence in the college curriculum by the end of the seventeenth century, it was not until 1726 that Harvard College established a professorship in mathematics; prior to that time the teaching of scientific and mathematical subjects had been in the hands of tutors. In 1753 President Samuel Johnson of King's College (later Columbia College) advertised the establishment of the College with a varied curriculum including surveying and navigation, but these subjects were not actually taught. They did find their way into the program of studies offered for the senior classes at the Wilmington (Delaware) Academy in 1786, however, along with Euclid, trigonometry, and astronomy. In 1788 a committee appointed to develop regulations for the Hollis Professorship of Mathematics and Natural and Experimental Sciences being established at Harvard specified the requirement for private lectures: "In Surveying in which branch there shall be a particular description of the construction and use of the various surveying instruments ———— In the application of plain Trigonometry to the mensuration of Heights and Distances, and to Navigation: with the uses of the several Instruments, and particularly, an explanation of the principles and construction of that very important instrument, Hadley's Quadrant." [27] There is no evidence, however, that such lectures were delivered either by Samuel Webber, who was appointed to the post shortly after the regulations had been formulated, or by his successors. It is difficult to reconcile this apparent lack of interest in the practical sciences with the fact that Reverend Samuel Williams, who had been appointed to the professorship in 1799, was granted leave of absence in 1786 to participate in the survey of the boundary between Massachusetts and New York with instruments borrowed from the College on an appointment made by the General Court of Massachusetts.[28]

Whereas the practical sciences were neglected in the colleges even after 1800, there was a growing awareness of their applications in community schools. A Massachusetts State Law of 1827 specified that "every city, town or district, containing five hundred families or householders . . . shall also be provided with a master . . . competent to instruct . . . geometry, surveying and algebra." [29]

In the postwar decades a change of emphasis occurred in the curricula of the secondary schools and evening schools with the introduction of astronomy and geography. Although astronomy had been the subject of popular lectures during the last quarter of the eighteenth century, its application for navigation and surveying became more and more apparent by the turn of the century, particularly in classes in the larger maritime cities. Joseph Failla of New York City, who styled himself "Professor of Mathematics and interpreter of languages" and taught navigation, offered "a new method of finding Latitude at sea by one altitude of the Sun, at any hour of the day, or by any Celestial body; the method of determining the longitude by a lunar observation; with a new correct method of ascertaining both Latitude and Longitude at once by a Celestial observation, according to the unerring laws of nature." [30]

In 1801 William Weatherill, also of New York City, featured navigation in the curriculum of his academy, and offered "Practical Astronomy" in addition to other related subjects. [31] In the same year Joseph Mallery advertised in his school on Peck-slip near the waterfront "the Elements of Geography and Astronomy and the Use of Margette's Longitude and Horary Tables, which were designed to contract, and render more general the practice of ascertaining the longitude at sea by lunar distances, among persons unversed in astronomical calculations. . . . He has been prevailed upon by a number of applicants to open, at this early season an Evening School for Seamen, and others, who wish to become proficient in nautical science." [32]

An important figure in science teaching at the beginning of the nineteenth century was George Baron, who from 1803 maintained an academy on Pine Street in New York City specifically for the training of seamen. He published tables of latitude and longitude for public sale. In 1804 he became editor-in-chief of the first American mathematical quarterly journal, *The Mathematical Correspondent*, of which only eight issues appeared. In the second issue he reprinted his lecture refuting Bowditch's *New American Practical Navigator* and also published the lecture separately. While continuing his navigational training program, Baron became involved in various other enterprises from time to time. Not the least of these was his chart for readily determining simple interest of any sum up to one million, copyrighted in 1811.[33]

Among the most competent and best-known science teachers in New England at the turn of the nineteenth century was Osgood Carleton of Nottingham-West, New Hampshire. After a career at sea, he settled in Boston. He had served in the French and Indian Wars and later as an officer in the Continental Army during the Revolution. In 1792 he produced an almanac which was published in Boston, and in the same year conducted a school at 11 Market Row in that city for teaching navigation and related subjects, with the occasional assistance of a science teacher named Robert Thomas. Carleton availed himself of every opportunity to advance his endeavors, publishing a number of maps and charts and several books on arithmetic and navigation. He shared the premises on Market Row with a maker of mathematical instruments, Charles Newell, who advertised on his own trade card "Navigation with the Lunar Observation, Taught at the above place by OSGOOD CARLETON." [34]

Despite the promise of the advertisements, evening schools were not always competent to provide the training necessary in navigation. According to one schoolmaster, "there are many who have thrown their money away to little or no purpose, by going to School to some Masters (of which art there are too many) that have only got a Smattering on the Theory, and a few Terms of Art by Rote, which enable them to talk in such a manner as to deceive those that go to learn of them." [35]

As the nineteenth century moved forward and the country moved westward, teachers followed the pioneers into the new lands and established in the new territories schools which included scientific curricula. One such teacher was Jeremiah Moriarity, who offered a mixed fare in Kentucky in 1789, advertising that in addition to dancing he "Teaches geography and the use of the globes, having a pair on a new construction with Captain Cook's discoveries." [36]

The new interest in geography and astronomy resulted in the production of a number of texts for use in school curricula. Many of these works emphasized the use of globes. The first American work on geography was *Geography Made Easy*, written by Jedediah Morse, a Congregational minister of Cambridge, Massachusetts.[37] It was published in 1784, the year after the author's graduation from Yale College, and he followed it by other geography texts and gazetteers which became immediately popular.[38] Two more elaborate works, published within the next two decades, were *The American Geography* and *The American Universal Geography*.[39] To the third edition of *The American Geography*, published in 1796, Morse added a substantial section describing the use of the globes in the study of geography.[40]

Morse's works were responsible for making geography part of the curriculum in the public schools and for supplementing the teaching texts with globes and atlases for detailed study. Morse's presentation, however, achieved even more. *The American Geography* projected the concept of "manifest destiny" for the emerging nation. In a section of his work concerned with the trans-Allegheny region and the western lands, Morse suggested that the seat of empire was moving continuously westward, eventually to come to rest in America, where conditions for the arts and sciences were eminently suitable. He went on to state that an American genius with the assistance of all the improvements of ages past "is to be exerted in humanizing mankind—in expanding and enriching their minds . . . with philosophical knowledge." [41]

Among Morse's first rivals in the production of geography texts were William Guthrie, whose *A New System of Modern Geography* included a section on astronomy prepared by David Rittenhouse,[42] and Nathaniel Dwight, who published in 1795 a geography text prepared in a question-and-answer form.[43] Following Morse's example, John Payne in 1798 produced a geography of the world utilizing globes.[44] Robert Davidson's *A Tour Round the World*, published in 1803, presented the novelty of a text written totally in verse.[45]

By 1815 geography had become a requirement for entrance to Harvard College, and a few years later it was made part of the public school curriculum in Massachusetts.

The growing popularity of the globe as a teaching device, and the high cost of imported globes, resulted in attempts to produce globes commercially in the United States. Occasional examples had been made by skilled jacks-of-all-trades, such as one produced in about 1760 by Samuel Lane of Stratham, Massachusetts, for his own use in surveying, but commercial production presented challenges that were difficult to meet. Lane was a shoemaker and tanner and worked also as a local surveyor. To assist him in his survey work, he made a globe turned from a solid wooden sphere 7 inches in diameter. He painted the surface white and cut the degree marks and land outlines into the wood, adding names in script. He then pinned the globe into an oak hoop which in turn he fitted into an opening made for it in the center of a pine table assembled in the form of a milking stool. Lane's work as a surveyor took him beyond the area in which he lived. One of the other towns he surveyed was Bow, Massachusetts. In 1751 he was in charge of an expedition to explore the Pemigewasset River for the purpose of establishing settlements in the region.[46] His homemade globe was a unique achievement, comparable to the early attempts of the first American commercial maker, James Wilson.

Wilson was a farmer in Francestown, New Hampshire, who moved to Bradford, Vermont, where he purchased his own farm in 1796. In the same year while on a visit to a friend at Dartmouth College in neighboring Hanover, New Hampshire, he was intrigued by a pair of globes in one of the buildings at the college. Although Dartmouth was a young institution, by 1774, five years after its founding, it had acquired a pair of 18-inch terrestrial and celestial globes. It also possessed a second pair of globes, made by John Senex, which were 16 inches in diameter, and a third pair of globes by an unknown maker.[47] It is not known which of the three pairs provided Wilson with his inspiration, but he decided to duplicate them and set to work at once after his return home. He turned two solid spheres of wood on a wood-turning lathe on his farm, covered the globes with paper glued to the surface, and finished them off by inscribing the meridian lines and the outlines of the continents in ink by hand. As he proceeded to produce other examples, he refined the process: the wooden balls were coated with several layers of paper; the coating was separated by cutting into two hemispheres; the wooden cores were removed to be used again; and the paper shells were pasted together to make globes of lighter weight. Wilson's meager knowledge of geography and astronomy hindered his project considerably, and he came to the conclusion that he needed an encyclopedia. Having no ready funds, he sold livestock until he had accumulated the price of a set of the third edition of the *Encyclopaedia Britannica*, $130.00, and purchased the work from a bookdealer in Ryegate, Vermont.[48] Reinforced with this fount of knowledge, Wilson next sought to master the technique of copperplate engraving. No one in his region could provide the training he needed, and he journeyed on foot to Boston and then to Newburyport to seek instruction. He was unable to pay the costs, and finally he walked from his home in Bradford to New Haven, Connecticut, to see Amos Doolittle, the engraver of the two maps that had been published as part of Jedediah Morse's *Geography Made Easy*. Doolittle proved amenable to Wilson's request and taught him the art of engraving on copper. Wilson improved his technique with self-instruction and practice and made his own tools. Having learned the trade of blacksmith earlier in life, he was able to make all the tools the work required, including lathes and presses. He not only did his own printing but also produced his own inks, glues, and varnishes and designed his own maps. Tradition relates that he spent 300 days on the production of his first large copper plate. Unable to determine the true proportion of meridians upon a globular surface, he walked to Charlestown, Massachusetts, to consult with Jedediah Morse, who helped him solve the problem.

It is not known with certainty when Wilson first sold globes commercially, but it is a matter of record that he sold two of his globes in January 1810 and that from that time forward his production and sales increased rapidly. The price he realized for his globes in that period was $50.00 a pair. He used the blacksmith shop on his farm premises as a manufactory, and there he also turned the wooden frame supports for the globes, generally in ash, on his lathe and made the brass quadrants and even the pine boxes in which his globes were packed. Wilson also ventured occasionally into such related endeavors as the compilation and printing of charts, such as a "Chronology Delineated to Illustrate the History of Monarchial Revolutions," which he co-produced with Isaac Eddy of Weathersfield, Massachusetts, in 1813.

Wilson's enterprise was sufficiently successful to enable him to establish a manufactory at 110 Washington Street in Albany, New York, in about 1815. He worked in partnership with his sons, Samuel and John Wilson, and later a third son, David, joined them for a brief period. Despite the successful development of the Albany manufactory, Wilson maintained his home at Bradford. He continued to direct the business until about 1826, at which time his future son-in-law, Cyrus Lancaster, became manager. Lancaster was a native of Acworth, New Hampshire, and had been a teacher at Bradford Academy and later a student at Dartmouth College. In 1833 Samuel and John Wilson died, and David left the firm to seek other endeavors, leaving Lancaster as the sole manager. Lancaster subsequently married Samuel Wilson's widow and continued the business independently until the Civil War.[49]

The products of the firm were promoted throughout the country, and in 1827 the Congress was invited to see a pair of Wilson globes displayed in Washington at "the United States Library." [50] As a supplement to the globes, the Wilson firm also published and sold a publication about them which had been prepared by Thomas Keith, an accountant at the British Museum. The original treatise was later revised and supplemented by Robert Adrain, a teacher of mathematics at Rutgers College, and published in a new edition by Wilson's New York agent.[51]

Wilson's globes were sold at prices substantially below those of globes imported from England and had other advantages as well. On the Wilson terrestrial globes the several states and territories of the United States were more accurately delineated than they were on the products of the most popular English makers, and the Wilson celestial globes utilized the most recent astronomical tables and were reduced in accordance with the precession of the equinoxes of that time. Even into advanced age, Wilson continued to be preoccupied with the development of science teaching devices. At the age of eighty-three he constructed a crank-operated planetarium which demonstrated, in addition to the motions of the heavenly bodies, the seasons and the precession of the equinoxes. He personally engraved and printed the plates for the signs of the zodiac and made all the parts of the apparatus himself.[52] In addition to a planetarium he made for his own use, he produced others for Bradford Academy and Thetford Academy.

One of Wilson's contemporaries and competitors was William B. Annin of Boston, an engraver trained under Abel Bowen, for whom he began to work in 1810. In partnership with George G. Smith, Annin produced a map of Boston in 1823 and 1824, as well as other engravings. In 1826 he was awarded a patent for his process for making "artificial globes," which appears to have been a method of printing paper gores or map sections, which were assembled on the globe core after printing. Annin's globes were sold by the Boston bookseller Joseph Loring under the latter's name and achieved great popularity in their time. In 1838 Loring was awarded a silver medal by the American Institute of the City of New York for the best specimens of terrestrial and celestial globes, which were in fact engraved for him by Annin. Annin also produced some of the engravings for Morse's work on geography, and he drew and engraved the gores for globes manufactured by Gilman Joslin of Boston. Joslin produced these teaching aids from 1837, and they continued to carry the legend "Drawn and engraved by W. B. Annin" long after Annin's death.[53]

Another American globe maker of the same period was George Pocock, who in 1830 proposed to produce a collapsible globe which was inflatable by means of an air pump and could be illuminated from within with a lamp, the heat of which would cause the globe to revolve.[54] A terrestrial globe made in the form of a paper balloon and inscribed "Ebe [nezer?] Pocock, delt. W. Day lithog. Bristol," in the collection of the Library of Congress, is similar to the type proposed by George Pocock; it depicts an expedition to Alaska made between 1825 and 1828.

As the use of globes became an accepted practice in science teaching, other globe makers sought to develop new types for commercial distribution. Unique examples produced by amateurs were often prototypes intended for commercial development but few were successful. Globes were made in some quantity by about 1830 by David Clark Murdock, a cabinet maker of West Boylston, Massachusetts. At first he produced them in his own cabinet-making shop, using cores of solid wooden spheres turned on a lathe which he covered with engraved paper gores, incorporating a paper horizon ring and mounted with a brass meridian circle on a frame support turned in fine woods. His second son Albert later joined him in a partnership to produce globes, which were thereafter marked "D. C. and A. Murdock." [55]

A new American maker who entered the scene in the 1840s was Gilbert Vale of New York City. He first came to public notice as a teacher of navigation, then as publisher of a periodical called *The Beacon*, which was distributed to a New York waterfront clientele. In about 1845 Vale began to advertise himself as a manufacturer of a special type of globe for which he had obtained a patent in 1843. The device combined a terrestrial and celestial globe in one to "form an exact model of nature as it appears to the inhabitants of the earth." By the middle of the nineteenth century other manufacturers in New England and New York were producing globes commercially for schoolroom use to meet the increasing demand.[56]

Paralleling the interest in geography was a preoccupation with astronomical studies, which had received considerable impetus with the publicity attending the orreries produced by David Rittenhouse just before the War for Independence. The orrery became practically mandatory for classroom teaching in the colleges of the late eighteenth and early nineteenth centuries, but the examples that could be obtained were generally English instruments imported at substantial cost. Although American makers attempted to produce such instruments, it was some time before they were undertaken on a commercial scale. When Pere Fobes, a Congregationalist minister, assembled instruments to be used for science teaching at Providence College (now Brown University), he loaned some items from his personal collection which had been constructed to his order by American makers. Among these were two instruments produced between 1790 and 1800—"a Platonic globe, Lunarium, solar system to shew the nodes & orbits of &c.," by an unknown American craftsman, and "a Brass Orrery, adjusted to an armillary sphere, constructed on a new & extensive plan, containing a system of mechanical astronomy," which had been constructed for the most part by Caleb Leach, a clockmaker of Plymouth, Massachusetts, with minor additional work by Asa Hall, a Boston clockmaker.[57]

One of the most notable efforts was the achievement of a Boston clockmaker, Joseph Pope, who worked on an orrery from 1776 to 1787 before completing it. He had received early training as a clockmaker and had traveled in Europe before settling in Boston. He devoted his leisure time to studies of mathematics and navigation with his brother, Robert Pope, and in the course of these studies he became fascinated with the concept of the mechanical universe demonstrated in the orrery. For a time he tried his hand at teaching the sciences, first at a writing school in Boston's South End and later at Fore Street, and after he began to work full time as a clockmaker, he continued teaching on a sporadic basis. Finally, in 1785 the Boston selectmen granted Pope permission to establish his own school in the South End, where he specialized in a science-related curriculum.[58] Throughout this period he continued construction of the great orrery which he intended should be acquired by Harvard College. It was an elaborate structure based on the design of the grand orreries produced by the great English makers of the period, measuring 6½ feet in diameter and 6½ feet in height. It was covered with a glass dome with the signs of the zodiac painted on the glass side panels, and was supported on a hexagonal frame of mahogany in the Chippendale style. Twelve figures adorned its corners; these were said to have been carved in wood by Simeon Skillin and cast in bronze by Paul Revere. The subjects were Franklin, James Bowdoin, and Sir Isaac Newton, each repeated four times.[59]

In 1787, shortly after the instrument was completed, Pope's house caught on fire, and Governor Bowdoin sent a cart with six men to rescue the orrery, which was then kept in the Governor's mansion for a time. An effort made by citizens of Boston to purchase it for Harvard by private subscription failed, and in 1788 an act was passed by the General Court of Massachusetts to grant a lottery for the purpose. When the lottery took place in March 1789, Pope received remuneration in the amount of 450 pounds and 3 shillings for the instrument. With the possible exception of Rittenhouse's orreries, Pope's instrument was the most elaborate piece of scientific apparatus constructed in America up to that time, and it received considerable attention from the public in the decades that followed its acquisition by the College.[60]

The rising public interest in astronomy was further stimulated by popular lectures with demonstrations of science equipment. Notable among the lecturers was Bartholomew Burges of Boston, a man with considerable maritime experience and knowledge of the practical sciences. He advertised in 1789 that he would present lectures on astronomy at Boston, and in the same year he published a short treatise on the solar system which was sold with a chart of "The Solar System Displayed" which had been engraved for him by John Norman, and which he dedicated jointly to the American Academy of Arts and Sciences and the "Philosophical Society of Pennsylvania."[61] The work, an impressive addition to American literature in the field, included not only an account of the solar system and of comets in general, but a special study of the comet of 1532 which was expected to reappear on April 27, 1789. Burges admitted that he had drawn freely from existing published works, including those of Alexandre Gui Pingré, William Whiston, and James Ferguson. In a closing note he advised that, in the section on the planets, "the words are partly the learned Ferguson's blended with some of my own. The Quotations I meant to have mark'd with Commas, but it having escap'd my memory, and unwilling anything that had the complexion of Plagiary should be submitted to the perusal of the Publick, I resolved on making this N.B."[62]

Early in 1789 Burges advertised in the local press that: "An Astronomical Apparatus by Bartholomew Burges, Will be exhibited this Evening, at Mr. Eliphalet Newall's Hall, in Charlestown. Two large Planispheres and Gilded Projectiles, displaying the Celestial Bodies, suspending in their due Proportion, and their Orbits; and their relative and mean Distances from the Sun, with their Moons or

Satellites. Likewise, the Path of the expected Comet through our System, will be shown, by a Wire Orbit; and an Artificial Comet circumvolving the Sun, together with the Angles the Planetary Orbits make with the Ecliptic, and their Eccentricities, &c. by means of Wire Hoops. The Diurnal and Apparent Motions of the Heavenly Bodies, will be shewn likewise, and the Heliocentric Positions of them at the said time; and Lessons given gratis to the Company, in order to show them the Use of Terrestrial Globes." [63]

Burges's apparatus does not appear to have become a subject of discussion among his contemporaries in the press or in published works, and nothing more is presently known about the orrery.[64] In the following year Burges published a volume of letters describing his sea voyages to Indostan [Hindustan], presumably in the employ of the East India Company.[65] Burges included in his solar system treatise the announcement: "The Author of the foregoing Pages is now preparing for the Press, an entire new Work, to be entitled, The American Seaman's Daily Assistant, Which, when compleated, will be submitted to the Examination of Men of known Abilities, for their Approbation—and if approved of as a Work of public Utility, the Patronage of the Publick will be solicited." [66] Whether Burges failed to complete the work, or whether it did not achieve the required approval when completed, cannot be determined, but there is no evidence that it ever reached publication. The last record of Burges is that he sailed with Captain Jonathan Buckford from Trinidad for Boston on March 8, 1807, in the brig *Hector* and was lost at sea.[67]

There is speculation as to whether the astronomical apparatus advertised by Burges may be identified with an unusual instrument having many similar features, which has survived. This is a portable planetary machine designed for public lectures or classroom teaching, incorporating a hand-operated planetary mechanism which is most unusual because it requires neither clockwork nor a hand crank, one of which is customarily found in such devices. The planetary attachment must be revolved by hand over the surface of an ecliptic table which is marked along its outer edge with angular divisions to 360 degrees, as well as with the 365 days and the 12 months of the year. Painted within this outer ring are the twelve signs of the zodiac rendered in a metallic paint in forms reminiscent of the woodcuts of these signs printed in early almanacs. The planetary mechanism is independently constructed and is fitted to the table surface by means of a peg which projects through a slot in the table so that the mechanism can be pinned into place. The mechanism consists of turned wooden and gilded spheres, or "Gilded Projectiles," representing the sun, the moon, and the planets Earth, Mercury, and Venus. Paintings of the sun, the moon, and a comet decorate the upper panel of the mechanism, the top and bottom plates of which are held together by means of wooden posts having threaded wooden nuts. The entire superstructure, when made to travel by hand along an ecliptic plane represented on the table surface, drives the mechanism by means of friction to make the planets revolve in their orbits. A scale for polar precession, which may be set by hand, is provided. An unusual feature is the use of inverseratio gearing; power is applied to the shaft of slowest speed, the earth's annual revolution, and all the other axes move at relatively higher speeds.[68]

This unusual apparatus represents not only an ingenious mechanism for science teaching, but also a superlative example of the replacement of metal with wood in the construction of scientific instrumentation. The instrument is entirely portable: the geared carriage can be separated by the removal of a single peg; the three legs supporting the table are designed to slide off for dismantling; and the table top is hinged to fold at the center. The woods used include common pine for the table top and legs, mahogany for the gears and plates, and pine and native woods for other parts. The supports for the turned wooden spheres, or "Wire Orbits," and some of the other parts are made of brass, and a few of the gears are cast in pewter.

Several other orreries designed for use in schools were produced in the United States at the end of the eighteenth and during the first quarter of the nineteenth century. Owen Biddle made a simple version of an orrery, or planetarium, and a much more elaborate example was produced by Aaron Willard, Jr., on order from the West Chester Academy at Chester, Pennsylvania, in 1821. This was a portable instrument, finely cased, and having two sets of accessories—a tellurion, or terrestrial attachment, and a celestial accessory—which could be interchanged at will.[69]

Produced at the same time as Willard's instrument, which appears to have been the only one of this type that he made, was a similar machine invented by a crippled Vermont farmer named Theodore Newell. Deprived of the use of his lower limbs by an accident,

Newell developed an interest in astronomy to pass the time and as a result of his studies constructed a simple planetarium for his own amusement. Encouraged by the interest shown by others in his device, he developed a more elaborate mechanical planetary machine, which, with the assistance of friends, he was able to bring to the attention of educators and others, including the New York State Legislature. The Assembly appointed a committee to investigate the merits of the invention with the possibility that it might be acquired for use in the State's institutions of learning. In 1819 the committee submitted a favorable report and the Assembly resolved that the trustees of the State Library "may purchase of Theodore Newell, one of his newly invented astronomical machines, and may from time to time make advances to him to procure the mechanical work to be done, on his giving good security for its completion, and for depositing the same in the library room in the capitol; and the legislature will appropriate a sum not exceeding one thousand dollars to meet the expense." [70] An act of the Assembly passed on January 14, 1820, made available the funds specified, but there is no evidence that Newell went into commercial production or that such an instrument was in fact acquired. [71]

Five years later Newell took his improved planetary machine to Middletown, Connecticut, with the intention of generating financial support to enable it to be produced commercially. Several gentlemen of Middletown and Hartford formed an association to support the venture, and since Newell's disability made it impossible for him to produce the instrument in quantity, a mechanician was employed for the purpose. He worked "under the immediate superintendence of two gentlemen attached to the Military Academy." When the project was well under way, the discovery was made that Newell had erred grossly in his calculations because of faulty knowledge of astronomy and mechanics and that the mechanism as designed incorporated serious errors. It had to be totally redesigned, resulting in an even more elaborate mechanism and one more expensive to produce. Whether in fact the Newell machine was actually manufactured is not known, but it came to the attention of Professor Benjamin Silliman at Yale, who described it in considerable detail and with great enthusiasm in his *American Journal of Science and Arts*. [72]

XVIII

☆ ☆ ☆ ☆ ☆ ☆ ☆ ☆ ☆ ☆ ☆ ☆ ☆

THE DIGNITY

OF

INDEPENDENCE

☆ ☆

> The time is now come, when the citizens of America should act entirely for themselves; when they should forever cease to depend on the caprices of foreigners. . . . The dignity of independence and the glory of usefulness should rouse the love of science from lethargic dispositions in America.
>
> Thomas Ewell, *Plain Discourses on the Laws or Properties of Matter* . . . (1806)

FORMALIZED EDUCATION in the sciences and technical training had become recognized needs at the time that interest in adult education was beginning to assert itself. The demand was partly met by popular lectures, and these, combining education and entertainment, became more and more prevalent in the larger communities. Presentations ranged from occasional single lectures to full series, and lecturers varied from teachers of specific subjects to popularizers who made lecturing their occupation. Relatively early examples included presentations by visiting foreigners.

Among the first of the latter was an Italian named Signor Falconi who became well known in New York City and whose series of popular lectures on natural philosophy was repeated over a period of more than a decade. He made his American debut in 1787 in Corre's Assembly Room, supplementing his lecture with a demonstration of experiments. In 1795 he performed again in the same room, with a repertoire that included numerous tricks of parlor magic in addition to the sciences. His last appearance was in 1797 in the John Street Theatre, where it was reported that his performance "seemed to have made primitive ideas of electricity beautiful and realistic." [1] In 1807–1808 a Monsieur Godon from France lectured on mineralogy in Boston.

Among the most popular of American lecturers was John Griscom, a New Jersey chemistry teacher who presented a series of publicly subscribed lectures in New York City in 1800. So successful were his first ventures that he rented part of the Friends' graveyard on Liberty Street and constructed there a brick building to serve as a lecture hall. He later moved to the Old Alms House, donated for his use by the New York City authorities, where he shared space with John Scudder's Museum, formerly the American Museum of Gardiner Baker. Griscom's lectures during 1807 and 1808 were attended by "upwards of one hundred persons, of both sexes, and have obtained a distinguished degree of approbation," according to the *Medical Repository*. [2] Members of his audiences volunteered to inhale nitrous oxide, occasions which were reported in the press with considerable interest. Griscom's lecture subjects ranged from chemistry and natural philosophy to astronomy, and the popularity of his presentations continued well into the second quarter of the nineteenth century. [3] Lecture series were presented in 1809 by Dr. John Gorham, a Harvard graduate just returned from study in Europe, whose most frequent topic was chemistry. The enthusiastic attendance at lectures on botany and natural history presented by the physician and Harvard professor Benjamin Waterhouse and the American physician and botanist Jacob Bigelow as well as by Joseph Correa de Serra, the Portuguese minister to the United States, testified to the avid public interest in scientific subjects.

Support of the popular lecturer came also from academic centers. Among the first to provide such support was Benjamin Silliman of Yale. Silliman himself enjoyed a most successful career as a lecturer on new fields and opportunities in the sciences, and he inspired others to undertake this method of educating the public. Amos Eaton was one of those induced by Silliman to leave the academic centers and lecture in local communities. Others followed Eaton's successful example, among the most notable being Josiah Holbrook, a country schoolteacher of Derby, Connecticut, who became interested in educational reform. Holbrook took advantage of the public curiosity about the sciences and the trend towards self-improvement. He established the first lyceum group in Millbury, Massachusetts, in 1826 and went on to organize the National American Lyceum, or Society for the Improvement of Schools and Diffusion of Useful Knowledge, in 1828. He became identified with the lyceum movement and concentrated with considerable success upon the practical aspects of teaching mathematics and the sciences. In 1829 his program for the American Lyceum described the teaching tools he had developed for instruction in geometry, arithmetic, chemistry, astronomy, geology, and natural philosophy. These materials included sheets of diagrams and geometrical cards for geometry; an orrery, a tidal dial, and an eclipsarium for astronomy; levers, pulleys, wedges, screws, for natural philosophy; and an assortment of scientific glassware for his courses in chemistry. He brought a new method and a new look to science teaching, which helped to revolutionize the field during the remainder of the century.[4]

The makers of almanacs were also frequently teachers and occasionally the authors of science textbooks. William Waring, a teacher of mathematics at the Friends' public school on Pear Street in Philadelphia, who calculated ephemerides for *Poor Will's Almanack*, published by Joseph Crukshank from 1787 to at least 1792, was the author of a journal designed for the use of seamen for making lunar observations for determining the longitude, which was published in 1791. Several years later he was co-author, with John Todd, Zachariah Jess, and Jeremiah Paul, of *The American Tutor's Assistant*. Waring was elected to membership in the American Philosophical Society in 1793, and several of his papers on the construction of mills were presented before the Society.[5]

Zachariah Jess, in addition to the work he co-authored, was independently the author of a popular and important textbook on surveying [6] and of texts on mathematics. His work on surveying was widely used until it was replaced to some degree by another by John Gunmere, a well-known schoolmaster of Burlington, New Jersey. Gunmere had established a classical academy which was unrivaled in its day. His pupils were chiefly the sons of leading local citizens and of wealthy planters from the West Indies, and the academy achieved distinction particularly for the public lectures delivered there from time to time on natural philosophy, chemistry, and other scientific subjects. A native of Willow Grove, Pennsylvania, Gunmere had studied at West Town with the mathematician Enoch Lewis, and had taught at various institutions before establishing his own academy in 1814. He subsequently became president of Haverford College and was a member of the American Philosophical Society and the Academy of Natural Sciences at Philadelphia. His treatise on surveying was published in 1814 and was reprinted in fourteen editions before the end of the nineteenth century.[7] The only popular surveying texts available at the time that Gunmere's appeared were the treatises by Robert Gibson and Zachariah Jess, and in his work Gunmere sought to correct the specific deficiencies in each of the others.[8] He considered that Gibson's work, although preferable to the text by Jess, did not provide a sufficient number of examples for classroom use, and that Jess's work suffered from want of adequate statement of the principles of the science of surveying. Gunmere later published a popular text on astronomy, which was widely used in the schools.[9]

Among other important works on the practical sciences that made their appearance soon after the beginning of the nineteenth century was *Essays, Mathematical and Physical* by Jared Mansfield, who subsequently achieved distinction in the survey of the western lands. The work was a compilation of essays on such varied subjects as the negative quantities in algebra, goniometrical properties, nautical astronomy, longitude, orbicular motion, fluxionary analysis, the theory of gunnery, and the theory of the moon. It was the first work of original mathematical research to be published in America and had considerable impact. The second edition, which appeared in 1802 and to which Mansfield had added an appendix of "New Tables, for computing the latitude and longitude at sea by means of double altitudes and lunar distances," attracted the attention of Thomas Jefferson during his presidency.[10] In part because of this work, Jefferson appointed Mansfield Surveyor-General of the Northwest Territory "for the purpose of determining astronomically certain lines of the lands north-west of the Ohio River and above the latitude, and of the principal meridians on which the surveys were thereafter to proceed, and in fact, have ever since proceeded." Jefferson provided for the purchase of the required astronomical instruments from a contingency fund, and they were used to furnish what became the earliest observatory erected west of the Allegheny Mountains. Mansfield was the first to run the meridian lines on which the system of public land surveys was based. In 1812 he was appointed to the chair of natural and experimental philosophy at West Point.[11]

Another text worthy of mention is one on surveying and navigation by Jeremiah Day, a Yale graduate who taught mathematics and natural philosophy at Yale College prior to 1801. Several works on mathematics, including algebra, mensuration of surfaces and solids, and plane trigonometry, preceded his book on surveying and navigation, which was published in 1817. The latter was elementary in scope and presentation but extremely practical for teaching novices.[12]

Meanwhile, a drastic change in American education was in process. The War for Independence had brought the declining grammar-school system almost to a total halt. Many of the schools were suspended and did not reopen after the war. Those that continued began to change, and by the beginning of the nineteenth century the entire school system in the United States was undergoing major reform. Less emphasis was given to college entrance requirements and more to practical subjects such as the various branches of the mathematics and others that would be helpful in daily life. The growth of numerous new industries gave rise to a class of merchants and tradesmen that formed a new middle class and achieved social control, effectively changing community life. The rapid growth in population resulted in the utilization of innovative ideas that effectively overthrew the established traditions of education. With the countless needs and problems facing the state governments at the conclusion of the war, primary and secondary education received less attention than was their due. The rapid disintegration of the grammar-school system left to the academies the responsibility for providing training in service and leadership which were so desperately required.

Several other influences had their impact on education. After the War of 1812, an even greater effort was made to shake off once and for always the remaining ties with the motherland. Americans began to think of their country as a totally new and separate entity, and a clear break was made with borrowed traditions, which affected the educational system as well as all other aspects of American life. The movement westward and the establishment of new communities with schools in each were important in the adoption of a revised system of education. The increasing overpopulation of the eastern coast, the development of new industries, and the adoption of a tariff system to protect these were other factors that signalized the passing of leadership from the conservative aristocratic element of society to the progressive middle class.

Thomas Jefferson had repeatedly emphasized the advantages to be gained by the application of science for the achievement of national goals, urging a deliberate and practical approach. Others joined him in emphasizing the advantages to be gained from knowledge of the natural world and the use of its resources. "Young Gentlemen" were urged, by an anonymous writer in 1790 in "A Charge which ought to be delivered to the Graduates of the Arts, in all the Colleges in the United States," not to "neglect yourself in arithmetic. It is the *ready change* of human life, and you cannot advance a step in any useful or profitable employment without it. ——— Make yourself as early as possible familiar with the works of nature, as they appear to us on our globe. You are not to live in the sun, nor moon, nor to ride upon the tail of a comet, and it will be of infinitely more consequence to you to know the names and uses of vegetable, animal, and mineral productions of your country, than to know the distances and revolutions of all the planets in the solar system. ———
A *few* astronomers are enough for an age, but *every* man should know the history of the substances from which his food — his clothing — his dwelling — his remedies in sickness — and his pleasures in health, are derived." [13]

One of the greatest achievements in this period of change was the establishment of the high school as a means of providing practical education to the greatest possible number of young people and simultaneously creating a controlled curriculum. The first American high school was conceived and initiated by citizens of Boston in 1821 to meet the needs of young Americans emerging chiefly from the ranks of merchants, artisans, and tradesmen. Within the next few decades the new form of educational institution spread rapidly.[14]

While high schools were coming into being and the lyceum movement was responding to the popular desire for self-improvement, regional industrial demands contributed to the changing direction and emphasis of the American educational system. An urgent need for specialized schools to train young people for careers in new industries led to the founding of technical schools. Such schools were established as independent foundations, not controlled by local or federal government.[15]

The first such endowed technical school was Rensselaer Polytechnic Institute, established at Troy, New York, by Stephen Van Rensselaer in 1824. It was opened to students in the following year with two courses, one in the natural sciences and the other in civil engineering, each of four years' duration. The head of the new school was Amos Eaton, already mentioned as a popular lecturer. Eaton was a failed lawyer of Catskill, New York, who found a new career in education. He had taught chemistry and geology at his alma mater, Williams College, and at Castleton Academy before becoming a lecturer. He wandered through Massachusetts and other New England states between 1817 and 1824, presenting lectures featuring simple homemade apparatus to demonstrate the sciences. His lectures were enthusiastically received. Eaton was the first to bring students out into the open to study nature in the field, and in due course others followed his example. He left his profitable lecture circuit to undertake land surveys for Stephen Van Rensselaer for several years prior to assuming leadership of the new Institute.[16]

One of Eaton's first achievements at the Institute was the installation of laboratories for use by the students to pursue experiments, another major innovation in science teaching. By this means the students took the place of the teacher and learned as they presented demonstrations and experimental lectures to their fellow students. Eaton's form of teaching, which combined the laboratory, the seminar, and the project, was eminently successful in training teachers, who went out from the Institute to distinguished careers in scientific investigation and science teaching. During the seventeen years that Eaton spent at Rensselaer, the school rose to a level of major importance in the field of technical education and served as an example for others. During the formative years, the largest number of students enrolled in a single year was eighteen. Many of these went into teaching but after the Institute added an engineering course in 1835, a greater number entered technical employment.

Other technical schools were established, sometimes as part of existing colleges or as separate schools in universities, and eventually as separate entities modeled on Rensselaer as a prototype. One of these was the Franklin Institute which was founded at Philadelphia in 1824.[17] The Mechanics Institute at Philadelphia was already well established, but its enrollment was limited specifically to apprentices of the trades. To provide facilities for mechanical training which would be made available to anyone became the mission of Samuel Vaughan Merrick, and he enlisted the assistance of Dr. William H. Keating, professor of chemistry at the University of Pennsylvania. At a meeting held in the hall of the American Philosophical Society in 1823, they obtained the support of a group of prominent citizens, and the following year they founded "The Franklin Institute of the State of Pennsylvania for the Promotion of the Mechanic Arts," which was chartered by the state legislature. Classes were begun in the spring of 1824 in the old Academy building, with offerings in mineralogy, chemistry, natural philosophy, mechanics, architecture, machine design, and mathematics. Among the speakers in the first series of lectures were such notables as Professor Robert Patterson and the electrician and inventor Robert Hare.[18]

The demand for technical education was so great that the pioneering technical schools could not meet it, and evening schools continued to flourish for some time to come. In 1820 William Elliott in the nation's capitol advertised that "at the White House north of the Capitol . . . his Evening School for teaching Mathematics" would reopen on the first Monday in November and continue until the first Monday in May, presenting a curriculum which included algebra and geometry "with their application to Surveying, Navigation, Mensuration, Astronomy, &c.," at a tuition cost of $15.00 per quarter.[19]

The advances made in education were accompanied by increasing involvement in educational pursuits of all types at all levels. The important influence of the American Philosophical Society on American intellectual life and the recognition it received from English and European intellectuals inspired the formation of a rival organization, the American Academy of Arts and Sciences, founded in Boston by John Adams in 1780. Its charter defined its aims to be: "To promote and encourage the knowledge of the antiquities of America and of the natural history of the country, and to determine the uses to which the various natural productions of the country may be applied; to promote and encourage medical discoveries, mathematical disquisitions, philosophical inquiries and experiments; astronomical, meteorological and geographical observations, and improvements in agriculture, arts, manufactures and commerce, and in fine, to cultivate every art and science which may tend to advance the interest, honor, dignity and happiness of a free, independent, and virtuous people." [20] The interest expressed by French academicians and men of science in the American Philosophical Society led to the appointment of a number of distinguished foreign scientists as honorary members of the new Academy during its early years.[21]

The Academy was launched with an impressive initial project. In cooperation with Harvard College it sponsored an expedition to Isleboro, Maine, to make observations of the solar eclipse which occurred on October 27, 1780. Although circumstances prevented the observation from being made, the expedition discovered the astronomical phenomenon now known as Baily's beads.[22] The first volume of the Academy's *Memoirs,* published in 1785, included papers dealing with astronomy, natural philosophy, medicine, and natural history. This first publication was not so much a major contribution to the sciences as it was evidence "that philosophical pursuits are carried on with vigour in the American States." [23] It also established the Academy, as one of the two major learned societies in the United States in a period when a substantial number of regional learned societies were being formed in the major cultural centers of the country. These took the forms of medical societies, state academies of arts and sciences, societies for the promotion of individual sciences, such as chemistry and geology, others formed primarily for the promotion of agriculture, arts, and manufactures, and historical societies.

All these organizations fostered the development of the museum movement in America.[24] Those concerned with the promotion of useful arts, agriculture, and related endeavors urged their members to contribute to the societies' collections materials useful for study. In time some of these special collections developed into major resources which led to the founding of museums.

The first important American public museum installation developed rather casually from a private gallery installed by Charles Willson Peale behind his home in Philadelphia for the purpose of displaying portraits he had painted of important men of his time. He found the facility useful for storing and exhibiting a variety of stuffed wild animals, some of which he had caught himself. Franklin once sent him the corpse of his French Angora cat and Washington provided some dead pheasants. When no other suitable repository was immediately available for the specimens brought back by Lewis and Clark, Jefferson had the materials sent to Peale, who added them to the displays in his museum. As the number of specimens of animals, birds, and reptiles increased, Peale attempted to display them against backgrounds depicting their natural habitats, producing stage sets and painting backdrops for the purpose. When in 1801 he read of the discovery of a group of large bones on a farm in New York State, he purchased them for $300 and with another $500 loaned by the American Philosophical Society and equipment borrowed from the Army and Navy, he excavated the bones, which were identified as mastodon. Not only were they displayed at the museum, but Peale depicted on a large canvas the recovery of the bones by what was in fact the first American paleontological expedition.[25]

The Peale displays catered to a public which sought freaks and showmanship. Peale visualized his enterprise as eventually developing into a government-sponsored institution preserved for posterity and built his museum deliberately with such a potential in mind. With the growth of its natural-history collections, the museum changed its character. In response to public interest, Peale added new dimensions, displaying curiosities ranging from the trigger finger of an executed murderer to a live eagle screaming from its perch on the ceiling rafters. He introduced such refinements as performances on the organ by one of his daughters and public lectures by his sons to accompany presentations of "moving pictures" created with a number of moving stage sets with sound effects. A Negro slave named Moses Williams produced silhouettes of visitors on a new invention of John Isaac Hawkins called the Physiognotrace. The public was constantly surprised by the variety of new exhibits and performances.[26]

Peale's operation inspired others to follow his example, usually on a much more modest scale and with emphasis on particular aspects of American life. Representative of the new national interest in the uses of technology was an attempt in about 1787 to establish a museum of models of manufacturing machines in Philadelphia.[27] The founder was a prominent clockmaker, inventor, and model maker named Robert Leslie, who advertised his wide range of activities in the local press, and who was associated with Thomas Jefferson from time to time in the latter's pursuit of technological projects. Curiously enough, the first public mention of Leslie's museum of models was in a communication from London published in a Philadelphia newspaper in 1789. The writer, after commenting on the advantages of the improvements of machines for manufacturing in England, which if produced in the United States would make the young nation more respected abroad, then went on to note "that the ingenious Mr. Robert Leslie, a native of Maryland, has commenced a MUSEUM in Philadelphia, for the purpose of collecting every model, drawing or description of any machine, implement or tool, which is employed in any foreign countries in manufactures of the useful arts." [28]

Leslie's Museum next achieved a full half-column announcement in a Philadelphia newspaper, in which Leslie, after describing the nature of the collection he proposed to make, stated that: "Such a Museum, beside gratifying the curiosity of ingenious men, will afford an opportunity of usefully investigating the comparative merits of a great variety of machines, by bringing them immediately into the same point of view; an advantage which could not be derived from drawings, or from the originals. Such an examination may reasonably be supposed to produce great improvements, in many of the machines now in use, either by simplifying the works, or by transferring the excellence of one machine advantageously to another." [29]

The museum was opened to the public with apparent success in the spring of 1790. An editorial note in the press described an operating model of Oliver Evans's flour mill, which was one of the first exhibits, as "a specimen of American ingenuity, worthy the attention of the curious." [30] Leslie, in addition to devising and patenting several innovations in clock and watch movements, also invented more than a dozen other useful machines, a few of which were for use with mills. The museum had a reasonable success during the short period of its existence. Early in 1793 Leslie decided to go to London to obtain British patents for his clock and watch inventions and liquidated his stock in his clock shop as quickly as possible to pay his expenses. At the same time he advertised that he would refund money for subscriptions received for visits to the museum and terminated that project also. He sailed for England with his family in April, taking with him the model of Evans's flour mill in which he hoped to interest the British. He also planned to obtain a British copyright and find an English publisher for Evans's book, *The Millwright's Guide*. [31]

Another pioneer museum effort, initiated in New York City in 1789 by John Pintard and associates, was named The American Museum of the Tammany Society. Gardiner Baker was appointed the first keeper and later became the owner of the museum. The early public notices encouraged the public to visit the "many articles on the historical and natural lines, highly deserving the notice of the curious" and noted that the museum would be open two days weekly. Baker developed a diversified series of displays, including a miniature guillotine "with a wax figure perfectly representing a man beheaded," an air gun which the visitor was permitted to discharge for an additional fee of sixpence, stuffed animals ranging from a porcupine to a "lamb with two perfect heads and necks compleat, and but one body from Brunswick, N. J.," as well as "A perfect Horn, between 5 and 6 inches in length, which grew out of a woman's head in this city." [32] Baker also assembled an impressive menagerie of live animals, birds, and reptiles and emphasized the relatively large number of exhibits that related to science or technology. He obtained from Scotland a model of a threshing machine which was turned by a single horse and was capable of simultaneously threshing and winnowing 150 bushels of wheat in six hours, a demonstration of continuous motion described by an English visitor as having "an activity that seemed likely to hold out for the time a spectator would stop to observe it." [33] Baker was personally involved in making astronomical observations, and he also maintained records of the weather in the city over a period of many years.[34] He utilized these personal interests as part of the public display and in 1794 advertised a "METEOROLOGICAL OBSERVATION, Made from a Thermometer kept in the cupola of the Museum at the Exchange." [35]

Baker also had an avid interest in mechanical devices and displayed a number of models of inventions by others and some he made himself.[36] From time to time he featured scientific experiments as part of the museum's exhibitions. Among such displays was one in 1796 announced as "a very pleasing Philosophical Experiment with Electrical Fluid united with Inflammable air, the Effect will be Shewn with a Brass Cannon." [37] In the same year Baker promoted Jean Pierre Baptiste Blanchard's forty-sixth balloon ascent, which was to be made in New York City. He advanced funds to Blanchard for his family's living costs in New York, produced a pamphlet explaining "The Principles, History and Use of Air-Balloons," and planned to make meteorological observations while airborne by recording changes on barometer, thermometer, hydrometer, electrometer, and other instruments with Blanchard during the ascent. However, the anticipated subscriptions to pay for the cost of the ascent came in slowly and insufficiently; the balloon was damaged by a thunderstorm before the date of the ascent and funds could not be found for making the necessary repairs; and an irreconcilable argument developed between Baker and Blanchard. The project ended in a fiasco which was widely aired in the public press over a period of many months.

Baker's museum survived the unpleasant publicity, and he continued to add new features to the displays from time to time. Unanticipated problems developed in other quarters, however. His wife's infatuation with a Frenchman led to a court case with the lover, and Baker abruptly took his family to Boston. He took along some of his cherished exhibits, but he contracted yellow fever and died shortly after his arrival in Boston. His wife returned to New York City with their four children to pursue her affair with the Frenchman. She continued the operation of her late husband's museum, and after she died in 1800, the museum was acquired by several successive owners, including a grocer, a historical painter, and finally one of its former curators, John Scudder, who not only improved the exhibits but moved the museum to a new location. In about 1853 Scudder's Museum was acquired by P. T. Barnum. During the period of its existence, the museum's incredible conglomeration of curiosities combined the functions of academy, art gallery, kindergarten, and college for the culturally oriented of the city.[38]

The formation of collections of objects of historical and scientific interest continued as private enterprises and eventually as government-sponsored projects. One of the most important private scientific collections of the times was formed by Charles Nicoll Bancker, a Philadelphia merchant and financier and member of the American Philosophical Society. He devoted many years to assembling apparatus for the cultivation of his personal scientific interests, and his collections included large arrays of minerals, glass and wooden models of crystalline forms, relief maps and charts illustrating geographical distribution, telescopes and other astronomical instruments, orreries and globes, various types of magnets and machines to demonstrate magnetism and electricity, and numerous models of machines, mills, and jets and other contrivances demonstrating the properties of fluids. The assemblage was particularly rich in collections of acoustical and optical apparatus, which the French mathematician François Moigno described as one of the most extensive and brilliant in the world. At Bancker's death in 1869, the widespread concern that such a comprehensive collection might be dispersed was voiced even by Joseph Henry, Secretary of the Smithsonian Institution. The entire collection was finally purchased intact by Professor Morton of the Stevens Institute of Technology at Hoboken, New Jersey, where it has been preserved.[39]

Government sponsorship of museum-type collections was slow in coming, and its development was an almost accidental result of a policy of the new American government. This was the decision to form a collection of patent models, sometimes known as "The American Museum of Arts," which became the nucleus from which was derived the larger collection that was subsequently transferred from the National Institute to the Smithsonian Institution in 1858. The National Institute, which had its genesis in an earlier organization "for the promotion of arts and sciences," was originally known as the National Institution for the Promotion of Science and was established in Washington, D.C. in 1840. The earlier collection of "The American Museum" was destroyed in the fire of the Patent Office Building in 1836.[40]

The proposal to establish a national museum under the federal government as part of a plan to found a federal university was first made by James Madison, although some authorities believe it to have been the suggestion of Dr. Benjamin Rush. This plan, which was first published in the *Pennsylvania Gazette* in 1788, included a statement in relation to the subject of natural history: "To render instruction in these branches easy, it will be necessary to establish a museum, and also a garden, in which not only all the shrubs, etc., but all the forest trees of the United States should be cultivated." [41] Another proposal for a national museum was made in 1806 by the American poet and diplomat Joel Barlow as part of his plan for what he described as a "National Institution" and provided for the maintenance and development of collections of minerals and philosophical instruments.[42]

The condition of the museum movement in America early in the nineteenth century was well summarized in a letter from Thomas Jefferson to G. C. de la Coste, who had written to Jefferson for a subscription to a museum enterprise being planned in Williamsburg. "In the particular enterprises for museums," wrote Jefferson, "we have seen the populous and wealthy cities of Boston and New York unable to found or maintain such an institution. The feeble condition of that in each of these places sufficiently proves this. In Philadelphia alone, has this attempt succeeded to a good degree. It had been owing there to a measure of zeal and perseverance in an individual [Peale] rarely equalled; to a population, crowded, wealthy, and more than usually addicted to the pursuit of knowledge." [43] Again, when the Peale Museum was being considered for acquisition and support by the federal government, Jefferson failed to respond favorably to the project. Despite his personal involvement in Peale's enterprise, he was convinced that interest on the part of the general public would not be adequate to support such an institution. Not until the second half of the nineteenth century, after the establishment of the Smithsonian Institution and its acquisition of the National Institute's collection, did the museum of science emerge as a full and permanent entity with the formation of the United States National Museum. This eventually was to become the repository that exhibited the achievements, practices, and tools of the early men of science, as well as the collections assembled by naturalists and specialists in the earth sciences.

With the emergence of the United States of America into a brave new world of nationhood concerned with its growing needs and opportunities, the pursuit of the practical sciences reached a point of culmination which opened up new frontiers, but at the same time led to the decline and demise of the role of the mathematical practitioners. Although the practitioners had emerged independently on both sides of the Atlantic and developed into strong movements through three centuries in England and two in America, the first three decades of the nineteenth century marked the end of the movement in both countries.

In Great Britain the practitioners were replaced by a group including the engineer, the industrial technician, and the sailor-scientist, which emerged slowly but strongly. In particular, the sailor-scientists, under the sponsorship of the British Royal Navy, initiated a program of hydrographical surveys for testing new instrumentation and for the collection and collation of data relating to the earth's physical properties. The detailed studies produced proved to have immeasurable importance in the development of navigational science.

A similar group of professions evolved more gradually in the

United States. The establishment of the U. S. Coast Survey and the United States Military Academy effectively combined the work of the cartographer, the navigator, and the surveyor in the new profession of engineering. The development of the American factory system and the production of machines that made machines, as well as the emergence of new industries, assimilated or supplanted the makers of mathematical instruments. The high schools, technical schools, and lyceums absorbed many of the independent science teachers and some amateurs of the sciences, while others found their way onto college faculties or into new scientific institutions, such as the early astronomical observatories. The fusing and merging of skills that resulted did not become visibly productive until government sponsorship of scientific effort became a reality.

Meanwhile, as those scientific skills which had literally shaped America were changing in focus from individual, independent efforts to more cooperative and organized activities, American achievement in general, and sometimes in the practical sciences specifically, did not find much appreciation overseas.

The British in particular continued to maintain a low opinion of the Americans, an opinion not substantially improved by their winning the War for Independence and forming a new nation. British disdain was leveled not only at all American achievements, but also at what was considered lack of quality in the Americans, as reflected in the language spoken and the form of government which had been established. The American language, the British claimed, retained all the local idioms and barbarisms of the country from which the inhabitants or their ancestors had emigrated, and as for the government, "they have borrowed the most beautiful and useful parts of their constitution from the English model." [44] Most particularly was British resentment directed at any evidence of American competence and success in manufacturing, industry, and science.

Comments representative of the British opinion and mood appeared in the published letters of Edward Thornton, secretary to George Hammond, the first British minister to the United States. In his correspondence with Sir James Bland Sturges, British Under-Secretary of State for Foreign Affairs, Thornton noted: "Your character of the Americans, from their writings in the magazine I sent you, is perfectly just; and you will perceive by several passages in different letters of mine that I have the happiness of coinciding in opinion with you. But there is one trait which you neglected to mention—it is impossible you could have overlooked it—their vanity as a nation. This tinctures the whole of their character. In arts, in arms, in literature, in political economy, they think that they take the lead, and have pointed out a new road to Europe. If they have any genius or original invention, I believe it is in the mechanic arts; but even then how far do they fall short of the discoveries of our manufacturing countries? They borrow, or rather steal, the models of our machinery, add some small improvement and call the whole their own invention. Nor is this vanity confined to the less informed class of people, but it extends to the highest. In his history of Virginia, Mr. Jefferson discovers the same spirit. Because Hadley and Godfrey, an American, invented, independently of each other, the instrument known by the name of Hadley's Quadrant, poor Hadley is a plagiary, and the American has been robbed of the merit of the discovery. It is in vain for an Englishman to allege that it is very possible two men might hit on the same idea without any previous communication, and to assert in proof of the possibility (which is an undoubted fact) that Sir Isaac Newton had the same idea, which he communicated to Dr. Halley, and which, for some curious circumstances, neither Hadley nor Godfrey could have known of. All this is of no avail, the verdict of plagiarism is given against Hadley, and he must abide by it. And because Rittenhouse made an orrery of his own, the man who really invented that instrument, I believe before Rittenhouse was in being, is a plagiary too. . . .

"For my part I can see nothing in this country of talents, in politics or literature, that can endure for an instant a comparison with those of the luminaries of the past and present day in England. Nor, however rapid the improvement may have been in civilization, can it be expected in a country whose very existence has not been known more than three centuries. If America assumes a rank in literature and arts to which she has no claim, she must not be surprised to be told that, on the scale of original invention, she is rated very low indeed." [45]

Thornton's view was justified. The Americans demonstrated all the assurance derived from their successful struggle for independence from the strongest power in the world and could anticipate no future challenge that could be greater. This feeling of confidence was essential if the young nation was to deal adequately with the mounting problems it faced in establishment of a new and untried form of government and the stabilization of a new economy. The postwar years were filled with confusion, as the embryonic democracy, straining to emerge from the debilitating effects of one war, found itself faced with another. Although such British criticism might have been anticipated and was deserved, it was nonetheless unfair to compare the achievements of the suppressed and struggling American colonies, with those of the motherland favored by many centuries of an established social and economic structure and dominance as a world power. The comparison made readily apparent, however, that the New World provided a fresh setting and an unparalleled impetus for human achievement, since it lacked the limitations on personal ambition and enterprise imposed by the traditions and restrictions of a feudal or an established society. To the American, every need posed a challenge which had to be met and overcome with the instinctive abilities and resources readily at hand, if the individual and the country were to survive and continue to achieve. Such challenges could not have been faced, however, had not the American colonists possessed a resource of immense value—the traditional British mathematical practices and aids in cartography, navigation, and surveying, as well as in science teaching—which they borrowed and utilized and adapted for their own needs and as the foundation on which to build independent resources. In the new democracy, even more than in the colonial period, the Americans were forced to rely on British achievement.

The emerging Americans were a target for criticism by the French as well. On every occasion that presented itself, Thomas Jefferson rose to contest the slurs, actual or implied, of English or European scholars. Indeed, his pronounced and acknowledged Anglophobia often inspired him to even excessive rebuttal. When the Abbé Guillaume Raynal, a French historian and philosopher, stated in one of his published works that America had yet to produce a poet, a mathematician, or indeed a man of genius in any single art and science, Jefferson immediately came to the defense with a published reply:

"When we shall have existed as a people as long as did the Greeks before they produced a Homer, the Romans a Virgil, the French a Racine or a Voltaire, or the English a Shakespeare or a Milton, then there will be cause to inquire the reason." [46] He pointed out that in war America had produced a Washington, in physics a Franklin, in astronomy a Rittenhouse second in genius to no living astronomer because he was self-taught. Comparing populations, Jefferson observed that since America had but 3 million inhabitants, France 20 million and the British Isles 10 million, France should have at least six geniuses to every American one, and Britain at least half that number.

Other French writers of the same period, less critical than Abbé Raynal, acknowledged the important fact that America and its people were different from the nations and people of the Old World and not necessarily in any negative sense.

"The discovery of America has not only been an interesting spectacle for politics and ambition," commented one French writer, "it has opened a new field to human knowledge; it has furnished new wealth to all parts of natural history; and the study of the inhabitants of that part of the globe has given us ideas on the nature of man which philosophy could never have supplied with its speculations. Everything is new in America, everything seems to have been arranged there after a different plan from that which provided at the formation of the rest of the earth." [47]

The spirit of confidence in the American ability to meet and overcome all challenges had manifested itself from the period of the first stubborn settlements throughout the creative era that resulted in an independent nation which lost no time in seeking recognition and a position among the other nations of the world. Ideas could not be and were not confined to the chosen or educated few, and this freedom of thought was to a large degree responsible for bold experimentation leading to startling departures from accepted standards in all fields of endeavor. Not least among the manifestations of this pervasive feeling was the output of the mathematical practitioners, whose collective efforts had significant impact both on the forming of the new nation and on its later technological growth. It may be an exaggeration to claim that the practitioner movement was the origin of the subsequent national scientific development, but there can be no question that it provided a strong foundation. Early in the nineteenth century Dr. Benjamin Rush commemorated the support of practical science as the beginning of a new era rather than the conclusion of another. "What may we not expect from this harmony between the sciences and government!" he wrote. "Methinks I see canals cut, rivers once impassable rendered navigable, bridges erected, and roads improved, to facilitate the exportation of grain. I see the banks of our rivers vying in fruitfulness with banks of the river of Egypt. I behold our farmers nobles; our merchants princes. . . . Patriotism and literature are here connected together; and a man cannot neglect the one, without being destitute of the other. Nature and our ancestors have completed their work among us; and have left us nothing to do but to enlarge and perpetuate our own happiness." [48]

Reference Notes

Glossary

Selected Bibliography

Acknowledgments

Illustration Credits

Index

REFERENCE
NOTES

I. In Their Beginnings

1. Derek J. de Solla Price, "The Mathematical Practitioners," *Journal of the Institute of Navigation*, vol. VIII, no. 1, January 1955, pp. 12–16; "Some early English instrument makers," *Endeavour*, vol. XVI, no. 54, April 1955, pp. 90–94; and *Science Since Babylon* (New Haven, Conn.: Yale University Press, 1961), p. 53.

2. E. G. R. Taylor, *The Mathematical Practitioners of Tudor and Stuart England* (Cambridge: Cambridge University Press, 1954), pp. 3–162.

3. The earliest works on the movement in America are Dirk J. Struik, *Yankee Science in the Making* (Boston: Little, Brown, 1948), and Silvio A. Bedini, *Early American Scientific Instruments and Their Makers* (Washington, D.C.: Smithsonian Institution, 1964). See also Price, *Science Since Babylon*, chapter 3: "Renaissance Roots of Yankee Ingenuity," pp. 45–67.

4. Samuel G. Goodrich, *Recollections of a Lifetime, or, Men and Things I Have Seen; In a Series of Familiar Letters to a Friend* (New York and Auburn: Miller, Orton and Mulligan, 1857), vol. I, pp. 95–98.

5. Gonzalo Fernandez de Oviedo y Valdes, *De la natural hystoria de las Indias* (Toledo, 1526) and *La historia general de las Indias* (Part I, Seville, 1535; Part II, Valladolid, 1557). The first was translated into English by Richard Eden, in 1555, with the title *The Decades of the newe world or West Indies, Containing the navigations of the Spaniards* (London: William Powell, 1955); a later translation appeared in Samuel Purchas, *Hakluttus Posthumus or Purchas His Pilgrims* (London, 1625).

6. Humphrey Gilbert, *A Discourse of a Discoverie for a New Passage to Cataia* (London: Jones for H. Middleton, 1576).

7. "Instructions to be observed by Thomas Bavin," British Museum, Add. Mss. 38823, ff. 3ᵛ–5ᵛ. See also E. G. R. Taylor, "Instructions to a Colonial Surveyor in 1582," *The Mariner's Mirror*, vol. XXXVII, 1951, pp. 48–62.

8. County Record Office, Chelmsford, Essex, England, Ms. D/DRh, M.I., discovered by county archivist F. G. Emmison and published by David B.

Quinn in "Preparations for the 1585 Virginia Voyage," *William and Mary Quarterly*, 3rd ser., vol. VI, no. 2, April 1949, pp. 208–236.

9. Rev. Increase N. Tarbox, ed., *Sir Walter Ralegh and His Colony in America*, The Publications of the Prince Society, vol. 15 (Boston: John Wilson & Son, 1884), pp. 38–39, 234.

10. Thomas Hariot, *A briefe but true report of the new found land of Virginia* (London, 1588); reprinted in facsimile edition entitled *A Brief and True Report of the New Found Land of Virginia by Thomas Hariot* (Ann Arbor, Mich.: Edwards Brothers, 1931, unpaginated). See also David Beers Quinn, ed., *The Roanoke Voyages 1584–1590* (London: The Hakulyt Society, 1955), vol. I, pp. 29–71, 375–376, 380–381; vol. II, pp. 841–872.

11. "Instructions to Bavin."

12. Edmond R. Kiely, *Surveying Instruments, Their History and Classroom Use*, (New York: Bureau of Publications, Teachers College, Columbia University, 1947), pp. 106, 186, 228–234, 375.

13. Theodore de Bry, *Grands et petits voyages* (Frankfurt, 1590); M. S. Giuseppi, "The Work of Theodore de Bry and His Sons, Engravers," *Proceedings of the Huguenot Society*, 1916, pp. 204–226.

14. Edward Arber, ed., *Capt. John Smith, President of Virginia and Admiral of New England, Works. 1608–1631* (Birmingham, England, 1884), pp. 396 ff. See also Charles Dudley Warner, *Captain John Smith* (New York: Henry Holt, 1881).

15. [Captain John Smith], *A Trve Relation of such occurences and accidents of noate as hath hapned in Virginia since the first planting of that Collony, which is now resident in the South part thereof, till the last returne from thence. Written by Captain Smith, Coronell of the said Collony, to a worshipful friend of his in England* (London: Printed for John Tappe, and are to bee solde at the Greyhound in Paules-Church-yard, by W. W., 1608).

16. The London Virginia Company, "Instructions by way of advice for the intended Voyage to Virginia" (1606), in E. D. Neill, *History of the London Virginia Company* (Albany, N.Y., 1869), p. 8.

17. Captain John Smith, *The Generall Historie of Virginia, New England, & The Summer Isles, The Third Book, on the Proceedings and Accidents of the English Colony in Virginia* (London, 1624). See also Philip L. Barbour, *The Three Worlds of Captain John Smith* (Boston: Houghton Mifflin, 1964), pp. 159–160.

18. Walter W. Ristow, "Captain John Smith's Map of Virginia," in Walter W. Ristow, ed., *A La Carte, Selected Papers on Maps and Atlases* (Washington, D.C.: Library of Congress, 1972), pp. 91–95; Coolie Verner, "The First Maps of Virginia, 1590–1673," *Virginia Magazine of History and Biography*, vol. 58, January 1950, pp. 3–15; C. Ford Worthington, "Captain John Smith's Map of Virginia, 1612," *Geographical Review*, vol. 14, July 1924, pp. 433–443.

19. Fairfax Harrison, *Landmarks of Old Prince William* (Richmond, Va.: The Old Dominion Press, 1924), vol. II, pp. 601–652.

II. In Surging Seas

1. *The Book of English Trades, and Library of Useful Arts* (London: For Sir Richard Phillips, 1823), p. 242.

2. [Captain John Smith], *An Accidence or the Path-way to Experience. Neces-*

sary for all Young Sea-men, or those that are desirous to goe to Sea, briefly shewing the Phrases, Offices and Words of Command, Belonging to the Building, Ridging and Sayling, a Man of Warre: And how to manage a Fight at Sea. Together with the Charge and Duty of every Officer, and their Shares: Also the Names, Weight, Charge, Shot and Powder, of all sorts of great Ordnance. With the use of the Petty Tally. Written by Captaine John Smith sometimes Governour of Virginia, and Admirall of New England (London: Printed for Jonas Man, and Benjamin Fisher, and are to be sold at the Signe of the Talbot in Aldersgate Streets, 1626); reprinted in 1627 and 1636.

 3. [Captain John Smith], *A Sea Grammar, With the Plaine Exposition of Smith's Accidence for Young Sea-men, enlarged. Divided into fifteene Chapters, what they are you may partly conceive by the Contents. Written by Captaine John Smith, sometimes Gouernour of Virginia, and Admirall of New-England* (London: Printed by John Haviland, 1627). Subsequent editions, issued in 1652–53, 1691, 1692, and 1699, were entitled *The Sea-man's Grammer.* . . .

 4. Theunisz Jacobsz., *The Lightning Columne, or Sea-Mirrour, containging The Sea-Coasts of the Northern, Eastern and Western Navigation: Setting fort in divers necessaire Sea-Cards, all the Ports, Rivers, Bayes, Roads, Depths and Sands; very curiously placed on its due Polus-height furnished. With the discoveries of the chief Countries, and on what cours and distance they lay from one another. Never there to fore so clearly laid open, & here & there very diligently bettered & augmented for the use of all Sea-men* (Amsterdam: C. Lootsman, 1680). Based on Lucas Janszoon Wagenaer, *Spieghel der Zeevaerdt, vande nauigitie der Westersche Zee, Innehoudende alle de Custe va Vranckrijck Spaignen eff t'principaelaste deel van Engelandt* . . . (Leiden: Christopher Plantin, 1585).

 5. Richard Eden, trans., *The Arte of Navigation, Contayning a briefe description of the Sphaere, with the partes and Circles of the same; as also the making and vse of certain Instruments. Very necessary for all sortes of Sea-men to vnderstand. First written in Spanish by Martin Curtis [sic], and translated into English by Richard Eden: and lastly corrected and augmented, with a Regiment of Table of declination, and diurse other necessary tables and rules of common Navigation. Calculated (this yeare 1596)*, 6th ed., revised by John Tapp (London, 1609); first published 1561.

 6. Edward Wright, *Certaine Errors in Navigation. Detected and Corrected by Edward Wright* (London, 1599); E. G. R. Taylor, *The Mathematical Practitioners of Tudor and Stuart England* (Cambridge: Cambridge University Press, 1954), pp. 53, 336, and *The Haven-Finding Art* (New York: Abelard-Schuman, 1957), pp. 222–225.

 7. John Davis, *The Seamans Secrets, Deuided into 2 partes, wherein is taught the three kindes of Sayling, Horizontall, Peradoxall, and sayling upon a great Circle: also an Horizontall Tyde Table for the essye finding of the ebbing and flowing of the Tydes, with a Regiment newly calculated for the finding of the Declination of the Sunne, and many other most necessary rules and Instruments, not heeretofore set foorth by any* (London: Thomas Dawson, 1595); reprinted in *The Voyages and Works of John Davis, the Navigator* (London: Hakulyt Society, 1880).

 8. William Gilbert, *De Magnete, magneticisque corporibus, et de Magno Magnete Tellure* (London, 1600). See also Silvanus P. Thompson, *Notes on the De Magnete of Dr. William Gilbert* (London, 1901), pp. 4–5.

 9. William Bourne, *A REGIMENT FOR THE SEA, CONTEINING VERY NECESSARY MATters, for all sorts of Sea-men and Trauailers, as Masters of ships, Pilots, Mariners & Marchauntes, NEWLY CORRECTED AND AMENded by the Author. Where-vnto is added a Hidrographical discourse to goe vnto Cattay, fiue severall ways* (London: T.

East, 1580). See also David W. Waters, *The Art of Navigation in England in Eliza-bethan and Early Stuart Times* (London: Hollis & Carter, 1958), p. 36.

10. Edmund Gunter, *The Description and Use of the Sector, The Cross-staffe and other instruments for Such as Are Studious of Mathematicall Practise* (London: John Thompson and John Tapp, 1623).

11. William Bourne, *An Almanacke and Prognostication for three yeares that is to saye for the yeare of our Lord 1571 and 1572 & 1573. nowe newlye added unto my late Rulles of Nauigation, Yt was printed iiii years past. Practised at Gravesend for the Meridian of London by William Bourne student of the Mathematicall science* (London: Thomas Pur-foote, 1571), Rules 3 and 4; John Seller, *Praxis Nautica: Practical Navigation; or, an Introduction to the whole Art* (London, 1669).

12. Seller, *Praxis Nautica;* Samuel Sturmy, *The Mariners Magazine: Stor'd with the following Mathematicall Arts: the Rudiments of Navigation and Geometry . . . (Surveying, Gauging, Gunnery, Astronomy, Dialling, Fortification)* (London: George Hurlock, Wm. Fisher, ed. Thomas and Dixy Page, 1669).

13. Eden, *Arte of Navigation.*

14. Wright, *Certaine Errors.*

15. John Tapp, *The Seamens Kalendar, or an Ephemerides of the Sun, and cer-tain of the most noble fixed Starrs. A table of the longitude and latitude of all the most emi-nent places of the world, an exact table of the North Starre, new tables of 65 of the principall fixed Starrs, the time of their coming upon the Meridian every day, with a discovery of the long hidden secret of the Longitude* (London, 1601–1631).

16. Nathaniel B. Shurtleff, ed., *Records of the Governor and Company of the Massachusetts Bay in New England* (Boston: William White, 1853), vol. I, pp. 122, 161, 168, 262, 266, 299, 400, 405; F. C. Pierce, ed., *Pierce Family* (Albany, N.Y., 1889), no. IV, Record of the Posterity of . . . Capt. William Pierce, pp. 11–17; Robb Sagendorph, *America and Her Almanacs, Wit, Wisdom and Weather 1639–1970* (Dublin, N.H.: Yankee, Inc., and Boston, Mass.: Little, Brown, 1970), pp. 30–32.

III. WHERE WOLVES NOW HOWL

1. E. G. R. Taylor, *Tudor Geography* (London: Methuen, 1930), pp. 140–161; and "The Surveyor," *Economic History Review,* vol. XVII, no. 2, 1947, pp. 121–133.

2. William Folkingham, *Feudographia: the Synopsis or Epitome of Surveying* (London, 1610); and [Richard Norwood], *Norwood's Epitomie: Being the Application of The Doctrine of Triangles in Certain Problems, concerning the use of the Plain Sea-Chart, and Mercator's Chart, Being the Two most useful kinds of Sailing, With a Table of Artificial Sines, Tangents, and the Complements Arithmetical of Sines supplying the use of Secants* (London: R. & W. Leybourn, 1659).

3. Aaron Rathborne, *The Surveyor in Foure Bookes* (London: W. Stansby, 1616).

4. [William Leybourn], *The Compleat Surveyor, Containing the Whole Art of Surveying of Land* (London: R. & W. Leybourn, 1653); rev. and enl. ed. of *Planome-tria, or the Whole Art of Surveying Land* (London: Oliver Wallinby, 1650).

5. John Love, *Geodaesia, or the Art of Surveying and Measuring of Land Made Easie* (London, 1688).

6. [Judge Tazewell], "The Mode of Acquiring Lands in Virginia in Early Times," *Virginia Historical Register and Literary Companion*, vol. 2, no. 4 [ca. 1849], pp. 190–194.

7. Alexander Brown, *Genesis of the United States: A Narrative of the Movement in England 1605–1616* (Boston: Houghton Mifflin, 1892), vol. II, pp. 778–779, "Brief Declaration of the Council for Virginia."

8. British State Papers. Colonial Papers, vol. II, no. 27 (1621), (Abstracts of the Proceedings of the Virginia Company of London), vol. I, p. 131.

9. William Waller Hening, ed., *The Statutes at Large; Being a Collection of All the Laws of Virginia . . .* , vols. I and II (Richmond, Va., 1809–1823); and Philip Alexander Bruce, *Economic History of Virginia in the Seventeenth Century* (New York: Peter Smith, 1935), vol. I, pp. 530–544. See also Richard Beale Davis, ed., *William Fitzhugh and His Chesapeake World* (Chapel Hill: University of North Carolina Press, 1963), pp. 146–191.

10. Hening, *Statutes*, vol. II, p. 102.

11. William H. Seiler, "Land Processioning in Colonial Virginia," *William and Mary Quarterly*, 3rd series, vol. VI, no. 3, July 1949, pp. 416–436.

12. Sarah Kemble Knight, *The Journal of Madam Knight, The Private Journal of a Journey from Boston to New York in 1704* (Boston: Small, Maynard, 1920; reprint, New York: Peter Smith, 1935), pp. 8–16, 69–72.

13. Hening, *Statutes*, vol. II, p. 103.

14. William B. Marye, "The Baltimore County 'Garrison' and the Old Garrison Roads," *Maryland Historical Magazine*, vol. XVI, no. 2, June 1921, pp. 125–127; no. 3, September 1921, p. 245.

15. Percy Scott Flippin, *The Royal Government in Virginia 1625–1775*, Studies in History, Economics and Public Law, vol. LXXXIV, no. 1, (New York: Columbia University Press, 1919), pp. 215–229.

16. W. K. Boyd, ed., *William Byrd's Histories of the Dividing Line Betwixt Virginia and North Carolina* (Raleigh, N.C.: North Carolina Historical Commission, 1929), p. xix.

17. Virginia Historical Society, Ludwell MSS. "A Journall of the Proceedings of Philip Ludwell and Nath[ll] Harrison Commissioners Appointed for seteling ye Limits betwixt Virg[a] & Carolina Begun July ye 18th 1719 by P.L."; published as "Boundary Line Proceedings, 1710," *Virginia Magazine of History and Biography*, vol. IV, no. 1, July 1896, pp. 30–42.

18. Bruce, *Economic History of Virginia . . .* , vol. I, p. 539.

19. George E. Bowman, "Plymouth's Wills and Inventories," *The Mayflower Descendant*, vol. IV, 1903, p. 76; David Pilsifer, ed., *Plymouth Colony Records* (Boston: William White, 1861), vol. I, Deeds, pp. 3–4, 7–13, 15.

20. [Valentine Leigh], *The Most Profitable and Commendable Way of Surveying . . . drawn up and collected by the Industrie of Valentine Leigh* (London, 1562).

21. A. W. Richeson, *English Land Measuring to 1800: Instruments and Practices* (Cambridge, Mass.: M.I.T. Press, 1966), p. 18.

22. Elizabeth M. Barrett, "The Angle Tree Monument," *Old-Time New England*, vol. XV, no. 3, January 1925, pp. 128–131.

23. Henry Wyckoff Belknap, *Trades and Tradesmen of Essex County, Massachusetts* (Salem, Mass.: Essex Institute, 1929), p. 3.

24. Cambridge, Mass., Middlesex Registry of Probate, Will of Captain John Sherman, 1690.

25. Charles H. Pope, ed., *The Plymouth Scrap Book*, (Boston: C. E. Goodspeed, 1918), p. 38.

26. Belknap, *Trades and Tradesmen*, p. 194.

27. Samuel Sewall, Diary, 1674–1729, vol. I, Collections of the Massachusetts Historical Society, 1878, 5th series, vol. V, pp. 180–181.

28. Hampton, Mass., Court Records, October 8, 1668; mentioned in Belknap, *Trades and Tradesmen*, pp. 76–77.

29. Roland Mather Hooker, *Boundaries of Connecticut* (Tercentenary Commission of the State of Connecticut. New Haven, Conn.: Yale University Press, 1933), pp. 16–25.

30. Belknap, *Trades and Tradesmen*, p. 80.

31. George Francis Dow, *The Arts and Crafts in New England*, 1704–1775 (Topsfield, Mass.: The Wayside Press, 1927), p. xxxi.

32. City of New Haven, Conn. Town Court Records, 1658; Richard Shelton Kirby, "Early Yale Engineers," *Inventors and Engineers of Old New Haven* (New Haven, Conn.: New Haven Colony Historical Society, 1939), pp. 37–39.

33. James Savage, *A Genealogical Dictionary of the First Settlers of New England* (Boston: Little, Brown, 1862), vol. II, p. 358.

34. Charles J. Hoadley, ed., *Public Records of the Colony of Connecticut, From August, 1689, to May, 1706* (Hartford, Conn.: Case, Lockwood and Brainard, 1868), Document 349, p. 325.

35. Ibid., Document 436, p. 445.

36. George Adams, *Geometrical and Graphical Essays, Containing a General Description of the Mathematical Instruments Used in Geometry, Civil and Military Surveying, Levelling, and Perspective; With Many New Problems, Illustrated by Thirty-Four Copper Plates*. 4th ed. corrected and enlarged by William Jones (London: C. Baldwin, 1813), p. 206, pl. 15, fig. 1.

37. Robert Gibson, *A Treatise of Practical Surveying; which is Demonstrated from its First Principles, wherein Every thing that is useful and curious in that art, is fully considered and explained* (Philadelphia: Joseph Crukshank, 1789), p. 160.

38. The map was entitled "Nova Terrae-Mariae Tabula" in Lord Baltimore's pamphlet, *A Relation of Maryland* (London, 1635). See also Lawrence C. Wroth, "The Maryland Colonization Tracts, 1632–1646," *Essays Offered to Herbert Putnam* (Baltimore: Johns Hopkins University Press, 1929), p. 554.

39. "Old Virginia and New," in *Virginia in America, Richly Valued: More especially the southern Parts. With the Tendure of the Vine and Silkworms, &c. Together with a Compleat Map of the Country from 35 to 41 Degrees of Latitude Discovered, and the West Sea* (London: Printed for John Stephenson, 1651). See also Coolie Verner, "The First Maps of Virginia, 1590–1673," *Virginia Magazine of History and Biography*, vol. 58, January 1950, pp. 13–14; and P. Lee Phillips, "Some Early Maps of Virginia and the Makers, Including Plates Relating to the First Settlement of Jamestown," *Virginia Magazine of History and Biography*, vol. XV, 1908, p. 73.

40. William P. Cumming, ed., *The Discoveries of John Lederer, with unpublished letters by and about John Lederer to Governor John Winthrop, Jr., With an essay on the Indians of Lederer's Discoveries by Douglas L. Rights and William P. Cumming* (Charlotttesville: University of Virginia Press, 1958), pp. 28–34.

41. Thomas Glover, *An Account of Virginia* (Oxford: Oxford University Press, 1904), pp. 9–10; reprinted from the *Philosophical Transactions of the Royal Society*, June 20, 1676.

42. John Ogilby, *America* (London, 1671). See also Arnoldus Montanus, *Die unbekante neue Welt* (Amsterdam, 1673).

43. "A New Description of Carolina. By Order of the Lords Proprietors, James Moxon, scul." (London, c. 1672).

44. "Virginia and Maryland. As it is Planted and In habited this present Year 1670. Surveyed and Exactly Drawne by the Only Labour and Endeavour of Augustin Herrman Bohemiensis. W. Faithorne Sculpt. London, 1673." Advertised and sold by John Seller, London.

45. Verner, "The First Maps," pp. 13–14; Phillip Lee Phillips, *The rare Map of Virginia and Maryland by Augustine Herrman* (Washington, 1911), p. 9; Edward B. Mathews, "The Maps and Map-Makers of Maryland," *Maryland Geological Survey* (Baltimore: Johns Hopkins University Press, 1898), vol. II, pp. 337–488; and Walter W. Ristow, "Augustine Herrman's Map of Virginia and Maryland," *Library of Congress Quarterly Journal of Current Acquisitions*, August 1960, pp. 27–29.

46. *John Carter Brown Library Annual Report*, 1929–1930, p. 10. See also Walter W. Ristow, "Augustine Herrman's Map of Virginia and Maryland, 1673, Acquired by the Library of Congress," *Surveying and Mapping*, vol. XXI, no. 3, September 1961, pp. 57–62.

47. "Nova Svecia Anno 1654 och 1655 Ardenna Novae Sveciae Carta Med dess Riviers och Landz Situation, ock beskassenhet aftagen och till Carts ford af P: Lindstrom, Ingin: fortif:" (Thomas Campanius Holm), *A Short Description of the Province of New Sweden, Now Called by the English, Pennsilvania, in America*. Trans. Peter S. Du Ponceau (Stockholm: J. H. Werner, 1834).

48. John Seller, *Atlas Maritimus or Coasting Atlas* (London, 1675).

49. Elizabeth Baer, *Seventeenth Century Maryland, A Bibliography* (Baltimore, The John Work Garrett Library, 1949), p. 89.

50. William A. Whitehead, *Documents Relating to the Colonial History of the State of New Jersey* (Newark, N.J.: Daily Advertising Printing House, 1881), vol. II, pp. 10–17, 34–36. See also Charles Harper Walsh, "The Earliest Copper Engraving Executed in the American Colonies," *Records of the Columbia Historical Society*, 1912, vol. XV, pp. 54–72.

51. *A New Mapp East and West New Jersey; Being an Exact Survey taken by Mr. John Worlidge* (London: John Thornton, [late 1600s]). See also Major E. M. Woodward and John F. Hageman, *History of Burlington and Mercer Counties, New Jersey, With Biographical Sketches of Many of Their Pioneers and Prominent Men* (Philadelphia, Everts and Peck, 1883), p. 161.

52. Homer Rosenberger, "Early Maps of Pennsylvania," *Pennsylvania History*, vol. XI, no. 2, April 1944, pp. 105–106; and Hazel Shields Garrison, "Cartography of Pennsylvania Before 1800," *Pennsylvania Magazine of History and Biography*, vol. LIX, no. 1, 1935, pp. 263–269.

53. *The Present State of New-England, being a Narrative of the Troubles With the Indians in New-England . . . , by the Rev. William Hubbard of Ipswich* (Boston: John Foster, 1677). See Randolph G. Adams, "William Hubbard's 'Narrative,' 1677, A Bibliographical Study," *Papers of the Bibliographical Society of America*, 1937, vol. 31, part I, pp. 25–39.

54. Richard Holman, "John Foster's Woodcut Map of New England," *Printing and Graphic Arts*, vol. VIII, 1960, pp. 53–96; and Walsh, "The Earliest Copper Engraving," pp. 54–72.

55. Fairfax Harrison, *Landmarks of Old Prince William* (Richmond, Va.: The Old Dominion Press, 1924), vol. II, pp. 607–612.

56. "Map of Virginia, Maryland, Pennsylvania, East and West Jersey," *The English Pilot* (London, 1706), Book 4, no. 13.

57. Nathaniel B. Shurtleff, ed., *Records of the Governor and Company of the Massachusetts Bay* (Boston: William White, 1854), vol. IV, 2, p. 182.

58. Obituary notice. *Boston News-Letter*, January 27–February 3, 1726.

IV. DARK HEMISPHERE

1. Jared Sparks, ed., *The Works of Benjamin Franklin* (Boston: Tappan & Whittemore, 1844), vol. VI, pp. 120–121.

2. *Proceedings of the Massachusetts Historical Society*, vol. XVI, 1878, pp. 224–225. Henry Oldenburg to John Winthrop, October 1667.

3. Royal Society Archives, Journal Book, vol. I, pp. 55–57; the paper was read before the Society July 9, 1662, and filed in Classified Papers, vol. I, p. 86; vol. III, no. 23.

4. Massachusetts Historical Society, Manuscripts Collections, Winthrop Papers. John Winthrop to Robert Morey, August 6, 1664.

5. Royal Society Archives, Letter Book I, pp. 147, 203, 204.

6. Isaac Newton, *Philosophiae Naturalis Principia Mathematica* (London, 1687), book III, prop. XLI, problem xxi. See also Francis Baily, *Supplement to His Account of the Rev. John Flamsteed* (London, 1837) p. 725n.

7. I. Bernard Cohen, *Some Early Tools of American Science* (Cambridge, Mass.: Harvard University Press, 1950), p. 28; E. G. R. Taylor, *The Mathematical Practitioners of Tudor and Stuart England* (Cambridge: Cambridge University Press, 1954), p. 273; Eugene Fairfield MacPike, ed., *Correspondence and Papers of Edmond Halley* (Oxford: Clarendon Press, 1932), pp. 3–6.

8. A manuscript map by Sir Edmond Halley entitled "A New Plan of the Harbour of Boston in New England . . . Observed An.° 1700" is in the collection of the American Antiquarian Society. See *A Society's Chief Joys* (Worcester, Mass.: American Antiquarian Society, 1969), p. 25.

9. [Thomas Brattle], "An Account of Some Eclipses of the Sun and Moon observed by Mr. Tho. Brattle, at Cambridge, four miles from Boston in New-England whence the Difference of Longitude between Cambridge and London is determin'd, from an observation made of one of them at London. J. Hodgson," *Philosophical Transactions of the Royal Society*, vol. 24, 1704–1705, no. 292, pp. 1633–1634.

10. Ibid., pp. 1633–1635.

11. Ibid., pp. 1636–1637; and Clifford K. Shipton, *New England Life in the Eighteenth Century* (Cambridge: Harvard University Press, 1963), pp. 198–212.

12. Theodore Hornberger, "The Date, the Source, and the Significance of Cotton Mather's Interest in Science," *American Literature*, vol. 6, no. 4, January

1935, pp. 413–420. See also K. B. Murdock, "Cotton Mather, Parson, Scholar and Man of Affairs," in Albert B. Hart, ed., *The Commonwealth History of Massachusetts* (New York: Russel and Russel, 1966), vol. II, pp. 323–354.

13. See Raymond Phineas Stearns, *Science in the British Colonies of America* (Urbana: University of Illinois Press, 1970), for a comprehensive study of the work of the naturalists and the members of the Royal Society of London in the New World.

14. George H. Daniels, *Science in American Society* (New York: Knopf, 1971), pp. 72–76.

15. George Lyman Kittredge, *The Old Farmer and His Almanack* (Boston: William Ware, 1904), pp. 52–61; Robb Sagendorph, *America and Her Almanacs, Wit, Wisdom and Weather 1639–1970* (Dublin, N.H.: Yankee, Inc., and Boston: Little, Brown, 1970), pp. 46–47, 55.

16. Charles L. Nichols, "Notes on the Almanacs of Massachusetts," *Proceedings of the American Antiquarian Society*, April 1912, pp. 15–48.

17. [Samuel Danforth], *An Astronomical description of the late Comet or Blazing Star, as it appeared in New England in the 9th, 10th, 11th and in the beginning of the 12th, moneth, 1664. Together with a brief theological application thereof.* By S.D. (Boston, 1665); and Charles Morton, "Compendium Physicae," *Collections of the Colonial Society of Massachusetts*, vol. XXXIII (Boston, 1940).

18. Increase Mather, *Heaven's Alarm to the World* (Boston, 1683).

19. Sidney Perley, *Historic Storms of New England* (Salem: The Salem Press Publishing and Printing Co., 1891), pp. 27–30, 105–114; Samuel Williams, "An Account of a Very Uncommon Darkness," *Memoirs of the American Academy of Arts and Sciences to the End of 1783*, 1785, pp. 236–237; William G. McLoughlin, "Olney Winsor's 'Memorandum' of the Phenomenal 'Dark Day' of May 19, 1780," *Rhode Island History*, vol. 26, no. 3, July 1967, pp. 88–90; and "Notes and Gleanings," *Old-Time New England*, vol. XXV, no. 4, April 1935, pp. 149–150; United States Forest Service Bulletin No. 117; and Franklin Bowditch Dexter, ed., *The Literary Diary of Ezra Stiles, D.D., LL.D.* (New York: Charles Scribner's Sons, 1901), vol. II, pp. 424–425.

20. Samuel Hazard, "New Style, 1752," *Pennsylvania Archives*, vol. II (Philadelphia: Joseph Severns & Co., 1853), pp. 68–70.

21. Clifford K. Shipton, *Sibley's Harvard Graduates. Biographical Sketches of Those Who Attended Harvard College in the Classes 1701–1712* (Boston: Massachusetts Historical Society, 1937), vol. V, p. 452; Fred G. Kilgour, "Thomas Robie (1689–1729), Colonial Scientist and Physician," *Isis*, vol. XXX, no. 82, August 1939, pp. 473–490; and N. W. Lovely, "Notes on New England Almanacs," *The New England Quarterly*, vol. VIII, 1935, p. 264.

22. Samuel Abbott Green, *John Foster, The Earliest American Engraver and the First Boston Printer* (Boston: Massachusetts Historical Society, 1909), pp. 50–53.

23. Oxford University. Bodleian Library. Manuscripts Collection. Simon Forman, "Treatise on Sea-Astrological Practice"; and E. G. R. Taylor, "Sir William Monson Consults the Stars," *Mariner's Mirror*, vol. 19, no. 1, January 1933, pp. 22–26.

24. George C. Mason, "The African Slave Trade in Colonial Times," *The American Historical Record*, 1872, vol. I, pp. 311–319, 338–345.

25. "A Table of the Astrological Houses of the Heaven" (London, 1654).

Quoted from Edward Eggleston, *The Transit of Civilization from England to America in the Seventeenth Century* (New York: D. Appleton, 1901), p. 5.

26. Relatively little has been published on the subject of astrology in early America. See Kittredge, *The Old Farmer and His Almanack*, chapter on "Astrology," pp. 39–52; and William D. Stahlman, "Astrology in Colonial America: An Extended Query," *William and Mary Quarterly*, vol. XIII, 1956, pp. 551–563.

27. Increase Mather, *Kometographia, Or a Discourse on Comets*, (Boston, 1683), p. 130.

28. David B. Field, "Statistical Account of the County of Middlesex in Connecticut," *Connecticut Academy of Arts & Sciences*, April 1819; reprinted by J. T. Kelsey, Haddam, Conn., 1892, p. 120.

29. Annie Russell Marble, "Early New England Almanacs," *New England Magazine*, n.s., vol. 19, (o.s., vol. 25), September 1898–February 1899, pp. 552–557.

30. John F. Watson, *Annals of Philadelphia, and Pennsylvania, in the Olden Times, Being a Collection of Memoirs, Anecdotes, and Incidents of the City and Its Inhabitants . . .* , Enlarged by Willis P. Hazard (Philadelphia: Edwin S. Stuart, 1898), vol. I, p. 77.

31. *The American Weekly Mercury*, January 17, 1721.

32. Whitfield J. Bell, Jr., "The Reverend Mr. Morgan, an American Correspondent of the Royal Society, 1732–1739," *Proceedings of the American Philosophical Society*, vol. XCV, 1951, pp. 255–256.

33. *The Almanack for 1727 by Nathanael Ames, Jun., Student in Physick and Astronomy* (Boston: B. Green, 1727), "Ingenious Reader."

34. *The Almanack for 1745 by Nathanael Ames* (Boston in New England: John Draper, 1745), "Courteous Reader."

35. Quoted in Oliver L. Fassig, "A Sketch of the Progress of Meteorology in Maryland and Delaware," *Maryland Weather Service* (Baltimore: Johns Hopkins Press, 1899), vol. I, p. 331. The English work is not identified.

36. E. B. Garriott, "Long Range Weather Forecasts," *Bulletin No. 35, Weather Bureau* (U.S. Department of Agriculture, 1904), pp. 37–43.

37. Henry Morley, *Character Writings of the Seventeenth Century* (London: George Routledge & Sons, 1891), pp. 55–56.

38. *Almanack for the Year 1667. By Samuel Brackenbury Philomath* (Boston, 1667).

39. John Albree, Jr., *The Tradition of the Weaver's Clock, A Study of Colonial Time-Keeping* (Medford, Mass.: privately printed, 1903), pp. 7–8.

40. John Gadbury, *Ephemerides for 1682 to 1701;* John Holwell, *Catastrophe Mundi: or Europe's many Mutations Until the Year, 1701* (London, 1682); Jacob Taylor, *Tenebrae in* [words missing in only known copy], *or, The Eclipses of the Sun and Moon Calculated for 20 Years* (Philadelphia: William Bradford, 1698); and [Vincent] *Wing's Ephemerides from 1672 to 1681* (London, 1670).

41. *Boston News-Letter*, November 20, 1704.

V. MEN OF INGENUITY

1. Rev. H. Hastings Weld, *Benjamin Franklin: His Autobiography; With a Narrative of His Public Life and Services* (New York: Derby & Jackson, 1859), pp.

116–118; and John F. Watson, *Annals of Philadelphia and Pennsylvania in the Olden Time: Being a Collection of Memoirs, Anecdotes and Incidents, of the City and Its Inhabitants,* Enlarged by Willis P. Hazard (Philadelphia: Edwin S. Stuart, 1898), vol. III, pp. 336–337.

2. Frederick B. Tolles, *James Logan and the Culture of Provincial America* (Boston: Little, Brown, 1957), pp. 202–206; see also "On the Invention of what is called Hadley's Quadrant," *American Magazine and Monthly Chronicle,* vol. I, 1758, pp. 475–476.

3. Letter from Thomas Godfrey to the Royal Society of London, November 9, 1732, Read before the Society January 31, 1733, Royal Society Archives, Letter Book Collection 20, fols. 415–419.

4. Depositions of George Steward, Edmund Wooley, and John Cox, sworn before Samuel Hassell, Mayor of Philadelphia, March 27, 1733, (Bureau of Land Records, Department of Internal Affairs, Commonwealth of Pennsylvania, Recorded in L of A, vol. D-2-2), pp. 200–102.

5. Letter from James Logan to Edmond Halley, President of the Royal Society, May 25, 1732 (Royal Society Archives, *Letter Book Minute Book*), Entry for the meeting of January 31, 1733.

6. Dr. Edmond Halley, "A Proposal for a method for finding the longitude at sea, within a degree or twenty leagues; with an account of the progress he hath made therein, by a continued series of accurate observations of the Moon," *Philosophical Transactions of the Royal Society,* vol. XXXVII, no. 421, 1731, pp. 185–195; paper read May 6, 1731.

7. "The Description of a new Instrument for taking Angles. By John Hadley, Esq. Vice-Pr. R. S. Communicated to the Society on May 13, 1731." *Philosophical Transactions of the Royal Scociety,* no. 420 for August and September 1731, vol. XXXVII (1733–1734), pp. 147–157, pl. XIII.

8. Isaac Newton, "Description of an Instrument for observing the Moon's distance from the Field Stars at Sea," *Philosophical Transactions of the Royal Society,* vol. XLII, 1742, p. 155.

9. "*An Account* of Mr. Thomas Godfrey's Improvement of Davis's Quadrant, *transferred to the* Mariner's-Bow, *communicated to the* Royal Society, by Mr. James Logan," *Philosophical Transactions of the Royal Society,* no. 435, vol. XXXVII, (1733–1734), pp. 441–450.

10. Edmund Stone, *Construction and Principal Uses of Mathematical Instruments,* translated from N. Bion (London: 1758, 2nd edition), "A Supplement concerning a further account of some of the more useful Mathematical Instruments as now improved," chapter III, pp. 274–275; and "*The Description of a new* Quadrant *for taking* Altitudes *without an Horizon, either at Sea or Land. Invented by Mr. John Elton,*" *Philosophical Transactions of the Royal Society,* no. 423, vol. XXXVII for the years 1731 and 1732 (1733), pp. 273–279. See also William Wales and Mr. William Bayley, *The Original Astronomical Observations, Made in the Course of a Voyage towards the South Pole, and Round the World, in his Majesty's Ships the Revolution and Adventure, in the Years MDCCLXXII, MDCCLXXIII, MDCCLXXIV and MDCCLXXV* (London: W. and A. Strahan, 1777), p. xxxiii.

11. *The DESCRIPTION and USE of a New Astronomical Instrument, For Taking ALTITUDES of the SUN and Stars at Sea, Without an HORIZON: Together with an Easy and Sure Method of Observing the Eclipses of Jupiter's Satellites, or any other PHOE-*

NOMENON of the like Kind, on Ship-board; In order to determine the DIFFERENCE OF MERIDIANS AT SEA. To which are added, TABLES for computing the Times when the Eclipses of the First Satellite of Jupiter happen under the Meridian of London (London, 1735), 32 pp., 1 pl.

12. Caleb Smith, *The Description, Use, and Excellency of a New Instrument, or Sea Quadrant, Invented by Caleb Smith, for Taking Altitudes of the Sun, Moon, and Stars, from the Visible Horizon (as well as any other Angular Distances at Land or Sea) without Impediment or Interruption from the Ship's Motion; Whereby the Latitude at Sea May be obtained with greater Certainty, and more frequently, than by Davis's or any other of the Common Instruments . . .* (London, c. 1735).

13. Old Salem, Inc., Winston-Salem, N.C., *Moravian Archives*, manuscript biography of Christian G. Reuter and Smith-Heath Sea Quadrant.

14. Benjamin Cole, Sr., *The Description and Use of a New Quadrant for Finding the Latitude at Sea: Invented and Made by Benjamin Cole; Also Instructions for the use of that instrument by Hadley* (London, 1748); George Adams, Sr., *The Description and Use of a New Sea Quadrant for Taking the Altitude of the Sun from the visible Horizon; Which is so contrived that the Observer will be liable to no Interruption, or Inaccuracy from the Ship's Motion. And the Latitude at Sea May be obtained with greater Certainty, and More frequently than by any Instrument of the Kind hitherto made Publick. Invented, Made and Sold by George Adams, Mathematical Instrument Maker to His Majesty's Office of Ordnance . . .* (London: John Hart, 1748); and Benjamin Cole, Sr., *The Description and Use of a New Quadrant for Finding the Latitude at Sea . . . , Second Edition. With an Appendix Shewing Some Useful Improvements on Cole's Quadrant. Particularly Godfrey's Horizon Vane improv'd. Which furnishes the Mariner with the Means of taking an Observation easily in Boisterous Weather. To which are added, Short and Plain Instructions for the Use of that most excellent Instrument, invented by John Hadley, Esq: with the Improvement of an Artificial Horizon* (London: Printed by John Hart, 1749).

15. *Boston Gazette*, September 18–25, 1738.

16. *The New-York Gazette*, January 23, 1749.

17. *The New-York Mercury*, June 11, 1753.

18. Clara Egli Le Gear, Manuscript list of the Southack charts on file in the Library of Congress; biographical sketch of Southack in *The Dictionary of American Biography;* "The New England Coasting Pilot of Cyprian Southack," *Imago Mundi*, vol. XI, 1954, pp. 137–144; and *Notes on the Southack Map (Boston 1717) to accompany the Facsimile issued by the John Carter Brown Library* (Providence: John Carter Brown Library, 1942). See also J. Franklin Jameson, *Privateering and Piracy in the Colonial Period* (New York: Macmillan, 1923), pp. 290–311.

19. John Green, *Explanation for the New Map of Nova Scotia and Cape Britain* (Boston, 1755), p. 5.

20. William Douglass, *Summary, historical and political . . . of the British Settlements in North America* (Boston, 1749), vol. I, p. 362.

21. *Boston News-Letter*, August 23, 1750; September 19, 1751; May 13, 1756; *Boston Evening Post*, May 21, 1753; and *Boston Gazette*, June 5, 1753, June 16, 1755, September 14, 1761, and November 1, 1762.

22. William Byrd, *History of the Dividing Line and Other Tracts. From the Papers of William Byrd, of Westover, in Virginia, Esquire*, ed. Thomas H. Wynne (Richmond, 1866), vol. II, "Journey to the Land of Eden . . . ," pp. 116–117.

See also Rosalind Strong Parker, "Colonel William Mayo, F.R.S., Surveyor and Promoter of the Virginia Piedmont, 1684–1744." M.A. thesis, University of Virginia, 1941, p. 68.

23. Edward B. Mathews, "The Maps and Map-Makers of Maryland," *Maryland Geological Survey* (Baltimore: Johns Hopkins University Press, October 1898), vol. II, pp. 337–488; and Arthur Pierce Middleton, *Tobacco Coast* (Newport News, Va.: The Mariner's Museum, 1953), pp. 73–75.

24. Fairfax Harrison, *Landmarks of Old Prince William* (Richmond, Va.: The Old Dominion Press, 1924), vol. II, pp. 629–634. See also Lois Fell Jackson Whitney, "Colonel Joshua Fry, Albemarle's Soldier-Statesman," M.A. thesis, University of Virginia, Corcoran School of History, 1941, pp. 8–21.

25. William P. Cumming, *The Southeast in Early Maps, With An Annotated Check List of Printed and Manuscript Regional and Local Maps of Southeastern North America During the Colonial Period* (Princeton, N.J.: Princeton University Press, 1958), pp. 52–54.

26. "The Humble Petition of Allane Jarrette To the Honble Peter Schuyler Esq' President & the Other Gentlemen of the Councell of the Province of New York, September 24, 1719," New York State Library, Albany, New York Colonial Manuscrpts, vol. LXI, pp. 187–189; and "New York Council Minutes" (manuscript), pp. xii, 26, 33, xiii, 62; and "The humble Memorial of the Proprietors of the Eastern and western Divison of Said Province of *New-Jersey*," October 12, 1719, New York Colonial Documents, vol. V, p. 531, and vol. LXXVI, p. 35. The foregoing are also repoduced in Daniel J. Pratt, compiler, *Report of the Regents of the University on the Boundaries of the State of New York* (Albany, N.Y.: The Argus Company, 1884), vol. II, pp. 618–649.

27. Office of the Surveyor General of the Board of Proprietors of the Eastern Division of New Jersey, Perth Amboy, Minutes of the Council of the Proprietors of East New-Jersey, Meeting of November 16, 1743, and of April 1 and October 19, 1745.

28. George J. Miller, *The Printing of the Elizabethtown Bill in Chancery. The Quadrant and Circumferentor, Flesh for Sale*, Pamphlet Series No. 1, Addresses Before the Board of Proprietors of the Eastern Division of New Jersey (Perth Amboy, N.J., 1942), pp. 23–33; based on the Minutes of the Council of Proprietors of East New-Jersey 1741–1746.

VI. The Witty Geometers

1. Edward B. Mathews, "History of the Boundary Dispute Between the Baltimores and Penns resulting in the Original Mason and Dixon Line," *Maryland Geological Survey* (Baltimore: Johns Hopkins University Press, 1908), vol. VII, part 3, pp. 103–203.

2. W. W. Spooner, "The Morris Family of Morrisania," *American Historical Magazine*, vol. 1, no. 1, January 1906, pp. 28–31.

3. Edward B. Mathews, ed., *Report on the Re-Survey of the Maryland-Pennsylvania Boundary. Part of the Mason and Dixon Line* (Harrisburg, Pa.: Harrisburg Publishing Co., 1909), pp. 135–138.

4. "Report of observation at Palmer's Island by James Conoway, Alexa. Dennett, Robert Jones," *Archives of Maryland*, vol. V, Proceedings of the Council of Maryland 1667–1687/8 (Baltimore: Maryland Historical Society, 1887), p. 394.

5. J. Carroll Hayes, "The Delaware Curve," *Pennsylvania Magazine of History and Biography*, vol. XLVII, 1923, pp. 238–258.

6. Historical Society of Pennsylvania. Penn Papers, Thomas Penn to Richard Peters, December 12, 1761. See also Thomas D. Cope, "The Jersey Quadrant Used in Pennsylvania," *Proceedings of the American Philosophical Society*, vol. 97, no. 5, October 30, 1953, pp. 565–570.

7. Historical Society of Pennsylvania. Penn Papers, Thomas Penn to Richard Peters, April 12, 1762.

8. Historical Society of Pennsylvania, Penn Papers, Thomas Penn to William Alexander, May 20, 1762.

9. C. Doris Hellman, "George Graham, Maker of Horological and Astronomical Instruments," *Vassar Journal of Undergraduate Studies*, vol. V, May 1931, pp. 234–243; H. Alan Lloyd, "George Graham, Horologist and Astronomer," *Journal of the Royal Society of Arts*, no. 4861, vol. C, 30 November 1951, pp. 41–46; and Henry C. King, *The History of the Telescope* (London: Charles Griffin & Co., 1955), pp. 108–118.

10. Historical Society of Pennsylvania, Penn Papers, Thomas Penn to Richard Peters, August 14, 1762.

11. Historical Society of Pennsylvania, Penn Papers, Thomas Penn to William Alexander, May 20, 1762; November 13, 1762.

12. Historical Society of Pennsylvania, Penn Papers, Thomas Penn to Governor Hamilton, August 14, 1762.

13. Historical Society of Pennsylvania, Penn Papers, Thomas Penn to the Proprietors of Pennsylvania, June 18, 1763.

14. Thomas D. Cope, "The Apprentice Years of Mason and Dixon," *Pennsylvania History*, vol. XI, no. 3, July 1944, pp. 155–170; and "Mason and Dixon and Franklin," *Proceedings of the Pennsylvania Academy of Science*, vol. XXV, 1951, pp. 167–170.

15. William Barton, *Memoirs of the Life of David Rittenhouse, L.L.D., F.R.S.* (Philadelphia: Edward Parker, 1813), p. 150.

16. U. S. National Archives. Charles Mason, Daily Journal. Entry, December 6, 1763. See also Thomas D. Cope and H. W. Robinson, "When the Maryland-Pennsylvania Boundary Survey Changed from a Political and Legal Struggle into a Scientific and Technological Project," *Proceedings of the American Philosophical Society*, vol. 98, no. 6, December 1954, pp. 432–441.

17. Thomas D. Cope, "Charles Mason and Jeremiah Dixon," *Scientific Monthly*, vol. LXII, 1946, p. 549.

18. Mason, Journal, Dec. 6, 1763; George A. Robertson, "The Original Notes of Mason and Dixon's Survey," *Magazine of Western History*, vol. V, 1886–1887, pp. 452–457.

19. Arthur E. James, *Chester County Clocks and Their Makers* (West Chester, Pa.: Chester County Historical Society, 1947), pp. 29–39.

20. American Philosophical Society, Ms. 264, William Darlington, M.D., to Franklin Bache, May 20, 1834.

21. "Introduction to the following Observations made by Messieurs Charles Mason and Jeremiah Dixon, for determining the Length of a Degree of Latitude, in the Provinces of Maryland and Pennsylvania, in North America; by the Reverend Nevil Maskeyne, B.D.F.R.S., Astronomer Royal"; "Observations for determining the Length of a Degree of latitude in the Provinces of Maryland and Pennsylvania, in North America, by Messieurs Charles Mason and Jeremiah Dixon"; "Astronomical Observations, made in the Forks of the River Brandiwine in Pennsylvania, for determining the going of a Clock sent thither by the Royal Society, in which to find the Difference of Gravity between the Royal Observatory at Greenwich, and the Place where the Clock was set up in Pennsylvania; to which are added, an Observation of the End of an Eclipse of the Moon, and some Immersions of Jupiter's First Satellite observed at the same Place in Pennsylvania: by Charles Mason and Jeremiah Dixon," *Philosophical Transactions of the Royal Society*, vol. LVIII, 1768 (London, 1769), pp. 270–335. See also Thomas D. Cope, "A Frame of Reference for Mason and Dixon," *Proceedings of the Pennsylvania Academy of Science*, vol. XIX, 1945, pp. 79–86.

22. Albany, N.Y., New York State Library, New York Council Minutes (Manuscript), vol. XXVI, pp. 417–418; Pennsylvania Department of Internal Affairs, Report of the Secretary of Internal Affairs, *Reports on the Survey and Resurveys of the Boundary Lines of the Commonwealth, Accompanied with Maps of the Same* (Harrisburg: Edwin K. Meyers, 1887), part I, pp. 493–495.

23. W. C. Hodgkins, "Report of the Engineer in Charge of the Resurvey of the Boundary Between Maryland and Pennsylvania, Part of the Mason and Dixon Line," *Report on the Resurvey of the Maryland and Pennsylvania Boundary, Part of the Mason and Dixon Line* (Harrisburg: Harrisburg Publishing Co., 1909), p. 40; and Thomas D. Cope, "Zenith Sectors, and Discoveries Made with Them, Linked with More Recent Events in Pennsylvania," *Proceedings of the Pennsylvania Academy of Science*, vol. XV–XVIII, 1941–1944, pp. 72–75.

24. Cope and Robinson, "Maryland-Pennsylvania Boundary Survey," p. 438; and Sharpe Correspondence, *Archives of Maryland* (Baltimore, Maryland Historical Society, 1895), vol. 3, pp. 124–129. Governor Horatio Sharpe to Cecelius Calvert, December 28, 1763.

25. Eric Doolittle, "Historic Discovery Made in Independence Hall," unidentified Philadelphia newspaper, September 18, 1912.

26. "Table of the Eclipses of Jupiter's First Satellite, observed at Norriton from February 16th to June 13th . . . ," *Transactions of the American Philosophical Society*, vol. 1, 1771, pp. 12, 21–22.

27. Brooke Hindle, *David Rittenhouse* (Princeton, N.J.: Princeton University Press, 1964), pp. 246–247.

28. Ohio Historical Society, Manuscript Collection. Worthington Papers, Box 1, Item 67, Rufus Putnam to Thomas Worthington, February 17, 1798.

29. "Report of William Nicoll and Gerard Bancker, surveyors of the boundary between New York and Massachusetts Bay, dated November 5, 1773," *New York Historical Collections* (New York: The New-York Historical Society, 1869), p. 325; and *Report of the Regents of the University on the Boundaries of the State of New York*, prepared by Daniel J. Pratt (Albany: The Argus Company, 1884), vol. II, pp. 177–179.

30. *The Virginia Gazette*, April 13, 1772; June 1, 1773.

31. "Thomas Marshall," *Bulletin of the Fauquier Historical Society*, July 1922, pp. 134–142.

32. Thomas Jefferson Memorial Foundation. Thomas Jefferson, Memo Books, Correspondence with James A. Bear, Jr.

33. John Russell Bartlett, ed., *Records of the Colony of Rhode Island and Providence Plantations, in New England* (Providence: Knowled Anthony & Co., 1860), vol. V, 1741–1756, pp. 322–325.

34. Rhode Island State Archives, Accounts Allowed by the Rhode Island General Assembly, June Session 1756.

35. Bartlett, *Records of the Colony of Rhode Island*, vol. V, p. 333.

36. Ibid., p. 512.

37. Caleb Smith, *The Description, Use and Excellency of a New Instrument, or Sea Quadrant, Invented by Caleb Smith, for Taking Altitudes of the Sun, Moon, and Stars, from the Visible Horizon, (as well as any other Angular Distances at Land or Sea) without Impediment or Interruption from the Ship's Motion; Whereby the Latitude at Sea May be obtained with greater Certainty, and more frequently, that by Davis's or any other of the Common Instruments* . . . (London, c. 1735).

38. Abbott Lowell Cummings, *Rural Household Inventories Establishing the Names, Uses and Furnishings of Rooms in the Colonial New England Home 1675–1775* (Boston: Society for the Preservation of New England Antiquities, 1964), pp. 234, 261.

39. Douglas Southall Freeman, *George Washington, A Biography* (New York: Charles Scribner's Sons, 1948), vol. I, p. 197 *fn.* 30.

40. Ibid., vol. I, p. 103.

41. John C. Fitzpatrick, ed., *Writings of George Washington* (Washington, D.C.: Government Printing Office, 1935), vol. 2, p. 354.

42. Ibid., vol. 2, p. 436.

43. Ibid., vol. 2, p. 463.

44. Benson J. Lossing, *The Home of Washington; Or Mount Vernon and its Associations, Historical and Biographical* (Hartford, Conn.: A. S. Hale, 1870), pp. 407–409; *Inventory of the Contents of Mount Vernon 1810*, with Prefatory Note by Worthington Chauncey Ford (1909), pp. 11–13.

45. Historical Society of Pennsylvania, Manuscripts Division. Parsons Papers. Day Book 1723–1727; Index to Surveys made in 1730; Field Book 1734; Receipt Book 1738–1749; Common Place Book, 1741. See also John W. Jordan, "William Parsons, Surveyor General, and Founder of Easton, Pennsylvania," *Pennsylvania Magazine of History and Biography*, vol. XXXIII, no. 2, 1909, pp. 340–346; and Hubertis Cummings, "William Parsons," *Bulletin of the Pennsylvania Department of Internal Affairs*, vol. XXX, no. 4, 1962, pp. 24–28.

46. Hazel Shields Garrison, "Cartography of Pennsylvania before 1800," *Pennsylvania Magazine of History and Biography*, vol. LIX, no. 1, 1935, pp. 269–274; Homer Rosenberger, "Early Maps of Pennsylvania," *Pennsylvania History*, vol. XI, no. 2, April 1944, pp. 107–109.

47. Lawrence A. Orrill, "Christopher Gist and His Sons," *Western Pennsylvania Historical Magazine*, vol. XV, August 1932, pp. 191–218.

48. American Philosophical Society, Manuscripts Division. The Benjamin Franklin Papers, Ledger D (1739–1748).

49. Adolph B. Benson, *The American of 1750: Peter Kalm's Travels in North America* (New York: Wilson-Erickson, 1937), pp. 28, 61, 149, 253, 292, 321, 351, 639, 653, 655, 725.

50. Walter Klinefelter, "Lewis Evans and His Maps," *Transactions of the American Philosophical Society*, n.s., vol. 61, Part 7, 1971, pp. 19–24; and Lawrence Henry Gipson, *Lewis Evans* (Philadelphia: The Historical Society of Pennsylvania, 1939), pp. 17–29.

51. *The Philadelphia Gazette*, January 2, 1749/50.

52. Gipson, *Lewis Evans*, pp. 33–41.

53. Garrison, *Cartography of Pennsylvania*, pp. 269–274; Rosenberger, "Early Maps of Pennsylvania," pp. 107–109.

54. [William Castell], "Extract from Castell's 'Discoverie' of America, 1644," *The New-York Historical Society Collections*, 2nd series, vol. 3, part 1, 1857, pp. 231–236.

55. Anna Wharton Smith, *Genealogy of the Fisher Family 1682–1896* (Philadelphia: privately printed, 1896), pp. 22–34.

56. Lawrence C. Wroth, *The Way of a Ship* (Portland, Maine: The Southworth-Anthoensen Press, 1937), p. 93, and "Joshua Fisher's 'Chart of Delaware Bay and River'," *Pennsylvania Magazine of History and Biography*, vol. LXXIV, no. 1, January 1950, pp. 90–109; Garrison, *Cartography of Pennsylvania*, pp. 279–281.

57. Capt. James Campbell, *Directions for Navigating up Delaware-Bay, from the Capes to Reedy-Island* (London: T. Faden, 1776); Lawrence C. Wroth, "Some American Contributions to the Art of Navigation 1519–1802," *Proceedings of the Massachusetts Historical Society*, vol. LXVIII, 1944–48, pp. 93–96; and M. V. Brewington, "Maritime Philadelphia 1609–1837," *Pennsylvania Magazine of History and Biography*, vol. LXIII, no. 2, April 1939, p. 98.

58. Lyman Carrier, "Dr. John Mitchell, Naturalist, Cartographer, and Historian," *Annual Report of the American Historical Association*, vol. I, 1918, pp. 201–219; and Herbert Thatcher, "John Mitchell, M.D., F.R.S. of Virginia," *Virginia Magazine of History and Biography*, vol. XXXIX, 1931, pp. 126–135; vol. XL, pp. 40–60, 268–279, 335–346; vol. XLI, pp. 60–70, 144–152.

59. Sir James Edward Smith, ed., *A Selection of the Correspondence of Linnaeus* (London, 1821), vol. I, p. 34.

60. Walter W. Ristow, comp., "John Mitchell's Map of the British and French Dominions in North America," *A la Carte, Selected Papers on Maps and Atlases* (Washington, D.C.: Library of Congress, 1972), pp. 103–113.

VII. To Rouse the Genius

1. E. G. R. Taylor, *The Mathematical Practitioners of Hanoverian England 1714–1840* (Cambridge: Cambridge University Press, 1966), pp. 14, 35–36.

2. A. W. Richeson, *English Land Measuring to 1800* (Cambridge, Mass.: The M.I.T. Press, 1966), pp. 90–92.

3. Robert Francis Seybolt, *The Evening School in Colonial America*, University of Illinois, Bureau of Educational Research, Bulletin No. 24 (Urbana, Ill.: University of Illinois Press, 1925), pp. 21–32, 58–59.

4. C. B. Hayes, *The American Lyceum. Its History and Contribution to Education*, Bulletin No. 12, Office of Education, U.S. Department of the Interior (Washington, D.C.: Government Printing Office, 1932); and S. I. Jackson, "Some Ancestors of the 'Extension Course'," *New England Quarterly*, vol. XIV, 1941, pp. 505–508.

5. Seybolt, *The Evening School*, pp. 49–54.

6. Stanley Morison, *American Copybooks: An Outline of Their History from Colonial to Modern Times* (Philadelphia, 1951). See also Ray Nash, "American Writing Masters and Copybooks," *Transactions of the Colonial Society of Massachusetts*, vol. XLII, 1952–1956 (1964), pp. 344–392.

7. George Fox, *Instructions for Right Spelling and Plain Directions for Reading and Writing True English. With Several Delightful Things Very Useful and Necessary, Both for Young and Old, to Read and Learn* (London: B. Clark, 1683); James Hodder, *Hodder's Arithmetick; or, that necessary art made most easy* (London, 1661); and Edward Cocker, *Cocker's Arithmetic* (London, 1677). See also [Isaac Greenwood], *Arithmetick, Vulgar and Decimal: With the Application thereof, to a variety of Cases in Trade, and Commerce* (Boston: S. Kneel and T. Green, for T. Hancock, 1729).

8. George Fisher, *The American Instructor: or, Young Man's Best Companion* (Philadelphia: Franklin & Hall, 1748); and John Jenkins, *The Art of Writing* (Boston: Thomas & Andrews, 1791).

9. Louis C. Karpinski, "The Elusive George Fisher 'Accomptant'—Writer or Editor of Three Popular Arithmetics," *Scripta Mathematica*, vol. 3, 1935, pp. 337–339.

10. B. Fernow, trans., *Minutes of the Orphan Masters of New Amsterdam*, 2 vols. (New York: F. P. Harper, 1902 and 1907), vol. II, pp. 115–116.

11. Jasper Dankers and Peter Sluyter, *Journal of a Voyage to New York in 1679–1680*, trans. Henry C. Murphy, from the original Dutch manuscript (New York: Long Island Historical Society, 1867), p. 128. See also Imogen Clark, *Old Days and Old Ways* (New York: Crowell, 1928), pp. 60–64; and W. H. Kilpatrick, *The Dutch Schools in New Netherlands and Colonial New York* (Washington, D.C., Government Printing Office, 1912), pp. 83.

12. Seybolt, *The Evening School*, pp. 49–54.

13. *Boston News-Letter*, March 14–21 and 21–28, 1709.

14. Samuel Sewall, "Diary," *Collections of the Massachusetts Historical Society*, 5th series, vol. V (1878), entry for 8 March 1719/20.

15. *Boston Gazette*, February 19–March 7 and March 21–22, 1719.

16. William Francis Guess, *South Carolina, Annals of Pride and Protest* (New York: Harper, 1957), pp. 95–96; Colyer Meriwether, "History of Higher Education in South Carolina, With a Sketch of the Free School System," *Contributions to American Educational History* [Circulars of Information 3, 4 and 7, 1888, 1, 1889] (Washington, D.C.: Government Printing Office, 1889), vol. II, pp. 13–15.

17. *American Weekly Mercury* (New York City), October 17–24 and 24–31 and October 31–November 7, 1723.

18. *Boston Gazette*, September 4–11 and 11–18, 1727; and *Boston Gazette and Country Journal*, September 13 and 26, 1756; *Essex Journal and New Hampshire Packet*, October 25 and November 1, 1776; and Robert Francis Seybolt, *The Public Schoolmasters of Colonial Boston* (Cambridge, Mass.: Harvard University Press, 1939), pp. 19, 24, and 29.

19. *New England Weekly Journal,* July 17 and 24, 1727; *Weekly News-Letter,* July 6–13 and 13–20, 1727.

20. *Boston Gazette,* March 26–April 2, and April 2–9, 1739.

21. Ibid., no. 684, February 5–12, 1733.

22. *Connecticut Journal,* May 27, 1768.

23. *Pennsylvania Gazette,* July 11, 1734.

24. *Pennsylvania Gazette and the American Weekly Mercury,* October 3–10, October 31–November 7, and December 5–13, 1734.

25. *American Weekly Mercury,* October 16–23, 1753.

26. *Pennsylvania Gazette,* October 30, 1740.

27. Lawrence Henry Gipson, *Lewis Evans* (Philadelphia: Historical Society of Pennsylvania, 1939), p. 146; Walter Klinefelter," Lewis Evans and His Maps," *Transactions of the American Philosophical Society,* n.s., vol. 61, part 7, 1971, p. 12.

28. *Pennsylvania Gazette,* November 24, December 1, 6, 15, and 20, 1743.

29. *Boston Weekly News-Letter,* October 2–9 and 9–16, 1735; and *Boston Weekly News-Letter,* July 7, 1737.

30. *Boston Weekly News-Letter,* July 7, 1737; Manuscript navigation book of Job Palmer in the Yale University Library.

31. *Boston Evening Post,* November 21 and 28, 1737.

32. *Boston Weekly News-Letter,* September 12, 1754.

33. Ibid., October 3, 10, and 17, 1754.

34. *Pennsylvania Gazette,* October 23 and November 6, 1755.

35. Ibid., October 2 and 9, 1760.

36. *New-York Gazette or Weekly Post-Boy,* January 12 and February 16, 1764.

37. Ibid., April 12, 1764.

38. *New-York Mercury,* May 6, 13, 20, September 30, and October 7, 1765.

39. *Pennsylvania Gazette,* August 7, 1766.

40. Ibid., October 9 and 16, 1766; *Boston Post-Boy* August 17, 24, and 31, 1767.

41. *New-York Gazette or Weekly Post-Boy,* December 12, 1768.

42. *Pennsylvania Gazette,* October 18, 1770.

43. *The Pennsylvania Chronicle,* August 26, 1771.

44. *Pennsylvania Gazette,* September 26, 1771.

45. Ibid., September 12, 1771.

46. Ibid., November 17, 1773.

47. Theodore G. Thayer, *As We Were, The Story of Old Elizabethtown* (Elizabeth, N.J.: Grassman Publishing Co., 1964), p. 109.

VIII. NEW PATHS IN SCIENCE

1. John A. Goodwin, *Pilgrim Republic* (Boston: Ticknor & Co., 1888), pp. 32, 243, 295, 298, 401, 412, 436–439; William Bradford, *History of Plimoth Plantation* (Commonwealth Edition) (Boston: Wright and Potter Printing Co., 1898), p. 316; George E. Bowman, "Plymouth Wills and Inventories," *The Mayflower Descendant,* vol. VI, pp. 168–174; and Nathaniel Morton, *New England's Memorial* (Boston: Crocker and Brewster, 1826, 5th edition), p. 102.

2. *The Description and Use of the Globes, Celestial and Terrestrial; With Variety for Examples for the Learner's Exercises: Intended for the Use of Such Persons as would attain to the Knowledge of those Instruments; But Chiefly designed for the Instruction of the Young Gentlemen at the Academy in Philadelphia. To which is added Rules for Working all the Cases in Plain and Spherical Triangles without a Scheme. By Theophilus Grew, Mathematical Professor* (Germantown: Printed by Christopher Sower, 1753), 60 pp.

3. Alfred Henry Smith, ed., *Writings of Benjamin Franklin* (London: Macmillan & Co., 1905), vol. III, pp. 89–91.

4. *Pennsylvania Gazette*, March 12, 1745.

5. *Boston Weekly News-Letter*, March 3 and 10, 1742/43; and *Boston Evening Post*, April 4, 1743.

6. Justin Winsor, ed., *The Memorial History of Boston, Including Suffolk County, Massachusetts 1630–1880* (Boston: Ticknor & Co., 1886), vol. IV, p. 492.

7. H. Alan Lloyd, "George Graham, Horologist and Astronomer," *Horological Journal*, vol. 93, 1951, pp. 708–717.

8. *The New-York Gazette*, July 8, 1734; *The New-England Weekly Journal*, June 24, 1734.

9. Chauncey Whittlesey, "A Description of an Orrery. . . ," *American Magazine and Historical Chronicle*, January 1744 (1743 O. S.), vol. I, pp. 202–203.

10. *The Pennsylvania Gazette*, December 6, 1750.

11. *The New-York Gazette Revived in the Weekly Post-Boy*, July 29, 1751.

12. William Barton, *Memoirs of the Life of David Rittenhouse, L.L.D., F.R.S.* (Philadelphia: Edward Parker, 1813), pp. 192–193.

13. J. Rowning, *A Compendious System of Natural Philosophy with Notes Containing the Mathematical Demonstrations and Some Occasional Remarks* (London: Saml. Harding, 1743), part IV, chapter 15, "The Description and the Use of the Orrery and the Globes," pp. 147–174; and Barton, *Memoirs of David Rittenhouse*, p. 198.

14. *Pennsylvania Gazette*, April 28, 1768; "A description of a new Orrery, planned and now nearly finished by David Rittenhouse, A. M. of Norriton in the county of Philadelphia. Communicated by Dr. Smith," *Transactions of the American Philosophical Society*, vol. I, 1789, pp. 1–3.

15. American Philosophical Society, Minutes, 3 January 1783; Archives Affaires Etrangeres, *Correspondence Polit. Etats-Unis*, vol. XXVI, pp. 252–253. Howard C. Rice, Jr., *The Rittenhouse Orrery Princeton's Eighteenth-Century Planetarium, 1767–1954* (Princeton, N.J.: Princeton University Press, 1954), pp. 21–75.

16. Leonard W. Labaree and Whitfield J. Bell, Jr., eds., *The Papers of Benjamin Franklin* (New Haven: Yale University Press, 1959), vol. I, p. 190. *The Pennsylvania Gazette*, January 19, 1731, advertisement for Godfrey's almanacs.

17. "Two Rare Imprints," *Pennsylvania Magazine of History and Biography*, vol. XXXI, 1907, p. 239.

18. Phillips Russell, ed., *Poor Richard's Almanack, Being the Almanacks of 1733, 1749, 1756, 1757, 1758 first written under the name of Richard Saunders by Benjamin Franklin* (Garden City: Doubleday, Doran, 1928), pp. xii–xiii.

19. *Poor Richard improved: Being An Almanack and Ephemeris of the Motions of the Sun and Moon . . . For the Year of Christ 1733*, p. 5; reprinted in ibid., 1734 and 1735, p. 6 in both.

20. *Poor Richard improved: Being an Almanack and Ephemeris of the Motions of the Sun and Moon . . . For the Year of Christ 1738*, p. 19.

21. Clarence S. Brigham, "An Account of American Almanacs and Their Value for Historical Study," *Proceedings of the American Antiquarian Society*, October 1925, p. 19; and Brooke Hindle, *David Rittenhouse* (Princeton, N.J.: Princeton University Press, 1964), pp. 91–92.

22. *Pennsylvania Chronicle*, November 7, 1772; Hindle, *Rittenhouse*, pp. 91–92.

23. Robb Sagendorph, *America and Her Almanacs, Wit, Wisdom & Weather 1639–1970* (Dublin, N.H.: Yankee, Inc., and Boston: Little, Brown, 1970), pp. 112–113.

24. "Biography of Benjamin West, L.L.D. A.A.S., Professor of Mathematicks, Astronomy, and Natural Philosophy, in Rhode-Island College—and Fellow of the Philosophical Society of Philadelphia, &c," *The Rhode-Island Literary Repository*, vol. I, no. VII, October 1814, pp. 137–160.

25. Frances Manwaring Caulkins, *History of New London, Connecticut, From the First Survey of the Coast in 1612, to 1860* (New London: H. D. Utley, 1895), p. 656; and Chester Noyes Greenough, "New England Almanacs, 1766–1775, and the American Revolution," *Proceedings of the American Antiquarian Society*, October 1935, pp. 317–320.

26. Greenough, "New England Almanacs," pp. 394–395.

27. Sagendorph, *America and Her Almanacs*, pp. 108–112.

28. Ibid., pp. 112–114.

29. Richard B. Holman, "Seventeenth Century American Prints," in John D. Morse, ed., *Prints in and of America to 1850* (Charlottesville, Va.: The University Press of Virginia, 1970), pp. 23–52; John Langdon Sibley, *Biographical Sketches of Graduates of Harvard University in Cambridge, Massachusetts* (Cambridge, Mass., 1881), vol. II, p. 222.

30. Harry Woolf, *The Transit of Venus, A Study of Eighteenth Century Science* (Princeton, N. J.: Princeton University Press, 1959), pp. 170–175.

31. Benjamin West, *An Account of the Transit of Venus Upon the Sun, The Third Day of June, 1769, at Providence, in New-England* (Providence, R. I., 1769), pp. 11–12.

32. Franklin B. Dexter, ed., *The Literary Diary of Ezra Stiles, D.D., LL.D.* (New York, Charles Scribner's Sons, 1901), vol. I, pp. 11–13.

33. John Winthrop, *Two Lectures on the Parallax and Distance of the Sun, as Deductible from the Transit of Venus* (Boston, 1769).

34. "Observation of the Contacts of the Limbs of VENUS and the SUN, June 3, 1769, made by Mr. William Poole at Wilmington, in Pennsylvania," Appendix to the Astronomical Papers, *Transactions of the American Philosophical Society*, vol. I, 1771, p. 20 of Appendix; "An Abstract of Mr. Benjamin WEST's Account of the Transit of Venus, as Observed as Providence, in New England, June 3, 1769," ibid., pp. 97–105.

35. David Rittenhouse, "Calculation of the Transit of Venus over the Sun as it happened June 3rd, 1769 in lat. 40 N. long. 5h. West from Greenwich," pp. 4–7; and William Smith, "An Account of the Transit of Venus over the Sun, June 3rd, 1769, as observed in Norriton, in Pennsylvania," pp. 8–39; and John Ewing, "An Account of the Transit of Venus over the Sun, June 3rd, 1769, and of the Transit of Mercury, Nov. 9th, both as observed in the State-House Square, Philadelphia," pp. 39–83; and Owen Biddle, "An Account of the Transit of Venus over

the Sun, June 3rd, 1769, as observed near Cape Henlopen, on Delaware," pp.
83–91; and William Smith, "An Account of the terrestrial measurement between the
Observatories of Norriton and Philadelphia; with the difference of longitude and latitude thence deduced," pp. 114–120; and William Smith, and J. Ewing, O. Biddle,
H. Williamson, T. Combe and D. Rittenhouse, "Apparent time of the Contacts of
the limbs of the Sun and Venus; with other circumstances of most note, in the different European observations of the Transit, June 3rd, 1769," pp. 120–126, *Transactions of the American Philosophical Society*, vol. I, 1771.

  36. Brooke Hindle, *The Pursuit of Science in Revolutionary America 1735–1789*
(Chapel Hill, N.C.: University of North Carolina Press, 1956), pp. 146–165.

  37. "New Method of placing a Meridian Mark, in a Letter to the Rev. Dr.
Ewing, Provost of the University. By D. Rittenhouse, Esq.," *Transactions of the
American Philosophical Society*, vol. II, 1786, no. XVII, pp. 181–183.

  38. *Boston Gazette*, October 6–13, 1729.

  39. Ibid., May 21, 1754.

  40. Ibid., June 9, 1760.

  41. *Boston News-Letter*, August 30, 1770.

  42. *The Virginia Gazette*, December 19, 1777.

  43. Edwin Wolf 2nd, "The Dispersal of the Library of William Byrd of
Westover," *Proceedings of the American Antiquarian Society*, April 1958, pp. 19–45.

  44. George C. Mason, *Annals of the Redwood Library, and Athenaeum* (Newport, R.I.: Redwood Library, 1891), pp. 9–11, 27–30.

  45. Howard Mumford Jones, *O Strange New World. American Culture; The
Formative Years* (New York: Viking, 1964), p. 285.

  46. Carl Bridenbaugh, *Cities in Revolt* (New York: Knopf, 1955), pp.
310–311.

  47. *Dictionary of American Biography* (New York: Charles Scribner's Sons,
1928–1936), vol. III, pp. 440–441; *The National Cyclopedia of American Biography*
(New York: J. T. White & Co., 1893–1966), vol. III, pp. 233–234.

  48. Cotton Mather, *Parentator, Memoirs of Remarkables in the Life and Death
of the Ever-Memorable Dr. Increase Mather* (Boston, 1724), p. 86.

  49. Smith, *Writings of Benjamin Franklin*, vol. I, pp. 298–299.

  50. Bernard Fay, *Franklin* (Boston: Little, Brown, 1929), pp. 88–92,
119–123.

  51. Library Company of Philadelphia, Minutes, vol. I, pp. 26–28, Communication from the founders to Thomas Penn, May 16, 1733.

  52. Library Company of Philadelphia, Minutes, vol. I, p. 74, 83, 86, 93,
102; and Edwin Wolf 2nd and Robert C. Smith, "A Press for Penn's Pumps," *The
Art Quarterly*, vol. XXIV, no. 3, Autumn 1961, pp. 277–248.

  53. Library Company of Philadelphia, Minutes, vol. I, p. 131; and I. Bernard Cohen, ed., *Benjamin Franklin's Experiments* (Cambridge, Mass.: Harvard University Press, 1941), p. 169.

  54. Austin K. Gray, *Benjamin Franklin's Library* (Philadelphia: Library
Company of Philadelphia, 1936), p. 137.

  55. Carl Van Doren, "The Beginnings of the American Philosophical Society," *Proceedings of the American Philosophical Society*, vol. LXXXVII, no. 3, 1943,
p. 277.

56. Lyon G. Taylor, "Virginia's Contribution to Science," *Proceedings of the American Antiquarian Society*, October 1915, pp. 364–365; "To David Rittenhouse, Esquire, from John Page, Esquire, December 4, 1799," *Transactions of the American Philosophical Society*, vol. II, 1786, pp. 173–174.

57. George Brown Goode, "Museum-History and Museums of History," *Report of the United States National Museum, Part II, Annual Report of the Board of Regents of the Smithsonian Institution . . . for the Year 1897* (Washington, D.C.: Government Printing Office, 1901), p. 70, and "The Beginnings of American Science," ibid., p. 425. See also Dirk J. Struik, *Yankee Science in the Making* (Boston: Little, Brown, 1948), p. 43; and John Adams, *Works*, ed. C. F. Adams (Boston, 1851–1856), vol. IV, p. 302n.

58. *South Carolina Gazette*, March 22, April 5, April 12, 1773; and *The South Carolina Gazette and Country Journal*, March 30 and April 6, 1773.

59. David Ramsay, *History of South Carolina* (Charleston, 1809), vol. II, p. 379.

60. J. L. E. W. Shecut, *Medical and Philosophical Essays* (Charleston, 1809), pp. 49–52. See also "The Collections of the Charleston Library Society from 1798 to 1815," *Bulletin of the College of Charleston Museum*, vol. 2, no. 6, October 1906, pp. 47–54; and Paul M. Rea, "Origin of the Museum," *Bulletin of the College of Charleston Museum*, vol. VIII, no. 4, April 1911, pp. 25–27; and Paul M. Rea, "A Contribution to Early Museum History in America," *Proceedings of the American Association of Museums*, vol. IX, July 6–9, 1915, pp. 53–65.

61. Ernest S. Dodge, "The Contributions to Exploration of the Salem East India Marine Society," *The American Neptune*, 1965, vol. XXV, no. 3, pp. 176–179; Walter Muir Whitehill, *The East India Marine Society and the Peabody Museum of Salem: A Sesquicentennial History* (Salem, Mass.: Peabody Museum, 1949), pp. 3–15.

IX. Such Pleasant Inventions

1. James Savage, *A Genealogical Dictionary of the First Settlers of New England* (Boston: Little, Brown, 1860), vol. II, p. 341.

2. Robert Francis Seybolt, *Apprenticeship & Apprenticeship Education in Colonial New England and New York*, Teachers College, Columbia University, Contributions to Education, No. 85 (New York: Teachers College, Columbia University, 1917), pp. 22–51. See also Ian M. G. Quimby, "Apprenticeship in Colonial Philadelphia," (M. A. thesis, University of Delaware, 1963).

3. Penrose R. Hoopes, *Connecticut Clockmakers of the Eighteenth Century* (Hartford, Conn.: Edwin Valentine Mitchell, 1930), p. 85.

4. Carl Bridenbaugh, *The Colonial Craftsman* (New York: New York University Press, 1950), pp. 160–161.

5. Arthur H. Cole, "The Tempo of Mercantile Life in Colonial America," *Business History Review*, vol. XXXIII, Autumn 1959, pp. 277–299.

6. Silvio A. Bedini, *Early American Scientific Instruments and Their Makers* (Washington, D.C.: Smithsonian Institution, 1964), pp. 85–89; Massachusetts Historical Society, Manuscripts Division, Thwing Catalogue, file on Thomas Greenough.

7. New London County Historical Society, Manuscripts Collection. Manuscript Journal of Clark Elliott, unpaginated.

8. Edward E. Chandlee, *Six Quaker Clockmakers* (Philadelphia: Historical Society of Pennsylvania, 1943), pp. 105–145.

9. Adolph B. Benson, ed., *The America of 1750: Peter Kalm's Travels in North America* (New York: Dover Publications, 1966), vol. I, p. 220.

10. *Boston Gazette*, August 22–29 and November 21–28, 1737.

11. Ibid., December 25, 1744.

12. Ibid., May 19–26, 1740.

13. *Boston News-Letter*, June 24–July 1, 1742, and December 26, 1745.

14. Elliott, Manuscript Journal.

15. *The Cabinet Maker's Assistant* (London, 1853).

16. F. Lewis Hinckley, *Directory of the Historic Cabinet Woods* (New York: Bonanza Books, 1960), pp. 115–116, 142–143, 151, 168–179.

17. Samuel G. Drake, *The History and Antiquities of Boston; the Capital of Massachusetts and Metropolis of New England, From Its Settlement in 1630 to the Year 1770.* 2 vols. (Boston: Luther Stevens, 1856), vol. II, p. 781; and Isaac J. Greenwood, ed., *The Revolutionary Services of John Greenwood of Boston and New York 1775–1783* (New York: privately printed, 1922), p. 93.

18. Penrose R. Hoopes, *Shop Records of Daniel Burnap, Clockmaker* (Hartford, Connecticut Historical Society, 1958), pp. 63–66. Connecticut Historical Society, Manuscript Division, Manuscript ledgers of Daniel Burnap.

19. *Massachusetts, Acts and Resolves, 1735–1736*, vol. II, chapter 22, p. 788. "An Act Granting to Rowland Houghton of Boston, in the County of Suffolk, Merchant, the Sole Privilege of Making and Vending a Certain Surveying Instrument Called "The New Theodolite."

20. *Boston Gazette*, January 17–24, 1737.

21. Bedini, *Early American Scientific Instruments*, p. 26.

22. Franklin Institute, Philadelphia.

23. Private collection.

24. New Hampshire Historical Society, Concord, N.H.

25. Samuel Sturmy, *The Mariners Magazine; Or, Sturmy's Mathematical and Practical Arts* (London: Printed by E. Cotes, 1669). This work is described in considerable detail in Cyril Ernest Kenney, *The Quadrant and the Quill* (London: Metcham and Son, n.d.).

26. Sturmy, *Mariner's Magazine*.

27. Ibid.

28. Ibid.

29. Joseph Moxon, *Mechanick Dialling* (London, 1668); and William Leybourn, *Dialling, Plain, Concave, Convex, &c* . . . (London: Awnsham Churchill, 1682).

30. Bedini, *Early American Scientific Instruments*, pp. 36–37; M. V. Brewington, *The Peabody Museum Collection of Navigating Instruments* (Salem: Peabody Museum, 1963), pp. 132.

31. [Rev. William Bentley], *The Diary of William Bentley, D. D.*, (Salem: Essex Institute, 1907), vol. 3, p. 130, entry for December 30, 1804; Essex County (Massachusetts) Probate Records, Docket 15785; and Henry W. Belknap, *Artists and Craftsmen of Essex County Massachusetts* (Salem: Essex Institute, 1927), p. 103.

32. Newport, R.I., Probate Court Records, book 6, p. 54, entry for March 10, 1820; p. 69, entry for March 17, 1820; Theodore Bolton, *Early American Portrait Painters in Miniature* (New York: Frederic Fairchild Sherman, 1921), p. 92; Franklin B. Dexter, ed., *The Literary Diary of Ezra Stiles, D.D., L.L.D.*, (New York: Charles Scribner's Sons, 1901), vol. III, pp. 131–132, 389; William B. Stevens, "Samuel King of Newport," *Antiques*, November 1969, pp. 729–733.

X. A Work Adorned

1. Silvanus P. Thompson, "The Rose of the Winds: The Origin and Development of the Compass Card," *Proceedings of the British Academy 1913–1914*, London, 1914, vol. 6, pp. 179–209.

2. Private collection.

3. Silvio A. Bedini, *Early American Scientific Instruments and Their Makers* (Washington, D.C.: Smithsonian Institution, 1964), pp. 81–83; and Charles E. Smart, *The Makers of Surveying Instruments in America since 1700* (Troy, N.Y. Regal Art Press, 1962), frontispiece.

4. Bedini, *Early American Scientific Instruments*, pp. 112–117; and Massachusetts Historical Society, Manuscripts Division, Paul Revere, Day Book.

5. Clarence S. Bingham, *Paul Revere's Engravings* (Worcester, Mass.: American Antiquarian Society, 1954), pp. 79–81, 84, 87, 117, 139.

6. Wilfred P. Cole, "Henry Dawkins, Engraver," thesis submitted for an M.A. degree, University of Delaware, 1966, pp. 9–26, 110–112; see also Wilfred P. Cole, "Henry Dawkins and the Quaker Comet," *Winterthur Portfolio 4*, pp. 33–46.

7. John Lowry Ruth, "Pages From the First Clockmaker's Catalogue of Record. The Pamphlet Issued by Jacob Gorgas of Lancaster County, Pa. c. 1765," *Timepieces Quarterly*, vol. I, no. 2, February 1949, pp. 66–67.

8. E. Wilfred Taylor, J. Simms Wilson, and P. D. Scott Maxwell, *At The Sign of the Orrery, The Origins of the Firm of Cooke, Troughton & Simms, Ltd.* [n.p., n.d.], pp. 18–23.

9. Leonard W. Labaree and Whitfield J. Bell, Jr., eds., *The Papers of Benjamin Franklin* (New Haven: Yale University Press, 1962), vol. 5, pp. 331–332.

10. William Barton, *Memoirs of the Life of David Rittenhouse, L.L.D., F.R.S.* (Philadelphia: Edward Parker, 1813), p. 139.

11. A. Hughlett Mason, ed., *The Journal of Charles Mason and Jeremiah Dixon, Transcribed from the Original in the United States National Archives, With an Introduction.* Memoirs of the American Philosophical Society, vol. 76, 1969.

12. Barton, *Memoirs of David Rittenhouse*, p. 155.

13. Ibid., p. 207.

14. Frederick William Hunter, *Stiegel Glass* (Boston: Houghton Mifflin, 1914), pp. 103–104.

15. John F. Amelung, *Remarks on Manufacturers, Principally of the New Established Glass-House, Near Frederick-Town, In the State of Maryland* (Printed for the Author, 1787); and *Maryland Journal and Baltimore Advertiser*, February 11, 1785.

16. Silvio A. Bedini, "Lens-Making for Scientific Instrumentation in the Seventeenth Century," *Applied Optics*, vol. 5, no. 5, May 1966, pp. 687–694, and "The Makers of Galileo's Scientific Instruments," in *Atti del Symposium Internationale*

della Storia, Metodologia, Logica e Filosofia della Scienza (Galileo Nella Storia e Nella Filosofia della Scienza, Vinci: Gruppo Italiano della Storia della Scienza, 1967), pp. 89–115; Silvio A. Bedini and Derek J. de Solla Price, "Instrumentation," in Melvin Kranzberg and Carroll W. Pursell, Jr., eds., *Technology in Western Civilization* (New York: Oxford University Press, 1967), vol. I, chapter 11, pp. 168–187; and Francis W. Glaze, "History of Optical Glass Production in the United States," *American Ceramics Society Bulletin*, January 1953, pp. 242–245.

17. Joshua Kelley, *Modern Navigator's Complete Tutor* (London, 1720).

18. Silvio A. Bedini, "The Tube of Long Vision" *Physis*, Anno XIII, fasc. 2, 1971, pp. 147–204; and Bedini and Price, "Instrumentation," pp. 172–175.

19. Nicholas Bion, *The Construction and Principal Use of Mathematical Instruments*, trans. Edmund Stone (London, 1758); 2nd ed. "An Appendix or Supplement Concerning a Further Account of Some of the Most Useful Mathematical Instruments as Now Improved," p. 307.

20. Peter Dollond, *Some account of the discovery made by the late John Dollond which led to the grand improvement of the reflecting telescopes, in order to correct some misrepresentation in foreign publications, of that discovery; with an attempt to account for the mistake in an experiment made by Sir Isaac Newton on which experiment, the improvement of the reflecting telescope, entirely depended* (London, April 15, 1789), pp. 216, 233.

21. *The New-York Gazette, or The Weekly Post-Boy*, May 21, 1753.

22. Barton, *Memoirs of David Rittenhouse*, p. 105.

23. Ibid., p. 171, p. 181.

24. Ibid., p. 171.

25. W. Smith, J. Lukens, D. Rittenhouse, and J. Sellers, "An Account of the Transit of Venus . . . ," *Transactions of the American Philosophical Society*, vol. I, 1771, p. 11.

26. Ibid., pp. 11–14.

27. American Philosophical Society, Manuscript Division. Benjamin Lightfoot to Samuel Coates, August 21, 1771.

28. American Philosophical Society, Manuscripts Division. Printed receipt of the Delaware and Schuylkill Canal Navigation Co., February 19, 1793.

29. Corra Bacon-Foster, "Early Chapters in the Development of the Potomac Route to the West," *Records of the Columbia Historical Society*, vol. 15, 1912, pp. 123–322; and George Washington Ware, "The Early Development of the Chesapeake and Ohio Canal Projects," *Johns Hopkins University Studies in History and Political Science*, (Baltimore: Johns Hopkins University Press, 1899), vol. XVII, pp. 9–14.

30. Cecil A. Meadows, *Trade Signs and Their Origins* (London: Routledge and Kegan Paul, 1957), p. 4.

31. Alice Morse Earle, *Stage-Coach and Tavern Days* (New York: Macmillan, 1901), pp. 141–142.

32. Charles Dickens, *Dombey and Son* (London, 1848; New York: Dodd, Mead, 1950), pp. 31–32.

33. Raymond J. Walker, "The Tavern Signs of Old Boston," *Hobbies*, vol. 38, no. 9, November 1933, pp. 87–88. See also Annie Haven Thwing, *The Crooked and Narrow Streets of the Town of Boston, 1630–1822* (Boston: Charles E. Lauriat, 1925), p. 136; Justin Winsor, *Memorial History of Boston* (Boston: Ticknor & Co., 1886), vol. II, p. xx; and Leroy Thwing, "The Four Carving Skillins," *Antiques*, June 1938, pp. 326–328.

34. *Boston Gazette*, March 12, 1770.

35. *The Salem Gazette and Newbury and Marblehead Advertiser*, Friday, July 15, 1774, vol. I, no. 3, p. 16. The figure also appeared in advertisements in *The Gentlemen and Ladies Town and Country Magazine*, April 1789, and in the *Columbia Centinel*, March and April, 1792.

36. In 1916 it was acquired by the Bostonian Society and it has been preserved and exhibited in its collection since that time. See "Report of the Committee on the Rooms," *Proceedings of the Bostonian Society*, 1917, no. 1, p. 16.

37. Nathaniel Hawthorne, "Drowne's Wooden Image," *Mosses from an Old Manse. The Collected Novels and Tales of Nathaniel Hawthorne* (New York: Random House, Modern Library, 1937), pp. 1116–1124.

38. Earle, *Stage Coach and Tavern Days*, p. 139.

39. Erwin O. Christensen, *The Index of American Design* (New York: Macmillan, 1950), p. 62.

40. Philip F. Purrington, "Taking Lunars on Water Street," *Bulletin of the Old Dartmouth Historical Society and Whaling Museum*, Spring 1959, pp. 2–4.

41. *The New Bedford [Mass.] Mercury*, 1878.

42. Purrington, "Taking Lunars . . . ," pp. 2–4.

43. M. V. Brewington, *The Peabody Museum Collection of Navigating Instruments* (Salem: Peabody Museum, 1964), p. 134. See also Christensen, *Index of American Design*, p. 70.

44. *New-York Mercury*, October 20, 1755; Cole, "Henry Dawkins," pp. 33–46.

45. Steven J. Shaw, "Colonial Newspaper Advertising: A Step Toward Freedom of the Press," *Business History Review*, vol. XXXIII, 1959, pp. 409–420.

46. Isaiah Thomas, *The History of Printing in America, With a Biography of Printers, and an Account of Newspapers* (Albany: Joel Munsell, 1874), vol. II, pp. 1–10.

47. *The Salem [Mass.] Gazette and Newbury and Marblehead Advertiser*, Friday, July 15, 1774, vol. I, no. 3, p. 16.

48. *Baltimore Daily Repository*, May 13, 1793.

49. *Philadelphia Gazette*, April 12, 1798.

XI. Of Liberty and Life

1. Brooke Hindle, *David Rittenhouse* (Princeton, N.J.: Princeton University Press, 1964), pp. 124–138.

2. William Barton, *Memoirs of the Life of David Rittenhouse, L.L.D., F.R.S.* (Philadelphia: Edward Parker, 1813), pp. 264–274.

3. Pennsylvania Archives, 2d series, vol. I, pp. 573–576, 647; Pennsylvania Colonial Records, vol. VII, p. 142; Daniel K. Cassell, *A Genea-Biographical History of the Rittenhouse Family and All Its Branches in America* (Philadelphia, 1893), pp. 224–226.

4. Hollis R. Bailey, ed., *The Bailey Genealogy. James, John and Thomas and Their Descendants* (Somerville, Mass.: The Citizen Company, 1899), pp. 350–352, 377–378; John S. Barry, *A Historical Sketch of the Town of Hanover, Mass., With Family Genealogies* (Boston: For the Author by Samuel G. Drake, 1853), pp. 199–206; Silvio A. Bedini, *Early American Scientific Instruments and Their Makers* (Washington, D.C.: Smithsonian Institution, 1964), p. 39.

5. Bedini, *Early American Scientific Instruments*, pp. 93–97.

6. Frank Smith, *The Genealogical History of Dover, Massachusetts* (Dover, Mass.: The Historical and Natural Society, 1917), p. 78.

7. Isaac J. Greenwood, ed., *The Revolutionary Services of John Greenwood of Boston and New York 1775–1783* (New York, 1922), Appendix, pp. 106–112. Isaac John Greenwood, *The Greenwood Family of Norwich, England, in America* . . . (New York, privately printed, 1934), pp. 94–98.

8. Esther Forbes, *Paul Revere and the World He Lived In* (Boston: Houghton Mifflin, 1942), pp. 289–292; and Bedini, *Early American Scientific Instruments*, pp. 40, 42.

9. Penrose R. Hoopes, *Connecticut Clockmakers of the Eighteenth Century* (Hartford, Conn.: Edwin Valentine Mitchell, 1930), pp. 70–73.

10. Ibid., pp. 48–49.

11. Ibid., pp. 92–93; and Bedini, *Early American Scientific Instruments*, pp. 118–122.

12. Theodore G. Thayer, *As We Were, The Story of Elizabethtown* (Elizabeth, N.J.: Grassman Publishing Co., 1964), pp. 228–234; and William E. Drost, *Clocks and Watches of New Jersey* (Elizabeth, N.J.: Engineering Publishers, 1966), pp. 98–104.

13. Bedini, *Early American Scientific Instruments*, p. 51.

14. Thompson Westcott, *Life of John Fitch, the Inventor of the Steamboat* (Philadelphia: J. B. Lippincott, 1857), pp. 42–54.

15. Henry D. Biddle, "Owen Biddle," *Pennsylvania Magazine of History and Biography*, vol. XIV, 1892, pp. 299–329.

16. *The Royal Pennsylvania Gazette*, April 19, 1778; and Harrold E. Gillingham, "Some Early Philadelphia Instrument Makers," *Pennsylvania Magazine of History and Biography*, vol. 51, no. 3, 1927, p. 303; and Bedini, *Early American Instrument Makers*, p. 59.

17. Hoopes, *Connecticut Clockmakers*, p. 120.

18. Private correspondence with Mr. Gerald D. Foss, Grand Historian, Grand Lodge of the Free and Accepted Masons, State of New Hampshire, September 26, 1966.

19. *New-York Gazette and Weekly Mercury*, May 5, 1777; and Bedini, *Early American Instrument Makers*, p. 66.

20. *New-York Mercury*, June 19, 1775; J. Hall Pleasants and Howard Sill, "Charles Oliver Bruff, Silversmith," *Antiques*, June 1941, pp. 309–311; and John E. Langdon, "New Light on Charles Oliver Bruff, Tory Silversmith," *Antiques*, June 1968, pp. 768–769.

21. Bedini, *Early American Instrument Makers*, p. 43; and Howard M. Chapin, "Davis Quadrants," *Antiques*, vol. 12, no. 5, 1927, pp. 397–399.

22. Bedini, *Early American Instrument Makers*, pp. 43–44; and Chapin, "Davis Quadrants," pp. 398–399.

23. Gillingham, "Some Early Philadelphia Instrument Makers," pp. 293–294; and Bedini, *Early American Scientific Instruments*, p. 59.

24. Hoopes, *Connecticut Clockmakers*, pp. 66–70.

25. Isaac Q. Leake, *Memoir of the Life and Times of General John Lamb, An Officer of the Revolution* . . . (Albany, N.Y., 1857; reprinted Glendale, N.Y.: Bench-

mark Publishing Co., 1970), pp. 9, 100–290; and Silvio A. Bedini, *Ridgefield in Review* (New Haven, Conn.: Walker-Rackliffe Co., 1958), pp. 71, 84.

26. Oliver Ayer Roberts, *History of the Military Company of the Massachusetts, Now Called the Ancient and Honorable Artillery Company of Massachusetts 1637–1888* (Boston: Alfred Mudge & Son, 1895), vol. I, p. 381; vol. II, pp. 16, 30–31, 44, 50, 188, 466; and Ruth Lawrence, *Colonial Families of America* (New York: National Americana Society, 1928), vol. VI, pp. 118–124.

27. "Thomas Marshall," *Bulletin of the Fauquier Historical Society*, July 1922, pp. 134–142; and *Dictionary of American Biography* (New York: Charles Scribner's Sons, 1933), vol. XII, pp. 328–329.

28. Joan Lynn Schidd, "Silversmiths of Rochester," *Guide Bulletin*, Rochester Museum of Arts and Sciences, no. 8, pp. 16–17; George L. Vose, *A Sketch of the Life and Works of Loammi Baldwin, Civil Engineer* (Boston: George H. Ellis, 1885), pp. 3–7; and Samuel Sewall, *The History of Woburn, Middlesex County, Mass.* (Boston: Wiggin & Lunt, 1868), pp. 385–389.

29. John Stuart Barrows, *Fryeburg, Maine, An Historical Sketch* (Fryeburg, Me.: Pequawket Press, 1938), pp. 28–48; Bedini, *Early American Scientific Instruments*, pp. 90–91, 137.

30. Denison Olmsted, "Roger Sherman," *American Literary Magazine*, vol. IV, no. 6, June 1849, pp. 699–708; Samuel Orcutt, *History of the Towns of New Milford and Bridgewater, Connecticut, 1703–1882* (Hartford, Conn.: Case, Lockwood & Brainard, 1882), pp. 617–618.

31. John C. Fitzpatrick, ed., *Writings of George Washington* (Washington, D.C.: U.S. Government Printing Office, 1935), vol. 3, pp. 320–329.

32. Ibid., vol. 5, pp. 109–110.

33. Benson J. Lossing, *The Pictorial Field-Book of the Revolution* (New York: Harper & Bros., 1860), vol. I, p. 704; Brooke Hindle, *The Pursuit of Science in Revolutionary America 1735–1789* (Chapel Hill, N.C.: University of North Carolina Press, 1956), pp. 241–242; Elizabeth S. Kite, *Brigadier-General Louis Lebeque Duportail, Commandant of Engineers of the Continental Army 1777–1783* (Baltimore: The Dolphin Press, 1933), pp. 27–30; 246–247.

34. Peter Guthorn, *American Maps and Map Makers of the Revolution* (Monmouth Beach, N.J.: Philip Freneau Press, 1966), pp. 9–12, 16, 22, 29–30, 34, 36.

35. U.S. National Archives, The Papers of the Continental Congress, 1777; Fitzpatrick, *Writings of Washington*, vol. 7, p. 65.

36. Lawrence Martin, ed., *The George Washington Atlas* (Washington, D.C.: George Washington Bicentennial Commission, 1932), passim.

37. J. C. Webster, *The Life of Joseph Frederick Wallet Des Barres* (New Brunswick: privately printed, 1923); and J. C. Webster, "Joseph Frederick Wallet Des Barres and the Atlantic Neptune," *Proceedings and Transactions of the Royal Society of Canada*, vol. 3, no. 21, 1927, Section II, pp. 21–40.

38. W. Chipman, "The Life and Times of Major Samuel Holland, surveyor 1764–1801," *Ontario Historical Society Papers and Records*, vol. 21, no. 11, 1924, pp. 11–98.

39. Joseph F. W. Des Barres, *The Atlantic Neptune* (London: For the British Admiralty, 1777).

40. James Cook and Michael Lane, *A Collection of the Charts of the Coasts of*

Newfoundland and Labrador, &c. (London: Thomas Jeffreys, 1765–1768); John Bennett and Robert Sayer, *American Atlas: or, A Geographical Description of the Whole Continent of America* (London, 1775), *The North-American Pilot and West India Atlas* (London, 1777), *The Western Neptune* (London, 1778), and *The American Military Pocket Atlas* (London, 1776); and William Faden, *The North American Atlas, Selected from the Most Authentic Maps, Charts, Plans, &c., Hitherto Published* (London, 1777).

41. G. L. Le Rouge, *Pilote Americain Septentrional* (Paris, 1778); *Neptune Americo-Septentrional Contenant les Côtes, Iles et Bancs, les Baies, Ports et Mouillages, et les Soundes des Mers de cette-partie du Monde* (Paris: Depôt des cartes et plans de la Marine, 1778–1780).

42. W. Bart Greenwood, compiler, *The American Revolution 1775–1783, An Atlas of 18th Century Maps and Charts* (Department of the Navy, Naval History Division, 1972); and Coolie Verner, *Maps of the Yorktown Campaign, 1780–1781, A Preliminary Checklist of Printed and Manuscript Maps Prior to 1800* (London: Map Collectors' Series, no. 18, 1965).

43. George S. Bryan, *The Spy in America* (Philadelphia: J. B. Lippincott, 1943), pp. 68–84. See also Guthorn, *American Maps*, pp. 38–40.

44. St. George L. Sioussat, "Dr. William Smith, David Rittenhouse, and the Canal Plate, September 7, 1777," *Proceedings of the American Philosophical Society*, vol. 95, no. 3, June 1951, pp. 223–231.

45. Thomas Gilpin, "Map of Chesapeake and Delaware Canals," *Transactions of the American Philosophical Society*, vol. I, 1771, plate 7; Ralph D. Gray, "Philadelphia and the Chesapeake and Delaware Canal 1769–1823," *Pennsylvania Magazine of History and Biography*, vol. LXXXIV, no. 4, 1960, pp. 401–423, and "Memoir of Thomas Gilpin," ibid., vol. XLIX, no. 4, 1925, pp. 289–348.

46. Library of Congress, Manuscripts Division, George Washington Papers; Fitzpatrick, *Writings of Washington*, vol. 7, p. 443.

47. U. S. National Archives, The Journal of the Continental Congress 1774–1789, entry dated July 25, 1777.

48. Library of Congress, Manuscripts Division. George Washington Papers, Robert Erskine to General Washington, August 1, 1777.

49. *Journals of the Military Expedition of Major General John Sullivan* (Auburn, N.Y.: New York State, Secretary of State, 1887).

50. T. Romeyn Beck, "Art. XV. Eulogium on the Life and Services of Simeon De Witt, Surveyor-General of the state of New-York, Chancellor of the University, &c.," *Transactions of the Albany Institute* (Albany, N.Y.: Joel Munsell, 1832–1835), vol. II, pp. 309–330. Walter W. Ristow, "Simeon De Witt, Pioneer American Cartographer," *Kartengeschichte und Kartenbearbeitung*, Festschrift honoring Dr. William Bonacker, Geographer and Professional Cartographer of Berlin, Germany on his eightieth birthday, ed. Karl-Heinz Meine (Bad Godesburg, West Germany: Kirschbaum Verlag, 1968), pp. 103–114.

51. Fitzpatrick, *Writings of Washington*, vol. 11, pp. 246.

52. *George Washington's Letters to G. and J. Clinton* (New York: George H. Richmond and the New York Cooperative Society, 1934), pp. 27–29.

53. A. H. Heusser, *The Forgotten General, Robert Erskine, F.R.S.* (Paterson, N.J.: Benjamin Franklin Press, 1928), pp. 209–210.

54. Ibid., p. 154.

55. U.S. National Archives, War Department Collection of the Revolutionary War Records, Peter R. Livingston to Col. Timothy Pickering, January 24, 1781.

56. *The New-York-Packet and the American Advertiser*, Fishkill, N.Y., August 30, 1781.

57. Fitzpatrick, *Writings of Washington*, vol. 23, pp. 68–69, 332.

58. Thomas Hutchins, *A Topographical Description of Virginia, Pennsylvania, Maryland and North Carolina* (London, 1778).

59. *New-York Daily Gazette*, May 20, 1789; *The American Museum*, April 1790.

60. Fitzpatrick, *Writings of Washington*, vol. 26, p. 496; U.S. National Archives, The Papers of the Continental Congress, Journal, 1783, pp. 401–402, 711.

61. Beck, "Eulogium of Simeon De Witt," p. 10.

62. Library of Congress, Manuscripts Division, Franklin Papers, Jefferson to Franklin, March 31, 1790. U.S. National Archives, Department of State general records, March 1790.

63. Hunter Miller, ed., *Treaties and Other International Acts of the United States of America* (Washington, D.C., 1933), vol. III, pp. 329–330.

64. I. N. Phelps Stokes and Daniel C. Haskell, *American Historical Prints: Early Views of American Cities, etc., from the Phelps Stokes and Other Collections* (New York: New York Public Library, 1933), pp. 33–34, pl. 28. See also P. L. Phillips, "Notes on the Life and Works of Bernard Romans," *Publications of the Florida State Historical Society*, no. 2 (1924), pp. 33 ff.; and *The Connecticut Journal* [Hartford], March 31, 1784.

65. *Pennsylvania Packet*, August 9, 1783, December 17, 1784, and April 18, 1785.

XII. WAR'S WEAPONS

1. John Muller, *A Treatise of Artillery*, Preface by Harold L. Peterson (Ottawa, Ontario: Museum Restoration Service, 1965).

2. William Bourne, *The Arte of Shooting in Great Ordnance* (London, 1578); Thomas Smith, *The Art of Gunnery* (London, 1641); William Eldred, *The Gunners Glasse* (London, 1646); and Nathaniell Ney, *The Art of Gunnery* (London, 1670). See also Major-General Sir John Headlam, "The Guns, Gunners and Gunnery of the English Renaissance," *The Journal of the Royal Artillery*, vol. LXVI, no. 4, January 1940, pp. 469–488.

3. John Robertson, *A Treatise of Such Mathematical Instruments, As Are usually put into a Portable Case . . .* 1st ed. (London: for T. Heath, 1757); ibid., 2d ed. *To which is now added an appendix containing the description of the gunner's callipers* (1757); *A Treatise of Such Mathematical Instruments As are usually put into a Portable Case, Shewing Some of their Uses . . . With an Appendix Containing the Description and Use of the Gunners Callipers . . .* 3rd ed. (London: for J. Nourse, 1775), pp. 148–215. See also Parker Brewis, "A Gunner's Compound Compass or English Callipers," *Archaeologia Aeliana, or Miscellaneous Tracts Relating to Antiquities*, 4th series, vol. VIII, 1932, pp. 213–218.

4. Silvio A. Bedini, *Early American Scientific Instruments and Their Makers* (Washington, D.C.: Smithsonian Institution, 1964), pp. 40–42, and *Proceedings of the Bostonian Society*, 1913, pp. 21–22.

5. Esther Forbes, *Paul Revere and the World He Lived In* (Boston: Houghton Mifflin, 1942), pp. 289–292.

6. The table is identical in almost all details with the one provided in Robertson's Appendix, *Treatise of Mathematical Instruments*, 2nd ed., p. 171. The same data appears in Muller, *Treatise of Artillery*, pp. 6–11, 111–112; and in Louis de Tousard, *The Artillerist's Companion* (Philadelphia: C. & A. Conrad, 1809), pp. 551–555; 566–568.

7. A. R. Hall, *Ballistics in the Seventeenth Century* (Cambridge: Cambridge University Press, 1952, pp. 33, 44–45.

8. Dean A. Fales, Jr., "Notes on Early American Brass and Copper," *Antiques*, December 1958, p. 538.

9. Harold L. Peterson, *The Book of the Continental Soldier* (Harrisburg, Pa.: Stackpole, 1968), pp. 134–135.

10. *New-York Gazette and Weekly Mercury*, May 5, 1777, p. 3; *New-York Mercury*, April 14, 1760.

11. Charles James, *A New and Enlarged Military Dictionary* (London, 1810), vol. I, unpaginated.

12. Benson J. Lossing, *The Home of Washington; or Mount Vernon and Its Associations, Historical and Biographical* (Hartford, Conn.: A. S. Hale & Co., 1870), pp. 407–409.

13. New-York Historical Society, Accession files.

14. *The Milwaukee Sentinel*, January 22, 1902; *Green Bay Press Gazette*, January 25, 1902; "Collector's Notes," *Antiques*, March 1965, vol. LXXXVII, no. 3, pp. 336–337; C. H. Lewis, "Lienard de Beaujean's Compass-Sundial," *Antiques*, vol. LXXXVII, no. 3, March 1965, pp. 336–337; and "Pocket Sundials," *Bulletin of the Fort Ticonderoga Museum*, pp. 63–64. See also Alice Morse Earle, *Sundials and Roses of Yesterday* (New York: Macmillan, 1902), p. 143.

15. *Boston Gazette*, October 14, 21, 1734.

16. *Boston News-Letter*, September 22, 1743.

17. *Boston Gazette*, May 21, 1754.

18. Ibid., April 3, 1758.

19. *Pennsylvania Evening Post*, August 30, 1777.

20. *Royal Gazette* [New York], May 27, 1778, p. 3.

21. *Inventory of the Contents of Mount Vernon 1810*, With a Prefatory Note by Worthington Chauncey Ford (1909), p. xvii; Kathryn C. Buhler, *Mount Vernon Silver* (Mount Vernon, Va.: The Mount Vernon Ladies Association of the Union, 1957), frontispiece. The original sketch is in the collection of the Maryland Historical Society.

22. John C. Fitzpatrick, ed., *Writings of George Washington* (Washington, D.C.: Government Printing Office, 1935), vol. 2, p. 343.

23. *Accounts of G. Washington with the United States, Commencing June 1775, and ending June 1783, Comprehending a Space of 8 Years* (Facsimile ed. 1783), pp. 15, 43.

24. Fitzpatrick, *Writings of Washington*, vol. 13, pp. 24, 192.

25. Bedini, *Early American Scientific Instruments*, p. 149.

26. [Helen Maggs Fede], *General Washington's Military Equipment* (Mount Vernon, Va.: The Mount Vernon Ladies Association of the Union, 1963), pp. 32–33.

27. [John Trumbull], *Autobiography, Reminiscences and Letters of John Trumbull, from 1756 to 1841* (New York: Wiley and Putnam, 1841), Appendix, pp. 435–436.

28. G. W. Parke Custis, *Recollections and Private Memoirs of Washington* (Washington, D.C.: William H. Moore, 1859); quoted in Lossing, *The Home of Washington*, pp. 238–239.

29. Douglas Southall Freeman, *George Washington, A Biography* (New York: Charles Scribner's Sons, 1948), vol. III, p. 323.

30. Peter Force, *American Archives: Fifth Series, Containing a Documentary History of the United States of America, From the Declaration of Independence, July 4, 1776, to the Definitive Treaty of Peace with Great Britain, September 3, 1783* (Washington, D.C., April 1848), vol. I, p. 1475.

31. Ibid., p. 1480.

32. Ibid., p. 1485.

33. Ibid., pp. 1478, 824, 853, 1488.

34. Columbia University Library, University Archives, Minutes of the Meetings of the Governours of the College.

35. William Parker Cutler and Julia Perkins Cutler, *Life, Journals and Correspondence of Rev. Manassah Cutler, L.L.D., By his Grandchildren* (Cincinnati: Robert Clarke, 1888), vol. II, pp. 239–240.

36. Lossing, *The Home of Washington*, p. 239; and *Inventory of the Contents of Mount Vernon 1810*, "An inventory of articles," p. 5.

37. Peabody Museum, Salem, Mass., The Fox Papers; also noted in M. V. Brewington, "American Navigation During the Revolution," in *Naval Documents of the American Revolution*, ed. William Bell Clark (Washington, D.C.: Government Printing Office, 1966), vol. II, p. 807.

38. Hepburn Collection, Philadelphia. Account of Stores Under the Care of the Several Officers Belonging to the Continental Ship Alliance Boston Nantasket Road 25 Decr. 1781 John Barry Esq. Commander at Sea.

39. Louis F. Middlebrook, *History of Maritime Connecticut During the American Revolution 1775–1783* (Salem, Mass.: Essex Institute, 1925), vol. II, pp. 39–40.

40. Thomas Haselden, *The Seaman's Daily Assistant* (Philadelphia: Joseph Crukshank, 1777); 2nd ed., 1778.

41. Samuel Buckner, *The American Sailor: A Treatise on Practical Seamanship* (Newport, R.I.: Peter Edes, 1790).

42. Thomas Truxton, *Remarks, Instructions and Examples relating to the Latitude & Longitude; also, the Variation of the Compass* (Philadelphia: T. Dobson, 1794).

43. *Essex Journal and New Hampshire Packet*, October 23 and November 1, 1776.

44. Nicholas Pike, *A New and Complete System of Arithmetic, Composed for the Use of the Citizens of the United States* (Newburyport, Mass.: John Mycall, 1788).

45. Silvio A. Bedini, *The Life of Benjamin Banneker* (New York: Charles Scribner's Sons, 1972), pp. 92.

46. Benjamin Workman, *A Treatise of Arithmetic in Theory and Practice* . . .

by John Gough. To Which are Added, Many valuable Additions and Amendments; More Particularly Fitting the Work for the Improvement of the American Youth (Philadelphia: Printed by J. M. M'Culloch for W. Young, 1788), and *Gauging Epitomized or, A Short Treatise of Gauging, In which that Branch is rendered familiar to the Meanest Capacity. To which are added, Accurate Tables for finding the Mean-Diameters of Casks by Inspection. Also, A comprehensive Ullage Table, and an accurate Method of Ullaging Casks, by an easy Rule adapted to it* (Philadelphia: W. Young, 1788).

47. Benjamin Workman, *The American Accountant, or School-master's New Assistant* (Philadelphia: John M'Culloch for W. Young, 1789); 2nd ed. revised by Robert Patterson, published by W. Young, 1793.

48. Nathan Daboll, *Daboll's Schoolmaster's Assistant. Being a Plain Practical System of Arithmetic; Adapted to the United States* (New London, Conn.: Samuel Green, 1800).

49. Bedini, *Banneker*, pp. 148–149.

50. Ibid., pp. 137–234.

XIII. ONE VAST REPUBLIC

1. Carl Van Doren, *The Great Rehearsal* (New York: Viking, 1948), pp. 239–251.

2. Leroy L. Thwing, "The Four Carving Skillins," *Antiques*, June 1938, pp. 326–328.

3. Mabel M. Swan, "Artisan Leaders of 1788," *Antiques*, vol. XXVII, no. 3, March 1935, pp. 90–91.

4. *The Daily Advertiser* [New York], July 26, 1797, and *The New-York Gazette and General Advertiser*, September 4, 1798.

5. *The New-York Gazette and Weekly Mercury*, January 6, 1777, and *The Diary*, February 20, 1796.

6. *The New-York Gazette and General Advertiser*, April 5, 1800, November 20, 1801, and January 12, 1803.

7. *The Columbia Gazeteer* [New York], December 5, 1793.

8. Advertisement of importer at 128 Pearl-Street, New York City, in *The Commercial Advertiser*, January 1, 1800; for John Grayson at 142 Pearl-Street in *The New-York Gazette and General Advertiser*, April 5, 1800; and repeated thereafter in the same newspaper on November 20, 1801, March 13, 1802, and January 12, 1803; for George Shipley at 191 Water-Street in New York City, and for Henry Gattey at 205 Water-Street, in *The Daily Advertiser*, March 31, 1801; and for William Seger at 74 Pine-Street in *The American Citizen*, December 12, 1803; for the ships chandlers Armstrong & Smith at 231 Water-Street in *The Mercantile Advertiser*, July 17, 1801; and for the firm Porri & Vecchio in New York City in *The Daily Advertiser*, October 13, 1801, and *The New-York Evening Post*, December 9, 1801, among others.

9. W. H. Quarrell and M. Mare, *London in 1710* (London: Faber & Faber, 1934), p. 145.

10. Robert Hooke, "Some Ways of Discovering y[e] various Pressures on y[e] Air at Sea," Royal Society, *Classified Papers*, vol. XX. item 48; Edmond Halley, "An Account of Dr. Robert Hook's [sic] Invention of the Marine Barometer, with its

Description and Uses, published by order of the R. Society, by E. Halley," *Philosophical Transactions*, vol. 22, 1701, pp. 791–794.

11. Guillaume Amontons, *Remarques et Experiences Physiques* (Paris, 1695), pp. 121–125.

12. Constantine John Phipps, *A Voyage Towards the North Pole Undertaken by His Majesty's Command* (London, 1773), pp. 123–124.

13. ·William Wales and Mr. William Bayley, *The Original Astronomical Observations, Made in the Course of a Voyage Towards the South Pole and Round the World, in His Majesty's Ships the Resolution and Adventure in the Years MDCCLXXII, MDCCLXXIII, MDCCLXXIV and MDCCLXXV* (London: W. & A. Strahan, 1777), pp. li–liii.

14. Silvio A. Bedini, *Early American Scientific Instruments and Their Makers* (Washington, D.C.: Smithsonian Institution, 1964), pp. 61–62.

15. Nicholas Goodison, *English Barometeres 1680–1860* (New York: Carkson N. Potter, Inc., 1966), pp. 71–96.

16. *The Pennsylvania Evening Herald*, March 17, 1787.

17. *The New-York Daily Advertiser*, October 17, 1787.

18. Harrold E. Gillingham, "Some Early Philadelphia Instrument Makers," *Pennsylvania Magazine of History and Biography*, vol. 51, 1927, no. 3, pp. 305–306; and Bedini, *Early American Scientific Instruments*, pp. 61–62.

19. *Pennsylvania Packet*, May 19, 1789; and *Federal Gazette*, April 20, 1790.

20. *The Diary, or Evening Register* [New York City], November 3, 1794.

21. *Philadelphia City Directory* for 1800; Gillingham, "Some Early Philadelphia Instrument Makers," p. 306, fn. 6; and *The Federal Gazette* [Philadelphia], May 31, 1796.

22. [James Six], "Account of an improved Thermometer. By Mr. James Six . . . , *Philosophical Transactions*, vol. 72, 1782, pp. 72–81.

23. *Mercantile Advertiser* [New York], September 18, 1800; and *American Citizen* [New York City], December 12, 1803.

24. Bedini, *Early American Scientific Instruments*, p. 31; Arthur E. James, *Chester County Clocks and Their Makers* (West Chester, Pa.: West Chester Historical Society, 1947), p. 304.

25. *Thomas' Massachusetts Spy, or Worcester Gazette*, February 25, 1817.

26. William Barton, *Memoirs of the Life of David Rittenhouse, L.L.D., F.R.S.*, (Philadelphia: Edward Parker, 1813), pp. 305–308; Brooke Hindle, *David Rittenhouse* (Princeton, N.J.: Princeton University Press, 1964), pp. 251–258.

27. Barton, *Memoirs of David Rittenhouse*, pp. 282–286.

28. *Pennsylvania Colonial Record*, vol. XIV, pp. 399, 454, 457; Historical Society of Pennsylvania, Pennsylvania Miscellaneous Papers, David Rittenhouse to Governor Dickinson, May 8, 1785.

29. *Pennsylvania Archives*, vol. X, p. 454; *Report of the Regents of the University on the Boundaries of the State of New York* (Albany, N.Y.: Argus Company, 1874), vol. I, p. 260; Historical Society of Pennsylvania, Manuscripts Division, David Rittenhouse to James Irvine, May 12, 1785.

30. *Report of the Superintendent of the U.S. Coast and Geodetic Survey Showing the Progress of the Work During the Fiscal Year Ending With June 1880* (Washington: Government Printing Office, 1882), pp. 18–19; U.S. National Archives, *Topographi-*

cal Bureau, Record Group 77. Letter from Simeon De Witt to Stephen Van Rennselaer dated November 6, 1826. Office of the Chief of Engineers, Letters Sent and Received.

31. Barton, *Memoirs of David Rittenhouse*, pp. 299–300; Hindle, *David Rittenhouse*, p. 246; and John C. Fitzpatrick, ed., *Writings of George Washington* (Washington, D.C.: Government Printing Office, 1935), vol. 26, pp. 27, 136; and vol. 27, p. 6.

32. Philadelphia College of Physicians, Gilbert Collection, David Rittenhouse to James Searle, August 13, 1780.

33. *Saggio del Real Gabinetto di Fisica, e di Storia Naturale di Firenze* (Rome: Stamperia di Giovanni Zempel, 1775), p. 6; noted in Giovanni Govi, "Della invenzione del micrometro per gli strumenti astronomici," *Bulletino di Bibliografia e di Storia delle Scienze Matematiche e Fisiche pubblicato da B. Boncompagni* (Rome), December 1887, Vol. XX, p. 619. See also G. Boffito, *Gli Strumenti della Scienza e la Scienza degli Strumenti* (Florence: Libreria Internazionale Seeber, 1929), p. 129.

34. "New Method of placing a Meridian Mark, in a Letter to the Rev. Dr. Ewing, Provost of the University. By D. Rittenhouse, Esq.," *Transactions of the American Philosophical Society*, vol. II, 1786, p. 183.

35. "Description of a Lamp-Micrometer and the Method of using it. By Mr. William Herschel," *Philosophical Transactions*, vol. LXXII, 1782, pp. 163–172.

36. J. T. Queckett, *Practical Treatise on the Use of the Microscope* (London: H. Bailliere, 1852), p. 29; John F. W. Herschel, "Observations of the apparent distances and positions of 380 double and triple Stars, made in the years 1821, 1822, and 1823 . . . ," *Philosophical Transactions*, 1824, Part III, pp. 9–14.

37. Lockwood Barr, "Spider Web . . . ," *Bulletin of the National Association of Watch and Clock Collectors*, vol. VIII, no. 9, April 1959, pp. 499–500.

38. Silvio A. Bedini, *The Life of Benjamin Banneker* (New York: Charles Scribner's Sons, 1972), pp. 113–119, 132.

39. Pierre Charles Le Monnier, *Histoire Celeste, ou Recueil de Toutes les Observations Astronomiques Faites par Ordre du Roy; Avec Un Discours Preliminaire sur le Progres de l'Astronomie, ou l'on Compare les plus recentes Observations à celles qui ont ête faites immediatement âpres la fondation de l'Observatoire Royal* (Paris: Chez Briasson, 1741), Discours preliminaire, pp. lxxv–lxxxvi.

40. J. S. Bailly, *Histoire de l'astronomie moderne* (Paris, 1785), vol. III, p. 17.

41. Charles W. Evans, *Biographical and Historical Accounts of the Fox, Ellicott and Evans Families, and the Different Families Connected with Them* (Buffalo, N.Y.: Baker, Jones, & Co., 1882), pp. 155–165.

42. Catherine Van Cortlandt Mathews, *Andrew Ellicott, His Life and Letters* (New York: Grafton Press, 1908), pp. 18–29.

43. Ibid., pp. 55–79.

44. Ibid., pp. 70–79.

45. Ibid., pp. 72–79.

46. Andrew Ellicott, *The Journal of Andrew Ellicott, Late Commissioner on Behalf of the United States . . . for Determining the Boundary Between the United States and the Possessions of His Catholic Majesty* (Philadelphia, 1803; reprinted Chicago: Quadrangle Books, 1962).

47. Mathews, *Andrew Ellicott*, pp. 200–247.

48. Dumas Malone, *Jefferson and His Time. Volume One, Jefferson The Virginian* (Boston: Little, Brown, 1948), pp. 40–45.

49. Thomas Jefferson, *Notes on the State of Virginia; written in the year 1781, somewhat corrected and enlarged in the winter of 1782, for the use of a Foreigner of distinction, in answer to certain queries proposed by him . . .* (Paris, 1782).

50. Thomas Jefferson, from an unidentified source.

51. William D. Pattison, *Beginnings of the American Rectangular Land Survey System, 1784–1800*, University of Chicago Department of Geography Research Paper No. 50 (Chicago: University of Chicago Press, 1964), pp. 10–39, 82–105.

52. Ibid., pp. 119–143; and Payson J. Treat, *The National Land System, 1785–1820* (New York: E. B. Treat & Co., 1910), pp. 31–38.

53. Lowell O. Stewart, *Public Land Surveys, History, Instruction, Methods* (Ames, Iowa: Collegiate Press, Inc., 1935), pp. 9–40.

54. Pattison, *American Land Survey System*, pp. 220–225.

55. Charles Whittlesey, "Origin of the American System of Land Surveys. Justice to the Memory of Thomas Hutchins," *Journal of the Association of Engineering Societies*, vol. III, November 1883 to October 1884, pp. 275–280.

56. Robert Patterson, "An Easy and Accurate Method of finding a true Meridian Line, and thence the Variation of the Compass," *Transactions of the American Philosophical Society*, vol. II, 1786, no. XXXIII, pp. 251–263.

57. Andrew Ellicott, A. M., *Several Methods by Which Meridional Lines May Be Found with Ease and Accuracy; Recommended to the Attention of the Surveyors In the United States* (Philadelphia: Thomas Dobson, 1796), 32 pp., 2 pl.

58. Ibid., pp. 25–26.

59. Daniel K. Cassel, *A Genea-Biographical History of the Rittenhouse Family and All Its Branches in America* (Philadelphia, 1893), pp. 221–226.

60. Edward E. Chandlee, *Six Quaker Clockmakers* (Philadelphia: Historical Society of Pennsylvania, 1943), pp. 105–145.

61. Ohio Historical Society, Manuscript Collection. Worthington Papers, Box 1, Item 60. Alexander White 3rd to Thomas Worthington at Chillicothe, Ohio, June 2, 1796.

XIV. The True Geography

1. Library of Congress, Manuscripts Division, Andrew Ellicott Papers. Andrew Ellicott to Sarah Ellicott, July 29, 1785.

2. Ibid., Andrew Ellicott to Sarah Ellicott, September 11, 1785.

3. Ibid., Andrew Ellicott to Sarah Ellicott, June 20, 1785.

4. Ibid., Andrew Ellicott to Sarah Ellicott, October 11, 1787.

5. Ibid., Andrew Ellicott to Sarah Ellicott, June 12, 1790.

6. Ibid., Andrew Ellicott to Sarah Ellicott, February 17, 1799.

7. New-York Historical Society, Manuscripts Collection. Andrew Ellicott Papers, Andrew Ellicott to Sarah Ellicott, dated September 11, 1795.

8. Library of Congress, Manuscripts Division, Andrew Ellicott Papers. Andrew Ellicott to Sarah Ellicott, August 24, 1785.

9. Catherine Van Cortlandt Mathews, *Andrew Ellicott, His Life and Letters* (New York: Grafton Press, 1908), p. 124.

10. Andrew Ellicott, "Manuscript Field Notebooks of Astronomical Observations," The National Museum of History and Technology, Smithsonian Institution.

11. Andrew Ellicott, *The Journal of Andrew Ellicott* . . . (Philadelphia, 1803; reprinted Chicago: Quadrangle Books, 1962), p. 104.

12. Ibid., p. 86.

13. Library of Congress, Manuscripts Division, Andrew Ellicott Papers, Andrew Ellicott to Albert Gallatin, Secretary of the Treasury, August 7, 1803, with annexed report of the same date.

14. Ibid., Undated memorandum in the hand of Andrew Ellicott, c. 1800.

15. Pierre Louis Moreau de Maupertuis, *Le figure de la terre determinée par les observationes de Messieurs de Maupertuis, Clairault, Camus, Le Monnier, de l'Académie Royale des Sciences* (Paris: Imprimerie Royal, 1738).

16. Andrew Ellicott, *Journal*, pp. 44–47.

17. Andrew Ellicott, "Manuscript Astronomical Notebook B.," The National Museum of History and Technology, Smithsonian Institution.

18. "A Letter from Andrew Ellicott to Robert Patterson in Two Parts. Part first contains a number of Astronomical Observation . . . April 2nd, 1795," *Transactions of the American Philosophical Society*, vol. IV, 1799, pp. 49–51.

19. Mayor H. W. Clark, *Report of the Regent's Boundary Commission* (Albany, N.Y., 1886). Report of Simeon De Witt, 1794.

20. Library of Congress, Manuscripts Division, Thomas Jefferson Papers, vol. 130, fol. 22446, Isaac Briggs, at Sharon, Md., to Thomas Jefferson, March 1, 1803.

21. Ibid., vol. 131, fol. 22716, Isaac Briggs to Thomas Jefferson, May 17, 1803.

22. U.S. National Archives, Records of the Department of the Treasury, Register of letters sent from and received in Philadelphia 1792–1835; and Gaillard Hunt, *Calendar of Application and Recommendation for Office During the Presidency of George Washington* (Washington, 1901), pp. 132–133.

23. Silvio A. Bedini, *Early American Scientific Instruments and Their Makers* (Washington, D.C.: Smithsonian Institution, 1964), pp. 62, 148–149, Fig. 10.

24. Library of Congress, Andrew Ellicott Papers, Andrew Ellicott to Thomas Jefferson, May 11, 1802.

25. Ibid., Andrew Ellicott to Thomas Jefferson, December 29, 1801.

26. Ibid., Thomas Jefferson to Andrew Ellicott, February 14, 1802; Andrew Ellicott to Thomas Jefferson, March 10, 1802.

27. Mathews, *Andrew Ellicott*, pp. 226–247.

28. U.S. National Archives, Bureau of Rolls, Jefferson Papers, series 2, vol. 51, Document 269, Jefferson's instructions to Meriwether Lewis, June 20, 1803; William H. Goetzmann, *Exploration and Empire* (New York: Knopf, 1967), pp. 6–8.

29. U.S. National Archives, Jefferson Papers, Jefferson's instructions, June 20, 1803.

XV. THE PROMOTION OF SCIENCE

1. [Tobias Mayer], *Theoria Luna Juxta Systema Newtonium* (London, 1767), and *Tabulae Motuum Solis et Lunae Novae et Correctae, Auctore Tobia Mayer: Quibus Accedit Methodus Longitudinum Promota, Eodem Auctore. Editae Jessu Praefectorum Rei Longitudinariae* (London: William and John Richardson, 1770).

2. Chevalier Jean-Charles de Borda, *Description et usage du cercle de reflexion* (Paris, 1787).

3. E. G. R. Taylor, *The Mathematical Practitioners of Hanoverian England 1714–1840* (Cambridge: Cambridge University Press, 1966), pp. 32, 45, 69, 199.

4. Nevil Maskelyne, *The British Mariner's Guide to the Discovery of the Longitude at Sea* (London, 1763).

5. *The Nautical Almanac and Astronomical Ephemeris* (London, 1766); and Nevil Maskelyne, *Tables Requisite to Be Used with the Astronomical and Nautical Ephemeris* (London, 1766).

6. Jesse Ramsden, *Description of an Engine for Dividing Mathematical Instruments* (London: Published by order of the Commissioner of Longitude, William Richardson, 1771).

7. Rev. Nevil Maskelyne, "The Use of Hadley's Quadrant," *Nautical Almanac for the Year 1774* (London, 1773).

8. Taylor, *Mathematical Practitioners of Hanoverian England*, p. 58.

9. John Hamilton Moore, *The New Practical Navigator* (London, 1807), p. 327.

10. Samuel Eliot Morison, *The Maritime History of Massachusetts 1783–1860* (Boston: Houghton Mifflin, 1921), p. 116. The documentary source is not provided.

11. Rev. John Ewing, "Improvement in the construction of Godfrey's (commonly called Hadley's) quadrant," *Transactions of the American Philosophical Society*, vol. I, 1770, Appendix, pp. 126–130.

12. American Philosophical Society, Minutes, vol. III, January 1774–June 1787, pp. 155–156, entry for December 9, 1784.

13. American Philosophical Society, MSS Communications, vol. I, folio A 18 and 19; and Minutes, August 17, 1788.

14. Robert Patterson, "An easy and accurate method of adjusting the Glasses of Hadley's Quadrant, on Land for the Back-Observation . . . in a letter to DAVID RITTENHOUSE, President of the Society, April 18, 1794," *Transactions of the American Philosophical Society*, vol. IV, 1799, pp. 154–161.

15. F. R. Brainard, *The Sextant and Other Reflecting Mathematical Instruments, With Practical Hints, Suggestions, and Wrinkles, on their Errors, Adjustment and Use* (New York: D. Van Nostrand, 1891); Specification of Letters Patent No. 18,701 dated November 24, 1857, issued to Robert Norris and Frederick Peters.

16. John Elton, "The Description of a New Quadrant for Taking Altitudes without an Horizon, either at Sea or on Land," *Philosophical Transactions* No. 423 (1732), pp. 273–279; Taylor, *Mathematical Practitioners of Hanoverian England*, p. 37; John Short, "An Account of an horizontal top invented by Mr. Serson," paper read before the Royal Society, February 6, 1752, *Philosophical Transactions*, vol. 47, 1753, pp. 352–353; (manuscript in the collections of the Science Museum, South

Kensington); and E. G. R. Taylor and M. W. Richey, *The Geometrical Seaman* (London: Hollis & Carter, 1962), pp. 79–81.

17. "American Patents for March," *Journal of the Franklin Institute*, June 1830, vol. V, no. 6, pp. 369–370.

18. John Fitch, *An Explanation for Keeping a Ship's Traverse At Sea, By the Columbian Ready Reckoner* (London: printed for, and published by the author, 1793), 12 pp.

19. Thompson Westcott, *Life of John Fitch, Inventor of the Steamboat* (Philadelphia: J. B. Lippincott, 1878), pp. 359–360.

20. Taylor, *Mathematical Practitioners of Hanoverian England*, pp. 11, 54–55, 62, 92, 141–142, 184–185, 369–370; Joseph Gilmore, *The Improvement of Navigation by two new invented Engines* (n.d.); and Charles Grant, *On Finding Latitude and Longitude* (London, 1808).

21. Francis Hopkinson, "Description of a Machine for Measuring a Ship's way through the Sea," *Transactions of the American Philosophical Society*, vol. II, 1786, no. XI, pp. 159–166.

22. Correspondence with the Arlington (Mass.) Historical Society, June 8, 1973.

23. *New-York Gazette and General Advertiser*, July 23, 1799.

24. Andrew Wilson, *Naval History of the United Kingdom* (Cork, 1807), Appendix.

25. "New patents lately enrolled: Mr. Gould, for a Sea-Log," *The Monthly Magazine; or, British Register*, London, vol. X, part III, for 1800, pp. 360–361; *Commercial Advertiser* [New York], April 26, 1800; *American Citizen and General Advertiser* [New York], June 1, 1801; and *The Daily Advertiser* [New York], June 23, 1803.

26. Bernard Romans, "Extract of a Letter from Bernard Romans, of Pensacola, dated August 20, 1773, on an improved sea-compass," *Transactions of the American Philosophical Society*, vol. II, 1786, pp. 396–399; reprinted in *The Annual Register, or a View of the History, Politics, and Literature, for the Year 1787* (London: J. Dodsley, 1789), vol. 29, pp. 83–85, and 1796, vol. 38, pp. 448–449.

27. *Mercantile Advertiser* [New York], September 18, 1800.

28. Langley's patent specifications in "American Patents," *Journal of the Franklin Institute*, vol. VI, no. 2, August 1828, pp. 129–130.

29. "Specification of a Patent for an improvement in the Mariner's and Surveyor's Compass Needle . . . ," *Journal of the Franklin Institute*, October 1830, vol. VI, no. 4, pp. 238–240.

30. U.S. National Archives, Classification Division 8669-x, 88. Optics, Compasses, vol. 21, p. 165, "J. Ball, Mariners Compass"; "American Patents for March, with Remarks," no. 17. "For an Improvement in the Mariners' Compass; Jonathan Ball, Buffalo, Erie County, New York, March 6," *Journal of the Franklin Institute*, vol. XVI, no. 1, June 1835, pp. 234–235.

31. Sir John Ross, *A Voyage of Discovery* (London, 1819), Appendix V, "Observations on the Variation, Made on Shore, or on the Ice, at a sufficient distance from the ships to be beyond the Influence of the Iron they contained."

32. "Items and Novelties. The Liquid Compass of N. S. Ritchie," *Journal of the Franklin Institute*, April 1868, vol. LV, no. 4, pp. 218–221; M. V. Brewington,

The Peabody Collection of Navigating Instruments (Salem, Mass.: Peabody Museum, 1963), pp. 62–63, 137–138.

33. Murdoch Mackenzie, *Treatise on Marine Surveying* (London, 1774).

34. [William Bolles], *A Description and Practical Application of Bolles' trigonometer* (New London, privately printed, 1824).

35. "Bolles's Trigonometer," *American Journal of Science and Arts*, vol. IX, 1825, p. 401, pl. IV; Brewington, ibid., 91, 120.

XVI. FROM HIS KNOWN SHORE

1. E. G. R. Taylor, *The Haven-Finding Art* (New York: Abelard-Schuman, 1957), pp. 151–155, 186–191, 203–212, 244–260; Charles H. Cotter, *A History of Nautical Astronomy* (London: Hollis & Carter, 1968), pp. 180–267.

2. E. G. R. Taylor, "A Reward for the Longitude," *The Mariner's Mirror*, vol. 45, 1959, pp. 59–66; Rupert T. Gould, *The Marine Chronometer, Its History and Development* (London: Holland Press, 1923; reprinted 1960), pp. 40–70; Humphrey Quill, *John Harrison, The Man Who Found Longitude* (New York: Humanities Press, 1966).

3. Quoted in M. V. Brewington, "American Navigation During the Revolution," in *Naval Documents of the American Revolution*, ed. William Bell Clark (Washington, D.C.: U.S. Navy Department, 1966), vol. II, p. 803. The original source is not stated.

4. *Maryland Gazette* [Annapolis], May 27, 1729. Noted also in Lawrence C. Wroth, "Some American Contributions to the Art of Navigation 1519–1802," *Proceedings of the Massachusetts Historical Society*, vol. LXVIII, 1944–1948, p. 88.

5. Historical Society of Pennsylvania. Manuscripts Division. Kirk Brown Papers, p. 104.

6. *The Pennsylvania Journal* [Philadelphia], September 8, 1777.

7. American Philosophical Society, Manuscripts Division. Ms Communications, Natural Philosophy, vol. I, p. 12. Communication from John Churchman to the American Philosophical Society; Minutes, February 16, 1787 [III]; *Proceedings of the American Philosophical Society*, vol. XXII, 1884, pp. 148–151.

8. Julian P. Boyd, ed., *The Papers of Thomas Jefferson* (Princeton, N.J.: Princeton University Press, 1955), vol. II, pp. 293–294.

9. Ibid., vol. II, pp. 397–398.

10. Ibid., vol. II, pp. 403–533.

11. Ibid., vol. II, p. 562.

12. Ibid., vol. XII, p. 5.

13. John Churchman, "An Address to the members of the different learned Societies in America and Europe, in support of the Principles of Magnetic Variation and their application in determining the Longitude at Sea," *The American Museum or Repository of Ancient and Modern Fugitive Pieces*, 1789, vol. V, pp. 496–500; John Churchman, *An Explanation of the Magnetic Atlas, or Variation Chart, Hereunto Annexed: Projected on a Plan Entirely New* (Philadelphia, 1790); Library of Congress, Manuscripts Division, Thomas Jefferson Papers, vol. 58, folio 9896; vol. 69, folio 11945; vol. 58, folio 9894.

14. Irving Brant, *James Madison, Father of the Constitution, 1787–1800* (Indianapolis, 1950), pp. 331–332. See also Brooke Hindle, *The Pursuit of Science in Revolutionary America 1735–1789* (Chapel Hill, N.C.: University of North Carolina Press, 1956), pp. 350–351.

15. John Churchman, *Magnetic Atlas or Variation Charts of the Whole Terraqueous Globe. Comprising a System of the Variation and Dip of the Needle, by which the observations being truly made . . . the Longitude may be ascertained* (London: Darton and Harvey, 1794).

16. *Nova Acta Academiae Scientiarum Imperialis Petropolitanae,* (1799–1802), vol. XV.

17. Ibid. (1791), vol. X, p. 16, and (1795–1796), vol. XIII, p. 14.

18. John Churchman, "Essay on the Improvement of Geography," *Transactions of the Society Instituted at London, for the Encouragement of Arts, Manufactutures, and Commerce; With the Premiums Offered in the Year 1804,* vol. XXII, 1804, pp. 221–229.

19. Boyd, *Jefferson Papers,* vol. II, p. 562.

20. American Philosophical Society, Manuscript Communications, Mathematics and Astronomy, vol. I, folios 22 and A 11.

21. Library of Congress, Manuscripts Division, Thomas Jefferson Papers, vol. 126, folios 21, 823, 21836, 21941.

22. *Mercantile Advertiser* [Boston], September 12, 1803.

23. H. A. Washington, ed., *The Writings of Thomas Jefferson* (Washington: Taylor and Maury, 1853), vol. V, pp. 374–375.

24. *Alexandria Gazette,* April 25, 1839, page 3, col. 3.

25. Samuel Eliot Morison, *The Maritime History of Massachusetts 1783–1860* (Boston: Houghton Mifflin, 1921), p. 116. Original source not stated.

26. *The Daily Advertiser,* June 15, 1802; *New-York Evening Post,* July 1, 1802, and *New-York Herald,* July 7, 1802.

27. *New-York Gazette and General Advertiser,* April 23, 1804.

28. Edward S. Holden, *Memorials of William Cranch Bond, Director of the Harvard College Observatory 1840–1859, and of His Son, George Phillips Bond, Director of the Harvard College Observatory 1859–1865* (San Francisco: C. A. Murdock & Co., and New York, Lemoke & Buechner, 1867), pp. 1–17.

29. *Annals of the Astronomical Observatory at Harvard College* (Cambridge, Mass.), vol. I, part 1, 1855; vol. II, part 1, 1856.

30. William J. Youmans, ed., *Pioneers of Science in America* (New York: D. Appleton, 1896), pp. 223–232.

31. W. Cranch Bond, "Observations on the Comparative Rates of Marine Chronometers," *Memoirs of the American Academy of Arts and Sciences,* 1833, n.s., pp. 84–89; and Charles S. Crossman, "A Complete History of Watch and Clock Making in America, Watch Case Making," *The Jewelers' Circular and Horological Review,* vol. XX, no. 10, November 1889, p. 101.

32. Charles S. Rogers, *American Superiority at the World's Fair* (Philadelphia, 1852), pp. 19–24.

33. Charles S. Crossman, "A Complete History of Watch and Clock Making in America, Marine Chronometers," *The Jeweler's Circular and Horological Review,* vol. XX, no. 11, December 1889, pp. 86–87.

34. Thomas Truxtun, *Remarks, Instructions and Examples relating to the Latitude & Longitude; also, the Variation of the Compass* (Philadelphia: T. Dobson, 1794).

35. John F. Campbell, *History and Bibliography of* The New American Practical Navigator *and* The American Coast Pilot (Salem, Mass.: Peabody Museum, 1964), pp. 29–40, 61–69, 101–114.

36. John Hamilton Moore, *New Practical Navigator and Seaman's New Daily Assistant, being an Epitome of Navigation* (London, 1772); actually a revision of John Robertson, *Elements of Navigation* (London, 1754), which had been produced for use in the Royal Mathematical School.

37. Nathaniel Bowditch subsequently published this material in an independent paper entitled "New Method of Working a Lunar Observation," *Memoirs of the American Academy of Arts and Sciences*, vol. II, 1804, p. ii.

38. Nathaniel Bowditch, *The New American Practical Navigator* (Newburyport, Mass.: Edmund M. Blunt, 1802).

39. Campbell, *History of* The New American Practical Navigator, pp. 13–25, 73–98.

40. George Baron, *Exhibition of the Genuine Principles of Common Navigation* (New York: Sage and Clough, 1803); and *The New-York Evening Post*, August 10, 1802.

41. *The New-York Evening Post*, April 1, 1803.

42. *Commercial Advertiser* [New York], April 23, 1803; and *The New-York Evening Post*, December 27, 1804.

43. The fifth and final volume of Laplace's work was not published until after Bowditch's death and consequently was not translated into English.

44. Benjamin Peirce, "Bowditch's Translation of the *Mécanique Celeste*," *North American Review*, vol. XLVIII, 1839, pp. 143–180; and Harold Bowditch, *Nathaniel Bowditch* (Salem, Mass.: Peabody Museum, 1945), pp. 7–8.

45. Ferdinand R. Hassler, *Principal Documents Relating to the Survey of the Coast of the United States, since 1816* (New York, 1834); and Nathan Reingold, comp., *Records of the Coast and Geodetic Survey*, National Archives Publication no. 59-3 (Washington, D.C.; The National Archives, Preliminary Inventories no. 105, 1958).

46. Russel Leigh Jackson, *Edmund March Blunt* (Salem, Mass.: Essex Institute, 1943), pp. 9–13; and Harold L. Burstyn, *At The Sign of the Quadrant* (Mystic, Conn.: The Marine Historical Association, Inc., 1957), pp. 32–41.

47. Florian Cajori, *The Chequered Career of Ferdinand Rudolph Hassler* (Boston: The Christopher Publishing House, 1929), pp. 45–49, 71–93.

48. *New York Evening Post*, February 23 and April 18, 1815.

49. *New York Gazette*, March 30, 1817.

50. *Niles Register*, June 7, 1828.

51. "Trials between Edmund M. Blunt vs. Isaac Greenwood For A Libel: and Edmund M. Blunt vs. Richard Patten, for Infringement of Copy Right," *Blunt's Edition of the Nautical Almanac and Astronomical Ephemeris, for the Year 1831* (New York: Edmund and George W. Blunt, March 1829). Blunt also issued the report as a separate publication in 1828.

52. Willis I. Milham, *Time and Timekeepers*, 2nd ed. (New York: Macmillan, 1947), p. 281; and M. V. Brewington, "The Observatory on Federal Hill," *Maryland Historical Quarterly*, June 1949, pp. 102–103.

53. Philip Astor, "The Centre of the World. How Time is Made," *Harmsworth Magazine*, vol. VI, no. 33, 1901, pp. 247–252.

54. *Executive Office Building*, General Services Administration Historical Study no. 3 (Washington, D.C: Government Printing Office, 1964), pp. 74–75; Charles Oscar Paullin, "Early Movements for a National Observatory 1802–1842," *Records of the Columbia Historical Society*, vol. 25, 1923, pp. 36–56; and A. N. Skinner, "The United States Naval Observatory," *Science,* vol. IX, n.s., January 6, 1899, pp. 1–16.

XVII. THE BOOK OF NATURE

1. Sidney Forman, *West Point* (New York: Columbia University Press, 1950), pp. 20–60; and R. E. Depuy, *The Story of West Point: 1802–1946, The West Point Tradition in American Life* (Washington, D.C.: The Infantry Journal, 1943), pp. 18–51.

2. Edward S. Holden, "Origins of the United States Military Academy, 1777–1802," *The Centennial of the United States Military Academy, at West Point, New York* (Washington, D.C.: Government Printing Office, 1904), vol. I, pp. 201–222.

3. *A Biographical Dictionary of American Engineers*. ASCE Publication no. 2 (New York: American Society of Civil Engineers, 1972), pp. 40, 64, 32, 109–110, 49, 132–134, 126–127, 114, 101.

4. "Isaac Roberdeau," *Dictionary of American Biography* (New York: Charles Scribner's Sons, 1935), vol. XV, p. 647; and Elisabeth S. Kite, *L'Enfant and Washington, 1791–1792* (Baltimore: Johns Hopkins University Press, 1929), pp. 21–23, 140.

5. Bernhard, Duke of Saxe-Weimar-Eisenach, *Travels Through North America* (Philadelphia, 1828), vol. I, p. 181.

6. Charles E. Smart, *The Makers of Surveying Instruments in America Since 1700* (Troy, N.Y.: Regal Art Press, 1962), pp. 170–171.

7. Ibid., pp. 11–13; and *Description of the E. & G. W. Blunt Dividing Engine* (New York: E. & G. W. Blunt, 1858), 8 pp., 5 pl.

8. *The New-York Evening Post*, November 28, 1815, p. 3, col. 5; and *New-York Gazette and General Advertiser*, March 20, 1817, p. 2, col. 3.

9. Smart, *Makers of Surveying Instruments*, pp. 114–115; and Roger G. Gerry, "Richard Patten: Mathematical Instrument Maker," *Antiques*, July 1959, pp. 56–58.

10. "Description of an Automatic Dividing Machine, arranged for use in the Coast Survey Office, by Joseph Saxton, Assistant in the Office of Weights and Measures, Washington, and constructed by William Wurdemann, mechanician, Coast Survey Office," *Journal of the Franklin Institute*, 3rd series, vol. 12, 1846, pp. 258–261.

11. Robert P. Multhauf, *A Catalogue of Instruments and Models in the Possession of the American Philosophical Society*. Memoirs of the American Philosophical Society, vol. 53 (1961), p. 46.

12. Smart, *Makers of Surveying Instruments*, pp. 172–176; and *Catalogue of Mathematical and Surveying Instruments of William J. Young & Sons*, 5th ed. (Philadelphia, 1878); 15th ed. (1896), p. 83.

13. Smart, *Makers of Surveying Instruments*, pp. 39–40.

14. *The Providence* [R. I.] *Daily Journal*, April 22, 1833.

15. William A. Burt, *A Key to the Solar Compass and Surveyor's Companion* (New York: D. Van Nostrand, 1909); and Alan S. Brown, "William Austin Burt, Michigan's Master Surveyor," *Michigan Academy of Science, Arts and Letters* (Western Michigan University), vol. XLVII, 1962, pp. 263–274.

16. Henry Wyckoff Belknap, *Artists and Craftsmen of Essex County, Massachusetts* (Salem, Mass.: Essex Institute, 1927), p. 102; and M. V. Brewington, *The Peabody Museum Collection of Navigating Instruments* (Salem, Mass.: Peabody Museum, 1963), pp. 130–131.

17. Brewington, *Peabody Museum Collection*, p. 119.

18. *The Bay of San Francisco: A History* (Chicago: Lewis Publishing Co., 1892), vol. II, pp. 142–144.

19. *Royal Gazette*, October 17, 20, 31, and November 21, 1781.

20. *New-York Gazette and Weekly Mercury*, January 7 and 14, October 14 and 21, 1782.

21. *Royal Gazette*, December 5, 1781.

22. *Independent Journal, or, the General Advertiser*, May 11, 21, and 28, 1785.

23. *The Complete Mariner: or A Treatise of Navigation trigonometrically, by Logarithmical Numbers, and the geometrical Construction of Scale and Compass. Also the Orthographic Projection of the Sphere astronomically.* (Williamsburg: Printed February the 18th, 1731. E. L. James Hubard). Owned by Colonial Williamsburg, Inc. Title-page possibly the work of William Parks. See also James Mulhern, "Manuscript School-Books," *Papers of the Bibliographical Society of America*, vol. XXII, 1938, pp. 17–37; and Lawrence C. Wroth, "Some American Contributions to the Art of Navigation 1519–1802," *Proceedings of the Massachusetts Historical Society*, vol. LXVIII, 1944–1948, p. 88.

24. American Philosophical Society, Manuscript Collections. Robert Patterson Papers, manuscript on Navigation.

25. Samuel Eliot Morison, *The Maritime History of Massachusetts 1783–1860* (Boston: Houghton Mifflin Co., 1961), p. 114 fn.

26. [William Bentley], *The Diary of William Bentley, D. D.* (Essex, Mass.: Essex Institute, 1907), vol. II, p. 423.

27. Harvard College Archives. Corporation Records, vol. III, pp. 325–327; I. Bernard Cohen, *Some Early Tools of American Science* (Cambridge, Mass.: Harvard University Press, 1950), pp. 12–14.

28. Harvard College Archives, Corporation Records, vol. III, p. 267; Cohen, *Some Early Tools*, p. 53.

29. Emit Duncan Grizzell, *Origin and Development of the High School in New England Before 1865* (Philadelphia: University of Pennsylvania Press, 1922), pp. 36–37; Edgar W. Knight, *Education in the United States* (New York: Greenwood Publishers, 1951), pp. 160–188.

30. *The Daily Advertiser*, January 1, 1800.

31. *American Citizen and General Advertiser*, January 1, 1801.

32. *Weekly Museum*, September 12, 1801, and *The Daily Advertiser*, November 25, 1801.

33. *New-York Evening Post*, October 18, 1803.

34. *Diary of William Bentley*, vol. II, p. 423; George Lyman Kittredge, *The Old Farmer and His Almanac* (Boston: William Ware & Co., 1904), p. 8.

35. M. V. Brewington, "American Navigation During the Revolution," *Naval Documents of the American Revolution*, ed. William Bell Clark (Washington, D.C.: U.S. Navy Department, 1966), vol. II, p. 803. The original source is not stated.

36. *Kentucky Gazette*, May 23, 1789.

37. Jedediah Morse, *Geography Made Easy* (Cambridge, Mass., 1784).

38. Clifton Johnson, *Old-Time Schools and School-Books* (New York: Macmillan, 1904; reprint, Dover Publications, 1963), pp. 318–362.

39. Jedediah Morse, *The American Geography; Or a View of the Present Situation of the United States of America* (Elizabeth Town, N.J., 1789), and *The American Universal Geography* (Boston: Isaiah Thomas and Ebenezer T. Andrews, 1793).

40. Jedediah Morse, *The American Geography*, 3rd ed. (Boston, 1796).

41. J. C. Parish, *The Emergence of Manifest Destiny* (Los Angeles and Berkeley: University of California Press, 1932), p. 16.

42. William Guthrie, *A New System of Modern Geography; or, A Geographical History and Commercial Grammar and Present State of the Several Nations of the World: The Astronomical Parts Corrected by Dr. Rittenhouse* (Philadelphia: Matthew Carey, 1793).

43. Nathaniel Dwight, *A Short But Comprehensive History of the Geography of the World: By Way of Question and Answer* (Albany, N.Y.: C. R. and G. Webster, 1795).

44. John Payne, *New and Complete System of Universal Geography . . . With Corrections by James Hardie* (New York: Low, 1799–1800), vol. I, pp. xxxiii–xxxviii.

45. Robert Davidson, *Geography Epitomized: or, A Tour Round the World; Being a Short But Comprehensive Description of the Terraqueous Globe, Attempted in Verse . . .* (Morristown, N.J.: For H. P. Russel, 1803); and Thomas Greenleaf, *Geographical Gazetteer of the Towns in the Commonwealth of Massachusetts* (Boston: Greenleaf and Freeman, 1784–1785).

46. Charles B. Nelson, *History of Stratham, New Hampshire, 1631–1900* (Somersworth, N.H.: New Hampshire Publishing Co., 1965), pp. 70–84.

47. Dartmouth College Library. Manuscript Journal of Jeremy Belknap. Description of the commencement exercises for 1774.

48. *Encyclopaedia Brittanica; or a Dictionary of Arts, Sciences and Miscellaneous Literature* (Edinburgh: A. Bell and C. Macfarlane, 1788–1797), 18 vols.

49. LeRoy E. Kimball, "James Wilson of Vermont, America's First Globe Maker," *Proceedings of the American Antiquarian Society*, n.s., vol. 48, April 1938, pp. 29–48.

50. *Albany Argus*, July 4, 1820, and August 21, 1821; *The New York Statesman*[Albany, N.Y.], August 21, 1821, and January 1, 1822; and *Albany Register*, January 15 and 22, 1822.

51. Thomas Keath [*sic*], *A New Treatise on the Use of the Globes* (Albany, N.Y.: James Wilson & Co., 1820); and Thomas Keith, *Treatise on the Use of Globes, Revised and corrected by Robert Adrain, L.L.D. etc., and Professor of Mathematics in Rutger's College, New Brunswick, New Jersey* (New York: Samuel Wood & Sons, 1826 and 1832).

52. L. P. Tucker, "A Vermont Genius, James Wilson, the First Globe-Builder," *The Vermonter*, August 1903, pp. 270–275; and John C. Huden, "James Wilson, Vermont Globe Maker," ibid., December 1943, pp. 241–246.

53. Alexander O. Vietor, "Some American Globemakers," *Antiques*, January 1943, pp. 21–23.

54. "To George Pocock, Gentleman, for improvements in making and constructing Globes for astronomical, geographical, or other purposes. Dated February 4, 1830," *Journal of the Franklin Institute*, vol. IV, no. 3, 1830, pp. 171–172.

55. Ena L. Yonge, *A Catalogue of Early Globes Made Prior to 1850 and Conserved in the United States* (New York: American Geographical Society, 1968), p. 114; and private correspondence with Mrs. Gladys Howe Cummings, Beaman Memorial Public Library, West Boylston, Mass., March 10, 1965.

56. Gilbert Vale, *Astronomy and Worship of the Ancients* (New York: The Beacon Press, 1855); and Vietor, "Some American Globemakers," pp. 21–23.

57. Brown University, John Hay Library, Fobes Mss. Statement from Pere Fobes to the Corporation of the College, August 25, 1802.

58. *Boston Gazette and Country Journal*, June 23 and June 30, July 7, 1786.

59. Harrold E. Gillingham, "The First Orreries in America," *Journal of the Franklin Institute*, vol. 229, 1940, pp. 92–97; and Cohen, *Some Early Tools*, pp. 64–65, 157.

60. David P. Wheatland, *The Apparatus of Science at Harvard 1765–1800* (Cambridge, Mass.: Harvard University Press, 1968), pp. 56–59.

61. *Boston Gazette*, December 8, 1788, and September 7, 1789.

62. Bartholomew Burges, *A Short Account of the Solar System, and of Comets in General: Together With a Particular Account of the Comet that Will Appear in 1789* (Boston: B. Edes & Son, 1789), 16 pp. + 3, 2 pl.

63. *Boston Gazette*, February 16, 1789.

64. Brooke Hindle, *The Pursuit of Science in Revolutionary America 1735–1789* (Chapel Hill, N.C.: University of North Carolina Press, 1956), pp. 334, 339.

65. Bartholomew Burges, *A Series of Indostan Letters by Bar. Burges Containing a Striking account of the manners & customs of the Gentoo Nations & of the Moguls & other Mahometan Tribes in Indostan with other polemical East India Tracts both amusing, interesting & perfectly original* (New York: for the author by W. Ross, 1790).

66. Burges, *Short Account*, unpaginated advertisement.

67. Essex Institute, Salem. "Salem Vital Statistics." Records kept by Benjamin Blanchard.

68. In the collections of the National Museum of History and Technology, Smithsonian Institution.

69. Henry D. Biddle, "Owen Biddle," *Pennsylvania Magazine of History and Biography*, vol. XVI, 1892, pp. 299–329; and William Ball, Jr., "Another American Orrery," *Antiques*, October 1938, pp. 184–185.

70. New York State Senate and Assembly Journal, 1819, pp. 884, 1072.

71. Laws of New-York. Forty-third Session, 1820, Chapter IV, p. 6.

72. "Art. XII. The Newellian Sphere," *American Journal of Science and Arts*, vol. XII, June 1827, pp. 103–115.

XVIII. THE DIGNITY OF INDEPENDENCE

1. G. C. D. Odell, *Annals of the New York Stage* (New York, 1927), vol. I, pp. 398, 474.

2. *The Medical Repository*, 3rd hexade, no. 2 (1811), p. 88; no. 11 (1812), p. 320.

3. Edgar F. Smith, *John Griscom 1774–1852 Chemist* (Philadelphia: privately printed, 1925).

4. [J. Holbrook], *American Lyceum, or Society for the improvement of schools and the diffusion of useful knowledge* (Boston: Perkins and Marvis, 1829). See also Dirk J. Struik, *Yankee Science in the Making* (Boston: Little, Brown, 1948), pp. 207–209.

5. John Todd, Zachariah Jess, William Waring, and Jeremiah Paul, *The American Tutor's Assistant; or, A Compendious System of Practical Arithmetic; Containing, the Several Rules of that Useful Science, Concisely Defined, Methodically Arranged, and Fully Exemplified . . .* (Philadelphia: Zachariah Poulson, Junior, 1791).

6. Zachariah Jess, *A Compendious System of Practical Surveying, and Dividing of Land: Concisely Defined, Methodically Arranged, and Fully Exemplified, the Whole Adapted for the Easy and Regular Instruction of Youth, in our American Schools* (Wilmington: Bonsal and Niles, 1799).

7. John Gunmere, *A Treatise on Surveying, Containing the Theory and Practice: to Which is Prefixed a Perspicuous System of Plane Trigonometry. The Whole . . . Particularly Adapted to the Use of Schools* (Philadelphia: Kimber and Richardson, 1814).

8. Robert Gibson, *A Treatise of Practical Surveying; Which is Demonstrated from its First Principles* (Dublin: Printed for William Ross, 1768; reprint, Philadelphia: Joseph Crukshank, 1789).

9. John Gunmere, *Elementary Treatise on Astronomy* (Philadelphia: Kimber, 1822).

10. Jared Mansfield, *Essays, Mathematical and Physical: containing new theories and illustrations of some very important and difficult subjects of sciences. Never before published . . .* (New Haven, [1800]; rev. and suppl. ed. 1802).

11. F. B. Dexter, *Biographical Sketches of the Graduates of Yale University* (New Haven, 1903), vol. III, pp. 691–694; and Edward D. Mansfield, *American Education* (New York, 1851), pp. 158–160.

12. Jeremiah Day, *The Mathematical Principles of Navigation and Surveying, with the Mensuration of Heights and Distances, Being the fourth part of a Course of mathematics. Adapted to the method of instruction in the American colleges* (New Haven: Steele and Gray, 1817).

13. "A Charge which ought to be delivered to the Graduates in the Arts, in all the Colleges in the United States," *The Universal Asylum, and Columbian Magazine*, August, 1790.

14. Emit Duncan Grizzell, *Origin and Development of the High School in New England before 1865* (Philadelphia: University of Pennsylvania Press, 1922), pp. 36–37.

15. T. C. Mendenhall, *Scientific, Technical and Engineering Education*. Nicholas Murray Butler, ed., *Education in the United States*, Monographs on Education in the United States no. 11 (Albany, N.Y.: J. B. Lyon, 1900), pp. 5–10.

16. P. C. Ricketts, *History of the Rensselaer Polytechnic Institute, 1824–1894* (New York: Wiley, 1895).

17. Mendenhall, *Scientific, Technical and Engineering Education*, pp. 8–15; Robert Middlekauf, *Ancients and Axioms: Secondary Education in Eighteenth-Century New England* (New Haven, Conn.: Yale University Press, 1963) pp. 155–162.

18. Thomas Coulson, "The Franklin Institute from 1824 to 1949," *Journal of the Franklin Institute*, vol. 249, no. 1, January 1950, pp. 1–48; [unsigned], "The First Hundred Years of Research at the Franklin Institute," ibid., vol. 256, no. 1, July 1953, pp. 1–25.

19. *Daily National Intelligencer* [Washington, D.C.], October 27, 1820.

20. *Memoirs of the American Academy of Arts and Sciences*, n.s., vol. XI, 1888, Charter of Incorporation, Granted May 4, 1780 . . . , pp. 77–79.

21. Ralph S. Bates, "The American Academy of Arts and Sciences," *Scientific Monthly*, vol. LIV, no. 3, March 1942, pp. 265–268.

22. Ralph S. Bates, "Baily's Beads or Williams' Beads," *Telescope*, vol. VIII, March–April 1961, pp. 36–38.

23. Brooke Hindle, *The Pursuit of Science in Revolutionary America 1735–1789* (Chapel Hill, N.C.: University of North Carolina Press, 1956), p. 266.

24. Ralph S. Bates, *Scientific Societies in the United States*, 3rd ed. (Cambridge, Mass.: M.I.T. Press, 1965), pp. 13–27.

25. Charles Coleman Sellers, *Charles Willson Peale* (New York: Charles Scribner's Sons, 1969), pp. 293–301.

26. Oliver Jense, "The Peales," *American Heritage*, vol. VI, no. 3, April 1955, pp. 40–50, 97–101.

27. *Freeman's Journal* [Philadelphia], August 27, 1788.

28. *Pennsylvania Packet*, May 28, 1789.

29. Ibid., June 23, 1789.

30. Ibid., November 6, 1790.

31. Greville and Dorothy Bathe, *Oliver Evans* (Philadelphia: Historical Society of Pennsylvania, 1935), pp. 28–30, 40–42, 50–53, 294.

32. *Dunlap's American Daily Advertiser*, April 15, 1793; *Pennsylvania Packet*, April 27, 1793.

33. Thomas Twining, *Travels in America 100 Years Ago* (New York, 1894), p. 155.

34. *New York Commercial Advertiser*, October 9, 1797.

35. *Columbian Gazeteer* [New York City], February 3, 1794.

36. Robert M. and Gale S. McClung, "Tammany's Remarkable Gardiner Baker," *The New-York Historical Society Quarterly*, vol. XLII, no. 2, April 1958, pp. 143–169.

37. *The Diary, or Loudon's Register* [New York City], February 16, 1792; *The New-York Weekly Museum*, December 21, 1793.

38. Isaac Newton Phelps Stokes, *Iconography of Manhattan Island* (New York: Robert H. Dodd, 1915–1928), January 25, 1796.

39. "Items and Novelties: The Bancker Collection," *Journal of the Franklin Institute*, 3rd ser., June 1871, pp. 375–376.

40. George Brown Goode, "The Origin of the National Scientific and Educational Institutions of the United States," *Annual Report of the American Historical Association for the Year 1889*, p. 7.

41. Ibid., pp. 66, 126.

42. [Joel Barlow], *Prospectus of a National Institution, To be Established in the United States* (Washington, D.C.: Samuel H. Smith, 1806); reprinted in the *National Intelligencer*, August 1, 1806, and November 24, 1806.

43. Andrew A. Lipscomb, ed., *The Writings of Thomas Jefferson* (Washington, D.C.: The Thomas Jefferson Memorial Foundation, 1904), vol. XI, pp. 206–207, Letter from Jefferson to G. C. de la Coste, May 24, 1807.

44. James Hutton, ed., *Selections from the Letters and Correspondence of Sir James Bland Burges, Bart., sometime Under-Secretary of State for Foreign Affairs, With Notices of His Life* (London: John Murray, 1885), pp. 222–224.

45. "The United States Through English Spectacles in 1792–1794," *Pennsylvania Magazine of History and Biography*, 1885, vol. IX, pp. 214–222.

46. Paul L. Ford, ed., *The Works of Thomas Jefferson*. Federal Edition (New York: G. P. Putnam Sons, 1892–1899), vol. III, pp. 458–460.

47. "Mémoires philosophiques, historiques, phisiques, concernant la découverte de l'Amérique . . . ," *Journal de médecine, chirurgie, pharmacie, &c., dédie à Monsieur, Frère du Roi*, vol. LXXI, April 1787, pp. 533–534. A review.

48. Benjamin Rush, "Natural History of Medicine Among the Indians . . . ," *Medical Inquiries and Observations*, 3rd ed. (Philadelphia, 1809), vol. I, p. 168.

GLOSSARY

The definitions of technical terms most frequently used in the text and the descriptions of mathematical instruments have been derived from consultation of a large number of published sources, the most important of which are included in the Selected Bibliography.

ABERRATION. In optics, the failure of rays of light to meet at a point expected by simple theory. In spherical aberration the marginal rays are brought to a focus closer to the lens or mirror than are the central rays; in chromatic aberration the images formed by different-colored components of light are of unequal sizes and are not brought to the same focus in one plane.

ACHROMATIC LENS, see LENS, ACHROMATIC.

ALIDADE. Wooden or brass rule with sighting vanes to measure or plot the direction or elevation sighted; also, the radial arm with sights customarily found on astrolabes and on early surveying instruments such as the circumferentor.

ALMANAC. Publication issued periodically, containing an ephemeris consisting of astronomical and meteorological data presented in calendrical form by the day, week, and month for a given year, in addition to meteorological information, distances, recipes, medical advice, monetary tables, and other items. See also EPHEMERIS.

ALTITUDE. The angular position of a celestial object measured in degrees vertically from the horizon. Observations of the altitude of selected objects, such as the sun or a star, can be used to determine the observer's latitude.

ARMILLARY SPHERE. Science-teaching device for demonstrating a cosmological theory, used since the Middle Ages. Generally made of wood or metal, it consists of a celestial sphere in skeletal form, with rings representing the meridian, equator, ecliptic, and tropics, on which fixed stars are marked by pointers. Within the frame of the sphere are representations of the planets.

ARTIFICIAL HORIZON. Device to enable observation of the altitude of objects when the true horizon is not visible. The most common form, dating from about 1790, con-

461

sists of an oblong trough containing mercury, which provides a level reflecting surface, and two panes of glass set at right angles to the observer's line of sight and held in a protective frame. In early examples various other liquids, including oil, treacle, and water, were used.

ASTROLABE. Instrument for astrological and astronomical computation, also employed in surveying, used from the Hellenistic period to the beginning of the eighteenth century. It is made of brass and consists of a thick round plate called a mater, having a depression into which are fitted plates engraved with stereographic projections for various latitudes, and a superimposed star map, or rete, which is rotatable. The reverse side of the mater, called the dorsum, is engraved with scales useful to the astrologer or astronomer.

ASTROLABE, MARINER'S. Simplified form of the stereographic astrolabe consisting only of a scale and an alidade, used at sea for taking the altitude of the sun or stars to determine the ship's latitude.

ASTRONOMICAL CLOCK, see CLOCK, ASTRONOMICAL.

ASTRONOMICAL COMPENDIUM. Collection of astronomical devices or instruments fitted into a box or container of a convenient size for travel.

ASTRONOMICAL QUADRANT, see QUADRANT, ASTRONOMICAL.

ASTRONOMICAL RING. Instrument for astronomical observation which could be used for timetelling and/or surveying. Based on the armillary sphere, it was revived in the early sixteenth century from an earlier form.

ASTRONOMICAL TRANSIT, see TRANSIT, ASTRONOMICAL.

AZIMUTH. The angular position of an object either on the horizon or in the sky, measured around the horizon in degrees from a starting reference point to a point directly under the object. For astronomical purposes the distance is measured westward from the south point of the observer's meridian; in surveying and navigation it is measured eastward from the north point.

AZIMUTH COMPASS, see COMPASS, AZIMUTH.

BACKSTAFF. Navigational instrument for observing the altitude of the sun at sea, consisting of a framework of wood with a large and a small arc and three vanes—a horizon vane at the common center, an eye vane on the large arc, and a shadow vane on the small arc. The shadow vane was maintained at a convenient angle less than the expected altitude. The observer, standing with the sun at his back, sighted the horizon through the eye vane and a small slit in the horizon vane, moving the eye vane along the arc until the edge of the shadow cast by the shadow vane was thrown upon the horizon vane and coincided with the line of the horizon. The angles indicated by the two vanes on the graduated scales of the arcs were then added together to obtain the altitude of the sun. In the version modified by Captain John Davis between 1600 and 1604 and known as DAVIS'S IMPROVED QUADRANT, visual distortion was eliminated. Later the shadow vane was replaced by a vane having a lens with a focal length equal to the radius of the lesser arc. See also MARINER'S BOW; PLOUGH; QUADRANT, ELTON'S.

BAILY'S BEADS. Phenomenon occuring during a total solar eclipse whereby at the moment preceding totality the disappearing crescent of the sun's light breaks up into a number of glowing points shining through the irregular surface of the moon and resembling a string of bright beads around the edge.

BAROMETER. Instrument which indicates atmospheric pressure on or near the surface of the earth by measuring the height of a column of mercury supported within a glass tube sealed at its upper end and terminating in a cistern of mercury; a scale attached near the top of the tube enables the barometric pressure to be measured.

BAROMETER, MARINE. A form designed for use at sea; the bore of the upper part of the tube is constricted and the instrument is supported on a gimbal attachment.

BINNACLE, BITTACLE. Free-standing, shelved, pillar-like cupboard placed directly in front of the ship's steersman and anchored firmly to the deck to house the ship's compass, which was thus protected from wind and sea spray and could be readily viewed by the steersman.

BOND'S ELECTRIC REGISTER, see BREAK-CIRCUIT, BOND'S.

BORDA CIRCLE, see CIRCLE, REFLECTING.

BOX SEXTANT, see SEXTANT, BOX.

BREAK-CIRCUIT, BOND'S. A break-circuit apparatus used with a battery-powered regulator clock to register astronomical observations. Also known as BOND'S ELECTRIC REGISTER.

BUBBLE LEVEL. Device used for defining the horizontal as an adjunct to instruments for astronomy, navigation, and surveying. It consists of a glass tube filled with a liquid and sealed to prevent evaporation, in which a bubble of air is trapped so that it stands at the center of a marked glazed opening in the tube when the instrument is exactly level. The bubble moves away from the center with the slightest slope or deviation.

BURT'S SOLAR COMPASS, see COMPASS, BURT'S SOLAR.

CALIPERS, GUNNER'S. Multipurpose instrument for artillery use, consisting of two flat brass plates joined at one end so that one plate could be moved around the other. It was used to measure the caliber of a cannon bore and the diameter of a cannonball and was inscribed with tables for the weight of shot, windage, tolerance, service charges of powder, specific gravities of various materials, etc.

CAMERA OBSCURA. Instrument with which objects at a distance can be viewed on a ground-glass screen by means of light passing through a double convex lens into an inclined plane mirror.

CELESTIAL GLOBE, see GLOBE, CELESTIAL.

CHAIN STAKES. Iron pins 14 inches in length, used to mark distances measured on the ground with surveying chains, particularly the point from which the succeeding chain would be measured. Also called MARKING PINS, TALLY PINS.

CHAIN, SURVEYING. Chain used to measure distances on the ground, consisting of a standard number of links of an established length (7.92 inches) made of wrought iron or steel. Its length was measured in multiples of perches or poles of 16.5 feet. The types most commonly used were the Gunter's Chain of four poles or perches, consisting of 100 links measuring a total of 66 feet, and the two-pole chain, consisting of 50 links and measuring a total of 33 feet.

CHART. Map delineated on parchment paper or similar substance, generally for the use of navigators, showing shores, harbors, headlands, and anchorages, with sailing directions, and generally oriented to the north or the lodestar. The simple form, or "plain chart," was drawn to scale and included a "trunk," or scale, of miles. It was traversed with the rhumb lines (lines extending from the points or rhumbs of the compass rose), often inscribed in a different color for each.

CHART, MERCATOR'S, see MERCATOR'S CHART.

CHIP LOG, see DUTCHMAN'S LOG.

CHRONOMETER, MARINE. Timepiece of relatively extreme precision carried on a ship to indicate the time at the port of sailing, which can be compared with the local time of any place at sea to determine the difference in longitude. The first successful chronometer was produced in 1762 by John Harrison, an English carpenter turned clockmaker, and tested successfully in 1764.

CIRCLE, GREAT. Circle on a sphere, the plane of which passes through the center of the sphere. The ecliptic, celestial equator, horizon, and meridian are great circles of the celestial sphere.

CIRCLE, REFLECTING. The earliest example of a type of navigational instrument designed specifically for measuring the greater angles required to determine the longitude by measurement of the lunar distances. Suggested by Tobias Mayer and first made by John Bird, the instrument was improved by Jean-Charles de Borda. Also called BORDA CIRCLE, FULL CIRCLE. Subsequently modified in the form known as REPEATING CIRCLE.

CIRCUMFERENTOR. Instrument for surveying, consisting of a round flat brass plate with its circumference graduated to 360°. An alidade with two or four sighting vanes separated from each other by 90° is pivoted at the center so that it swivels over the plate. A magnetic compass protected with a glass covering is usually inset in the center of the plate. Also called HOLLAND CIRCLE. The English later called this instrument a graphometer and gave the name circumferentor to the instrument which was commonly known in America as the plain surveying compass. See also COMPASS, PLAIN SURVEYING; GRAPHOMETER.

CLOCK, ASTRONOMICAL. Timepiece used by astronomers and surveyors for establishing the time of true noon and other events. These are tall-case clocks with a dead-beat escapement which eliminates recoil; they have a seconds pendulum and frequently incorporate a compensating device to correct against the expansion and contraction of the pendulum rod due to temperature changes.

COMING-UP TELESCOPE, see TELESCOPE, COMING-UP.

COMPASS, AMPLITUDE. Instrument to determine the magnetic compass variation by observation of the sun's bearing at sunrise or sunset and comparison with amplitude tables. It incorporates a compass card pivoted inside an enclosed square compass box. Two opposite sides of the box are open and glazed and have sights for taking solar bearings. Amplitude tables were first published early in the seventeenth century by the Portuguese.

COMPASS, AZIMUTH. Instrument for calculating the true azimuth of the sun; it incorporates a large flat brass ring which rotates around the edge of a dry-card compass and has a sighting bar attached perpendicularly and pivoted to the outer edge of the ring. The sighting bar has a vertical vane at the pivot with a wire from the top of the bar to the horizontal arm. When a bearing is to be taken, the ring is rotated until the two cross wires coincide with the cardinal points of the fly and the sighting bar is then turned until the shadow of the wire is thrown upon the center of the vertical vane by the sun.

COMPASS, BURT'S SOLAR. Modified version of the vernier surveying compass, designed to overcome difficulties experienced with magnetic declination in regions where iron deposits were prevalent. The instrument is similar to the railroad compass except that the magnetic needle is supplemented with a solar apparatus which enables the surveyor to determine the meridian from the position of the sun instead of by the needle.

COMPASS CARD. The dial of a marine compass, usually made of paper and engraved with the thirty-two points of the wind rose, or nautical circle of the horizon.

COMPASS, DRY-CARD. Magnetic compass for use at sea, in which, instead of a compass needle pivoted above the compass card, the card itself pivots to indicate the ship's course with respect to the center line of the vessel. The engraved or printed compass card, which has a magnetized iron wire or bar attached to its under surface by glued paper strips, is pivoted on a brass pin projecting from the compass bowl's base, and the bowl is suspended on gimbals within a square wooden box.

COMPASS FLY. The name given by English seamen to the compass card of a dry-card compass.

COMPASS, LIQUID. Marine compass designed to withstand derangement from sudden movement or shock, consisting of a brass bowl filled with liquid in which a waterproof compass card is suspended.

COMPASS, MARINE. Instrument for establishing a ship's course. See COMPASS, DRY-CARD; COMPASS, LIQUID.

COMPASS, PLAIN SURVEYING. Instrument used by the surveyor to take bearings from one survey station to another. It is particularly useful when multiple angle measurements are required, especially through areas obscured by underbrush. It consists of a single plate, usually of heavy cast brass, formed with a round center to accommodate a raised compass ring and having arms extending north and south along the center line. A compass dial, sometimes silvered, is inscribed within the round compass ring, with a graduated circle divided to half degrees, the whole degrees being also cut into the inside circumference, inscribed 0° to 90° on each side of the center line of zero. A steel needle approximately 6 inches long is suspended on a central brass pivot and the compass ring covered with a glass plate, usually set in putty to protect it from the elements and having a removable cover. Removable sighting bars having two sets of slotted sights one above the other are attached at each end of the main plate by a sliding notched arrangement or by means of screws. In rare examples the sighting bars are permanently attached. Also known in America as the single-plate compass and common compass, the instrument was called a circumferentor by the English. See also CIRCUMFERENTOR.

COMPASS, RAILROAD. Modified version of the plain surveying compass having a graduated circle and a vernier scale, developed to enable an engineer making railroad surveys to determine a number of angles in less time and with more accuracy than is possible with the needle of the plain surveying compass or the vernier compass. It is provided with a vernier reading inside the compass dial.

COMPASS ROSE. The thirty-two points of the compass, or the nautical circle of the horizon. The eight major points signify the eight winds, and their halves and their quarters. The most dominant are the four cardinal points indicating the four principal directions—north, south, east, and west—and the next series of four points are the sub-cardinal points. The remaining twenty-four points are not individually named. The points were also known as the "rhumbs of the winds." Also called WIND-ROSE, ROSE OF THE WINDS.

COMPASS, TELL-TALE. Form of marine compass in which the bowl is inverted to enable the card to be read from the underside. The inverted bowl is attached to a ceiling fixture in the captain's cabin by means of a simple universal joint. The bowl is customarily covered with a brass frame shaped like a heavy crown, and the compass card, on which the East and West points are necessarily reversed, is suspended at the tip of a pivot needle and is visible through a half-dome of glass even when the observer is reclining. The universal joint permits the compass to hang free despite the ship's motion. Also called OVERHEAD COMPASS, HANGING COMPASS.

COMPASS, VARIATION. Instrument used with a dip needle on shore for determining minute changes in the variation of the compass by measuring the earth's magnetism and the changes in the magnetic poles. The instrument usually consists of a trough compass attached to a brass horizontal frame having a scale marked twice from zero degrees at the center to thirty degrees. An index arm having a vernier scale with a precision screw is moved along the graduated arc. See also DECLINATION.

COMPASS, VERNIER. Modification of the standard plain surveying compass, in which the graduated compass ring can be rotated a few degrees in relation to the line of sight to the center line and the compass card, and the difference can be read to considerable accuracy by means of a vernier scale against which the ring is rotated. In some examples the ring can be locked into place at a given angle in relation to the sights. An arc fixed to the main plate is generally graduated in half-degrees and is in the same plane as the vernier, which is usually provided with thirty equal divisions. The instrument was useful for laying off the magnetic declination because of the range of the arc, but this was considerably reduced in later examples. This instrument is traditionally credited to David Rittenhouse, and as having been made between 1770 and 1776, but no supporting documentation has been found. Also called MAGNETIC VARIATION COMPASS.

CROSS HAIRS. A pair of fine threads, placed at right angles to each other to bisect an axis and inserted into the eyepiece of an optical instrument, where they are held firmly in place. Materials used for this purpose included silk, human hair, metal wire, and natural fibers, but all these were either too thick to attain the precision required or reacted too much to temperature and humidity. The most successful cross hairs are produced from spider silk.

CROSS-STAFF. Navigational instrument for taking the altitude of the sun or a star in order to obtain the latitude. The main component was a wooden staff of varying length having a square cross section of ½ inch. The length varied, but most examples were 30 or 36 inches in length. This staff is used with three or four cross-pieces, also called "transoms," "transversaries," or "crosses," of the same thickness as the staff and usually about 2.5 inches in width and 12 to 26 inches in length. A square mortise cut through the center of a transom enabled it to be fitted snugly on the staff and to slide backward and forward as required. The transoms are known as the 10, 30, 60, and 90 crosses and are used one at a time on the staff, selected in accordance with the height of the sun or star in the sky at the time that the observation was to be made. In use, the terminal end of the cross-staff is pointed at the sun while the nearest end rested on the bone beside the observer's eye, with the bottom edge of the bar aligned on the horizon and the top edge on the lower limb of the sun, achieved by sliding the cross-piece backward or forward along the bar to the point where the alignment occurs. The altitude of the sun or star is then read on the scale marked along the side of the staff at the juncture of the staff and cross-piece on the side to which that particular cross belongs; from this reading in degrees the latitude is established. Also called FORE-STAFF.

CROSS, SURVEYING. Sighting instrument of simple form, consisting of a cylindrical unit with slit sights at 90 degrees, and sometimes at 45 degrees as well, to measure those angles. It is frequently combined with a compass and used in the field with a jacob staff or tripod.

DAVIS'S IMPROVED QUADRANT, see BACKSTAFF.

DAY-AND-NIGHT TELESCOPE, see TELESCOPE, DAY-AND-NIGHT.

DEAD RECKONING, DEDUCED RECKONING. Art of calculating the position of a vessel from a record of its continuously changing speed and course. The results are rather crude, and the error increases considerably with the duration of the voyage from a previously noted landmark.

DECLINATION. In astronomy, the position of a celestial object, such as the sun or a star, north or south of the celestial equator, which is important to the determination of the observer's latitude. In navigation and surveying, declination is the difference between magnetic north and true north at a particular location expressed in degrees. The change in the declination, over time, is the variation, although the two terms are often used interchangeably.

DECLINATION OF THE COMPASS, see MAGNETIC VARIATION.

DECLINATION SOCKET. Adjustable socket for accommodating the plain surveying compass upon a jacob staff or tripod. The only examples known are part of such instruments made by Benjamin Rittenhouse and appear to have been standard equipment for the plain surveying compasses which he produced. This device consists of a cast brass sleeve in cylindrical form, the top of which fits into the base of the surveying compass which has a socket to accommodate it. The opposite end fits over the jacob staff or terminal of a tripod and is held in place by brass screws. The sleeve encloses a ratchet wheel held tightly in place by a strong brass spring, and the two elements are activated by a knurled knob which projects from the side of the sleeve. The knob enables the surveyor to turn the plate of the compass easily and slowly to the fine adjustment which he requires without having to reset the instrument upon the staff or tripod, or having to reposition the latter in the ground. This device may have been a precursor of the vernier compass or developed simultaneously as a less expensive substitute.

DEEP-SEA LINE, see LEAD-AND-LINE.

DIAL. The face of a timepiece or scientific instrument on which the hours or a graduated scale are marked; also a sundial.

DIALING. Art of constructing any instrument, portable or fixed, which determines the divisions of the day by the shadow of some object or part upon which the sun's rays fall.

DIP CIRCLE. Instrument for determining the dip of the magnetic needle from the plane of the horizon. It consists of a graduated circle attached vertically to a pedestal base and having a magnetic needle so attached at the center that it moves freely against the graduated circle. A horizontal line or marking bisecting the circle represents the horizon.

DIVIDERS. Drafting instrument for measuring distances on maps and charts and marking them by pricking. It consists of a pair of identical limbs made of metal, usually brass, which are joined at one end in such a manner that the limbs can be spread or withdrawn as required. The opposite ends terminate in needle-sharp points, usually made of steel inset into the brass limbs. A form commonly used in navigation is known as single dividers or one-handed dividers and has existed since Roman times. In this form each limb is made as a single piece with the spacers and connecting pins also made of brass. Designed for use with one hand, these are particularly useful at sea for work with charts and for taking off and laying off distances and course bearings, and for use with a plain scale, Gunter's scale, or sector.

DIVIDING ENGINE, see MACHINE GRADUATION.

DOUBLE-ALTITUDE. Method for finding the latitude and the longitude from two observations of the altitude of the sun or a star. From the observations and the interval of time between them the latitude may be computed by spherical trigonometrical calculation. Many versions for finding the latitude by this method have been devised from the sixteenth century to the present.

DRAFTING COMPASS. Instrument for marking the circumference of a circle or marking points and distances on charts, maps, and other drawings. It consists of a pair of identical limbs joined at one end so that the legs could be spread or withdrawn as desired. One limb terminates in a needle-sharp point, and the other is equipped with a holder into which a craylon or piece of black lead (later a pencil) was placed.

DRY-CARD COMPASS, see COMPASS, DRY-CARD.

DUTCHMAN'S LOG. Device used to mark the speed of a ship, a predecessor of a log-ship-and-line. It consists of a wooden stick or chip of wood which is thrown overboard at a given point on the ship's bow; the time required for it to pass a marked point at the ship's stern is noted on a time glass having 14 or 28 seconds running time. The estimate provided is converted to distance by means of a table called a Dutchman's Log Timer. Also called CHIP LOG.

DUTCHMAN'S LOG TIMER. Brass tobacco box, oval in form, on the top lid of which is engraved a perpetual calendar and on the bottom a speed table to be used with the Dutchman's log or the log-ship-and-line. It was designed and first produced by Pieter Holm, a teacher of navigation in Amsterdam c. 1729. Also known as SEA-MEASURE, ZEE-MEETER.

"DUTCH SHOE." Brass or wood attachment for the cross-staff, which replaced the short cross; used for taking an observation when the observer's back was to the sun. See CROSS-STAFF.

ECLIPTIC. The sun's apparent path among the stars during the year, as viewed from the earth. In astronomy, the great circle made by the intersection of the plane of the earth's orbit with the celestial sphere, drawn upon a terrestrial globe at an angle of about 23° 27′ with the equator, which is used to illustrate astronomical problems.

ELECTROSTATIC MACHINE, see FRICTION MACHINE.

ELTON'S QUADRANT, see QUADRANT, ELTON'S.

EPHEMERIS. Table of the positions of celestial bodies for regular intervals or specified dates, including the times of sunrise and sunset, the phases of the moon, eclipses, and related data. See ALMANAC.

EQUAL ALTITUDES. Method of determining the precise time of the meridional passage of a celestial body such as the sun or a star, by means of a series of observations made before and after the event. A transit and equal altitude instrument is particularly useful to measure a series of altitudes before passage of a celestial body across the meridian and another series of timed observations when the object later reaches the same altitudes. The time observations, reduced mathematically, could precisely determine, for example, the time of noon required to check or adjust the rate of timepieces in the field. See also TRANSIT AND EQUAL ALTITUDE INSTRUMENT.

EQUATION OF TIME, see TIME, EQUATION OF.

EQUATOR, CELESTIAL. The great circle of the celestial sphere halfway between the celestial poles and 90 degrees from each. It is the projection of the plane of the terrestrial equator onto the celestial sphere.

ESTABLISHMENT OF THE PORT. The times of high-water at a port on the days of the full and the new moon in terms of the compass bearing of the moon and the moment of high water. Since the highest high waters, or spring tides, occur at about the time of the full moon and new moon, or "full and change," the times of their occurrence become the establishment of the port.

FATHOM. A unit of measure of the depth of water, equal to 6 feet.

FORE-STAFF, see CROSS-STAFF.

FRICTION MACHINE. Device for demonstrating electricity and for generating both positive and negative static electrical charges for research and for popular entertainment. First developed about 1660, it became popular from the middle of the eighteenth century. Also called ELECTROSTATIC MACHINE.

FULL CIRCLE, see CIRCLE, REFLECTING.

GLASS, PERSPECTIVE. Sighting instrument consisting of a cylindrical tube held to the eye to observe celestial phenomena or objects at a distance, which may not have included optical lenses. It was a precursor of the telescope developed and used prior to the beginning of the seventeenth century, but there is confusion concerning its origin and method of its construction. Also called PERSPECTIVE TRUNK, PROSPECT GLASS.

GLASS, TIME. Device using the passage of sand to measure a unit of time. It is commonly constructed from a pair of blown cylindrical glass vessels sealed at one end at atmospheric pressure, joined at the narrow open neck, and mounted vertically within a wooden frame with one vessel above the other. The period of time is determined by the "time" that it takes for a quantity of fine, dry sand to pass from one vessel to the other when the vessel filled with sand is above the empty one. Only one "time" can be determined with a time glass; the sizes, in terms of time measured, range from 15 seconds to 2 hours. Also called SAND GLASS. See RUNNING GLASS; SEA-CLOCK.

GLOBE, CELESTIAL. Sphere representing the constellations on a background of the sky, and including the principal circles of the celestial sphere. The stars are represented as if seen from the outside of the heavenly vault.

GLOBE, TERRESTRIAL. Sphere representing a map of the known world, inclined and oriented to demonstrate a true model of the earth at the point of observation.

GRADUATION, COMMON. Technique of graduating, or dividing, circular or linear scales on the surface of a mathematical instrument, performed by hand by means of a combination of simple tools. The principal tools are a dividing plate, an index or straight edge attached to the plate's center, with which the divisions are made, a dividing knife, and a scraper used for inscribing. Circular lines are achieved with a beam compass, a dividing gauge, and a dividing square. See also GRADUATION, MACHINE; GRADUATION, ORIGINAL.

GRADUATION, MACHINE; GRADUATION, ENGINE. Division of a circle or some part thereof into degrees and their subdivisions on the limb of any mathematical instrument designed for measuring angles, by means of a machine known as a DIVIDING ENGINE. The first such machine is credited to a Yorkshire clockmaker named Henry Hindley in 1740 for cutting the teeth of clockwheels. In 1768 Jesse Ramsden developed a machine which was automatic in its movements, for graduating circular scales with considerable precision. In 1773 he produced an improved second machine for which he received an award from the Board of Longitude. All subsequent circular dividing engines have embodied the principles of construction of the Ramsden machine, derived from a descriptive work with explanatory drawings which he produced at the direction of the Board of Longitude.

GRADUATION, ORIGINAL. Individual methods of dividing and marking limbs of mathematical instruments designed for measuring angles into degrees and their subdivisions, employed by astronomers and instrument makers prior to the advent of the dividing engine. These methods, applied generally for instruments of large size such as mural quadrants, required excessive skill. John Bird's method, considered to be the highest state of the art, consisted of laying off chords or arcs, which he then divided in turn by continuous bisection. He was the first to realize that the contraction and expansion of metals due to heat and cold affected the inscription of the scales and to develop means to counteract it.

GRAPHOMETER. Semicircular version of the circumferentor used for surveying, taking bearings, and measuring horizontal angles. Its flat brass circle is divided in degrees along the edge from o at the center to 90 to both edges. It is equipped with an inset trough compass and a needle indicating north and south and has an alidade, bearing sighting bars at each end, which slides over the surface. The instrument is used on a jacob staff or tripod. Also called SEMI-CIRCLE. See also CIRCUMFERENTOR.

GUNNER'S CALIPERS, see CALIPERS, GUNNER'S.

GUNNER'S QUADRANT, see QUADRANT, GUNNER'S.

GUNTER'S CHAIN, see CHAIN, SURVEYING.

GUNTER'S SCALE, see SCALE, GUNTER'S.

HADLEY'S REFLECTING QUADRANT, see OCTANT.

HANGING COMPASS, see COMPASS, TELL-TALE.

HODOMETER, see ODOMETER.

HOLLAND CIRCLE, see CIRCUMFERENTOR.

HORARY QUADRANT, see QUADRANT, HORARY.

HORIZON. The true horizon is a great circle on the celestial sphere, situated halfway between the observer's zenith and the nadir, and 90° from each. The visible horizon is the boundary between the visible landscape, or the surface of the sea, and the sky. See ARTIFICIAL HORIZON.

HYDROGRAPHY. The charting, study, and description of bodies of water, such as seas, lakes, and rivers, including the flow and behavior of streams with reference to the control of their waters.

HYGROMETER. Instrument to determine the amount of water vapor in the atmosphere, from the readings of which the likelihood of rain can be estimated by registering the amount of expansion and contraction of substances such as catgut, human hair, or hemp, which readily react to changes of humidity.

JACOB STAFF. Long straight wooden rod, usually of round section, on which a surveying instrument is supported in use in the field. The lower terminal, which is sunk into the ground, is bound in an iron ferule or shoe and pointed with steel; the upper terminal is fitted with a brass head into which the instrument is mounted. The staff was frequently made by the surveyor from a suitable sapling selected in the forest, or by a wheelwright. Also, an instrument known from classical times for measuring the angle of sight of a given object, believed to have been first used by Archimedes and Hipparchus for astronomical observation. Also called Jacob's staff.

KENNING. A unit of measure—old English term for the average linear distance or length of coastline visible to an observer on board a sailing vessel, used to estimate the distance sailed from a particular point of origin. In English waters a kenning was 20 miles; in Scottish waters 14 miles.

KENNING GLASS. Sighting tube without optical lenses, used to estimate distances or for sighting the Pole Star or related celestial objects; used at sea prior to the advent of the telescope.

KNOT. The rate of speed required for a ship to travel one nautical or sea mile, which is standardized at 6080 feet (the statute or land mile is 5280 feet). A knot signifies a speed of 1 nautical mile per hour.

LATITUDE. The distance north or south of the equator; measured in degrees. It can be determined by observation of the sun or stars.

LEAD-AND-LINE. A means of measuring the depth of water in which a ship is running near shore. At first an unmarked hand line with a lump of lead at its end was used, and the leadsman was required to measure the length between the lead and the ship's waterline with each cast, using the span of his outstretched arms which was approximately 6 feet. As a result, this unit, known as a fathom, came into use for measuring depth. When depths greater than the capacity of the hand line required measurement, a DEEP-SEA LINE of 120 fathoms was used in which every tenth fathom above 20 fathoms was marked with knots, the knots representing the number of tens of fathoms.

LENS. A piece of transparent material, usually glass, having two opposite regular surfaces, either both curved or one curved and the other plane, used singly or in combinations in an optical instrument for focusing rays of light to form an image.

LENS, ACHROMATIC. Compound lens consisting of more than one piece of glass, designed to produce an image as free as possible from chromatic and spherical aberration providing an image that is sharp and free from the prismatic colors. It is constructed of at least two lenses, one of crown glass and one of flint glass, of different refractive indexes and therefore of different focal lengths, cemented or spaced together and mounted in an objective cell.

LENS, OBJECT-, see OBJECT-LENS.

LENS, OCULAR. The lens of an optical instrument, such as a telescope or microscope, which is situated closest to the observer's eye and forms part of the eyepiece.

LEVEL. Simple instrument for determining the difference in height between two points distant from each other. The primitive form was a rule fastened to a cord stretched between the two points, with a plumb bob suspended from the rule.

LEVELING ROD, see ROD, LEVELING.

LIQUID COMPASS, see COMPASS, LIQUID.

LODESTONE, LOADSTONE. A piece of magnetite, or magnetic iron ore, shaped or ground symmetrically and mounted in a brass frame having a suspension ring. The magnetic strength of the device was strengthened by having steel or iron pole pieces and a keeper, which consisted of a small block of iron attached to the ends of the poles by magnetic force to preserve the lodestone's power.

LOG, SHIP'S; LOG BOOK. Bound volume in which a diary of a vessel's voyage is kept, including data concerning speed traveled, weather, the winds, currents, shoals, and incidents on board. It was often illustrated by the shipmaster with sketches of coast lines, headlands, other vessels encountered, and similar data. At sea, entries are made for each astronomical day, which extended from noon to noon; on shore, they are made in conformity to the civil day, from midnight to midnight.

LOG-SHIP-AND-LINE. Device to determine the speed of a ship, or the distance a ship has run in a given period of time, which appears to have been an English invention first introduced in the mid-sixteenth century. It consists of a piece of wood weighted at one end and attached to a line over the ship's stern. As the wooden billet, or Log-Ship, floats on the surface of the water astern of the vessel, the length of time required for the line to run out is the distance it travels in a given period. See also PATENT LOG.

LOG SLATE. Device used by American seamen for keeping a record of a ship's course. It generally consists of a double-faced wooden panel or piece of black slate with a flat smooth surface, enclosed in a wooden frame. One side of the slate is permanently marked with seven or eight columns, each headed by a letter or other indication for the information to appear thereon, such as H for Hour, F for Fathoms, C for Course, W for Wind, LW for Lee Way.

LONGITUDE. The distance east or west of a known place or reference point, measured in degrees. The longitude is usually expressed in degrees east or west of the prime meridian at Greenwich, England. For the most common methods used for determining the longitude at sea, see DEAD RECKONING; LUNAR DISTANCES; SATELLITES OF JUPITER; CHRONOMETER.

LOXODROMIC CURVE, see RHUMB LINE.

LUBBER'S LINE. Line drawn across the face of the steering compass of a vessel to indicate the fore-and-aft line of the ship for the convenience of the steersman.

LUNAR DIAL, see MOON DIAL.

LUNAR DISTANCES. Method for determining the longitude which utilizes the moon's movement around the earth as a clock, the moon serving as the hand or index and the sun, planets, and stars as the markers or indicators.

LUNARIUM, see MOON DIAL.

MAGNETIC NEEDLE. Instrument used to indicate the direction of the north magnetic pole. The needle is pivoted or suspended at its center of gravity, either by balancing the center of the needle on a sharpened pin, or by laying it on the surface of a bowl of water. The needle is usually constructed from a thin strip of iron or steel, either flat or cylindrical in cross section, and is magnetized by stroking along its length with a permanent magnet or lodestone. Its length varies from 1 to 6 inches. Since the needle is affected by the presence of any nearby magnetic materials in the earth it often becomes inaccurate in use.

MAGNETIC VARIATION. The angle at which the compass needle points away from the true north. Also known as DECLINATION OF THE COMPASS.

MAGNETIC VARIATION COMPASS, see COMPASS, VERNIER.

MARINER'S ASTROLABE, see ASTROLABE, MARINER'S.

MARINER'S BOW. Version of the backstaff consisting of a wooden staff similar to that for a cross-staff or plough, terminating in an arc of 90°, having a semicircular "bow" and horizon, shade, and sight vanes. The horizon vane is attached to the opposite terminus of the staff. In use the instrument is held upright by the staff and the shade vane set at about 25° as a trial, the sight vane is moved up or down along the staff as the observer looks through the sight vane until the shadow of the upper edge of the shade vane becomes visible in the slit of the horizon vane, at the same time that the horizon is visible. See also BACKSTAFF; CROSS-STAFF; PLOUGH.

MARKING PINS, see CHAIN STAKES.

MARSHALL'S INSTRUMENT. Instrument for finding the variation of the compass needle, invented by Thomas Marshall of Fauquier County, Virginia, c. 1772, and recommended to Virginia surveyors during that period.

MEASURING ROD, see ROD, MEASURING.

MENSURATION. The application of geometry for the measurement of lengths, areas, or volumes from given dimensions or angles; also, the branch of mathematics dealing with the quantitative measurement of length, areas, and volumes.

MERCATOR'S CHART. Chart or planisphere of the world with straight-lined rhumbs, produced in 1569 by Gerhard Mercator for use in navigation. The basis of Mercator's projection is a network of lines of latitude and longitude in which the meridians and parallels are drawn as parallel straight lines at right angles, which exaggerates the length of the degree of longitude progressively increasing toward the poles in proportion to the line representing the latitude and compensates by progressively increasing the degree of latitude toward the poles in the same proportion.

MERCATOR'S SAILING. The geometrical solution of navigational problems plotted on a Mercator's chart. It is concerned essentially with the differences of meridional parts and of longitude—the angular distance sailed east or west.

MERIDIAN. In astronomy the celestial meridian is the great circle through the poles and the zenith, which intersects the horizon at the north and south points; it is the projection on the celestial sphere of the plane of the observer's terrestrial meridian. Geographical meridians are the great circles drawn on the earth's surface which pass through the poles and thus through all places having the same longitude. Terrestrial longitudes are reckoned from the zero, or prime, meridian at Greenwich, England.

MERIDIAN, PRIME. Arbitary datum line at a right angle to the equator, which serves as the base point (0°) for the measurement of the longitude east or west of it.

Various prime meridians have been used in the past, including several within the United States, but by international agreement since 1884 the meridian at Greenwich, England, has been adopted by all countries.

MICROMETER. Device for measuring small angles or dimensions, usually employing the principle of the screw to obtain high accuracy; first used in the seventeenth century.

MICROSCOPE. Optical instrument for magnifying images of minute objects, generally objects not visible to the naked eye. Invented early in the seventeenth century, the microscope was used by early naturalists as well as by the medical profession.

MOON DIAL. Dial for determining the time at night from the moon's direction as it changes position because of its revolution about the earth. These changes result in a retrogression of 50 minutes of solar time, compensation for which is provided on the dial. Also called LUNARIUM and LUNAR DIAL.

MURAL QUADRANT, see QUADRANT, ASTRONOMICAL.

NADIR. The point on the celestial sphere which a plumbline would meet if extended through the earth. It is directly beneath the observer and directly opposite, or 180° from, the zenith, which is the point directly overhead.

NAPIER'S BONES, NAPIER'S RODS. Pocket calculating aid for multiplication and division, based on an ancient method of multiplication known as *gelosia* and invented by John Napier, the inventor of logarithms. It consists of a set of loose, square-sectioned rods which have a series of numbers divided by diagonal lines along each of their four sides. They are housed on a small tray which can be enclosed in a sliding case.

NOCTURNAL. Instrument for determining the time at night by sighting the pole star. It consists of a disk with the days of the year inscribed on the rim, and a handle to hold it by; a smaller time disk and an index arm are attached to the center by a rivet with an opening through it. The smaller disk is set to the appropriate date, and as a sighting is taken of the pole star through the central opening, the index arm is moved to the point where its edge bisects the particular star of the Great Bear or Little Bear when it will indicate the time.

NONIUS. Method devised by Pedro Nuñez in 1542 for dividing the arc of a circle into a given number of parts. Within the outer arc of a quadrant, which is graduated in degrees, 44 concentric arcs are drawn and respectively divided into 89, 88, 87 . . . 46 equal sections. The angle can then be determined by means of a simple proportion.

NUTATION. A deviation of the terrestrial pole from its mean position, caused by inequalities in the action of the sun and moon on the equatorial protuberance of the earth. A motion of the pole in a circle of 9-seconds radius over a period of 18.6 years is the main part of the nutation.

OBJECT-LENS. The light-gathering lens of an optical instrument, such as a telescope or microscope; it is the lens nearest the object to be observed. Also called OBJECTIVE.

OCCULTATION. The hiding of one object in the sky by another. As distinguished from eclipse, occultation usually refers to the passing of the moon in front of a star or a planet; the term is also applied to the passing of a satellite behind a planet.

OCTANT. Instrument for observing the altitude of the sun or a star at sea. It consists of a single arc representing one-eighth of the circumference of a circle, whereas the backstaff or Davis's improved quadrant (see BACKSTAFF) combines two arcs to represent one-fourth of the circumference of a circle, or a quadrant. The invention of the octant was claimed simultaneously in about 1731 by Thomas Godfrey of Philadelphia and John Hadley of London. The instrument underwent radical design changes from its large and cumbersome early forms to the versions produced after the War of Independence, which were substantially reduced in size and refined in detail. In its most advanced and common form, the octant is made of ebony and consists of two limbs permanently joined at an angle of 45° and reinforced with two cross members assembled with mortise-and-tenon joints. The arc between the two members is inscribed, usually on an inset panel of ivory, with a scale graduated to 90°. A brass index arm attached at the apex of the radius swivels over the surface of the arc; at the end of the arm is an opening which laps over the limb and through which the degrees can be read. Attached to the index arm is a silvered index glass in a brass frame which moves with the arm. A fixed horizon glass, half silvered and half clear, is attached to the left limb, and either a telescope or a pinnule sight is provided on the right limb, a short distance from the index glass. To take an observation of the altitude of the sun, the observer holds the instrument vertically and sights through the pinnule sight and through the horizon glass. The observer sights at the horizon directly through the clear half of the horizon glass and at the sun or a star reflected by the index mirror on to the silvered half of the horizon glass. To accomplish this the angle between the two mirrors must be half the altitude of the object being observed. The index mirror, moved by means of the index arm, doubles the angle through which it is moved to give the altitude, which is read on the arc through the opening in the index arm. Also called REFLECTING QUADRANT and HADLEY'S REFLECTING QUADRANT.

ODOMETER. Instrument which measures distances by counting and numbering the revolutions of a wheel of specified circumference. Eighteenth-century examples made for English landowners consisted of hand-directed devices which were customarily fitted with brass parts and mahogany frames. A brass wheel generally about 1.5 feet in diameter was geared to a registering mechanism with dial and pointers which indicated the distance traveled in the number of links, poles, chains, furlongs, and miles. In some forms of the instrument the motion of the rotating axle of the wheel was transmitted to a perpendicular shaft running along one bearing fork by a pair of bevel wheels, and from the shaft to the recording mechanism by a worm and worm wheel. Occasionally the dial was marked in yards and poles, with a pointer making a complete revolution every furlong of distance traversed, while a second dial was graduated in furlongs and miles and read by a second hand or index. Also called HODOMETER, PERAMBULATOR, or WAYWEISER.

ORRERY. A form of planetarium which demonstrates the solar system in three-dimensional form, showing the annual as well as the diurnal motion of the earth around the sun and the motion of the moon around the earth. The instrument was invented between 1705 and 1709 and named in honor of the fourth Earl of Orrery. It sometimes includes the other planets and their motions. It is generally hand-cranked or clockdriven and was popular for science-teaching demonstrations.

OUTKEEPER. Counting device which forms part of certain surveying compasses and enables the surveyor to keep a current record of the number of times a surveying chain has been laid out to measure distances. It consists of a click wheel marked from one through sixteen which is visible from a window opening on the dial of the compass and is operated manually from the underside.

OVERHEAD COMPASS, see COMPASS, TELL-TALE.

PANTOGRAPH. Mechanical instrument which makes a pen or pencil copy of letters, signatures, drawings, designs, symbols, etc., at the same time that the original is produced. The basic mechanism consists of four thin wooden or metal arms bolted loosely together to form a flexible parallelogram, and two extended arms to which pens or styluses can be attached. The motion of the pen in the user's hand is transferred by the parallelogram to the pen attached to the second arm, faithfully duplicating the original.

PARALLAX. The angle between the directions of two celestial bodies seen from two different points of view.

PARALLEL RULERS. Plotting aid primarily for use with charts, which consists of two straightedges kept in parallel alignment by connecting links. One arm of the ruler is laid along the course line drawn on the chart, and the ruler is moved, in as many successive steps as necessary, until one edge cuts through the center of the chart's compass rose. Then the course can be read, either in points or degrees, on the circumference of the compass rose.

PATENT LOG. Device to measure the speed of a ship within a given time period, which replaced the log-ship-and-line in the late eighteenth century. The successful later versions consisted of a rotator and register which was cast overboard and then hauled aboard again to be read.

PEDOMETER. Mechanical counter for recording paces taken or distance walked. Invented in the sixteenth century, it is carried in the pocket or attached to the walker's waist and connected to one foot by means of a cord; a small rocking lever to which the upper end of the cord is attached actuates the pedometer's gearing through a spring pawl and a ratchet wheel and thus records on a dial with a hand or index the number of double strides.

PERAMBULATOR, see ODOMETER.

PERCH. The basic English unit of measure in surveying. One perch is equal to 16.5 feet (5.5 yards) and represents the length of one rod. Surveying chains are customarily made in two- or four-rod lengths. Also called POLE.

PERSPECTIVE GLASS, see GLASS, PERSPECTIVE.

PERSPECTIVE TRUNK, see GLASS, PERSPECTIVE.

PILOT, see RUTTER; WAGGONER.

PLAIN SAILING, PLANE SAILING. Method of determining a ship's position, based on the theory that it is moving on a plane. A plane chart, on which the meridians and the parallels of latitude are represented by equidistant straight lines, is used. Also that part of navigation which treats a ship's course as an angle, and the distance, difference of latitude, and easting or westing as the sides of a right-angled triangle.

PLAIN SURVEYING COMPASS, see COMPASS, PLAIN SURVEYING.

PLANE TABLE. Plotting instrument for making maps or charts. It consists basically of a smoothly finished wooden panel with an attachment on the underside for mounting it on a jacob staff or a tripod, and a provision for leveling. It is furnished with a removable metal bar (alidade), pivoted at the center so that it can be swiveled and having sighting bars attached to each end. The bars can be removed and the alidade used as a ruler for drawing lines or as a straight edge. Corner clamps hold a sheet of paper tightly in place on the panel. One edge of the panel or "table" is marked into a scale of equal parts, and another of its edges is inscribed with the divisions of the semicircle. A portable compass can be fixed to the edge of the table so that the North-South points are parallel to one of its sides.

PLANETARIUM. Mechanical model of the universe in which the earth and the other planets, represented by three-dimensional orbs, are moved around the sun in appropriate ratios of distance, size, and speed. The model represents a diametrical section of the universe in which the upper and lower hemispheres are suppressed. The upper plate takes the place of the ecliptic and is inscribed with the days of the month and the signs of the ecliptic in opposite circles by means of which the planets may be set to their mean places in the ecliptic for any day of the year. The sun and the planets are represented by brass or ivory orbs attached to metal stems or arms and are rotated by means of a clockwork or hand-cranked gearwork. See also ORRERY.

PLANISPHERE. Engraved chart of the northern and/or southern skies, based on celestial globes, such as Mercator's globe of 1551.

PLAT. Map of a portion of land on which topographical and other features may be indicated. A plat may be a part of or a complete survey executed by a surveyor in the field.

PLOUGH. Navigational instrument used for observing the altitude of the sun at sea, a version of the backstaff. Prevalent in the sixteenth and early seventeenth centuries, it survived in use into the eighteenth century. See BACKSTAFF; MARINER'S BOW.

PLUMMET. Ball of lead suspended on a thread or line used to establish the vertical direction for a level.

POCKET SEXTANT, see SEXTANT, BOX.

POLE, see PERCH.

POLE STAR, POLARIS. The star nearest the pole in the northern hemisphere. It is the brightest star in the constellation Ursa Minor (Little Bear) and is used in observations made with the nocturnal for determining time at night.

PORTULANO, PORTOLANO. Italian pilot book, either manuscript or printed, which included sailing directions, place names, distances and bearings, and other information necessary to the pilot or shipmaster. Charts included in the book were called Portulan charts. See RUTTER.

PRECESSION OF THE EQUINOXES. The very slow westward motion of the equinox points among the constellations, an effect connected mainly with a gradual change in the direction of the earth's axis of rotation, which describes a cone like a spinning top. The north pole of the celestial sphere describes a circle of $23.5°$ radius among the constellations, making a revolution in approximately 26,000 years. The cause, described by Isaac Newton, is the attraction exercised by the sun and the moon on the equatorial protuberance of the earth, the moon being responsible for about two-thirds and the sun for one-third of the motion, in the same proportion as the lunar and solar tides.

PROSPECT GLASS, see GLASS, PERSPECTIVE.

PROTRACTOR. Instrument, usually forming part of a set of drafting instruments, which is used to measure angles on a drawing, map, or chart and consisting of a graduated semicircle with an inch scale marked along the straight side. Protractors are generally made of brass, but examples in boxwood and ivory or horn were commonly produced.

QUADRANT. Instrument for determining angular elevations of heavenly bodies in astronomical observations or in surveying. It consists of a flat plate of wood or metal having two straight edges at a right angle and a curved edge which is a quarter of a circle. The curved edge is inscribed along its perimeter with a scale of $90°$, which is read from a plumb line with a small plummet suspended from the apex of the right angle. One of the straight edges is fitted with two peep sights. See also SEA-QUADRANT.

QUADRANT, ASTRONOMICAL. Instrument for determining the positions of stars and their coordinates, and for measuring altitudes. Large examples, 6 feet or more in diameter, which were constructed for observatory installations, were called MURAL QUADRANTS because their size required that they be supported against a wall. Smaller portable versions were produced in the eighteenth century for the use of astronomers and surveyors in the field. The instrument is usually formed of a heavy brass quadrant with supporting cross-members, having a telescope attached to its upper horizontal length and a second and longer telescope serving as an index along its vertical surface. The second telescope is equipped with a clamp and fine adjustment screw.

QUADRANT, ELTON'S. Modification of the backstaff, devised by Captain John Elton in about 1730 consisting of the addition of a vernier scale and two bubble levels to a frame made in two parts, one having a graduated arc of $30°$ subdivided into six equal parts and the other a chord of $60°$ divided into two equal parts, which combined to form a quadrant of $90°$. An index arm attached at the center of the frame moved the width of the full arc; it combined a nonius plate with a vernier scale which moved with the index, an eye vane and a tubet or bubble level. See BACKSTAFF.

QUADRANT, GUNNER'S. The most commonly used of artillery instruments, the form of which varied extremely little over centuries. It consists of an L-shaped brass bar with an arc joining the two arms. The long arm is laid along the bottom of the bore of a cannon with the shorter arm pointed downward. A weight or plumb bob suspended from a string is pivoted from a center point at the juncture of the arms and the reading on the arc where the string crosses it provides the angle at which the cannon is to be elevated. The arc is inscribed in degrees from 0 to 90, divided in minutes.

QUADRANT, HORARY; QUADRANS VETUS. A form of the quadrant made as a wooden or brass plate forming a right-angle sector of a circle with its arc graduated in degrees, and having a pair of brass pinnule sights attached along one of the radial arms. It is inscribed with a diagram of the planetary hours above the graduated arcuate scale. A sliding bead on a plumb line, and later an adjustable zodiacal scale, make it possible to ascertain solar declination.

QUADRANT, SINICAL. A form of altitude quadrant developed in the second half of the seventeenth century for use at sea. It was designed to provide a graphical solution for trigonometrical problems involved in the calculation of a ship's estimated position from the course steered and the distance traveled. Two lines at right angles to each other and parallel to the quadrant's straight edge run from each degree marked on the arcuate scale, forming a rectangular grid over the instrument's face representing the meridians and parallels. The navigator sets off his course along the correct bearing with a scale and measures the north-south and east-west distances with the same scale.

QUINTANT. A form of the sextant in which the arc is extended to 150° or more instead of the usual 120°. It was introduced in the first quarter of the nineteenth century in England. See SEXTANT.

RAILROAD COMPASS, see COMPASS, RAILROAD.

REFLECTING CIRCLE, see CIRCLE, REFLECTING.

REFLECTING QUADRANT, see OCTANT.

REPEATING CIRCLE, see CIRCLE, REFLECTING.

RESECTION. Method utilized in hydrographical surveying, in which the position of the observing station, which is frequently unstable, is established by angular observations made with a sextant upon three fixed points and plotted by means of a station pointer.

RHUMB. A point of the compass rose.

RHUMB LINE. Line on the surface of a sphere which makes equal oblique angles with all meridians. It is used to record the path of a vessel sailing always obliquely to the meridian in the direction of one and the same point of the compass. Also called LOXODROMIC CURVE.

RIGHT ASCENSION. The angular distance of a celestial object determined by dividing the celestial sphere into twenty-four hours counted from the vernal equinox.

RING DIAL. A form of sundial having a ring with a sliding collar made with a small opening. The collar is adjusted to the solar declination and the ring suspended toward the sun to enable sunlight to pass through the opening to indicate the time on an hour scale engraved inside the ring. A more complicated form is the equinoctial ring dial which combines a meridian ring and an equinoctial ring to indicate the time.

RING-DIAL, UNIVERSAL. Instrument used at sea for ascertaining the time from the sun. It consists of two metal rings, usually brass. The equatorial ring pivots inside the meridian ring and can be folded flat when not in use. A flat metal strip called a bridge is fixed as a diameter to the meridian ring and can be pivoted to fold flat. It has a central slot with a small slide having a pinnule sight. The ring-dial is used by suspending it from the thumb by means of a ring which can slide around the perimeter of the meridian ring. The slide is set to the correct position according to the date scale on the bridge, and the sun shines through the pinnule onto a line on the inside of the meridian ring.

ROD, LEVELING. Wooden rod, 6 feet long and usually 1.25 inches wide, the face of which is graduated and marked along its whole length in inches divided to tenths and also in hundreths of a foot. A second rod is sometimes added, which is of smaller section and made to slide along the back of the first rod and is retained in position by a metal band, so that it can serve as an extension of the first, without graduations. Used with a surveying instrument.

ROD, MEASURING. Wooden rod commonly used for measuring land. It was held in the hand of the land-measurer by its middle and placed successively along the line to be measured by turning it over on the forward end. The rod was made of well-seasoned wood, either square or oval in section, 3, 4, or 5 meters in length, marked off in meters or feet along its length. It was generally varnished to limit variation caused by moisture.

ROSE OF THE WINDS, see COMPASS ROSE.

RULE, RULER. Strip of wood or metal having a straight edge engraved with a scale; used as a guide for pencil or pen on paper or for measuring distances on a map or chart.

RULE, SLIDE, see SLIDE RULE.

RULERS, PARALLEL, see PARALLEL RULERS.

RUNNING-GLASS. Time glass, generally of a half-hour duration, for keeping a record of the distance run by the ship, and for gauging the passage of the watches. See GLASS, TIME; SEA-CLOCK.

RUTTER. A compilation of sailing directions and notations of landmarks with their distances and bearings, including studies of the tides and soundings. The name is derived from the French term for such compilations, *routier*.

SAND GLASS, see GLASS, TIME.

SATELLITES OF JUPITER. Observations at the instant in which one of Jupiter's satellites is eclipsed by the planet provide a method of determining the longitude. Inasmuch as the position of any of the earth's meridians is known in relation to the sun and stars, and the observer's meridian is located by means of his local time, the difference in the two times constitutes the difference in the longitude. If the observer's latitude is known, he can determine the local time from a simple observation of the meridian altitude of a celestial body, such as the sun or a star. This method was first attempted by Galileo Galilei in 1616 and 1617.

SCALE. A series of spaces indicating degrees or quantities marked by lines in a process of equal division known as graduation. Scales are a basic component of all instruments of measurement required in map making, surveying, and navigating.

SCALE, GUNTER'S. Set of logarithmic scales of natural numbers and trigonometrical functions set off on a 2-foot staff made of boxwood or brass. By using a pair of dividers, problems relating to distance and bearing could be transferred from scale to scale on the staff. The scales inscribed included the line of numbers (common logarithms), the line of artificial sines (log sines), the line of artificial sines of the rhumbs, the artificial tangents of the rhumbs, the meridian line in Mercator's chart, and the scale of equal parts. See also SECTOR.

SCALE OF EQUAL PARTS. Scale inscribed on an instrument used for drawing lines and angles, such as a sector or an alidade for a plane table, and usually marked to 200 equal parts. The scale is formed by dividing a line of any given length into equal portions by the process of repeated subdivision.

SCALE, VERNIER. Small sliding scale moved by a fine-threaded screw attached to the main scale, which marks off fractions of the latter. Invented by a French military engineer, Pierre Vernier, in 1631, the vernier scale was commonly applied to the octant, sextant, and other navigational and astronomical instruments.

SEA-CLOCKE. Large time glass fitted with grommets or eyelets above and below so that it could be hung from a hook on shipboard and readily turned. This form of time glass was favored on British naval vessels and remained in use into the early nineteenth century.

SEA-QUADRANT. Name given to several instruments of the early seventeenth century, with consequent confusion. In about 1610 Edward Wright devised a sea-quadrant which featured a large scale on a single arc of large radius and had sliding vanes and an aid for taking a sight on the pole star. The instrument proved to be impractical because of its size. Several years later George Waymouth proposed another form of sea-quadrant, which was attached to a staff and had an alidade at its center, but this was probably not produced for general use. The name was also used for the simple hand-held quadrant in popular use at sea from the mid-fifteenth through the early seventeenth century.

SECTOR. Drafting instrument, 12 inches in length, made of ivory, hardwood, or brass, in two equal parts hinged at the center to fold together. The forms most commonly used in English and colonial American navigation were Gunter's sector or Gunter's scale, and a subsequent refined version known as the sliding Gunter. Gunter's sector or scale was customarily made of boxwood, but sometimes of brass and was hinged with a brass joint. When open, it measured exactly 2 feet in length and approximately 1.25 inches in width. The later version was inscribed on one side with Gunter's line of numbers, or common logarithms, the line of artificial sines or log sines, the line of artificial tangents, of the rhumbs, the meridional line in Mercator's Chart, and the scale of equal parts. See also SCALE, GUNTER'S; SLIDE RULE; SLIDING GUNTER.

SEMI-CIRCLE, see GRAPHOMETER, SEMI-CIRCUMFERENTOR.

SEMI-CIRCUMFERENTOR. Surveying instrument made with a cast brass plate, sometimes mounted on wood, in the form of a half circle instead of a full circle as in the circumferentor or plain surveying compass. The half circle's periphery is graduated in degrees from 0 to 90 to 0. An alidade having sighting bars at its terminals swivels around the half circle from a central point, and a trough compass with magnetic needle is set into the base of the half circle. The underside is fitted with a socket for attachment to a jacob staff or tripod. Also called SEMI-CIRCLE.

SEXTANT. Instrument designed to measure large angles by reflection, particularly useful for measuring lunar distances to determine longitude at sea. Basically a refinement of the octant, the sextant is equipped with a scale of a little more than 60° instead of the 45° scale of the octant, thus enabling readings to be made of angular distances to 120°. To overcome some of the problems experienced with the octant, which was customarily made of wood with brass fittings and index arm, the sextant has a heavy cast-brass frame and index arm to provide greater rigidity. The index arm terminates in an opening to enable the scale to be read on the arc of the sextant; and the inner edge of the opening is inscribed with a vernier scale. A screw on the underside of the terminal of the index enables the index to be fixed at any given point. Later improvements were the addition of a finely threaded side screw and a fixed magnifying glass for reading the scale with greater accuracy and the replacement of the peepsight for observing the fixed mirror with a small telescopic sighting tube.

SEXTANT, BOX. Compact form of the sextant, used chiefly for surveying on land but also applicable at sea. The instrument consisted of a circular brass case approximately 3 inches in diameter, with an index having a radius of 1.5 inches on its upper surface. The index is moved by a rack and pinion within the case turned by a projecting hand screw instead of the tangent screw of the customary sextant. A telescope is attached to the side of the case by a screw thread, but a sight vane is also provided for making observations without the telescope. The limb is usually graduated from 0° to 150° with a vernier reading to 1 minute. The glasses are contained within the case, which has an upper lid of brass that screws into place and can be screwed into the bottom of the case when the instrument is in use. Also known as POCKET SEXTANT.

SIGHT, OPTICAL. Device having a small aperture through which objects are viewed; usually a component of an instrument for astronomical observation, navigating, or surveying. The commonest form consists of a brass bar or pair of aligned bars with an aperture which guides the observer's eye to the object or target.

SINICAL QUADRANT, see QUADRANT, SINICAL.

SLIDE RULE. Instrument used for rapid calculation, consisting of a ruler and a medial slide both graduated with similar logarithmic scales and labeled with corresponding antilogarithms. It was based on the logarithms invented by John Napier in 1614. Slide rules were usually constructed of boxwood, brass, or ivory. See also SLIDING GUNTER.

SLIDING GUNTER. A form of the slide rule made for use at sea, introduced in the seventeenth century. It consists of three graduated scales, the outer two bound together by brass attachments and the middle scale sliding back and forth between them. See also SECTOR.

SOLAR COMPASS, see COMPASS, BURT'S SOLAR.

SOUNDING LEAD. Lead weight with an eyelet for attaching to a rope, used to measure the depth of water. A hand-lead for small vessels weighs approximately 6 pounds and is attached to a line 20 fathoms long. A deep-sea lead, used by large vessels and military vessels, weighs as much as 80 pounds and is attached to a considerably longer line. The lead lines are marked in fathoms at intervals of 6 feet with pieces of leather or colored cloth so that depths can be readily identified. The base of the lead has a hollow space filled with tallow, which can pick up bits of gravel, sand, and other materials and so inform the seafarer of the nature of the bottom, an important factor when following sailing directions and charts. The lead is heaved over the side and forward in accordance with the movement of the vessel so that the line is plumb with the observer as the lead strikes the bottom. Sounding leads have been used from antiquity with relatively little change.

SPYGLASS, see TELESCOPE.

STATION POINTER. Instrument designed to mark a ship's position on a chart from three shore landmarks. It consists of a semicircular scale approximately 6 inches in diameter to which are attached three chamfered radial rules. One rule is fixed at the 0° position of the scale, while the other two are moved about on the surface of the chart and locked into the positions selected. Angular distances between three identified shore points are taken with a sextant and laid off on the pointer's scale by moving the pointer until the three rules pass through the three points noted. A pin thrust through an opening in the center of the scale then marks the ship's position.

SUNDIAL. Instrument used from Hellenistic times to the present to indicate time by means of the sun's shadow. In its simplest form, the horizontal dial, it consists of a flat plate, which may be round, square, or some other form, with a horizontal scale inscribed around the outer edge, and a projecting gnomon or index.

SURVEYING CHAIN, see CHAIN, SURVEYING.

SURVEYING COMPASS, see COMPASS, PLAIN SURVEYING.

SURVEYING CROSS, see CROSS, SURVEYING.

SURVEYING TRANSIT, see TRANSIT, SURVEYING.

TALLY PINS, see CHAIN STAKES.

TELESCOPE. Instrument for terrestrial and/or astronomical observation, consisting of an ocular lens and an object lens fitted into a long tube, with the ocular lens placed nearest the eye of the observer. Hand-held versions of the instrument are also called spyglasses, and instruments mounted on a base are known as pedestal telescopes.

TELESCOPE, "COMING-UP." Hand telescope of the achromatic type to which has been added a Rochon micrometer (a double refracting prism of rock crystal) fitted into a sliding case placed between the eyepiece and object-lens so that two images of the object being observed are formed. The images are brought into contact by adjusting the distance of the prism from the eyepiece and varying the optical angle subtended at the eye by the object as indicated on a divided vernier scale engraved on the eyepiece end of the tube. The instrument enables an observer to distinguish the approach or retreat of a ship at a distance.

TELESCOPE, DAY-AND-NIGHT. Hand telescope or spyglass which can be used at night as well as in daytime by change of aperture of the object lens. The brass cap covering the object lens is made in two parts; the center disk is removed for daytime observation and both center disk and annular ring removed to provide a larger aperture for use at night.

TELESCOPE, EQUATORIAL. Telescope for the general study of the sky. It can be set in two coordinates, declination and right ascension, by means of an equatorial mounting, which enables the instrument to swing around an axis directed toward the pole of the sky and graduated in hour angles. In declination, the mounting can pivot up and down perpendicular to the equator; in right ascension, it is driven by a sidereal clockwork that keeps it pointed toward the desired object.

TELESCOPE, REFLECTING. Optical instrument for observing objects at a distance, consisting of a cylindrical body equipped with lenses and a mirror. Observation is achieved by the reflection of light rays, accomplished by means of a concave mirror incorporated within the tube.

TELESCOPE, REFRACTING. Optical instrument for viewing distant objects by means of the refraction of light rays through a lens. It consists of a cylindrical tube with an object-lens at the terminal closest to the object and an ocular lens in an eyepiece closest to the observer. An improvement was made by adding a compound or achromatic lens for the object-lens.

TELLURIUM. Wheeled device with cords operated by hand motion, which demonstrates the annual and diurnal motion of the earth, the change of the seasons, the revolution of the moon around the earth in an orbit inclined to that of the ecliptic, and eclipses. The sun and planets are represented by orbs rendered in relative proportion.

TERRELLIA. Lodestone shaped into a small sphere. The name, which means "small earth," was derived from its shape.

TERRESTRIAL GLOBE, see GLOBE, TERRESTRIAL.

THEODOLITE. Instrument for measuring vertical and horizontal angles, the altitude, and the azimuth. Its invention, in a form known as a polimetrum, is credited to Leonard Digges in 1555, but the instrument did not become practical until a telescope was added by Jonathan Sisson about 1720 to replace open sights. The early theodolite consisted of a brass circle 10 or 12 inches in diameter having a limb divided into 360° and again subdivided. A circumferentor is fixed to the center with a compass and needle, and over the circumferentor is a pair of sights fixed to a movable index which turns on the center of the instrument and upon which the circumferentor box is placed. The instrument is used to take the angles of the field or the bearing of each stationery distance line from the meridian. Vertical angles are measured by means of verniers and a graduated circle on the axis of the telescope perpendicular to the axis of the horizontal plate. Bubble levels are often attached to both the telescope and the horizontal plates to aid in alignment prior to use. The bubble levels attached to the telescope also permit the instrument to serve as a level. A magnetic compass is usually positioned in the center of the horizontal circle for taking bearings with magnetic north. The instrument is mounted on a tripod.

THERMOMETER. Instrument for recording temperature. It consists of a fine glass tube terminating in a bulb. Colored alcohol or mercury is sealed inside the tube and rises and falls in a column in accordance with the change of temperature. The temperature is read on a scale marked either on the outside of the glass tube or on its support, which generally consists of a wooden panel.

TIDE CALCULATOR. Device to indicate by mechanical means the high water for a given port on a given day. The instrument is generally made with three dials: a clock dial of the twenty-four hours shown I through XII twice; a dial of the sixteen compass points; and a dial graduated in the twenty-nine and one-half divisions of the ages of the moon, with a moon pointer attached. The calculator is set to a port location indicated by the moon pointer on the appropriate compass point, and the moon dial is adjusted so that the proper age of the moon lies beneath the sun pointer, which thereupon indicates the time of high water on the appropriate number of the clock dial.

TIME BALL. Visual signal of time measurement to enable shipmasters aboard vessels in harbor and in the roads to correct their chronometers. It consists of a large ball, often 5 feet in diameter, in a wooden or basket framework covered with leather and painted either black or gold. The time ball is installed at a high elevation overlooking a harbor so that the descent of the ball will be clearly visible some distance away. At 5 minutes before 12 o'clock noon the ball is raised by means of a windlass to a halfway position along the pole as a warning to shipmasters to have their chronometers in readiness. At 2 minutes before the hour the ball is raised to the top and held by a catch connected to a simple trigger mechanism. At exactly the hour observed by the operator on the observatory clock, the ball is released and begins its descent. The instant that the ball starts down marks the hour.

TIME, EQUATION OF. The difference in minutes at any moment between the apparent solar time and the mean solar time. It represents a correction factor in minutes that during the year must be either added to or subtracted from solar time, or the time shown by a sundial, to convert the apparent solar time to the mean time customarily indicated by clocks and watches.

TIME GLASS, see GLASS, TIME.

"TOUCHING." Process of remagnetizing the steel needle of a compass, accomplished either by rubbing the needle against a lodestone or by floating it in a bowl of water and holding the lodestone near it. In the latter method the needle is attracted to the lodestone, which is then revolved around the bowl at increasing speed. When the stone is removed, the needle points to the north. The process was also known as "giving virtue."

TRADE CARD. Engraved or printed advertisement identifying a product and its pur-veyor. Widely used by makers of mathematical instruments in England and in the Americans colonies from the early eighteenth century to modern times, the trade card was first produced on good-quality paper and later on card stock. It was glued inside cases and carrying boxes of instruments.

TRANSIT. The passing of a celestial body over or in front of another, or across a line or circle, as the transit of an inferior planet across the disc of the sun, the transit of a Jovian satellite over the disk of Jupiter, or the transit of a star or other astronomical body across the meridian.

TRANSIT AND EQUAL ALTITUDE INSTRUMENT. Instrument for taking equal altitudes of the sun for the purpose of establishing the time and for fixing meridians and running straight lines. It consists of a movable telescope on a horizontal axis on a portable tripod.

TRANSIT, ASTRONOMICAL. Instrument for observing the passage of celestial objects across the observer's meridian, consisting primarily of a telescope, with one or more sets of cross hairs, securely fastened in a rigid mount which restricts the instrument to vertical movement along the observer's meridian. It can be used for determining the exact time, or the difference of right ascension of the stars observed, and pro-vides a means for determining the difference in longitude between any two points where corresponding observations are made. This type of transit instrument was in-vented in 1716 by Roger Cotes, professor of astronomy at Cambridge University, as a simple instrument for determining the exact time.

TRANSIT OF VENUS. The planet Venus moves around its orbit in greater rapidity than does the earth, with the result that the sun, Venus, and earth periodically lie more or less in a straight line, although the planes of the orbits of Venus and the earth are not identical. In orbiting, Venus crosses the plane of the earth's orbit, and when the earth happens to be at the appropriate point, Venus appears as a dark disk moving across the face of the sun. Observation of this "transit" from several terrestrial lati-tudes made it possible to establish the true scale of the solar system.

TRANSIT, SURVEYING. Modification of the plain surveying compass with the sighting bars replaced by a telescope, by means of which the horizontal and vertical angles are measured simultaneously with reference to an assumed plane and azimuth direc-tion. It has an advantage over the theodolite in that the telescope can be "transited," or made to revolve completely on its horizontal axis. The telescope is generally fit-ted with cross hairs, is equipped with a bubble level and scale, and has a vertical circle connected with its axis.

TRAVERSE BOARD. Device providing a visible method for recording the course of a ship during the watch. Of ancient derivation, it may have been Scandinavian in ori-gin. In its most common form it consists of a wooden panel on which are marked the thirty-six points of the compass rose, each point having eight holes drilled equidistantly along the line from the center of the rose to the point's extremity. Wooden pegs are accommodated in these holes. The lower half of the board is ordi-narily marked into a rectangle, having from thirteen to nineteen series of four holes each drilled along its length. The ship's course is noted each half hour of the ship's watch and a peg inserted into the hole nearest the center of the course which the ship was sailing. The holes are successively filled with pegs from the top toward the center so that the course is apparent at a glance. The series of holes on the lower part of the board serve to record the speed of the ship at every hour as noted by means of the running glass. The hour units one through twelve are marked from the left, while the holes at the right are used to mark the quarters or tenths.

TRIGONOMETER. Instrument used in mensuration of distances and heights; in surveying; in plane, parallel, middle-latitude, and Mercator's sailing; and in right-angle and oblique trigonometry. Made entirely of brass, it consists of two protractors of 180° with diameters of 5.5 inches. The protractors are divided in degrees and quarter compass points and are attached to one end of a base 12 inches long divided from its center to the terminal in 100 equal segments.

UNIVERSAL RING-DIAL, see RING-DIAL, UNIVERSAL.

VARIATION COMPASS, see COMPASS, VARIATION.

VERNIER; VERNIER COMPASS, see COMPASS, VERNIER.

VERNIER SCALE, see SCALE, VERNIER.

WAGGONER. Name given to a type of combined nautical manual and chart book imported from Holland and widely used by English shipmasters from the late sixteenth into the eighteenth century. The term is derived from the name of Lucas Wagenaer, author of the first such work, published in 1584 and entitled *Spieghel der Zeevaerdt* (translated into English as *The Mariner's Mirror*).

WAYWEISER, see ODOMETER.

WATCH-CLOCK. Timepiece for determining the longitude at sea by a predicted eclipse of the sun. Described in the instructions compiled in 1582 for Thomas Bavin, watch-clocks were spring-driven, of a flat or table-clock type, with the wheelwork gilded to prevent rusting and were equipped with a dial indicating minutes as well as hours, and operating for twenty-four or forty hours at a winding. The watch-clocks were to be adjusted by means of readings of the time from the sun with a universal ring-dial.

ZENITH, ASTRONOMICAL. The point in the sky directly above the observer, which a plumbline would meet if extended upward.

ZENITH SECTOR. Telescopic instrument for measuring the zenith distances that come within its arc, and for discovering the aberrations of the stars and the nutation of the earth's axis. It consists of a tube of brass suspended by trunnions at the top within a framework. The focal length of the sector made by David Rittenhouse for Andrew Ellicott was 63.7 inches and the aperture 2.1 inches; it had a lens made by Nairne of London. It swung against a graduated arc extending north and south, with a radius of 61 inches, enabling the observer to measure zenith distances in the meridian to 5° north and south of the zenith. The sector is employed to determine the parallels of latitude by repeated observation of a number of fixed stars near the zenith as they cross the meridian at differing hours.

SELECTED
BIBLIOGRAPHY

EUROPEAN AND ENGLISH

Daumas, Maurice. *Les instruments scientifiques aux XVII et XVIII siècles*. Paris: Presses-universitaires de France, 1953.

Guye, Samuel, and Michel, Henri. *Time & Space, Measuring Instruments from the 15th to the 19th Century*. New York: Praeger, 1971.

Hill, H. O., and Paget-Tomlinson, E. W., *Instruments of Navigation*. London: Her Majesty's Stationery Office, 1958.

Maddison, Francis R. "Early Astronomical and Mathematical Instruments, A Brief Survey of Sources and Modern Studies," *History of Science*, vol. 2, 1963, pp. 17–50.

———. "Medieval Scientific Instruments and the Development of Navigational Instruments in the XVth and the XVIth Centuries," *Revista Universidada de Coimbra*, vol. XXIV, 1969, 60 pp.

Michel, Henri. *Scientific Instruments in Art and History*. Translated by R. E. W. Maddison and Francis R. Maddison. New York: Viking, 1967.

Richeson, A. W. *English Land Measuring to 1800*. Cambridge, Mass.: M. I. T. Press, 1966.

Rohde-Hamburg, Alfred. *Die Geschichte der Wissenschaftlichen Instrumente vom Beginn der Renaissance bis zum Ausgang des 18. Jahrhunderts*. Leipsig: Verlag von Klinkhardt & Biermann, 1923.

Smith, Alan G. R. *Science and Society in the 16th and 17th Centuries*. London: Thames and Hudson, 1972.

Taylor, E. G. R. *The Mathematical Practitioners of Tudor and Stuart England*. Cambridge: Cambridge University Press, 1954.

———. *The Haven-Finding Art*. New York: Abelard-Schuman, 1957.

———. *The Mathematical Practitioners of Hanoverian England 1714–1840*. Cambridge: Cambridge University Press, 1966.

Taylor, E. G. R., and Richey, M. W. *The Geometrical Seaman*. London: Hollis & Carter, 1962.

Turner, Gerard L'E. "The History of Optical Instruments: A Brief Survey of Sources and Modern Studies," *History of Science*, vol. 8, 1969, pp. 53–93.

Waters, David W. *The Art of Navigation in England in Elizabethan and Early Stuart Times*. London: Hollis & Carter, 1959.

Zinner, Ernst. *Deutsche und Niederlandische Astronomische Instruments Des 11.–18. Jahrhunderts*. Munich: C. H. Beck'sche Verlangbuchhandlung, 1956.

AMERICAN

Bedini, Silvio A. *Early American Scientific Instruments and Their Makers*. Washington, D.C.: Smithsonian Institution, 1964.

Bell, Whitfield J., Jr. *Early American Science, Needs and Opportunities*. Williamsburg, Va.: Institute of Early American History and Culture, 1955.

Brewington, M. V. *The Peabody Museum Collection of Navigating Instruments, With Notes of Their Makers*. Salem, Mass.: Peabody Museum, 1963.

Cajori, Florian. *The Early Mathematical Sciences in North and South America*. Boston: Richard G. Badger, 1928.

Cohen, I. Bernard. *Some Early Tools of American Science*. Cambridge, Mass.: Harvard University Press, 1950.

Hindle, Brooke. *The Pursuit of Science in Revolutionary America 1735–1789*. Chapel Hill, N.C.: University of North Carolina Press, 1956.

Jaffe, Bernard. *Men of Science in America*. New York: Simon & Schuster, 1944.

Kiely, Edmond R. *Surveying Instruments, Their History and Classroom Use*. New York: Columbia University, Bureau of Publications, Teachers College, 1947.

Price, Derek J. de Solla. *Science Since Babylon*. New Haven, Conn.: Yale University Press, 1961.

Ristow, Walter W., comp. *A La Carte, Selected Papers on Maps and Atlases*. Washington, D.C.: Library of Congress, 1972.

Smart, Charles E. *The Makers of Surveying Instruments in America Since 1700*. Troy, N.Y.: Regal Press, vol. I, 1962; vol. II, 1967.

Stearns, Raymond Phineas. *Science in the British Colonies of America*. Urbana, Ill.: University of Illinois Press, 1970.

Struik, Dirk J. *Yankee Science in the Making*. Boston: Little, Brown, 1948.

Wheatland, David P. *The Apparatus of Science at Harvard College 1765–1800*. Cambridge, Mass.: Harvard University Press, 1968.

ACKNOWLEDGMENTS

I wish first to express my appreciation to the American Philosophical Society for a grant from the Johnson Fund which made possible the completion of this work, and for the assistance of its library staff during the many years that the research was in progress.

There are few libraries, historical societies, or museums in the United States, or indeed in the British Isles, which have not in some measure contributed to the compilation of this volume over a period of many years. To the staffs of all those organizations, and to the numerous town and county clerks and local historians who have participated in my research, I am extremely grateful. In addition to the Library of the American Philosophical Society, I would like to mention especially the cooperation I have received from the John Carter Brown Library, the Connecticut State Library, the Historical Society of Pennsylvania, the Library Company of Philadelphia, the Manuscripts Division of the Library of Congress, the Massachusetts Historical Society, and the New-York Historical Society.

Several individuals deserved special mention for their assistance in the preparation of this work. Derek J. de Solla Price, Avalon Professor of the History of Science at Yale University, first coined the phrase "little men of science" and was largely responsible for leading me to study them. Both Jacob Ernest Cooke, McCracken Professor of History at Lafayette College, and Warren J. Danzenbaker of the Smithsonian Institution read the manuscript in its several forms and made many useful suggestions. My wife, Gale, has been intimately involved with every aspect of this work from preliminary research to the final manuscript and also compiled the index.

It is not possible to name all the individuals who have co-operated in this research, but their contributions are sincerely appreciated. Among those deserving particular acknowledgment are the following:

Thomas R. Adams, Librarian, The John Carter Brown Library, Brown University

Frank P. Albright, Director, Old Salem, Inc., Winston-Salem, North Carolina

Michele L. Aldrich, Joseph Henry Papers, Smithsonian Institution

Edwin A. Alexander, The Henry Francis Du Pont Winterthur Museum, Winterthur, Del.

Roy Basler, Chief of the Manuscripts Division, Library of Congress

Preston R. Bassett, Ridgefield, Conn.

Edwin A. Battison, Associate Curator of Timekeeping and Light Machinery, The National Museum of History and Technology, Smithsonian Institution

James A. Bear, Jr., Curator, Thomas Jefferson Memorial Foundation, Charlottesville, Va.

Whitfield J. Bell, Jr., Librarian, Library of the American Philosophical Society

Charles G. Berger, Smithsonian Institution Libraries

Robert G. Billingsley, Smithsonian Institution Libraries

Rose T. Briggs, Plymouth Antiquarian Society, Buzzards Bay, Mass.

David J. Bryden, Curator, Whipple Museum of the History of Science, Cambridge University

Mrs. H. Ropes Cabot, Bostonian Society, Boston, Mass.

Marion P. Carson, Philadelphia, Pa.

Jane L. Cayford, Director, New Hampshire Historical Society, Concord, N.H.

Howard I. Chapelle, Curator (Emeritus) of Transportation, The National Museum of History and Technology, Smithsonian Institution

I. Bernard Cohen, Professor of the History of Science, Harvard University

P. Wilfred Cole, National Portrait Gallery, Smithsonian Institution

Herbert R. Collins, Associate Curator of Political History, The National Museum of History and Technology, Smithsonian Institution

Karen J. Danzenbaker, Annandale, Va.

Ernest S. Dodge, Director, Peabody Museum of Salem, Salem, Mass.

Elizabeth Donagley Garrett, Director-Curator, Daughters

of the American Revolution Museum, Washington, D.C.

Edith Douglass, Tucson, Ariz.

Charles Ellis Ellicott, Jr., Baltimore, Md.

P. William Filby, Director, Mayland Historical Society, Baltimore, Md.

Elizabeth R. Fitzhugh, Garrison, Md.

Herman R. Friis, Chief, Polar Archives, U. S. National Archives

Craddock R. Goins, Jr., Associate Curator of Military History, The National Museum of History and Technology, Smithsonian Institution

Hamilton P. Greenough, Santa Barbara, Calif.

James Gregory, Librarian, The New-York Historical Society, New York, N.Y.

Per E. Guldbeck, Research Associate, New York State Historical Association, Cooperstown, N.Y.

Thompson R. Harlow, Director, Connecticut Historical Society, Hartford, Conn.

Lilla M. Hawes, Director, Georgia Historical Society, Savannah, Ga.

James J. Heslin, Jr., Director, The New-York Historical Society, New York, N.Y.

Gertrude D. Hess (retired), The Library of the American Philosophical Society

Brooke Hindle, Director, The National Museum of History and Technology, Smithsonian Institution

J. Paul Hudson, Head Curator, Colonial National Historical Park, Jamestown, Va.

Donald W. Holst, The National Museum of History and Technology, Smithsonian Institution

Charles P. Hummel, Curator, The Henry Francis Du Pont Winterthur Museum, Winterthur, Del.

Donald A. Hutzlar, The Museum and Library of the Ohio Historical Society, Columbus, Ohio.

John T. Kelly, Department of the History of Science, Harvard University

Robert L. Klinger, The National Museum of Science and Technology, Smithsonian Institution

Elizabeth B. Knox, Curator, The New London County Historical Society, New London, Conn.

C. H. Lewis, Toronto, Canada

Nancy R. Long, College Park, Md.

Francis R. Maddison, Curator, Museum of the History of Science, Oxford University.

Dorothy D. Merrick, Plymouth Hall, Plymouth, Mass.

Uta C. Merzbach, Curator of Mathematics, The National Museum of History and Technology, Smithsonian Institution

Clifford P. Monahon, Director, The Rhode Island Historical Society, Providence, R.I.

Harold L. Peterson, Chief Curator, U.S. National Park Service, Washington, D.C.

Frank A. Pietropaoli, Librarian, Smithsonian Institution Libraries

Philip F. Purrington, Curator, Old Darmouth Historical Society and Whaling Museum, New Bedford, Mass.

R. Joyce Ramey, Fairfax, Va.

Stephen D. Riley, Director, Massachusetts Historical Society, Boston, Mass.

Walter W. Ristow, Chief, Geography and Map Division, Library of Congress

Albert L. Rogers, Smithsonian Institution Libraries

Carolyn V. Scoon (retired), The New-York Historical Society

Charles E. Smart, Troy, N.Y.

Huldah M. Smith, Curator, Essex Institute, Salem, Mass.

Alan N. Stimson, Assistant Keeper, Department of Navigation, National Maritime Museum, Greenwich, England.

Dirk J. Struik, Department of Mathematics, Massachusetts Institute of Technology

Nicholas B. Wainwright, Director, Historical Society of Pennsylvania, Philadelphia, Pa.

William L. Warren, Chief Curator, Old Sturbridge Village

John Wartnaby, Keeper, Astronomy and Geophysics, The Science Museum, South Kensington, London

Wilcomb E. Washburn, Office of American Studies, Smithsonian Institution

David W. Waters, Deputy Director, National Maritime Museum, Greenwich, England

John A. Watson, Curator of History, New York State Museum, Albany, N.Y.

Elizabeth G. West, Maine State Museum, Augusta, Maine

John Whitelaw, Jr., Bowie, Md.

Alfred F. Whiting, Dartmouth College, Hanover, N.H.

Charlotte M. Wiggin, Litchfield Historical Society, Litchfield, Conn.

Norman Wilson, California State Library, Sacramento, Calif.

Edwin Wolf 2nd, Librarian, Library Company of Philadelphia

Sydney L. Wright, President, Newport Historical Society, Newport, R.I.

Illustration Credits

Grateful acknowledgment is made to the following individuals and institutions for permission to use the materials listed here by illustration number:

1   The President and Fellows of Trinity College, Oxford University

2, 3   The Trustees of the British Museum

4, 45   The New-York Historical Society, New York, N.Y.

5, 7, 19, 24, 34, 41, 65, 69, 73, 74, 75, 76, 77, 79, 80, 83, 87, 91, 92, 93, 96, 99   The National Museum of History and Technology, Smithsonian Institution, Washington, D.C.

6, 8, 11, 14, 16, 18, 72   The Trustees of the National Maritime Museum, Greenwich, England

9, 17   Burndy Library, Inc., Norwalk, Conn.

10, 85   The Old Gaol Museum Committee, York, Maine

12, 58   Preston R. Bassett, Ridgefield, Conn.

13, 15, 53   Peabody Museum, Salem, Mass.

20   The Connecticut Historical Society, Hartford, Conn.

22, 23   C. H. Lewis, Toronto, Canada

25, 27, 28, 37, 55, 59, 84, 102   Private collections

29, 47, 48, 60, 86   American Philosophical Society, Philadelphia, Pa.

30, 98   The Trustees of Harvard University, Cambridge, Mass.

35, 43, 44   Old Salem, Inc., Winston-Salem, N.C.

36, 50   The John Carter Brown Library, Brown University, Providence, R.I.

37   Russell Ward Nadeau, Winchester, Mass.

38   Fogg Art Gallery, Harvard University, Cambridge, Mass.

39   Ohio Historical Society, Ohio State Museum, Columbus, Ohio

40   The Franklin Institute, Philadelphia, Pa.

42   Charles Ellis Ellicott, Jr., Baltimore, Md.

INDEX

497